HAPPINESS

RANDY
ALCORN

 Tyndale House Publishers, Inc., Carol Stream, Illinois

Library of Congress Cataloging-in-Publication Data

Alcorn, Randy C.
  Happiness / Randy Alcorn.
    pages cm
  Includes bibliographical references.
  ISBN 978-1-4143-8934-9 (hc)
  1. Happiness—Religious aspects—Christianity. I. Title.
  BV4647.J68A43 2015
  248.4—dc23   2015022242

ISBN 978-1-4964-1124-2 ITPE edition
Printed in the United States of America

21   20   19   18   17   16   15
7   6   5   4   3   2   1

To Nanci Annette Noren Alcorn, on our fortieth anniversary:
You are my soul mate. Our God of grace has brought me extraordinary happiness
through you, and delight in you. I love you more than ever. I can hardly wait to see our
happy King face-to-face and explore his New Heaven and New Earth with you!

The people of God ought to be the happiest people in all the wide world!
People should be coming to us constantly and asking the source of our joy and delight.

A. W. TOZER

CONTENTS

WHAT IS HAPPINESS?

Be happy and full of joy, because the LORD has done a wonderful thing.
JOEL 2:21, NCV

In him the day-spring from on high has visited the world;
and happy are we, for ever happy, if that day-star arise in our hearts.
MATTHEW HENRY

I FIRST HEARD ABOUT Christ as a teenager, visiting a church youth group. Initially, Bible stories seemed to me like the Greek mythology and comics I loved. Then I read the Gospels, and I came to believe that Jesus was real, and superheroes are his shadows. I felt a profound happiness I'd never known.

My heartfelt gladness was the result of being born again, forgiven, and indwelt by God's Spirit. This "joy of your salvation" (Psalm 51:12) stood in stark contrast to the emptiness I'd felt before hearing the gospel's "good news of great joy" (Luke 2:10). My parents immediately noticed the change. (Mom liked it; Dad didn't.)

I never considered the things I gave up to follow Christ as sacrifices—mainly because they hadn't brought me real happiness. My worst days as a believer seemed better than my best days before knowing Christ. Jesus meant everything to me. I wasn't attempting to be happy; I simply *was* happy.

Having known Jesus for more than four decades now, I realize that my story isn't universal. Not everyone who comes to Christ experiences the dramatic increase in happiness that I did. Many do, but some see that happiness gradually fade.

Nothing is more annoying than reading a book by a naturally gleeful person who's a cheerleader for happiness. I've known a few people with perpetually sunny dispositions, but my own nature is reflective and, at times, melancholic. I've experienced seasons of depression, both before and since coming to faith in Christ—some due to my personality type and emotional makeup (and perhaps genetics), some triggered by my long-term physical illness (insulin-dependent diabetes), and some the result of adverse circumstances.

I'm no stranger to unhappiness—in this world under the curse of evil and suffering, something would be wrong if I were. I've researched the Holocaust, walked through the Killing Fields of Cambodia, written at length on persecution and the problem of evil and suffering, and have walked alongside people who have experienced profound tragedy and grief. In short, I'd be the last person to write a breezy book on happiness that ignores life's difficulties and denies the struggles of living in a fallen world. But by God's grace, as the years have passed, I've experienced a more consistent heartfelt gladness and delight in Christ. That—not perpetual and unsustainable ecstasy—is what this book is about.

Rest assured, this book is not about pasting on a false smile in the midst of heartache. It's about discovering a reasonable, attainable, and delightful happiness in Christ that transcends difficult circumstances. This vision is realistic because it's built on God's all-encompassing sovereignty, love, goodness, grace, gladness, and redemptive purposes in our lives.

Until Christ completely cures us and this world, our happiness will be punctuated by times of great sorrow. But that doesn't mean we can't be predominantly happy in Christ. Being happy as the norm rather than the exception is not wishful thinking. It's based on solid facts: God secured our eternal happiness through a cross and an empty tomb. He is with us and in us right this moment. And he tells us to be happy in him.

"Positive thinking" says we can always be happy if we look on the bright side and don't deal with negative things (such as sin, suffering, judgment, and Hell). I don't believe that. Nor do I embrace the God-as-genie prosperity gospel preached by name-it-and-claim-it folks, which promises happiness through perpetual health, wealth, and success—if only we muster enough faith.

This health-and-wealth philosophy isn't unique to Christians. In *The Secret*, Rhonda Byrne tells about Colin, a ten-year-old boy who was dismayed by long waits for rides at Disney World. He'd seen *The Secret* movie, so he focused on the thought that tomorrow he wouldn't have to wait in line. What happened? Colin's family was chosen to be Epcot's "First Family" for the day, putting them first in every line.[1]

Of course, we should be grateful when God sends us fun surprises. But it's one thing to be happy when such things occur and another to expect, demand, or lay claim to them.

Our models should be people such as Amy Carmichael (1867–1951), who brought the gospel to countless children she rescued from temple prostitution in India. She experienced a great deal of physical suffering and never had a furlough in her fifty-five years as a missionary. Yet she wrote, "There is nothing dreary and doubtful about [life]. It is meant to be continually joyful. . . . We are called to a settled happiness in the Lord whose joy is our strength."[2]

This book is about the surprising "settled happiness" that God makes possible despite life's difficulties. Rich and durable, this happiness is ours today because Christ is here; it's ours tomorrow because Christ will be there; and it's ours forever because he will never leave us.

What I'm writing of is *not* a superficial "don't worry, be happy" philosophy that ignores human suffering. The day hasn't yet come when God will "wipe away every tear from [his children's] eyes" (Revelation 21:4). But it *will* come. And this reality has breathtaking implications for our present happiness.

WE ALL KNOW HAPPINESS WHEN WE SEE AND EXPERIENCE IT.

Webster's Dictionary defines happiness as—wait for it . . . "the state of being happy."[3] Synonyms include *pleasure, contentment, satisfaction, cheerfulness, merriment, gaiety, joy, joyfulness, joviality, delight, good spirits, lightheartedness,* and *well-being*.[4]

The *Dictionary of Bible Themes* gives a more biblical definition of happiness: "A state of pleasure or joy experienced both by people and by God. . . . True happiness derives from a secure and settled knowledge of God and a rejoicing in his works and covenant faithfulness."[5]

Among Christ-followers, *happiness* was once a positive, desirable word. Only in recent times have happiness and joy been set in contrast with each other. I believe this is biblically and historically ungrounded and has significant downsides, as we'll see later.

Are laughter, celebration, and happiness God-created gifts, or are they ambushes from Satan and our sin nature that incur God's disapproval? Our answer determines whether our faith in God is dragged forward by duty or propelled by delight.

My best times with my wife, Nanci, and our family and friends are filled with Christ-centered interaction and heartfelt laughter. These two experiences aren't at odds but are intertwined. The God we love is the enemy of sin *and* the creator and friend of fun and laughter.

LIKE ALL GOD'S GIFTS, HAPPINESS CAN BE TWISTED.

Many Christians in church history knew that happiness, gladness, feasting, and partying are God's gifts. Can these good things be warped, selfish, superficial, and sinful? Of course. In a fallen world, what *can't* be?

Believers and unbelievers alike recognize that there's a negative form of happiness, which is all about self-gratification at others' expense. The philosophy "do whatever makes you happy" gets considerable press, but people who live that way end up pathetic and despised.

Is there selfish and superficial happiness? Sure. There's also selfish and superficial love, peace, loyalty, and trust. We shouldn't throw out Christ-centered happiness with the bathwater of self-centered happiness.

Although the quest to be happy isn't new, people today seem to be particularly thirsty for happiness. Our culture is characterized by increasing depression and anxiety, particularly among the young.[6] Studies show that more people feel bad than good after using social media; photos and updates of everyone else having a great time leave observers feeling left out—like they don't measure up.

Numerous Christians live in daily sadness, anger, anxiety, or loneliness, thinking these feelings are inevitable given their circumstances. They lose joy over traffic jams, a stolen credit card, or increased gas prices. They read Scripture with blinders on, missing the reasons for happiness expressed on nearly every page.

Research indicates that there is "little correlation between the circumstances of people's lives and how happy they are."[7] Yet when people respond to the question "Why aren't you happy?" they tend to focus on their current difficult circumstances. In our fallen world, troubles and challenges are constants. Happy people look beyond their circumstances to someone so big that by his grace, even great difficulties become manageable—and provide opportunities for a deeper kind of happiness.

HAPPINESS IS OFTEN ELUSIVE.

For many people, happiness comes and goes, changing with the winds of circumstance. Such happiness isn't solid or grounded. We can't count on it tomorrow, much less forever.

We say to ourselves, *I'll be happy when* . . . Yet either we don't get what we want and are unhappy, or we do get what we want and are still unhappy.

Sometimes happiness eludes us because we demand perfection in an imperfect world. It's the Goldilocks syndrome: everything must be "just right," or we're unhappy. And nothing is ever just right! So we don't enjoy the ordinary days that are a little, quite a bit, or even mostly right.

Sometimes happiness eludes us because we fail to recognize it when it comes or because we fail to contemplate and treasure it. Some people are only happy when they're unhappy. If they have nothing to complain about, they don't know what to do with themselves. But habitual unhappiness is a pitiful way to live.

Our happiness will remain unstable until we realize our status in the light of eternity. The truth is—and the Bible makes it clear—this life is temporary, but we will live endlessly somewhere, in a place that's either far better or far worse than here.

We can find lasting and settled happiness by saying yes to the God who created and redeems us and by embracing a biblical worldview. When we look at the world and our daily lives through the lens of redemption, reasons for happiness abound. And while these reasons are at times obscured, they remain permanent.

EVERYONE HAS A THEOLOGY OF HAPPINESS—BUT IS YOURS ANY GOOD?

Theologian J. I. Packer writes, "Every Christian is a theologian. Simply by speaking of God, whatever you say, you become a theologian. . . . The question then is whether you are good or bad at what you are doing."[8]

In order to be competent theologians when we speak about God and happiness, we need to go back centuries and millennia rather than months or decades. My many quotations from centuries past may appear to make this book less relevant, but they actually make it far *more* relevant. That's because they've stood the test of time. They aren't trending on Twitter today, only to disappear into tomorrow's graveyard of triviality.

C. S. Lewis (1898–1963) spoke of "chronological snobbery," the flawed belief that newer ideas are inherently better. The people of God who went before us lived the Christian life in difficult times and places. What Augustine, Thomas Aquinas, John Calvin, John Bunyan, John Wesley, and Charles Spurgeon said about happiness cries out for attention. Let the Puritans serve as a wake-up call as well—they often experienced and spoke of profound happiness in seemingly unbearable circumstances. Like skilled blacksmiths, they forged happiness on Scripture's anvil, under the severe hammer of life . . . all the while smiling at the bountiful beauties of God's creation and providence.

My hope is that this book will bring balance to your worldview and your walk with Christ by correcting—through Scripture and Christian history—widespread and deep-seated misconceptions about happiness.

Why such a big book? Because what God's Word says about happiness, and what God's people have said about it, is not a puddle, a pond, or even a lake. It is an ocean.

I invite you to join a long line of God-worshipers in celebrating the Creator's happiness, his design for his image bearers to enter into his happiness, and his willingness to take extreme measures to purchase our happiness.

AN OVERVIEW OF THIS BOOK'S DIRECTION.

Many people spend their lives waiting to be happy. *If only* they can enter the perfect relationship, graduate, move, lose weight, find a better job, buy that new car, get married, have children, win the lottery, have grandchildren, or retire—*then* they'll be happy.

Anyone who waits for happiness will never be happy. Happiness escapes us until we understand why we should be happy, change our perspective, and develop habits of happiness. In researching this book, I've experienced a deeper, more biblical, more Christ-centered happiness than I've ever known. I hope reading it will make you as happy as writing it has made me.

Knowing where we're headed will help you make sense of this journey.

Part 1 examines our longing and search for happiness.
We'll address God's desire for our happiness and how he has wired us to seek happiness—a wiring that remained after Adam and Eve's fall. We'll explore sin's land mines and discover happiness at its only true source.

We'll see that statements such as "God isn't concerned about our happiness, only our holiness" and "God calls us to joy, not happiness" are misguided and unbiblical.

We'll look at the modern evangelical Christian skepticism concerning happiness and see how it skews our worldview and undermines our effectiveness in sharing the gospel.

Part 2 explores the happiness of the triune God.
Though I was happy as a young Christian, there's a paradigm-shifting doctrine I was never taught in church, Bible college, or seminary: the happiness of God himself. I've read many Christian books on joy that make no mention of God's joy. It's something I now believe should be at the heart of a Christian worldview.

This is why I give considerable attention to the biblical teaching that God is happy. Only when we understand this can we believe that God wants *us* to be happy. Scripture makes this statement about imitating Jesus: "Whoever says he abides in him ought to walk in the same way in which he walked" (1 John 2:6). If Jesus walked around mostly miserable, we should be miserable too. If he was happy, we should be happy. (If we're to be Christlike, we'd better learn what Christ is like!)

If God is happy, then this world's unhappiness is a deviation from God and his original design. Scripture reveals that even our present struggles, which trigger unhappiness, are part of his larger plan to bring greater and everlasting happiness. Even here and now, God's children have every reason to be the world's happiest people.

Part 3 surveys the numerous biblical passages that speak of happiness, joy, and gladness.
We'll observe the astounding scope and frequency of the Hebrew and Greek words for happiness, which demonstrate how the Bible repeatedly shows that our Creator wants us happy. Here are just a few:

- May all those who seek you be happy and rejoice in you! (Psalm 40:16, NET)
- You are the LORD's people! So celebrate and praise the only God. (Psalm 97:12, CEV)
- Shout triumphantly to the LORD, all the earth! Be happy! Rejoice out loud! (Psalm 98:4, CEB)
- You also should be happy and full of joy with me. (Philippians 2:18, NCV)
- Rejoice always, pray without ceasing, in everything give thanks. (1 Thessalonians 5:16-18, NKJV)

We'll discover that some of the Hebrew and Greek words used to convey the meaning of *happy* or *happiness* aren't translated as such in most English Bible versions. We'll see how words translated *joy*, *gladness*, and *delight* are synonyms of *happiness*.

Part 4 addresses ways to live a Christ-centered life of happiness.
When we seek holiness at the expense of happiness or happiness at the expense of holiness, we lose both the joy of being holy and the happiness birthed by obedience. God commands holiness, knowing that when we follow his plan, we'll be happy. He also commands happiness, which makes obeying him not only duty, but also pleasure.

Many Christians live as if their faith has drained their happiness! But the same Jesus who calls for sacrifice, promising that we'll share in his suffering, also tells us to lay our burdens at his feet. We're to take up our crosses daily, yet he promises that his burden is light. Life isn't easy, but believers have the benefit of walking the hard roads side by side with a loving Father, a Son who's our friend, and a comforting Holy Spirit.

Thomas Watson (1620–1686), a Puritan preacher and author, said, "He has no design upon us, but to make us happy. . . . Who should be cheerful, if not the people of God?"[9] Did you catch that? A Puritan is saying that God's design is to make us happy. What did Watson know that we don't?

British preacher Charles Spurgeon (1834–1892) said, "Those who are 'beloved of the Lord' must be the most happy and joyful people to be found anywhere upon the face of the earth."[10] Our happiness makes the gospel contagiously appealing; our unhappiness makes it alarmingly unattractive. But is the church today known for its happiness or unhappiness?

We'll discover how we as individuals and the church as a whole can be known for being genuinely happy. When we search for happiness apart from Christ, we find loneliness, confusion, and misery. When we focus on God and others, we find untold happiness.

I hope that as you read you'll ask God to speak to you and you'll contemplate the Scripture at the book's core. May you find greater happiness in God than you've ever known. And may you experience more delight in sharing with others the startlingly "good news of great joy": eternal happiness in Jesus . . . starting right now.

PART 1

Our Compelling Quest for Happiness

CHAPTER 1

WHY DO WE LONG
FOR HAPPINESS?

The people the LORD has freed will return and enter Jerusalem with joy. Their happiness will last forever. They will have joy and gladness, and all sadness and sorrow will be gone far away.
ISAIAH 51:11, NCV

The most essential and active desire in human nature is to happiness. . . . There is nothing more uniform and inviolable than the natural inclination to happiness.
WILLIAM BATES

THE SHAWSHANK REDEMPTION contains a poignant scene in which a prisoner, Andy, locks himself into a restricted area and plays a record featuring opera singers. Beautiful music pours through the public address system while prisoners and guards stare upward, transfixed.

Another prisoner, Red, played by Morgan Freeman, narrates:

> I have no idea to this day what those two Italian ladies were singing about. . . . I'd like to think they were singing about something so beautiful, it can't be expressed in words, and makes your heart ache because of it. I tell you, those voices soared higher and farther than anybody in a gray place dares to dream. It was like some beautiful bird flapped into our drab little cage and made those walls dissolve away, and for the briefest of moments, every last man in Shawshank felt free.[1]

The music liberated those prisoners, stirring feelings of a better reality and instilling hope that true beauty exists. We, too, though we live in a fallen world, dare to hope for a transcendent happiness that's out there . . . somewhere.

The feverish pursuit of happiness in our culture might lead us to believe it's a passing fad, the worldview equivalent of bell-bottoms or Beanie Babies. Not so. The desire for happiness isn't, as many misrepresent it, the child of modern self-obsession. The thirst for happiness is deeply embedded both in God's Word and in every human culture.

Timothy Keller says, "While other worldviews lead us to sit in the midst of life's joys, foreseeing the coming sorrows, Christianity empowers its people to sit in the midst of this world's sorrows, tasting the coming joy."[2]

MY ACHE FOR SOMETHING GREATER BEGAN IN CHILDHOOD.

There's a cartoon that makes a profound statement about happiness. The first panel shows happy schoolchildren entering a street-level subway station—laughing, playing, tossing their hats in the air. The next panel shows middle-aged adults emerging from the station looking like zombies—dull, joyless, unenthusiastic.

A study indicates that children laugh an average of four hundred times daily, adults only fifteen.[3] So what happens between childhood and maturity that damages our capacity for happiness?

I have some fond memories of my childhood and the idealistic dreams of my early life. But by the time I was a teenager, I was disillusioned and empty—though most who knew me wouldn't have guessed.

I grew up knowing almost nothing of Jesus, God, the gospel, the Bible, and the church. My father owned taverns and operated Alcorn Amusements, which supplied and serviced game machines for taverns. Before computers and video games, I grew up in a home filled with foosball and pool tables, pinball and bowling machines. I even had two jukeboxes in my bedroom. (My house was a popular place for my friends to hang out!) These amusement machines were designed to make people happy . . . yet *nobody in my family was happy*.

This was a second marriage for both my parents. Every time Dad came home drunk and he and Mom yelled at each other, I lay in bed wondering whether this fight would end in divorce.

In junior high I got good grades, won awards, played quarterback, and was named team captain and student body president, but I wasn't happy. I had brief tastes of happiness, but I spent far more time seeking happiness and longing for it than experiencing it. I bought comic books by the hundreds, subscribed to fantasy and science fiction magazines, and spent nights gazing through my telescope, pondering the universe.

The night sky filled me with awe—and a small taste of happiness. I yearned for something bigger than myself. (Since I knew nothing of God, aliens were the primary candidates.) One unforgettable night, I gazed at the great galaxy of Andromeda, 2.5 million light-years away, with its trillion stars. I longed to explore it someday, to lose myself in its immensity.

But my wonder was trumped by an unbearable sense of loneliness and separation. I wept because I felt so incredibly small. Unknown to me, God was using the marvels of his universe to draw me to himself. Through God's creation, I was seeing "his invisible attributes . . . his eternal power and divine nature" (Romans 1:20).

That gnawing emptiness grew until eventually I set the telescope aside. If the universe had meaning—if I had meaning—I had no clue what it was.

Sometimes I'd sit on my bed for hours, staring into the jukebox, immersed in the sounds of the '60s. I felt a sense of urgency listening to John Lennon sing "Help!" As I sang the words, "I need somebody," I didn't realize that "somebody" was Jesus.

I later learned that at the height of his success, Lennon wrote a personal letter to an evangelist. After quoting a line from a Beatles song, "Money can't buy me love," he said, "It's true. The point is this, I want happiness. I don't want to keep on with drugs. . . . Explain to me what Christianity can do for me. Is it phoney? Can He love me? I want out of hell."[4]

Lennon knew he didn't have what philosophers and theologians have long claimed we all want—happiness.

As for me, I looked for ways to fill that hungry void, but unhappiness and loneliness prevailed. I found distraction, but never fulfillment.

When I first read the Bible, it was new, intriguing, and utterly disorienting. I opened it and discovered these words: "In the beginning, God created the heavens and the earth" (Genesis 1:1). Then I read the greatest understatement ever: "He made the stars also" (Genesis 1:16, KJV). Countless stars in a universe one hundred billion light-years across are a mere add-on: "also."

I realized that this book was about a person who made the universe, including Andromeda and Earth—and me.

Because I had no reference points when I read the Bible, it wasn't just Leviticus that confused me. But when I reached the Gospels, something changed. I was fascinated by Jesus. Everything about him had the ring of truth, and soon I came to believe he was real. Then, by a miracle of grace, he transformed me.

This life change was characterized by many factors, but the single most noticeable difference was my newfound happiness. My father, enraged that I'd turned to a belief he disdained, predicted I would "outgrow" my conversion. I'm grateful that forty-five years later, I haven't. (I'm also grateful that at age eighty-five, my dad trusted Christ.) Like most of us, I've experienced suffering and heartaches. Still, I regularly find happiness in the one who reached out to me with his grace decades ago—and continues to do so every day.

Though I live in a world that sells false happiness at newsstands, websites, and big-box stores, I thank God for authentic happiness in Jesus.

SEEKING HAPPINESS IS AS NATURAL AS BREATHING.

Augustine, considered by many the most influential theologian in church history, wrote 1,600 years ago, "Every man, whatsoever his condition, desires to be happy."[5]

In the fourth century AD, Augustine asked, "For who wishes anything for any other reason than that he may become happy?"[6] He also said, "There is no man who does not desire this, and each one desires it with such earnestness that he prefers it to all other things; whoever, in fact, desires other things, desires them for this end alone."[7]

(I will quote many sources here to demonstrate that this view of happiness isn't a narrowly held belief but a consensus throughout church history.)

Nearly 1,300 years after Augustine, the French philosopher and mathematician Blaise Pascal (1623–1662) wrote, "All men seek happiness. This is without exception."[8]

Pascal's contemporary, English Puritan Thomas Manton (1620–1677), said, "It is as natural for the reasonable creature to desire to be happy, as it is for the fire to burn." Manton followed with the bad news: "But we do not make a right choice of the means that may bring us to that happiness that we desire." He went on to say that human beings "choose means quite contrary to happiness."[9]

English theologian Richard Sibbes (1577–1635) echoed this sentiment: "Happiness being by all men desirable, the desire of it is naturally engrafted in every man; and is the centre of all the searchings of his heart and turnings of his life."[10]

In 1639, Puritan Robert Crofts wrote, "All men naturally desire happiness. All their plots, purposes, and endeavors aim at this end only."[11]

Scottish churchman Thomas Boston (1676–1732) said, "Consider what man is. He is a creature that desires happiness, and cannot but desire it. The desire of happiness is woven into his nature, and cannot be eradicated. It is as natural for him to desire it as it is to breathe."[12]

Puritan preacher Jonathan Edwards (1703–1758) said, "There is no man upon the earth who isn't earnestly seeking after happiness, and it appears abundantly by the variety of ways they so vigorously seek it; they will twist and turn every way, ply all instruments, to make themselves happy men."[13]

Evangelist George Whitefield (1714–1770) said, "Is it the end of religion to make men happy, and is it not every one's privilege to be as happy as he can?"[14] Whitefield asked an audience, "Does [Jesus] want your heart only for the same end as the devil does, to make you miserable? No, he only wants you to believe on him, that you might be saved. This, this, is all the dear Savior desires, to make you happy, that you may leave your sins, to sit down eternally with him."[15]

None of these men of God had an argument against happiness-seeking. Their message was simply that true happiness could be found only in Christ.

If we don't understand what these figures from church history knew, we'll imagine that we have a choice whether or not we want to pursue happiness. In fact, *we don't*. Seeking happiness is a given—a universal constant. It's present in every person of every age, era, and circumstance. So it's entirely unrealistic and counterproductive for Christians to tell people they shouldn't want to be happy. They can't help it!

Any pastor who tries to motivate people to stop seeking happiness, any parent who tries to make his or her child repent of being motivated by happiness, is fighting a losing battle. Neither will succeed, and both will do damage by distancing the gospel from the happiness everyone craves.

WHAT IF WE WANT TO BE HAPPY NOT BECAUSE WE'RE SINNERS BUT BECAUSE WE'RE HUMANS?

Based on the books I've read, the sermons I've heard, and the conversations I've had, I'm convinced that many Christians believe our desire for happiness was birthed in humankind's fall.

But what if our desire for happiness comes from God? What if he wired his image bearers for happiness before sin entered the world? How might this perspective change our approach to life, parenting, church, ministry, business, sports, and entertainment?

Augustine asked rhetorically, "Is not a happy life the thing that all desire, and is there any one who altogether desires it not?" Then he added a critical question: "But where did they acquire the knowledge of it, that they so desire it? Where have they seen it, that they so love it?"[16]

Not only has God written his law on our hearts (see Romans 2:15); he has written a love of happiness on them.

Blaise Pascal, who said that "all men seek happiness," wrote these words in his collection of thoughts on theology:

> What else does this longing and helplessness proclaim, but that there was once in each person a true happiness, of which all that now remains is the empty print and trace? We try to fill this in vain with everything around us, seeking in things that are not there the help we cannot find in those that are there. Yet none can change things, because this infinite abyss can only be filled with something that is infinite and unchanging—in other words, by God himself. God alone is our true good.[17]

In other words, the Fall didn't generate the human longing for happiness—it derailed and misdirected it.

Scripture portrays our connection to the sin of Adam in a way that transcends time—as if we were there in Eden with him (see Romans 5:12-21). Similarly, I believe we inherited from our Eden-dwelling ancestors a sense of their pre-Fall happiness. This explains why our hearts refuse to settle for sin and suffering and we long for something better.

Were we merely the product of natural selection and survival of the fittest, we'd have no grounds for believing any ancient happiness existed. But even those who have never been taught about the Fall and the Curse intuitively know that something is seriously wrong.

Why else would we long for happiness and sense what a utopian society should look like even if we've never seen one? We are nostalgic for an Eden we've only seen hints of.

Medieval scholar Anselm of Canterbury (1033–1109) lamented humanity's fall and the loss of the happiness that comes from knowing God: "O wretched lot of man, when he hath lost that for which he was made! . . . He has lost the blessedness [happiness] for which he was made, and has found the misery for which he was not made."[18]

Anglican bishop J. C. Ryle (1816–1900) wrote, "Happiness is what all mankind want to obtain—the desire for it is deeply planted in the human heart."[19]

If this desire is "deeply planted" in our hearts, who planted it? Our answer to that question will dramatically affect the way we see the world. Did Adam and Eve want to be happy before they sinned? Did they enjoy the food God provided because it tasted sweet? Did they sit in the sun because it felt warm and jump into the water because it felt refreshing? If we believe God is happy (a topic we'll explore in part 2), then wouldn't he make us with the desire and capacity to be happy?

Christ-followers say things like, "God wants you blessed, not happy";[20] "God doesn't want you to be happy. God wants you to be holy";[21] and "God doesn't want you to be happy, he wants you to be strong."[22] But does the message that God doesn't want us to be happy promote the Good News or obscure it?

When we separate God from happiness and from our longing for happiness, we undermine the Christian worldview. We might as well say, "Stop breathing and eating; instead, worship God." People must breathe and eat and desire happiness—and they can worship God as they do so!

PUTTING GOD ON THE SIDE OF HOLINESS AND SATAN ON THE SIDE OF HAPPINESS IS A DANGEROUS MANEUVER.

The devil has mastered this strategy. His lie from the beginning was that God doesn't care about our good. The truth is, God wants us to seek real happiness in him, while Satan wants us to seek imitation holiness stemming from our self-congratulatory pride. The Pharisees had a passionate desire to be holy on their own terms. Christ's response? "You are of your father the devil, and your will is to do your father's desires" (John 8:44).

Satan hates God, he hates us, and he hates happiness as much as he hates holiness—God's and ours. He isn't happy and has no happiness to give. He dispenses rat poison in colorful, happy-looking wrappers. The devil has no power to implant in us a desire for happiness. Satan is not about happiness; he is about sin and misery, which come from seeking happiness where it can't be found. God is the one who planted our desire for happiness.

Baptist pastor and professor John Broadus (1827–1895) put it this way:

> The minister may lawfully appeal to the desire for happiness and its negative
> counterpart, the dread of unhappiness. Those philosophers who insist that we
> ought always to do right simply and only because it is right are not philosophers
> at all, for they are either grossly ignorant of human nature or else indulging in
> mere fanciful speculations.[23]

The modern evangelical antipathy to happiness backfires when it portrays Christianity as being against what people long for most. (True, we chronically seek happiness in sin, but the core problem isn't seeking happiness but choosing sin instead of God.)

FEW FIND THE LASTING HAPPINESS THEY CRAVE.

Anselm wrote what seems tragically obvious: "Not everyone who has the will for happiness has happiness."[24] Adam and Eve fell away from God and happiness because of their disobedience. However, they never lost their desire to be happy.

Why are many people so unhappy? Pascal suggested, "Who is unhappy at not being a king, except a deposed king?"[25]

Because we were made for greatness, the world's superficiality is unsatisfying. We sense that unhappiness is abnormal, and we ache for someone, somehow, to bring us lasting happiness. That someone is Jesus, and that somehow is his redemptive work.

A. W. Tozer (1897–1963) said, "Man is bored, because he is too big to be happy with that which sin is giving him."[26]

As Adam and Eve's descendants, we inherited their separation from God, and therefore from happiness. Ages later, we retain a profound awareness that we were once happy—and that we should be happy.

This compelling desire for genuine happiness, while at times painful, is God's grace to us. Longing for the happiness humankind once knew, we can be drawn toward true happiness in Christ, which is offered us in the gospel.

God used my persistent desire for happiness to prepare me for the gospel message. The "good news of great joy" in Christ was exactly the cool water my thirsty young soul craved.

The gospel is good news only to those who know they need it. Had I been happy without Jesus, I never would have turned to him.

CHAPTER 2

WHAT DOES OUR LONGING FOR HAPPINESS REVEAL ABOUT US?

Happy are the people who know the joyful shout; Yahweh, they walk in the light of Your presence.
PSALM 89:15, HCSB

Give me an explanation, first, of the towering eccentricity of man among the brutes; second, of the vast human tradition of some ancient happiness.
G. K. CHESTERTON

PSYCHOTHERAPIST LYNNE ROSEN and motivational speaker John Littig cohosted an hour-long radio show on WBAI in New York called *The Pursuit of Happiness*. But this Brooklyn couple's final act was putting plastic bags over each other's heads and committing suicide.[1]

Rosen and Littig were experts in pursuing happiness yet failures in catching it. This tragic couple epitomizes the irony that the more we advertise and purchase products, events, and books intended to make us happy, the unhappier we may become.

In 1997, thirty-nine members of the cult Heaven's Gate, led by Marshall Applewhite, participated in a mass suicide. They'd been taught that once they exited their earthly bodies, they would land on a spaceship following the Hale-Bopp comet. At the time of their death, each member carried a five-dollar bill and three quarters. Why? To pay an interplanetary toll.

Most of us shake our heads in amazement at this kind of gullibility. Yet we fail to see the futility of our own attempts to find happiness. Many people try the age-old practices of turning to money, sex, power, beauty, sports, nature, music, art, education, work, or celebrity for happiness. In the end, each of these proves as big a lie as a spaceship on a comet's tail.[2]

The problem for the Heaven's Gate followers wasn't that they trusted too much; it was that they trusted the wrong person. Only Jesus was worthy of their trust. Only he could have granted them, in this life and for eternity, the deep and lasting happiness they sought.

11

ASK PEOPLE WHAT THEY WANT OUT OF LIFE, AND THEY'LL ANSWER, "TO BE HAPPY."

The same is true for the most superficial materialist and the most devout saint: all of us are wired to seek happiness.

The Greek philosopher Aristotle (384–322 BC) wrote, "Happiness, then, is something final and self-sufficient, and is the end of action."[3]

Centuries later, French philosopher Denis Diderot (1713–1784) said essentially the same thing: "There is only one passion, the passion for happiness."[4]

Even Charles Darwin (1809–1882), best known as the father of evolutionary theory, wrote, "All sentient beings have been formed so as to enjoy, as a general rule, happiness."[5]

William James (1842–1910), the philosopher and psychologist, wrote, "How to gain, how to keep, how to recover happiness, is in fact for most men at all times the secret motive of all they do, and of all they are willing to endure."[6]

The quest for happiness transcends gender, age, and life circumstances. Holocaust victim Anne Frank (1929–1945) wrote as a teenager, "We all live with the objective of being happy; our lives are all different and yet the same."[7]

In an 1898 article arguing against religion, L. K. Washburn said, "There is a constant mental pilgrimage towards that Mecca of the human heart—happiness. . . . Everybody wants to be happy, and thinks, strives, wishes, and lives to that end."[8]

How many subjects do Puritans, philosophers, atheists, and agnostics emphatically agree on? One of the few is our innate longing for happiness.

WHERE DOES OUR DESIRE FOR HAPPINESS LEAD US?

In *The Discarded Image*, C. S. Lewis references a vivid simile in Chaucer's "The Knight's Tale" to illustrate that human beings have "some inkling of the truth," even if they go about seeking it in the wrong way. The knight describes the human journey this way: "All men know that the true good is Happiness, and all men seek it, but, for the most part, by wrong routes—like a drunk man who knows he has a house but can't find his way home."[9]

The human race is homesick for Eden, which only two humans have ever known. We spend our lives chasing peaceful delight, following dead ends or cul-de-sacs in pursuit of home.

We know intuitively that we've wandered. What we don't know is how to return. Our lives are largely the story of the often wrong and occasionally right turns we take in our attempts to get home to Happiness with a capital H—God himself.

WE ANTICIPATE GREATER HAPPINESS THAN LIFE SEEMS TO OFFER.

Aren't we all weary of the onslaught of politicians, religious leaders, and commercials promising more than they can deliver? We have our expectations raised only to be crushed time and time again. Yet we continue to hope for better things than life's track record suggests possible.

A. A. Milne (1882–1956), creator of Winnie the Pooh, conveyed the joy of anticipation:

"Well," said Pooh, "what I like best—" and then he had to stop and think.
Because although Eating Honey was a very good thing to do, there was a
moment just before you began to eat it which was better than when you were,
but he didn't know what it was called.[10]

C. S. Lewis called this anticipation *Sehnsucht*, a German word for "yearning."[11] *Sehnsucht* is used to describe a longing for a far-off country that's, for now at least, unreachable. Lewis connected the yearning itself and the foretastes of it with the joy that is longed for.

Before the Fall, Adam and Eve undoubtedly anticipated good food, but instead of falling short of expectations, the food in Eden likely tasted *better* than imagined. After the Fall, however, the opposite is true. We expect something more of food, entertainment, and relationships, and we are inevitably disappointed. Though we live in a fallen world, we still retain the expectations and hopes of a better one.

A. W. Tozer wrote, "For whatever else the Fall may have been, it was most certainly a sharp change in man's relation to his Creator. He . . . destroyed the proper Creator-creature relation in which, unknown to him, his true happiness lay." Without that understanding of the Fall, we can't appreciate the gospel's reinstatement of our lost happiness: "Essentially salvation is the restoration of a right relation between man and his Creator, a bringing back to normal of the Creator-creature relation."[12]

When I was young, fantasy stories appealed to my desire for something great and wondrous outside my experience. I longed for Eden before I understood there had been an Eden. I ached for God before I believed in God.

I embraced the gospel because it so perfectly corresponded with what I longed for. I've studied many worldviews, but none comes close to the biblical worldview in accounting for all the facts of our existence—including our longing for happiness.

HUMAN HISTORY IS LARGELY THE STORY OF OUR SEARCH FOR HAPPINESS.

Magazines have "happiness editors," whose sole job it is to create or find happiness-related articles. Google "happy hour," and you get somewhere around 100 million hits. (People don't flock to happy hour because they want to be unhappy.) The online world is rife with people who've dubbed themselves "happiness gurus" or who offer "three [or five or ten] simple steps to happiness."

Writer Thomas Wolfe (1900–1938), after years of seeking happiness, articulated his gloomy assessment of life:

The whole conviction of my life now rests upon the belief that loneliness, far
from being a rare and curious phenomenon, peculiar to myself and to a few other
solitary men, is the central and inevitable fact of human existence . . . and that
morning—bright, shining morning with its promise of new beginnings—will
never come upon the earth again as it did once.[13]

From a biblical perspective, the loneliness Wolfe described is the result of being separated from God. His assessment is penetrating, but it fails to acknowledge the open arms of Christ. Like all of us, Wolfe desperately needed Jesus, but coming to him requires confession and submission. Without the miraculous intervention of God, our default is to choose our imaginary self-sufficiency over dependence on God . . . which requires humility.

In the final section of this book I'll talk about choices we can make that will bring us greater happiness now. But the truth is, many people from every demographic have quietly given up hope of ever finding joy.

Psychiatrist Paul D. Meier writes,

> I have had millionaire businessmen come to my office and tell me they have big houses, yachts, condominiums . . . , nice children, a beautiful mistress, an unsuspecting wife, secure corporate positions—and suicidal tendencies. They have everything this world has to offer except one thing—inner peace and joy. They come to my office as a last resort, begging me to help them conquer the urge to kill themselves.[14]

In the midst of such hopelessness, God offers the good news of his transforming grace, mercy, love, and eternal happiness: "Let the one who is thirsty come; let the one who wants it take the water of life free of charge" (Revelation 22:17, NET).

ONLY A GOD-SIZED GOSPEL CAN ENABLE US TO FIND TRUE HAPPINESS.

Satan is aware of a truth we often fail to see: *sin sabotages happiness.* According to Spurgeon, "Man was not originally made to mourn; he was made to rejoice. The Garden of Eden was his place of happy abode, and as long as he continued in obedience to God, nothing grew in that Garden that could cause him sorrow."[15]

The apostle John, aided by an angel, time-traveled to the New Earth. There he saw "the water of life, as clear as crystal, flowing from the throne of God and of the Lamb down the middle of the great street of the city. On each side of the river stood the tree of life." He went on to explain what life will be like for those who live in the New Earth: "No longer will there be any curse. The throne of God and of the Lamb will be in the city, and his servants will serve him. They will see his face" (Revelation 22:1-4, NIV).

That's how much God wants us to be happy—he'll re-create the universe, raise us from the dead, and give back the wonders of Eden multiplied a thousand times over. There we'll live in joyful, never-ending communion with him . . . all bought and paid for with his own blood.

THE BIBLE PROMISES EVERLASTING HAPPINESS FOR GOD'S PEOPLE.

World peace and universal happiness seem like utopian dreams, but these dreams are not far fetched, because according to God's Word, utopia once existed and will again. (What is far fetched is believing we are capable of creating this utopia ourselves!)

It should delight us to hear that the future involves a return to Paradise. Jesus promised his disciples that one day there will be a "renewal of all things" (NIV), which the English Standard Version translates as "the new world" and the Complete Jewish Bible renders as "the regenerated world" (Matthew 19:28).

Just as we'll take on our eternal, resurrected bodies, the world itself will be resurrected. Peter preached that Christ would not return "until the time for restoring all the things about which God spoke by the mouth of his holy prophets long ago" (Acts 3:21). The New Century Version translates this as "when all things will be made right again." Our entire experience on the New Earth will be of happiness far greater than Adam and Eve could have ever imagined!

The past will be remembered as that temporary period of rebellion when God's creatures turned from him. We'll celebrate endlessly that Jesus entered our history to redeem us and to restore the shared happiness of God and his people.

As God's children, we have a history of his faithfulness in the past and an assurance of a secure future, which should define how we view our present. This perspective can infuse us with happiness even in what would otherwise be the unhappiest times of our lives. "So we fix our eyes not on what is seen, but on what is unseen, since what is seen is temporary, but what is unseen is eternal" (2 Corinthians 4:18, NIV).

THERE'S NO TRUE HAPPINESS WITHOUT GOD.

Charles Darwin, near the end of his life, spoke of what he called his "loss of happiness":

> Up to the age of thirty, or beyond it, poetry of many kinds . . . gave me great pleasure, and even as a schoolboy I took intense delight in Shakespeare. . . . Formerly pictures gave me considerable, and music very great delight. But now for many years I cannot endure to read a line of poetry: I have tried lately to read Shakespeare, and found it so intolerably dull that it nauseated me. I have also almost lost my taste for pictures or music. . . . I retain some taste for fine scenery, but it does not cause me the exquisite delight which it formerly did. . . . My mind seems to have become a kind of machine for grinding general laws out of large collections of facts. . . . The loss of these tastes is a loss of happiness, and may possibly be injurious to the intellect, and more probably to the moral character, by enfeebling the emotional part of our nature.[16]

Darwin may not have traced his diminished happiness to his gradual change in worldview, but it's likely that the naturalistic perspective he embraced gradually undermined his early delight in studying God's creation, resulting in a joyless, machinelike indifference.

Thomas Traherne (1636–1674), an English poet and theologian, wrote, "Till you can sing and rejoice and delight in God . . . you never enjoy the world."[17] Yes, unbelievers can experience limited joy, but when we know and love the Creator, our heartfelt delight is magnified.

Seeking happiness without God is like seeking water without wetness or sun without light. Since God himself is the happiness that overflows into his creation, every attempt to separate him from happiness is futile.

In an 1847 letter to his father, Scottish author George Macdonald (1824–1905) wrote of the barriers he faced in turning to Christ:

> One of my greatest difficulties in consenting to think of religion was that I thought I should have to give up my beautiful thoughts & my love for the things God has made. But I find that the happiness springing from all things not in themselves sinful is much increased by religion. God is the God of the Beautiful, Religion the Love of the Beautiful, & Heaven the House of the Beautiful— nature is tenfold brighter in the sun of righteousness, and my love of nature is more intense since I became a Christian. . . . God has not given me such thoughts, & forbidden me to enjoy them. Will he not in them enable me to raise the voice of praise?[18]

Loving nature and beauty should indeed be enhanced by loving the God who made them and reveals himself in them—how could it be otherwise?

Living in Oregon, surrounded by stunning natural beauty and people who love and sometimes worship it, I often ponder the irony that my state and our neighbor, Washington, have among the lowest percentages of Christ-followers anywhere in the United States. For the present, by God's grace and kindness, people can reject God but still receive the benefits of his common grace, including the enjoyment of loving relationships, natural and artistic beauty, and pleasure. However—and we need to be so warned—we live on borrowed time. This temporary situation will come to an abrupt end (see Hebrews 9:27-28; Revelation 20:11-15).

After the termination of this life, we can have one of two combinations:

1. both God and happiness
2. neither God nor happiness

What we won't be able to have is God without happiness or happiness without God.

CHAPTER 3

DOES GOD WANT US TO BE HAPPY?

Sing, Jerusalem. Israel, shout for joy! Jerusalem, be happy and rejoice with all your heart.
ZEPHANIAH 3:14, NCV

God made human beings as He made His other creatures, to be happy.
. . . They are in their right element when they are happy.
CHARLES SPURGEON

IN MY NOVEL *Safely Home,* I tell the story of two Harvard roommates reunited in China twenty years after graduation. One is American businessman Ben Fielding, an entrepreneur in international high-tech corporate partnerships. The other is Li Quan, a brilliant academic who, when Ben last saw him, was headed home to be a professor at a Chinese university.

When Ben reconnects with Li Quan on a business trip to China, he's shocked to find his old friend living in poverty, working as a locksmith's assistant, and involved with a house church often raided by the police. Shortly after the two become reacquainted, Quan is imprisoned. Yet even in prison, to Ben's astonishment, Quan remains cheerful, trusting God and rejoicing in his goodness despite enduring cruel treatment.

The longer Ben stays in China and the more time he spends with Li Quan and his wife and son, the more he envies his old friend. Even with everything he has going for him and everything working against Quan, Ben realizes he wishes he could trade places with his former roommate. Why? Because Quan has what Ben doesn't: love and happiness.

Li Quan drew his happiness from God, who was with him even in prison. Ben Fielding attempted to find happiness in everything the world had to offer . . . and failed miserably.

HAPPINESS IS GOD'S COMMAND—AND A PLEASANT CALLING— FOR HIS PEOPLE.

C. S. Lewis said, "It is a Christian duty . . . for everyone to be as happy as he can."[1] Happiness is a privilege. However, since God repeatedly calls upon us to rejoice, delight, and be glad in him, we have an obligation to actually do so.

This makes sense only if the God we love is happy, if the gospel message we embrace and proclaim is happy, and if Heaven is a happy place. It makes sense if we understand that people long to be happy and won't turn to Jesus if they believe there's no happiness in him. Others will judge whether there's happiness in Jesus by whether they see happiness in his followers. Hence, our happiness is, indeed, a Christian duty.

But what an incredibly wonderful responsibility it is . . . like being required to eat Mom's apple pie! We're accustomed to thinking of duty as drudgery, not happiness. But a person's duty to love his or her spouse or to care for a son or daughter, and a soldier's duty to defend his country—when done with the right heart and perspective—all bring satisfaction, contentment, and happiness.

Paul's words in Philippians 4:4 are often translated "Rejoice in the Lord always, and again I say rejoice." They could also be translated, "Be happy in the Lord always, and again I say be happy." Commenting on this verse, Spurgeon said, "It is intended that we should be happy. That is the meaning . . . that we should be cheerful."[2]

This passage commands us twice to be glad in God. A command carries with it the duty to obey, and when it's repeated, that expectation is intensified. Fortunately, when God commands us to rejoice, his Holy Spirit empowers us to obey.

God could have stated, "You have cause to rejoice." But a command is different from a statement. A command doesn't leave us the option to passively wait for joy, hoping it comes to us. Rather, we must take action to lay hold of joy in God.

The command to be sexually pure and abstain from immorality requires proactive choices (see 1 Thessalonians 4:3). Similarly, to glorify God in all we do, love our neighbor, care for our families, help the poor, and resolve conflicts requires actions on our part. The same is true of the command to rejoice.

The fact that "rejoice" is followed by "always" and is repeated ("*again* I say rejoice") makes it one of the most emphatic directives in Scripture. If our lives are not characterized by rejoicing, or if we've given up on happiness, we're missing out on what God intends for us. We must go to him and ask for his help and empowerment to find joy in him.

Only if we truly want to experience the happiness-driven desires of our hearts will we be drawn to God by verses such as this: "Seek your happiness in the LORD, and he will give you your heart's desire" (Psalm 37:4, GNT). Judging by what we hear, we might expect Scripture to say, "Obey God, and say no to your heart's desire." Not so!

Jesus says, "Until now you have asked nothing in my name. Ask, and you will receive, that your joy may be full" (John 16:24).

The Contemporary English Version and God's Word Translation both render the final clause in John 16:24 this way: so that we will be "completely happy."

Can our joy be full if we're not happy? No.

The CEV, a translation from the original biblical languages (not a paraphrase), says:

- Be happy and shout to God who makes us strong! (Psalm 81:1)
- Be happy and excited! You will have a great reward in heaven. (Matthew 5:12)

The Bible clearly *commands* us to be happy. "But that's just one English version," someone might say. Correct. But every other version echoes the same command even when using other words. The CEV isn't alone in its translation of these and similar passages. The Good News Translation says:

- Be happy with your wife and find your joy with the woman you married. (Proverbs 5:18)
- Go ahead—eat your food and be happy; drink your wine and be cheerful. It's all right with God. (Ecclesiastes 9:7)
- Be happy with those who are happy, weep with those who weep. (Romans 12:15)

You may not be accustomed to thinking that God commands us to be happy. But it's a fact. And I'm betting it's a command most of us would like to obey!

Some have an intuitive resistance to the notion that happiness is unbiblical, and so we should. A blogger says, "Happiness isn't in the Bible? But what about all the commands to rejoice? What about laughter? Please tell me I'm not supposed to always be heavy-hearted, trudging along and begrudging obedience. I want to be a happy Christian!"[3]

SCRIPTURE CONFIRMS THAT GOD WANTS US HAPPY.

I've studied more than 2,700 Scripture passages where words such as *joy, happiness, gladness, merriment, pleasure, celebration, cheer, laughter, delight, jubilation, feasting, exultation,* and *celebration* are used. Throw in the words *blessed* and *blessing,* which often connote happiness, and the number increases.

God is clear that seeking happiness—or joy, gladness, delight, or pleasure—through sin is wrong and fruitless. But seeking happiness in him is good and right.

The ESV, which I most often cite in this book, doesn't use the word *happy* nearly as often as many translations, but it's still there:

- Happy are you, O Israel! Who is like you, a people saved by the LORD? (Deuteronomy 33:29)
- Judah and Israel were as many as the sand by the sea. They ate and drank and were happy. (1 Kings 4:20)
- Happy are your men! Happy are your servants, who continually stand before you and hear your wisdom! (1 Kings 10:8)
- How beautiful upon the mountains are the feet of him who brings good news, who publishes peace, who brings good news of happiness. (Isaiah 52:7)

Even without the word *happiness,* the concept is unmistakable in passages such as these:

- Enjoy life with the wife whom you love. (Ecclesiastes 9:9)
- All the days of the afflicted are evil, but the cheerful of heart has a continual feast. (Proverbs 15:15)

Most translations render the phrase "cheerful of heart" or "cheerful heart." Two say "glad heart," and one says "gladness of heart." Four, including the King James Version, say "merry heart." Five, including the New Living Translation, render it "happy heart." Which is correct? All of them. These words are synonyms.

Even Jeremiah, who's called "the weeping prophet" since he was brokenhearted over the tragic suffering of God's people, spoke prophecies of happiness. He saw the future—some of it in this world's Jerusalem and much of it in the New Jerusalem to come—and in it he was given glimpses of God's promised happiness:

> Hear the word of the LORD. . . . [My people] will come and shout for joy on the heights of Zion; they will rejoice in the bounty of the LORD. . . . They will be like a well-watered garden, and they will sorrow no more. Then young women will dance and be glad, young men and old as well. I will turn their mourning into gladness; I will give them comfort and joy instead of sorrow. JEREMIAH 31:10, 12-13, NIV

That's a lot of joy for a weeping prophet!

Consider the Psalms, which reflect both great sorrow and great happiness:

- I will be happy and rejoice in you! I will sing praises to you, O sovereign One! (Psalm 9:2, NET)
- You will fill me with joy when I am with you. You will make me happy forever at your right hand. (Psalm 16:11, NIrV)
- God, your love is so precious! . . . [People] eat the rich food in your house, and you let them drink from your river of pleasure. (Psalm 36:7-8, NCV)
- I will go to your altar, O God; you are the source of my happiness. I will play my harp and sing praise to you, O God, my God. (Psalm 43:4, GNT)

As Jeremiah and Jesus wept, we, too, will sometimes weep—and so we should. But if we're not experiencing happiness in God, then we're not obeying God's commands and we're missing out on the abundant life Jesus came to give us (see John 10:10).

MODERN CHRISTIANS NEED TO SPEAK MORE, NOT LESS, ABOUT HAPPINESS.

Francis of Assisi (1181–1226) said, "Let us leave sadness to the devil and his angels. As for us, what can we be but rejoicing and glad?"[4]

I talked with a young woman who viewed the Christian life as one of utter dullness. She knew that following Christ was the right thing to do, but she was certain it would mean sacrificing her happiness.

Unless her view changes dramatically, her spiritual future is bleak. It isn't in our nature to continually say no to what we believe would make us happy—or to say yes to something that would make us unhappy. (Don't mistake perseverance for choosing unhappiness—the man who faithfully loves his wife suffering from dementia is not choosing unhappiness but rather choosing the happiness of honoring his wife, keeping his vows, and hearing God's "well done.")

So where did this young woman, who was raised in a fine Christian family and church, acquire such an unbiblical notion? What are we doing—what are we missing—that leaves many of our children and our churches laboring under such false impressions? Why do we think it would be unspiritual for the Christian life to be centered on what God calls the good news of happiness?

Celebration and gladness of heart have characterized the church, including the suffering church, throughout history. Scripturally, the culture of God's people is one of joy, happiness, gratitude, eating and drinking, singing and dancing, and making music. It's not the people who know God who have reason to be miserable—it's those who *don't*.

When our face to the world is one of anger, misery, shame, cowardice, or defensiveness, the gospel we speak of doesn't appear to be the good news of happiness. And we shouldn't be surprised if people, both outside and inside the church, aren't attracted to it. *Why should they be?*

JOY AND LAUGHTER SHOULD BE THE CHURCH'S NORM, NOT THE EXCEPTION.

Children who grow up seeing church as a morose, hypercritical place will turn their backs on it in their quest for happiness. Those who have found happiness in the church will usually stay or return.

Sadly, many non-Christian young adults today view Christ's followers as "hypocritical," "insensitive," and "judgmental."[5] These words all describe unhappy people. (If the world judges us, so be it, but it shouldn't be because we're chronically unhappy.)

It seems to me there are two extremes of Christians when it comes to happiness. Some change the channel from the coverage of a hurricane, refuse to think about sex trafficking and abortion, and ignore the sufferings of this world while grabbing on to superficial living. They look the other way when their marriages are in trouble or when their children choose wrong friends, yet they keep claiming Jesus' promise of easy lives without suffering. (Never mind that Jesus never made such a promise!)

Other Christians are perpetually somber, never laughing or poking fun at themselves, rarely celebrating, and quick to frown when they see someone having fun. Shoulders sagging, they believe that happiness is ungodliness.

The Bible presents a more balanced perspective. Paul said he was "sorrowful, yet always rejoicing" (2 Corinthians 6:10). Sorrow and joy can and do coexist, for now. (Note that the "always" in this verse is applied to rejoicing, not being sorrowful.)

If we constantly focus on all that's wrong with the world, then sorrow or anger will be our default. But the apostle Paul, writing from prison in Rome, calls on us to rejoice in the Lord not periodically, but always.

It's not insensitive, unkind, or wrong to be happy. By being happy in Christ, we lay claim to the fact that God is bigger than the Fall and affirm that our Lord and Savior Jesus Christ will reverse the Curse and reign over a new universe. Our happiness shouts that our God is present with us and at work in the world every minute of every hour of every day. The narrower our view of God's presence in this world—and in our daily lives—the less happiness we'll experience.

Parents repeat instructions to children because kids tend to miss it the first time. Hence Paul said, "Again I will say, rejoice" (Philippians 4:4). He wanted to make sure we'd get it. Synonyms for happiness appear repeatedly throughout Scripture. If God says it enough, shouldn't we get it? Still, most of us have failed to notice the cumulative force of the biblical revelation that we are to be consistently happy in God.

GROWING IN OUR HAPPINESS IN CHRIST IS A PROCESS.

The bride of Christ matures incrementally. As we "grow in the grace and knowledge of our Lord and Savior Jesus Christ" (2 Peter 3:18), we grow in joy.

Paul depicted the gradual process of growth in Christlikeness this way: "We all, who with unveiled faces contemplate the Lord's glory, are being transformed into his image with ever-increasing glory, which comes from the Lord, who is the Spirit" (2 Corinthians 3:18, NIV). With ever-increasing glory comes ever-increasing happiness in our Lord. Sin loses its hold on us—largely because we see the misery it brings. We begin to ask ourselves, "How could I believe for a moment that sin could bring me happiness?"

We also learn from adversity. When our perspective and our faith are put to the test, our happiness can flourish. That's why so many passages surprise us by connecting rejoicing with trials (see James 1:2-4; 1 Peter 1:6-9; 2 Corinthians 8:2-3; Hebrews 10:34).

OUR PURSUIT OF GENUINE HAPPINESS IN GOD HONORS HIM.

When Puritan Jonathan Edwards was only nineteen years old, he made a resolution that speaks volumes: "Resolved, to endeavor to obtain for myself as much happiness in the other world as I possibly can, with all the power, might, vigour, and vehemence . . . I am capable of."[6]

Like most of the Puritans, Richard Sibbes did not demean the quest for happiness; rather, he saw Jesus as the proper object of that quest: "Only to a true Christian, by a supernatural light, is discovered both the right object, and the right way to felicity."[7]

In the movie *The Stepford Wives*, husbands program "perfect" wives. Of course, these robotic wives are perfect only in the sense that they do whatever their husbands want. But what any good man really desires is a relationship with a real person who responds out of heartfelt love and happiness. Fake, programmed love or happiness is empty—in fact, it's unreal. God doesn't force happiness on us. He invites us to enter his happiness and find it in him.

C. S. Lewis said, "The happiness which God designs for His higher creatures is the happiness of being freely, voluntarily united to Him and to each other in an ecstasy of love and delight compared with which the most rapturous love between a man and a woman on this earth is mere milk and water."[8]

In 2014, Victoria Osteen, wife of megachurch pastor Joel Osteen, made a statement that went viral and was highly criticized on hundreds of Christian blogs. She said,

> I just want to encourage every one of us to realize when we obey God, we're
> not doing it for God—I mean, that's one way to look at it—we're doing it for

ourselves, because God takes pleasure when we're happy. . . . That's the thing that gives Him the greatest joy. . . . Just do good for your own self. Do good because God wants you to be happy. . . . When you come to church, when you worship Him, you're not doing it for God really. You're doing it for yourself, because that's what makes God happy. Amen?[9]

She didn't get many amens online. The statement "When we obey God, we're not doing it for God" is certainly misguided. Whatever we do, we should do it out of love for God (see Matthew 22:37), fear of God (see 1 Peter 2:17), a desire to glorify God (see 1 Corinthians 10:31), and a longing to please God (see 1 John 3:22).

But had Victoria Osteen said, "When we obey God we do it first for him, but *also* for ourselves," that would be biblical. We should seek to please and find pleasure in God, and we're right to oppose the superficial self-centered happiness of prosperity theology. But we're wrong to suppose that God doesn't care about our happiness.

Most critics failed to recognize the nugget of truth in her statement. Obeying God and worshiping him really *should* make us happy! And God finds pleasure in that kind of happiness. "Praise the LORD, for the LORD is good; sing praises to His name, for it is pleasant" (Psalm 135:3, NKJV). Whom is it pleasant for? Hopefully for God, but the inspired text speaks of *our* pleasure in worshiping God.

SCRIPTURE'S GOOD NEWS IS OF "GREAT JOY," NOT "GREAT DUTY."

Mike Mason writes, "No one would become a Christian if this hard decision were not accompanied by stupendous joy."[10]

The Puritans, never accused of being trendy, talked a great deal about Christian happiness. Scottish theologian Samuel Rutherford (1600–1661) wrote to Lady Kenmure, "I have neither tongue nor pen to express to you the happiness of such as are in Christ."[11]

Baptist pastor Octavius Winslow (1808–1878) said, "The child of God is, from necessity, a joyful man. His sins are forgiven, his soul is justified, his person is adopted, his trials are blessings, his conflicts are victories, his death is immortality, his future is a heaven of inconceivable, unthought-of, untold, and endless blessedness—with such a God, such a Saviour, and such a hope, is he not, ought he not, to be a *joyful* man?"[12] It was a rhetorical question—who could possibly have more reason to rejoice than one who knows Jesus?

When the gospel is viewed primarily as laying burdens and obligations on people, the Good News gets buried. Burdens and obligations are not good news; good news is about liberation, deliverance, newfound delight, and daily celebration. Sure, duty is real and the gospel calls us to a life of obedience, but it's *glad* duty and *joyful* obedience.

There's an age-old tradition of Christ-followers who have found their deepest happiness in their Lord. We should eagerly join them and say with English Puritan John Flavel (1627–1691), "Christ [is] the very essence of all delights and pleasures, the very soul and substance of them. As all the rivers are gathered into the ocean . . . so Christ is that ocean in which all true delights and pleasures meet."[13]

CHAPTER 4

WHY DOES OUR HAPPINESS MATTER?

All the people of Judah were happy because they had made this covenant with all their heart.
They took delight in worshiping the LORD, and he accepted them and gave them peace on every side.
2 CHRONICLES 15:15, GNT

Affirming that by transgression of God's commandments [Adam and Eve] might attain to
felicity and joy . . . [the devil] caused them to seek life where God had pronounced death to be.
JOHN KNOX

CHRISTOPHER PARKENING, CONSIDERED by many to be the world's greatest classical guitarist, achieved his musical dreams by the age of thirty. By then he was also a world-class fly-fishing champion.

However, his successes failed to bring him happiness. Weary of performances and recording sessions, Parkening bought a ranch and gave up on the guitar. But instead of finding happiness after getting away from it all, his life became increasingly empty. He wrote, "If you arrive at a point in your life where you have everything that you've ever wanted and thought would make you happy and it still doesn't, then you start questioning things. It's the pot of gold at the end of the rainbow. I had that and I thought, 'Well, what's left?'"

While visiting friends, he attended church and put his faith in Christ. Parkening developed a hunger for Scripture and was struck by 1 Corinthians 10:31: "Whatever you do, do it all for the glory of God" (NIV).

He explains, "I realized there were only two things I knew how to do: fly fish for trout and play the guitar. Well, I am playing the guitar today absolutely by the grace of God. . . . I have a joy, a peace, and a deep-down fulfillment in my life I never had before. My life has purpose. . . . I've learned first-hand the true secret of genuine happiness."[1]

THE WORLD HAS DIVORCED CHRISTIANITY FROM HAPPINESS . . . AND CHRIST-FOLLOWERS ARE PARTLY RESPONSIBLE.

G. K. Chesterton (1874–1936) has been widely credited with saying, "Jesus promised His disciples three things—that they would be completely fearless, absurdly happy, and in constant trouble." It might be argued that most Western Christians aren't any of these three . . . but least of all "absurdly happy."

Christianity is perceived to be about tradition and morality, not happiness. I've taught college courses on biblical ethics, and I make no apologies for believing in morality. But some Christians, in the name of moral obligation, go around with frowns on their faces, dutifully living a paint-by-the-numbers religious existence, and proudly refraining from what "lesser" people do to be happy. They seem to wear their displeasure as a badge of honor.

Hannah Whitall Smith (1832–1911), author of *The Christian's Secret of a Happy Life*, was raised in a religious home. She recorded these thoughts about churchgoers in her journal, years before coming to Christ:

> Some look almost as if they think it is a sin to smile or speak a pleasant word. It appears to me that religion is supposed to make one happy, not miserable and disagreeable. . . . Instead of a cheerful voice there is a long, drawing, melancholy whisper . . . instead of love and concern for those who have not yet found the path of life . . . there is a cool standoffishness, a feeling of "I'm better than you"— that effectually closes off the slightest opening. Instead of a winning gentleness and loving kindness to those around them, there is a kind of hidden snappishness and a continual comparing of oneself with them, followed by a disagreeable dictatorianism. And so, instead of the noble, beautiful, humble, liberal-minded, and happy religion I have so often pictured to myself, I see it as cross, gloomy, proud, bigoted, and narrow minded.[2]

Sadly, some people still misrepresent Christianity this way, and equally sadly, some attempt to solve the problem not by drawing near to Christ but by watering down biblical truth to make it more appealing. The gospel is attacked on both fronts—on the one hand, stripped of its intrinsic happiness and on the other, stripped of its holy uniqueness and ability to deliver happiness.

After her conversion, Smith wrote to her son, "The Gospel is good news, something to make people happy; not a law to bind them."[3]

Gloomy Christians don't win friends or attract others. C. S. Lewis said, "Morality or duty . . . never yet made a man happy in himself or dear to others."[4]

British preacher J. C. Ryle put it this way:

> Will it increase a man's happiness to be converted? . . . [People] have a secret, lurking fear, that if they are converted they must become melancholy, miserable, and low-spirited. Conversion and a sour face, conversion and a gloomy brow, conversion and an ill-natured readiness to snub young people, and put down all mirth . . . conversion and sighing and groaning—all these are things which they seem to think must go together! No wonder that such people shrink from the idea of conversion![5]

There are valid reasons why unbelievers fear that becoming a Christian will result in their unhappiness. They've known—as many of us churchgoers have also known—professing Christians who go out of their way to promote misery, not gladness. I've seen Bible-believing, Christ-centered people post thoughts on a blog or on social media only to receive a string of hypercritical responses from people who wield Scripture verses like pickaxes, swiftly condemning the slightest hint of a viewpoint they consider suspicious. Others quickly join the fray, and soon it appears that no one has bothered to read what the blogger actually said. Responders assume the worst, not giving the benefit of the doubt and engaging in shotgun-style character assassination. If I were an unbeliever reading such responses, I certainly wouldn't be drawn to the Christian faith.

I wonder why it's not immediately recognized by those engaging in such behavior that what they're doing is utterly contrary to the faith they profess and the Bible they believe. How is it that perpetual disdain, suspicion, unkindness, and hostility are seen as taking the spiritual high ground? Perhaps the message that Christians shouldn't be happy has really been taken to heart! Hence, curmudgeon Christianity abounds.

In refreshing contrast, J. C. Ryle said, "I assert without hesitation, that the conversion described in Scripture is a happy thing and not a miserable one, and that if converted persons are not happy, the fault must be in themselves. . . . I am confident the converted man is the happiest man."[6]

Spurgeon loved to connect the gospel and happiness: "There is nothing that more tends to strengthen the faith of the young believer than to hear the veteran Christian, covered with scars from the battle, testifying that the service of his Master is a happy service, and that, if he could have served any other master, he would not have done so, for His service is pleasant, and His reward everlasting joy."[7]

Ryle and Spurgeon cared about biblical orthodoxy and sound doctrine, but they were full of not only truth but also grace.

TOO OFTEN, BELIEVERS REINFORCE THE STEREOTYPE THAT CHRISTIAN LIVING BRINGS UNHAPPINESS.

Some professing Christians feel morally superior to those who engage with culture, and as a result, they major on making world-condemning judgments. They refrain from laughing not just at immoral jokes but *any* jokes. They assume that barbecues and ball games are the spawn of sin. Grim-faced pharisaical "Christians" make Satan's propaganda campaign far easier by undermining the Good News and promoting a negative view of happiness.

Who would ever be drawn to the worldview of decidedly unhappy people? Consider satirist and journalist H. L. Mencken's (1880–1956) definition of Puritanism as "the haunting fear that someone, somewhere, may be happy."[8] (On the contrary, Puritans, judging by their writings, were some of the happiest people who have ever lived! *Considerably* happier, judging by their writings, than H. L. Mencken.)

In 1898, during an era when debunking Christianity was becoming fashionable, an article in the *Freethinker* made this claim about the Bible:

There is one fact connected with the Bible which condemns it. . . . It is this: There is not a smile in it. . . . Life, fashioned after the teachings of the Bible, would have no sweetness in it. . . . You cannot find a text in the Bible for a sermon on real human happiness. In fact, I believe that the word "happiness" is not to be found anywhere in the volume. One cannot find any helps to happiness in a book which says nothing about happiness.[9]

Part 3 of this book is filled with what the Bible says about happiness, proving how ludicrous this statement is. Yet I've heard people today—believers and unbelievers alike—make the same claim!

John Piper says, "If you ask me, 'Doesn't the world need to see Christians as happy in order to know the truth of our faith and be drawn to the great Savior?' my answer is 'Yes, yes, yes!' And they need to see that our happiness is the indomitable work of Christ in the midst of our sorrow."[10]

Happiness in Christ is one of our most powerful evangelistic tools.

BECAUSE EVERY TEMPTATION INVOLVES A PROMISE OF HAPPINESS, THE IDEA OF HAPPINESS SUFFERS GUILT BY ASSOCIATION.

Former NFL quarterback and ESPN commentator Joe Theismann explained to his soon-to-be-ex-wife why he'd had an affair: "God wants Joe Theismann to be happy."[11]

Theismann's story demonstrates why happiness suffers a bad reputation. Those who say, "It's my turn to be happy now" can rationalize nearly any sin.

Anyone who has tasted rotten fruit is right to object to rottenness. But they're wrong to object to fruit itself! There's good fruit and bad fruit. There's righteous happiness and sinful happiness.

God created the physical world and happiness. But the devil doesn't have a single shred of happiness to give. We won't want a thing he offers unless we are deceived into thinking it will make us happy. The devil specializes in rearranging price tags, making the cheap look valuable and the miserable appear happy. (For example, if, before the purchase, people saw photos of themselves after five years of using methamphetamines, would they still buy them?)

UNBELIEVERS OFTEN SEE CHRISTIANITY AS A DREARY FAITH.

Paul returned to Jerusalem to discuss with church leaders the explosive issue of whether Gentiles should be required to keep the Jewish law, including rules about circumcision and dietary restrictions. This was a heated issue in the early church, with generations of tradition on the line. Luke describes what could have been a tense encounter: "When we had come to Jerusalem, the brothers received us gladly" (Acts 21:17). A Bible translation lexicon states, "The word *asmenos* here means 'pertaining to experiencing happiness, implying ready and willing acceptance—happily, gladly.'"[12]

This exuberant welcome is followed by stories of the gospel's impact on the Gentiles and a celebration of how the Holy Spirit was strengthening Christ's church. Such a happy gathering is a timeless model for believers in any era who face difficult issues.

The pervasive happiness of the New Testament church stands in stark contrast to what the English poet Algernon Swinburne (1837–1909) said about Jesus: "Thou hast conquered, O pale Galilean: The world has grown grey from thy breath."[13] Swinburne believed Jesus sucked the life out of the supposed vibrancy paganism had infused into the world.

G. K. Chesterton commented on Swinburne's words:

> I rolled on my tongue with a terrible joy, as did all young men of that time, the taunts which Swinburne hurled at the dreariness of the creed. . . . But when I read the same poet's accounts of paganism . . . I gathered that the world was, if possible, more gray before the Galilean breathed on it than afterwards. The poet maintained . . . that life itself was pitch dark. . . . The very man who denounced Christianity for pessimism was himself a pessimist . . . and it did for one wild moment cross my mind that, perhaps, those might not be the very best judges of the relation of religion to happiness who, by their own account, had neither one nor the other.[14]

In most unbelievers' perceptions, Christianity hasn't brought much joy to the world. As a religion, it's primarily known for its rules, self-righteousness, and intolerance—none of which convey gladness and merriment.

This is not the whole story, of course. Throughout history, the Christian worldview has accounted for such happiness-generating developments as hospitals and schools, science and industry, music, drama, and the arts. And on a more personal level, nearly every community includes people with quiet confidence in Christ who are extraordinarily loving, kind, helpful, and cheerful. They gladly give of their time and money to those in need. Such people are rarely in the public eye, but they certainly exist. Sadly, however, to many people, they seem to be the exception rather than the rule.

FINDING OUR GREATEST HAPPINESS IN GOD FREES US TO ENJOY AND APPRECIATE HIS CREATION.

C. S. Lewis wrote,

> If there lurks in most modern minds the notion that to desire our own good and earnestly to hope for the enjoyment of it is a bad thing, I submit that this notion . . . is no part of the Christian faith. Indeed, if we consider the unblushing promises of reward and the staggering nature of the rewards promised in the Gospels, it would seem that Our Lord finds our desires, not too strong, but too weak. We are half-hearted creatures, fooling about with drink and sex and ambition when infinite joy is offered us, like an ignorant child who wants to go on making mud pies in a slum because he cannot imagine what is meant by the offer of a holiday at the sea. We are far too easily pleased.[15]

When I first read these words, having known Christ for only a few years, it was paradigm shifting. In my brief church experience, I'd come to believe that God was opposed to our pursuit of happiness. When I delighted in something "secular," such as music or science fiction, I felt vaguely guilty, as if my pleasure displeased God.

But Lewis had a different perspective. He wasn't saying that alcohol, sex, and ambition were wrong, only that God—who created these things—deserves the highest place in our hearts. While we can enjoy the gifts God has given us in the appropriate time and place, they will never be able to give us the deep happiness and satisfaction we find in him. Finding our greatest pleasure in God elevates our enjoyment of those happiness-giving things. They're transformed from mud pies to mouthwatering desserts to be fully enjoyed—at the proper time and place—at the celebratory table of God's goodness.

When I was a young Christian, one of the hymns often sung at my church featured these words:

> *Turn your eyes upon Jesus,*
> *Look full in his wonderful face,*
> *And the things of earth will grow strangely dim,*
> *In the light of his glory and grace.*[16]

If the things of Earth were all sinful, those words would make sense. But shouldn't drawing close to our Creator make the beauties and wonders of his Earth brighter to us, not dimmer?

After coming to Christ, Jonathan Edwards commented on that very topic:

> The appearance of everything was altered; there seemed to be, as it were, a calm, sweet cast or appearance of divine glory in almost everything. God's excellency, his wisdom, his purity and love, seemed to appear in everything; in the sun, moon, and stars; in the clouds and blue sky; in the grass, flowers, trees; in the water and all nature.[17]

As I've walked with God over the years, the sin-centered and shallow attractions of this Earth have indeed grown dimmer, but the happy-making beauty of this Earth's animals, trees, flowers, oceans, and sky, and of friends, family, good stories, music, and food have grown brighter.

Thomas Aquinas (1225–1274), the most influential theologian of the Middle Ages, said, "No one can live without delight, and that is why a man deprived of spiritual joy goes over to carnal pleasures."[18] We crave joy, delight, pleasure—in a word: happiness.

Being happy in God and living righteously tastes far better for far longer than sin does. When my hunger and thirst for joy is satisfied by Christ, sin becomes unattractive. I say no to immorality not because I hate pleasure but because I want the enduring pleasure found in Christ.

THE GREAT THEOLOGIANS HAVE ALWAYS BEEN HAPPINESS ADVOCATES.

I don't agree with all the beliefs of various historical figures I cite. But given their stature as serious thinkers of great influence on church and culture, they serve as proof that preoccupation with happiness is not just a modern development.

Ignatius of Antioch (35–117), believed to be a student of the apostle John, wrote a letter beginning with these words: "To the Church which is at Ephesus . . . deservedly most happy. . . . Abundant happiness through Jesus Christ, and His undefiled joy."[19] Another letter is addressed, "To her who is worthy of happiness; to her who is at Ephesus, in Jesus Christ, in joy which is unblameable: abundance of happiness."[20]

Ignatius wishes the same "abundance of happiness" when he writes to the early church bishop and eventual martyr Polycarp.[21] He closes that letter saying, "I pray for your happiness for ever in our God, Jesus Christ."[22]

What would we think of a modern Christian who begins and ends his letters fixated on happiness? Ignatius, in the first century, must have understood something about happiness in Christ that we don't.

The pre-Christian Augustine was an intellectual who chose an immoral life for the same reason others did and still do—happiness. Yet happiness eluded him. Augustine said, "Certainly by sinning we lost both piety and happiness; but when we lost happiness, we did not lose the love of it."[23] Augustine insisted that this longing is as true for Christ-followers as it is for anyone else: "If I should ask you why you believe in Christ, and why you have become Christians, every man will answer truthfully by saying: for the sake of a happy life. The pursuit of a happy life is common to philosophers and to Christians."[24]

If Augustine was right, then whether people go to church, a coffee shop, a ball game, a crack house, or a strip club, they go in search of happiness. Augustine didn't mean that their search is always successful. He said, "Indeed, man wishes to be happy even when he so lives as to make happiness impossible."[25]

This description is true for every culture after the Fall. We wish to be happy above all, even while making choices that rob us of exactly what we seek.

Cyprian of Carthage (672–735) wrote of God, "He opens to us the way of life; He brings us back to paradise. . . . We Christians shall be . . . always rejoicing with perpetual pleasures in the sight of God, and ever giving thanks to God. For none can be other than always glad and grateful who, having been once subject to death, has been made secure in the possession of immortality."[26]

Thomas Aquinas wrote, "Man is unable not to wish to be happy."[27] This means that all attempts by Christians to disregard or demean happiness are misguided and unfruitful. By creating distance between the gospel and happiness, we send the unbiblical (and historically ungrounded) message that the Christian faith is dull and dreary. We should speak against sin but hold up Christ as the happiness everyone longs for. If we don't, then we are responsible for the world's perception that Christianity takes away happiness instead of bringing it.

THROUGHOUT HISTORY, GOD'S PEOPLE HAVE AGREED THAT OUR QUEST FOR HAPPINESS CAN BE FULFILLED IN CHRIST.

The belief that Christ is the answer to our deep longing for happiness can be credited to scholars, preachers, and teachers from every generation and from all denominational backgrounds.

German Reformer Martin Luther (1483–1546) said, "It is pleasing to the dear God whenever thou rejoicest or laughest from the bottom of thy heart."[28]

French Reformer John Calvin (1509–1564) wrote, "Human happiness . . . is to be united with God. . . . The chief activity of the soul is to aspire thither."[29]

Jonathan Edwards said, "Jesus knew that all mankind were in the pursuit of happiness. He has directed them in the true way to it, and He tells them what they must become in order to be blessed and happy."[30] Edwards expounded on his point further: "What could the most merciful being have done more for our encouragement? All that he desires of us is that we would not be miserable, that we would not follow those courses which of themselves would end in misery, and that we would be happy."[31]

These are not the words of a suntanned, jewelry-laden inspirational speaker. This is a Puritan pastor, steeped in Scripture, speaking nearly three hundred years ago! And what was he saying? That God's desire is to deliver us from misery and make us happy.

Any objections?

Puritan Thomas Watson wrote, "God has twisted together his glory and our good." He argued that God says to us, "The more happiness you have, the more I shall count myself glorified."[32]

Blaise Pascal, who said, "All men seek happiness," continued with these words:

> Whatever different means they employ, they all tend to this end. The cause of some going to war, and of others avoiding it, is the same desire in both, attended with different views. The will never takes the least step but to this object. This is the motive of every action of every man, *even of those who hang themselves.*[33]

Pascal is saying that those who commit suicide are actually seeking happiness—or to be relieved of unhappiness. That claim is compelling and shocking, but it rings true.

I suspect that Pascal had been reading Aquinas, who six hundred years earlier said, "The last end [goal] of human life is . . . happiness." Aquinas went on to say, "No man wills and works evil to himself, except he apprehend it under the aspect of good. For even they who kill themselves, apprehend death itself as a good, considered as putting an end to some unhappiness or pain."[34]

Thoughtful Christ-followers have long addressed the great lengths people will go to pursue what they *think* will bring them happiness.

CHRISTIANS OF DIFFERENT DOCTRINAL TRADITIONS EMPHASIZE THE HAPPINESS OF LIFE IN CHRIST.

English evangelist John Wesley (1703–1791), perhaps the most prominent leader in the Arminian tradition, wrote, "Give a man every thing that this world can give . . . something *is wanting!* That *something* is neither more nor less, than the knowledge and love of God; without which no spirit can be happy either in heaven or earth."[35]

I can relate to Wesley when he spoke of his state as an unbeliever:

Having plenty of all things, in the midst of sensible and amiable friends . . . still I was not happy. I wondered why I was not, and could not imagine what the reason was. The reason certainly was, I did not know God, the Source of present as well as eternal happiness.[36]

Notice Wesley's emphasis. Happiness doesn't merely await God's children in the future. Even in a world filled with hardship and suffering, God's presence brings incomparable happiness to all who know him. Christ-followers don't preach the flimsy kind of happiness that's built on wishful thinking. Instead, we have rock-solid reasons to be happy people— reasons that remain true, and sometimes become clearer, in suffering.

Wesley said, "Nothing is so small or insignificant in the sight of men, as not to be an object of the care and Providence of God; before whom, nothing is small that concerns the happiness of any of his creatures."[37]

Calvinist Charles Spurgeon wrote,

The thought of *delight* in religion is so strange to most men, that no two words in their language stand further apart than "holiness" and "delight." . . . They who love God with all their hearts, find that his ways are ways of pleasantness, and all his paths are peace. . . . We are not dragged to holiness, nor driven to duty. No, our piety is our pleasure, our hope is our happiness, our duty is our delight.[38]

Though Wesley and Spurgeon represented different theological persuasions, they agreed with these ideas:

1. All people desire happiness.
2. The gospel of Jesus Christ offers people both eternal happiness *and* present happiness.
3. People are drawn to Christ when they see true happiness in his followers and are pushed away when they see us chronically unhappy.
4. God is the sole origin of true happiness, and we should wholeheartedly seek our delight in him.

THE VALUE OF OUR HAPPINESS DEPENDS ON WHAT WE COMPARE IT TO.

If we weigh the value of our happiness against the needs of a suffering world, we may suppose we have no right to be happy. But the fact is, miserable Christians have nothing to offer a suffering world. Our happiness in Christ, which involves not indifference but heartfelt compassion, allows us to help others and share with them the joy in Christ. It is this same happiness that energizes and sustains us as we serve God and others.

Of course, if we compare the value of our happiness to the value of God and his glory, our happiness is infinitely outweighed. But the same is true of everything else. Just because God and his glory are infinitely more important than our families, friendships, churches, and jobs, that doesn't mean any of those are unimportant. Indeed, God himself tells us they are important.

Such a comparison also makes the false assumption that God's glory and our happiness fall on two different sides of a balance, to be weighed against each other. On the contrary, they are inextricably linked—both are parts of his design and plan. God is glorified when we are happy in him, so our happiness shouldn't be weighed against his glory but seen as part of it.

Rather than minimizing our happiness in comparison to him, we should see God as desiring our happiness—being the source of it and going to inconceivable lengths to bring his happiness to us.

This is what makes our happiness in God immensely important. Not first and foremost because *we* want to be happy (though of course we do), but because *God* made us to want to be happy and because he himself truly wants us to be happy.

CHAPTER 5

WHAT'S THE DIFFERENCE BETWEEN JOY AND HAPPINESS?

The godly are happy; they rejoice before God and are overcome with joy.

PSALM 68:3, NET

My dear brothers and sisters, if anybody in the world ought to be happy, we are the people. . . . How boundless our privileges! How brilliant our hopes!

CHARLES SPURGEON

IN THE THREE years I've spent researching and writing this book, I've had dozens of nearly identical conversations.

Someone asks, "What are you writing about?"

I respond, "Happiness."

Unbelievers are immediately interested.

Believers typically give me an odd look, as if to say, "Don't you usually write on *spiritual* themes?"

They often say, "You said *happiness*—did you mean *joy*?"

A pastor friend wrote to tell me why it would be a big mistake to write a book about happiness: "Happiness changes from moment to moment and is reflected by our moods and emotions. Joy is a spiritual peace and contentment that only comes from God and is strong even during times of sadness. God's desire is not to make us happy in this life but to fill our lives with joy as a result of our relationship with Christ."

Since many readers have been taught to think the same way as my pastor friend, I'll start the conversation now, then finish it in part 4.

WHY USE THE TERM *HAPPINESS* RATHER THAN *JOY*?

First, happiness covers more ground—it's the broader, more familiar term, used in philosophy, theology, and common speech.

Second, an ungrounded, dangerous separation of joy from happiness has infiltrated the Christian community. In this book, I'm trying to do my part to reclaim the territory Christians have relinquished in the conversation about happiness, which is vitally important in any worldview.

Third, the word *happiness* has historically had a common meaning for both believers and unbelievers—and for many it still does. Until recent decades, it's been a bridge between the church and world—one we can't afford to burn.

Joy is a perfectly good word, and I use it frequently. But there are other equally good words with overlapping meanings, including *happiness*, *gladness*, *merriment*, *delight*, and *pleasure*.

John Piper writes, "If you have nice little categories for 'joy is what Christians have' and 'happiness is what the world has,' you can scrap those when you go to the Bible, because the Bible is indiscriminate in its uses of the language of happiness and joy and contentment and satisfaction."[1]

The Bible often employs parallelisms: words with similar meanings used in close proximity to reinforce their meaning. We do the same. If someone says, "I expected the party to be fun and exciting, but it turned out dull and boring," the words *fun* and *exciting* are synonyms, as are *dull* and *boring*; they reinforce each other.

To demonstrate the close relationship between joy and happiness, I've chosen a small sampling of the more than one hundred verses in various translations that use joy and happiness together. None of these versions are paraphrases; each was translated by highly skilled teams of Hebrew and Greek scholars who finally agreed on the wording of each verse. As you read, note that *joy* and *happiness* in these passages are clearly synonyms. In each case I've italicized these words for emphasis:

New International Version
- For the Jews it was a time of *happiness* and *joy*, gladness and honor. (Esther 8:16)
- May the righteous be glad and rejoice before God; may they be *happy* and *joyful*. (Psalm 68:3)
- This is what the LORD Almighty says: "The fasts . . . will become *joyful* and glad occasions and *happy* festivals for Judah." (Zechariah 8:19)

Holman Christian Standard Bible
- The *joy* of the wicked has been brief and the *happiness* of the godless has lasted only a moment. (Job 20:5)
- *Happy* are the people who know the *joyful* shout; Yahweh, they walk in the light of Your presence. (Psalm 89:15)
- The young women will rejoice with dancing, while young and old men rejoice together. I will turn their mourning into *joy* . . . and bring *happiness* out of grief. (Jeremiah 31:13)

New Living Translation
- Give your father and mother *joy*! May she who gave you birth be *happy*. (Proverbs 23:25)

- Eat your food with *joy*, and drink your wine with a *happy* heart, for God approves of this! (Ecclesiastes 9:7)
- Be glad; rejoice forever in my creation! And look! I will create Jerusalem as a place of *happiness*. Her people will be a source of *joy*. (Isaiah 65:18)

God's Word Translation
- You didn't serve the LORD your God with a *joyful* and *happy* heart when you had so much. (Deuteronomy 28:47)
- The people ransomed by the LORD . . . will come to Zion singing with *joy*. Everlasting *happiness* will be on their heads as a crown. They will be glad and *joyful*. They will have no sorrow or grief. (Isaiah 35:10)
- You don't see [Christ] now, but you believe in him. You are extremely *happy* with *joy* and praise. (1 Peter 1:8)

New English Translation
- You, O LORD, have made me *happy* by your work. I will sing for *joy* because of what you have done. (Psalm 92:4)
- Rejoice in the LORD and be *happy*, you who are godly! Shout for *joy*. (Psalm 32:11)
- Satisfy us in the morning with your loyal love! Then we will shout for *joy* and be *happy* all our days! (Psalm 90:14)

New Century Version
- Solomon sent the people home, full of *joy*. They were *happy* because the LORD had been so good. (2 Chronicles 7:10)
- [The believers] ate together in their homes, *happy* to share their food with *joyful* hearts. (Acts 2:46)
- If I have to offer my own blood with your sacrifice, I will be *happy* and full of *joy* with all of you. (Philippians 2:17)

Good News Translation
- Hannah prayed: "The LORD has filled my heart with *joy*; how *happy* I am because of what he has done!" (1 Samuel 2:1)
- When they saw [the star], how *happy* [the wise men] were, what *joy* was theirs! (Matthew 2:9-10)
- That day many sacrifices were offered, and the people were full of *joy* because God had made them very *happy*. (Nehemiah 12:43)

The relationship between joy and happiness in these passages refutes two common claims: (1) that the Bible doesn't talk about happiness, and (2) that joy and happiness have contrasting meanings.

In fact, the Bible overflows with accounts of God's people being happy in him. (These examples only skim the surface, as part 3 will demonstrate.)

WHY TAKE THE HAPPINESS OUT OF JOY?

The "weeping prophet" experienced times of great gladness: "I belong to you, LORD God Almighty, and so your words filled my heart with joy and happiness" (Jeremiah 15:16, GNT). Not joy instead of happiness, but joy *and* happiness.

Depicting joy in contrast with happiness has obscured the true meaning of both words. Joyful people are typically glad and cheerful—they smile and laugh a lot. To put it plainly, they're *happy*!

The following is typical of the artificial distinctions made by modern Christians:

Joy is something entirely different from happiness. Joy, in the Biblical context, is not an emotion. . . . Joy brings us peace in the middle of a storm. Joy is something that God deposits into us through the Holy Spirit. . . . There is a big difference between joy and happiness. Happiness is an emotion and temporary; joy is an attitude of the heart.[2]

Judging from such articles (and there are hundreds more out there), you'd think the distinction between joy and happiness is biblical. It's not.

THERE'S A LONG, RICH HISTORY OF EQUATING JOY WITH HAPPINESS IN CHRIST.

Jonathan Edwards cited John 15:11 ("that [Jesus'] joy might remain in you," KJV) to prove this point: "The happiness Christ gives to his people, is a participation of his own happiness." Edwards wrote of "the joy and happiness that the church shall have in her true bridegroom"[3] and spoke of believers as "these joyful happy persons."[4] Edwards used the words *joyful* and *happy* to reinforce, not contrast, each other.

Puritan pastor Richard Baxter (1615–1691) said, "The day of death is to true believers a day of happiness and joy."[5] William Law (1686–1761), an Anglican church leader, said believers should "never want [lack] the happiness of a lively faith, a joyful hope, and well-grounded trust in God. If we are to pray often, 'tis that we may be often happy in such secret joys as only prayer can give."[6]

These highly influential writers used joy and happiness as synonyms.

Charles Spurgeon made the following statements about happiness and joy:

- The more often I preached, the more joy I found in the happy service.[7]
- Despite your tribulation, take full delight in God your exceeding joy this morning, and be happy in Him.[8]
- O cheerful, happy, joyous people, I wish there were more of you! . . . Let the uppermost joy you have always be "Jesus Christ, Himself."[9]
- May you so come, and then may your Christian life be fraught with happiness, and overflowing with joy.[10]

Spurgeon's views of happiness and joy, evident in hundreds of his sermons, are completely contrary to the artificial wall the contemporary church has erected between joy and happiness.

Susanna Wesley wrote to her son John in 1735, shortly after his father died, "God . . . is so infinitely blessed [happy], that . . . every perception of his blissful presence imparts a vital gladness to the heart. Every degree of approach toward him is, in the same proportion, a degree of happiness."[11] Notice the interchangeability of these words of delight. Susanna Wesley piled synonyms one upon another—"blissful presence," "vital gladness," and "happiness"—to express her overflowing pleasure in God. Not once in her statement did she use the word many today consider most spiritual: *joy.*

OPPOSITION TO THE WORD *HAPPINESS* IS A RECENT DEVELOPMENT IN THE CHURCH.

In stark contrast to believers prior to the twentieth century, many modern Christians have portrayed happiness as, at best, inferior to joy and, at worst, evil. Oswald Chambers (1874–1917), whom I greatly respect, is one of the earliest Bible teachers to have spoken against happiness. Chambers wrote, "Happiness is no standard for men and women because happiness depends on my being determinedly ignorant of God and His demands."[12]

After extensive research, I'm convinced that no biblical or historical basis exists to define happiness as inherently sinful. Unfortunately, because Bible teachers such as Chambers saw people trying to find happiness in sin, they concluded that pursuing happiness was sinful.

My first pastor often cited Oswald Chambers's *My Utmost for His Highest*, and I eagerly read that great book as a young Christian. But at the time I didn't know enough to disagree with his statement: "Joy should not be confused with happiness. In fact, it is an insult to Jesus Christ to use the word happiness in connection with Him."[13] I certainly didn't want to insult Jesus, so after reading this and many similar statements, I became wary of happiness.

These proclamations were common enough that it seemed they must be right. But they made me uneasy, because before reading such things and hearing them from the pulpit, I had celebrated my newfound happiness in Christ. Now I was being told that happiness was at least suspect and apparently even unspiritual, and shouldn't be part of a serious Christian life.

To me, this was counterintuitive. Of course, we shouldn't turn to sin for happiness—but happiness was something I gained when I came to Christ, not something I gave up! If it was God who made me happy to be forgiven and gave me the joy of a right relationship with him and the privilege of walking with him and serving him, was God really against my happiness?

Chambers said, "Joy is not happiness; there is no mention in the Bible of happiness for a Christian, but there is plenty said about joy."[14] The problem with that statement is that it simply isn't true. Along with the twenty-one passages cited previously, there are hundreds of other verses that disprove it.

In the King James Version, which Chambers used, Jesus tells his disciples, "If ye know these things, happy are ye if ye do them" (John 13:17). The apostle Paul wrote these words to Christians: "Happy is he that condemneth not himself in that thing which he alloweth" (Romans 14:22). Speaking of faithful Christians, James said, "We count them happy which endure" (James 5:11). Peter said to fellow believers, "If ye suffer for righteousness' sake, happy are ye," and "If ye be reproached for the name of Christ, happy are ye" (1 Peter 3:14; 4:14).

How then could Oswald Chambers, a truly great Bible teacher and Christ-follower, claim that "there is no mention in the Bible of happiness for a Christian"?

It's important to understand that Chambers isn't alone—it's common to hear people make claims like this: "Joy is in 155 verses in the KJV Bible, happiness isn't in the Bible."[15] That may be technically true, but as we've just seen, *happy* is found in the King James Version—a total of twenty-nine times. Just as *holy* speaks of holiness and *joyful* speaks of joy and *glad* speaks of gladness, obviously *happy* speaks of happiness!

So why did Chambers say, "Holiness of character, chastity of life, living in communion with God—that is the end of a man's life, whether he is happy or not is a matter of moonshine"?[16]

Regardless of the arguments made from the pulpit and Christian books and in personal conversations, *people have always wanted to be happy—and they always will*. So when we hear that we shouldn't want to be happy, it doesn't change a thing, except to make us feel guilty and hopeless as we continue to desire and pursue happiness.

Forcing a choice between happiness and holiness is utterly foreign to the biblical worldview. If it were true that God only commands us to be holy, wouldn't we expect Philippians 4:4 to say, "Be holy in the Lord always" instead of "Rejoice in the Lord always"?

A. W. Tozer said, "The people of God ought to be the happiest people in all the wide world!"[17] He offered this explanation:

> Goodness is that in God which desires the happiness of His creatures and that irresistible urge in God to bestow blessedness [happiness]. The goodness of God takes pleasure in the pleasure of His people. . . . For a long time it has been drummed into us that if we are happy, God is worried about us. We believe He's never quite pleased if we are happy. But the strict, true teaching of the Word is that God takes pleasure in the pleasure of His people, provided His people take pleasure in God.[18]

IS IT TRUE THAT JOY IS NOT AN EMOTION?

A Christian writer says, "We don't get joy by seeking a better emotional life, because joy is not an emotion. It is a settled certainty that God is in control."[19] Another says, "Joy is not an emotion. It is a choice."[20]

The idea that "joy is not an emotion" (a statement that appears online more than 17,000 times) promotes an unbiblical myth.

A Bible study says, "Spiritual joy is not an emotion. It's a response to a Spirit-filled life."[21] But if this response doesn't involve emotions of happiness or gladness, what makes it joy?

Some claim that joy is a fruit of the Spirit, not an emotion. But in Galatians 5:22, *love* and *peace* surround the word *joy*. If you love someone, don't you feel something? What is peace if not something you feel?

Hannah Whitall Smith gave her son this advice:

> Say night and morning, and whenever through the day you think of it, "Dear Lord make me happy in you," and leave it there. All the rest will come out right

when once you are happy in Him. And this happiness will be the beginning; remember; "love, joy and peace" are the first fruits mentioned.[22]

A hundred years ago, every Christian knew the meaning of joy. Today, if you ask a group of Christians, "What does joy mean?" most will grope for words, with only one emphatic opinion: that joy is different from happiness. This is like saying that rain isn't wet or ice isn't cold. Scripture, dictionaries, and common language don't support this separation.

I googled "define joy," and the first result was this dictionary definition: "a feeling of great pleasure and happiness." This definition harmonizes with other dictionaries and ordinary conversations, yet it contradicts countless Christian books and sermons. The church's misguided distinction between joy and happiness has twisted the words. Christian psychiatrist George Vaillant says, "Happiness is secular, joy sacred."[23] So we should be joyful but not happy when reading the Bible, praying, and worshiping? Is the Christian life really divided into the secular and sacred, or is every part of our lives, even the ordinary moments, to be centered in God?

Here's just a tiny sampling of this misguided thinking:

- A book on Christian ministry has a chapter called "Happiness vs. Joy." It says, "Joy and happiness are very different."[24]
- In a chapter titled "Joy versus Happiness" a different Christian author states, "Happiness is a feeling, while joy is a state of being."[25]
- Another claims, "Joy is distinctly a Christian word and a Christian thing. It is the reverse of happiness."[26]
- In an article called "Jesus Doesn't Want You to Be Happy," the author states, "As you read through the gospels you'll see plenty of promises of joy, but none of happiness. And they are infinitely different things."[27]

Happiness is the *reverse* of joy? The two are *infinitely different*? Is there nothing more to joy than "a state of being"? Is emotion something we should reject, or is it a gift of God, part of being made in his likeness?

God created not only our minds but also our hearts. Sure, emotions can be manipulated, but so can intellects. God designed us to have emotions, and he doesn't want us to shun or disregard them. It's ill advised to redefine joy and happiness and pit them against each other rather than embracing the emotional satisfaction of knowing, loving, and following Jesus.

HAPPINESS IS NOT A FLUFFY IMITATION OF JOY BUT A SYNONYM FOR IT.

Consult English dictionaries and you'll see how contrived and artificial this supposed contrast between joy and happiness is. The first definition of joy in Merriam-Webster's dictionary is "a feeling of great happiness." Secondarily, it's defined as "a source or cause of great happiness."[28] The *American Heritage Dictionary* defines joy as "intense and especially ecstatic or exultant happiness."[29] The *Collins English Dictionary* defines joy as "a deep feeling or condition of happiness or contentment."[30]

What about Christian dictionaries? The *Evangelical Dictionary of Biblical Theology* defines joy as "happiness over an unanticipated or present good."[31] It says, "On the spiritual level [joy] refers to the extreme happiness with which the believer contemplates salvation and the bliss of the afterlife."[32]

The *Dictionary of Bible Themes* defines happiness as "a state of pleasure or joy experienced both by people and by God."[33] It also defines joy as "a quality or attitude of delight and happiness."[34] Happiness is joy. Joy is happiness. Virtually all dictionaries, whether secular or Christian, recognize this.

Consider our common expressions:

- "He jumped for joy."
- "That child is a bundle of joy."
- "He is our pride and joy."
- "I wept for joy."

Diagram 1 depicts the contrast between joy and happiness as portrayed by many Christians. Joy, they suppose, is something substantial yet lacking emotional dimension. Happiness is seen as lightweight and temporary—a cloud soon blown away by the wind of circumstances.

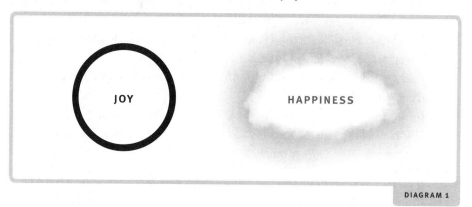

DIAGRAM 1

The contrast can be further portrayed as in diagram 2, with joy as three dimensional—something with depth. Happiness, meanwhile, is allegedly one dimensional and superficial.

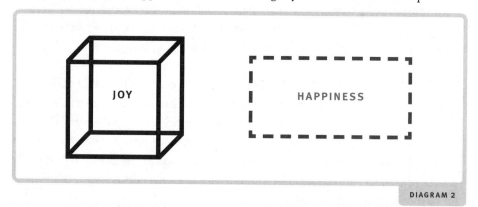

DIAGRAM 2

Diagram 3 shows joy and happiness as commonly seen by evangelical Christians (but few others). The two separate circles show joy in the upper position—closer to Heaven, further from Earth—and thereby superior to happiness. Happiness is lower, smaller, demoted, and inferior—earthly, not heavenly. (Again, this is not my position but the predominant one among many Christians.)

If these three views of the relationship between joy and happiness are wrong—and I'm convinced they are—then what is the right view? According to the vast majority of the usages of these two words in (1) English history, (2) English literature, (3) Bible translations, and (4) English dictionaries, the words are synonyms with predominantly overlapping meanings. They have far more in common with each other than not. Hence, I depict them as two predominantly overlapping circles.

This portrayal in diagram 4 stands in stark contrast to the modern evangelical belief about happiness—the one I was taught as a new Christian and have read and heard throughout my life. (I am an evangelical, so my issue isn't with evangelical theology in general but with this particular viewpoint on joy and happiness.)

This final illustration of overlapping word meanings includes not only *happy* and *joyful*, but also *glad*, *cheerful*, *delighted*, and *merry*. In part 3, I will show diagrams of Hebrew and Greek words used in Scripture that are similar to the English words in diagram 5. Later we'll also deal with the issue of semantic domains, or word families, which are vital to understand as we read our English Bibles.

If what I'm saying is true, and the sharp distinctions between joy and happiness are arbitrary and subjective, why do so many Christian authors, pastors, and teachers depart from the long-held understanding, as well as the common dictionary definitions, of joy and happiness?

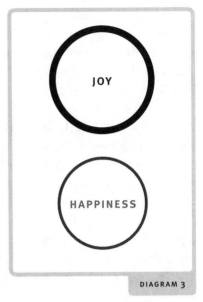

DIAGRAM 3

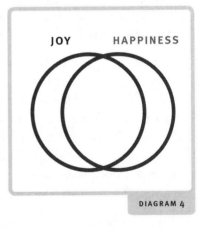

DIAGRAM 4

DIAGRAM 5

Many people I've talked with have the distinct impression that Scripture distinguishes between joy and happiness. They think the Bible depicts all joy as godly and all happiness as ungodly. In part 3, I will demonstrate, with a thorough study of the Bible's original languages, that this is a false impression. In fact, Scripture itself refutes the artificial distinction between happiness and joy.

WE CAN'T AFFORD TO DISTANCE HAPPINESS FROM A RELATIONSHIP WITH GOD.

Historically, philosophically, and practically, *happiness* is a vital word. The Greek and Latin counterparts were used by Aristotle, Plato, Augustine, and Aquinas. Its French equivalent was used by Pascal to speak of humankind's universal longing.

Jonathan Edwards said, "Happiness is the highest end [purpose] of the creation of the universe. . . . How happy . . . will be those intelligent beings that are to be made eternally happy!"[35] In other words, human beings are hardwired to long for happiness, and a relationship with God is the only way to truly fulfill that longing.

While writing this book, I read a devotional by Joni Eareckson Tada, whom I respect as a biblical thinker. I've become so accustomed to reading misstatements by contemporary Christians about joy and happiness that I cheered aloud when I read her words.

Tada opens by citing Psalm 68:3: "May the righteous be glad and rejoice before God; may they be happy and joyful" (NIV). She then writes:

> We're often taught to be careful of the difference between joy and happiness. Happiness, it is said, is an emotion that depends upon what "happens." Joy by contrast, is supposed to be enduring, stemming deep from within our soul and which is not affected by the circumstances surrounding us. . . . I don't think God had any such hair-splitting in mind. Scripture uses the terms interchangeably along with words like delight, gladness, blessed. There is no scale of relative spiritual values applied to any of these. Happiness is not relegated to fleshly-minded sinners nor joy to heaven-bound saints.[36]

Tada is absolutely right. Modern distinctions between happiness and joy are completely counterintuitive. This is no minor semantic issue. For too long we've distanced the gospel from what Augustine, Aquinas, Pascal, the Puritans, Wesley, Spurgeon, and many other spiritual giants said God created us to desire—and what he desires for us—happiness.

To declare joy sacred and happiness secular closes the door to dialogue with unbelievers. If someone is told that joy is the opposite of happiness, any thoughtful person would say, "In that case, I don't want joy!"

If we say the gospel won't bring happiness, any perceptive listener should respond, "Then how is it good news?"

We need to reverse the trend. Let's redeem the word *happiness* in light of both Scripture and church history. Our message shouldn't be "Don't seek happiness," but "You'll find in Jesus the happiness you've always longed for."

CHAPTER 6

DO MODERN STUDIES CONFIRM THE BIBLICAL PERSPECTIVES ON HAPPINESS?

You were so happy! What has happened?
GALATIANS 4:15, GNT

The Christian owes it to the world to be supernaturally joyful.
A. W. TOZER

GARY HAUGEN, FOUNDER and president of International Justice Mission, learned an important lesson on a family vacation as a boy. His father wanted the family to hike over a rock formation on Mount Rainier, but ten-year-old Gary, feeling afraid, stayed behind in the visitor's center. He loved the exhibits and inspirational videos, but he was soon bored by the looping footage. He was safe but totally stuck—and unhappy. Finally, his family returned from their adventure triumphant and exhausted, covered with scrapes from the rocks and ice, and bursting with great stories to tell. Gary sums up his experience: "I went on the trip and missed the adventure."[1]

How many people avoid an adventurous happiness in favor of the safe, routine, boring, unhappy life they've settled into?

The former chapel dean at Duke University tells about a recruiter coming from Teach For America, an organization that strives to place talented graduates as teachers in some of the lowest-rated public schools. She told them she'd probably come to the wrong place. After all, these successful students would predictably go on to pursue profitable careers.

She described the schools in the program and how two of their teachers were killed on the job in the past year. After surmising that none of the students would be interested, she ended by saying, "So go on to law school or whatever successful thing you plan on doing." She closed the meeting, mentioning where students could find brochures.

Students rushed to grab the limited number of brochures, some literally fighting to get one. The dean learned a lesson that day: "People want something more out of life than even happiness. People want to be part of an adventure. People want to be part of a project greater than their lives."[2]

This revealing story, while capturing something interesting about these students' longing for meaning, overlooks something critical. Those young people weren't happy people willing to give up their happiness in exchange for noble service. Many were almost certainly unhappy people who were moved to do something great and fulfilling with their lives—something that wouldn't take away happiness, but bring it! Yes, they were considering turning their backs on safety, prestige, and affluence. But they had no plans to turn their backs on happiness.

Secular research confirms the benefits of happiness and the downsides of unhappiness. Consider, for instance, the finding that "unhappy employees take more sick days, staying home 15 extra sick days a year."[3] It also shows that there are steps we can take to raise our level of happiness, including our need for adventure and fulfillment. When scientific studies confirm the observations of the wise and are in harmony with Scripture, they're worth noting.

RESEARCH REPEATEDLY PARALLELS BIBLICAL PRINCIPLES.

In the late 1990s, Martin Seligman, the president of the American Psychological Association, noted psychology's emphasis on the negative side of life, including depression and anxiety, while ignoring the positive, including happiness and well-being. His observation spurred new research and hundreds of articles on happiness.

One of the central topics addressed in these studies is this simple question: Can people become happier? The resounding answer is yes—to a degree. Researchers say there are limits on human happiness, some genetic and some relating to humanity's general condition (which, from the Christian worldview, is caused by sin and the Curse).

Though in this book I emphasize an understanding of happiness based on the Bible, theology, and church history, I've also read a dozen or so secular books on happiness. Many writers document remarkable discoveries about happiness that conform to biblical teachings—though few appear to realize the connection.

For instance, modern happiness studies demonstrate that wealth, success, power, and popularity are not indicators of happiness. People who choose gratitude and engage in respectful, others-centered relationships are happier than those who are self-focused and driven by feelings of entitlement.[4]

With their talk of being thankful, serving others, and giving generously of time and money—accompanied by the assurance that money, sex, and power won't buy happiness—progressive secular psychologists sound remarkably like old-fashioned preachers!

Consider the results of a Duke University study that concluded happiness is fostered by eight factors:

1. Avoiding suspicion and resentment. Nursing a grudge was a major factor in unhappiness.

2. Not living in the past. An unwholesome preoccupation with old mistakes and failures leads to depression.

3. Not wasting time and energy fighting conditions that can't be changed. People are happier when they cooperate with life instead of trying to run from it.

4. Staying involved with the living world. Happiness increases when people resist the temptation to become reclusive during periods of emotional stress.

5. Refusing to indulge in self-pity when handed a raw deal. It's easier for people to achieve happiness when they accept the fact that nobody gets through life without some sorrow and misfortune.

6. Cultivating old-fashioned virtues—love, humor, compassion, and loyalty.

7. Not expecting too much of oneself. When there is too wide a gap between self-expectation and a person's ability to meet the goals he or she has set, feelings of inadequacy are inevitable.

8. Finding something bigger to believe in. Self-centered, egotistical people score lowest in any test for measuring happiness.[5]

While reading this study, I found myself often writing Bible verses in the margins, summarizing the findings: "Love your neighbor as yourself" (Matthew 22:39), "Give thanks in all circumstances" (1 Thessalonians 5:18), "[Forgive] each other . . . as the Lord has forgiven you" (Colossians 3:13).

Compare this list point by point to the study's eight-part conclusion:

1. Jesus said this about not holding grudges: "Whenever you stand praying, forgive, if you have anything against anyone, so that your Father also who is in heaven may forgive you your trespasses" (Mark 11:25).

2. The apostle Paul embraced not living in the past: "One thing I do: forgetting what lies behind and straining forward to what lies ahead, I press on toward the goal for the prize of the upward call of God in Christ Jesus" (Philippians 3:13-14).

3. Jesus instructed us not to worry about things we can't change: "Do not be anxious about your life, what you will eat or what you will drink, nor about your body, what you will put on. . . . Which of you by being anxious can add a single hour to his span of life?" (Matthew 6:25, 27).

4. Solomon spoke of the importance of engaging in human relationships: "Two are better than one, because they have a good reward for their toil. For if they fall, one will lift up his fellow" (Ecclesiastes 4:9-10).

5. Paul knew that contentment is the antidote to self-pity: "I have learned in whatever situation I am to be content. I know how to be brought low, and I know how to abound. In any and every circumstance, I have learned the secret of facing plenty and hunger, abundance and need" (Philippians 4:11-12).

6. The list of virtues described by the secular psychologists looks very similar to this one: "Make every effort to supplement your faith with virtue, and virtue with

knowledge, and knowledge with self-control, and self-control with steadfastness, and steadfastness with godliness, and godliness with brotherly affection, and brotherly affection with love" (2 Peter 1:5-7).

7. We're reminded of our limitations and that we're constantly in need of mercy and grace. God has willingly showered these gifts on us: "Let us then with confidence draw near to the throne of grace, that we may receive mercy and find grace to help in time of need" (Hebrews 4:16).

8. Jesus said we should focus on what's bigger than ourselves: "Seek first the kingdom of God and his righteousness" (Matthew 6:33). Furthermore, we are better off with others-centered humility than self-centered arrogance: "Do nothing out of selfish ambition or vain conceit. Rather, in humility value others above yourselves" (Philippians 2:3, NIV).

ONLY THE CROSS CAN BRIDGE THE GULF BETWEEN MODERN PSYCHOLOGY AND TRUE HAPPINESS IN GOD.

Secular studies, naturally, say nothing about our need to know and love the God of the Bible.

Sonja Lyubomirsky may be the best-known happiness researcher in the world. She admits, "I don't have a religious or spiritual bone in my body."[6] But, she says, the studies clearly show that religious people are happier. Her advice? "If it seems natural for you to practice religion and spirituality, then by all means do it."[7]

She's speaking in the best interest of people's happiness. But of course, the solution isn't pretending to believe something if we don't. Without a personal relationship with God, we won't enjoy true peace and happiness.

A naturalistic worldview that embraces randomness, ultimate meaninglessness, and survival of the fittest doesn't lend itself to happiness. People can borrow certain values from a Christian worldview, but without faith in Christ and the indwelling Spirit as an agent of change, they're left without a solid foundation for happiness.

Psychologists and self-help books offer proven methods for increasing our subjective sense of happiness. However, this marginal contentment can numb people into complacency. A self-achieved, tolerable happiness can anesthetize us into becoming mere sin managers, distancing us from our desperate need for God. Even when this strategy appears sufficient for now, it can't survive the Day of Judgment.

The question of how to reconcile evil people with a God who hates evil is the greatest problem of history. It calls for no less than the greatest solution ever devised—one so radical it appears foolish to the sophisticated—and that is the cross of Christ. "The word of the cross is folly to those who are perishing, but to us who are being saved it is the power of God" (1 Corinthians 1:18).

Psychologist David Powlison says, "Don't ever degenerate into giving good advice unconnected with the good news of Jesus crucified, alive, present, at work, and returning."[8]

Good advice is always better than bad advice. Yet those trapped in a burning building need more than advice—they need good news coupled with practical action. People who are Hell bound need someone who will brave the searing flames, rescue them from sin's destruction, and bring everlasting happiness.

OUR DESIRE FOR HAPPINESS POINTS TO OUR NEED FOR CHRIST.

The human deficiency of both holiness and happiness points to our separation from God. Though people don't intuitively realize their desperate need for atonement and redemption, they do instinctively know that they want to be happy—and they are troubled when they aren't. Happiness, then, is a bridge we can cross to present the gospel. People certainly need to gain holiness through a right standing before God. But the prospect of happiness, peace, and contentment can lead them toward a need that's beneath the surface and less obvious to them: holiness.

J. C. Ryle said something as true today as when he wrote it in the 1800s: "A cheerful, kindly spirit is a great recommendation to a believer. It is a positive misfortune to Christianity when a Christian cannot smile. A merry heart, and a readiness to take part in all innocent mirth, are gifts of inestimable value. They go far to soften prejudices, to take stumbling-blocks out of the way, and to make way for Christ and the Gospel."[9]

This doesn't mean the Christian life will be smooth or easy. God promises, "All who desire to live godly in Christ Jesus will suffer persecution" (2 Timothy 3:12, NKJV). We're not to be surprised when we face great difficulties (see 1 Peter 4:12).

Yet many of the same passages that promise suffering also offer joy (see James 1:2-3). Jesus says, "In the world you will have tribulation; but be of good cheer, I have overcome the world" (John 16:33, NKJV).

Nothing in this book suggests that God's people won't suffer or grieve. But throughout the ages, God has infused his followers with supernatural happiness even in sorrow and adversity.

HAPPINESS IS AN ESSENTIAL COMPONENT TO THE GOSPEL.

The angel's message to the shepherds at the birth of Jesus condenses the gospel to its core. He said, "I bring you good news of great joy that will be for all the people" (Luke 2:10). The gospel isn't for some; it's for all. The Greek adjective translated "great" here is *megas*—this isn't just news, but good news of "mega-joy." It's the best news there has ever been or ever will be.

What characterizes this good news is a deep, everlasting joy for any who will receive it. The Contemporary English Version renders the verse this way: "good news for you, which will make everyone happy."

Though the English Standard Version uses *happiness* and its derivatives only thirteen times, it joins the New American Standard Bible and several other translations in using the word in Isaiah 52:7: "How beautiful upon the mountains are the feet of him who brings good news, who publishes peace, who brings good news of happiness."

This important messianic proclamation begins with "thus says the LORD" (Isaiah 52:3), meaning that God himself is directly responsible for each word. All Scripture is inspired, so all the words are ultimately from God, but it seems that the Holy Spirit typically worked through the vocabulary and speech patterns of the human writer (see 2 Peter 1:21). Here in Isaiah, God tells us directly that our mission is bringing everyone the "good news of happiness."

Paul clearly refers to Isaiah 52:7 in Romans 10:15 as he references the gospel, demonstrating that this "good news of happiness" is in fact nothing else but the gospel of salvation in Jesus Christ.

This means the Bible tells us explicitly that the gospel is very much about happiness. If the gospel we preach isn't about happiness, then it contradicts the direct words of God in Isaiah 52:7. The gospel offers an exchange of misery-generating sin for happiness-giving righteousness provided by Jesus himself. In bowing to him, the shepherds bowed to joy incarnate, happiness in human flesh.

Each stanza of "O Come All Ye faithful" contains sentiments of true happiness: "joyful and triumphant," "sing in exultation," "born this happy morning."

Joy, exultation, and happiness are proper responses to Jesus. A gospel not characterized by such overwhelming gladness isn't the gospel.

Think about it—delivery from eternal damnation is delivery from eternal misery. Eternal life grants eternal happiness. The happiness humans lost when our sin alienated us from God can be regained in Christ. What better qualifies as the "good news of happiness" in Isaiah 52:7?

Those who trust and serve Christ receive this mind-boggling invitation: "Come and share your master's happiness!" (Matthew 25:21, NIV). Those who trust in riches, in contrast, are told, "Weep and howl for the miseries that are coming upon you" (James 5:1).

The true gospel cannot be improved upon. Theologian J. Gresham Machen (1881–1937) said, "In the gospel there is included all that the heart of man can wish."[10] What do we wish for most? Happiness.

Our happiness is certainly not the only thing the gospel is about. However, it's one of the wonderful things Christ accomplished through his redemptive work.

As a young believer, I often heard testimonies in which people happily recalled the day of their conversion. Years later, it dawned on me that instead of only being happy about what Jesus did in the past (on the cross and at my conversion) and what he'll one day do (at his return), I should be happy in what he's doing *today*. The psalmist was onto something when he said, "This is the day that the LORD has made; let us rejoice and be glad in it" (Psalm 118:24). Yes, he spoke of one particular day, but God has ordained all our days.

How much happier we'll be if we rejoice for what God is doing here and now, every day and every hour of our lives. Why wait many years—or until we're with the Lord—to look back and say, "God, I finally see that you were at work even in those hard times; I wish I would have trusted you then"?

I have a friend who genuinely believes that nearly every meal, get-together, retreat, or vacation is the best he has ever experienced. This makes him fun to be with. His capacity to enjoy the moment and savor present happiness becomes a treasured memory of past happiness. After every time we've been with him, it seems, he texts me, saying, "That was the BEST dinner and most FUN time we've ever had." I smile and enter into his happiness.

The present is the only place we live. Happiness in God should be more than memories and anticipation. Circumstances constantly change, and good news comes and goes, but we should look to God for happiness now. Why? Because the Good News of happiness has come, it is still here, and it will never go away!

ENJOYING GOD IS OUR CHIEF PURPOSE.

The Westminster Shorter Catechism was written in 1646 by a group of English, Irish, and Scottish Reformed theologians. It begins with the question, "What is the chief end of man?" and offers the reply, "Man's chief end is to glorify God and to enjoy Him forever."

For theologians to come up with "glorify God" is no surprise. But to *enjoy* him forever? Why not obey or fear him forever?

The composers of the catechism weren't firing off an e-mail in which they chose words on the fly. They were writing a painstakingly deliberate statement of belief and practice that generations to come would memorize and seek to live by. Each word was judiciously selected.

These seventeenth-century theologians and pastors stated that we exist not only to glorify God but also to find pleasure and happiness in him. This doesn't fit the stereotype of stodgy religious Scotsmen from nearly four hundred years ago.

Remarkably, the English Parliament officially endorsed this confession not long after it was written. What did theologians and even Parliament realize that has somehow been obscured over the centuries?

And what does it mean to enjoy God? Puritan Thomas Watson said, "What is enjoying God for ever but to be put in a state of happiness? . . . God is the summum bonum, the chief good; therefore the enjoyment of him is the highest felicity."[11]

The catechism writers understood that God created people not only to glorify him but also to be happy in him—to be in a personal relationship with him that's deep, satisfying, and everlasting. They understood that the Good News includes more than one dimension. There's the God who deserves to be glorified, and there are the people he created not only to glorify him but to enjoy him and delight in him unendingly.

HAPPINESS IS OUR NATURAL RESPONSE TO GOOD NEWS.

When we hear good news, what's our reaction? Happiness, excitement, wonder, and celebration, right?

Consider the iconic kiss between two strangers, a sailor and nurse, in Times Square on August 15, 1945. The photo, first published in *Life* magazine, shows a crowd of faces surrounding the couple, all of whom are filled with sheer delight over President Truman's announcement that World War II had ended. Good news can be huge, such as "The war is over," or smaller, such as "Your best friend is coming to visit you." The news might be small to someone else but big to you, such as, "You and your spouse are going to have a baby." The better the news, the happier you'll be.

The gospel is a concrete, reality-grounded call to happiness. Jesus really did become a man, go to the cross, and rise from the grave. He truly is with us and in us now and will return again one day. These facts are what separate the gospel from wishful thinking.

Jesus said, "I came that they might have life and have it abundantly" (John 10:10). The word translated "abundantly" suggests something profuse or extraordinary in quantity and quality—a surpassingly happy life. Similarly, Scripture describes eternal life not just as life that doesn't end but as full and satisfying: "God gave us eternal life, and this life is in his Son" (1 John 5:11). The phrase "eternal life" appears forty-three times in the New Testament. It means far more than eternal existence—it means eternal *happiness!*

In Hebrews 3:13, God calls us to happiness this way: "Encourage each other daily, while it is still called today" (HCSB). If God wants us to be happy in him, today (not tomorrow) is the time to experience Christ-centered happiness.

If we believe in the sovereign God who offered us the redemptive grace of Jesus and we aren't happy, we should ask ourselves why.

Choosing to rejoice by rehearsing reasons to be happy and grateful even in the midst of suffering is an affirmation of trust not only in what God has done but also in our belief that he will bring a good end to all that troubles us. The gospel infuses hope and joy into our circumstances because it acknowledges God's greatness over any crisis we'll face.

It is now, not at some vague point in the future, that "the LORD gives strength to his people; the LORD blesses his people with peace" (Psalm 29:11, NIV). The fruit of the Spirit is not something we wait until Heaven to enjoy; it's available to us in this life (see Galatians 5:22). "So my heart rejoices and I am happy" (Psalm 16:9, NET). Did you catch that the psalmist is speaking in the present tense? He isn't just anticipating rejoicing—he's doing it now.

Today's happiness in Christ is drawn from an infinite deposit of happiness that God has already placed in our account. It isn't something we have to wait to experience after death, though only then will we experience it completely. "The LORD is near to all who call upon Him" (Psalm 145:18).

If the gospel doesn't bring us true happiness, then what we believe is not the gospel. When a pastor or author says, "God never intended for humans to be happy,"[12] it may sound spiritual. But unless being happy is a sin, it's not true.

Unfortunately, we diminish the Bible's overflowing happiness when we separate "holy" things that give us joy, such as prayer, Bible reading, and church, from "worldly" things that bring us happiness, such as pets, hobbies, barbecues, vacations, and sports. This turns us into spiritual schizophrenics, creating false divisions between "Jesus time" and "world time," "God time" and "me time."

How can we glorify God in everything and pray without ceasing if we can't glorify God and pray while working, riding a bike, playing games, or watching a movie?

The truth is, the Good News should leak into every aspect of our lives, even if we're not consciously talking about God or witnessing to someone. Every time we ponder the gospel, live by it, share it, and anticipate its culmination in a world without sin and death, "good news of happiness" will permeate our lives with . . . well, *happiness.*

That's exactly what happened when Paul and Barnabas took the gospel to the Gentiles. Paul said, "We bring you the good news [glad tidings (KJV)]. . . . And when the Gentiles heard this, they began rejoicing [the Gentiles were very happy to hear this (CJB)]. . . . The disciples were filled with joy and with the Holy Spirit [The disciples were overflowing with happiness (CEB)]" (Acts 13:32, 48, 52).

God proved his boundless love for us when he sent his only Son to die in our place so those who believe in him can have everlasting life (see John 3:16). God is for us, and not even death can separate us from God's love (see Romans 8:31-39). If we really believe these truths, how can we not be happy?

What better sums up the proper response to the good news of God's goodness, loving-kindness, grace, mercy, salvation, rebirth, renewal, and gift of the Holy Spirit through Jesus (see Titus 3:5-7) than the word *happiness*?

Fred Sanders writes, "A gospel which is only about the moment of conversion but does not extend to every moment of life in Christ is too small. A gospel that gets your sins forgiven but offers no power for transformation is too small."[13] I would add that a gospel incapable of making you happier than you have ever been is too small.

If the gospel doesn't make us happy, we're not believing the truly good news—perhaps we've embraced a burdensome bad-news religion. We need to remind ourselves of what the gospel really means. As Jerry Bridges says, "Preach the gospel to yourself every day."[14]

Elton Trueblood (1900–1994), a chaplain who served at both Harvard and Stanford, said, "Any alleged Christianity which fails to express itself in cheerfulness, at some point, is clearly spurious."[15]

Octavius Winslow wrote, "The religion of Christ is the religion of JOY. Christ came to take away our sins, to roll off our curse, to unbind our chains, to open our prison-house, to cancel our debt. . . . Is not this joy? Where can we find a joy so real, so deep, so pure, so lasting? There is every element of joy—deep, ecstatic, satisfying, sanctifying joy—in the gospel of Christ. The believer in Jesus is essentially a happy man."[16]

THE GOSPEL CAME INTO A WORLD DOMINATED BY HAPPINESS-SEEKING PHILOSOPHIES STILL PRESENT TODAY.

The world Jesus entered desperately needed a redeemer from sin, hopelessness, and unhappiness. The mythological Greek gods (which the Romans had renamed) were seldom taken seriously. In daily life, Greek and Roman worldviews were centered more on Stoicism or Epicureanism, both of which professed to be means of obtaining happiness.[17]

The Stoics believed in truth and virtue. They exercised mental disciplines that allowed them to overcome emotions and rise above difficulties, similar to some forms of Buddhism today. Scholar William Morrice states, "There was no joy in it. Stoicism was essentially pessimistic in spirit, and its outlook upon life was dark and foreboding."[18]

Epicureanism, on the other hand, taught that happiness was found in enjoying life's pleasures. According to Epicurus, "There was no place at all in religion for joy—except in the case of the gods themselves, who lived a life of perpetual happiness and bliss. The self-appointed task of the philosopher was to free men from the terrors and degradations of religion."[19]

Stoicism and Epicureanism have close counterparts in contemporary Western culture. As a religion, modern Christianity is viewed, sometimes unfairly and sometimes not, much like Stoicism: as a duty-driven, negative, joyless way of life.

The secular backlash against Christianity today has much in common with Epicureanism. Its message is to be happy however and whenever you can—don't allow guilt and worry about moral standards to interfere with your happiness.

The so-called "mystery religions" in Greek and Roman culture affirmed that happiness could be found only in the gods, who alone were truly happy. Today's New Age beliefs have some similarities to these religions. They correctly see that happiness is found in a higher spiritual being or force, but they don't acknowledge the true God.

When Christianity emerged, the appeal of Jesus' teachings was widespread. He emphasized truth and virtue, as did Stoicism, and the goodness of pleasures and happiness—including eating and drinking—as did Epicureanism. He also offered a true relationship with God, which the mystery religions fruitlessly sought. Just as he does today, Jesus offered the genuine happiness everyone wanted but had not found.

GOD TIMED THE INCARNATION OF JESUS—JOY PERSONIFIED—PERFECTLY.

"When the set time had fully come, God sent his Son, born of a woman . . ." (Galatians 4:4, NIV). God's timing in sending Jesus wasn't just perfect for the world in general; it was ideal for Israel in particular. The hand of Rome was heavy on the Jewish people, and life under an emperor who claimed to be god was particularly oppressive to those who believed in the one true God.

Though the Jews had long hoped for God's intervention, the promises of redemption and judgment on their enemies seemed no closer to fulfillment. Discouragement and pessimism were rampant.

The average Jew was equally burdened by the stern, unhappy requirements placed on him by religious leaders. Many Pharisees were obsessed with the law and emphasized self-righteous human merit over God's grace. Jesus said, "They tie up heavy burdens, hard to bear, and lay them on people's shoulders, but they themselves are not willing to move them with their finger" (Matthew 23:4).

This was the weary and hopeless world into which God brought "good news of great joy" (Luke 2:10). The God of holiness and happiness came to Earth to deliver us from eternal sin and misery—that's why calling the gospel "good news of great joy" is no overstatement.

WISE HAPPINESS-SEEKERS ACCEPT GOD'S OFFER OF ETERNAL, UNENDING HAPPINESS.

Jesus tells two stories about great parties thrown by God: the wedding feast (see Matthew 22:1-14) and the great banquet (see Luke 14:15-24). In both celebrations, the hosts (who represent God) invite guests to join in.

People in that culture certainly knew how to put on parties, and nothing was more festive and fun than a wedding feast—lots of free food, drinks, music, and laughter.

In the second story, when a good, happy king with vast wealth and unlimited resources threw a party—well, nobody in his or her right mind would decline! If you're too busy for a great wedding feast and a banquet put on by the king, you're too busy.

Yet the people the king invited made all kinds of excuses for not coming. They said no to the party, choosing instead to go to work, take a trip, inspect livestock, or stay home. *They said no to happiness.* When those who were invited refused to come, the king sent invitations to anyone his servants could find. So the wedding hall was filled with grateful people.

These parables exemplify God's sincere invitation to happiness and our tendency to turn down his invitation to pursue things we believe will make us happier.

We couldn't be more wrong. Refusing the King's invitation to endless celebration in his presence is refusing happiness itself.

The moral of the story? *When God invites you to a party, say yes.* You'll be happy you did!

CHAPTER 7

IS HAPPINESS UNSPIRITUAL?

I will rejoice in the LORD. I will be glad because he rescues me. With every bone
in my body I will praise him: "LORD, who can compare with you?"
PSALM 35:9-10, NLT

The faint, far-off results of those energies which God's creative rapture implanted in matter when
He made the worlds are what we now call physical pleasures. . . . What would it be to taste at
the fountainhead that stream of which even these lower reaches prove so intoxicating? Yet that,
I believe, is what lies before us. The whole man is to drink joy from the fountain of joy.
C. S. LEWIS

W HEN MY BOOK *Heaven* was published in 2004, one of my favorite professors
from Bible college had serious objections. In the book I develop the doctrines of
the Resurrection and the New Earth, and I envision what I believe Scripture teaches: an
embodied life of loving and serving God as we reign over the New Earth.

I point out that we will eat and drink on the New Earth. Depictions in Scripture lead
logically to the conclusion that most of what we do in our current bodies on Earth we will
do with greater happiness in our new bodies on the New Earth.

I speculate that as resurrected people on a resurrected Earth, we might invent, write, read,
play games, and ride bikes. This troubled my professor. Over coffee together, this godly man
furrowed his brow and said, "When we can see God, why would we ever want to ride a bike?"

Both his countenance and his tone of voice told me that in his mind, seeing God was
spiritual, while riding a bike was secular—almost sinful.

Respectfully, I asked him what Scripture means when it gives us this command: "Whether
you eat or drink, or whatever you do, do all to the glory of God" (1 Corinthians 10:31).
Eating and drinking are not only necessities but also physical pleasures that we're to do
for God's glory. I told him that I ride my bike to God's glory in this life. And I worship
God while joyfully playing tennis and snorkeling, just as I worship him while enjoying
music, reading God's Word, and playing with dogs. If we can worship God here, as we eat,
drink, work, and enjoy hobbies, nature, and art, why would we not be able to do that on the

resurrected Earth? Couldn't a bike ride in the wondrous beauty of a new creation, alongside other worshipers of the King, lift our hearts to great praise, drawing us closer to him?

That conversation ended with prayer, love, and mutual respect. But our divergent perspectives weren't resolved. We see the material world and our material bodies, both the present ones and the ones to come, through differing worldviews.

My professor and I are just two voices in a larger conversation about the role of the physical versus the spiritual when it comes to faith. For centuries, believers have wrestled with questions about how tangible, concrete, and physical our eternal happiness will be. When we see God, will we spend all our moments motionless, simply gazing at him? Or will we go about our days also serving him, enjoying each other's company, and exploring the wonders of his creation while praising and worshiping him?

WHY DO SOME CHRISTIANS DENY THE GOODNESS OF PHYSICAL, BODILY PLEASURE?

Some Christians are wary of physical pleasure because of an unbiblical belief that the spirit realm is good while the material world is bad. I call this *Christoplatonism*, a term I coined in my book *Heaven*.[1] It is a widespread belief, sometimes spoken and sometimes not, that has plagued countless Christians and churches over the years, convincing people that physical pleasures are unspiritual and therefore that many of the things that make people happy are unworthy and suspect.

Plato was among the first Western philosophers to claim that reality is fundamentally something ideal or abstract. He considered the body "a hindrance, as it opposes and even imprisons the soul."[2] Plato wrote, "Our body is the tomb in which we are buried."[3] In his statement "*Soma sema*" ("a body, a tomb"), Plato suggested that the spirit's highest destiny is to be free from the body.

Scripture contradicts this antagonism between body and spirit. God created body *and* spirit; both were marred by sin, and both are redeemed by Christ. Our bodies aren't prisons. Nor are they something we can occupy or abandon at will as a hermit crab does a shell. They're essential and God-designed aspects of our being. Our bodies weren't created to distract from our Creator but to disclose him. Bodies and spirits can, under the Fall, sometimes work at odds with each other (hence the references to the flesh in Romans 7:14-24), but this is not their natural, God-created relationship, nor is it a permanent one.

Likewise, Earth—long disparaged by some Christians—is not a second-rate location from which we must be delivered. Rather, it was custom made by God for us. Earth, not some incorporeal state, is God's choice as humankind's original and ultimate dwelling place. God made the material world not to hinder our walk with him but to facilitate it.

God could have given us tasteless nutrients to keep us healthy instead of filling the world with great-tasting food and giving us the taste buds to enjoy it. He could have easily devised some mechanistic means of conceiving children; instead, he devised the elaborate and pleasurable process of sexual relations. He could have looked at all he created and said, "It is functional." Instead he said, "It is very good!"

GOD WANTS US TO ENJOY BOTH HIMSELF *AND* HIS GIFTS.

Unfortunately, Platonic ideas made inroads into Christian theology through the writings of Philo (circa 20 BC–AD 50). In contrast to the literal interpretations favored by most rabbis, he made a point of allegorizing Scripture.[4]

Clement of Alexandria (150–215) and Origen (185–254), influential church fathers, also embraced Greek philosophy and argued that Scripture should be understood allegorically. They believed the Bible's references to eating and drinking in resurrection bodies on a redeemed Earth weren't to be taken literally—after all, in the view of Christoplatonism, the body is bad and only the pure spirit is good. So, they argued, when the Bible talks about earthly pleasures and delights, it can't be taken literally.

Isaiah's prophetic statements about life on a perfect New Earth and the portrayal of resurrected people living on a New Earth in Revelation 21–22 were considered mere symbols of the supposed ideal of a disembodied spiritual world. This viewpoint stood in stark contrast to Scripture's emphatic affirmation of the importance of literal physical resurrection (see 1 Corinthians 15).

Ever since the Greek philosophers, this hyperspiritualized approach to Scripture and the Christian life has infected segments of the Western church. It has crippled people's ability to understand what Scripture says about the goodness of God's creation, as well as the delight and happiness he intends for us in the physical dimension. (Once, after I preached about the Resurrection and the New Earth, a fine Christian man said to me, "This idea of having bodies and eating food and living in an earthly place . . . it just sounds so *unspiritual*.")

Why did God make our taste buds for us to enjoy food and dopamine to be generated in the "pleasure centers" of our brains? Why did he give us our ability to find joy in a cool swim and a hot shower, in listening to music and audiobooks, in hitting a golf ball, skiing down a slope, or running through a park? Why did he give us physical senses if not to know him better and to be far happier in him than we ever could be if he had instead made us disembodied spirits who couldn't enjoy physical pleasures?

If we buy into, even subconsciously, the misguided perspective that bodies, the Earth, material things, and anything "secular" are automatically unspiritual, we will inevitably reject or spiritualize any biblical revelation about bodily resurrection or finding joy in God's physical creation.

Christoplatonism falsely assumes that spiritual people should shun physical pleasures. But who invented pleasure? Who made food and water, eating and drinking, marriage and sex, friendship and games, art and music, celebration and laughter? Hint: it wasn't Satan!

The devil cannot create; he can only twist and pervert what God has created. In his book *The Screwtape Letters*, C. S. Lewis depicts a correspondence between two demons. The "Enemy" the demon refers to is God.

> Never forget that when we are dealing with any pleasure in its healthy and normal and satisfying form, we are, in a sense, on the Enemy's ground. I know we have won many a soul through pleasure. All the same, it is His invention, not ours. He

made the pleasures: all our research so far has not enabled us to produce one. All we can do is to encourage the humans to take the pleasures which our Enemy has produced, at times, or in ways, or in degrees, which He has forbidden.[5]

We must be careful not to make idols out of God's provisions. But God is happy when we, with the proper perspective, enjoy his gifts to us. He's not in Heaven frowning at us, saying, "Stop it—you should find joy only in me." This would be as foreign to our heavenly Father's nature as it would be to mine as an earthly father if I gave my daughters Christmas gifts, then pouted because they enjoyed them too much.

BODILY RESURRECTION DEMONSTRATES THE GOODNESS OF GOD'S PHYSICAL CREATION.

It's no coincidence that the apostle Paul's detailed defense of the physical resurrection was written to the church at Corinth. Corinthian believers were immersed in the Greek philosophies of Platonism and dualism, which perceived a dichotomy between the spiritual and physical realms.

God intended for our bodies to last as long as our souls. Platonists see a disembodied soul as the ideal. The Bible, meanwhile, sees this division as unnatural and undesirable. We are unified beings. That's what makes bodily resurrection so vital and why Job declared, "After my skin has been thus destroyed, yet in my flesh I shall see God" (Job 19:26). That's also why Paul said that if there is no resurrection, "we are of all people most to be pitied" (1 Corinthians 15:19).

Any views of the afterlife that settle for less than a full bodily resurrection—including Christoplatonism, reincarnation, and transmigration of the soul—are explicitly anti-Christian. The early church waged doctrinal wars against Gnosticism and Manichaeism, dualistic worldviews that associated God with the spiritual realm of light and Satan with the physical world of darkness. These heresies contradict the biblical account, which says that God was pleased with the entire physical realm, all of which he created and called "very good" (Genesis 1:31). Christ's resurrection repudiates Gnosticism and Manichaeism, and discredits the heresy of Christoplatonism.

GOD CREATED PHYSICAL PLEASURES AND NATURAL DELIGHTS FOR OUR ENJOYMENT.

If we believe the physical world is evil, inferior, or unspiritual, we'll inevitably be suspicious of everything in it. We'll look down our noses at good food and wine, art and music (unless they're explicitly Christian), sports and culture, hobbies and recreation, drama and amusements. We will berate the notion of happiness because, after all, happiness is "worldly." We'll come to the conclusion that God's people should be concerned only about holiness and perhaps some unemotional, transcendent concept called "joy" that never makes its way to their faces.

But this is not consistent with a biblical worldview. Scripture is clear that physical pleasures and even temporal happiness, such as what we experience from a good meal, fine art, and adventure, are from God, not Satan.

To refute this idea, some people quote James 4:4: "Do you not know that friendship with the world is enmity with God?" But this verse doesn't condemn the physical world as a whole; it only rejects the godless aspects of it—those things that have been twisted by sin until they're robbed of their God-intended beauty.

Christoplatonism frowns on the pleasures of the physical world, mistaking asceticism for spirituality. In contrast, Scripture says that God provides us with material things "for our enjoyment" (1 Timothy 6:17, NLT). Paul said it is demons and liars who portray the physical realm as unspiritual (see 1 Timothy 4:1-3). He wrote, "Everything God created is good, and nothing is to be rejected if it is received with thanksgiving, because it is consecrated by the word of God and prayer" (1 Timothy 4:4-5, NIV). It's a serious mistake to divorce God from the pleasures he created.

GOD INTENDS US TO WHOLEHEARTEDLY ENJOY PHYSICAL PLEASURES IN THEIR PROPER PLACE AND TIME.

To paraphrase Proverbs 5:18-19, God tells us, "I made you to be happy. I invented sex for the marriage relationship, and I intend for you to enjoy it!"

Many Bible-believing churches have taught or implied a quite different message. An anti-pleasure mentality still permeates the thoughts of many believers. They think that God has drawn a line between himself and the world. On God's side is Bible reading, prayer, fasting, evangelism, and church attendance. On the world's side is sex, eating, alcohol, parties, sports, art, drama, movies, careers, games, and concerts.

The world, it seems, offers an unending smorgasbord of promised happiness. Seekers move from one false promise to another, ending in ruins before they discover what Solomon learned—that all these promises of happiness are empty. They are wind and vapor, not substance and reality.

Suppose churches taught that God is happy and that he is the source of all happiness. Suppose Christians believed that God calls them to view work, play, music, food, and drink as gracious gifts from God's hand to be responsibly enjoyed within the parameters of his commands. If this were the reality, the call to holiness would not be mistaken for a call to unhappiness!

GOD USES THE PHYSICAL WORLD TO DRAW PEOPLE TO HIM AND TO REFLECT HIS CHARACTER.

By distancing ourselves from the pleasures and beauties of the natural world, we disregard one of the two books God gave humanity to draw sinners to himself. One book is the Word of God, which theologians call "special revelation"; the other is nature, or "general revelation." General revelation covers everything from electrons and quarks to solar systems and quasars. It includes not only the natural world but much of human culture, in which God's image bearers reflect their maker.

In Romans 1:20, Paul writes that God's attributes have been clearly revealed in his creation. Psalm 19:1 says, "The heavens declare the glory of God, and the sky above proclaims his handiwork." These verses clearly show that God reveals his attributes through nature. We can see in creation the greatness and beauty of God. All who love mountains and waterfalls and oceans, all who climb and dive and photograph the wonders of nature, all who love animals—even if these people attribute these things entirely to natural causes—see God. This is the natural bridge to theism, a belief in God. It is not the gospel, but it can prepare people to hear it.

Sadly, Christoplatonism tears down that bridge to unbelievers by negating the value and goodness of not only the natural world but also his image bearers' creativity—their ability to build parks, playgrounds, zoos, dams, reservoirs, roads, monuments, greenhouses, and sculptures. People are sinners, to be sure, but is all human achievement nothing but sin?

Such thinking leaves believers with a shriveled view of both the present and the future. They envision spirits stripped of bodies, whose heavenly lives consist only of worship and service in a "higher plane" of disembodied angelic spirituality. The Bible teaches no such thing.

FOR HUMANS, TRUE JOY CAN'T EXIST IN A SPIRITUALIZED, DISEMBODIED FORM.

Much of what I've read about joy, when contrasted with happiness, attempts to raise it to such a peak of spirituality that it disappears from the realm of mortals. In *Mere Christianity*, C. S. Lewis wrote, "There is no good trying to be more spiritual than God. God never meant man to be a purely spiritual creature. That is why He uses material things like bread and wine to put the new life into us. We may think this rather crude and unspiritual. God does not: He invented eating. He likes matter. He invented it."

Lewis went on to say,

> I know some muddleheaded Christians have talked as if Christianity thought
> that sex, or the body, or pleasure, were bad in themselves. But they were wrong.
> Christianity is almost the only one of the great religions which thoroughly
> approves of the body—which believes that matter is good, that God Himself
> once took on a human body, that some kind of body is going to be given to us
> even in Heaven and is going to be an essential part of our happiness, our beauty
> and our energy.[6]

The movie *Babette's Feast* depicts a conservative Christian sect that scrupulously avoids "worldly" distractions. They live out the unhappy philosophy of Christoplatonism—quick to judge, slow to rejoice, and convinced that celebration, pleasure, and laughter must be sinful.

Then Babette, once a gourmet cook in France, is forced by war to become a maid for the two women who lead this small group of austere believers. Babette unexpectedly inherits a significant sum of money, and out of gratitude for their kindness to her, she spends it all to prepare a fabulous dinner party for the elderly sisters and their friends.

Babette's Feast is a picture of God's extravagant grace. Touched by Babette's generosity and the great feast she prepared, the community's false guilt dissipates and they begin to laugh, take delight, and truly enjoy the richness of God's provision. The movie illustrates the beauty of enjoying God's lavish, creative gifts with heartfelt gratitude. As these legalists come to understand gradually over the many courses of this meal, feasting and laughter and beauty can draw us not away from God, but to him, when he and his gifts are the objects of our happiness.[7]

GOD PROMISES AN ETERNALLY EMBODIED LIFE ON A PHYSICAL NEW EARTH.

In *The Four Loves*, C. S. Lewis described redeemed relationships and culture: "We may hope that the resurrection of the body means also the resurrection of what may be called our 'greater body'; the general fabric of our earthly life with its affections and relationships."[8] Scripture describes the New Earth in these terms: "The kings of the earth will bring their splendor into [the New Jerusalem]. On no day will its gates ever be shut. . . . The glory and honor of the nations will be brought into it" (Revelation 21:24-26, NIV; see also Isaiah 60; 65; Revelation 21–22). What splendors? Tributes to the King of kings.

There's nothing more solid, more earthly, and less ghostly than city walls made of rocks and precious stones. If there will be redeemed architecture, music, and art on the New Earth, why not science, technology, entertainment, writing, reading, and exploration, all done to the glory of God? We're told that "his servants will serve him" (Revelation 22:3, NIV). We'll engage in meaningful work serving our King. And we will enjoy rest and relaxation (see Hebrews 4:1-11; Revelation 14:13).

Will we eat and drink as resurrected beings? Scripture couldn't be more emphatic on this point (see Revelation 2:7; 19:9; Matthew 8:11). Jesus said, "People will come from east and west, and from north and south, and recline at table in the kingdom of God" (Luke 13:29). Isaiah 25:6 says, "On this mountain the LORD of hosts will make for all peoples a feast of rich food, a feast of well-aged wine." How good a meal will that be? I can only imagine: "My compliments to the chef: the Lord God!"

Despite Scripture's evidence to the contrary, even Christians end up thinking, *If I can't live my dreams now, I never will.* Or, *You only go around once . . .* But if we know Jesus, we go around twice—and the second time lasts forever. It's called eternal life, and it will be lived in a redeemed universe, on a New Earth, with King Jesus!

The typical view of Heaven—eternity in a disembodied state—is not only completely contrary to the Bible, but it also obscures the far richer truth: that God promises us eternal life as healthy, embodied people who have said a final good-bye to sin and suffering and are *more* capable of worship, friendship, love, discovery, work, and play than we have ever been—and therefore far happier than we've ever been.

In part 4 we'll more fully address our final deliverance from unhappiness and the delight and pleasures awaiting us in the New Heaven and the New Earth—where happiness will be the air we breathe.

CHAPTER 8

CAN GOOD THINGS BECOME IDOLS THAT STEAL OUR HAPPINESS?

No one can serve two masters, for either he will hate the one and love the other,
or he will be devoted to the one and despise the other. . . . But seek first the kingdom
of God and his righteousness, and all these things will be added to you.

JESUS (MATTHEW 6:24, 33)

"Accepting Jesus" is not just adding Jesus. It is also subtracting the idols.

RAY ORTLUND

O NE SUNDAY A visiting minister substituted for Henry Ward Beecher (1813–1887), a famous and controversial pastor who commanded sizable fees for speaking around the country.

A large audience had assembled to hear Beecher at his New York church. When the visiting minister entered the pulpit, some people in the congregation headed toward the doors.

The minister called out, "All who have come here today to worship Henry Ward Beecher may now withdraw from the church! All who have come to worship God, keep your seats!"[1]

Idolatry comes in many forms. Even churches that condemn idolatry sometimes practice it without even realizing that's what they're doing. Whether they worship their pastor, the church building, tradition, their denomination, or the pew with their name on it, churchgoers can be as idolatrous as pagans.

EVERY CULTURE WORSHIPS IDOLS, AND OURS IS NO EXCEPTION.

Despite shows such as *American Idol* and celebrities that earn the nickname "teen idols," most twenty-first-century Americans don't believe we're a nation of idol worshipers. The word *idol* conjures up images of primitive people offering sacrifices to crude carved images. Surely we're above that. Aren't we?

Even when God's people didn't worship physical idols, they were still capable of idolatry. God said to the prophet Ezekiel concerning some who professed to serve him, "These men have set up their idols in their hearts" (Ezekiel 14:3, NKJV).

When the apostle John wrote to Christ-followers near the end of the first century, most had nothing to do with carved idols. Still, his final words to them were, "Little children, keep yourselves from idols" (1 John 5:21). The New Living Translation captures the meaning this way: "Keep away from anything that might take God's place in your hearts."

In *Counterfeit Gods*, Tim Keller writes,

> Our contemporary society is not fundamentally different from these ancient ones. Each culture is dominated by its own set of idols. . . . We may not physically kneel before the statue of Aphrodite, but many young women today are driven into depression and eating disorders by an obsessive concern over their body image. We may not actually burn incense to Artemis, but when money and career are raised to cosmic proportions, we perform a kind of child sacrifice, neglecting family and community to achieve a higher place in business and gain more wealth and prestige.[2]

HUMANKIND'S DESIRE FOR INDEPENDENCE IS AT THE HEART OF IDOLATRY.

The apostle Paul portrayed humanity's sins as idolatrous acts: "[They] exchanged the glory of the immortal God . . . and worshiped and served created things rather than the Creator" (Romans 1:23, 25, NIV).

The prophet Isaiah said of a human king who appears to also represent the devil, "How you have fallen from heaven, morning star, son of the dawn! You have been cast down to the earth" (Isaiah 14:12, NIV). Jesus was actually there when this event happened. He told his disciples, "I saw Satan fall like lightning from heaven" (Luke 10:18). The devil has been unhappy ever since he rebelled against the God of happiness and was evicted from Heaven, the home of happiness.

Satan forfeited his own happiness, and he bitterly hates us—the objects of God's love. As committed as he is to making us just as miserable, the devil tempts us toward what will dishonor God by telling persuasive lies to convince us that the things that make us miserable will actually make us happy. After thousands of years of doing this, he's remarkably good at it. Jesus said of Satan, "When he lies, he speaks his native language, for he is a liar and the father of lies" (John 8:44, NIV).

The devil's first temptation of Eve and Adam demonstrates his attempt to persuade them to find greater happiness apart from God. That first human sin became the mother of all human unhappiness. Anything we desire more than God—anything that preoccupies our thoughts or diverts us away from him—is an idol.

IDOLATRY BEGAN IN EDEN AND HAS YET TO END.

In the first chapters of Genesis, God had no competition for the affection of his creatures. Humanity found its meaning, purpose, and happiness in God. God was God; everything else wasn't. And everyone knew it.

The Fall tragically changed that.

An idol is anything we praise, celebrate, fixate on, and look to for help that's not the true God. Scripture speaks strongly about the sin of idolatry: "Woe to those who go down to Egypt for help, and rely on horses, who trust in chariots because they are many, and in horsemen because they are very strong, but who do not look to the Holy One of Israel, nor seek the LORD!" (Isaiah 31:1, NKJV).

Egypt, horses, chariots, and horsemen became God-substitutes. Ironically, the Israelites looked for help from a nation that had once enslaved them. As strange as that sounds, we often do the same, idolizing things that have brought us harm and hoping in vain that they'll come through for us this time.

Puritan Thomas Boston wrote, "When God and the creature come in competition, we must renounce the creature, and cleave to God only. . . . We must . . . not prefer [creatures, possessions, or life itself] to the glory of God, which we ought always to study as our main end, and account our chief happiness and joy."[3]

Moses' brother, Aaron, made a golden calf for the Israelites when Moses was on the mountaintop meeting with God. There was no illusion that this was anything other than false worship—it was an idol from the beginning (see Exodus 32:4-8). In contrast, Moses made the bronze serpent when God commanded him to, and God used it to deliver many from death (see Numbers 21:4-9). But instead of worshiping God, the people started worshiping the bronze serpent. Even though God himself wanted the bronze serpent made for a good purpose, it became an idol, and it had to be destroyed (see 2 Kings 18:4).

Tim Keller says,

> To live for anything else but God leads to breakdown and decay. When a fish leaves the water, which he was built for, he is not free, but dead. Worshiping other things . . . cannot deliver satisfaction, because they were never meant to be "gods." They were never meant to replace God.[4]

Because we all sinned in Adam (see Romans 5:12-14), we all became idolaters in Adam. Idolatry is woven into our very nature. Calvin said, "The human heart is a factory of idols." He added, "Everyone of us is, from his mother's womb, expert in inventing idols."[5]

To grasp a biblical theology of happiness, we must understand the nature and extent of our constant temptations toward idolatry.

HAPPINESS-SEEKING MAKES US VULNERABLE TO IDOLATRY.

In the Christian worldview, created things are means to help us delight in God. The problems start when we believe we can find more happiness in God's creation than in God himself.

Consider this description of idolatry: "They served their idols, which became a snare to them. They sacrificed their sons and their daughters to the demons; they poured out innocent blood, the blood of their sons and daughters, whom they sacrificed to the idols of Canaan, and the land was polluted with blood" (Psalm 106:36-38). Those who seek happiness in false gods end up sacrificing their integrity, their families, their culture, and the very happiness they crave.

ALL IDOLS APPEAL TO OUR DESIRES AND TRAP US BY TWISTING WHAT'S GOOD.

C. S. Lewis portrayed this conversation between two demons, concerning God:

He's a hedonist at heart. All those fasts and vigils and stakes and crosses are only a façade. Or only like foam on the seashore. Out at sea, out in His sea, there is pleasure, and more pleasure. He makes no secret of it; at His right hand are "pleasures for evermore." Ugh! . . . There are things for humans to do all day long without His minding in the least—sleeping, washing, eating, drinking, making love, playing, praying, working. Everything has to be *twisted* before it's any use to us.[6]

Lewis pointed out a great irony, one we shouldn't miss: since the devil only has God's good creation to use as temptation, he must twist it to his evil purposes. He never acts for our good, since he hates us just as he hates God, who made us in his likeness.

When the fulfillment of a desire is seen as a gift and is gratefully enjoyed for God's glory, we find satisfying happiness. When it's not, we become miserable, enslaved to the very thing that was intended to be a gift.

Idolatry isn't just wrong—it doesn't work.

Those who argue over whether to use cheese or peanut butter in a mousetrap agree on one thing: the stronger the attraction, the better the chance of catching what you're going after. Every temptation uses false happiness as bait. A woman told me, "I left my family to find happiness. It didn't last, but I sacrificed for it the greatest happiness I'd ever known." In the name of momentary happiness, she made choices that brought her despair.

This is always how the devil works. Like someone baiting a trap, he offers false happiness to bring utter ruin. How else could he get us to bite?

The devil has been trapping and devouring people for millennia—he's good at it. "Be alert. . . . Your enemy the devil prowls around like a roaring lion looking for someone to devour" (1 Peter 5:8, NIV).

J. R. R. Tolkien (1892–1973) wrote, "It does not do to leave a live dragon out of your calculations, if you live near him."[7] Walking this planet, we dare not be ignorant of Satan's strategies (see 2 Corinthians 2:11). And one of his favorite strategies, sometimes unwittingly aided by believers, is constructing an imaginary chasm between Jesus and happiness.

RECOGNIZING OUR CRAVINGS HELPS US AVOID THE TRAP OF IDOLATRY.

Augustine said, "This is the happy life, to rejoice to Thee, of Thee, for Thee. . . . For they who think there is another, pursue some other and not the true joy."[8]

The happy life is to worship God as God—and not put anything or anyone else in his place. But in this fallen world, we can't simply affirm God as the source of happiness without dealing with the competition. Take a look at this list of potential idols. All can be legitimate sources of happiness when enjoyed in their rightful position below God, but they become toxic when we elevate them above him.

- loving family relationships
- supportive friendships
- intellectual advancement, education, and learning
- reputation, popularity, and fame
- meaningful work
- serving others
- self-expression (artistic, musical, literary, etc.)
- leisure, hobbies, and entertainment
- sports
- politics, power, influence, and success
- leaving a legacy
- faith, spirituality, religion, and philosophy
- health and fitness
- beauty and youthfulness
- comfort
- food and drink
- sex
- wealth

God isn't listed because he's the only one we can worship without committing idolatry. If God is at the center, almost anything on this list can help us enjoy happiness in him.

Resisting the Christoplatonism I spoke of earlier, we should remind ourselves, "Every good thing given and every perfect gift is from above, coming down from the Father of lights" (James 1:17, NASB). The problem with idols is not that they're intrinsically wrong. God created wood, stone, and gold, which can be fashioned into heathen idols. Likewise, he created family, friendships, work, music, art, sex, food, drink, and all that we rightly value. But all of these can still become idols—God-substitutes.

Idolaters are condemned by God because "they exchanged the truth about God for a lie and worshiped and served the creature rather than the Creator" (Romans 1:25). Creation and creatures are not the problem; the problem is fallen human hearts that worship these false gods instead of the holy and happy God.

Let's take a closer look at each item on this list. (I'll deal with the final four in the next chapter, where I focus on idols of pleasure.)

Loving Family Relationships; Supportive Friendships
God put within each of us a need to relate to others.

Spouses can be God's gifts, but when they're elevated to the place of God in our lives, they become idols. This is not only wrong but also unfair to them and destructive to our relationships, because no human being is able to meet the needs only God can meet.

Similarly, children are damaged when parents idolize them and smother them in "love," depriving them of opportunities to experience growth. By loving God more than anyone else, we can love others in ways that help them rather than harm them (see Matthew 22:37-39).

Tim Keller writes,

> When we make something into an idol, it continually makes us miserable. If we fall short of it . . . it robs us of joy. If our children are our false god, when their lives are troubled, we will lose our joy; and even when their lives might become troubled (which is all the time!), we will worry, and lose our joy.[9]

Human friendship is one of God's greatest gifts to us—a reflection of the relational goodness of his triune self. God said, "It is not good that the man should be alone; I will make him a helper fit for him" (Genesis 2:18). This statement isn't simply about marriage; it is also about the intrinsic human need for friendship and companionship. It's not good for any of us to be alone. Notice that God didn't say, "I'm all you need," though in one sense that's true. Rather, he said, "I'll give you all you need—and I made you to need others of your kind."

The greater the good—and friendship is a great and powerful good—the greater our potential to pervert and exalt it as if it were God. When we do that, we damage others and ourselves. While few things in life are better than a good friendship, few things are worse than a bad one. And no friendship is worse than an idolatrous one.

Intellectual Advancement, Education, and Learning

The fear of the Lord is the beginning of both knowledge and wisdom (see Proverbs 1:7; 9:10). When centered on God, study and learning can bring great happiness. However, when knowledge-seeking is separated from God, it brings pride and smugness. If we trust in academics and intellect, with their inherent limits and temporary nature, they'll eventually fail us—as will everything we treat as a god that's not God.

King Solomon, the wisest, most knowledgeable man of his day, said, "I have acquired great wisdom, surpassing all who were over Jerusalem before me. . . . I perceived that this also is but a striving after wind. For in much wisdom is much vexation, and he who increases knowledge increases sorrow" (Ecclesiastes 1:16-18). Unless we keep intellectual pursuits in their proper place, they will become mere strivings after the wind.

Reputation, Popularity, and Fame

God has given each of us a platform with our own unique spheres of influence. Recognition can be used for his glory, but it is fleeting—soon the next big thing or important person comes and pushes us out of the way.

It's a pathetic life that's devoted to the pursuit of fame. Few idols are crueler. Ninety-nine percent of people who pursue the fame god are disappointed because they never achieve what they live for. The remaining one percent find themselves more unhappy than ever—not to mention shallow, superficial, insecure, and unloved as a result of what they've done to become famous.

Attempts to find our worth in the eyes of others bring other temptations, especially pride. "Pride goes before destruction, and a haughty spirit before a fall" (Proverbs 16:18). When we live for others' approval, we'll eventually stop seeking to hear God's "Well done." Jesus said, "The righteous will shine like the sun in the kingdom of their Father" (Matthew 13:43). Ironically, if we live for the praise of others now, we leave no room for God's reward later.

A pervasive cultural idol is being "cool." The cult of cool is so ingrained that sometimes we aren't aware of it any more than a fish is aware of water. As is true of most students headed off to college, we want to fit in and be progressive and modern—sometimes so desperately that conformity to the world becomes our god.

One consequence of being a people pleaser is failing to say what's true because it's unpopular. Paul said, "What I want is God's approval! Am I trying to be popular with people? If I were still trying to do so, I would not be a servant of Christ" (Galatians 1:10, GNT).

Meaningful Work

Many people find happiness in their work. This is not inherently a bad thing, as Solomon discovered: "I saw that there is nothing better for a person than to enjoy their work, because that is their lot" (Ecclesiastes 3:22, NIV).

However, it's important that we remind ourselves whom we really work for. That will keep our work from becoming idolatrous: "Whatever you do, work at it with all your heart, as working for the Lord, not for human masters, since you know that you will receive an inheritance from the Lord as a reward. It is the Lord Christ you are serving" (Colossians 3:23-24, NIV). When we do our work independently of Christ, our work easily *becomes* our Christ. However, when we work for him, we experience the right measure of happiness in that work, recognizing it as his gift to us, which pleases him.

Serving Others

Serving others isn't just noble; it's a matter of self-interest, since pouring ourselves out for the good of others brings happiness. But it's important to evaluate whether we're helping others as a way to worship Christ or as a means to receive praise for ourselves and to feel important. We can serve God and others in love, as Jesus commanded us to, but we can also serve so that others will say of us, "What a great servant!"

Jesus spoke these words to the Jewish leaders, but they serve as a valid warning for us as well: "You like to have your friends praise you, and you don't care about praise that the only God can give!" (John 5:44, CEV).

Serving others is a good thing, but if we disconnect it from God, it feeds our egos and makes us imagine we're working our way to Heaven.

The most humble servant of God who faithfully and thanklessly cleans bathrooms or works a factory assembly line has a far greater purpose in life than a king who doesn't honor God. The Lord will lift up those who serve him now in obscurity, making them visible to all (see 1 Peter 5:6).

Artistry and Self-Expression

God shared his artistic abilities with the people he created: "[God] has filled them with skill to do every sort of work done by an engraver or by a designer or by an embroiderer . . . or by a weaver—by any sort of workman or skilled designer" (Exodus 35:35).

Creative skill in art, craftsmanship, music, and literature comes from being made in God's image. When we consciously credit God as the source of these skills, we experience great happiness as we do what he has made us for. When we place our gifts and skills above God, however, they become nothing more than wood, hay, and straw (see 1 Corinthians 3:12)—in other words, flammable gods that won't survive the fire of God's holiness on the Day of Judgment.

Leisure, Hobbies, and Entertainment

Our leisure time can be used in ways that please God—by studying and meditating on his Word (see 2 Timothy 2:15), by resting in Christ (see Matthew 11:28-30), and by recuperating from life's busyness, as Christ commanded his disciples (see Mark 6:31).

Hobbies and God-honoring entertainment can be an enriching part of an abundant, satisfying, and happy life. But leisure time can also deteriorate into hours and days wasted watching mind-numbing television, endlessly browsing the Internet, or indulging in illicit fantasies, whether through pornography, explicit romance novels, or video games.

We'd be wise to take these verses into account as we choose how to spend our time: "Look carefully then how you walk . . . making the best use of the time" (Ephesians 5:15-16); "Be self-controlled and vigilant" (1 Peter 5:8, PHILLIPS).

Sports

Sports can't be inherently bad, or the apostle Paul wouldn't have used them to provide positive analogies: "Every athlete exercises self-control in all things. . . . I do not box as one beating the air. But I discipline my body and keep it under control" (1 Corinthians 9:25-27).

I've participated in sports and enjoy watching them. I've learned that competition can bring health and some happiness. But it can also bring disappointment, bitterness, and self-obsession if not kept in check. Cheering for a team can be harmless fun, but when our enthusiasm isn't yielded to Christ, it can degenerate into an obsessive idol that consumes our limited time and passions, and feeds anger and depression.

It's a fair and idol-exposing question to ask ourselves how much time and money we spend on equipment, tickets, TV packages, fantasy picks, and gear to celebrate our team compared to the time and money we invest in teams that are taking the gospel to the world. If we care more about what's happening on the playing field than the mission field, sports have become an idol. While the happiness they yield comes and goes, happiness in Christ celebrates gains but isn't crushed by losses.

Politics, Power, Influence, and Success

When people put their hope in political parties and beliefs, these can become gods. Christians sometimes view political leaders and their platforms with a degree of faith that should be reserved only for God and his Kingdom. And sometimes they display a degree of hatred and scorn that should be reserved for Satan and his demons.

There's nothing wrong with power in itself, but the fact is, power often corrupts, whether it's in politics, business, or even churches and families.

Political influence is good, provided our focus is Christ centered, with policies that honor God's Word. Success is good, if it's achieved in godly ways. If not, it's thinly disguised idolatry, which is always a failure, no matter how widely we're praised.

Leaving a Legacy

We all leave a legacy—the question is, what kind? Humble, Jesus-centered people leave a legacy of love and godliness, and their children and grandchildren are fortunate indeed. Many wealthy people leave a large inheritance but a poor heritage. Legacies of materialism, cynicism, moral corruption, and self-adulation would be better never left.

Only the legacy of service to Christ leads to true happiness. Most people who die with regrets wish they'd spent more time *with* their children, not more money *on* them.

Faith, Spirituality, Religion, and Philosophy

Studies on happiness show that religious people are happier than those who are nonreligious.[10] The Bible commends true religion, which helps orphans and widows and involves holiness before God (see James 1:27).

But the Bible also shows that religious people, such as the Pharisees, often find their pleasure in self-righteousness (see Matthew 23:25-28) or through oppressing others (see Matthew 23:4, 13-15). Religion can be a vain attempt at glorifying ourselves and trying to work our way to God.

Spirituality can be God centered. But it's also possible to consider ourselves "spiritual" while living in a way that's contrary to Scripture. Rather than trust in our spirituality, we should put our faith in God and thereby become spiritually minded.

Health and Fitness

When I exercise regularly, I'm more energetic and happy, so I try to make it a priority. But obsession with exercise can easily become idolatry. Keeping fit may slow down the physical effects of the Curse, but it can't eliminate them. Some people imagine that if they can just sculpt their bodies to look attractive, they'll be happy. The truth is, we're created with a longing for eternal life that will never be fulfilled before our death and resurrection, no matter how long we manage to live.

It's wise to make reasonable efforts to be healthy by managing our weight and avoiding harmful foods. But when our perspective is off, health can become a god. Some people are obsessive about food and evangelistic about diet plans and supplements, always seeking the magic formula to prevent cancer or make pounds disappear. The goal may be good, but the time, energy, and money invested can end up dominating our conversations and our entire lives.

David prayed, "My health may fail, and my spirit may grow weak, but God remains the strength of my heart; he is mine forever" (Psalm 73:26, NLT). Good health is a blessing. We should be grateful for whatever health we have and take reasonable efforts to maintain it. But health can last only so long, and even the physically fit can experience chronic unhappiness and depression, proving that health isn't a guarantee of happiness and is utterly unworthy of our worship.

Beauty and Youthfulness

Beauty is desirable. Obsession with beauty, however, is ugly. "Charm is deceitful, and beauty is vain, but a woman who fears the LORD is to be praised" (Proverbs 31:30). Our culture praises physical appearance, while God has a different perspective: "Man looks on the outward appearance, but the LORD looks on the heart" (1 Samuel 16:7). After offering a warning about preoccupation with clothes and jewelry, Scripture says, "Let your adorning be the hidden person of the heart with the imperishable beauty of a gentle and quiet spirit, which in God's sight is very precious" (1 Peter 3:4).

In Western cultures, people cling desperately, sometimes pathetically, to youth and beauty. But plastic surgery, Botox, and implants don't contravene mortality. Growing old—and looking it—is part of life. People whose happiness depends on looking good become shallow and pretentious, worshiping youth and mourning its loss but never finding the happiness they seek. Youthfulness is temporary, which means the faith we place in it is temporary too.

When we look at God first and beauty second, we see God in the beauty around us. In the Resurrection, he promises eternal beauty, including contentment with the way he has made us. We've never been as healthy or as beautiful as we'll always be in our resurrection bodies. Eternal youth (accompanied by sage wisdom) awaits God's children. Meanwhile, we should put our trust not in youth or beauty but in the God who by his redemptive grace will grant these things to us.

THERE'S ROOM FOR ONLY ONE OBJECT OF WORSHIP IN OUR LIVES.

Evangelist George Whitefield said, "Could [Satan] give you the whole world, yea, that could not make you happy without God. It is God alone . . . that can give solid lasting happiness to your souls; and he for this reason only desires your hearts, because without him you must be miserable."[11]

Everything that threatens to occupy the throne that only God can fill is an idol, and God calls us to ruthlessly dethrone these false gods: "This is what you are to do to them: Break down their altars, smash their sacred stones, cut down their Asherah poles and burn their idols in the fire" (Deuteronomy 7:5, NIV).

John Piper says, "We all make a god out of what we take the most pleasure in."[12] The one way to avoid idolatry is to take the most pleasure in the one true God. As Christ-followers, we shouldn't be more tolerant of our idols than God was of Israel's. Once we recognize those idols, we can destroy them, exalting God alone.

Only then can we know true and lasting happiness—the kind that all lesser pleasures are but shadows of.

CHAPTER 9

WHAT HAPPENS WHEN WE PUT PLEASURE IDOLS IN GOD'S PLACE?

*Oh, the joys of those who trust the LORD, who have no confidence
in the proud or in those who worship idols.*

PSALM 40:4, NLT

*I feel greater pity for someone who takes delight in a sinful deed than for
someone else who seems to suffer grievously at the loss of pernicious pleasure
and the passing of a bliss that was in fact nothing but misery.*

AUGUSTINE

YOUSSUF ISHMAELO, THE "Terrible Turk," was an international wrestling phenomenon in the 1890s who was known for demolishing his opponents. A suspicious man, he demanded his winnings in gold and strapped them into his belt, which he never removed.

Then, while he was heading home from a victory in America, his ship sank. Survivors remember Ishmaelo acting "like a wild beast." With a dagger in hand, he forced his way through the frightened crowds who were waiting to board the lifeboats. He came to a fully loaded boat that was already being lowered. Ignoring the shouts of the crew, he jumped into it. His significant weight, together with the force of his leap, overturned the boat, and all its occupants were thrown into the sea. Ishmaelo, though a good swimmer, was dragged down under the weight of his $10,000 gold belt.[1]

Contrast this example of one who turned wealth into an idol with Stanley Tam, who used wealth as a tool to worship God.

As a young door-to-door salesman, Tam met a farmer's wife who told him about Jesus. He soon placed his faith in Christ. With twenty-five dollars in his pocket, plus twelve dollars added by his father, he launched the United States Plastic Corp. Tam later sensed that God wanted to run the business with Tam as his employee. So he legally made God the majority owner of the business, gifting 51 percent of the company's stock to a nonprofit.

As the business prospered, Tam used all his profits to spread the gospel. His salary was a small fraction of what CEOs typically earn. He was careful not to rob God's glory, and he continually sought to give more to missions, ultimately contributing more than $140 million.

Tam was inspired to give through Jesus' story of the merchant who sold everything to purchase a pearl of great value (see Matthew 13:45-46). Like the man in Christ's story, Tam joyfully placed 100 percent ownership of United States Plastic Corp. into a foundation that established churches in developing countries.

He guarded himself against idolatry by giving God prominence in his life. As I write this, Stanley Tam is a happy ninety-nine-year-old who is anticipating the words, "Well done, my good and faithful servant."[2]

ANY TRUST TRANSFERRED FROM THE INFINITE, HOLY GOD TO CREATED THINGS INVOLVES DRAMATIC LOSS.

God gave Moses the Ten Commandments, the first and second of which are, "You shall have no other gods before me" and "You shall not make for yourself a carved image, or any likeness of anything.... You shall not bow down to them or serve them" (Exodus 20:3-5).

Meanwhile, the Israelites were worshiping a golden calf. When Moses descended from the mountain, we're told that he "took the calf that they had made and burned it with fire and ground it to powder and scattered it on the water and made the people of Israel drink it" (Exodus 32:20). This is a graphic example of being made to taste the bitter, nauseating reality of idol worship. It symbolizes how all idolaters end up with the terrible aftertaste and stomach-wrenching consequences of worshiping idols that promised them happiness.

In the idol-worshiping cultures described in the Bible, when the gospel took hold of hearts, idols were collected and destroyed. The new converts in Ephesus burned their books of sorcery (see Acts 19:19). The books weren't idols of wood or gold with graven images, but the content they contained dishonored God.

The challenge we face today is our often unconscious worship of idols. These idols may be less obvious than golden calves or statues of Baal, but they are idols nonetheless.

We need to train ourselves and future generations to see how idols manifest themselves in our culture. These things usually aren't intrinsically bad—everything from food and clothes to celebrities, video games, sports, and sex. A significant part of following Christ is learning to identify and tear down idols—figuring out how to enjoy his creations while worshiping God alone.

Young Scottish theologian Henry Scougal (1650–1678) said that God's love is "that alone which can make [the soul] happy. The highest and most ravishing pleasures, the most solid and substantial delights . . . arise from . . . a well-placed and successful affection."[3]

We place our affections where we choose—whether on God or on God-substitutes. Joshua called on the Israelites to follow God intentionally: "Choose for yourselves this day whom you will serve, whether the gods which your fathers served that were on the other side of the River, or the gods of the Amorites, in whose land you dwell. But as for me and my house, we will serve the Lord" (Joshua 24:15, NKJV). People will not turn from idols to the true God unless they know how great and satisfying God is and recognize, in contrast, the destruction and misery idols bring.

WE TURN TO IDOLS WHEN WE LOSE SIGHT OF GOD.

Everything about God is suited to fill us with wonder and amazement, but some deny him as Creator. Naturalism, taken at face value, is the enemy of awe, explaining the physical universe as the random product of time and chance. Even so, there's still plenty of wonder in many naturalists. Carl Sagan is remembered for the awe he demonstrated as he spoke about the cosmos. He didn't believe in a creator, and sadly the cosmos itself became the object of his devotion. He was right to admire the universe, but he stopped short of experiencing the greatest wonder of all: the holy and loving God who created it.

We are like blind people standing before a glorious sunset. But we're not completely blind, since Romans 1:19-20 tells us that God has shown himself to us in his creation.

People sometimes credit the creation of this world to random forces or even to the stars, aliens, or mythical gods. That's idolatry. We can't deny the marvels of the night sky, the Grand Canyon, or Niagara Falls. But rather than worshiping their Creator, we tend to create fictional alternatives that exclude a holy God to whom we're morally accountable.

To compensate for God's supposed absence, culture manufactures its own sources of awe: the Super Bowl, concerts, thrill rides, 3-D movies, gourmet food, fine wines, runners' highs, chemical highs, and sexual highs. The term *awesome*, once reserved for God, is now applied to new music downloads or a good pizza.

The transcendence in this universe should remind us that there's someone outside the universe who works inside it. Too often we refuse to turn to the true God of the Bible, who is full of grace and truth. But we must turn somewhere—and if we don't turn to God, then we inevitably turn to idols. (We are made to worship, just as we're made to seek happiness—it isn't a matter of whether we'll worship but who or what we'll worship.)

Tim Keller states, "Sin isn't only doing bad things, it is more fundamentally making good things into ultimate things. Sin is building your life and meaning on anything, even a very good thing, more than on God. Whatever we build our life on will drive us and enslave us. Sin is primarily idolatry."[4]

Comfort

When we put comfort above serving God, we turn that pleasure into an idol. In contrast, those who find their delight in God are motivated to follow him, even if that means leaving their recliner, remote, computer, and the securities of home in order to engage with others.

The God of providence and common grace grants us innumerable pleasures. A good night's sleep, a hot bath, chocolate, laughing with friends, a warm house, a classic movie, playing catch with children, fresh biscuits with melting butter, mountain biking, walking the dog—these pleasures and a thousand others are gifts from God we can thank him for, exalting him as our creator and benefactor and source of happiness.

When Paul instructed Timothy to teach people to share their wealth, he said they should "put their hope in God, who richly provides us with everything for our enjoyment" (1 Timothy 6:17, NIV). God has provided for us in his creation a wealth of pleasures and comforts he desires us to enjoy. Unfortunately, because we're fallen creatures and don't see clearly, we can focus our lives on otherwise legitimate pleasures, turning them into idols.

Some "pleasures" are harmful and addictive. People take drugs to relieve boredom, to escape, to relax, to fit in, or to rebel. Instead of providing a solution to unhappiness, drugs—like other quick hits of pleasure—bring the very unhappiness we hope they'll relieve.

Food and Drink

Food can honor God when it fuels our bodies and brings us pleasure. But when food becomes the focus of our lives, as demonstrated by compulsive overeating, binging, or self-starvation, it turns into an idol that robs people of happiness. Though the sin of gluttony is rarely discussed these days, Paul spoke against those whose "god is their stomach" (Philippians 3:19, NIV).

Likewise, people can enjoy alcohol in moderation, or it can become an addiction. A member of Alcoholics Anonymous wrote a list of reasons for drinking. His first two statements:

1. We drank for happiness and became unhappy.
2. We drank for joy and became miserable.[5]

Food commercials rarely show overweight people. Wine and beer commercials never show drunks and ruined families. Cigarette ads don't show people dying of lung cancer.

Food and drink find their proper place when we live out 1 Corinthians 10:31: "Whether you eat or drink, or whatever you do, do all to the glory of God."

Sex

Sex as God intended—in marriage, between a man and a woman—is a pleasure to be celebrated (see Proverbs 5:15-19). Sex outside of marriage brings serious negative consequences—emotional, physical, and spiritual. Promising long-term pleasure it can't deliver, addiction to sex and pornography enslave and degrade everyone involved. "[The adulterer] follows her, as an ox goes to the slaughter. . . . He does not know that it will cost him his life" (Proverbs 7:22-23).

Research data from 16,000 American adults who were asked confidentially how many sex partners they'd had in the preceding year proved the same point made in the book of Proverbs: "Across men and women alike, the data show that the optimal number of partners is one."[6] Other research similarly revealed that "people with more sexual partners are less happy."[7]

Satan would like us to believe that people who have sex outside marriage are happier, but that's a lie.

The unhappiest-looking person I've ever seen—face drawn and haggard, eyes vacant—was holding a sign that said, "Gay and happy about it." I'm not suggesting, of course, that homosexuals can never be happy. God's common grace offers some happiness to all. But Romans 1:27 speaks of those making these choices as "receiving in themselves the due penalty for their error." Romans lists many other sins God hates, yet that one is singled out as particularly self-punishing.

I've had long, honest talks with those living the "gay lifestyle" who are decidedly miserable—just like many heterosexuals who have idols of their own.

Teenagers and single adults often face heavy pressure to pretend they're having a great time sleeping around, when privately they're filled with self-loathing and disillusionment, because reality never lives up to the promises. Likewise, there's pressure on gay people to project an image of fulfillment. Some people—both heterosexuals and homosexuals—go out of their way to publicly celebrate their promiscuous behavior, all while trying to ignore the emptiness and pain. With the Satan-scripted obligatory claim, "[Fill in sin] makes me happy," they offer false advertising for the father of lies, who relishes their self-destruction.

The god of lust dominates countless lives in our culture. Jesus said, "I tell you that anyone who looks at a woman lustfully has already committed adultery with her in his heart" (Matthew 5:28, NIV). Then he added, "If your right eye makes you stumble, tear it out and throw it from you. . . . If your right hand makes you stumble, cut it off and throw it from you" (Matthew 5:29-30, NASB). How decisively do we deal with the idol of lust? To find true happiness, radical steps are required to dethrone it and put God in his proper place.

In *Future Grace*, John Piper writes that we "must fight fire with fire. The fire of lust's pleasures must be fought with the fire of God's pleasures. . . . We must fight it with a massive promise of superior happiness. We must swallow up the little flicker of lust's pleasure in the conflagration of holy satisfaction."[8]

Wealth

While many would say that money can't buy happiness, nearly everyone wants to test the theory!

Most people believe they would become happy if only they had more money. However, lottery winners provide a telling case study of what happens when people's financial dreams come true.

As I write, 130,000 Powerball tickets are sold each *minute*. Buyers have high hopes, yet the track record of happiness for winners is shockingly dismal. After a group of coworkers won $450 million in the lottery in 2013, Willie Seeley—a memorable figure with long beard, tinted glasses, and a battered straw hat—took the microphone at a press conference. Beaming, he said, "We are very happy, happy, happy." He and his wife appeared on NBC's *Today* show, where he said he was going to fish, hunt, and do as he pleased.

After only two months, Willie and his wife were full of regrets. He said, "There are days I wish we were back to just getting paid every two weeks. You have to change your whole way of life, but we didn't want to change the way we lived."

His wife, Donna, called their winnings "the curse." Seeley offered this advice for the new winner of a $400 million lottery: "Just disappear. . . . Get lost while you still can." Feeling sorry for the winner, he said, "The drama is nonstop."[9]

Individual experiences may differ, but it's fair to say that over the long haul, personal happiness is rarely increased by gaining a windfall of money. Here are summaries of eight winners' stories:

- Charles Riddle won a big lottery in 1975. After getting divorced and facing several lawsuits, he was arrested for selling cocaine.[10]
- William "Bud" Post won $16.2 million in 1988. He was sued by a former girlfriend who wanted the money, and his brother hired a hit man, hoping to murder him and inherit his fortune. After a year, he was $1 million in debt and then went to jail for shooting a gun over a bill collector's head. Post called winning the money a "nightmare." He died in 2006, after declaring bankruptcy.[11]
- Jeffrey Dampier won $20 million in 1996 and bought homes for his relatives. Several years later, his sister-in-law and her boyfriend kidnapped him and murdered him to get the money.[12]
- Billie Bob Harrell Jr. won $31 million in 1997. Harrell used the money to purchase a ranch, several homes, and cars for himself and his family. His spending and lending spiraled out of control, and not long after, he divorced. Just twenty months after winning, Harrell killed himself with a shotgun.[13]
- Jack Whittaker won $315 million in 2002. His life after the win involved arrests, shattered relationships, lawsuits, and the death of loved ones, including one from a drug overdose. Whittaker's ex-wife later said she wished she'd "torn up the ticket."[14]
- Callie Rogers won $3 million in 2003. Sixteen-year-old Rogers, one of England's youngest winners, spent the money on fancy cars, gifts, lavish vacations, and plastic surgery. An ex-boyfriend got her hooked on cocaine, and she attempted suicide twice.[15]
- Keith Gough won about $18 million in 2005. He used the money to buy racehorses, and he divorced his wife. It wasn't long before his life started falling apart: he was conned by a girlfriend, he developed cirrhosis of the liver from alcoholism, and he died in 2010. He told a newspaper, "My life was brilliant but the Lottery ruined everything. My dreams turned to dust. . . . What's the point of having money when it sends you to bed crying?"[16]
- Abraham Shakespeare won $31 million in 2006. Shakespeare went missing in 2009 after spending most of the money. A few months later, his body was found under a slab of concrete.[17]

People dream of winning the lottery because they're certain it will bring them lasting happiness. As long as they don't win, hope remains. But once they do and they still don't find lasting happiness, hope vanishes. When money is exposed as the idol it is, those who have worshiped it are devastated. Unfortunately, we're experts at ignoring wealth's track record.

THE RICHEST MAN IN THE WORLD HAD EVERYTHING BUT HAPPINESS.

King Solomon's life was full of all the finest things—beauty, education, productive work, art, music, women, the finest food and wine, entertainment, success, power, and wealth. He didn't just find a new spouse when he became rich and powerful; he acquired seven hundred wives and three hundred mistresses. "I refrained from nothing that my eyes desired. I refused my heart no pleasure" (Ecclesiastes 2:10, CEB). Solomon possessed nearly everything on our list of potential idols—the things we seek for happiness.

What was his appraisal once he obtained all this? "But when I surveyed all that my hands had done, and what I had worked so hard to achieve, I realized that it was pointless—a chasing after wind" (Ecclesiastes 2:11, CEB).

Here is Solomon's summary of one of the most seemingly enviable lives in history: "Utterly meaningless! Everything is meaningless" (Ecclesiastes 1:2, NIV).

Solomon started well, asking the Lord for wisdom (see 2 Chronicles 1:7-13), but he lost his way. In the end, after experiencing the emptiness of idolatry in dozens of forms, he offered this seasoned advice: "Remember also your Creator" and "Fear God and keep his commandments, for this is the whole duty of man. For God will bring every deed into judgment, with every secret thing, whether good or evil" (Ecclesiastes 12:1, 13-14).

EMBRACING A WRONG VIEW OF GOD IS IDOLATRY.

We worship whatever we believe will ultimately make us happy. But it's possible to worship the God of the Bible while believing things about him that aren't true. So we worship a false object in a way that makes even what we call "God" into an idol.

It's common to hear people say, "I like to think of God not as my judge but as my papa," or "I like to think of Jesus as my friend, not my master." But he's all the things Scripture reveals him to be, all the time, including judge, father, friend, and master. His attributes aren't a smorgasbord for finicky Christians to choose what they want and leave the rest untouched.

If we take one attribute of God—his love, for instance—and divorce it from his other attributes, including his holiness, we end up worshiping our own distorted concept of love instead of the true God. He is indeed love, but he has many other qualities as well. We're to worship the God of love *and* holiness, grace *and* truth, justice *and* compassion, wrath *and* mercy, jealousy *and* happiness.

Jesus is not only the Lamb of God or the Good Shepherd. He's those and much more. The gentle, compassionate Jesus is also the Jesus who drove the merchant-thieves from the Temple and spoke condemnation against self-righteous religious leaders. Were Jesus as meek and mild as many think, he never would have been crucified. But his less popular qualities so outraged people that they nailed him to a cross.

We should believe all that Scripture says about God—the parts that make sense to our finite, little minds and those that don't. Only then can we avoid idolatrous thoughts about him.

HAPPINESS BECOMES AN IDOL WHENEVER WE FAIL TO LOOK FOR IT IN GOD.

Puritan preacher George Swinnock (1627–1673) said, "What joy is there in being with Christ. . . . How happy are they that enjoy the fountain, if some small streams are so pleasant!"[18] Every stream we enjoy should move our thoughts back to the ultimate source.

Since I've been speaking so positively about happiness, it may seem surprising to say it can be an idol. But that shouldn't be unexpected for two reasons. First, nearly everything else that can become an idol in a fallen world is also good. Second, the happiness I've been praising has been happiness *in God*. Happiness in God is never an idol, because by definition it recognizes God as God and is grounded in him and the gospel of Jesus.

The search for happiness is behind all God-honoring worship, just as it's at the root of all idolatry. What motivates people to worship stones and statues? They hope to receive benefits. Rain gods are worshiped because people want rain. Likewise, there are fertility gods for having children, harvest gods for bringing in crops, and war gods for gaining power and strength.

Worshipers sincerely believe that idols will bring them happiness. Isn't that the same reason more "civilized" cultures worship ideologies and material wealth?

In 1629 Edward Leigh wrote, "The happiness of man consists in the enjoying of God. All other things are no otherwise means of happiness or helps to it, then as we see and taste God in them."[19] This wise Puritan was saying that the very things God has given us to make us happy succeed in doing that only when we are first and foremost finding our happiness in God.

The person without Christ can see a little of God's grace in the secondaries without recognizing it, while the committed Christ-follower sees him in every lesser joy.

HAPPINESS IS DIFFERENT FROM OTHER IDOLS.

Our desire for happiness moves us toward idols or toward God—depending on where we think we can find that happiness.

Things become idols not because they're wrong in themselves but because we put them in God's place. This is true of happiness also. We need to say no to things that cause harm, like drugs or stealing, but the solution is never to say no to happiness. What we should say no to are false notions of happiness—but this is not saying no to happiness; in fact, it requires saying yes to true happiness.

If someone idolizes the stars of the night sky, we shouldn't try to convince that person that the stars aren't beautiful or wondrous! Rather, we should point to the one who made them—the most beautiful, most wondrous being in the universe. If people worship the forests, the ocean, or animals, we should help them see that they're right to love these things but that the one who made them warrants their exclusive worship and can give them the happiness they crave.

Tony Reinke perceptively states, "The serious problem with atheism is not *intellectual atheism*, denying God's existence. The real problem is *affectional atheism*, finding God to be an obstruction in the path of personal joy. This practical atheism is the fundamental root problem of humanity and it plagues the hearts of atheists, agnostics, and even professing deists alike."[20]

C. S. Lewis wrote in *The Weight of Glory*,

> The books or the music in which we thought the beauty was located will betray us if we trust to them; it was not *in* them, it only came *through* them, and what came through them was longing. . . . If they are mistaken for the thing itself, they turn into dumb idols, breaking the hearts of their worshippers. For they are not the thing itself; they are only the scent of a flower we have not found, the echo of a tune we have not heard, news from a country we have never yet visited.[21]

If gambling, alcohol, soccer, or fantasy football has become an idol to us—as nearly anything can—we'd be wise to give it up. But we can't give up our desire for happiness. Instead, we need to turn it to its proper object—God—putting him first by seeking our greatest happiness in him.

WHAT WE REALLY WANT IS WHAT NO IDOL CAN GIVE US: NEVER-ENDING HAPPINESS.

Historian Mark Noll writes, "The cross, in sum, was God's everlasting 'no' to the most fundamental human idolatry of regarding the self as a god. It was God's final word of condemnation for all efforts to enshrine humanity at the center of existence."[22]

Any pleasure that enslaves brings minutes of happiness, but prolonged unhappiness inevitably follows, just as the pleasure of overeating lasts about as long as that second helping of ice cream.

We want joy to last our whole lives. (We also want our lives to last—which becomes a problem!) But what does "lasting" mean? Suppose you live to be one hundred and manage to enjoy plentiful happiness. How "lasting" will your happiness be if it ends in death?

Consider the expression YOLO: "You only live once." It rightly recognizes we will die, but it assumes we'll never live again *after* we die.

The Good News is radically different from this temporal mind-set. Christ promises that those who believe in him will not perish but will have everlasting life (see John 3:16). He says, "Whoever believes in me, though he die, yet shall he live" (John 11:25). The gospel has power that not only affects this life but transcends it.

This idea of hope for the future is where every secular happiness guru, book, and seminar falls fatally short. It's one thing to speak to a thirty-year-old about hope, but what about a ninety-year-old who can no longer walk? We want everlasting relationships, health, wealth, beauty, significance, success, and security.

For those who haven't embraced Christ's promise of eternal life as resurrected people on a New Earth, there's no hope for a body and mind that will be forever young. The Christian worldview offers the majority of things on our current happiness list in an embodied life without end, in a transformed culture, on a resurrected Earth—where none of these things will ever again tempt us toward idolatry.

A life characterized by an eternal perspective focuses on long-term happiness. In saying no to idolatrous pleasures and saying yes to the pleasures of God—present and future—we choose what is for both his glory and our good.

CHAPTER 10

WHAT (OR WHO) IS OUR PRIMARY SOURCE OF HAPPINESS?

You make known to me the path of life; in your presence there is fullness of joy; at your right hand are pleasures forevermore.
PSALM 16:11

As there is the most heat nearest to the sun, so there is the most happiness nearest to Christ.
CHARLES SPURGEON

C. S. LEWIS WROTE this caution about what happens when we promote a good thing in our lives to the main thing:

> The woman who makes a dog the centre of her life loses, in the end, not only her human usefulness and dignity but even the proper pleasure of dog-keeping. . . . Every preference of a small good to a great, or partial good to a total good, involves the loss of the small or partial good for which the sacrifice is made. . . . You can't get second things by putting them first. You get second things only by putting first things first.[1]

When *60 Minutes* correspondent Steve Kroft interviewed superstar quarterback Tom Brady of the New England Patriots, an obviously unhappy Brady said, "Why do I have three Super Bowl rings, and still think there's something greater out there for me? I mean, maybe a lot of people would say, 'Hey man, this is what is.' I reached my goal, my dream, my life. Me, I think: 'God, it's gotta be more than this. . . .'"

"What's the answer?" Kroft asked.

Brady responded, "I wish I knew. I wish I knew."[2]

While countless other athletes believe they would be happy if they had Brady's achievements, he knows differently. He has all the secondary things people long for. But without what's primary, he remains unfulfilled.

THE SATISFIED SOUL LOOKS UPWARD AND OUTWARD.

Happiness can't be bigger than its source. God is primary; all other forms of happiness—relationships, created things, and material pleasures—are secondary. If we don't consciously see God as their source, these secondary things intended for enjoyment can master us.

Things such as winning a game, a promotion, or the lottery; taking a new job or a vacation are too small to bring big happiness. God, on the other hand, "satisfies the longing soul, and the hungry soul he fills with good things" (Psalm 107:9). We're finite and fallen, and we lack what's required for happiness. All those who look within themselves for pleasures and delight are doomed to misery.

Christ-followers enjoy what God provides first and foremost because they enjoy the God who provides them. Unlike us, God is infinite and without flaws. Secondary things bring some joy, but God alone is our "exceeding joy" (Psalm 43:4). Samuel Rutherford wrote, "It is the infinite Godhead that must allay the sharpness of your hunger after happiness, otherwise there shall still be a want of satisfaction to your desires."[3]

Secondary things are not incidental or unimportant—they're God's gifts to draw us to him—so we should never disdain the created world. But by putting God first and his creation second, the world and its beauties become instruments of joy and worship. We love them better when we love God more than them.

Why do we watch the World Series or the Olympics? Why do we go to the Grand Canyon, the Alps, or the ocean? Why do we want to get near bigness and beauty and magnificence? Because we find happiness in beholding what's greater than ourselves. It's what we're made for: an infinitely great, happy-making God.

TO LOVE GOD IS TO KNOW HAPPINESS.

Augustine wrote, "He is happy who possesses God."[4] Taking that idea one step further, he said, "[God] is the fountain of our happiness, He the end of all our desires."[5]

Augustine was right: "It is the decided opinion of all who use their brains that all men desire to be happy. . . . The happy life which all men desire cannot be reached by any who does not cleave with a pure and holy love to that one supreme good, the unchangeable God."[6]

For Augustine, God and happiness were inseparable. He said, "Following after God is the desire of happiness; to reach God is happiness itself."[7] He also said, "The greatest commandment, therefore, which leads to happy life . . . is this: 'Thou shalt love the Lord thy God with all thy heart, and soul, and mind.'"[8] He added, "In order that we may attain this happy life, he who is himself the true Blessed [happy] Life has taught us to pray."[9]

What would you think if you heard a modern pastor say, "Jesus encouraged us to pray so that we'll be happy"? To Augustine this made perfect sense, not because his spirituality was shallower than ours, but because it was deeper. He viewed God as the source of all happiness, so he viewed all God's commands as leading to our happiness.

Many Christians are convinced that happiness is a foreign term that slipped into the church from contemporary culture; hence, they labor to keep it at bay. But Augustine lived in the fourth century—his thoughts weren't the product of modern trends.

GREAT THINKERS THROUGHOUT HISTORY HAVE UNDERSTOOD THAT ALL HAPPINESS ORIGINATES IN GOD.

God is happiness in the same sense that God is love (see 1 John 4:8). He is the *essence* of love and happiness.

Puritan preacher Thomas Brooks (1608–1680) said, "Nothing can make that man truly miserable that hath God for his portion, nor nothing can make that man truly happy that [lacks] God for his portion. God is the author of all true happiness; he is the donor of all true happiness; he is the maintainer of all true happiness, and he is the centre of all true happiness. . . . He that hath him for his God, for his portion, is the only happy man in the world."[10]

Puritan Jeremiah Burroughs (1600–1646) spoke about the futility of finding happiness in anything other than God:

That is just as if a man were hungry, and to satisfy his craving stomach he should gape and hold open his mouth to take in the wind, and then should think that the reason why he is not satisfied is because he has not got enough of the wind; no, the reason is because the thing is not suitable to a craving stomach.[11]

In 1611, the same year the King James Version of the Bible was published, Robert Bolton (1572–1631) wrote that God "alone is the highest perfection of bliss, a river of infinite pleasures, the well of life, and endless rest of all created desires."[12]

John Bunyan (1628–1688), the author of *The Pilgrim's Progress*, wrote,

God alone is able by himself to put the soul into a more blessed, comfortable, and happy condition than can the whole world; yea, and more than if all the created happiness of all the angels of heaven did dwell in one man's bosom.[13]

Nearly all the Puritans affirmed God as the birthplace of human happiness. They didn't mean that the Earth and its inhabitants had no beauty and value and shouldn't be enjoyed. Instead, they understood that when cut off from their primary source, the beauty and joy of the secondary diminishes and ultimately disappears.

John Calvin said, "If it is the very summit of happiness to enjoy the presence of God, is it not miserable to [lack] it?"[14]

HAPPINESS CAN ALWAYS BE TRACED BACK TO GOD.

If an atheist enjoys the cool breeze of a sunny autumn day as he writes his treatise on God's nonexistence, the source of his pleasure is God. For God is the author of the universe itself: the Earth, cool breezes, sunny days, the atheist made in God's image, the physical sensations that give the capacity to enjoy nature, and even the powers of rational thought the atheist uses to argue against God.

In diagram 6, the person depicted as experiencing happiness may not realize that the entire circle of human happiness exists within the infinitely larger circle of God and his happiness.

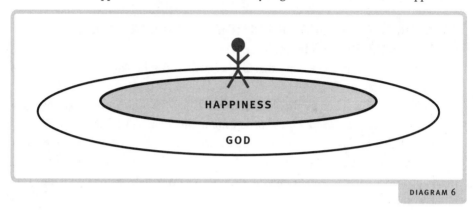

DIAGRAM 6

One of the keys to enjoying the Christian life is connecting the dots between our happiness and God as its provider, as well as between our happiness and God's own happiness.

When I run with my dog or look at Jupiter dominating the sky over Mount Hood, I experience happiness. Unbelievers are capable of enjoying happiness in exactly the same things, but their happiness can't be as immense or enduring, because they stop short of recognizing the one whose overflowing reservoir of happiness has spilled over into his creation.

This helps us understand what Asaph says in Psalm 73: "Whom have I in heaven but you? And there is nothing on earth that I desire besides you" (verse 25). Is Asaph saying he doesn't desire food, water, clothes, shelter, friendship, and laughter? No. He's saying, in essence, "Of the many things I desire, at the core of all of them is God himself. Therefore, all that I desire is summed up in God alone."

Dutch Reformer and Rotterdam pastor Wilhelmus à Brakel (1635–1711) said essentially the same thing when he wrote, "Such is our God, who . . . with His all-sufficiency can fill and saturate the soul to such an overflowing measure that it has need of nothing else but to have God as its portion. The soul so favored is filled with such light, love, and happiness, that it desires nothing but this."[15]

In the mid-1600s, Puritan John Gibbon said, "God alone is enough, but without him, nothing [is enough] for thy happiness."[16] Whether or not we're conscious of it, since God is the fountainhead of happiness, the search for happiness is *always* the search for God.

Aquinas said, "Of God alone is it true that His Being is His Happiness."[17] Creatures are finite and limited in every way, including in our capacity to generate happiness. God alone need not look outside himself for happiness. But as fallen and rebellious creatures, while we still want happiness, we don't even *want* to want God. In our spiritual darkness, we attribute our happiness to anything and everything but God.

GOD CAN'T MAKE US HAPPY WITHOUT IMPARTING SOMETHING OF HIMSELF.

Puritan William Bates (1625–1699) asked a penetrating question: "Can we frame a fuller conception of happiness than to be perfectly loved by the best and most blessed [happy]

Being, and perfectly to love him?"[18] Scripture and human history, as well as the hearts of all who love God, emphatically answer no.

Considering the vast cultural differences between the Puritans and the atheist-turned-agnostic-turned-Christian C. S. Lewis, the fact that his words so complement the Puritans' writings testifies to the truth they both recognized. In *Mere Christianity*, Lewis wrote:

> What Satan put into the heads of our remote ancestors was the idea that they could "be like gods"—could set up on their own as if they had created themselves—be their own masters—invent some sort of happiness for themselves outside God, apart from God. And out of that hopeless attempt has come nearly all that we call human history—money, poverty, ambition, war, prostitution, classes, empires, slavery—the long terrible story of man trying to find something other than God which will make him happy.[19]

Every sin we commit, every shortcoming we display is an attempt to be happy through a God-substitute. Lewis, who spent much of his life trying to find happiness outside God, finally realized he'd been deceiving himself. He wasn't alone.

But it's not only unbelievers who try to find happiness outside God. Every time believers are tempted to sin, we're contemplating whether greater happiness can be found without God. If we imagine it can, we'll succumb to the temptation.

Lewis continued his argument:

> God made us: invented us as a man invents an engine. A car is made to run on petrol, and it would not run properly on anything else. Now God designed the human machine to run on Himself. He Himself is the fuel our spirits were designed to burn, or the food our spirits were designed to feed on. There is no other. That is why it is just no good asking God to make us happy in our own way without bothering about religion. God cannot give us a happiness and peace apart from Himself, because it is not there. There is no such thing.[20]

Lewis also said, "There is a difficulty about disagreeing with God. . . . It is like cutting off the branch you are sitting on."[21]

We're free to be unhappy. We're free to search for happiness where it can't be found. What we're not free to do is reinvent God, the universe, or ourselves so that what isn't from God will bring us happiness.

GOD IS NEVER DISTANT FROM THE HAPPINESS HE GIVES US.

After God made the world, he entrusted it to human care, yet he insists that it still belongs to him: flowers, pinecones, butterflies, planets, nebulae, prairies, mountains, waterfalls. And people.

God is hands-on with what he owns, and he takes full credit for it:

- The earth is the LORD's, and everything in it, the world, and all who live in it. (Psalm 24:1, NIV)

- To the LORD your God belong the heavens, even the highest heavens, the earth and everything in it. (Deuteronomy 10:14, NIV)
- The silver is mine, and the gold is mine, declares the LORD of Hosts. (Haggai 2:8)
- Every animal of the forest is mine, and the cattle on a thousand hills. I know every bird in the mountains, and the insects in the fields are mine. . . . The world is mine, and all that is in it. (Psalm 50:10-12, NIV)
- Whatever is under the whole heaven is mine. (Job 41:11)

The cumulative weight of these verses is staggering. God made *every* source of pleasure, *every* reason for happiness. There has never been nor will there ever be any happiness in the universe that isn't from God.

The more people enjoy good pleasure, the closer they get to seeing God. In *The Screwtape Letters*, the demon Wormwood reports to Screwtape that he has lost his subject to God ("the Enemy"). Screwtape asks, "Could you not have seduced him?" He points out Wormwood's error:

> You . . . allowed the patient to read a book he really enjoyed, because he enjoyed it and not in order to make clever remarks about it to his new friends. In the second place, you allowed him to walk down to the old mill and have tea there— a walk through country he really likes. . . . In other words you allowed him two real positive Pleasures. Were you so ignorant as not to see the danger of this?[22]

Genuine pleasures, even such simple ones, can point people to God. Satan's strategy is to divorce pleasure from its logical connection with God. In doing so, he robs God of glory and us of happiness!

I've heard it said, "We should set our minds on God—no one and nothing else." It sounds spiritual, but is it accurate? Clearly not, since Scripture commands us to think about "whatever is true, whatever is honorable, whatever is just, whatever is pure, whatever is lovely, whatever is commendable, if there is any excellence, if there is anything worthy of praise, think about these things" (Philippians 4:8). Things exist that aren't God but are nonetheless true, honorable, just, pure, lovely, commendable, excellent, and praiseworthy. They are rooted in God's character. We should trace them back to him as we'd trace a sunbeam back to the sun.

So by all means, we should contemplate and enjoy all goodness that isn't God. But when we do so, we should thankfully worship him as the source, so that in thinking of and delighting in every good thing, we'll be thinking of and delighting in God himself.

We err in seeing God as the only happiness and thereby failing to see the countless secondary sources of happiness he has graciously provided.

PUTTING GOD FIRST ENHANCES EVERYTHING BENEATH HIM.

In *Eyes Wide Open*, Steve DeWitt says, "Christians who properly place God as the source and goal of the things they enjoy will find themselves enjoying those things even more.

In truth, the way we as believers relish created beauties ought to outstrip that of unbelievers, since we neither find our identity in them nor hold on to them as ultimate."[23]

Secondary happiness, which is found in something or someone God has created, ultimately leads back to him. Have you ever pointed to something you want a child to see and then watched the child look at your finger instead of what you're pointing at? The secondary only fulfills its purpose when people follow it to the primary.

The man who knows his wife is secondary to God can find great happiness in a relationship with her. In contrast, the man who makes his wife primary will be continuously disappointed because she can't meet his deepest needs. Because he tries to make her into more than any human can be, both will suffer.

Robert Crofts wrote, "Let these earthly pleasures and felicities excite and encourage us to thankfulness, to all duties of virtue and piety, to look higher to their fountain, to God himself, to heaven, to love and enjoy in him, to contemplate his infinite goodness, love, beauty, sweetness, glory, and excellency."[24]

Paul said, "What is our hope, our joy, or the crown in which we will glory in the presence of our Lord Jesus when he comes? Is it not you? Indeed, you are our glory and joy" (1 Thessalonians 2:19-20, NIV).

But, wait—didn't Paul know that God is our only joy? No, he knew that God is our *primary* joy. It's fine for me to say that my wife, my children, my grandchildren, and my friends are joys if I remember that God made them and works through them to bring me happiness. They're not lesser joys to me, but greater ones—precisely because I know whom these gifts come from!

In the movie *The Avengers*, Thor's brother, the evil Loki, weary of the Incredible Hulk, says to him in a commanding voice, "Enough! . . . I am a god, you dull creature!" The Hulk, unimpressed, picks up Loki with one hand and gives him a merciless thrashing, pounding him into the ground. As he walks away, the Hulk turns back toward Loki, looking disgusted, and mutters, "Puny god." Loki, utterly defeated, gives a pathetic little squeak.

All the idols I've talked about are not only false gods but also puny gods. The very gifts of God that can bring us great joy become dismally small when we make them primary. A couch that's plenty big to sit on suddenly becomes tiny when you need someplace to land a plane.

What's big enough to bring us a little happiness from the hand of an infinitely big God isn't nearly big enough to bear the weight of all our happiness. Only the true God is that big, and the larger we see him, the bigger our happiness in him.

DETERMINE TO DRINK FROM THE WELL OF HAPPINESS.

The world is full of desperate people thirsting for happiness. They eagerly drink from contaminated water surrounded by huge signs with neon letters flashing "Happiness." What they long for and desperately need can be found solely in the one and only "fountain of living waters"—God himself. God laments over the poor choices we make: "My people have committed two evils: they have forsaken me, the fountain of living waters, and hewed out cisterns for themselves, broken cisterns that can hold no water" (Jeremiah 2:13).

When I'm thirsty, I don't look up *water* on Wikipedia. I don't go to social media to find out what other people say about water. I don't drink out of the nearest puddle. I go to the faucet and satisfy my thirst by drinking some of the world's best water from the Bull Run water system in Oregon.

I find God to be pure, refreshing, and satisfying. My happiest days are those I drink most deeply of him. I also know that *if I don't drink of him, I will drink something else*—something that will leave me thirsty, dissatisfied, and sick. For idols cannot satisfy. George Whitefield wrote, "I drank of God's pleasure as out of a river. Oh that all were made partakers of this living water."[25]

Jonestown was a socialist community in South America. In 1978, after murdering a US congressman and four others, Jim Jones gathered his cult members, who had relocated from the United States to Guyana, and served them a grape-flavored drink laced with cyanide, thereby killing himself and 912 of his followers.

Hence the expression "Don't drink the Kool-Aid," which means, "Don't follow anyone blindly." This is good advice for gullible people who are prone to believe that counterfeits will really deliver happiness.

Most offers of happiness are deceptions. People were wrong to trust Jim Jones. But we are not wrong to trust Jesus, God's Son, who went to the cross to meet our deepest need: to be reconciled to God. Jesus is fully worthy of our trust, and he makes this offer: "If anyone thirsts, let him come to me and drink. Whoever believes in me, as the Scripture has said, 'Out of his heart will flow rivers of living water'" (John 7:37-38).

Are you thirsty for happiness—for meaning, peace, contentment? Jesus invites you to join millions throughout history and across the globe, and a multitude of those now living in the visible presence of the fountain of living waters, to come to him and drink the best water in the universe—the only refreshment that will ever truly and eternally satisfy.

CHAPTER 11

DO SECONDARY GIFTS HAVE REAL VALUE APART FROM THEIR SOURCE?

Whether you eat or drink, or whatever you do, do all to the glory of God.

I CORINTHIANS 10:31

God is the only source of happiness and joy, and no creature is or can be a source
of happiness independently of Him. But He can and does make use of creatures
to adorn, perfect, and complete the happiness of the whole man.

FLORENTIN J. BOUDREAUX

———————— ❦ ————————

TWO SERIOUSLY ILL men occupied the same hospital room. The man next to the window was able to sit up, while the other couldn't.

Each day the man by the window described in picturesque detail what he saw—including a lake, ducks, and children sailing model boats. This meant the world to his roommate, who had no outside view. Seeing these magnificent sights in his mind's eye brought him daily happiness.

Eventually the man by the window died. His saddened roommate requested a move to the bed by the window. He eagerly looked outside for the first time . . . only to see nothing but an old brick wall.

This story tells of imagination's power to envision true reasons for happiness, even if they're not currently visible. There really are lakes, ducks, and children playing in this world. And behind all these there really is a God who created us, loves us, and has a plan for us. There really is a Heaven, and there will be a New Earth, where all things are made right. This isn't just pretense.

SOMETIMES IT'S DIFFICULT TO SEE REASONS FOR HAPPINESS IN THIS WORLD.

Ever since sin entered the world, we humans have been working at a tremendous disadvantage. Before the Fall, it was natural for Adam and Eve to see God in everything—how could they not? Then came the rebellion, and unnatural sin became the new normal. Now our sinful natures, the fallen world, and the devil conspire to obscure and misrepresent God.

Too often we try to gain happiness with no understanding of how we lost it and why it seems so evasive. The first three chapters of the Bible provide the answer. If we don't embrace the biblical account, this life simply won't make sense. We'll try to fill our emptiness by relentlessly grabbing at secondary means of happiness. John Wesley said, "As there is one God, so there is one religion and one happiness for all men. God never intended there should be any more; and it is not possible there should."[1]

Some prisoners, surrounded by bare walls, see in their mind's eye the world's beauty. Other people, mostly free, are surrounded by rich beauty yet fail to see it at all. The difference is perspective.

J. R. R. Tolkien put it beautifully in *The Fellowship of the Ring*: "The world is indeed full of peril, and in it there are many dark places; but still there is much that is fair, and though in all lands love is now mingled with grief, it grows perhaps the greater."[2]

WHEN WE SEE GOD FOR WHO HE IS, WE CAN SEE THAT HAPPINESS IS ALL AROUND US.

By recognizing God as primary, we maximize our enjoyment of the secondary with no danger of idolizing it. Tim Keller says, "If you uproot an idol in your life and fail to plant the love of Christ in its place, the idol will grow back."[3]

The better I know Jesus, the more I see him all around me—in people, animals, places, and objects. But if I hadn't studied his Word and reflected on his character over the years, I wouldn't have known what to look for. A student of insects or birds can see dozens of fascinating specimens on a short walk. Another person on the same walk, not having learned to observe, can miss them all.

The person who sees God is happy. In ancient church history, seeing God was labeled "the beatific vision," from a Latin expression meaning "the happy-making sight."[4] Revelation 22:4 says that God's servants "will see his face." We won't see God's face until death, but the wonderful news is that we glimpse his face daily while playing with a child, reading a story, or experiencing the exhilaration of a job well done. As we express conscious thanks to God, we can experience the "happy-making sight" here and now in countless ways.

Scripture paints a picture of how we should think about God in our daily lives: we should be talking about (and to) God throughout the day, teaching ourselves and our children to see him in everything (see Deuteronomy 6:1-7). Two of my grandsons love football and speak tirelessly of professional players. So Nanci and I enter into their world. We name those we consider the best players and say, "Isn't it amazing that God has given each person special gifts to use for his glory, and the rest of us get to enjoy it?" In this way, we see God for who he is in the beauty of life. When we see an athlete who honors Christ, we encourage our grandsons with his or her example. When we see ugliness in an athlete who glorifies himself, we see the Curse at work, and it's another teaching opportunity.

These were Moses' last recorded words before he died: "Happy are you, O Israel! Who is like you, a people saved by the LORD, the shield of your help, and the sword of your triumph!" (Deuteronomy 33:29).

Moses was old, nearing death, and he left his people with this message: *be happy in God.* What gave them cause for happiness wasn't their merit or accomplishments, but that they were "saved by the LORD," who was the shield that protected them and the sword that gave them victory. Moses died with perspective because he lived with perspective—centered on the goodness and greatness of God, the rock-solid foundation of happiness. Moses could call on others to be happy in God, because he'd been happy in God.

WE CAN EXPERIENCE GREATER HAPPINESS IN A SECONDARY SOURCE IF WE RECOGNIZE ITS ORIGIN IN WHAT'S PRIMARY.

Mystery writer David Rosenfelt and his wife, Debbie, visited an animal shelter and saw a dirty but adorable terrier about to be euthanized. They took the dog home, named her Princess, bathed her, and listed her for adoption.

Not long after, a couple and their mentally challenged adult son came to look at dogs. The parents favored a golden retriever, but the son, Richard, visibly brightened when he saw Princess. The two connected instantly, and Princess went home with the family.

Three weeks later, the couple called the Rosenfelts, explaining that, as an infant, Richard had been in an accident that left him brain damaged. His behavior was so erratic that for thirty years he had to receive residential care and could only come home on weekends.

But Princess had already transformed Richard. She calmed him, so the doctors agreed that he could move back home with his parents. The couple called the Rosenfelts to say, "Thank you for giving us our son back."

"We were too choked up to say it," David writes, "but of course Princess deserved the credit."[5]

I'm touched by this story. And while it might touch anyone regardless of his or her worldview, its effect on me is greatly enhanced by my beliefs about God's love and providence. This story didn't happen without design. My worldview matches Matthew Henry's (1662–1714), who wrote, "Whatever is the matter of our joy, God must be acknowledged as the Author of it."[6]

Even if the Rosenfelts believed this connection was nothing more than dumb luck, it would still make them happy. For them to be the instruments uniting the boy and dog must have been especially gratifying. I use the term *instrument*, but of course if there were no God and no design, then neither the Rosenfelts nor the dog, neither the son nor his parents, were part of any larger plan. So if the primary happiness of this story is a man and his dog and the people who gave him the dog, then it's at best a good story, touching yet with limited long-term value. However, when the players are supporting actors and God is the screenwriter and director, the people and the dog don't become less important, but more. The happiness of the story ascends from an accidental and passing sentimentality to a transcendent, purposeful, and enduring story of God's grace and kindness.

When the primary is put in the proper place, the secondary is dethroned—yet in being dethroned, it becomes more significant.

SECONDARY SOURCES REFLECT GOD'S HAPPINESS, AS THE MOON REFLECTS THE SUN.

Consider the brightest "stars" in the sky—which are actually the planets Venus, Jupiter, Mars, and Saturn. Unlike the true stars we see, which are far away and therefore dimmer, these planets don't shine with their own light; they are bright only because they reflect the sun. Likewise, the moon is a beautiful sight, but it doesn't generate light on its own. It merely reflects it. *Merely* makes the reflection sound trivial, but this is actually a magnificent phenomenon. The moon was made to glorify the sun, and when it does, it shares in the sun's glory. (If the moon were able to talk, wouldn't we think it foolish if we heard it congratulate itself for how brightly it shines?)

And so it is with secondary sources of happiness. Things such as art, music, literature, sports, careers, and hobbies generate no light of their own. The light they bring comes from "the Father of lights with whom there is no variation or shadow" (James 1:17).

I don't value the planets and moon less because they don't shine by their own light. Likewise, I don't devalue my wife, my children, my grandchildren, my coworkers, or my dog because they're secondary to God. I value them more because the God who is primary has made them who and what they are, and he has endowed them with value that makes them far more important than if they were merely random accidents.

Richard Baxter exalted God as the primary fount of gladness and spoke of the derivative joy that comes from others: "What should be rejoiced in, if not the Lord of life himself, who is the everlasting joy and glory of the saints? If felicity itself cannot make us happy, and life itself is insufficient to quicken us, and the sun itself cannot illuminate us, it is in vain to expect this light, this life, this happiness and joy from any other. . . . Other things may be means of the conveyance, but God is the matter of our joy."[7]

Consider this fatherly advice given in an ancient culture without refined sugar, in which nature's greatest treat was honey: "My son, eat honey, for it is good, and the drippings of the honeycomb are sweet to your taste" (Proverbs 24:13).

The father doesn't warn his son to stay away from honey because he might love honey more than God. If we're thinking biblically, we realize that God created bees to make honey not only for them but for us. He designed our taste buds to enjoy the sweetness of honey—it's a gift to the people he loves. To enjoy that gift is to enjoy the God who gives it to us.

Could someone turn honey into an idol? Of course. This proverb warns, "If you find honey, eat just enough—too much of it, and you will vomit" (Proverbs 25:16, NIV). Enough honey makes us happy. Too much honey makes us sick.

The father's advice to his son requires no explanation as to how it relates to God because that was self-evident to the original audience. The Hebrew worldview saw creation as the expression of the Creator's mind and heart. Therefore, to be happy with honey was to be happy with God. And people's happiness with God's abundant gifts, they knew, made God happy too.

Our modern Western worldview, in which God seldom gets credit for natural processes or the countless little treasures of life, requires us to think more deliberately and to train our children more explicitly to see God's giving hand present everywhere in his creation.

WE SHOULDN'T SEEK THE GIVER *INSTEAD* OF THE GIFTS; WE SHOULD SEEK THE GIVER *THROUGH* THE GIFTS.

Many believers have spiritualized church, preaching, and prayer, and in doing so they have distanced God from creation, pleasure, and happiness. As a young Christian I was told, "Seek the giver, not the gift." In certain contexts that can be an apt warning, but as a general rule it's misguided.

What we should say is, "Seek the giver *through* the gift." I should appreciate and enjoy a wonderful meal consciously aware that it, and my capacity to enjoy it, are God's gifts to me. By enjoying food and drink, I am enjoying him. John Calvin wrote, "In despising the gifts, we insult the Giver."[8]

Dissociating God from his gifts isn't the solution; it's the problem. Instead of viewing God's gifts as demonic temptations, we should view them as benevolent extensions of his love and grace. His gifts to us are not gods—but they are God's. And God himself is the greatest gift he gives us. As long as we realize that and see God in his gifts to us, we need not be suspicious of them or fearful that we are appreciating them too much.

Idolatry becomes a threat whenever we divorce God from pleasure and happiness. It's God's very presence in pleasure, happiness, and the beauty of his creation that should lead us to love him! The message that we must turn away from pleasure, happiness, and creation in order to worship God is fundamentally false and ensures spiritual disaster. Why? Because in the end, people will always love pleasure, happiness, and creation—and so we should. And we will hate unhappy religion; dutiful drudgery; and feelings of guilt for enjoying good food, funny stories, and a great party—and so we should.

In fact, if we don't appreciate the inspired invitation to taste and enjoy delicious food, including honey—and cookies, cake, or ice cream (in moderation)—will we really appreciate God's invitation to "taste and see that the LORD is good" (Psalm 34:8)? This verse is a directive to go to God and experience pleasure and happiness in him. When you taste honey—and Winnie the Pooh will back me up on this—you naturally want more of it. When you taste God, you naturally want more of him!

Instead of reducing pleasure to either cosmic accidents or demonic temptations, we should see them through a biblical worldview: the God who wants us to take pleasure in him made a world filled with pleasures to point us toward him. Having tasted such pleasures and seen that they are good, we can better taste the God who made them and see that he is good. If we don't see their goodness, we won't see his.

WHEN WE WORSHIP AND SERVE THE CREATED RATHER THAN THE CREATOR, OUR HAPPINESS IS ECLIPSED.

In the context of God revealing himself in creation, Paul said, "Although they knew God, they did not honor him as God or give thanks to him. . . . [They] worshiped and served the creature [secondary] rather than the Creator [primary]" (Romans 1:21, 25).

A solar eclipse occurs when the moon passes in front of the sun. In that moment, the moon is seen for what it truly is on its own: *dark*. If the moon always blocked the sun, there would be no light on this planet.

Likewise, when people put secondary things above God and worship created things, what follows is the darkness of an eclipse. We see this daily in our fallen world.

Because of the Fall, creatures are tempted to elevate created things, including themselves, to the status reserved only for the Creator. Eden was right side up, but the Fall turned the world upside down.

In the proud Greek city of Thessalonica, people looked at followers of Jesus and said, "These men who have turned the world upside down have come here also" (Acts 17:6). Ironically, when you flip an already upside-down world, you turn it right side up. The Christian worldview offers a massive correction by acknowledging the true God as primary.

Bonaventure, a thirteenth-century theologian, described how to think backward from what we see: "Finite realities, such as . . . a tree, or a mountain, can be taken as points of departure for the ascent insofar as each of them, in its own way, mirrors God as the creator. . . . God's infinite being then becomes visible, audible, touchable as displayed . . . in the mirror of finite entities."[9] So look at a tree, and worship God.

THERE'S NOTHING WRONG WITH BEING THE EFFECT, NOT THE CAUSE; THE CREATURE, NOT THE CREATOR.

Being finite isn't a sin. The problem with created things is not what they are but what we turn them into: gods.

When we worship God as God, everything else falls into place—good food and drink are delightful; friendship is fulfilling; sex with a marriage partner can be deeply satisfying; and work, hobbies, sports, music, and entertainment can all enrich our lives as intended. That's when those things shine as happy-making gifts from God, "who generously gives us everything for our enjoyment" (1 Timothy 6:17, GNT).

In *Letters to Malcolm*, C. S. Lewis said, "We—or at least I—shall not be able to adore God on the highest occasions if we have learned no habit of doing so on the lowest."[10] If I am not happy in God when I see a waterfall or hear a great symphony or see a child playing in a mud puddle or watch a dog chasing his tail, then I will not be happy in God when I attend church, read the Bible, or pray.

When we treat the secondary as if it were primary, however, we undercut its ability to make us happy. These things can only do so when they stay in their proper place under God. Idolatry is looking to the secondary as the source of happiness rather than as a conduit. What's good ceases to be good only when we give it the prominence that should be reserved for God.

The child who loves to play basketball as one facet of life can one day look back with fond memories and look forward to what's next. The adult who makes basketball the center of his life still ruminates on his childhood successes and failures, and is devastated when his kids don't make the team or when his favorite team loses. The problem isn't basketball; the problem is turning basketball (or anything else) into the main thing.

As long as we see God completing our happiness through his creations, they'll never eclipse his glory.

SECONDARY SOURCES SERVE THEIR HIGHEST PURPOSE WHEN THEY POINT OUR HEARTS TO THE PRIMARY.

Is it really okay for me to enjoy Nanci, my daughters, my grandsons, taco salad, books, biking, snorkeling, and underwater photography? Yes, if they are *part of* enjoying God, and not alternatives to him. As long as they remain under him and I thank him for the happiness he brings through them, they can't compete with him. But if they gain ascendancy over God, they become idols, and I need to renew my mind and put them back in their proper place.

While taking a break from writing this book, I experienced a series of events that illustrated the relationship between the secondary and primary.

First, I stood on our deck and looked up at the cold night sky, filled with the familiar stars I've known and loved since childhood. Then I returned to the warm house and pondered the immensity and beauty of the universe.

I looked at a chair with Nanci's Bible beside it and thanked God for her, a woman of the Word. She's part of a church team that writes and edits lessons for a weekly women's Bible study, and that day she'd led the study. I pondered how Nanci and I have known each other for forty-five years and that I love her more than ever. I marveled at God's grace in bringing us together and thanked him for our two wonderful daughters and our grandchildren.

At that moment Maggie, our golden retriever, sidled up and put her paw on my knee. I stroked Maggie's head, and she gazed into my eyes and sighed deeply. I thanked God for dogs and for Maggie in particular, and I contemplated how God reveals glimpses of himself through his creation. Maggie is loyal to me; God is loyal. She's beautiful; God is the maker of all beauty. Maggie makes me happy many times a day. But because I understand Maggie's true nature and role, I realize it is God, in his kindness, who makes me happy through her. So I poured out my heart in gratitude to him.

All these secondary things are important because they point me to God, the primary. The creation and creatures spontaneously prompt my worship of the Creator. During a break from writing a book about happiness, I realized that I am profoundly happy!

GOD'S SECONDARY GIFTS GIVE US MORE REASONS TO ENJOY AND PRAISE HIM.

Suppose I sit down to enjoy a slice of warm pecan pie à la mode. Should my pleasure in eating it point my heart to God? Absolutely!

I'm not spiritualizing pecan pie; I'm simply following the biblical directive to glorify

God as we eat and drink and do whatever else we do (see 1 Corinthians 10:31). We're to see God and glorify him in even the smallest pleasures of life by consciously recognizing him as the creator and source of all delights. It could be argued that pie tastes just as good with no recognition of God, but experience teaches me otherwise.

I love snorkeling and taking underwater photos of God's sea creatures. I look at photos years later, some of them hanging in our living room and my office, and they take me back to those magical moments of discovery. Raccoon butterfly fish and Christmas wrasses reach out and pull me back to their home in the reef. The photos rekindle my original delight when, peering into the dark shadows of a reef, I saw a puffer fish peeking back with huge eyes and a frogfish masterfully disguising itself as part of the reef. I remember the sudden discovery of a moray eel lurking behind two giant sea turtles and the thrill of seeing one shark, then five, emerging from a cave below me. I recall swimming in the open ocean and suddenly becoming part of a school of dolphins as they wove their way around me. What wonder and worship!

Many people who don't know God love to snorkel. But a large part of my happiness is knowing the God who made all these wonders and sensing his presence with me—both when I'm out in his ocean and as I sit in my home remembering his presence, then and now. This is a shared experience between my God and me, and even as I type, the memories of countless hours spent in the water together, enjoying his beautiful underwater kingdom, bring joyful tears to my eyes.

When we invite God into our happiness, we become aware of how he invites us into his. The happiest times of my life are when I've entered into the happiness of God—not only through Bible study, prayer, and church, but also when reading a good book, laughing with a friend, running, biking, and enjoying the wonders of creation.

CONTINUALLY RECOGNIZING GOD'S PRESENCE IS THE PATH TO HAPPINESS.

Happiness can be sought in thousands of places, but it can be found in only one. And that source, incredibly, is "Christ in you" (Colossians 1:27). He is big enough to create the galaxies, yet he dwells in each of us who know him.

Brother Lawrence (1614–1691) wrote *The Practice of the Presence of God* about his constant, conscious rehearsal of God's presence. He saw his relationship with God not as a mountaintop experience that fades in memory as years pass but as a moment-by-moment lifestyle. His service to God involved contentment with what he called little things:

> Nor is it needful that we should have great things to do. . . . We can do little things for God. I turn the cake that is frying on the pan for the love of Him. When that is done, if there is nothing else to call me, I prostrate myself in worship before Him, who has given me grace to work—afterwards, I rise happier than a king. It is enough for me to pick up but a straw from the ground for the love of God.[11]

The simple, daily cultivation of God-consciousness has had a central role in the increasing happiness I've experienced over the years. I often have coffee with God, and sometimes

I have a meal alone with him. Occasionally when I'm praying, I pull out a chair for him and think of Jesus occupying it (not only did he sit in chairs; he also built them!). I talk to him. I'm not pretending Jesus is with me at lunch or when I pray; I simply believe his promise that he really is with me and I act in keeping with it. If you want to be happy, put meaning to the sometimes empty phrase "spending time with God."

A king's advisers hesitate to interrupt him, but his children are always welcome. God tells us, "Whenever we are in need, we should come bravely before the throne of our merciful God. There we will be treated with undeserved kindness, and we will find help" (Hebrews 4:16, CEV).

We can't spend time with many of the world's famous people, but I have a hunch we'd often be disappointed if we could. We can, however, spend time with God daily—hour by hour. To "pray without ceasing" (1 Thessalonians 5:17) is not an impossible chore but an ongoing delight.

Imagine if we came to God as dogs come to their masters—with tail-wagging enthusiasm, overflowing joy, and complete vulnerability. What if we came bounding into his presence, conveying with everything in us, "I just want to be with you!"?

God wants us to recognize his constant presence and goodness, and thank him not only when things go our way but "in all circumstances" (1 Thessalonians 5:18). This is as close as Scripture gets to a formula for happiness. But it's more than a prescription; it's a happiness-permeated reality for those who live it out.

In order to be happy, we must regain the ground we've forfeited. We've lost our way, sacrificed our relationship with the wellspring of happiness, and violated our purpose for living. We've lost our happiness by seeking it in a million secondary places instead of in the one and only primary source. Left to ourselves, we are desperate and hopeless, and happiness is but an empty dream.

But the good news is that God has not left us to ourselves. What we never could have done by our own strength, the Creator in his grace has done for us: "God shows his love for us in that while we were still sinners, Christ died for us. . . . We have now been justified by his blood. . . . While we were enemies we were reconciled to God by the death of his Son. . . . We also rejoice in God through our Lord Jesus Christ, through whom we have now received reconciliation" (Romans 5:8-11).

This is why the gospel of Jesus Christ is truly, among other things, about both God's happiness and ours. It's about restoring our relationship with the Creator who promises he is with us, in us, and for us—the God from whom happiness flows as freely as pure water from a mountain spring.

PART 2

The Happiness of God

CHAPTER 12

IS GOD HAPPY?

God . . . in eternal felicity alone holds sway. He is King of kings and Lord of lords.
I TIMOTHY 6:15, NEB

Where others see but the dawn coming over the hill, I see the soul of God shouting for joy.
WILLIAM BLAKE

IN THE MOVIE *Chariots of Fire*, Olympic hopeful and eventual gold medalist Eric Liddell is challenged by his sister, Jennie, about his decision to train for the Olympics. He plans to leave for the mission field but delays so he can attempt to qualify in the 400-meter race. In doing so, Jennie thinks he's putting God second. But Eric sees things differently. He explains, "God . . . made me fast, and when I run I feel his pleasure."[1]

Eric and Jennie believe in the same God . . . yet they don't. Both fear and love God. Both are committed to serving Christ. But Eric, who smiles warmly and signs autographs while his sister looks on disapprovingly, has something she lacks: a relaxed, heartfelt awareness of God's happiness—in his creation, in his people, and in all of life, including sports and competition.

Eric wants to serve God as much as his sister does, but he senses God's delight and purpose in making him a fast runner. If God finds pleasure in the majesty of a horse (see Job 39:19-25), surely he finds even greater pleasure in Eric's running for the pure joy of it. Because of the God-centered joy this gift brings him, Eric tells Jennie that giving up running "would be to hold [God] in contempt."

Both Eric and his sister want to reach the world with the gospel. But Eric's good news is far better news. Why? Because it's about more than deliverance from Hell—he understands that God's mind and heart are delightfully engaged in *all* he has created, not just church and ministry. Liddell's belief in a happy God makes his life profoundly attractive.

WHY AREN'T MORE CHRISTIANS MARKEDLY HAPPIER THAN UNBELIEVERS?

We can spend our lives moving our eyes (and our forks) all over our plates, searching for the next bite to eat, instead of enjoying the bite currently in our mouths.

Armand Nicholi observes that despite their dramatically different perspectives, Sigmund Freud and C. S. Lewis agreed that happiness-seeking is universal and central to the human condition. Nicholi comments,

> No aspect of life is more desired, more elusive, and more perplexing than happiness. People wish and strive for what they believe will make them happy—good health, attractive looks, an ideal marriage, children, a comfortable home, success, fame, financial independence—the list goes on and on. Not everyone who attains these goals, however, finds happiness.[2]

Indeed, it could be argued that *most* people who attain these goals find only transitory happiness, because circumstantially determined happiness, by its very nature, cannot last in a world where circumstances fluctuate. From a naturalistic worldview such as Freud's, if death means the end of human existence, then each person's happiness—whether small or great—dies with that person.

But what about those of us who share Lewis's worldview? Though believing there's a sovereign God who loves us theoretically offers a happiness we wouldn't otherwise have, the fact remains that many who affirm this truth aren't much happier than their unbelieving friends. This is puzzling, particularly since God's people have long affirmed the importance of finding happiness in Christ.

What accounts for Christians not experiencing the happiness and joy the Bible often speaks of? I'm convinced a central reason—perhaps *the* central reason—is that many people who believe in God do not believe that God himself is happy. And how could anyone expect that knowing and serving an unhappy God would bring us happiness?

WHY DOES IT MATTER WHETHER WE BELIEVE GOD IS HAPPY AND KIND?

I don't always agree with Terence Fretheim's theology, but here he asks good questions:

> The church has stressed the unhappiness of God—most famously in God's anger at human sin—more than the divine happiness. Does such an emphasis have a negative effect on how people think of God and live their lives? . . . Does the lack of attention to *divine* happiness contribute to the often dour and stern countenance of so many Christians? How might an increased emphasis on divine joy positively affect the teaching and preaching of the church and the well-being of Christians?[3]

Jesus said, "Anyone who loves me will obey my teaching. My Father will love them, and we will come to them and make our home with them" (John 14:23, NIV). Would you prefer to share a home with someone who brings you misery or happiness? Scripture speaks of God's anger, but is his anger a temporary response to sin, or is it his eternal and default condition? Nearly all Christians believe that God is good, but many don't believe that he's good natured.

When we think of God as happy, we see how his happiness overflows in all he does. If your grumpy neighbor asks, "What are you up to?" you'll see it as a suspicious, condemning question. But if your cheerful neighbor asks the same thing, you'll smile and talk about your plans. We interpret people's words according to how we perceive their character and outlook. So it is with our view of God.

Given most people's opinion of God, no wonder they read the Bible negatively, selectively focusing on his anger and judgment while missing his mercy, grace, and happiness. God seems restrictive and condemning because they believe he's against us and our happiness.

The same Scriptures, when read by those who see God as loving and happy, emphatically show that he has our best interests at heart. For them, the Bible becomes a warm, living document instead of a set of harsh, arbitrary rules. If we believe that "God is for us" (Romans 8:31), then even when Scripture exposes our sin, we still trust him, because he desires to address our sin with his forgiving and empowering grace. We realize that the happiness we feel in gratitude for what he's done for us makes God happy too.

WHERE DOES HAPPINESS ORIGINATE?

Some people suppose happiness is uniquely human, unrelated to God's nature: as he gave us a body and hunger, which he doesn't have, he gave us a capacity for happiness, which he also doesn't have. I believe something radically different—that God wants us happy because he's happy! He treasures his happiness and treasures us, and therefore he treasures our happiness!

Old Testament professor Brent Strawn writes, "In the Bible, God is happy, and God's happiness affects and infects the rest of the non-God world, humans included."[4] The last part of the sentence hinges on the first: if God isn't happy, he has no happiness with which to "infect" us.

To be godly is to resemble God. If God is unhappy, we'd need to pursue unhappiness, which is as likely as developing an appetite for gravel. If following Jesus means having to turn away from happiness, and we're wired to want happiness, then *we can only fail as Christians.*

Looking at Scripture carefully, we find a happy God who desires us to draw happiness from him. Yet how many Christians have ever heard a sermon, read a book, had a discussion about, or meditated on God's happiness?

Not once at church, Bible college, or seminary did I hear about God's happiness. I have no doubt it would have been surprising, memorable, and encouraging. What better explanation for the flood of happiness that overwhelmed my life after coming to Christ than that my God, who created, redeemed, and indwelt me, was happy?

Though I studied the Bible continuously, somehow the hundreds of Scriptures indicating God's pleasure, delight, and joy didn't register. They were nullified by unbiblical statements I heard from pastors and authors, such as "God calls us to holiness, not happiness."

I've always been a voracious reader, inhaling books, including theological works, by the hundreds. But I didn't read anything about the happiness of God until the late 1980s, after

I'd been a pastor for ten years. John Piper's books *Desiring God* and *The Pleasures of God* introduced me to a subject I should have heard about in my first few months attending church as a teenager.

Why did it take so long for me to hear what Scripture clearly teaches? Because God's happiness simply wasn't on my radar, nor that of my church or school. God's love, mercy, and grace were affirmed—not just his justice and wrath—so perhaps I should have deduced that God was happy. But the thought never occurred to me.

I believe it's vital that we not leave our children and future generations of Christians to figure out for themselves that God is happy. Most never will. How can they, unless their families and churches teach them and demonstrate God-centered happiness in their own lives? We need to tell them that sin, suffering, shame, and unhappiness are temporary conditions for God's people. We'll once and for all be righteous, healthy, shame free, and happy. Once we're in his presence, we'll never again experience the anger, judgment, and discipline of God we see in Scripture (all of which are appropriate and important, but even now do not nullify his happiness or love).

I'm convinced that in the new universe—called in Scripture the New Heaven and the New Earth—the attribute of God's happiness will be apparent everywhere. Upon their deaths, Christ won't say to his followers, "Go and submit to your master's harshness" but "Come and share your master's happiness!" (Matthew 25:21, NIV). Anticipating those amazing words can sustain us through every heartbreak and challenge in our present lives.

UNDERSTANDING GOD'S HAPPINESS IS LIFE CHANGING.

A teenage boy came to me with questions about his faith. He'd attended church all his life, but now had some doubts. I assured him that even the writers of the Bible sometimes struggled. He wasn't questioning any basic Christian beliefs, and he didn't need six evidences for Christ's resurrection, so I talked to him about holiness and happiness.

"What does God's holiness mean?" I asked.

His clear, biblical answer: "He's perfect, without sin."

"Absolutely true. Does thinking about God's holiness draw you to him?"

He responded sadly, "No."

I asked him whether he wanted to be holy 100 percent of the time.

"No."

"Me neither. I should, but I don't."

Then I surprised him. "Guess what you want 100 percent of the time."

He didn't know.

"Have you ever once thought, *I don't want to be happy?*"

"No."

"Isn't that what you really want—happiness?"

His expression said, "Guilty as charged." Friendships, video games, sports, academics— every activity, every relationship—played into his desire to be happy. But I could see he felt that this longing was unspiritual.

I told him the word translated "blessed" in 1 Timothy 1:11 and 6:15 speaks of God being happy (more on that in chapter 14). I asked him to memorize these verses, replacing "blessed God" with "happy God."

Then I asked him to list whatever points him to God's happiness—backpacking, music, playing hockey, favorite foods. I said, "God could have made food without flavor, but he's a happy God, so he created a world full of happiness. That means you can thank him for macaroni and cheese, for music, for Ping-Pong, and above all, for dying on the cross so you can know him and be forever happy."

This boy had seen Christianity as a list of things he should do that wouldn't make him happy and a list of things he shouldn't do that would make him happy.

I'd never diminish the importance of God's holiness. As we'll see in chapter 37, holiness and happiness are inseparable. Yet most Christians have heard, "God is holy" countless times but haven't heard, "God is happy." They don't look at the world through the lens of God's happiness. That's why this chapter and those following (including chapter 18, "Was Jesus Happy?") are essential. If—but only if—you believe them, the rest of the book falls logically into place.

IF GOD ISN'T HAPPY, HOW CAN HE MAKE US HAPPY?

Since we'll inevitably seek what we believe will bring us happiness, what subject is more important than the source of happiness? Just as we'll live a wealth-centered life if we believe wealth brings happiness, so we'll live a God-centered life if we believe God will bring us happiness. No one shops for milk at an auto parts store or seeks happiness from a cranky God.

As much as I believe in the holiness of God, I also believe highlighting God's happiness is a legitimate and effective way to share the gospel with unbelievers or to help Christians regain a foothold in their faith.

Some imagine that following Christ boils down to, "Just say no to happiness!" Christian homes and churches need to counteract that misconception with a biblical doctrine of happiness, built upon the happiness of God.

In his classic book *The Knowledge of the Holy*, which influenced me profoundly as a new believer, A. W. Tozer wrote, "What comes into our minds when we think about God is the most important thing about us. . . . No religion has ever been greater than its idea of God. . . . The most portentous fact about any man is not what he at a given time may say or do, but what he in his deep heart conceives God to be like."[5]

It's narcissistic to think of God only in terms of how loving, angry, forgiving, just, or patient he is in relation to *us*. We're but creatures, latecomers, and incredibly small. He's the Creator, without beginning and end, continuously vibrant and energetic. His identity and character don't depend on us. He had a life before we met him, and had we never met him, he would have retained his identity. So the question isn't merely whether God is happy with us but whether God, in himself, is happy.

Jonathan Edwards said, "It is of infinite importance . . . to know what kind of being

God is. For he is . . . the only fountain of our happiness."[6] Edwards knew that just as an unloving God couldn't bring us love, an unhappy God couldn't be our source of happiness.

GOD IS A PERSONAL BEING WITH REAL EMOTIONS, INCLUDING HAPPINESS.

Centuries ago, theologians formulated a doctrine called God's impassibility. They argued that God was "without passions," as stated in "The Westminster Confession of Faith," a 1646 document written by the leaders of the Church of England. Their motive was to be true to Scripture passages that say that "God is not a man" (Numbers 23:19, KJV) and that in him "there is no variation or shadow due to change" (James 1:17).

They were right to distance God from erratic human emotions. Unfortunately, many understood this to mean that God has *no* emotions. J. I. Packer takes a different view:

> [Impassibility] means, not that God is . . . unfeeling . . . , but that no created beings can inflict pain, suffering and distress on him at their own will. In so far as God enters into suffering and grief . . . it is by his own deliberate decision; he is never his creatures' hapless victim. . . . God is [not] a stranger to joy and delight. . . . His joy is permanent, clouded by no involuntary pain.[7]

God feels love, compassion, anger, and happiness. He's never overwhelmed by unsettling emotions, nor is he subject to distresses imposed by others. But he does feel his children's suffering deeply.

If your human father said he loved you but never showed it through his emotions, would you believe him? If we think God has no emotions, it's impossible to believe he delights in us or to feel his love. That's one reason believing in God's happiness can be a breakthrough for people in their love for him.

GOD EXPERIENCES A BROAD RANGE OF EMOTIONS WITHOUT LOSING HIS HAPPINESS.

When I say I'm happy and my dog is happy, I don't mean our experiences are indistinguishable. I'm happy in my human way; she is happy in her doggy way. Likewise, when I say God is happy, I don't mean his experience is identical to ours, but comparable.

Scripture sometimes speaks of God in anthropomorphisms, meaning he's described as if he has a human form. For example, the Bible talks about him having a hand, a face, and eyes (see Exodus 7:5; Numbers 6:25; Psalm 34:15), even though he has no body (see John 4:24). Similarly, some speak of *anthropopathisms*, indicating that Scripture ascribes emotions to God to show he relates to humans, though he doesn't really have emotions himself.

But we know that when Scripture speaks of God having eyes, it means that he sees, and the mention of his ears means that he hears our prayers. While God is not a physical being, he is a spiritual being, and he does have attributes of personhood. Passages that ascribe to him emotional qualities he doesn't have would mislead us.

God commands us not to "grieve" the Holy Spirit (Ephesians 4:30). God is said to be "angry" (Deuteronomy 1:37), "moved to pity" (Judges 2:18), and "pleased" (1 Kings 3:10).

This passage about God's compassion contains a remarkable statement: "In all their distress he too was distressed" (Isaiah 63:9, NIV). A form of the same word is used to describe both Israel's distress and his own. Yes, our distress can involve feelings God doesn't have, such as helplessness or uncertainty. But clearly God intends us to see a similarity between our emotional distress and his. If God experiences the full range of non-sinful human emotion, as indicated by Scripture, it stands to reason that he would feel happiness, too.

Spurgeon explained:

> We have been educated to the idea that the Lord is above emotions, either of sorrow or pleasure. That He cannot suffer, for instance, is always laid down as a self-evident postulate. . . . For my part, I rejoice to worship the living God, who, because He is living, does grieve and rejoice! . . . To look upon Him as utterly impassive and incapable of anything like emotion does not, to my mind, exalt the Lord, but rather brings Him down to be comparable to the gods of stone or wood which cannot sympathize with their worshippers.[8]

Ellen Charry writes, "If the doctrine of God cannot countenance God's emotional life, there is something wrong with the *doctrine*—it is not fully responsive to the fullness of the biblical witness."[9]

GOD'S HAPPINESS NEVER PREVENTS HIM FROM GRIEVING FOR AND WITH HIS PEOPLE.

If you're going through great suffering right now, the message "God is always happy" may disturb you. You might react the way you would if you told a friend, "My daughter was just diagnosed with leukemia," and your friend replied, "I'm always happy, so I won't let that bother me."

God's happiness, though uninterrupted, should never be misconstrued as indifference. Here are a few examples of God's empathy for his people:

- The people of Israel groaned because of their slavery and cried out for help. Their cry . . . came up to God. And God heard their groaning. (Exodus 2:23-24)
- Then the LORD said, "I have surely seen the affliction of my people who are in Egypt. . . . I know their sufferings, and I have come down to deliver them." (Exodus 3:7-8)
- He has pity on the weak and the needy, and saves the lives of the needy. (Psalm 72:13)
- The LORD was moved to pity by their groaning because of those who afflicted and oppressed them. (Judges 2:18)
- In all their affliction he was afflicted. . . . In his love and in his pity he redeemed them; he lifted them up and carried them all the days of old. (Isaiah 63:9)

But if God is so moved by our sorrows, how can he still be happy while we're suffering? He's all knowing, so nothing takes him by surprise. He's all powerful, so there's nothing he wants to do but can't. He's completely loving and good, and he's capable of—and committed to—bringing ultimate goodness to his children.

God himself models his inspired command to rejoice always. He sympathizes with all his suffering children, but he rejoices in purchasing our redemption and making us more like Jesus. He joyfully prepares a place for us, and he has eternally happy plans. He has the power to accomplish everything, as well as the sure knowledge that it will happen.

While I'm grateful that God cares deeply for me, I'm also grateful that when I'm miserable, it doesn't mean God is. As any good father will be moved by his daughter's pain when her boyfriend breaks up with her, God can feel our pain while retaining his own happiness. God the Father has an infinitely larger picture of eventual, eternal good that he will certainly accomplish. Nothing is outside his control. Therefore, nothing is a cause for worry. God does not fret.

WHEN UNHAPPINESS ENTERED THE WORLD, IT DIDN'T THWART GOD'S PLAN FOR OUR ETERNAL HAPPINESS.

Complete happiness for his entire creation was God's original design. Yes, Satan rebelled. Yes, Adam and Eve freely chose sin, and with it death and suffering. And yes, the all-powerful, happy God could have intervened to prevent those choices. If that intervention would have brought him more glory and us more good, no doubt he would have done it. But God, in his wisdom, determined that not even rebellion and sin could thwart his plan to further his happiness and that of his people.

Once sin separated Adam and Eve from the happy God, all the happiness left to them was secondary or derivative. Savory food, fragrant flowers, stunning sunsets—mere glimpses of the intimate, perfect relationship with God they'd once enjoyed. Even when they repented, the death sentence of the Fall and the weight of the Curse made their experience of God's own happiness cloudy and distant.

English novelist George Orwell (1903–1950), who was skeptical of the biblical account, wrote, "Of course, no honest person claims that happiness is *now* a normal condition among adult human beings."[10] Orwell's "now" suggests precisely what the Bible reveals—that happiness was once a normal condition.

Puritan William Bates argued, "God permitted the fall of man, to raise him to a more excellent and stable felicity. Adam was dignified with dominion over the lower world, and seated a prince in paradise; but his happiness depended upon his obedience. . . . But the pardon of sin is the foundation of eternal happiness."[11]

GOD'S HAPPINESS WILL SHINE, UNRESTRAINED, IN EARTH'S RE-CREATION.

God joyfully anticipates his new creation—for the sake of his own happiness and that of his people. Note the intermixing of his joy with human joy in this passage:

> Behold, I create new heavens and a new earth. . . . Be glad and rejoice forever in
> that which I create; for behold, I create Jerusalem to be a joy, and her people to

be a gladness. I will rejoice in Jerusalem and be glad in my people; no more shall be heard in it the sound of weeping and the cry of distress. ISAIAH 65:17-19

In the New Earth, God will be happy with us, and unhappiness will disappear once and for all. There will be no more alienated relationships, cancer, war, betrayal, or car accidents; no more sin or suffering.

English churchman and historian Thomas Fuller (1608–1661) said, "He does not believe who does not live according to his belief."[12] If this is true, I think it's fair to say that many Christians don't believe God is happy.

If we did believe it, wouldn't we be happier?

CHAPTER 13

WHAT DOES THE BIBLE SAY ABOUT GOD'S HAPPINESS?

I am so happy I found my lost sheep. Let us celebrate!
LUKE 15:6, GNT

You must live as God lives—in peace and joy, and happiness.
CHARLES SPURGEON

I'VE NEVER BEEN to Iguazu Falls, on the border of Brazil and Argentina. But I've watched astounding videos that offer a glimpse of its wonders.

The falls are 1.7 miles across, with many small islands dividing the torrent of water into separate cataracts and waterfalls. Depending on the water level, there are between 150 and 300 of these falls, varying from about 200 to 270 feet high. I've witnessed the power of Niagara Falls firsthand, but the volume of the cascading waters of Iguazu Falls can be up to twenty times greater. (Upon visiting Iguazu Falls, Eleanor Roosevelt reportedly exclaimed, "Poor Niagara!"[1])

For those who believe in God, wonders like these are compelling evidence of the one who takes delight in his creation.

WHY SHOULD GOD'S HAPPINESS AND OTHER EMOTIONS MATTER TO US?

If we are going to fully trust God, it's vital that we believe in a happy God who cares deeply for our welfare and is active in creation and redemption. Jesus says, "The thief comes only to steal and kill and destroy. I came that they may have life and have it abundantly" (John 10:10). The thief exchanges misery for what he steals, kills, and destroys. In stark contrast, Jesus offers abundant, overflowing life, giving us ultimate happiness.

Only God is infinitely happy. Finite beings can't be infinitely anything. But we can draw upon God's power to rejoice in him. As we're transformed by the renewing of our minds (see Romans 12:2), we become closer to our happy God.

CREATION WAS THE RESULT OF GOD'S OVERFLOWING GOODNESS AND HAPPINESS.

God created a world of goodness. "And God saw everything that he had made, and behold, it was very good" (Genesis 1:31). In other words, "What I've made makes me very happy."

Jonathan Edwards wrote, "Happiness is the end [purpose] of the creation. . . . For certainly it was the goodness of the Creator that moved him to create . . . that he might delight in seeing the creatures he made rejoice."[2]

God asked Job, "Where were you when I laid the foundation of the earth? Tell me, if you have understanding . . . when the morning stars sang together and all the sons of God shouted for joy?" (Job 38:4, 7). Most translations render the phrase "angels" instead of the literal "sons of God." While this passage is almost certainly referring to angels, something in the original Hebrew is lost when they aren't called God's sons.

Though angels aren't said to be made in God's image, being called "sons of God" implies a resemblance to him. For God's sons to shout for joy at the Creation suggests they were responding to their Father God, whose own gladness overflowed in the magnificence of what he'd made.

ALL CREATION REFLECTS GOD'S HAPPINESS.

A. W. Tozer depicted the happiness of God as seen in his creation:

> God is not only pleased with Himself, delighted with His own perfection and happy in His work of creating and redeeming, but He is also enthusiastic. There is an enthusiasm in the Godhead, and there is enthusiasm in creation. . . . This infinite God is enjoying Himself. Somebody is having a good time in heaven and earth and sea and sky. Somebody is painting the sky. Somebody is making trees to grow . . . causing the ice to melt . . . and the fish to swim and the birds to sing. . . . Somebody's running the universe.[3]

Is God happy about the animals he has made? Take a look at this: "Do you give the horse his might? Do you clothe his neck with a mane? . . . He paws in the valley and exults in his strength. . . . He laughs at fear and is not dismayed. . . . With fierceness and rage he swallows the ground; he cannot stand still at the sound of the trumpet. When the trumpet sounds, he says 'Aha!'" (Job 39:19, 21-22, 24-25).

Isn't God's utter delight in horses obvious? Since he finds pleasure and happiness in animals, we shouldn't feel "unspiritual" when we do. To animal-loving unbelievers, we can say, "I believe in a God who not only made those animals but also delights in them!"

Does God have a sense of humor? He created the giraffe, the camel, the hippopotamus, and the duck-billed platypus. If you need more proof, look at online photos of animals such as the proboscis monkey, the star-nosed mole, the pink fairy armadillo, the Dumbo octopus, the sucker-footed bat, the blobfish, or my personal favorite, the axolotl.[4] I've done this several times with my grandsons, enjoying shared laughter and great conversations about God's happiness and sense of humor.

Had we been able to watch God spin the galaxies into existence, fashion this planet, and make animals and the first humans (perhaps one day we will go back and see all this), we'd surely have seen his happiness and the pleasures he intended for us.

Our view of God's happiness with and in his creation will inevitably determine our view of the gospel's depth and breadth. Mike Goheen and Craig Bartholomew argue, "The gospel as recorded in Scripture is as broad as creation. Since the church has been sent to make known this good news in all of life, in actions and in words, the church's mission is, likewise, as broad as creation."[5]

The implications are far reaching. If God is happy only with limited aspects of his creative work and hostile or indifferent to most of it, including the culture developed by his image bearers, then there's far less left to bring him glory. But suppose he still loves his fallen creation and desires not to destroy it but to redeem it so that he and we might forever take delight in it. This supposition is precisely what Scripture teaches (see Matthew 19:28; John 3:17; Acts 3:21; 2 Peter 3:13).

Charles Spurgeon said,

The Gospel is like wine which makes us glad. Let a man truly know the Grace of our Lord Jesus Christ, and he will be a happy man! And the deeper he drinks into the spirit of Christ, the more happy will he become! That religion which teaches misery to be a duty is false upon the very face of it, for God, when He made the world, studied the happiness of His creatures. You cannot help thinking, as you see everything around you, that God has diligently, with the most strict attention, sought ways of pleasing man. He has not just given us our absolute necessities, He has given us more—not simply the useful, but even the ornamental! The flowers . . . the stars . . . the hill and the valley—all these things were intended not merely because we needed them, but because God would show us how He loved us and how anxious He was that we should be happy!

Now, it is not likely that the God who made a happy world would send a miserable salvation! He who is a happy Creator will be a happy Redeemer![6]

GOD REJOICES OVER HIS PEOPLE WITH GLADNESS AND SINGING.

In Zephaniah 3:14, God calls upon his people to be glad using four different Hebrew words that convey happiness: "Sing aloud [with joy, or *rinnah*[7]], O daughter of Zion; shout [for joy, or *ruah*[8]], O Israel! Rejoice [*samach*] and exult [*alaz*] with all your heart."

The gladness described here is over the top—surely a God who isn't happy would never call his people to such happiness. But three verses later, in Zephaniah 3:17, we see an even more remarkable statement, which also contains four happiness words. This time, however, all four terms are used not of God's people but of God himself: "The Lord your God is in your midst, a mighty one who will save; he will rejoice [*sus*] over you with gladness [*simchah*]; he will quiet you by his love; he will exult over you [*gyl*] with loud singing [*rinnah*]."

There's more of the happiness, tenderness, and love of God for us in this single verse than we can wrap our minds around. In fact, this understanding about God's delight in us is the rock-solid foundation for the fourfold happiness he calls on his people to experience three verses earlier. We're accustomed to thinking of God as angry or saddened by us. But here we're told, four times over, of God's happiness over us! Tozer said of this passage, "God is happy if nobody else is."[9]

While Zephaniah was speaking to his fellow Israelites, it's no stretch to say that today's believers, the church, are also God's people. Certainly God's nature hasn't changed, so everything Zephaniah 3:17 says about God's happiness remains true. Since he rejoiced over Israel, he also rejoices over us.

This verse alone, even if there weren't hundreds of others that affirm it, should be sufficient to convince us that God is happy with us.

MANY SCRIPTURES SUGGEST GOD'S HAPPINESS BY AFFIRMING THAT WE CAN FIND HAPPINESS IN HIM.

If I take delight in someone, it's normally because that person has delightful qualities.

Psalm 2:12 offers a clear picture of the happiness of those who turn to the Lord for their protection:

- Happy are all who go to him for protection. (GNT)
- All those who take refuge in Him are happy. (HCSB)

The oldest and most literal English translations render the verse this way:

- Happy be all they, who trust in him. (WYC)
- O the happiness of all trusting in Him! (YLT)

Other verses describe the happiness awaiting God's people:

- Happy is the person whom the LORD does not consider guilty. (Psalm 32:2, NCV)
- Happy is the nation whose God is Yahweh. (Psalm 33:12, HCSB)
- Happy are those whom you choose. (Psalm 65:4, NRSV, GNT)

These passages don't directly state, "God is happy," but they make no sense whatsoever unless he is.

WHY WOULD A GOD WHO ISN'T HAPPY CARE WHETHER WE ARE HAPPY?

Think of people who have made you truly happy over the course of your life. Were any of them unhappy?

"In your presence there is fullness of joy; at your right hand are pleasures forevermore" (Psalm 16:11). As love and holiness are found in God's presence because God is loving and holy, so joy and happiness are found in God's presence because God is joyful and happy. How could it be otherwise?

God created the universe out of nothing, but he doesn't create love, holiness, and happiness as separate entities; those ever-existing attributes emanate from his own nature. Nine qualities are listed as the fruit of the Spirit, the first being love and the second joy (see Galatians 5:22-23). There is "joy in the Holy Spirit" (Romans 14:17). Jesus was "full of joy through the Holy Spirit" (Luke 10:21, NIV). Joy is not merely something God brings; joy is something God *is*.

If we see God as happy, suddenly the command for us to "find your joy in him at all times" (Philippians 4:4, PHILLIPS) makes sense. God is saying, in essence, "Be as I am." Paralleling "Be holy, because I am holy" (1 Peter 1:16, NIV), the answer to the question "Why should God's children be happy?" is "Because our Father is happy."

GOD IS HAPPY WHEN PEOPLE REPENT FROM SIN AND EMBRACE HIS FORGIVENESS.

In Luke 15:6, Jesus pictures God as a shepherd who "calls together his friends and his neighbors, saying to them, 'Rejoice with me, for I have found my sheep that was lost.'" The Good News Translation renders this verse, "I am so happy I found my lost sheep. Let us celebrate!" In Christ's parable of the lost son, who is it that runs to his son, embraces him, and forgives him? The father, who represents God. Who orders a feast and fills the home with music and dancing? God. Whose laughter is deepest and richest at the party? God's.

The younger son falls for the lie that happiness can be found by leaving his father's presence. He embarks on a futile search for happiness and lands in misery. Desperate, he comes home, only to receive from his father the very happiness he'd hunted for elsewhere.

The younger son is *temporarily* miserable, but everything changes when he's reconciled with his father. The older son is *permanently* miserable, like the self-righteous religious leaders Jesus told the story to who knew nothing of grace and forgiveness—and therefore nothing of happiness.

The elder brother resents his father for graciously celebrating his brother's repentance. The father explains, "But we had to celebrate and be happy, because your brother was dead, but now he is alive; he was lost, but now he has been found" (Luke 15:32, GNT).

Why did the father say he *had* to celebrate and be happy? God only has to do what's true to his nature—his happiness compels celebration. He grieves over sin—even dying on a cross—to restore his relationship with his children. When they repent, he throws a party and all Heaven joins in (see Luke 15:7; 22-24). *This all transpires because God is happy!*

In *The Screwtape Letters*, a demon whines about the love of God for his people:

We must never forget what is the most repellent and inexplicable trait in our Enemy; He *really* loves the hairless bipeds He has created. . . . He really *does* want to fill the universe with a lot of loathsome little replicas of Himself— creatures whose life, on its miniature scale, will be qualitatively like His own, not because He has absorbed them but because their wills freely conform to His. We want cattle who can finally become food; He wants servants who can finally become sons.[10]

Tozer said something that, if we believe it, should fill our hearts with delight: "God is going to be as pleased to have you with Him in heaven as you will be to be there with Him."[11] Think about *that* for a few million years!

GOD DELIGHTS IN US, WHICH MEANS WE MAKE HIM HAPPY.

Scripture repeatedly says that God delights in and takes pleasure in us. I delight in my wife, which means I treasure her and she makes me happy. *It's impossible to take delight in someone without being happy with that person.*

Moses said, "The LORD will again be happy with you, just as he was with your ancestors" (Deuteronomy 30:9, NCV).

David wrote, "Let those who are happy when I am declared innocent joyfully sing and rejoice. Let them continually say, 'The LORD is great. He is happy when his servant has peace'" (Psalm 35:27, GW).

Other verses also speak to God's delight in the people he has made:

- Not by their own sword did they win the land, nor did their own arm save them, but your right hand and your arm, and the light of your face, for you delighted in them. (Psalm 44:3)
- Lying lips are an abomination to the LORD, but those who act faithfully are his delight. (Proverbs 12:22)
- The LORD takes pleasure in those who fear him, in those who hope in his steadfast love. (Psalm 147:11)

Ponder this amazing statement: "As the bridegroom rejoices over the bride, so shall your God rejoice over you" (Isaiah 62:5). Can you imagine anyone with more reason to be happy than a groom who delights in his bride? God rejoices over us the same way.

Based on such passages, Robert Duncan Culver (1916–2015) said, "God transcendent in heaven and immanent in all creation is supremely happy . . . always has been so, and for ever will be."[12]

GOD IS HAPPY ABOUT OUR HAPPINESS.

Scripture makes it clear that God doesn't keep his happiness to himself; he delights in sharing it with us. "How precious is your steadfast love, O God! The children of mankind . . . feast on the abundance of your house, and you give them drink from the river of your delights" (Psalm 36:7-8).

In 1868, American theologian Albert Barnes commented,

The following things . . . are taught by this verse: (1) that God is happy; (2) that religion makes man happy; (3) that his happiness is of the same kind or nature as that of God; (4) that this happiness is satisfying in its nature, or that it meets the real wants of the soul; (5) that it is abundant, and leaves no want of the soul unsupplied; and (6) that this happiness . . . is closely connected with the public worship of God.[13]

The psalmist recognized the pleasure God takes when we find joy in him: "May my meditation be pleasing to him, for I rejoice in the LORD" (Psalm 104:34).

Jonathan Edwards said God has extended his happiness to his children: "All his beauty is their portion, and his dying love is theirs, his very heart is theirs, and his glory and happiness in heaven are theirs . . . for he has promised it to them, and has taken possession of it in their name."[14]

Edwards also said that God "delight[s] as much in communicating happiness to another as in enjoying of it himself."[15] He maintained that God's children will enjoy without end his infinite happiness and love: "They have a fountain of infinite good for their comfort, and contentment, and joy. . . . He is also an infinite fountain of love; for God is love, yea, an ocean of love without shore or bottom!"[16]

Think about it: now and forever, God delights in our streams of happiness while we delight in his ocean of happiness!

If that doesn't fill our hearts to overflowing, what will?

ONE DAY GOD WILL INVITE EACH OF HIS CHILDREN TO FULLY ENTER INTO HIS HAPPINESS.

Consider Jesus' words: "Come and share your master's happiness!" (Matthew 25:23, NIV). At least nine translations use the term *happiness* in this verse, while others use *joy*. Correctly understood, they mean the same thing.

When Jesus spoke to the disciples, his message was unmistakable: *God is happy.* Furthermore, we don't have to make ourselves happy—God invites us to enter into *his* happiness! We'll be free to enjoy him and all his estate offers and to share in everything that makes God happy.

In first-century Palestine, entering into someone's home and happiness meant removing filthy sandals to bathe and put on clean clothes and then enjoy a delicious feast with a delightful host. Visualize an estate owner and host who somehow exists in three persons. Suppose his guests witness, with utter delight, these three persons enjoying each other with eternal and infinite happiness. Now imagine that the guests don't just observe this delightful relationship but are invited to join it.

What we've just supposed is what God has actually done. Along with countless other sons and daughters of the King, we'll celebrate God without end and be happy *with* him and *in* him.

Edwards said, "The happiness of the Deity, as all other true happiness, consists in love and society."[17] In other words, the God who is three in one has always been engaged in happy relationships. So he didn't first enter into a happy society through creating and loving us—he already had that society, but he graciously includes us in his happiness.

Jesus took this idea one step further when he prayed to his Father "that [my followers] may be one even as we are one, I in them and you in me, that they may become perfectly one . . . that the love with which you have loved me may be in them, and I in them" (John 17:22-23, 26).

It would be easy to suppose that the perfect Father, Son, and Spirit wouldn't want to include others in their inner circle of happiness. Who would believe they would open their arms to invite us, mere creatures, to sit with them at their table and share the benefits of their eternal relationship?

Try to wrap your mind around that, and as you do, experience the sheer delight God desires for you.

CHAPTER 14

IS GOD HAPPY, OR IS HE BLESSED?

You [God] make [King David] happy with the joy of your presence.
PSALM 21:6, CEB

Joy is the most infallible sign of the presence of God.
PIERRE TEILHARD DE CHARDIN

ABRAHAM LINCOLN'S ADVISERS recommended that he include a particular man in his presidential cabinet. When he refused, they asked why.

"I don't like the man's face," Lincoln replied.

Surprised, someone insisted, "But the poor man isn't responsible for his face."

Lincoln responded, "Every man over forty is responsible for his face."[1]

Lincoln wasn't talking about a person's physical beauty; he was saying that the heart's condition always makes its way to the face. "A happy heart makes the face cheerful" (Proverbs 15:13, NIV). If that's true of us, isn't it true of the God whose image we bear?

Typically we associate God's face with holiness. But doesn't it also reflect his love, compassion, and yes, happiness?

God says of his people, "Their faces will shine with happiness about all the good things from the LORD" (Jeremiah 31:12, NCV). This suggests that God's face shines with a happiness so great it spills onto the faces of those who love him. Certainly an unhappy God wouldn't make his people's faces shine with happiness.

God told Moses what Aaron and the priests were to say to the people: "The LORD bless you and keep you; the LORD make his face shine on you and be gracious to you; the LORD turn his face toward you and give you peace" (Numbers 6:24-26, NIV). How do you envision a face that shines on you and is gracious to you and gives you peace? Would such a face be stern and hostile or pleasant and happy?

THE BIBLE DIRECTLY DESCRIBES GOD AS HAPPY.

At this point you might suppose the most we can do is conclude that God is happy simply by deduction—for instance, from his commands to his people to rejoice and the pleasure he takes in his sons and daughters. But Scripture doesn't leave us with only deductions; it gives us direct statements that God is happy.

Paul spoke of "the gospel of the glory of the blessed God with which I have been entrusted" (1 Timothy 1:11). At the end of 1 Timothy he refers to God as "he who is the blessed and only Sovereign, the King of kings and Lord of lords" (1 Timothy 6:15).

How do these verses relate to God's happiness? The fact that this is even a question displays a fundamental obstacle to our understanding of Scripture. As I'll demonstrate, the meaning of the Greek adjective *makarios*, translated here as "blessed," is "happy." So both verses explicitly say that God is happy.

The Greek word *eulogatos*, often properly translated "blessed," is also used to describe God (see Luke 1:68; Romans 1:25; 2 Corinthians 1:3; Ephesians 1:3; 1 Peter 1:3). However, in 1 Timothy 1:11 and 6:15, the word is *makarios*. A prominent Greek lexicon defines *makarios* as "pertaining to being happy";[2] another defines it as "fortunate, happy";[3] another says, "happy, blessed."[4]

What would *makarios* mean in 1 Timothy if it didn't mean that God is happy? Fortunate? But how could the self-sufficient, all-powerful God be fortunate? Greek scholar A. T. Robertson translated 1 Timothy 6:15 this way: "The happy and alone Potentate."[5] Here's how other experts explain these verses:

- "The word translated 'blessed' here [1 Timothy 1:11] . . . means 'happy.' . . . We have a happy God, a happy Ruler . . . altogether happy and altogether powerful."[6]
- "The term itself means . . . 'happy' and therefore here designates 'God as containing all happiness in Himself and bestowing it on men.'"[7]
- "The term 'blessed' indicates . . . *supreme happiness*."[8]

Rather than assuming God can't be happy, shouldn't we look at the usual meaning of *makarios*, find the closest English word, and simply let God describe himself as he chooses?

THE EPISTLES DESCRIBE GOD AS "THE HAPPY GOD."

John Piper has written more about God's happiness than nearly any modern author. In *The Pleasures of God*, he states, "There is a beautiful phrase in 1 Timothy 1:11 buried beneath the too-familiar surface of Bible buzzwords. Before we dig it up, it sounds like this: 'The gospel of the glory of the blessed God.' But after we dig it up, it sounds like this: 'The good news of the glory of the happy God.'"[9]

Referring to the "blessed God," Piper says, "It is astonishing that only here [1 Timothy 1:11] and in 1 Timothy 6:15 in the entire Old Testament and New Testament does the word refer to God. Paul has clearly done something unusual, calling God *makarios*, happy."[10]

Paul didn't simply talk about the gospel; he referred to the "good news of . . . the happy God." This good news comes from God and relates to his glory—but the adjective *makarios* gives a single description of what characterizes this God who brings us good news. He is not just any god but the *happy* God. God's happiness is included here as part of the gospel's good news. This corresponds to the gospel being prophesied as the "good news of happiness" (Isaiah 52:7).

Charles Spurgeon said of 1 Timothy 1:11, "The Gospel . . . is the Gospel of happiness. It is called, 'the glorious Gospel of the blessed God.' A more correct translation would be, 'the happy God.' Well, then, adorn the Gospel by being happy!"[11]

After Paul writes in 1 Timothy 6:15 that God is happy, he says, only two verses later, that God "richly provides us with everything for our enjoyment" (verse 17, NIV). If verse 15 were translated "the happy God," it would be obvious to us that verse 17 flows naturally from that description.

Fred Sanders writes, "God in himself is perfect, and perfectly happy. Being perfect, he cannot essentially improve. . . . He can make happiness and blessedness available to [his] creatures because he always already has it."[12]

Commenting on 1 Timothy 1:10-11, Piper says,

> A great part of God's glory is his happiness. It was inconceivable to the apostle Paul that God could be denied infinite joy and still be all-glorious. To be infinitely glorious was to be infinitely happy. He used the phrase, "the glory of the happy God," because it is a glorious thing for God to be as happy as he is. God's glory consists much in the fact that he is happy beyond our wildest imagination.[13]

As the only infinite being in the universe, God has within himself not only infinite holiness, love, and goodness but also peace, joy, and delight. He truly is the happy God. God's unhappiness with sin is temporary, because sin itself is a temporary aberration—one dealt with by Christ. Happiness, however, is the underlying nature of the timeless God. His happiness, without beginning, eternally preceded sin's birth and will forever continue after sin's death.

WHY NOT CALL GOD'S HAPPINESS BY NAME?

Of the forty-five translations I consulted, forty-two of them render *makarios* in 1 Timothy 1:11 and 6:15 as "blessed." One uses "honored," another "wonderful." Though dozens of translations use "happy" to translate *makarios* in the vast majority of other places in Scripture, I've found none that do so in these passages referring to God. The only one that uses a happiness synonym is the New English Bible, with the word *felicity*.

Remarkably, even Young's Literal Translation, which translates *makarios* as "happy" forty-two out of fifty times, renders *makarios* as "blessed" only twice—the two times the word describes God!

Why is "happy" considered the literal translation of *makarios* . . . except when it's used in reference to God?

It's understandable that John Wycliffe, William Tyndale, and the translators of the King James Version rendered this phrase "the blessed God," since in the 1300s–1600s the word *blessed* included a clear notion of happiness. But that's no longer the case (more on this in chapter 21). Not only do people rarely use the word *happiness* in relation to God, but they also don't attach the meaning of happiness when they see "blessed God."

The Pulpit Commentary describes *makarios* as meaning "happy" when used of human beings. Yet of the two occurrences in 1 Timothy, the same source says, "It does not appear how or why the apostle here applies μακάριος [happy] to God."[14] Could it be that the reason Paul used a word meaning "happy" to describe God is that it's what he intended to say?

Occam's razor is the philosophical rule that the simplest explanation is most likely true. It argues that the more assumptions required, the more unlikely the account. In the two cases in 1 Timothy, the simplest explanation is that Paul called God happy because God *is* happy.

Most people appear to have a mental block against thinking of God as happy . . . even though God's Word reveals it's true.

If our English Bibles clearly showed what the original language conveys, *pastors would preach on God's happiness.* Children would grow up with Bibles that clearly say what most scholars agree is the God-inspired original meaning.

Sadly, few churches teach that God is happy—or wants us to be happy. We are unintentionally silencing the biblical revelation of one part of God's nature, at great loss to the church, families, and individuals.

WHY DO THEOLOGIANS SAY "THE BLESSEDNESS OF GOD" RATHER THAN "THE HAPPINESS OF GOD"?

None of the many systematic theologies I've consulted names a chapter or even a heading "The Happiness of God." Since *blessedness* was once a synonym for *happiness,* modern theologies sometimes use the word for the sake of continuity. Unfortunately, the term is archaic, and to most it doesn't convey the original meaning.

A friend of mine was recently teaching on the attributes of God. He told me, "I'm going to include God's happiness, but of course I'm not going to refer to it as that—it'll be 'the blessedness of God.'"

"Why?" I asked.

"Well, no one actually calls it 'God's happiness.'"

Since nearly every modern theologian and commentator who uses the word *blessedness* immediately explains that blessedness means happiness, why not simply say "God's happiness" in the first place?

Consider that even though the word was used for centuries, medical textbooks no longer refer to pulmonary tuberculosis as "consumption." It's curious that modern systematic theologies either don't deal with God's happiness or don't call it by that name. That's likely for the same reason translators don't render the phrase in 1 Timothy as "the happy God": it sounds awkward, unfamiliar, and to some, even blasphemous. But do you know any happy people who would be insulted if others called them happy? Doesn't God want us to recognize all his attributes, as specifically revealed in his Word?

I've heard people say that calling God happy makes them uncomfortable. Others maintain that using the word *blessed* instead of *happy* imparts more dignity to God. But when it comes to Bible translations, is the point to make us feel comfortable or to reflect as accurately as possible the meaning of the original languages? Should we refuse to call God what he, in his inspired Word, calls himself? Isn't that censoring God?

In Jesus' parable, when the prodigal's father runs across the field to greet his repentant son, commentators point out that it was undignified for men in the ancient Middle East to run.[15] But in his overflowing happiness, the father, who represents God, disregards his dignity to shower grace upon his repentant son.

God sees no incompatibility between his dignity and his happiness. Why should we?

WE DON'T HAVE TO CHOOSE BETWEEN GOD AND HAPPINESS.

Would you rather have a roommate who's happy or one who's cranky? What if you had to live with that person forever? Many would prefer annihilation to living unendingly with an omnipotent being subject to unpredictable mood swings or incapable of feeling affection or gladness.

If God isn't happy, living with him forever can't appeal to us. God's happiness has great implications for whether the gospel will be seen as truly good news.

If we offer people a choice between God and happiness, they'll choose happiness. But it's a false dichotomy. Instead, we should demonstrate that happiness can be found only in an eternally happy God who willingly sacrificed himself to purchase our eternal happiness.

Thomas Oden writes in his systematic theology,

> The One who in the fullest sense is happy is the eternally happy One: God. All creatures are in some way capable of sharing in that eternal happiness. Thus the glory of the Creator and the happiness of creatures are inseparable. Human happiness is not an incidental part of the original purpose of God in creation.[16]

When I've shared from Scripture the truth of God's happiness, people who have long been Christians are sometimes initially skeptical, assuming this is a modern attempt to twist the Bible's meaning. But once they see the truth, they're both surprised and delighted. Here are some responses I've heard to the claim that God is happy:

- "No kidding?"
- "Seriously?"
- "I've never even thought about God being happy."
- "If that's true, it would really change my view of God."

The most difficult question is this one: "I've been a Christian for many years; I grew up in the church. If this is true, why have I never heard it?"

John Wesley said, "A sour religion is the devil's religion."[17] The sure way to have a sour religion is to believe in a sour God. We play right into the devil's hands when we fail to recognize and teach the happiness of God.

My heartfelt belief that God is happy motivates me to love him more and know him better. I like being with happy people—who doesn't? The idea of spending extended time with someone who is unhappy sounds daunting and disheartening. Yet that's what "eternal life" means to many people—living forever with an unhappy God.

I'd much rather spend not only eternity but also my present life accompanied by, indwelt by, and empowered by a happy God—one who understands my desire for happiness because he, too, experiences and thoroughly enjoys his happiness.

And if that isn't enough, he has gone to unimaginable lengths to secure mine.

CHAPTER 15

WHAT MAKES THE TRIUNE GOD HAPPY?

This is my beloved Son, with whom I am well pleased.

MATTHEW 3:17

There is a concurrence of all the persons of the Holy Trinity in the happiness of heaven: the Father, Son and Holy Ghost are equally the fountain of that eternal blessedness the saints enjoy.

WILLIAM BATES

"TEAM HOYT," A father-son duo, was recently inducted into the Ironman Hall of Fame. Dick Hoyt and his son Rick, who was born with cerebral palsy, started competing together in marathons and triathlons in 1977, when Rick was fifteen. They participated in more than 1,100 events spanning four decades. In triathlons, Dick swam, pulling Rick in a special boat; he bicycled with Rick attached to a custom-made seat; and he ran, pushing Rick in a wheelchair. They participated in seventy-two marathons and six Ironman triathlons together. They biked and ran across the United States, completing 3,735 miles in forty-five days.

The Hoyts continued to compete until 2014, when Dick was in his midseventies and Rick was in his midfifties. They inspired millions of people who watched them race. The bond this father and son experienced in a sport known for its individualism was a source of great joy for both of them.[1]

COMMUNITY LIES AT THE VERY HEART OF GOD'S HAPPINESS.

The most ancient team in the universe consists of three persons: Father, Son, and Holy Spirit.

The concept of the Trinity is difficult for us finite human beings to comprehend. How is it possible for one God to consist of three distinct persons, each of whom is God? Somehow God has three centers of consciousness distinct enough to allow individual identities and intercommunication with each other, *and* so unified as to constitute one— and only one—God.

Theologians and scholars have wrestled with this conundrum for centuries. Yet it's possible to say, "Huh?" to the mysterious mathematics of the Trinity while appreciating its inexplicable wonders.

A. W. Tozer wrote of the triune God, "Such a truth had to be revealed; no one could have imagined it."[2]

Charles Spurgeon, at age twenty, began a sermon with these words:

> The most excellent study for expanding the soul is the science of Christ and
> Him crucified and the knowledge of the Godhead in the glorious Trinity. . . .
> Oh, there is, in contemplating Christ, a balm for every wound! In musing on the
> Father, there is a quietus for every grief and in the influence of the Holy Spirit,
> there is a balsam for every sore. . . . Plunge yourself in the Godhead's deepest
> sea—be lost in His immensity. And you shall come forth as from a couch of rest,
> refreshed and invigorated. I know nothing which can so comfort the soul, so
> calm the swelling billows of grief and sorrow—so speak peace to the winds of
> trial—as a devout musing upon the subject of the Godhead.[3]

If that invitation doesn't stir your soul with anticipation, ask God to move your heart and give you a sense of how every happiness should be seen in relationship to the triune God.

In his book *Delighting in the Trinity*, Michael Reeves writes, "The Trinity is the governing center of all Christian belief, the truth that shapes and beautifies all others. The Trinity is the cockpit of all Christian thinking."[4]

The Trinity is the crux of all happiness. Yet strangely, the Trinity is rarely discussed in the many Christian books on happiness I've read.

GOD'S ETERNAL LOVE AND HAPPINESS MAKE NO SENSE APART FROM THE TRINITY.

Theologian William Shedd (1820–1894) wrote, "God is blessed [happy] only as he is self-knowing and self-communing. A subject without an object could not experience either love or joy. Love and joy are social. They imply more than a single person."[5]

The only way God's happiness or love could be without beginning is if there exists within God himself a reason for and object of his happiness and love. Baptist pastor and theologian Augustus Strong (1836–1921) said, "Love is an impossible exercise to a solitary being."[6]

God is one, but he is not solitary. Since God is loving and happy within himself, he didn't create the world out of need. It's easy to imagine that a God full of love and happiness might wish to express those emotions in the form of a universe, angels, people, and animals. They could enjoy his happiness, and he could enjoy them. But God does not need his creation in order for his happiness to be complete. Puritan Stephen Charnock (1628–1680) wrote, "God cannot have an infinite satisfaction in anything besides himself, because nothing is infinite but himself."[7]

THE TRINITY SPOTLIGHTS THE DIFFERENCE BETWEEN FALSE GODS AND THE GOD OF SCRIPTURE.

No other religion has an eternally relational Creator God. Some claim that Islam's Allah is simply another name for the God of historic Christianity. But the Quran denies this: "Say not 'Trinity': desist: . . . For Allah is one Allah: Glory be to Him: (far exalted is He) above having a son."[8]

The Quran also makes this statement against the Trinity: "They say: '(Allah) Most Gracious has begotten a son!' Indeed ye have put forth a thing most monstrous!"[9]

Christians agree that God didn't beget a son through sexual union. However, the statement is often used to refute the claim that Jesus is God's physically procreated son—a straw man misrepresentation of Christianity, since Christians don't believe that.

Allah is a monolithic deity who doesn't consist of the persons of Father, Son, and Holy Spirit. When Christians affirm their belief in one God without considering the relational richness within his triune self, they're seeing not the God of Scripture but a Christianized form of Allah.

One of Allah's titles is "The Loving." Michael Reeves poses this question:

> How could Allah be loving in eternity? Before he created there was nothing else in existence that he could love. . . . If Allah needs his creation to be who he is in himself ("loving"), then Allah is dependent on his own creation, and one of the cardinal beliefs of Islam is that Allah is dependent on nothing. Therein lies the problem: how can a solitary God be eternally and essentially loving when love involves loving another?[10]

The doctrine of the Trinity beautifully resolves the apparent problem of God's love preexisting any object of his love. Likewise, as we'll see, his happiness has always been fully satisfied within his triune being.

THE TRIUNE GOD'S HAPPINESS IS REVEALED IN THE LIFE OF JESUS.

Twice in Matthew's Gospel—at Jesus' baptism and at the Transfiguration—we see extraordinary exhibitions of the triune God's happiness:

> When Jesus was baptized . . . behold, the heavens were opened to him, and he saw the Spirit of God descending like a dove and coming to rest on him; and behold, a voice from heaven said, "This is my beloved Son, with whom I am well pleased." MATTHEW 3:16-17

The Father, Son, and Holy Spirit all participate here. The Father audibly expresses his pleasure and happiness in the Son, while the Spirit affirms their threefold unity through an outward manifestation of his presence, descending on Jesus like a dove.

At the Transfiguration, the Father's statement is repeated: "This is my beloved Son, with whom I am well pleased; listen to him" (Matthew 17:5). For the Father to be well pleased with his Son means he is happy with him. The Father and the Son take boundless pleasure in each other, just as they do in the Holy Spirit.

Steve DeWitt writes, "Before you ever had a happy moment, or your great-grandparents had a happy moment, or Adam and Eve had a happy moment—before the universe was even created—God the Father and God the Son and God the Spirit were enjoying a perfect and robust relational delight in one another."[11]

A good way to think about God's infinite enjoyment of his own glory is to contemplate the delight he has in his Son, who is the perfect reflection of that glory (see John 17:24-26; 2 Corinthians 4:4). The Father says, "Behold my servant, whom I uphold, my chosen, in whom my soul delights" (Isaiah 42:1).

Likewise, the Son and the Holy Spirit had every reason for total delight in one another and with the Father from before the dawn of time (see John 17:24; 1 Peter 1:20).

God's communal happiness has significant implications for our own happiness. It means happiness didn't begin with the first human who experienced it. It also explains how God could be displeased with his creatures and their sin without disrupting his innate happiness. (Creatures aren't the central reason for his happiness, so his happiness doesn't rise and fall based on our attitudes and actions.)

Puritan William Bates envisioned human beings in the presence of God, basking in his triune happiness:

> There is a concurrence of all the persons of the Holy Trinity in the happiness of heaven: the Father, Son and Holy Ghost are equally the fountain of that eternal blessedness the saints enjoy in their glorified state. O consider how happy the creature must be when it receives all from God's blessed treasury.[12]

Some religions portray God as a master who created humans for the sole purpose of serving him while remaining uncaring about their welfare. In this philosophy, the master's happiness is important but not the servant's. Indeed, the master's happiness is maintained through the sacrifices made by the servant, but there is no personal, joyful relationship.

The biblical portrayal of God is profoundly different. The master's happiness and love preexisted his creatures. Not only does God have infinite happiness in himself, but the happiness that overflows to his creatures can fully satisfy them.

GOD'S DEFAULT DISPOSITION IS HAPPINESS.

I'm convinced that most people view God's typical emotional state as one of unhappiness. They think, *Yes, maybe he has occasional moments of happiness when his creatures do something right. But this happiness is always short lived, because we sin and God becomes unhappy again.* The logic is that since people are full of sin, God must be full of unhappiness.

But this logic begins in the wrong place—with ourselves. We flatter ourselves by imagining we're the primary source of God's happiness, tilting him one way or the other by what we think, do, and say.

Sure, God can be happy or unhappy with a creature's thoughts or actions, just as a man who is thoroughly happy with his wife and child can be unhappy with an employee or neighbor. But the analogy breaks down, because even a beloved spouse or child is a sinner. However, the Father, Son, and Holy Spirit can never disappoint or be disappointed by one another. They'll always have happiness in one another, and they'll always bring only happiness to one another.

The possible dramatic and brief interruption in God's eternal triune happiness (and there is considerable debate about this) is when the Son of God appeared estranged from his Father, while darkness covered the land for his final three hours on the cross (see Matthew 27:45). Jesus cried out to the Father, "My God, my God, why have you forsaken me?" (Matthew 27:46). The Father was displeased with the sin Jesus took on himself: "For our sake he made him to be sin who knew no sin" (2 Corinthians 5:21). Yet at the same time, God was well pleased with Jesus' willing sacrifice (see Isaiah 53:10), which he made with ultimate joy in view (see Hebrews 12:2).

If there has been any day, any time in history when the happiness of Father, Son, and Holy Spirit was disturbed, surely it would have been on what we call Good Friday. But even if that were the case, the unhappy suffering and death of Jesus ultimately guaranteed the death of death (see Revelation 21:4). It also guaranteed the eternal happiness of all who believe and trust in Jesus and his unfathomable suffering—and in turn that of his beloved Father and the Holy Spirit—all for our eternal good and his eternal glory.

THE TRIUNE GOD'S HAPPINESS HAD NO BEGINNING AND WILL HAVE NO END.

German theologian Meister Eckhart (1260–1328) said, "In the core of the Trinity the Father laughs and gives birth to the Son. The Son laughs back at the Father and gives birth to the Spirit. The whole Trinity laughs and gives birth to us."[13] Jonathan Edwards wrote, "The beloved Son of God is [the Father's] most precious treasure, in which God's infinite riches, and infinite happiness and joy, from eternity to eternity, does consist."[14] The point is that the happiness enjoyed by the members of the Trinity has always existed and always will.

Since the triune God had no beginning, neither did his happiness. Had God first experienced happiness at a particular point in time, we couldn't know whether his happiness would continue a million years from now. We would be left to wonder, *What if God was happy once and maybe still is, but one day he no longer will be?*

This is where the doctrines of God's eternal existence and unchanging nature are critical. Moses wrote, "From everlasting to everlasting you are God" (Psalm 90:2). The happy and holy God had no beginning and will have no end. He will never change (see Malachi 3:6; James 1:17). When we read, "God is love" (1 John 4:8), we typically think of this as a declaration about how much God loves us. But it is first and foremost a statement about God's character. Yes, he loves us, but love is intrinsic to his eternal nature. As a triune being, he demonstrated and received love endless ages before he created the first human.

We'll only see the universe as it really is—centered on God and not us—if we discipline ourselves to think of God as God before we think of him in relationship to ourselves. Then God becomes more than a means to an end—aiding us on our self-help journey. He becomes the worship-worthy heart and soul, the Alpha and Omega of the "good news of great joy."

James Houston says,

> God delights in himself. Happiness is his essential nature. He is therefore the ground and source of all goodness and happiness.... Christians throughout the ages have said that by contemplating the Trinity they have found the ultimate essence, expression, and exercise of happiness.[15]

If we combine the doctrine of God's happiness with the doctrine of his immutability (his unchangeable nature), we'll understand that he must always remain happy. We needn't fear that one day God's happiness will wane or disappear. On the contrary, once sin, the enemy of happiness, is forever conquered, the happiness of God now evident in this world will expand exponentially and overwhelm us with its constant, pervasive brightness. When that day comes, we'll never need to try to be happy again—we'll be incapable of anything less.

DOES GOD'S HAPPINESS SOMETIMES INCREASE?

When God said that creation was "very good," was he even happier than on the preceding days, when he said, "It is good"? And was he happier in that moment than he was before his creation? If Jesus endured the cross for the "joy set before him" (Hebrews 12:2, NIV), doesn't that mean he knew his joy would increase?

These questions boil down to one underlying quandary: How can what's infinite increase? Logically, it can't. But there's a danger in construing this argument in a way that depersonalizes God. If God rejoices at the conversion of each sinner (see Luke 15:7), doesn't this mean he has more joy after each conversion and still more after millions of conversions than before? Sure, we can say he's always had joy because he knew each conversion would happen. But this doesn't diminish the fact that God participates in our moments with genuine delight.

God entered space and time with the incarnation of Jesus, but the timeless, transcendent God is still with us, partaking in our happiness in special times such as graduations, weddings, and childbirth, as well as the small joys of daily living.

We shouldn't minimize the father's joy in seeing his prodigal son return. Though God knew from eternity past exactly when he'd bring me to faith as a teenager, I think he rejoiced in some special way on that day—as he did when Nanci and I were married; when our daughters, Karina and Angie, were born; and as he does in the special moments of our grandchildren's lives. And I believe he likewise rejoices in those moments of celebration in your life.

SCRIPTURE SAYS WE CAN PLEASE GOD—WHICH MEANS WE CAN MAKE HIM HAPPY.

We're told we can please God with our faith, worship, and obedience. Jesus said he did "those things that please [the Father]" (John 8:29, KJV). "Pleasing God" is one of those phrases we see and often use without fully understanding. What does it mean to please someone? When you try to please your parents, your teacher, your coach, your boss, your spouse, or your children, isn't that synonymous with seeking to make them happy?

Every Scripture that speaks of pleasing or delighting God proves that God can be happy. He wouldn't command us to do what pleases him unless he (1) values his happiness and (2) desires us to make him happy. So when we read Scripture, we can accurately paraphrase "pleasing God" as making him happy.

Here are a few of many Scriptures that talk about God being pleased with his children:

- God "takes pleasure" in those who fear him and hope in his mercy. (Psalm 147:11, NKJV)
- God is pleased when we trust and seek him: "Without faith it is impossible to please him." (Hebrews 11:6)
- God is pleased when we're spiritually minded rather than fleshly minded, in which case we "cannot please God." (Romans 8:8)
- God takes "great delight" when we obey him. (1 Samuel 15:22)
- David said to God, "I know that you . . . are pleased with people of integrity. . . . Your people . . . have been happy to bring offerings to you." (1 Chronicles 29:17, GNT)

God's happiness in us and our happiness in him are inseparable. We're all familiar with the question, *What do you give the person who has everything?* Who better fits that description than God? Yet we're told we *can* please God, delight him, and make him happy. God made us in his likeness. Doesn't it follow that just as I'm happy to give Nanci, my family, and my friends what makes them happy, so God is happy when his gifts make us happy (see Psalm 36:8)?

DESPITE GOD'S INFINITE GREATNESS, WE CAN EXPERIENCE TRUE RELATIONSHIP AND MUTUAL HAPPINESS IN HIM.

American army chaplain Robert Dabney (1820–1898) wrote, "The Holy Trinity will ever be the central and chief object, from which the believer's bliss will be derived."[16] Mutual joy is bonding. No relationship is deep and meaningful without it. But how can God, who is eternally accustomed to experiencing delight in his triune self, find delight in us, his creatures? Perhaps God gave us stewardship over creation partly so we'd better understand what giving love to—and receiving love from—lesser beings is like.

If my golden retriever, Maggie, is hurt, I help her; if she's hungry, I feed her. I do it not primarily out of obligation but out of love. My care for her doesn't depend upon her appreciation, yet her appreciation brings me joy. Seeing her enjoy me increases my delight. We're not equal beings, but the relationship of mutual happiness doesn't hinge on that. So it is with God and us.

As I look out my kitchen window, I watch Maggie play in the yard, her eyes wide and her nose to the ground, as if she expects something wonderful to appear. Then suddenly she stops and stares at something. It's a thick branch from a rhododendron she's been happily tearing to pieces. (Since we love her more than the bush, it's not a problem.)

Maggie pounces on this treasure, then marches around the yard with her prize, strutting like a conquering hero. If you asked me to describe my dog's state of mind, I would say, "Happy." From head to tail, she shows clear evidence that her delight is heartfelt.

When my wife, Nanci, gets out Maggie's leash, it's a sight to behold. She gleefully runs in circles (Maggie, not Nanci—though Nanci is happy too). Maggie can't wait for her beloved owner to take her outside. During their walk, they enter into each other's joy, feeding off the happiness of the one they love.

As God sees us from Heaven, doesn't he delight in us the way Nanci and I delight in Maggie? The fact that God is infinitely smarter and greater than we are doesn't diminish his ability to find pleasure in us any more than our superior intelligence or worth interferes with our enjoyment of Maggie.

While there's a major difference between humans and animals, we're both living creatures, and the same Hebrew word *nephesh* is used to call both "living beings" (see Genesis 2:19). My dog and I have a common source for our happiness capacity: our Creator. God is the source of his own happiness and ours, and as his image bearers, both our capacity for happiness and our desire for it are modeled after his.

God's Spirit indwells believers (see 1 Corinthians 6:19). Jesus, too, indwells us (see Colossians 1:27). What about the Father? Scripture says of the risen Christ, "In him the whole fullness of deity dwells bodily" (Colossians 2:9). Jesus said, "I am in my Father, and you in me, and I in you" (John 14:20). Jesus' prayer to the Father "I in them and you in me" (John 17:23) suggests that his presence in us entails the Father's presence in us.

Scripture makes it plain that we are indwelt with two of the three persons of the Godhead, and by inference, we are indwelt with the third. This means that within us we have the triune God and his eternally joyous interrelationship. This is an astounding reality—we've been brought into an ancient and transcendent circle of happiness before and above all others. If we contemplated this truth daily, wouldn't it infuse our lives with wonder and delight?

We should recognize, welcome, and tap into that joy. It's one thing to understand that God is happy. But as great a beginning as that is, believing in a happy God who is not distant but always with us and interested in our lives is better still. If we're convinced he is *in* us, enjoying the eternal happiness of his interrelationship in his triune self, then this engages us in a circle of gladness that defies comprehension.

Dick and Rick Hoyt, as father and son, delight in each other not just in triathlons but also in life. They are a beautiful reflection of God the Father and his Son. We are called God's children, and just as Dick provides the strength Rick lacks, our Father provides the strength we lack. His love for us fuels ours for him.

Jesus prayed, "I in them and you in me, that they may become perfectly one, so that the world may know that you sent me and loved them even as you loved me" (John 17:23). The Father, Son, and Holy Spirit are infinitely greater than we are, yet they share their love and happiness, enter into our happiness, and empower us to enter into theirs.

Who better than the triune God, who has always known happiness, to offer us, in him, the happiness we so deeply crave and could never experience on our own?

CHAPTER 16

IS GOD HAPPY WITH HIMSELF? (AND SHOULD HE BE?)

Well done, good and faithful servant! . . . Come and share your master's happiness!
MATTHEW 25:23, NIV

The God of salvation, the God of the Covenant, is to be worshipped with joy!
He is the happy God and He loves happy worshippers.
CHARLES SPURGEON

N ORMAN COUSINS GAVE an amazing account of the therapeutic value of laughter in *Anatomy of an Illness*.[1] Diagnosed with an untreatable terminal disease, his chance for recovery was one in five hundred.

Cousins believed that worry, depression, and anger had contributed to his illness. So he decided to immerse himself in laughter, watching the Marx Brothers and other funny movies. He found that laughing for ten minutes relieved his pain for several hours. Eventually he made a full recovery and lived for another twenty years. Cousins was convinced the laughter and his sustained focus on the bright side brought about his healing.

I find this story impossible to explain from a naturalistic worldview. Did this powerful, heart-energizing, body-healing thing called laughter come from random chemicals, protons, and neutrons? Can natural selection and survival of the fittest account for humor, laughter, and happiness?

Or are humor and laughter gifts to us? And if they're gifts, where could they originate but in God? And if God gives us the gifts of humor and laughter in this fallen world, what does it tell us about God himself?

DOESN'T GOD'S HAPPINESS WITH HIMSELF SEEM SMUG OR SELF-CENTERED?

Humans who are happy with themselves are often considered arrogant and self-obsessed. So how can it be a compliment to say that God is happy with himself?

For a time, C. S. Lewis struggled with God's demand that we praise him and give him glory. Eventually Lewis realized that he'd misunderstood the truth:

The most obvious fact about praise—whether of God or anything—strangely escaped me. I thought of it in terms of compliment, approval, or the giving of honour. I had never noticed that all enjoyment spontaneously overflows into praise . . . just as men spontaneously praise whatever they value, so they spontaneously urge us to join them in praising it: "Isn't she lovely? Wasn't it glorious? Don't you think that magnificent?" The Psalmists in telling everyone to praise God are doing what all men do when they speak of what they care about. My whole, more general, difficulty about the praise of God depended on my absurdly denying to us, as regards the supremely Valuable, what we delight to do, what indeed we can't help doing, about everything else we value.[2]

If God is indeed the primary source of all that's good and praiseworthy, wouldn't it be unloving for him to withhold from us the happiness of praising him?

Lewis concluded,

I think we delight to praise what we enjoy because the praise not merely expresses but completes the enjoyment; it is its appointed consummation. It is not out of compliment that lovers keep on telling one another how beautiful they are; the delight is incomplete till it is expressed. . . . Fully to enjoy is to glorify. In commanding us to glorify Him, God is inviting us to enjoy Him.[3]

WHAT'S FOR GOD'S BEST IS ULTIMATELY FOR OUR BEST TOO.

God says, "For my name's sake I defer my anger, for the sake of my praise. . . . For my own sake, for my own sake, I do it. . . . My glory I will not give to another" (Isaiah 48:9, 11). A human being who repeatedly says "for my own sake" demonstrates selfishness. But we didn't create the universe. When people seek glory for themselves, it rubs us the wrong way because they aren't worthy of that glory. It's different with God: he *is* worthy of all the glory—more worthy than we can possibly comprehend.

When an audience gives a standing ovation after a concert, don't we expect the composer, the director, and the orchestra members to be happy? And doesn't the fact that the performers find happiness in the audience's happiness—which is so great that they erupt into spontaneous praise—negate the idea that the performers are selfish? Is it selfish to want to make people happy? Similarly, why should it disappoint us that God would be happy to receive the praise that makes us so happy when we offer it to him?

The doctrine of the Trinity explains how God can appropriately be God-centered. First, because he's worthy. Second, because he properly exalts what's worthy. Third, because in delighting in the other members, each person of the Trinity is others-centered. The Father is Son- and Spirit-centered. The Son is Father- and Spirit-centered, and the Spirit is Father- and Son-centered.

God's desire for us to please him is not only for his good but also for ours. Spurgeon said, "The chief end of man . . . in this life and in the next, is to please God, his Maker. If any man pleases God, he does that which conduces most to his own temporal and eternal welfare. Man cannot please God without bringing to himself a great amount of happiness."[4]

John Piper says, "God is the one being in the universe for whom self-exaltation is not the act of a needy ego, but an act of infinite giving. The reason God seeks our praise is not because he won't be fully God until he *gets* it, but that we won't be happy until we *give* it. This is not arrogance. This is grace."[5]

BECAUSE GOD IS TRIUNE, HE CAN DESIRE AND LOVE US WITHOUT NEEDING US.

Why would a happy God create us if he didn't need us in order to be happy? Jonathan Edwards offered this succinct answer: "It is no defect in a fountain that it is prone to overflow."[6]

God is a creator. But that doesn't mean he *has* to create to be happy. Rather, he creates *because* he is happy.

God has always engaged in a loving relationship with the other members of the Trinity. Jesus said, "Father . . . you loved me before the creation of the world" (John 17:24, NIV).

English theologian John Owen (1616–1683) offered this commentary about love within the Trinity:

> "God is love." . . . God's love of himself—which is natural and necessary unto the Divine Being—consists in the mutual [contentment] of the Father and the Son by the Spirit. And it was to express himself, that God made any thing [outside] himself. He made the heavens and the earth to express his being, goodness, and power. He created man "in his own image," to express his holiness and righteousness; and he implanted love in our natures to express this eternal mutual love of the holy persons of the Trinity.[7]

WHEN GOD GRANTS HAPPINESS TO US, HE REVEALS HIS OWN HAPPINESS.

After the exiles had returned to Jerusalem and the wall had been rebuilt, Nehemiah told the people to feast and celebrate. He said, "The joy of the LORD is your strength" (Nehemiah 8:10). The Good News Translation renders this verse, "The joy that the LORD gives you will make you strong." The passage isn't simply about our joy in God but about the way God imparts his joy to us.

Note the jubilant enthusiasm of God when he says of his children, "I will rejoice in doing them good, and I will plant them in this land in faithfulness, with all my heart and all my soul" (Jeremiah 32:41). Imagine the warmth and gladness you feel when you do something special for someone you love deeply. Now magnify that feeling exponentially to appreciate God's love and happiness toward us!

In 1754, Horace Walpole coined the word *serendipity*, based on a Persian fairy tale of the Middle Ages called "The Three Princes of Serendip." Serendipity is "an aptitude for making desirable discoveries by accident."[8]

Serendipity is a pleasure for anyone. But it should have special meaning for people who believe that those seemingly accidental delights are actually planned by the sovereign God, who purposefully interjects unexpected pleasures into our lives.

One of my Bible college professors often shared illustrations of Christ's presence in the small events of his day. I asked myself why those things didn't happen to me. As time passed, God showed me that they did—I just hadn't noticed!

Since God is sovereign in even the smallest things of life, shouldn't we think of the leaves falling from the trees, the rabbit bounding across the trail, the old friend we see in the store, or the unexpected word of encouragement as God sharing with us his happiness?

The fact that God provides us with causes for happiness in our lives serves as further proof of his happy and pleasure-giving nature.

ALL OUR HAPPINESS, DIRECT AND INDIRECT, COMES FROM GOD.

One day on the New Earth, when we see God's face, our happiness will be direct (see Revelation 22:4). God will still give us happiness in secondary ways, such as through fellowship with other saints, heavenly creatures, natural wonders, and animals. But our blinders will be off—we'll never again fail to see God as the chief happiness behind every lesser happiness.

On that day we'll take a bite of great food and give praise to the Creator and Provider. We'll laugh with others, never forgetting that God himself is the source of laughter and delights to share in it. (And as I suggest in chapter 19, there's every reason to believe that Jesus will have the most contagious laugh.) His delight will be our delight, and our delight will be his.

Only the God who is so vast as to be Father, Son, and Holy Spirit can conceive of and implement such good news of great joy, which is the foundation of our eternal happiness.

THE SON LOVES AND IS HAPPY WITH HIS FATHER.

Jesus said, "The Father loves the Son and has given all things into his hand" (John 3:35). The Son also loves the Father: "I do as the Father has commanded me, so that the world may know that I love the Father" (John 14:31).

As a loving Son, Jesus says, "My food is to do the will of him who sent me and to accomplish his work" (John 4:34). Our food not only keeps us alive; it brings us pleasure. What is Christ's food, his source of happiness? To accomplish his Father's will. Doing the will of his Father is a delight, not a burden, to Jesus—even though the Cross was the greatest burden in the history of the cosmos, one that makes all others seem insignificant.

When we're happy with ourselves, the object is singular and limited and unworthy of glory. When God is happy with himself, the source and objects of his happiness include two other persons, unlimited in nature and worth.

THE FATHER'S LOVE FOR JESUS EXTENDS TO HIS REDEEMED SONS AND DAUGHTERS.

Not only does Jesus call God his Father, but he also extends God's fatherhood to his disciples: "I am ascending to my Father and your Father, to my God and your God" (John 20:17).

We also see glimpses of this astonishing truth in the Old Testament: "Thus says the LORD, Israel is my firstborn son" (Exodus 4:22). "You have seen how the LORD your God carried you, as a man carries his son" (Deuteronomy 1:31). Moses says of God, "Is not he your father, who created you, who made you and established you?" (Deuteronomy 32:6). The psalmist echoes this idea: "As a father has compassion on his children, so the LORD has compassion on those who fear him" (Psalm 103:13, NIV).

Consider the ultimate cost paid by Jesus. When he cried, "My God, my God, why have you forsaken me?" (Matthew 27:46), it indicated that the perfect, loving relationship he and his Father had enjoyed from eternity past was broken. He who could only please his Father became the sin they both hated—all so that thieving, murderous, ungrateful rebels could enter into an intimate, happy relationship with God!

Victor Hugo (1802–1885) wrote in *Les Misérables*, "The supreme happiness of life consists in the conviction that one is loved."[9] The greater the person who loves us, the greater our happiness. That's why every child of God should fixate on biblical promises such as, "No power in the sky above or in the earth below—indeed, nothing in all creation will ever be able to separate us from the love of God that is revealed in Christ Jesus our Lord" (Romans 8:39, NLT).

Though God grieves over the pain we experience here on Earth, he's content with his perfect plan, knowing it will prove best. He radiates love toward his children and patience toward the unsaved, yet he's angry at sin. He who was happy before the world began will be happy in the world to come, and he is happy now.

OUR WORLDVIEW IS TRANSFORMED WHEN WE REALIZE THAT GOD WANTS US TO SHARE IN HIS HAPPINESS—NOW AND FOREVER!

John Bunyan was a Puritan and an English preacher who lived in the 1600s. While imprisoned for preaching the gospel, he wrote *The Pilgrim's Progress*, which is widely considered the most influential piece of literature other than the Bible. He said, "God is the chief good. . . . He is in himself most happy . . . and all true happiness is only to be found in God, as that which is essential to his nature."[10] To Bunyan, human happiness is inseparable from God and impossible unless God himself is happy.

Nanci and I know the delight of sharing in the happiness of each other and our family and dear friends during vacations and reunions. Years later, those happy times still have the power to yield warm memories. But why should we think these wonderfully happy times are limited to our human relationships? If we believe Scripture, we can reverently seek to enjoy happiness and laughter with God himself. I often remind myself that God is always with me. He wants us to know we can be happy both *in* him and *with* him—not only after we die, but as we live today. When I'm alone, whether I'm meditating or reading or looking at photos or watching a movie, any happiness or laughter I experience is a laugh I share with God because, in fact, I am *not* alone!

Charles Spurgeon personally experienced periodic depression.[11] He also warned students training for ministry they would be vulnerable to depression, saying, "Who can bear the weight of souls without sometimes sinking to the dust?"[12] Nevertheless, he said, "Let us get into our right position; children of the happy God should, themselves, be happy."[13] As his children, we're to bear our Father's likeness.

Paul said of God's suffering children, "We cry, 'Abba! Father!'" (Romans 8:15). *Abba* is an intimate term meaning "Papa" or "Daddy." We want to be like our Father, and his happiness gives birth to ours.

What higher compliment could God pay us than to desire us to spend eternity participating in his happiness, and he in ours? Our unworthiness is not an obstacle for him. He's passionate about showing us his love and sharing his happiness with us.

WHAT WE BELIEVE ABOUT GOD'S HAPPINESS—AND HIS FRIENDLINESS— AFFECTS HOW MUCH WE TRUST HIM.

In all his justice and holiness, God is also, to use Tozer's phrase, "a friendly, congenial God."[14] God is friendly? Congenial? If asked to list God's characteristics, how many of us would come up with those words?

We don't think of God as friendly and congenial precisely because we don't think of him as happy. That he truly is and wants to be our friend is a revolutionary concept to many Christians. If we believe it, we understand how Jesus' disciples must have felt when he said, "No longer do I call you servants . . . but I have called you friends" (John 15:15).

A happy God is friendly and approachable. "Let us then with confidence draw near to the throne of grace, that we may receive mercy and find grace to help in time of need" (Hebrews 4:16). Christ's redemptive work allows us to go boldly to God's throne—he paid the price for us because of his desire to be our Father and friend.

Princeton theologian Archibald Alexander (1772–1851) wrote, "God is good. His goodness is manifest in every work of his wisdom, for he hath so continued and arranged all things in the best manner, to promote the happiness of his creatures."[15]

Some assume that calling God happy remakes him in our image. Yet the truth is the opposite—it's because a happy God made us in his image that we want to be happy. We're so accustomed to looking for happiness in the wrong places that we've come to believe that happiness is sinful. In reality, sin resides in our refusal to seek our happiness in God. C. S. Lewis wrote, "Do not let your happiness depend on something you may lose."[16]

If we trust God when he says he loves us (see John 3:16) and he wants us to cast our cares on him (see 1 Peter 5:7), we must first believe that those promises genuinely reflect his happiness and his desire for us to be happy.

David, speaking of himself as the king, said to God, "You make him happy with the joy of your presence" (Psalm 21:6, CEB). David's happiness is wrapped up in (1) God being joyful and (2) the joyful God being with him.

Suppose I told you that if you were to drop by the house of someone I know, that person would make you happy with the joy of his or her presence. What sort of person could live up to such a claim? *Only a genuinely happy one.* We can't understand what these passages are saying if we don't believe in God's happiness!

IF YOU THINK GOD'S HAPPINESS FLUCTUATES, YOU'LL BE SKEPTICAL ABOUT BEING ETERNALLY HAPPY IN HIM.

It's not enough to believe that God *can* be happy or is *occasionally* happy. Children withdraw from emotionally inconsistent parents. If Mom or Dad is happy and loving one moment but angry and hostile the next, kids learn to keep their distance.

Of course, even a consistent, loving parent will be unhappy about a child's sin and rebellion. But a gracious parent extends forgiveness and seeks to restore the relationship.

If I believe God's happiness will disappear with my every doubt, mistake, or failure, I'll simply give up and look elsewhere for my happiness. But if I believe that God—despite all my sins and failures—is continually, deeply, and eternally happy, eager to forgive me and comfort me—and, when necessary, discipline me as his beloved child—I'll approach him confidently for the love and happiness I crave.

If his happiness depends on me, neither he nor I can ever be happy. If it's independent of me, both he and I can be happy.

This is why the doctrine of God's happiness is essential. Our failure to believe in God's continual happiness can close our hearts to the reassurances of Jesus when he says things like this: "Come to Me, all who are weary and heavy-laden, and I will give you rest. Take My yoke upon you and learn from Me, for I am gentle and humble in heart, and you will find rest for your souls. For My yoke is easy and My burden is light" (Matthew 11:28-30, NASB).

If we want our children and grandchildren and future generations to seek God as the answer to their deepest longings, we must teach them that he is by nature happy. They need to see that the God who brings them the Good News really can (and longs to) "change their sadness into happiness" (Jeremiah 31:13, NCV).

When we understand that the God of the Bible is both happy and powerful enough to overcome our greatest grief and suffering and to give us cause for eternal happiness, Satan's arguments against trusting God will lose their power.

If we embrace him as a happy God, the cloud of gloom and complaint that pervades some churches and believers will dissipate. Knowing that Scripture reveals to us God's happiness, Spurgeon took issue with the moodiness and lack of cheer among some Christians: "Now it would be an exceedingly strange thing if, in proportion as we became like a happy God, we grew more and more miserable. It would be a singular and unaccountable thing indeed if, by acting like the Giver of all good, whose bliss is perfect, we should increase in wretchedness."[17]

One day this God who dealt with our sins on the Cross will fully, once and for all, "turn [our] wailing into dancing" (Psalm 30:11, NIV).

Robert William Dale (1829–1895), an English pastor, wrote:

It was not the pleasant things in the world that came from the Devil, and the dreary things from God.... God Himself is the ever-blessed [happy] God. He dwells in the light of joy as well as of purity, and instead of becoming more like him as we become more miserable . . . we become more like God as our blessedness [happiness] becomes more complete. The great Christian graces are radiant with happiness.[18]

GOD CAN'T GIVE US WHAT HE DOESN'T HAVE.

God often speaks to me through his Word, as he does to all seeking believers. On Sunday, June 2, 2013, some thoughts regarding God's happiness came to me with unusual clarity. What follows is certainly not equivalent to inerrant Scripture. But I've tested it against God's Word, and I believe it's true.

Does it matter whether we believe that God is happy? It matters more than anything has ever mattered, or ever will. It determines whether we can believe Romans 8.

An unhappy God would never have done what Romans 8 says he did—come to deliver us, groan as he prays for us, secure our resurrection and eternal life, be *for* us and not against us, work all things together for our good, and never under any circumstances allow anything to separate us from his love.

If God isn't happy, he can't be our source of happiness. An unhappy God would never value nor assure the everlasting happiness of his creatures. We would never ask for grace from an ungracious God, kindness from an unkind God, or happiness from an unhappy God. It would be like asking a poor man for a million dollars. He can't give what he doesn't have.

If God were not happy, the fact that all people seek to be happy would be a cruel tragedy, since it would mean that God cannot give us what we most deeply desire. At best he might deliver us from the miseries of Hell. But Heaven can overflow with happiness only if God himself overflows with happiness.

Our Creator's happiness guarantees a happy ending to the story that will never end.

CHAPTER 17

HAS THE CHURCH HISTORICALLY
SEEN GOD AS UNHAPPY OR HAPPY?

Yahweh your God is among you, a warrior who saves. He will rejoice over you with gladness.
He will bring you quietness with His love. He will delight in you with shouts of joy.
ZEPHANIAH 3:17, HCSB

The beholding of God's happiness will increase the joy, to consider that he is so happy. . . .
Those who shall see God, will . . . exceedingly . . . rejoice in the happiness of God.
JONATHAN EDWARDS

IN THE OPENING chapter of *The Adventures of Huckleberry Finn*, Huck lives with Miss Watson, a Christian spinster. She takes a dim view of Huck's fun-loving spirit and threatens Huck with the fires of Hell. She speaks of Heaven as a place everyone should want to go, but Huck sees it this way:

> She went on and told me all about the good place. She said all a body would have to do there was to go around all day long with a harp and sing, forever and ever. So I didn't think much of it. . . . I asked her if she reckoned Tom Sawyer would go there, and she said not by a considerable sight. I was glad about that, because I wanted him and me to be together.[1]

It wasn't only an unhappy Heaven that Miss Watson projected. It was an unhappy *present* life, full of obligation and self-inflicted misery. And although she may not have made such a claim out loud, the clear subtext is that if God is the author of a Christian life that's unhappy, God himself must be unhappy too.

Had Huck seen in Miss Watson a deep, cheerful affection for Jesus and consequent grace that overflowed toward him and Tom and others, perhaps he would have also seen Christ, the church, and Heaven as attractive.

Huck's view of God reflected that of author Samuel Clemens, also known as Mark Twain.[2] I wonder if anyone told Clemens that the God he saw as so stern and humorless was, yes, a holy God, but he was also a happy God who invented playfulness, fun, laughter, and whitewash—and was the source of Twain's wit and humor.

In his book *Is God Happy?*, Marxist philosopher Leszek Kołakowski answers no to his title question. He says that God can't be happy and that as long as there's pain and death, humans can't be happy either. If happiness were utterly incompatible with sin and sorrow, I'd have to agree. But despite present conditions in the universe, God's unchanging nature includes underlying happiness—and the power to give us reasons for happiness too.

Though a long line of ancient philosophers, theologians, and regular folks once believed in God's happiness, this concept has shrunk and sometimes disappeared from modern Christian thought. It's time to rediscover what believers before us knew and taught for centuries.

THE EARLY CHURCH FATHERS AND BELIEVERS IN THE MIDDLE AGES SPOKE OF GOD'S HAPPINESS.

The *Epistle of Barnabas*, written late in the first century AD, is a noncanonical (i.e., not part of Scripture) book quoted favorably by a number of church fathers. It says, "Understand, therefore, children of joy, that the good Lord revealed everything to us beforehand, in order that we might know to whom we ought to give thanks and praise for all things" (7:1).[3] Why call Christ-followers "children of joy" instead of "children of God"? Because God is joyful—he is the very essence of joy.

Gregory of Nyssa (335–394), a bishop, wrote of God's happiness, "Blessedness [happiness] is that unsullied life: the ineffable and inconceivable good, the indescribable beauty, essential grace and wisdom and power, true light, fount of all goodness . . . perpetual delight, eternal joy."[4] Ask the typical believer today to describe God, and you'd be unlikely to get an answer that includes "indescribable beauty," "perpetual delight," and "eternal joy."

Anselm was a Benedictine monk who became the archbishop of Canterbury. Arguably, he was the greatest theologian between Augustine and Aquinas. In the opening of his philosophical treatise *Monologion*, Anselm spoke of the things "we must believe about God." One of those was God's happiness: "There is one nature, supreme among all existing things, who alone is self-sufficient in his eternal happiness, who through his omnipotent goodness grants and brings it about."[5] Few of us would be surprised that Anselm included God's omnipotence and goodness, but most modern Christians tend to bypass God's happiness.

French philosopher Peter Abelard (1079–1142) said, "God's happiness and glory is greater than any human happiness or glory."[6] (Anselm and Abelard are among many I cite that I sometimes disagree with.)

Thomas Aquinas stated, "Of God alone is it true that His Being is His Happiness,"[7] and "He not only desires happiness, as we do, but enjoys it. Therefore He is happy."[8] He also said, "Grace makes man an adopted child of God because it gives man a share in the Divine life and happiness."[9] When we have a share in God's happiness, what does this mean but that the pleasure we experience is a pleasure that first exists within God?

Aquinas wrote, "God is happiness by His Essence: for He is happy not by acquisition

or participation of something else. . . . On the other hand, men are happy . . . by participation."[10] He recognized that someday, in his presence, we'll "enjoy the same happiness
wherewith God is happy, seeing Him in the way which He sees Himself."[11] Aquinas
reasoned that since God is the epitome of happiness, our happiness is all about God:
"Happiness is called man's supreme good, because it is the attainment or enjoyment of the
supreme good [God]."[12]

Sounding unlike the stereotypical medieval religious scholar, Aquinas spoke to God
concerning his people: "They shall be inebriated by the plenty of thy house, and thou wilt
make them drink of the torrent of thy pleasure."[13]

German clergyman Thomas à Kempis (1380–1471) prayed, "Come, O come, for without You there will be no happy day or hour, because You are my happiness and without
You my table is empty. I am wretched, as it were imprisoned and weighted down with
fetters, until You fill me with the light of Your presence, restore me to liberty, and show
me a friendly countenance."[14]

THE REFORMERS IN THE SIXTEENTH AND SEVENTEENTH CENTURIES AFFIRMED GOD'S HAPPINESS.

Martin Luther wrote of Christ, "When I possess Him, I surely possess all; for He is pure
righteousness, life, and eternal blessedness [happiness], and Lord over death as well."[15]
According to John Calvin, God isn't simply going to make his children happy in eternity;
he will also "admit them to a participation in his happiness."[16] The happiness of God was
a doctrine long before the Reformation, but the emphasis on free grace during this period
recovered and exalted God's happiness as a vital concept. Though he's rarely portrayed
with a smile, Calvin believed in a happy God who calls his people to eternal happiness.

The Westminster Confession of Faith states, "God hath all life, glory, goodness, blessedness [happiness] in and of himself."[17]

Puritan Stephen Charnock wrote of God, "If, therefore, he did not perfectly know
himself and his own happiness, he could not enjoy . . . happiness."[18] Charnock argued,
"Were he not first infinitely blessed [happy] and full in himself, he could not be infinitely
good and diffusive to us; had he not an infinite abundance in his own nature, he could not
be overflowing to his creatures."[19]

Citing 1 Timothy 1:11 and 6:15, Swiss Reformed theologian Benedict Pictet (1655–
1724) suggested, "This life of God is most happy [*felicissima*]. . . . For who would not call
a Being happy, who wants nothing, has entire complacency in himself, and possesses all
things; who is free from all evil, and filled with all good."[20]

Pictet's reasons for God's happiness are reasons for God's children to be happy also—not
because we have God's attributes, but because our lives are safely held by the one who does!

Puritan Matthew Henry (1662–1714), the greatest Bible commentator of his era,
wrote, "The eternal God, though infinitely happy in the enjoyment of himself, yet took a
satisfaction in the work of his own hands."[21] God was all-happy before Creation, yet he
delighted in his creation in a special way.

Presbyterian pastor William Bates said, "God is infinitely happy, to whom no good was ever new."[22] He emphasized that God's own happiness gives him the ability to make us happy: "God was from eternity a heaven to himself, infinitely glorious and joyful in himself. . . . If God hath that infinite excess of happiness to make himself happy, he can easily make those happy that desire it."[23] Bates saw what few Christians today see—that our capacity for human happiness is solidly based on the happiness of God: "If God lives and is eternally happy, we shall be happy for ever."[24]

In 1646, English Puritan Edward Leigh wrote a remarkable book on happiness that includes many pages about the happiness of God. I recommend that you look online at the images of his original book to get a sense of how old it really is.[25] The antiquated Old English lettering is difficult to read, but seeing this historical book reminds us that even if we've never heard of "the happiness of God," it is, in fact, a very old doctrine—and far older than Leigh's book!

Leigh wrote:

God's happiness is that Attribute whereby God hath all fullness of delight and contentment in himself, and needeth nothing out of himself to make him happy. . . . He is truly blessed which of himself and from his own nature is always free from all evils and abounds with all goods, perfectly knowing his own felicity [happiness] and desiring nothing out of himself, but being fully content with himself.[26]

Leigh said of God, "He . . . is the fountain. . . . He that is the cause of all welfare to other things, and makes them in their several kinds happy, he must needs be therefore most happy himself."[27]

We might say that a friend was extremely sad over the death of her husband. But we can still think of her as a happy person. While weeping, she might suddenly smile or even laugh at a precious memory. If such paradoxical feelings of happiness and unhappiness can coexist within God's image bearers, surely there's room for them in the infinite vastness of God's being.

The Puritans and others affirmed that our happy God grieves for his people and is displeased by sin and injustice. Yet these reactions don't have the power to dislodge his happiness. This is what Leigh meant when he said, "God is *happy*. . . . He is immutably happy because he is essentially so. Happiness is a stable or settled condition."[28]

Many Puritan writers spoke of our happiness, which can be full of pleasure and emotion, as having its origin in God's happiness. They believed that God's happiness is not sterile or distant, but a greater version of our happiness, involving genuine pleasure and delight.

CHRISTIANS IN THE EIGHTEENTH CENTURY BELIEVED THAT HAPPINESS WAS ONE OF GOD'S KEY ATTRIBUTES.

Many Puritans spoke of God's happiness. While I quote others throughout the book, I'll cite two examples here.

John Gill (1697–1771) sang God's praise in ways that may seem surprising for a "body of divinity" written by a Hebrew scholar, pastor, and serious theologian:

Happy, thrice happy, are the people whose God is the Lord! Who, besides the good things he bestows on them here, he has laid up such goodness for them hereafter, which the heart of man cannot conceive of. How blessed and happy then must he himself be! Name whatsoever it may be thought happiness consists in, and it will be found in God in its full perfection.[29]

Jonathan Edwards, linking our happiness with God's, wrote, "He has created man for this very end, to make him happy in the enjoyment of himself, the Almighty, who was happy from the days of eternity in himself."[30]

Edwards believed that our own happiness reaches its peak in contemplating God's greater happiness: "The beholding of God's happiness will increase the joy, to consider that he is so happy."[31]

Edwards said, "The whole of God's internal good or glory, is in . . . his infinite knowledge, his infinite virtue or holiness, and his infinite joy and happiness. . . . There are a great many attributes in God . . . but all may be reduced to these."[32] Edwards put God's happiness on the short list of God's attributes, while many recent books leave it out entirely.

NINETEENTH-CENTURY CHRISTIANS PROCLAIMED THE HAPPINESS OF GOD.

In his book *Essays and Reviews*, written in 1857, theologian Charles Hodge said that God's benevolence is "the disposition to promote happiness."[33] God promotes in his image bearers a quality true of himself.

Charles Spurgeon was one of history's most prolific authors, a pastor, and a lover of theology who preached to an estimated ten million people. He said, "He is the happy God, and He loves happy worshippers."[34] Spurgeon called believers "children of the happy God."[35]

Spurgeon spoke of God's smile, saying, "There is not one step in the whole divine experience of the believer, not one link in the wonderful chain of grace, in which there is a withdrawal of the divine smile or an absence of real happiness."[36]

Theologian William G. T. Shedd wrote that the goodness of God is a quality "issuing forth from the Divine nature, and aiming to promote the welfare and happiness of the universe."[37]

H. D. M. Spence-Jones (1836–1917) was a Cambridge graduate who taught Hebrew and was the general editor of *The Pulpit Commentary*. I was struck by his observation on Jeremiah 32:41, where God says, "I will rejoice in doing them good, and I will plant them in this land in faithfulness, with all my heart and all my soul."

Spence-Jones wrote,

God has joy. He is not indifferent, nor is he morose; we are to think of him as the "blessed" God, *i.e.* as essentially happy. . . . The brightness and beauty of the world are reflections from the blessedness of God. Because he is glad, nature is glad, flowers bloom, birds sing, young creatures bound with delight. Nothing is more sad in perversions of religion than the representations of God as a gloomy tyrant. . . .

These fragrant meadows, broad rolling seas of moorland heather, rich green forest-cities of busy insect life, flashing ocean waves, and the pure blue sky above, and all that is sweet and lovely in creation, swell one symphony of gladness, because the mighty Spirit that haunts them is himself overflowing with joy. Our God is a *Sun*. And if divinity is sunny, so should religion be. The happy God will rejoice in the happiness of his children. . . . God is so joyous that he finds joy even in us.[38]

BELIEVERS IN THE TWENTIETH AND TWENTY-FIRST CENTURIES WEIGHED IN ON GOD'S HAPPINESS.

Countless Christ-followers, even in the last hundred years, have clearly affirmed God's happiness. Unfortunately, their voices are rarely heard today.

Biblical scholar A. W. Pink (1886–1952) commented on God as "the blessed and only Potentate" in 1 Timothy 6:15 (KJV): "God himself, the triune God, is the source of all blessedness and joy. God is self-sufficient, infinitely blessed and happy in Himself."[39]

Philosopher and theologian Cornelius Van Til (1895–1987) stated, "We may say, in all reverence, that God himself is happy."[40]

Martyn Lloyd-Jones (1899–1981) wrote, "What does Paul mean when he refers to God as 'blessed'? Well, he means . . . He rejoices in Himself. He delights in Himself. . . . God is, according to the Scriptures, well-pleased within Himself and His glorious being."[41]

A. W. Tozer wrote, "God takes pleasure in Himself and He rejoices in His own perfection. The divine Trinity is glad in Himself!"[42]

Some of the Christian thinkers I cite next say things similar to those who preceded them in church history. My purpose is to demonstrate the breadth and continuity of belief in God's happiness into the modern era.

One of the most widely read modern systematic theologies today is by Calvinist Wayne Grudem, who served on the overseeing committee of the English Standard Version of the Bible. In his section on God's attributes, he includes "blessedness." Grudem begins by saying, "To be 'blessed' is to be happy in a very full and rich sense."[43]

Grudem gives a clear and beautiful statement of the biblical doctrine of God's happiness:

God's blessedness means that God delights fully in himself and in all that reflects his character . . . as the focus of all that is worthy of joy or delight. This definition indicates that God is perfectly happy, that he has fullness of joy in himself. . . . God takes pleasure in everything in creation that mirrors his own excellence. . . .

We imitate God's blessedness when we find delight and happiness in all that is pleasing to God . . . [and] by rejoicing in the creation as it reflects various aspects of his excellent character. And we find our greatest blessedness, our greatest happiness, in delighting in the source of all good qualities, God himself.[44]

Similarly, Arminian theologian Thomas Oden writes, "To say that God is eternally blessed means that God rejoices eternally in the outpouring of goodness, mercy, and love upon creatures. . . . The blessedness of God, or divine beatitude, means that God's life is full of joy, both within the Godhead and in relation to creatures."[45]

Both Grudem and Oden, representing different theological traditions, affirm not only that God is happy but also that there's a direct link between God's happiness and our own.

Old Testament scholar Terence Fretheim states, "Happiness is, first of all and most importantly, *a characteristic of the divine life*. God is happy—or pleased, delighted, joyful."[46]

Writer John McReynolds says, "God is happy. His happiness is an intrinsic part of who He is. He was happy in eternity past, He is happy now, and He will be happy for all eternity. . . . His happiness, like all of His other attributes, is infinite and absolute."[47]

It's hard to overstate the liberating, gladness-producing result when God's people recognize his happiness. Knowing a God who is so happy that his delight spills out in the universe and in us changes everything—now and forever.

CHAPTER 18

WAS JESUS HAPPY?

I have told you this to make you as completely happy as I am.
JESUS (JOHN 15:11, CEV)

The best work is done by the happy, joyful workman. And so it is with Christ.
He does not save souls as of necessity—as though He would rather do something
else if He might—but His very heart is in it, He rejoices to do it, and therefore
He does it thoroughly and He communicates His joy to us in the doing of it.
CHARLES SPURGEON

M Y WIFE LED a women's Bible study group in discussing a lesson she'd written about the happiness of Jesus. One woman who'd grown up a churchgoer was startled. She shared how horrified she'd been once to see a picture of Jesus smiling. Why? Because she believed it was blasphemous to make Jesus appear happy!

Actor Bruce Marchiano, who played Jesus in a movie based on Matthew's Gospel, received this remarkable letter:

> A few weeks ago I was halfway watching TV and happened to look up, and there was "Jesus" (you) walking along the banks of the Sea of Galilee.... He slowly looked over His shoulder, smiled a big smile, and motioned to follow Him. My heart leaped right out of my chest! . . . It was Jesus like I'd never considered Him to be, and in a moment I was convinced in my heart that Jesus just had to be this way—completely different from everything I'd ever thought! Glowing with excitement from His face—from His eyes. A strong, energetic, passionate, joyous man! It instantaneously transformed my relationship with Him—so much so, I grieve to think of all the decades I've wasted knowing Him, but not *knowing* Him; loving Him and receiving His love from some distant place, but never being "in love" with Him. Well . . . I am now![1]

When believers demonstrate genuine happiness, it draws people to God and the gospel. A young woman tells her story about coming to know Jesus:

> Before I met him my life was going down the drain. I had nothing to live for, let alone die for. There was no light at the end of my tunnel. In fact, there wasn't

even a tunnel. Only a deep, damp grave. Those days passed long ago, but I can't ever let myself forget them. . . .

I had never been in a church my whole life and I was unsure about what I should do. My heart began to panic. As we took our seats I relaxed a little. . . . I also noticed everyone's faces were so lit up with happy expressions. I never knew church made people happy.

After the service . . . I wanted to go back again and again and find out what all the happiness was about. I soon learned that it wasn't the church that made people happy, but rather, it was God and his son Jesus. They were the reason for the happy expressions on people's faces.[2]

Countless believers have similar stories. People are attracted to Jesus when they see his attributes in others' lives. They've observed kindness, graciousness, and happiness, and as a result, they want to know the source of those qualities.

I didn't meet a lot of "cool" people in the church where I first heard the gospel. I met some regular people who displayed profound peace, contentment, and happiness. When I saw these qualities, I couldn't ignore them. These were qualities I wanted, too, and they drew me toward the Christ they worshiped. And when I came to know Jesus myself, the happiness I found in him was deeper than I'd ever dreamed.

THE NEW TESTAMENT AND THE OLD TESTAMENT BOTH CLEARLY AFFIRM CHRIST'S HAPPINESS.

Most portrayals of Jesus show him as rather stoic and unemotional, but Scripture says otherwise. Jesus often expressed his emotions. The shortest verse in the English Bible is one of the most powerful: "Jesus wept" (John 11:35). And that isn't the only time God's Word shows him crying (see Luke 19:41). Many other passages demonstrate his compassion (see Matthew 9:36; Luke 7:13), his pity (see Matthew 20:34), his anger (see John 2:15-17), and his agony, which was so intense that his capillaries burst (see Luke 22:44). It shouldn't surprise us to discover that Jesus also experienced happiness.

Christ is called "the wisdom of God" (1 Corinthians 1:24). Jesus referred to himself as "wisdom" when he said, "The Son of Man came eating and drinking, and they say, 'Look at him! A glutton and a drunkard, a friend of tax collectors and sinners!' Yet wisdom is justified by her deeds" (Matthew 11:19). I believe Jesus is speaking of himself here as the well-known personification of wisdom in Proverbs 8. (Note that wisdom is called "she" in Proverbs 8. Jesus associates himself with wisdom, saying wisdom is justified by "her" deeds—a clear connection to the one teachers called "Lady Wisdom" in Proverbs 8.)

Puritan John Gill said the chapter is about "Christ, under the name of Wisdom."[3] Charles Bridges (1794–1869) claimed that the wisdom referred to in Proverbs 8 is "the voice of the Son of God."[4] Scottish clergyman Ralph Wardlaw (1779–1853) said, "The majority . . . of those regarded as evangelical expositors, interpret what is said in this chapter by Wisdom as the words of the Second Person of the ever-blessed Trinity."[5] Modern

Anglican scholar Derek Kidner (1913–2008) took this position,[6] as does Old Testament professor Tremper Longman III: "Jesus claims [in Matthew 11:19] that his behavior represents the behavior of Woman Wisdom herself."[7]

In Proverbs 8, then, we almost certainly see the words of Christ, speaking of the Father: "When he established the heavens, I was there. . . . When he marked out the foundations of the earth, then I was beside him, like a master workman" (verses 27, 29-30). Jesus says of the Father, "I was constantly at his side. I was filled with delight day after day, rejoicing always in his presence, rejoicing in his whole world and delighting in mankind" (verses 30-31, NIV).

Dylan Demarsico says of this passage, "Rejoicing is a conservative translation of the Hebrew word *sachaq*. More accurate would be *laughing* or *playing*. We're understandably reluctant to ascribe *laughing* and *playing* to Almighty God. Still, you can see for yourself in any Hebrew lexicon what the word means—and subsequently what God and wisdom were doing when they created the world: laughing and playing."[8]

The Common English Bible captures these words of God's all-wise Son: "I was *having fun, smiling* before him all the time, *frolicking* with his inhabited earth and delighting in the human race" (Proverbs 8:30-31, emphasis added). The Good News Translation says, "I was his daily source of joy, always happy in his presence—happy with the world and pleased with the human race."

Creation is attributed to Christ (see John 1:1-3; Colossians 1:16). But here he's seen as playfully interacting with his Father and his creation. What an amazing portrayal of the preincarnate happiness of Jesus!

Demarsico says of this passage, "If you had witnessed this transcendent Being-in-Three-Persons letting out roaring laughter as he played, thus creating the universe, you probably would have shouted and cried out with joy. . . . The joy of the Lord is not something trifling. It's a playfulness that created and sustains the universe, a laughter that guides history to its glorious end."[9]

Since we're told that the angels shouted for joy when the triune God created Earth (see Job 38:4, 7), surely we would have done the same. Perhaps we will someday on the New Earth—maybe God will open the past and delight us with a front-row seat beholding his original creation!

If, as compelling evidence suggests, Jesus was referring to himself as incarnate wisdom in Proverbs 8, then Scripture affirms not only the happiness but also the playfulness of God's Son. It's not a stretch to believe there was beautiful laughter among the triune God before the creation of the first human beings.

JESUS IS DEPICTED WITH A GLAD HEART.

In the first-ever gospel message of the newborn church, the apostle Peter preached that Psalm 16 is about Christ: "David says concerning him, 'I saw the Lord always before me, for he is at my right hand that I may not be shaken; therefore my heart was *glad*, and my tongue *rejoiced*. . . . For you will not abandon my soul to Hades, or let your Holy One see corruption. . . . You will make me *full of gladness* with your presence'" (Acts 2:25-28, emphasis added). This effusive statement, attributed to the Messiah, is a triple affirmation of his happiness!

The passage Peter ascribed to Jesus includes Psalm 16:11: "In your presence there is fullness of joy; at your right hand are pleasures forevermore." The New Life Version says, "Being with You is to be full of joy. In Your right hand there is happiness forever."

I'm convinced we should view this first apostolic sermon as a model for sharing the gospel today. Peter, full of the Holy Spirit, preached a prototype gospel message, asserting three times the happiness of the one who is at the center of the gospel—Jesus. Yet how many people, unbelievers and believers alike, have ever heard a modern gospel message that makes this point? Peter preached that Jesus was "full of gladness"; why shouldn't we?

What if we regularly declared the happiness of our Savior? Imagine the response if we emphasized that what Jesus did on that terrible cross was for the sake of never-ending happiness—ours and his (see Hebrews 12:2). We would be proclaiming a part of the gospel that's not only exceedingly attractive but also entirely true.

JESUS WAS—AND IS—THE HAPPIEST OF PEOPLE.

Psalm 45:6-7 is quoted in direct reference to the Messiah, in Hebrews 1:8-9, where the Father says of his Son: "You have loved righteousness and hated wickedness; therefore God, your God, has anointed you with the oil of gladness beyond your companions." The Contemporary English Version renders it, "your God . . . made you happier than any of your friends."

Who are Jesus' companions in this passage? This could refer to his immediate group of friends, all believers, or all his fellow human beings. If it's the latter, he has gladness that exceeds that of all people (which makes sense, because he created us). If we were to ask a random group of believers and unbelievers, "Who is the happiest human being who ever lived?" few people would give the correct answer: "Jesus."

Reflecting on these passages in Psalm 45 and Hebrews 1, John Piper writes, "Jesus Christ is the happiest being in the universe. His gladness is greater than all the angelic gladness of heaven. He mirrors perfectly the infinite, holy, indomitable mirth of his Father."[10]

Since the subject in the following verses in Psalm 45 doesn't change, these references, too, presumably point to Jesus: "From ivory palaces stringed instruments make you glad"; "Music comes to make you happy" (NCV). Does music sometimes make you happy? It makes Jesus, the one who is glad beyond all others, happy too.

THE BIBLE REPEATEDLY SUGGESTS THAT JESUS EXEMPLIFIED THE JOY OF LIVING.

If it were true that "it is an insult to Jesus Christ to use the word happiness in connection with Him,"[11] then Proverbs 8, Psalm 16, Acts 2, Psalm 45, and Hebrews 1 would all be insults to Jesus!

Scripture contains many additional indications of Christ's happiness. It takes a joyful person to instruct his disciples in the art of rejoicing. Jesus said, "Do not rejoice in this, that the spirits are subject to you, but rejoice that your names are written in heaven" (Luke 10:20). The CEV renders the verse, "Be happy that your names are written in heaven!"

The next verse connects his disciples' joy to Jesus' joy: "In that same hour he rejoiced in the Holy Spirit" (Luke 10:21). The Weymouth New Testament reads, "Jesus was filled by the Holy Spirit with rapturous joy."

Consider this part of the verse: "At that very time [the Son] rejoiced greatly in the Holy Spirit, and said, 'I praise You, O Father . . .'" (Luke 10:21, NASB). This verse clearly affirms the Trinity's gladness—Jesus overflows with joy from the Holy Spirit, and the Father finds pleasure in revealing himself to his children.

Puritan David Clarkson (1622–1686) said of this text, "We find Christ in an ecstasy, almost transported with joy. . . . Christ seemed to make man, of all earthly things, his chief joy on earth; this was it which revived him, joyed his heart in the midst of his sorrows and sufferings, that man should be thereby made happy."[12]

Imagine this scene: "Children were brought to him that he might lay his hands on them and pray. The disciples rebuked the people, but Jesus said, 'Let the little children come to me and do not hinder them, for to such belongs the kingdom of heaven.' And he laid his hands on them and went away" (Matthew 19:13-15). This passage leaves no doubt about Jesus' love for children. And the fact that children flocked to him is telling: children are drawn to happy adults, not unhappy ones.

The words Jesus spoke reveal his happiness. He says "Peace! Be still!" in the midst of a storm (Mark 4:39); "Do not be anxious" (Matthew 6:25); and "Blessed [happy] are the merciful, for they shall receive mercy" (Matthew 5:7). All these statements clearly flow out of a God-centered happiness.

Jesus says, "These things have I spoken unto you, that my joy might remain in you, and that your joy might be full" (John 15:11, KJV). The *Greek-English Lexicon of the New Testament* says that *chara*, the word translated here as "joy," means "a state of joy and gladness—joy, gladness, great happiness."[13] The CEV renders the verse, "I have told you this to make you as completely happy as I am." What a great life goal: to become as happy as Jesus!

Commenting on this passage, Spurgeon wrote, "The joy of Jesus is, first, the joy of abiding in His Father's love. He knows that His Father loves Him. . . . That is the joy which Christ gives to you—the joy of knowing that your Father loves you . . . even as Jesus Christ is loved."[14]

JESUS' HAPPINESS SET HIM APART FROM THE RELIGIOUS LEADERS OF HIS TIME.

First-century Pharisaism, with its endless rules, often negated the joy that God intended through feasts, celebrations, Sabbath days, and everyday life. But Jesus stood in stark contrast to "holy people" of his time. Serious rabbis were never in danger of being accused of gluttony and drunkenness, because they never went to parties. (They probably didn't get many invitations!) Jesus wasn't serious enough for their tastes, so they imagined he couldn't be holy.

James Martin writes, "Think of how happy those on the fringes of society—tax collectors, prostitutes, 'sinners'—would have been to be included in the community. The joy around the table was magnified by their gratitude."[15]

John Piper says,

> The glory and grace of Jesus is that he is, and always will be, indestructibly happy. . . . My capacities for joy are very confined. So Christ not only offers himself as the divine object of my joy, but pours his capacity for joy into me, so that I can enjoy him with the very joy of God. . . . Christ has never been gloomy.[16]

Given his incredible insight and wit, along with his loving heart, people who ate dinner with Jesus had to be thinking, *What's he going to say next?*

When I wrote my first graphic novel, *Eternity*, I had to decide how I wanted the artist to portray Jesus' face in a typical scene. Having read the Gospels many times and known Jesus for forty years, I knew his default look should be one of happiness. Yes, I asked the artist to portray him as angry when facing off with the Pharisees and sad when heading to the cross. But the man who held children in his arms, healed people, fed the multitudes, and made wine at a wedding was, more often than not, happy!

If we picture Jesus walking around in perpetual sadness or anger, grumbling and looking to condemn rather than to extend grace, we're not seeing the Jesus revealed in the Bible.

JESUS WAS BOTH A MAN OF SORROWS *AND* A MAN OF JOY.

It is written of the Messiah, "He was despised and rejected by men; a man of sorrows, and acquainted with grief; and as one from whom men hide their faces he was despised" (Isaiah 53:3). Note that he's called "a man of sorrows" specifically in relationship to his redemptive work.

When he was headed to the cross, Jesus said, "My soul is deeply grieved to the point of death" (Mark 14:34, NASB). But this was the worst day of his life—he was heading to a worse death than any human has ever faced. It doesn't indicate the typical, day-to-day temperament of Jesus.

Given the price he paid for our sins, does being "a man of sorrows" contradict the notion that Jesus was happy? Absolutely not. Sorrow and happiness can and do coexist within the same person. Jesus knew, as we, too, can know, that the basis for our sorrow is temporary, while the basis for our gladness is permanent. In Christ's case, he'd known unbounded happiness since before the dawn of time, and he knew that it awaited him again. That had to infuse his days with gladness even in the face of suffering and grief.

William Morrice writes, "The very fact that Jesus did attract hurting people to himself shows that he cannot have been forbidding in his manner. It suggests that the 'man of sorrows' conception of his personality has been overrated in the past. Had he been a gloomy individual and a kill-joy, he would not have had such an appeal to common people and to children."[17]

In Luke 4:17, Jesus unrolls the scroll of Isaiah and reads the first few verses of Isaiah 61, after which he says, "Today this Scripture has been fulfilled in your hearing" (Luke 4:21). Isaiah 61 continues with its prophecy about Jesus: "I will greatly rejoice in the LORD; my soul shall exult in my God, for he has clothed me with the garments of salvation; he has covered me with the robe of righteousness" (Isaiah 61:10). This passage tells us that the Father is the Son's source of joy. The New Century Version renders the verse, "The LORD makes me very happy; all that I am rejoices in my God." Again, God's Word explicitly affirms the everyday happiness of Jesus.

Take another look at a remarkable verse: "For the *joy* that was set before him [Christ] endured the cross, despising the shame, and is seated at the right hand of the throne of God" (Hebrews 12:2, emphasis added).

What was the joy set before him?

- the joy of pleasing the Father and the Holy Spirit
- the joy of redeeming his beloved people
- the joy of working together with the Spirit to sanctify his people
- the joy of granting his people entrance to Heaven
- the joy of saying to his people, "Well done" and "Come and share your master's happiness" (Matthew 25:23, NIV)
- the joy of granting his people positions of service in his Kingdom
- the joy of eternally reigning as the "last Adam" over the New Earth (1 Corinthians 15:45)
- the joy of seeing his people raised from the dead and watching them celebrate and laugh, never to weep again

On Good Friday, Jesus experienced the terrible burden of atonement, the trauma of dying on the cross, and the anguish of being temporarily alienated from his Father when he became our sin (see Matthew 27:46; 2 Corinthians 5:21). But this suffering was overshadowed by the joy of *our* salvation. When Jesus walked the Earth, he lived every moment with divine happiness in his past, the happiness of an eternal perspective in his present, and the anticipation of unending happiness in the future.

WHEN PEOPLE REJOICE, THEIR FACES SHOW IT, AND JESUS WAS NO EXCEPTION.

Scripture includes dozens of passages in which it's hard to imagine Jesus not smiling broadly: as he holds children in his arms (see Matthew 19:13-15), as he raises a boy and a girl from the dead (see Luke 7:11-17; Mark 5:35-43), as he talks about the birds of the air and flowers of the field (see Matthew 6:26, 28), as he makes his outrageous statement about swallowing a camel (see Matthew 23:24), and as he contemplates the love he and his Father have for each other and extend to us (see John 15:9).

Proverbs 15:13 says, "A happy heart makes the face cheerful" (NIV). Did Jesus have a happy heart and cheerful face much of the time? I believe he did. Not every moment of every day, of course, but certainly more often than not.

Most versions translate Luke 10:21 as saying that Jesus "rejoiced [*agalliao*] in the Holy Spirit." The Easy-to-Read Version translates it, "Then the Holy Spirit made Jesus feel very happy." How could Jesus rejoice in the Holy Spirit without feeling happy?

CHRIST'S HAPPINESS IS INTRINSIC TO BOTH HIS DEITY AND HIS HUMANITY.

As the early church was establishing its identity, it faced a few significant heresies. Some denied Christ's deity; others denied his humanity. Scripture affirms both.

Some suppose that Jesus had a capacity for happiness because he's human. But that's not the place to start, since he was God before he was man. God didn't become happy for the first time after the Incarnation! As we've seen in Scripture, the triune God has always experienced joy within himself.

Scripture also makes it clear that Jesus experienced the gamut of human emotions: "Our high priest is able to understand our weaknesses. He was tempted in every way that we are, but he did not sin" (Hebrews 4:15, NCV).

Have you ever thought about the eternally happy Son of God enjoying happiness as a human being for the first time? I have to believe that his smiles, his laughter, and the words he spoke to his Father would have been full of delight as he marveled at his incarnation, which, because of his resurrection, will never end!

A. W. Tozer wrote, "[God] meant us to see Him and live with Him and draw our life from His smile."[18] The smile of Jesus is not like the smile of Buddha—disconnected from suffering. Jesus smiles as one who, having been happy from eternity past and fully knowing the cost, chose to take on the worst suffering imaginable to secure our everlasting happiness.

We view Jesus as the deity who miraculously puts an end to all suffering—and so he will—but meanwhile we need to see him as the one who understands and experiences both joy and suffering, and is committed to using both for his glory.

A wise man once observed, "The early Christians did not say in dismay, 'look what the world has come to,' but in delight, 'look what has come into the world.'"[19]

"What has come" is Jesus Christ, a person so attractive, so magnetic, and so joyful that he changed the world not only by his death but also by his life.

SINCE JESUS IS HAPPY, HIS DISCIPLES SHOULD FOLLOW HIM HAPPILY.

Ethics professor Paul J. Wadell writes,

> We are novices in the habits of happiness, and novices need a teacher. In the Christian life our primary teacher in the way of happiness is Christ. He is our mentor; we are his disciples. And it is by observing him, listening to him, learning from him, following his teachings, and imitating his example that we grow in happiness. The mortal life is a *training in happiness*, and, for Christians, happiness is intrinsically connected to Christ. In Christ one sees the path to happiness and discovers the virtues and practices constitutive of happiness. For Christians, happiness is a way of life by which we gradually are conformed to the love, goodness, and beauty of God revealed to us in Christ.[20]

Francis de Sales, the bishop of Geneva (1567–1622), said, "I cannot understand why those who have given themselves up to God and his goodness are not always cheerful; for what possible happiness can be equal to that? No accidents or imperfections which may happen ought to have power to trouble them, or to hinder their looking upward."[21]

One explanation for our cheerlessness is simple: many of God's people don't believe that the Christ we serve is cheerful.

Spurgeon said, "We are happy to think Christ is happy. I do not know whether you have ever drank that joy, Believer, but I have found it a very sweet joy to be joyful because Christ is joyful."[22]

Scripture commands us to follow in Jesus' footsteps (see 1 Peter 2:21). When we become convinced that our Savior walked this Earth not only experiencing suffering and sorrow but also doing so with an ancient yet forever-young happiness in his heart and a smile on his face, it will inspire us to love him more deeply and follow him more cheerfully.

CHAPTER 19

DID JESUS LAUGH, PLAY, AND HAVE A SENSE OF HUMOR?

You blind guides, straining out a gnat and swallowing a camel!
JESUS (MATTHEW 23:24)

If there is a single person within the pages of the Bible that we can consider to be a humorist, it is without doubt Jesus.
DICTIONARY OF BIBLICAL IMAGERY

A FRIEND AND I spent three hours with Carol King, a godly woman in her fifties who was dying of cancer. She'd read a few of my books and wanted to talk about Heaven. What struck me that day was an unexpected gift—the gift of laughter.

"I need some new clothes," Carol said, "but why buy them? I used to get jumbo-sized shampoo, but now I get small bottles. I don't even buy green bananas, because by the time they ripen I'll probably be gone!" Carol laughed as she spoke. It wasn't a morbid or cynical laugh, but one that naturally flowed from heartfelt peace. She anticipated being with Jesus in a better world. She'd already suffered great pain and had no romantic notions about death. Yet she faced the end of her time on Earth with quiet joy and Christ-honoring laughter that invited us to laugh as much as she did.

In his novella *A Christmas Carol*, Charles Dickens wrote,

> It was a great surprise to Scrooge . . . to hear a hearty laugh . . . his own nephew's and to find himself in a bright, dry, gleaming room, with the Spirit standing smiling by his side, and looking at that same nephew. . . . There is nothing in the world so irresistibly contagious as laughter and good-humour. When Scrooge's nephew laughed . . . Scrooge's niece, by marriage, laughed as heartily as he. And their assembled friends, being not a bit behindhand, roared out lustily.[1]

Nanci and I find that lightheartedness and laughter help us work through heavy and difficult situations without burning out or losing our perspective. Humor is our release, our safety valve. Laughter is therapeutic. It heals. It gives hope and vitality.

WHERE DOES THIS THERAPY CALLED LAUGHTER COME FROM?

Did Satan create laughter? Was it fashioned by humans? No. Scripture says of God, "He will yet fill your mouth with laughter, and your lips with shouts of joy" (Job 8:21, NRSV).

Scripture says of Jesus, "By him all things were created" (Colossians 1:16). Laughter comes from the Creator, who made us in his image! His laughter preceded our own laughter and is the ongoing source of it. We can be happy only because he's happy; we can laugh because he laughs.

GOD'S HAPPINESS

HUMAN HAPPINESS (FROM GOD)

DIAGRAM 7

Human beings are recipients of happiness, not sources of it. All our delight and gladness come from God.

We cannot divorce our happiness from God's happiness, because his happiness is foundational to ours.

WE CAN'T HAVE A CORRECT VIEW OF JESUS UNLESS WE EMBRACE HIS HAPPINESS.

Despite so much biblical evidence pointing to Jesus' happiness, many Christians believe otherwise. An evangelical pamphlet says, "Jesus never laughed."[2] Pastor and seminary professor Mike Abendroth says that growing up in Christian circles, he was taught as fact that Jesus didn't laugh.[3]

True, the Bible never directly states that Jesus laughed, but that doesn't prove anything. We're told that the vast majority of what Jesus said and did isn't recorded in Scripture (see John 20:30; 21:25). Arguing that Jesus didn't laugh because the Bible doesn't mention it is like saying Jesus didn't breathe, yawn, sneeze, or run since the Bible doesn't mention him doing so. It doesn't have to—we can safely assume he did those things because Scripture tells us Jesus was fully human (see Hebrews 2:14-18).

Human beings laugh. We don't have depictions of the disciples sitting around campfires telling stories or teasing each other. But I'm certain they did, because *that's what people do.*

Did Jesus joke with his friends? The better question is, Why wouldn't he? Jesus knew what Solomon did: there is "a time to weep, and a time to laugh; a time to mourn, and a time to dance" (Ecclesiastes 3:4).

Growing up in a faithful Jewish family, Jesus would have enjoyed many feasts and holidays, as well as the weekly Sabbath, all celebratory experiences (see chapter 33). One of the psalms that Jesus would have meditated on from his childhood says, "When the LORD brought us back to Jerusalem it was like a dream! How we laughed, how we sang for joy! . . . Indeed he did great things for us; how happy we were!" (Psalm 126:1-3, GNT).

Laughter is not only human, it's explicitly *biblical* and pleasing to God. It's therefore inconceivable that Jesus didn't laugh!

CHRIST'S HUMOR WOULD HAVE BEEN OBVIOUS TO ANY FIRST-CENTURY MIDDLE EASTERNER.

Few of us are familiar with the culture Jesus lived in. In our culture, most humor is based on joke telling, verbal ambiguities, and physical comedy. Jewish humor often employed witty hyperbole—clever, startling, over-the-top statements—to get a laugh. Though some comedians today do this and we laugh, when we see Jesus use the technique in the Gospels, we usually don't get it. Jesus certainly never employed the caustic humor of late-night comedians who ridicule the weak minded or the unfortunate. But he did make hypocrites in positions of power the brunt of his wit.

In *The Humor of Christ*, Elton Trueblood argued,

> There are numerous passages . . . which are practically incomprehensible when regarded as sober prose, but which are luminous once we become liberated from the gratuitous assumption that Christ never joked. . . . Once we realize that Christ was not always engaged in pious talk, we have made an enormous step on the road to understanding.[4]

Did humor come into the universe as the result of sin? No. We have a sense of humor because as his image bearers, we are similar to God, who enjoys laughter.

The *Dictionary of Biblical Imagery* says, "Jesus was a master of wordplay, irony and satire, often with an element of humor intermixed."[5] Jesus makes many serious points in humorous ways. "Are grapes gathered from thornbushes?" he asks, "or figs from thistles?" (Matthew 7:16). People who worked the ground in that culture surely smiled at the self-evident answers.

When encountering a verse such as this one, which instructs us not to "cast your pearls before swine" (Matthew 7:6, NKJV), a modern reader might wonder why anyone would even think to do such an outlandish thing. But that's the whole point—no sane person would! Therefore, Jesus was saying, don't do the spiritual equivalent of that ridiculously stupid thing.

Jesus told people, "When you give to the needy, sound no trumpet before you, as the hypocrites do in the synagogues and in the streets, that they may be praised by others" (Matthew 6:2). No one would do anything so obviously self-promoting. Instead, they'd draw attention to themselves by walking slowly and piously, making their money clearly visible. These self-congratulatory actions, which Jesus characterized as "sounding a trumpet," undoubtedly produced numerous smiles, smirks, and chuckles.

Can't you imagine folks looking at each other with amazement and nervous glee when Jesus said, "Woe to you, scribes and Pharisees, hypocrites! For you are like whitewashed tombs, which outwardly appear beautiful, but within are full of dead people's bones and all uncleanness" (Matthew 23:27)? Jesus was not telling jokes but painting mental pictures with a humorous, satirical sting. Think of the religious leaders' outrage when Jesus said, "The harlots go into the kingdom of God before you" (Matthew 21:31, KJV). Then think of the approving smiles of the poor and oppressed in the crowds who finally saw someone unafraid to confront these pseudospiritual false shepherds.

Jesus referred to the shrewd and ruthless political leader Herod as "that fox" (Luke 13:32). Since a fox is cunning, this may appear to be a compliment, but it certainly wouldn't have been lost on the crowd that those pointy-eared varmints were nuisances, not terrors. Jesus was poking fun at a vicious, immoral, murderous tyrant by comparing him not to a lion or a bear but to a fox! Imagine people going home and telling their friends, "You won't believe what Jesus called Herod!"

Jesus said, "And when you fast, do not look gloomy like the hypocrites, for they disfigure their faces that their fasting may be seen by others" (Matthew 6:16). ("Do not look gloomy" would be a great memory verse for some churchgoers!) The self-righteous religionists of Jesus' day liked to call attention to their fasting by rubbing ashes on their faces to make them look gaunt and deprived. The more miserable, the more spiritual—or so they supposed. Christ made fun of them for it, and they didn't like it—but no doubt many of his listeners enjoyed hearing the self-righteous leaders taken to task.

Jesus said of the religious leaders, "They are blind guides. And if the blind lead the blind, both will fall into a pit" (Matthew 15:14). This graphic word picture might have prompted outright laughter. Of course, Jesus wasn't making fun of the blind; he was critiquing the wealthy, powerful, influential people who prided themselves on their supposed clarity of spiritual vision.

JESUS USED EXAGGERATION FOR COMEDIC EFFECT.

Jesus told the religious leaders they were sightless, missing the whole point of following God: "You blind guides, straining out a gnat and swallowing a camel!" (Matthew 23:24). Straining out a gnat would have been hard work for anyone—but impossible for the blind. And what could be more ridiculous than swallowing a camel? This odd and pithy statement undoubtedly caused laughter to erupt.

The *Dictionary of Biblical Imagery* says, "The most characteristic form of Jesus' humor was the preposterous exaggeration."[6] It's important to understand that this form of exaggeration is not falsehood in any sense, because the hearer knows it's overstatement. The speaker is not misleading anyone; rather, he is appealing to the hearer's humor to make his point.

Consider the parable of the talents in Matthew 25. Jesus depicts a wealthy man who hands over one to five talents to various servants. Five talents would have been the equivalent of nearly a hundred years' wages.[7] In a culture where many people lived hand to mouth, this extreme amount of money would equate to saying, "There was a man who ate one thousand gourds." The storyteller deliberately paints an absurd picture, with a gleam in his eye, to emphasize his point.

Jesus took hyperbole—a rhetorical art form—to a new level in his story about the king who loaned one of his servants ten thousand talents (see Matthew 18:23-35), an amount so ludicrous it defied comprehension, since the average person made one talent every twenty years.[8] Imagine the listeners' expressions when they tried to calculate the sum that the king forgave his servant.

Then Jesus said another servant owed the forgiven servant one hundred denarii (see

Matthew 18:28). A denarius was a day's wage, and although a hundred days' wages was significant, it was the tiniest fraction compared to the forgiven servant's debt. The parallel to each person's debt to God, which is beyond measure, must have had a deep impact. It wasn't stand-up comedy (which might not have been funny to them anyway), but Jesus' humor certainly would have resonated with his original audience.

Consider when Jesus asked, "Why do you see the speck that is in your brother's eye, but do not notice the log that is in your own eye? . . . You hypocrite, first take the log out of your own eye, and then you will see clearly to take the speck out of your brother's eye" (Matthew 7:3, 5). Surely the ridiculous picture of a log sticking out of a man's eye produced not only a sense of conviction but also broad smiles.

Elton Trueblood recounted how he noticed Christ's humor for the first time. He was reading Matthew 7 aloud when his young son burst into laughter at Jesus' words about a log in the eye. Until then, Trueblood had failed to see Christ's obvious wit.[9]

Those who heard Jesus speak knew his keen humor—and they were endeared to him.

CHRIST USED HUMOROUS STORIES OF FOOLISH ACTIONS TO MAKE HIS POINT.

Jesus told a parable about the wise man who built his house on the rock and the foolish man who built his house on the sand (see Matthew 7:24-27). The moment they heard the part about the man building on sand, the audience would have laughed, because they saw where the story was going!

When Jesus told the parable about sewing a piece of new cloth on an old garment (see Luke 5:36), every housewife would have smiled knowingly, realizing what a bad plan that was.

When he said, "Neither is new wine put into old wineskins. If it is, the skins burst and the wine is spilled and the skins are destroyed" (Matthew 9:17), no doubt people in the crowd grinned and nodded, having learned that very thing the hard way. Fermentation expands wine, causing a sealed wineskin to explode. This creates a mess, drenching everyone nearby, sending people off to find rags to wipe off their faces, and perhaps causing permanent stains on a table or clothes that can only be laughed at later.

In making a spiritual point about purity of heart, Jesus said, "Do you not see that whatever goes into the mouth passes into the stomach and is expelled?" (Matthew 15:17). The English Standard Version's note about this verse says the Greek means "is expelled into the latrine." The note refers to what Jesus actually said, and his words surely would have caused smirks among his hearers. Most English versions obscure the meaning for fear it might come across as bathroom humor (like 1 Kings 18:27). But shouldn't we let God decide what he wants included in Scripture?

Jesus was a master of the clever turn of phrase: "Those who are well have no need of a physician, but those who are sick. I came not to call the righteous, but sinners" (Mark 2:17). Imagine healthy people lined up to see a doctor—how laughable.

Or ponder this example: "If the householder had known at what hour the thief was coming, he would have been awake and would not have left his house to be broken into"

(Luke 12:39, RSVCE). Imagine a thief scheduling his robbery with the householder! Haven't you laughed at "stupid criminal" stories, such as the bank robber who handed a threatening note to the teller on the back of his own check stub . . . and was arrested at his apartment thirty minutes later?

Jesus asked, "Is a lamp brought in to be put under a basket, or under a bed, and not on a stand?" (Mark 4:21). In Jesus' day, lamps had open flames, and a bed was not a metal frame but a straw mattress! The imagery is absurd, and therefore humorous.

The humor of Jesus is far more apparent if we understand his culture and engaging personality. There's nothing disrespectful about noticing that many of Jesus' statements are, by design, happily outrageous.

LAUGHTER THAT'S GOOD, PURE, AND GOD-HONORING IN HEAVEN CAN ALSO BE ENJOYED HERE AND NOW.

Jesus says, "Blessed are you who weep now, for you shall laugh" (Luke 6:21). In context, he's talking about people having great reward in Heaven. In other words, he's saying, "You will laugh in Heaven." Surely Jesus will join in the laughter—and be the source of much of it. And when Jesus laughs, it's always the laughter of both God and man.

Jesus goes on to say, "Woe to you who laugh now, for you shall mourn and weep" (Luke 6:25). The laughter he opposes is laughter at injustice, immorality, and other things that dishonor God. Obviously, laughter can be twisted by sin, just as eating, drinking, and everything else can.

As believers, we need to laugh a great deal more and a great deal less: more at ourselves and the incongruities of life, and less at immorality and mockery of what pleases God.

The Bible says that Jesus dwells within his people (see Galatians 2:20). I've laughed at myself and many experiences, and I believe I've truly sensed Jesus' laughter joining mine. As long as no one gets hurt by them, I end up laughing at my stupid mistakes regularly, which allows me to find happiness in what otherwise could become frustration or embarrassment. I don't laugh at my sin; I do laugh at my limitations and mistakes, often whispering to myself, "You're an idiot." (It's not self-hatred; it's being entertained by my innocent blunders.) Laughing at ourselves can please God, relieve stress, and reflect humility—after all, proud people can't laugh at themselves and are outraged when others laugh at them.

Jesus may have laughed at some of the limitations of his own humanity. He didn't sin or make foolish decisions, but did he ever fall down, spill milk, or hit his thumb while hammering? He who made the heavens with his fingers (see Psalm 8:3) surely got splinters in them while working with wood all day. I doubt he complained, but I do think he marveled at what it means to be human. Remember, Jesus brought into the world not only the grace and truth of God but also the happiness, delight, humor, and laughter of God.

DID JESUS PLAY?

Play is happiness in motion. Why do otters keep going down waterslides hour after hour? Why do they swim on their backs munching abalone the way we sit in recliners munching popcorn? Because God put something of himself into them, revealing his attributes in what he created (see Romans 1:20). God must love play; otherwise, nothing he created would have the instinct to play. Study otters and learn something about God.

Play didn't start with fallen humanity; God wove it into animals and people, especially children, coming straight from his heart. God, speaking to Job, says of the sea monster Leviathan, "Will you play with him as with a bird, or will you put him on a leash for your girls?" (Job 41:5). God is implying he can do what Job can't—play with his beloved creature. God made creatures to play in the waters: "There go the ships, and Leviathan, which you formed to play in it" (Psalm 104:26). Their play makes God happy—in fact, the vast majority of underwater play is seen by no one but God (though perhaps an audience of angels watches too).

In his response to Job, God talks about delighting in his creation. He says, "The mountains yield food for him where all the wild beasts play" (Job 40:20). His creatures play because their Creator enjoys play and built it into them.

Since God is playful, and because he wired his image bearers and even animals to enjoy play, of course Jesus must have played. As we saw previously, Proverbs 8:22-31 tells us that God's Son, wisdom personified, played even before his incarnation. But even without that reference, we would know he played; he was once a child! Did he play and race and joke with the disciples? Obviously. I have no doubt he will play and joke with us on the New Earth too.

A new world is coming where we'll play with animals that are now dangerous, without threat of harm: "The nursing child shall play over the hole of the cobra, and the weaned child shall put his hand on the adder's den" (Isaiah 11:8). Whether this is the Millennium, the New Earth, or both, God promises that we'll one day be able to play with animals that are now dangerous.

God describes children playing as a fruit of his presence. He promises a time of great happiness: "The streets of the city shall be full of boys and girls playing" (Zechariah 8:5). What a beautiful and hope-giving picture! Play is part of a perfect world.

Since Jesus will always remain incarnate, living with his people on the New Earth (see Revelation 21:3), surely the spirit of play he created and built into people will be reflected in his own nature and actions. What will it be like for people and animals to play with the one who made them to love play? Nothing short of glorious.

HOW DOES THE HAPPINESS OF JESUS CARRY OVER TO OUR LIVES?

Why isn't Christ's playfulness and humor clear to us? Perhaps because we think it's an insult to imagine that God has a sense of humor. But how could he not? If God doesn't have the ability to laugh and find things funny, where did we get those inclinations? And why would it insult him to credit God and God's Son with something so delightful as play and laughter? On the contrary, doesn't it insult him *not* to credit him for these wonderful gifts?

Before I came to faith in Christ, I laughed and had some tastes of happiness. But once I knew Jesus, I found myself smiling and laughing far more often.

My life hasn't always been easy. At times I've fought depression, but as a teenager, before knowing God, I had nothing much to fight it with. Now I have far better tools—first and foremost an awareness of the presence and grace of God. I thank him that as the years have gone on, he has enabled me to experience more frequent times of happiness even in the midst of difficulties. God's gift of laughter is a huge part of that; in fact, sometimes it's like a ladder that helps me climb out of deep holes. A close friend once told me, "I always know when you're hurting. You joke and laugh more." (There are medications that help some people, and I'm grateful for that, as they're part of his common grace.)

When the weather is nice, Nanci and I often keep the side door open while we eat or watch a movie. Every few minutes, we see Maggie run by, carrying a huge branch. We laugh at her repeatedly, and she never tires of the game. She can play for hours—with us, with our grandkids, with other dogs, and by herself. And God, I believe, is with her.

Maggie frequently comes to me while I work and nestles her head against me. If I don't respond quickly enough, she realizes I'm distracted by what she considers less important concerns (including writing this book), and she knocks my hand off the keyboard with her big paw. I laugh at her, then play with her. I know that in those moments she's being the way God made her. I'm consciously aware that Jesus is causing me to smile through her. And I believe he's smiling at us both. If I didn't believe this, my happiness would be diminished.

Such happiness is available for all of us. As ripe fruit drops easily from the branches, so happiness drops easily from Jesus' hand to ours. If we're not sensing happiness in him, we need to ask if we're seeing him as the delightful and happy-making person he really is—and whether we're failing to see the multitude of daily expressions of his happiness he has built into the world and into each of our lives. (Many who are poor and live in hardship, even in slums or prisons, will testify that they have learned to see God in countless details of their lives.)

Though you won't discover happiness in most books about God's attributes, and you may never find books about his humor, isn't it obvious that these are intrinsic parts of his character? Surely the one who says, "Rejoice and be exceedingly glad" (Matthew 5:12, NKJV) knows how to rejoice and be glad.

WHY IS GOD'S HAPPINESS IMPORTANT?

Nazi death camp survivor Viktor E. Frankl (1905–1997) wrote, "Happiness [is] the unintended side-effect of one's personal dedication to a cause greater than oneself or as the by-product of one's surrender to a person other than oneself."[10] This explains why so many of us aren't happy—we're our own biggest cause, the most important people in our lives. And we're way too small and powerless to create or sustain our own happiness.

Too often we envision a small God, not the incomparably great God—the happy, smiling God—and his boundless, treasure-laden Kingdom. So we devote ourselves to our puny little mini kingdoms instead of his mega Kingdom. We need to stop being content with anything less than what we're made to experience in God. We'll do that when we believe our greatest happiness resides in him.

Jeremiah Burroughs said, "God is the only source of real happiness. He does not need anything or anyone to make him happy: even before he made the world, the three persons of the Trinity were completely happy with each other. What God does for Christians is to make them as happy as he is."[11] Wow!

God is infinite, so our quantity of happiness won't ever be as great as his. But as God is fully happy, one day we will be fully happy. Meanwhile, our happiness in God can grow significantly. If you don't go to God for happiness, you'll certainly go elsewhere. But you won't go to him if you don't believe he's happy. No wonder the devil hates the happiness of God and labors to hide it from us.

Charles Spurgeon realized that the doctrine of God's happiness can't be separated from our own experience: "If you knew anything of the joy of the happy God, you would understand that a truly Christian life cannot be an unhappy one!"[12] In a fallen world, our happiness will be—in fact, must be—punctuated by times of sorrow. But happiness in God can and should be the norm rather than the exception.

One day in the presence of Jesus, we'll know what it means to have entered our Master's happiness. And on the New Earth, as we play and feast and joke and tell stories together, always looking to the one who redeemed us, I truly believe that no laugh will be louder, and no happiness larger, than his.

PART 3

The Bible's Actual Words for Happiness

CHAPTER 20

HAPPINESS, JOY, AND GLADNESS IN THE BIBLE

They come with happiness and joy; they enter the king's palace.
PSALM 45:15, NCV

All your security, freedom, rest, peace, and happiness consist in the goodness and love of your Maker towards you.
WILHELMUS À BRAKEL

I'VE WATCHED PEOPLE in several countries view the *JESUS* film for the first time. They beam as Jesus befriends children and performs miracles, groan and weep at his crucifixion, and smile or cry out with delight when they witness his resurrection. The reality of who Jesus is overwhelms them. (I'm told that at one showing, tribal warriors spontaneously jumped to their feet and riddled the screen with blowgun darts in an attempt to stop the soldiers from nailing Jesus to the cross.)

I've also watched videos of tribal groups hearing about eternal life in Jesus for the first time. People repent, turn to Jesus, then break out in shouts of rejoicing and dancing, which continues for hours.[1]

A video of the Kimyal tribe in Indonesia conveys the overwhelming happiness of those receiving the first Bible in their own language. The occasion, marked by joyful tears, broad smiles, and spontaneous dancing, demonstrates the contagious happiness of people who delight in reading God's words in their heart language.[2]

Remarkably, happiness from reading and hearing God's words is available to us every day.

SCRIPTURE OFFERS A SWEET REWARD FOR THOSE WHO STUDY IT.

The Bible is a vast reservoir of happiness, consisting of not dozens but hundreds of related passages. This section of the book is arguably the most important because it contains more of God's words than mine. (The primary exception to this is the following chapter, dealing with the meaning of *blessed*.) God says, "My word that goes out from my mouth . . . will not return to me empty, but will accomplish what I desire and achieve the purpose for which I sent it" (Isaiah 55:11, NIV). That promise is for his words, not mine or yours.

My goal in these next chapters is to let God speak for himself concerning happiness, joy, and gladness. What he has to say is surprising and delightful, and differs radically from what many people—unbelievers and believers alike—assume.

I need to give three warnings. The many Scripture passages in this section may make it your favorite part of the book, but to some, it may seem like too much. If, after reading the first several chapters, you feel like you're drinking all that living water out of a fire hose, take a break and move to part 4. Just mark where you stopped so you can return and finish later. God's words will still be here when you're ready for more!

The second warning is this: you may be put off by the Hebrew and Greek words and the quotations from scholars about what they mean. These might seem technical or academic at first. However, I encourage you not to undersell your ability to understand. I've written many books, and this is the first one in which I've felt that if I don't discuss the words in their original languages, I'll leave readers in the dark. We simply can't understand what the Bible says about happiness unless we cut through the modern misconceptions and go back to the particular Hebrew and Greek words God chose.

I'm focusing extensively on two Hebrew words and two Greek words. You will also find nineteen additional Hebrew words and fourteen Greek words in the appendices if you want to learn more. I'm using only as much technical language as I consider vital to demonstrate how happiness-rich God's Word truly is—a fact that isn't evident in many English translations.

If we don't explore the actual happiness-related words God put in the Bible, we will miss the richness of happiness in Christ lying beneath the surface of Scripture. Stick with me in this section, and I think you'll be glad you did.

A final warning: the words and verses I've chosen focus, naturally, on the subject of this book: happiness. They're not the whole story, any more than books I've written on evil and suffering are the whole story. Still, just as I talk about joy in those books, I fully acknowledge sorrow in this one.

All the psalms of lament, the entire book of Lamentations, and many other Scripture passages reveal the importance of realism and sorrow in the Christian life. No treatment of joy and happiness should deny or minimize such texts. Indeed, a truly biblical worldview and an authentic doctrine of joy and happiness fully recognize and embrace the realities of suffering in this present age. Happiness in Scripture is all the deeper and richer because it doesn't require denial or pretense, and can be experienced in the midst of severe difficulty.

SCRIPTURE SPEAKS A LANGUAGE OF HAPPINESS.

James Swanson, my friend and the compiler of the *Dictionary of Biblical Languages*, points to eighteen different Hebrew root words in the Old Testament related to joy, happiness, and gladness, making Hebrew one of the most happiness-rich languages in the world.[3]

William Morrice writes that the many Greek synonyms for *joy* appear a total of 326 times in the New Testament.[4] Robert J. Dean says, "A number of Greek and Hebrew words are used to convey the ideas of joy and rejoicing. We have the same situation in English with such nearly synonymous words as joy, happiness, pleasure, delight, gladness, merriment, felicity, and enjoyment."[5]

I looked up all references to these words in the English Standard Version: *happiness, joy, enjoy, rejoice, gladness, merry, pleasure, delight, celebration, cheerful, please, pleasant, laugh, laughter, smile, jubilant, jubilee, relax, rest, feast, festival,* and *exult.* These and their related words appear more than 1,700 times. When we add the times the word *blessed* is used to translate words that mean "happy," the total comes to about two thousand.

While you may be surprised by how many biblical passages I cite in the following chapters, what's remarkable to me is how many I've left out!

WHY ARE BIBLE TRANSLATIONS SO VARIED?

English versions of the Bible, or versions in any other language, differ simply because *that's the nature of language and translation!* Words rarely have exact equivalents in other languages. And though paraphrases such as The Message take considerable liberties, actual translations from the original languages convey far more similar meanings than different ones.

The Bible was written entirely in Hebrew and Greek, with the exception of a few Aramaic chapters in Ezra and Daniel. The original languages are translated into others, including English, each using words carefully chosen by teams of rigorously trained scholars.

For example, consider Ecclesiastes 9:7. The New American Standard Bible reads, "Eat your bread in happiness [Hebrew *samach*] and drink your wine with a cheerful [*tob*] heart; for God has already approved your works." Other than different pronoun choices ("thy" and "your"), the English Standard Version and the King James Version are identical: "Eat your bread with joy, and drink your wine with a merry heart." So the two most literal modern translations render the same Hebrew word differently—one as "happiness" (NASB) and the other "joy" (ESV). And in the same verse, one renders a second word "cheerful," the other "merry."

The New International Version says, "Eat your food with *gladness,* and drink your wine with a *joyful* heart" (emphasis added). So you might think these three translations don't agree on a single rendering of the original Hebrew words. But in fact, the three translations align closely. Why? Because the two Hebrew words are synonyms, and each can be accurately rendered by any of the chosen English words—which are also synonyms.

The New Living Translation, the Complete Jewish Bible, and the New English Translation all agree on still another rendering of Ecclesiastes 9:7: "Drink your wine with a *happy* heart" (emphasis added).

Is only one translation right? No, because *exact* equivalents rarely exist in differing languages, and Hebrew into English is no exception. As long as the translations effectively capture the original's intent, all are correct.

To understand this vital concept, we need to learn about semantic domains. A semantic domain is a family of closely related words. Suppose you say, "It's a bright day." The semantic domain for *bright* includes these words: *sunny, luminous, light, clear,* and *unclouded.*

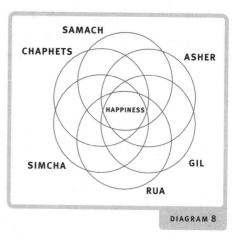

Diagrams 8 and 9 reflect the overlapping meanings of the Hebrew and Greek words for *happiness* in Scripture. There are far more words for happiness than depicted in each diagram. To be complete, the Hebrew diagram would need three times more circles, and the Greek about two times more. (Never mind the nuances of these words for now; we'll get to that later.) The main point of the diagrams is to give an idea of the overlapping nature of words in the Bible's happiness semantic domain.

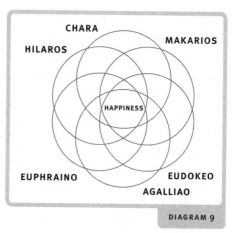

With these diagrams in mind, let's take another look at Ecclesiastes 9:7. The Holman Christian Standard Bible echoes the NASB's advice to drink with a cheerful heart but adds, "Eat your bread with pleasure." So should we eat with gladness (WYC, NIV), joy (KJV, ESV), happiness (NASB, GNT), or pleasure (HCSB)? Think about it—is there any significant difference?

Consider Charles Spurgeon on his conversion experience: "How blessed [happy-making] it was when first we felt it! My heart did leap for joy! I was never so happy before and I sometimes think that I have scarcely ever been quite as jubilant as I was on that day of holy excitement and exhilaration."[6]

Blessed, joy, happy, jubilant, excitement, and *exhilaration*—just as Spurgeon "piled on" these synonyms in English, the same technique occurs in Scripture.

CONTEXT IS THE KEY TO UNDERSTANDING WORD MEANINGS.

Hebrew scholar James Barr (1924–2006) established that relying entirely on dictionaries or lexicons to discover a word's meaning is dangerous because a word doesn't acquire a specific meaning until it's used in a sentence.[7] Dictionaries only tell us what a word can mean or what it sometimes means, not what it *actually* means in a particular context. The surrounding sentences must be examined to offer clues to the author's meaning.

Likewise, a particular Hebrew or Greek word doesn't always mean happy, joyful, glad, or anything else. Context is king—this is the challenge of translation.

In this section, I'll present passages utilizing particular Hebrew and Greek words that linguists and translators have most often associated with the concepts expressed by the English words *happiness, joy,* and their synonyms.

In the course of my research, I interacted with various Hebrew scholars, including Dr. Reinier de Blois, whose specialty is Hebrew lexicography based on cognitive linguistics, a field offering new perspectives on word meanings.[8] Dr. de Blois explains,

> You cannot get the meaning of a biblical term without seeing it within the context of the entire semantic domain to which it belongs. . . . Hebrew has a lot of synonyms. . . . Because of the abundance of parallelisms and word pairs many Hebrew terms have counterparts. In those constructions there is relatively little focus on the differences between these words. It is the repetition that gives extra emphasis to the entire construction. That is why you often hear about "righteousness and justice," "loving-kindness and truth," and "rejoice and be glad."[9]

I cite various translations because familiarity with a preferred version can lead to believing other translations are wrong. We imagine sharp distinctions between Hebrew and Greek synonyms and also the chosen English words, such as *joyful, glad,* or *happy.* Only when we recognize how meanings overlap in words from the same semantic domain will we be saved from making artificial distinctions between the corresponding English words.

While I normally use more literal Bible translations for my own study and rarely cite dynamic (less literal) translations in the books I write, this one is a notable exception. When it comes to renderings of the Hebrew and Greek words in the joy and happiness semantic domain, I believe some of the more dynamic translations are more faithful to the original meanings than the literal versions, which tend to follow translation tradition, obscuring some of the central Hebrew and Greek words for happiness.

Whenever I use a particular translation in this book, I do so because I believe it accurately renders the verses I'm citing, particularly in relation to the specific Hebrew or Greek words we're exploring.

This should *not* be interpreted as an unqualified endorsement of any and all versions I cite! While I believe the New Century Version, for instance, often accurately renders *asher* and *makarios,* that doesn't mean I always agree with how the version renders other words in other contexts. Similarly, though The Message often interjects the author's particular interpretations in ways I think depart from the original meaning, in some cases it beautifully and accurately paraphrases the heart of the biblical text. In two such instances I cite The Message even though I wouldn't recommend it as a primary Bible for meditation and study.

I'm well aware that authors who cite a variety of translations may be guilty of theological cherry-picking—that is, choosing versions that support their interpretive bias. My citing many translations in this book to make my point guarantees the same criticism. My request is that anyone who questions the use of multiple versions would carefully study the Hebrew and Greek texts or consult trusted commentators who know the original languages and then evaluate the meanings of those texts. If you do this, I believe you'll see merit in my translation choices.

My focus in these word studies is on the entire sentences used by the biblical writers. If you ponder these passages, not only will you understand God's Word better but you'll also likely find yourself happier—indeed, that's the reason God gave them to us!

DIFFERENT TRANSLATIONS REFLECT THE FLUIDITY OF THE ORIGINAL LANGUAGES.

Before we dig deeper into the usage of specific Hebrew and Greek words, let's take a look at a few translation examples. The ESV says, "We are writing these things so that *our joy may be complete*" (1 John 1:4, emphasis added). The Contemporary English Version renders the verse, "We are writing to tell you these things, *because this makes us truly happy*" (1 John 1:4, emphasis added). How different are these meanings? Given the common use of the words in our culture, not much.

Now let's consider Psalm 149:2. (Note that I've italicized the key happiness words here for easier comparison.)

- Let Israel *rejoice [samach]* in their Maker; let the people of Zion *be glad [gayal]* in their King. (NIV)
- Let Israel *be glad* in his Maker; let the children of Zion *rejoice* in their King! (ESV)
- Let the Israelites *be happy* because of God, their Maker. Let the people of Jerusalem *rejoice* because of their King. (NCV)

Is one translation right and the others wrong? No. As the words *samach* and *gayal* are Hebrew synonyms, so "rejoice," "be glad," and "be happy" are English synonyms. Translation teams of Hebrew scholars had different but not contradictory preferences.

Psalm 149:4 says that the Lord . . .

- takes *delight [ratsah]* in his people. (NIV)
- takes *pleasure* in his people. (ESV)
- is *happy* with His people. (NLV)

Isaiah 65:18 begins similarly in multiple translations: "*Be glad* and *rejoice* forever in what I will create." Four versions render the second half of the verse as follows:

- I will create Jerusalem to be a *delight* and its people a *joy*. (NIV)
- I create Jerusalem to be a *joy*, and her people to be a *gladness*. (ESV)
- I will create Jerusalem as a place of *happiness*. Her people will be a source of *joy*. (NLT)
- The new Jerusalem I make will be full of *joy*, and her people will be *happy*. (GNT)

All differ, but not much. And none misrepresents the meaning of the inspired original.

The use of various synonyms in a target language is not a sign of bad scholarship. It reflects the fluid nature of both the source language and the target language. Seeing the words chosen by various Hebrew and Greek translation committees, often after hours of dialogue and debate, can broaden, enrich, and deepen our sense of the Bible's original words, which we will study in the coming chapters.

This section is different from the rest of the book—think of it as the Bible study portion. I won't do a lot of interpreting or use many illustrations here. Ask God's Holy Spirit to be your teacher, renew your mind, and warm your heart (see John 14:26; 1 John 2:27). Since the Bible alone is God breathed, see this as an opportunity to hear directly what God has to say about happiness.

Let God's Word do what it intends: let it delight you!

WHY DOES IT MATTER WHETHER WE TRANSLATE THE ORIGINAL WORDS AS "BLESSED" OR "HAPPY"?

Happy [are] the peacemakers—because they shall be called Sons of God.
JESUS (MATTHEW 5:9, YLT)

The Lord Himself invites you to a conference concerning your immediate and endless happiness, and He would not have done this if He did not mean well toward you.
CHARLES SPURGEON

G ROWING UP IN an unbelieving home, I never heard the word *blessed*. After I came to Christ and had been part of a church several years, I'd heard the word *blessed* countless times. I didn't know what it meant, and I never asked. I just knew it sounded holy and spiritual. It was part of the church's "white noise"—those words whose meanings are masked due to constant use.

Years later, I heard someone say that *blessed* in the Bible often really means "happy." My response was, "Huh?"

The thought had never occurred to me; I was certain it must be wrong. In the many years since, I've dug for the truth, and my search has yielded rich and surprising discoveries.

IT'S CRITICAL TO UNDERSTAND THE ORIGINAL WORDS ALTERNATELY TRANSLATED "BLESSED" OR "HAPPY."

Before we dig into Scriptures dealing with happiness in the subsequent chapters, we need to address the widespread confusion related to the word *blessed* in our English Bibles.

To understand the happiness God offers his creatures, there's no word in Scripture more important than the Hebrew *asher*.

Those who use Bible reference books are accustomed to reading that *asher* means "happy" and the English word *blessed* used to translate it means "happy." Standard Hebrew dictionaries routinely give "happy" as the closest English equivalent for *asher*.[1]

Judging by some reference works, it would be easy to conclude that *blessed* captures the happiness meaning of *asher*. For instance, Webster's dictionary says *blessed* can mean "blissfully happy."[2] *The International Standard Bible Encyclopaedia* defines *blessedness* as "the happy state or condition of a man to whom Christ's righteousness is imputed by faith."[3] This definition is followed by the note, "See HAPPINESS."

Proverbs 28:14 is one of many examples of *asher* translated "blessed":

- Blessed is the one who always trembles before God. (NIV)
- Blessed is the one who fears the LORD always. (ESV)

The Bible Knowledge Commentary says of that passage, "A person who has that kind of dread [of sin's consequences] will be happy (blessed; cf. Psalm 1:1)."[4] *The English Standard Version Study Bible* notes, "Such a person [the blessed God-fearer] receives mercy and is therefore truly happy."

Such notations are nearly universal. Had *asher* been translated "happy" in these verses, as it is in over twenty others, the reader would see the meaning without the need for commentary or study notes.

However, there's a major problem. If you played Password or Catch Phrase and the word was *happy*, you could expect clues such as "joyful," "glad," and "cheerful." But if someone offered the clue *blessed*, would "happy" pop into your mind? More likely you'd say "sacred" or "holy."

Before delving deeper into the meaning of *asher*, let's consider the word *blessed* in our contemporary context.

WHAT DOES THE WORD *BLESSED* MEAN TODAY?

Everyone knows it's good to be blessed, but what does that word actually mean?

Someone wrote me, "Your books have blessed me." I think they meant, "Your books have been of spiritual benefit." Though I hope it's also true, I doubt they meant, "Your books made me happy." Otherwise, they simply would have said that.

I googled "blessed," and the first hit was this definition: "Adjective: made holy; consecrated." Followed by "Noun: those who live with God in Heaven."

There are more than 2.5 million online references to the "blessed virgin Mary." Does anyone suppose this phrase means the "*happy* virgin Mary"? No. The reference is to her sanctity, not her gladness.

The third most popular hit for "blessed" was "Synonyms and antonyms for blessed."[5] Here are the listed synonyms: "adored, beatified, consecrated, divine, enthroned, exalted, glorified, hallowed, redeemed, resurrected, revered, rewarded, saved, among the angels, holy, inviolable, sacred, sacrosanct, spiritual, unprofane."

In the *Merriam-Webster Unabridged Dictionary*, the first synonym listed in the definition of *blessed* is "of, relating to, or being God."[6] Then the following synonyms are listed: "divine, godlike, godly, heavenly, sacred, supernatural." Under "related words," the dictionary adds, "eternal, everlasting, immortal; all-powerful, almighty, omnipotent, omniscient, supreme." The second definition of the word *blessed* is "set apart or worthy of veneration by association with God." The synonyms here include "consecrate, consecrated, hallowed, sacral, sacred, sacrosanct, sanctified."

Notice that every definition and synonym cited for *blessed* relates to holiness. Virtually nothing relates to happiness.

The *Oxford English Dictionary*'s first definition of *blessed* is "consecrated, hallowed, holy; consecrated by a religious rite or ceremony." The second is "the object of adoring reverence, adorable, worthy to be blessed by men."[7] Only a third and remote definition involves happiness. Shorter modern dictionaries don't even list "happy" as a possible definition of *blessed*. Happiness is, for the most part, completely off the *blessed* radar.

MOST PEOPLE DON'T ASSOCIATE *BLESSED* WITH *HAPPY.*

I couldn't locate an official poll concerning what people today think *blessed* means, so I asked people on my Facebook page, "What comes to mind when you hear the word *blessed*?"

More than 1,100 responses followed, with 904 people offering specific meanings for *blessed*.

Some associated *blessed* with being "covered," "favored," or having peace and contentment. Five percent said that *blessed* meant "lucky" to them, while 21 percent thought *blessed* means "lucky" to unbelievers.

About 30 percent of responders mentioned "undeserved favor" from God, as most would define *grace*.

Here's a sampling of verbatim responses to what the term *blessed* brought to mind:

- Things going well.
- Someone who has it all and has had an easy life.
- Talented; privileged.
- Having my needs met.
- A showering of mercies from God.
- Being protected by God.
- To have something others want.
- Before I knew God, I thought *blessed* was creepy . . . like a cult term.
- Some kind of anointing.
- To be set apart/holy.
- Disguised bragging, as in, "Look at my new, expensive car. I'm so blessed."
- Being comfortable—a vaguely positive, churchy word.

Only 12 percent of those who answered the question made any mention whatsoever of happiness, gladness, or joy. In two cases where happiness was mentioned, respondents said they'd heard this connection from a pastor, but they were skeptical. One person said, "I think of blessed as being happy, but I know that isn't right."

One respondent said, "If my unbelieving friends hear me say 'blessed,' it doesn't have any concrete meaning to them; it's just part of a different worldview." Another said, "To unbelievers, it is Christianese. I doubt the current meaning attracts them to the gospel."

NEARLY EVERY COMMENTARY BY HEBREW SCHOLARS EXPLAINS THAT THE BEST TRANSLATION OF *ASHER* IS "HAPPY."

Asher is consistently translated in the Greek Old Testament (the Septuagint) with the word *makarios*. *Makarios*, in turn, is used fifty times in the New Testament—more than half by Jesus. One scholar told me, "When you read *makarios* in the New Testament, think *asher*. That's how closely the words are related."[8]

One of the central and most definitive terms in the entire book of Psalms is the word *asher*. In fact, it's the first word of the entire book. In his highly acclaimed exegetical handbook on the Psalms, Hebrew and Old Testament professor Mark Futato demonstrates how Psalms 1 and 2 set forth the major themes of the entire book. He affirms that the two central themes of Psalms are "instruction for happiness" and "instruction for holiness."[9]

Since some see the English word *happy* as having a limited emotional connotation, Futato proposes that, with its implication of well-being, "truly happy" is a better rendering.[10]

Since *asher* occurs in all five sections within the Psalms (twenty-six times in all), Futato concludes, "The book of Psalms is an instruction manual for living a truly happy life."[11]

Here are examples of other scholars' comments to demonstrate the consensus about the meaning of *asher*:

- "Both [Psalm 119 and Psalm 1] begin with the word *Blessed*, a word that could be best translated as 'happy.'"[12]
- "The word 'blessed' means 'happy.'"[13]
- "Blessed—literally, 'oh, the happiness'—an exclamation of strong emotion."[14]
- "The Hebrew word . . . means that such a person is happy, or fortunate, deserving congratulations."[15]
- "[*Asher*] can be literally rendered 'happy.'"[16]
- "An emphatic *Happy* . . . describes the righteous person. The meaning is 'O the blessedness, the joy, the good fortune!'"[17]

I've come across dozens of similar statements from leading commentaries and Hebrew scholars who explain that *asher* means "happy." Many of these sources also comment that the English *blessed* means "happy."

Preaching on Psalm 1, which begins with the Hebrew word *asher*, Spurgeon said, "It is an old saying, and possibly a true one, that every man is seeking after happiness. If it is so, then every man should read this Psalm, for this directs us where happiness is to be found in its highest degree and purest form!"[18]

But if the scholars agree that *asher* means "happy," then why isn't it translated "happy"? That's an important question.

Some Bible versions use the formal equivalency method of translation, which is a literal, word-for-word approach. Others follow the functional equivalency method, which is a dynamic, thought-for-thought approach.

The most word-for-word translation of all, Young's Literal Translation, renders *asher* and *makarios* as "happy" the vast majority of the time. It translates *asher* as "blessed" only twice, one of which refers to God (see Isaiah 30:18). Similarly, it renders *makarios* "blessed" only twice, both of which refer to God (see 1 Timothy 1:11; 6:15).

The three translations that choose "happy" over "blessed" most frequently are the New Revised Standard Version, the Holman Christian Standard Bible, and Young's Literal Translation—all more literal, not dynamic, translations.

In maintaining the word *blessed* from centuries-old English translations, the New International Version, the English Standard Version, and the New American Standard Bible, as well as other translations, are more traditional but not more literal.

WHEN THE KJV TRANSLATORS RENDERED *ASHER* AND *MAKARIOS* "BLESSED," THEIR AUDIENCES KNEW IT MEANT "HAPPY."

John Wycliffe's first English translation of the Bible, hand printed and published in 1382, translated *asher* as "blessed" in Proverbs 28:14. The King James Version, published in 1611, usually translates *asher* as "blessed," but Proverbs 28:14 reads, "Happy is the man that feareth . . ."

Since *happy* was a synonym for *blessed* in those eras, it didn't make much difference which term was chosen. Today, however, it makes a great difference. When people read this verse as "Blessed is the one who fears the Lord always" or "Blessed is the one who always trembles before God" (NIV), they naturally understand *blessed* to mean something closer to "holy" than "happy."

Approximately 80 percent of the time, translators of the KJV followed the wording of Tyndale's translation.[19] In passage-to-passage text comparisons, the ESV and the NASB follow the KJV roughly 70 percent of the time.[20] Tyndale could have translated *asher* as "happy." He could have done the same with *makarios* in Matthew 5: "Happy are the poor in spirit" instead of "Blessed are the poor in spirit." Since the word *blessed* at that time conveyed the concept of happiness, his translation was accurate. But is it still accurate today?

THE EARLY TRANSLATORS INTENDED *BLESSED* TO CONVEY HAPPINESS.

The Letters of the Martyrs includes this passage written by Bishop Nicholas Ridley (1500–1555) shortly before he was burned at the stake in Oxford:

> For his truth's sake, then are ye happy and blessed, for the glory of the Spirit of God resteth upon you. If for rebuke's sake, suffered in Christ's name, a man is pronounced by the mouth of that holy apostle blessed and happy, how much more happy and blessed is he that hath the grace to suffer death also.[21]

Like other English clergy of his day, Ridley, a contemporary of William Tyndale, used *blessed* and *happy* as synonyms to reinforce each other's meanings.

At least 120 times in his writing, Puritan Thomas Brooks used the phrase "happiness and blessedness," just as we might describe a day as "bright and sunny." He spoke of "soul-happiness and blessedness"[22] and said, "So shall I know God according to my capacity . . . face to face; and this is the greatest height of blessedness and happiness."[23]

William Shakespeare (1564–1616) wrote of a man who discovered happiness in his misfortune. Notice how he paralleled happiness and blessedness: "His overthrow heap'd happiness upon him; For then, and not till then, he felt himself, And found the blessedness of being little."[24]

For several centuries thereafter, *blessedness* and *happiness* remained nearly interchangeable in common speech. Cambridge University professor and evangelical pastor Charles Simeon (1759–1836) said, "'Well done, good and faithful servant, enter thou into the *joy* of thy Lord;' if, further, you could behold it in the very bosom of its God, invested with a *happiness* which can never be interrupted, and a glory that shall never end; then you would say that its *blessedness* is truly wonderful"[25] (emphasis added).

I found this in the 1828 edition of Noah Webster's dictionary:

BLESS'ED, pp. Made happy or prosperous; extolled; pronounced happy.
BLESS'ED, a. Happy; prosperous in worldly affairs; enjoying spiritual happiness and the favor of God; enjoying heavenly felicity.[26]

Likewise, Webster defined *blessedly* as "happily" and *blessedness* as "happiness." Two hundred years ago, people still understood *blessed* to mean "happy." That's a striking contrast to the results of my poll on what *blessed* means to people today.

BLESSED IS ONE OF MANY ENGLISH WORDS THAT HAVE CHANGED THEIR MEANINGS SINCE 1611.

It's common for word meanings to change over the centuries. For instance, the KJV says that the head of John the Baptist was put on a "charger" (Mark 6:25). Nearly every modern translation says "platter." In 1611 the word *charger* meant "platter"—so it was accurate.

Titus 2:14 speaks of Christ, "who gave himself for us, that he might redeem us from all iniquity, and purify unto himself a peculiar people" (KJV). Some of us Christ-followers may indeed be strange, but four hundred years ago, *peculiar* meant "singular" or "unique."

KJV scholars were usually correct to translate as they did in 1611. However, modern translators are also correct to depart from the King James when words no longer reflect the meaning of the Hebrew and Greek text to modern readers. Translations should convey the *original* meaning of the source language most closely expressed by words in the target language. That's why it doesn't make sense to continue to translate the Hebrew and Greek words that mean "happy" into the English word *blessed*.

Here's another illustration that shows the importance of this issue: Psalm 127:5 says, "Blessed [*asher*] is the man who fills his quiver with [children]!" (NASB). The NIV and the ESV also translate *asher* as "blessed." The KJV, the RSV, and YLT render it "happy."

Read the following translations and ask yourself whether *happy* conveys a significantly different understanding than *blessed* in this context. Remember, the "arrows" spoken of are children:

- *Happy* is the man who has many such arrows. (Psalm 127:5, GNT)
- The person who fills a quiver full with them is *truly happy!* (Psalm 127:5, CEB)

Readers who see "blessed" might think, *Sure, God views children as a blessing and parents may too—when they're getting enough sleep! But in the meantime, having lots of children is nothing but sacrifice and stress!*

The God-inspired text, however, connects child rearing with happiness. While this in no way suggests that having children is easy or is the *only* happiness, this text affirms that we should find great happiness in children.

"Blessed" may feel as comfortable as old slippers in such passages, especially for readers who are accustomed to the KJV. But surely the job of Bible translation is not to hang on to spiritual-sounding words when doing so cloaks the original meaning.

A DIFFERENT HEBREW WORD TRANSLATED "BLESSED" ACTUALLY MEANS BLESSED.

The Hebrew word *barak* (or *baruk*) appears 327 times in the Old Testament, more than three hundred of which are translated "blessed" in the KJV and most modern translations. For example, "King Solomon shall be blessed, and the throne of David shall be established before the LORD forever" (1 Kings 2:45).

"Bless" is the predominant translation of this word in nearly every version—literal or dynamic. The lexicons define it this way: "to kneel, bless or praise."[27] It has a further meaning: to "speak words invoking divine favor, with the intent that the object will have favorable circumstances."[28]

"Blessed" is an excellent translation of *barak*. Even when not precisely understood, it conveys a sense of divine favor, in that God "blesses" by providing for us and we in turn "bless" God by praising him. Though this is a happy-making process, the word usually doesn't directly mean happiness.

When the Hebrew word *asher* is translated "blessed," the English reader naturally thinks of it just like the hundreds of appearances of *barak* that are properly translated "blessed." But all Hebrew readers know that *barak* and *asher* are distinct concepts. The words are not synonyms, but fall under two different semantic domains. English readers do not know this—and will not—unless the translations help us to understand the different meanings of the two words by using different words to translate them.

The problem also works the other direction. Upon learning that *asher* means "happy," English readers may see the word *blessed* and think it always means "happy." But when it's the translation of *barak*, it doesn't.

My question isn't whether *blessed* is a good or biblical word but whether it's the best translation of *asher* or *makarios*.

SOME ARGUE THAT THE WORD *HAPPY* IS TOO SHALLOW OR UNSPIRITUAL TO BE USED IN THE BIBLE.

Leon Morris says that *makarios* "points to happiness, but not happiness in a general, secular way. It means the joy that comes from the presence and approval of God."[29]

But if we see happiness in our Bibles, isn't it self-evident that it's a God-centered and God-honoring happiness, not a general, secular one? Don't all Bible readers know that when Scripture speaks of peace, hope, justice, and love, it routinely attaches deeper and more Christ-centered meanings to those words than our culture does?

One commentator says that *makarios* "is a deeper word than 'happy,' implying that deep and lasting joy that comes only as a gift from God."[30] How does using *blessed* instead of *happy* convey a deep and lasting joy to readers? Arguably, to the great majority of people, it conveys no joy or happiness at all.

Regarding the Beatitudes in Matthew 5, John Stott (1921–2011) said, "The Greek word *makarios* can and does mean 'happy.'"[31] Nonetheless, he argued, "It is seriously misleading to render *makarios* 'happy.' For happiness is a subjective state, whereas Jesus is making an objective judgment about these people."[32] But doesn't objectively declaring these people happy imply that they should subjectively *experience* the happiness God is imparting to them? If happiness is not experienced, in what sense could it be happiness?

Happy isn't the only word with baggage. The word *holy* has lots of baggage too. Since countless people routinely misunderstand it, should we avoid the word—or explain it? *Love* is commonly used in superficial ways, as popular music has long demonstrated. People say they love hamburgers, hairstyles, and YouTube. They "make love" to someone they barely know. Since the word *love* has been so trivialized, should we remove it from Bible translations and stop using the word?

Of course not. Instead, we should clarify what Scripture actually means by love, holiness, hope, peace, pleasure, and yes, happiness. We should contrast the meaning in Scripture with our culture's superficial and sometimes sinful connotations.

Rather than reluctantly admit that *makarios* typically means "happy" yet reject that translation, doesn't it make more sense to translate it "happy" and explain that this is referring to a deep and true happiness in God?

How much more explanation is required by using instead a word like *blessed*, which for most people doesn't convey the Bible's original meaning at all?

THE FEAR THAT *HAPPY* SOUNDS UNSPIRITUAL IS A POOR ARGUMENT FOR NOT USING IT.

About thirty years ago, my friend John R. Kohlenberger III, a biblical languages scholar and the author of dozens of original language reference books,[33] handed the newly updated NIV to the religion editor of a major newspaper. She immediately turned to the Beatitudes in Matthew 5 to see whether it used the familiar word *blessed*, in contrast to *happy*, which she knew some modern translations used. She was relieved to see that it said *blessed*—it passed her test. To her, *happy* was unfamiliar, and perhaps unspiritual.

Her concern didn't seem to be what the original language actually *meant*, but how the English translation *sounded*.

A pastor posted this response to the Common English Bible: "I turned to Matthew 5:3-11 and almost started crying. . . . In place of the theologically pregnant word 'Blessed' the CEB reads 'Happy.'"

His argument? "The beatitudes are not about a cheesy, tiptoe-through-the-tulips kind of emotional high. . . . 'Happy' simply destroys the meaning of the entire context. . . . God wants all men and women everywhere to be blessed. . . . But God never said he wanted everyone to be happy."[34]

The extent of bias here against the word *happy* is remarkable. And I'm not sure that the word *blessed* is as "theologically pregnant" as some suppose. What I am certain of, based on my countless conversations and poll of a thousand people, is that for those who find *blessed* to be pregnant with meaning, it's almost always the *wrong* meaning!

The pastor goes on to say, "There is a huge difference between being blessed and being happy! And to introduce the false idea of happiness into the Sermon on the Mount or Psalm 1 is to do significant damage to the concept of spiritual (and even physical) blessedness."[35]

He's absolutely right when he points out that in English, *blessed* and *happy* are very different words. What he fails to realize is that *happy* is the better translation of the original inspired words. In fact, the very English word he's objecting to, *happy*, is the primary lexical meaning of both *asher* and *makarios*!

I use this illustration because this pastor does what many people do. They act as if the inspired Bible really says *blessed* and therefore shouldn't be "changed" to *happy*. But the inspired words are neither *blessed* nor *happy*—*neither word exists in Hebrew or Greek*. The job of translation is to find the closest English equivalent to the actual inspired words *asher* and *makarios*—which nearly every scholar affirms is not "blessed," at least in the way most understand it today.

In his blog, this pastor says, "God is greatly concerned about our blessedness or lack of blessing, but God is truly disinterested about our happiness or unhappiness."[36] However, if the lexicons and scholars are correct about the meaning of *asher* and *makarios*, then God is in fact very interested in our happiness!

NO MODERN BIBLE TRANSLATION WOULD RENDER *ASHER* OR *MAKARIOS* "BLESSED" IF NOT FOR THE LONG HISTORY OF DOING SO.

My extensive research and dialogue with Hebrew and Greek scholars and translators left me perplexed about why most translators continue to use the word *blessed* as a translation of *asher* and *makarios*. Had the Bible never been translated into English, would any "first translations" today consider rendering *asher* or *makarios* as "blessed"? I can't imagine they would.

The literally inclined NASB translates Romans 14:22 as "Happy [*makarios*] is he who does not condemn himself in what he approves." Tyndale translated *makarios* as "happy" in Romans 14:22, and the KJV is identical.

But if "happy" is a good translation of *makarios* here, then why isn't it translated the same way in the Beatitudes, where Jesus used it with exactly the same sentence construction: "*Makarios* is . . ."? The clearest answer is that the KJV translated it "blessed," and it is a commonly known and memorized passage. That means that many people familiar with the traditional wording would balk at the change (just as the religion editor would have rejected the NIV had it said "happy" instead of "blessed" in the Beatitudes).

Both William Tyndale and the KJV translated the word *makarios* in 1 Corinthians 7:40 as saying that the widowed woman may be "happier" to remain single. Most modern translations followed suit. It seems obvious that "happier" is the right word. Then why is it not also the right word in other contexts, including the Beatitudes?

Consider 1 Peter 4:14, which the King James translates, "If ye be reproached for the name of Christ, happy are ye." *Makarios* here would immediately make readers think of Christ's parallel words, "[*Makarios*] are those who are persecuted because of righteousness" (Matthew 5:10, NIV). It's almost certain Jesus' words were echoing in Peter's mind as he wrote.

When we look at the context leading up to this passage, the subject of happiness is evident, as long as we don't buy into the false distinction between joy and happiness:

> Dear friends, don't be surprised at the fiery trials you are going through, as if something strange were happening to you. Instead, be very glad [*chairo*]—for these trials make you partners with Christ in his suffering, so that you will have the wonderful joy [*agalliao*] of seeing his glory when it is revealed to all the world. So be happy [*makarios*] when you are insulted for being a Christian, for then the glorious Spirit of God rests upon you.   I PETER 4:12-14, NLT

I asked Dr. Reinier de Blois, editor of the *Semantic Dictionary of Biblical Hebrew*,[37] to explain what *asher* describes in Psalm 1:1. He replied, "Someone who is privileged and has every reason to be exceptionally happy."[38] Dr. de Blois adds, "I personally like 'blessed' because I understand it, but for many readers it may have a somewhat esoteric meaning."

This may help explain why many Hebrew and Greek experts favor translating *asher* and *makarios* as "blessed." Not only does it have the longest history in translation, but *blessed* doesn't trip them up since they see through the word to *asher* and *makarios*, which they know connote happiness. Unfortunately, the vast majority of English readers don't know this.

Tyndale sometimes translated *makarios* as "happy," as in James 1:12: "Happy is the man that endureth in temptation." Had Tyndale translated *makarios* "happy" in the Beatitudes—which he easily could have, just as he did in the parallel structure of James 1—then the King James translators likely would have done the same. In turn, others would have followed the King James. Had this happened, today the Beatitudes would be known as those verses beginning with "Happy are . . ." and no modern Christians would be talking about the word *happy* being unspiritual!

WHILE MOST BELIEVERS DON'T KNOW WHAT *BLESSED* MEANS, MOST UNBELIEVERS DON'T *CARE* WHAT IT MEANS.

In contrast to *blessedness*—whatever we imagine it means—*happiness* is something we all think about, desire, and seek. As happiness seekers, what Christ actually says in the Beatitudes is of great interest to most unbelievers. If they saw, "Happy are those who mourn, for they shall be comforted," they might ponder the paradox. *Happiness and mourning at the same time? How is that even possible?*

No unbeliever says, "What I most want in life is to be blessed." Nor is there danger of that familiar song being sung as "Blessed Birthday to you."

While the secularization of culture has shrunk the common vocabulary of believers and unbelievers, *happiness* is a word that conveys meaning to both groups. Would the concept of a happy God and the offer of a deep, abiding happiness in Christ that begins now and goes on forever attract people to the gospel? I'm convinced it would. Of course, as sinners, we are rebels against God, and the offer of happiness alone won't persuade rebels to change their allegiance. But since God himself calls the gospel the good news of happiness, surely we shouldn't leave happiness out of it!

Suppose an unbeliever, struggling with depression and suicidal thoughts, sees a Bible open to Psalm 1 and reads, "Blessed is the man who . . ." Will that person feel a compulsion to read further?

But suppose instead that person reads one of the dozen or more Bible translations that render *asher* not as "blessed" but as "happy." He or she would be introduced to God's Word this way: "How happy is the man who does not follow the advice of the wicked or take the path of sinners or join a group of mockers!" (Psalm 1:1, HCSB).

Do you see how this wording might appeal to someone who has gone down the wrong roads, searching in vain for happiness, and is now world weary?

WHAT'S AT STAKE IN THE WAY WE TRANSLATE *ASHER* AND *MAKARIOS*?

Like every other word, *asher* and *makarios* should be translated so readers understand the original meaning in context. These words are especially important, because the language of happiness was, and still should be, common to both the world and the church. The word *happiness* is an important bridge, and again, my plea is that we not burn it!

The world and the church once agreed that happiness was good and that all people seek it. The prophet Isaiah called the coming gospel the "good news of happiness" (Isaiah 52:7), not the good news of blessedness. Pascal didn't say, "All men seek blessedness." Imagine if his English translators had used that term! Such a statement today would mean something like "All men seek holiness."

We desperately need holiness, but it's happiness we long for, and the church shouldn't retreat from such an important word. On the contrary, we should give it a biblical context, celebrate it, and embrace it as part of the gospel message.

CHAPTER 22

GOD FAVORS HIS PEOPLE WITH HAPPINESS: AN OVERVIEW OF *ASHER* AND *MAKARIOS*

How happy are those who reside in Your house, who praise You continually.

PSALM 84:4, HCSB

True religion was never meant to make men melancholy. On the contrary, it was intended to increase real joy and happiness among men.

J. C. RYLE

CHRISTIANA TSAI WAS born into a wealthy home in China. When attending a high school run by missionaries, she came to Christ. In her autobiography, she tells of how her Buddhist family reacted to her conversion with extreme anger. They tore her Bible to pieces and threw it in her face. But eventually her brother asked her about Christianity. The reason he gave was simple: "You seem much happier than you used to be."[1]

It wasn't messianic prophecies or dynamic preaching that opened him to the gospel—it was his sister's happiness.

"Good news of great joy" should produce happiness, and when it does, people notice. They're drawn to happiness like iron filings to a magnet.

ASHER EXPRESSES GOD-CENTERED HAPPINESS.

As Hebrew students know, I could have chosen a form other than *asher* to represent the original word, which sometimes appears in English as *asre, ashre, ashrei, ashrey,* or *esher.* They all refer to the same Hebrew word. I've chosen *asher* due to the ease of pronunciation, the commonness of use, and the familiarity of the name Asher, which means "happy one."

The happiness that comes from knowing and serving God typifies *asher*: "*Happy* is he whose help is the God of Jacob, whose hope is in the LORD his God" (Psalm 146:5, RSV, emphasis added).

According to the *Theological Wordbook of the Old Testament*, *asher* means "O the happiness of."[2]

The Brown-Driver-Briggs Hebrew and English Lexicon defines *asher* as "happiness, blessedness . . . intensive exclamation. . . . O happiness, blessedness of."[3] (Note that *blessedness* here refers to its past English meaning: happiness.)

The following table demonstrates how *asher* is translated in thirteen different Bible versions, with the numbers representing the number of times that *asher* is translated "blessed" as opposed to "happy":

asher (אֶשֶׁר) (44 uses)				
Version	blessed	happy	joyful	other
New American Standard Bible (NASB)	41	3		
New International Version (NIV)	38	6		
English Standard Version (ESV)	37	7		
King James Version (KJV)	27	17		
New Living Translation (NLT)	8	6	28	2
Jerusalem Bible (JB)	5	39		
New American Bible (NAB)	4	39		1
New Century Version (NCV)	4	35		5
Common English Bible (CEB)	3	41 (26 "truly happy")		
Young's Literal Translation (YLT)	2	42		
Good News Translation (GNT)	1	38		5
New Revised Standard Version (NRSV)	1	43		
Holman Christian Standard Bible (HCSB)	1	41	2	

Bible translation committees consist of skilled linguists who invest their lives working in the original languages. They carefully weigh how best to convey the original intent in English. Every team of Bible translators for these thirteen versions—with only one exception—uses both "blessed" and "happy" as the two preferred translations of *asher*. (The New Living Translation uses "joyful," a synonym for *happy*.) It's worth noting the significant number of translations that predominantly use *happy*.

The King James Version is the only translation that uses both words frequently, translating *asher* as "blessed" twenty-seven times and "happy" seventeen.

PSALM 1:1 CONTAINS THE FIRST AND MOST DEFINING OCCURRENCE OF *ASHER* IN THE PSALMS.

More than half of *asher*'s occurrences are in the Psalms. "How *happy* is the man who does not follow the advice of the wicked or take the path of sinners or join a group of mockers! Instead, his delight [*hepes*] is in the LORD's instruction, and he meditates on it day and night" (Psalm 1:1-2, HCSB).

Happiness is found in what this person does not do (hang out with the wrong people and take the wrong advice) and also in what he does do (meditate on God's Word). The key to happiness, it suggests, is allowing the right people to influence our thoughts and actions. If it's God and his Word, we'll find happiness; if it's mockers of God and his Word, we'll find unhappiness.

The Jerusalem Bible renders these verses, "*Happy* the man who never follows the advice of the wicked . . . but finds his *pleasure* in the Law of Yahweh" (emphasis added). The New American Standard Bible uses both "happiness" and "joy" in this passage: "*Happy* those who do not follow the counsel of the wicked. . . . Rather, the law of the Lord is their *joy*; God's law they study day and night" (emphasis added).

While some fine Bible translations, following the KJV, render *asher* as "blessed" in Psalm 1:1, the different meanings of *happy* and *blessed* today completely alter our understanding of the passage. An original languages scholar told me, "Likely they render *ashre* as 'blessed' because the translator wants to clean up and sanctify 'happy' to the next spiritual level."[4] But over time, especially to the general public, *happy* and *blessed* have become disconnected words. Hence, to most people, "Blessed is the man" doesn't convey happiness at all—sanctified or otherwise.

Countless Christians believe that Bible reading is their duty—something *holy* people do. What many don't understand is exactly what the passage really tells us: that meditating on God's Word can and should delight us, infusing us with heartfelt happiness. "Blessed" reinforces the stereotype of holy duty, while "happy" expresses a sense of eager privilege, telling the reader that what he or she most wants can be found through contemplating God and his goodness, as revealed in his Word.

MAKARIOS EXPRESSES CHRIST-CENTERED HAPPINESS.

Makarios appears fifty times in the New Testament. Louw and Nida's *Greek-English Lexicon of the New Testament* defines *makarios* as "a state of happiness . . . pertaining to being happy."[5] Because *makarios* is consistently used to translate *asher*, it's nearly inseparable from that word and its meaning of happiness.

The table on the following page shows how *makarios* is translated in different English versions.

You'll see how dramatically the versions are split in their rendering. If *blessed* were a synonym of *happy* for modern readers, this wouldn't matter much. (It would be no more significant than some versions using *sanctified* and others *holy*.) But because *blessed* is no longer a synonym for *happy*, the happiness connotations of *makarios*, like *asher*, are lost in many English translations, buried under the word "blessed."

Greek scholar Carl Holladay comments,

Perhaps the greatest challenge relating to Matthew and Luke's use of language is how to render the term *makarios*. . . . Some worry that "happy" fails to do justice to the richness and experiential depth connected by *makarios*, while others insist that "blessed" too narrowly restricts the word's semantic range to religious realms.[6]

makarios (μακάριος) (50 uses)			
Version	blessed	happy	other
English Standard Version (ESV)	48	1	1
New American Standard Bible (NASB)	47	2	1
New International Version (NIV)	44	1	5
King James Version (KJV)	44	6	
Common English Bible (CEB)	9	33	8
Jerusalem Bible (JB)	6	41	3
J.B. Phillips New Testament (Phillips)	6	35	9
Good News Translation (GNT)	5	40	5
Young's Literal Translation (YLT)	2	42	6

THE BEATITUDES REFER TO GOD-GIVEN HAPPINESS.

In the Beatitudes (see Matthew 5:2-12 and Luke 6:20-23), the word *makarios* occurs repeatedly. It's significant that Jesus didn't say, "Happy in God are the following . . ." and then give a grocery list including "the poor in spirit," "mourners," and "the meek." Instead, he repeated *makarios* with each statement, revealing this word as his central emphasis.

Greek scholar J. B. Phillips rendered Luke 6:22-23, "How happy you are when men hate you and turn you out of their company; when they slander you and detest all that you stand for because you are loyal to the Son of Man. Be glad when that happens and jump for joy—your reward in Heaven is magnificent" (PHILLIPS).

A senior translation director at a Bible translation ministry wrote me,

> From the Greek contexts, *makarios*, as used in the Sermon on the Mount, means, essentially, "be truly happy because of God's favor on you." God's favor is a big reason for the state of happiness. . . . The terms in our English translations are certainly legacy issues in translation. . . . Terms like blessed took on new meanings but are still maintained in our translations.[7]

Completed in the nineteenth century, Young's Literal Translation is the work of a Hebrew and Greek scholar, "an extremely literal translation that attempts to preserve the tense and word usage as found in the original Greek and Hebrew writings."[8] Young's text isn't known for being lyrical. It *is* known for taking the fewest linguistic liberties.

Here's Matthew 5:3-12, in its most literal translation:

> Happy the poor in spirit—because theirs is the reign of the heavens.
> Happy the mourning—because they shall be comforted.

Happy the meek—because they shall inherit the land.

Happy those hungering and thirsting for righteousness—because they shall be filled.

Happy the kind—because they shall find kindness.

Happy the clean in heart—because they shall see God.

Happy the peacemakers—because they shall be called Sons of God.

Happy those persecuted for righteousness' sake—because theirs is the reign of the heavens.

Happy are ye whenever they may reproach you, and may persecute, and may say any evil thing against you falsely for my sake—rejoice ye and be glad, because your reward [is] great in the heavens.

Young's translation of Luke 6:20-23 similarly renders *makarios* as "happy" throughout. It's intriguing that Young's translation, the "king of literal translations," and a number of the more dynamic (nonliteral) translations share a common rendition of *makarios* as "happy." The key may be that they are less prone to follow translation tradition. They aren't trying to appeal to those raised on the KJV and therefore don't ask whether they will lose readers as a result of using *happy* instead of *blessed*.

The word *happy* isn't just the literal meaning of *asher* and *makarios*—it's also a commonly used word that most people understand. First-century readers of the Gospels of Matthew and Luke also knew the meaning of *makarios*. So in the Beatitudes, the downtrodden, weary, and sorrow-laden listeners heard Jesus say, nine times in a row, "Happy are you . . ." These statements must have stunned them. (Though Jesus probably spoke Aramaic, Greek was the common written language of the day. The Gospel writers selected *makarios* as the closest Greek equivalent.)

JESUS CONNECTED SOME SURPRISING CONDITIONS WITH HAPPINESS.

Jesus' use of paradox is precisely what made his words so surprising, powerful, and paradigm-shifting. If we miss the startling nature of his words, we miss his meaning.

Paul Franklyn, associate publisher of the Common English Bible, writes, "*Makarios* actually belongs to a large semantic domain in Greek, reflecting Greco-Roman discussion about what constitutes genuine happiness." He gives an enlightening response to readers' complaints about the use of "happy" in their translation of the Beatitudes:

Several readers of the CEB have written to say that they do not approve of the term *happy* in this passage [Matthew 5]. We don't get good reasons why this word is wrong, other than some like the KJV word, *blessed*. Perhaps some Christians are suspicious of words that evoke human emotion because they prefer a faith that is based on fact or reason. Perhaps others mistakenly assume that happiness as a human condition is about human self-esteem and not something that God does or wants.

We might concede that it is possible to trivialize the meaning of happiness in our culture, to mistake happiness for personal self-gratification, but the CEB editors are not willing to let a trivial misapplication of the word derail the correct use of the meaning from the Greek.[9]

I agree with the conclusion of these translators and editors, since they are putting in the English Bible exactly what almost all linguists and commentators agree is the closest English translation of *makarios*.

Jonathan Edwards, a Greek scholar who was well aware of the meaning of *makarios*, commented on the Beatitude "Blessed are the pure in heart, for they shall see God," (Matthew 5:8) saying, "It is a thing truly happifying to the soul of man to see God."[10] (Don't you love the word *happifying*?)

In his commentary on Matthew 5, William Barclay (1907–1978) said of Christ's use of *makarios*:

> The beatitudes say in effect, "O the bliss of being a Christian! . . . O the sheer happiness of knowing Jesus Christ as Master, Saviour and Lord!" The very form of the beatitudes is the statement of the joyous thrill and the radiant gladness of the Christian life. In the light of the beatitudes, a gloom-encompassed Christianity is unthinkable.[11]

DURING DIFFICULT TIMES, WE CAN ANTICIPATE THE NEVER-ENDING HAPPINESS WE'LL EXPERIENCE IN GOD.

The Christ who indwells us now is the same Christ who will bring us joy throughout eternity. We have God's Word, through which he speaks happiness into our lives, and God's people, who despite their imperfections are often his instruments of love and encouragement. Many have found happiness in times of hardship by anticipating the glory and goodness that await us, compared to which our present troubles are called "light and momentary" (2 Corinthians 4:17, NIV).

A trapped miner, in pain from broken bones, can be overwhelmed with joy as he hears his rescuers making their way toward him—even though the actual rescue may not take place for hours or even days. Though knowing he'll still be suffering awhile, he rejoices that help is on its way. The husband at war overseas can write to his bride, who is facing difficult circumstances, "Be happy because I love you, and I'll come back for you." Her condition may be unpleasant and the separation difficult, but she can still be happy *now* because of her beloved's promise and her anticipation of his return.

Matthew 5:10 in the Worldwide English New Testament reads, "God makes happy those who have trouble for doing what is right. The kingdom of heaven is for them." This is what theologians sometimes call the "already and not yet." We can be happy now; we can experience being part of God's Kingdom now, because of our faith that God will bring his righteous Kingdom to Earth. This is the "already." But at the same time, we are "not yet" nearly as happy as we'll be in his presence, where happiness will be unqualified and unending.

Jesus follows up with an even stronger statement: "God makes you happy [*makarios*] when people say wrong things about you, when they trouble you, and when they say all kinds of lies about you" (Matthew 5:11, we).

When *makarios* is translated "blessed," the astounding paradox that Jesus expresses—that those who know him can experience happiness even as they face life's most difficult moments—is hard to see.

The paradox continues in verse 12, when Jesus says, "Rejoice [*chairo*] and be glad [*agalliao*], for your reward is great in heaven, for so they persecuted the prophets who were before you." Here, joy and gladness share the weight that has been carried by their synonym *makarios*. Present joy and gladness are dependent on believing the promise of Jesus that great reward awaits us in Heaven.

Despite the typical meaning of the word *makarios*, many claim that happiness is utterly incompatible with the Beatitudes. After all, how can the poor, mourning, meek, merciful, pure, peacemaking, and falsely accused be happy? But in saying this, they ignore the other parts of the verses! Jesus said the poor in spirit will inherit God's Kingdom, the mourners are comforted, the meek will inherit the Earth, the peacemakers will be called God's children, the ones who are hungry and thirsty for righteousness will be satisfied, and the pure in heart will see God, the source of all happiness. It's our Savior's certain promise of all these "not yets" that lift hearts to happiness "already."

GOD'S BLESSING OF HAPPINESS OVERFLOWS THE PAGES OF THE NEW TESTAMENT.

I've italicized the translation of *makarios* in each of the following verses. I encourage you to spend time contemplating these verses and taking pleasure in them.

Happy are those who believe in Jesus.

After Jesus' resurrection, Thomas wanted tangible proof that Jesus was alive. Jesus gave him the evidence he was looking for, but he also made a profound statement about the happiness that belongs to those who have faith in what they haven't seen with their physical eyes:

- Jesus said to him, "Thomas, because you have seen Me, you believe. Those are *happy* who have never seen Me and yet believe!" (John 20:29, nlv)
- How *happy* are those who believe without seeing me! (gnt)

An imprisoned and disappointed John the Baptist was confused that Jesus hadn't asserted his messianic ruling power. He sent a question to Jesus: "Are you the one who is to come, or shall we look for another?" (Matthew 11:3). Jesus explained that he was fulfilling Scripture in ways that didn't include political overthrow. Then he said to John: "How *happy* are those who have no doubts about me!" (Matthew 11:6, gnt). John was a holy man, but Jesus didn't offer him holiness here. By using the word *makarios*, the Lord was telling John (and us), "If you trust me, even when I don't do what you expected, you'll be *happy!*"

Happy are those facing trials for Jesus' sake.
James 1:12 offers a counterintuitive perspective on the kind of happiness that comes with suffering and persecution:

- *Happy* [is] the man who doth endure temptation. (YLT)
- *Happy* are those who remain faithful under trials. (GNT)
- *Happy* is the one who endures testing. (NET)

In language that closely parallels the Beatitudes, 1 Peter 3:14 (KJV) says, "But and if ye suffer for righteousness' sake, *happy* are ye." The CEB renders this verse, "But *happy* are you, even if you suffer because of righteousness!" By translating *makarios* as "happy" (as do the New Living Translation, Young's Literal Translation, the Orthodox Jewish Bible, and the J. B. Phillips New Testament), this verse corresponds with the way Peter begins his letter—rejoicing in trials (see 1 Peter 1:6).

When *makarios* is translated "blessed" in 1 Peter 3:14—as it is in thirty-six translations I looked at—most readers will suppose it means that God sanctifies or purifies us through persecution. He certainly does, but that's not the point of this particular verse, which is about happiness, not holiness!

Happy are those who see and hear Jesus for who he is.
Jesus said to his disciples, "*Happy* are your eyes because they see, and your ears because they hear" (Matthew 13:16, YLT). On another occasion, Jesus told them, "*Happy* the eyes that are perceiving what ye perceive" (Luke 10:23, YLT).

When Peter identified Jesus as the Messiah, Jesus said to him, "Simon son of Jonah, you are a *happy* man! Because it was not flesh and blood that revealed this to you but my Father in heaven" (Matthew 16:17, TJB).

Happy is the person who recognizes the real Jesus! It was true of his disciples then, and it's true of his disciples now.

Happy are those who serve God faithfully.
In a parable, Jesus said, "How *happy* that servant is if his master finds him doing this when he comes home!" (Matthew 24:46, GNT). Luke's account is rendered, "How *happy* are those servants whose master finds them awake and ready when he returns! I tell you, he will take off his coat, have them sit down, and will wait on them" (Luke 12:37, GNT).

Nothing makes a good servant happier than knowing his beloved master finds him faithful. Note how different and comparatively vague the word *blessed* seems (NASB, ESV, KJV). The term *happy* offers readers a clearer, more attractive motivation.

Happy are those who trust God's promises.
When Mary visited her relative Elizabeth shortly after she received the news that she was to bear the Messiah, Elizabeth proclaimed:

- *Happy* is she who believed that the Lord would fulfill the promises he made to her. (Luke 1:45, CEB)
- *Happy* [is] she who did believe, for there shall be a completion to the things spoken to her from the Lord. (YLT)

Elizabeth told Mary not that she was "blessed," as many translations render it (which appears to mean "sanctified"), but that she had reason to be happy because she trusted the Lord to do what he'd promised in a wonderful yet difficult situation.

Happy are those who obey God's Word.

Jesus made this profound statement about true happiness: "While Jesus was saying these things, a certain woman in the crowd spoke up: '*Happy* is the mother who gave birth to you and who nursed you.' But he said, '*Happy* rather are those who hear God's word and put it into practice'" (Luke 11:27-28, CEB).

James wrote this to believers facing great adversity: "The one who keeps looking into God's perfect Law and does not forget it will do what it says and be *happy* as he does it" (James 1:25, NLV).

Note the apparent difference in meaning in this translation: "One who looks intently at the perfect law . . . and abides by it . . . this man will be blessed in what he does" (NASB).

Those who don't understand *blessed* to mean "happy" simply can't comprehend these passages. The great appeal of James 1:25 is its offer of happiness through reading God's Word (the same is true in Revelation 1:3). It's only when we grasp God's genuine offer of happiness to us, even in the most challenging circumstances, that we can truly delight in obeying him.

Happy are those who help and serve others.

Happiness and service are inextricably linked in Scripture. Jesus told us to reach out to the poor and needy, then said,

- You *will* be *happy* if you do this. They cannot pay you back. You will get your pay when the people who are right with God are raised from the dead. (Luke 14:14, NLV, emphasis added)

When we serve those who can't pay us back, God promises to do so through rewards in Heaven. Meanwhile, today we experience happiness in our hearts for serving God and others.

In Paul's final words to the Ephesian church leaders, he said, "You must help the weak, remembering the words of the Lord Yeshua himself, 'There is more *happiness* in giving than in receiving'" (Acts 20:35, CJB). Eugene Peterson paraphrases this verse in The Message, "Our Master said, 'You're far *happier* giving than getting.'"

The translation—and even the paraphrase—captures the meaning we'll miss if we think "more blessed" means "more spiritual" rather than "more happy-making."

Happy are those who have been forgiven by the Lord.
Those who believe in Jesus have been forgiven of sins and saved from eternal punishment. Even in the midst of hardships, this forgiveness offers an unending source of joy.

· *Happy* those whose crimes are forgiven, whose sins are blotted out; *happy* the man whom the Lord considers sinless. (Romans 4:7-8, TJB)
· *Happy* they whose lawless acts were forgiven, and whose sins were covered; *happy* the man to whom the Lord may not reckon sin. (YLT)

The NLT's use of *makarios* as "joy" also captures what "blessed" doesn't: "Oh, what *joy* for those whose disobedience is forgiven, whose sins are put out of sight. Yes, what *joy* for those whose record the LORD has cleared of sin."

Note that this happiness is rooted in something real and permanent—our forgiven sins, which God will never hold against us. While finishing this chapter, I listened to a message by a popular Christian leader whom I respect. He said, "All it takes is one thing and your happiness is gone. . . . I am not interested in boosting, encouraging or helping your happiness. Because I believe it is cheap and will not sustain you for the journey God has for you. . . . What I am for . . . is your joy."

Thirty years ago, I would have said something similar. But I would never say it now, because the biblical texts, Hebrew and Greek scholars, a variety of good translations, church history, the God-given human longing for happiness, and God's promise of both present and eternal happiness in Christ all testify that while it's a well-intentioned statement, it's nonetheless misguided and misleading.

Happy are those who see unhappiness as a warning sign.
Paul reminded the Galatians of their satisfaction with him and their relationship: "You were very *happy* then, but where is that *joy* now? I am ready to testify that you would have taken out your eyes and given them to me if that were possible" (Galatians 4:15, NCV). He's saying, "Take notice of your loss of happiness. What has happened between us? God is sending you a message!"

Our degree of joy in relating to God and our fellow believers is a litmus test for the health of our Christian life. If the happiness is gone, we're wise to ask God and ourselves what has changed. We should join David in praying, "Restore to me the joy of your salvation" (Psalm 51:12). This is a prayer God is eager to answer.

Happy are those who are prepared for Christ's return.
The New Testament is full of promises of happiness for believers who anticipate the Lord's second coming:

· Listen! I am coming like a thief! *Happy* is he who stays awake. (Revelation 16:15, GNT)
· See! I am coming soon. The one who obeys what is written in this Book is *happy*! (Revelation 22:7, NLV)

- As we wait for the *happy* fulfillment of our hope in the glorious appearing of our great God and Savior, Jesus Christ. (Titus 2:13, NET)

Here "hope" means not a wish, but a certain promise. Since Christ's return will usher in eternal happiness, the very thought of it should infuse us with happiness today!

Happy are those who will spend eternity with God.

Scripture makes frequent reference to the happiness that awaits God's children:

- *Happy* are those who wash their robes clean and so have the right to eat the fruit from the tree of life and to go through the gates into the city. (Revelation 22:14, GNT)
- The angel said to me, "Write this: *Happy* are those who have been invited to the wedding feast of the Lamb." (Revelation 19:9, GNT)
- *Happy* [are] they who to the supper of the marriage of the Lamb have been called. (YLT)
- I heard a voice from heaven saying, "Write this: *Happy* are those who from now on die in the service of the Lord!" "Yes indeed!" answers the Spirit. "They will enjoy rest from their hard work, because the results of their service go with them." (Revelation 14:13, GNT)
- "*Happy* are the dead who die in the Lord!" "*Happy* indeed," says the Spirit. (PHILLIPS)

Are we, whom God has invited to his wedding feast, blessed? Absolutely. But that's not the meaning here. We are—as *makarios* indicates—happy, glad, joyful, and delighted to be so loved by God! The source of all happiness has invited us to join in the greatest celebration in the history of the universe, past or present! That wedding feast won't be the end of anything except suffering and sorrow. It'll be the beginning of our new and eternal life with Christ, our beloved bridegroom and the securer of our happiness, who has gone ahead to prepare a place for us so that "you also may be where I am" (John 14:3, NIV).

Happy are those who are also holy.

In Revelation 20:6, *makarios*, the common word for "happy," is joined with *hagios*, the common word for "holy" in the New Testament. The following versions are among the surprisingly few that fully capture this beautiful combination:

- Those who are raised from the dead during this first time are *happy* and holy. The second death has no power over them. (Revelation 20:6, NLV)
- *Happy* and holy [is] he who is having part in the first rising again. (YLT)
- *Happy* and holy is the one who shares in the first resurrection! (PHILLIPS)

Most translations read "blessed and holy," with the result that most readers understand the verse as containing two adjectives of consecration. But when the Greek is rendered "happy and holy," readers have the opportunity to think, *Wow, those who know God are not only holy, they're happy? Happiness is what I've been searching for! Maybe I should stop dividing my life into "church me," in which I try to be holy, and "world me," in which I seek to be happy!*

I asked Hebrew scholar Reinier de Blois his thoughts about the popular evangelical contrast between joy and happiness. His reply was striking. Taking "happiness" to correspond to the Hebrew word *asher*, he says,

> In Hebrew "happiness" is a more profound concept than "joy," as the former is usually directly related to God's intervention. [*Asher*] is a happiness caused by God. I am inclined to turn the whole discussion around. Christians are happy people because God is with them. This situation does not change. It is constant due to God's faithfulness and grace. It is joy that comes and goes depending on the situation, though Christians have every reason to rejoice because of their *asher* status![12]

Let this thought sink in: through the gospel, God extends to us his own happiness and invites us to join him in that happiness. When by faith we receive his gift, we who are undeserving, poor, and sometimes miserable are granted a new and everlasting status that can be expressed in a single startling word: *happy.*

CHAPTER 23

WE FIND LASTING HAPPINESS IN GOD: A CLOSER LOOK AT THE HEBREW WORD *ASHER*

Happy is the person whose sins are forgiven, whose wrongs are pardoned.
Happy is the person whom the LORD does not consider guilty.

PSALM 32:1-2, NCV

Oh Happiness! our being's end and aim.

ALEXANDER POPE

———— ⌘ ————

*A*SHER DESCRIBES THE happiness that comes from God and is experienced by God's people who put the Lord first, align themselves with his ways, and experience his goodness.

The Creator favors such people and promises them forgiveness—and some forms of prosperity. Eventually, in eternity, he promises the end of all suffering, with absolute and unqualified prosperity. Note the distinction between this and the health-and-wealth gospel (addressed in chapter 35), which some try to give credence to by citing verses containing *asher*. However, in both the Old and New Testaments, this extreme is corrected by examples and even promises of the present suffering and persecution of God's people.

THOSE WHO WORSHIP THE LORD AND OBEY HIS COMMANDS ARE HAPPY.

Psalm 84:5 describes the happiness of those who worship God in his house:

- *Happy* are the people whose strength is in You, whose hearts are set on pilgrimage. (HCSB)
- O the *happiness* of a man whose strength is in Thee. (YLT)
- Those who put their strength in you are *truly happy*. (CEB)
- How *happy* are those who live in your house. (CJB)

Proverbs 29:18 talks about the delight we can find in obedience to God's commands:

- Where there is no vision, the people are unrestrained, but *happy* is he who keeps the law. (NASB)

- Whoever obeys instruction is *happy*. (CEB)
- *Happy* are those who keep God's law! (GNT)
- One who listens to instruction will be *happy*. (HCSB)

God's law is lifesaving. Those who choose to rebel against his Word may do so in their desperate search for happiness, but the Bible clearly demonstrates that happiness is found in God and in submitting ourselves to live within the boundaries he provides for our protection. Job 5:17 says,

- Behold, *happy* is the man whom God correcteth: therefore despise not thou the chastening of the Almighty. (KJV)
- Behold, how *happy* is the man whom God reproves. (NASB)
- *Happy* is the person whom God corrects! (GNT)

If humbly submitting to God's correction makes us happy, then proudly resisting his correction makes us unhappy and sets us up for destruction (see Proverbs 16:18). Psalm 119:1-2 uses *asher* in both verses:

- *Happy* are those whose lives are faultless, who live according to the law of the LORD. *Happy* are those who follow his commands, who obey him with all their heart. (GNT)
- How *happy* are those whose way of life is blameless, who live by the Torah of ADONAI! How *happy* are those who observe his instruction, who seek him wholeheartedly! (CJB)
- Those whose way is blameless—who walk in the LORD's Instruction—are *truly happy*! Those who guard God's laws are *truly happy*! They seek God with all their hearts. (CEB)

Many translations render *asher* as "happy" in both verses. Some, including the English Standard Version, render it "blessed" in both.

The New Century Version translates *asher* as "happy" in verse 1 and "blessed" in verse 2. Readers today won't recognize what every reader or hearer of the original would have: it's exactly the same word in both places, a word depicting a state of happiness.

Likewise, Psalm 128:1-2 has echoes of happiness that come with obedience:

- How *joyful* are those who fear the LORD—all who follow his ways! You will *enjoy* the fruit of your labor. How *joyful* and prosperous you will be! (NLT)
- *Happy* are those who obey the LORD, who live by his commands. . . . You will be *happy* and prosperous. (GNT)
- Everyone who honors the LORD, who walks in God's ways, is truly *happy*! (CEB)

The fact that the King James Version, Revised Standard Version, English Standard Version, New American Standard Bible, and New International Version all sometimes translate *asher* as "happy" demonstrates their translators' recognition that happy is a legitimate rendering. Their choice not to do so more often is a judgment call and is not due to a more literal translation philosophy (as the consistent use of *happy* in Young's Literal Translation proves).

PEOPLE WHO LIVE BY GOD'S WISDOM ARE HAPPY.
Proverbs 3:13 emphasizes the connection between exercising wisdom and experiencing happiness:

- *Happy* is the man that findeth wisdom, and the man that getteth understanding. (KJV)
- *Happy* is the man who finds wisdom. (RSV, HCSB)
- *Ashrei* (happy) is the man . . . that getteth *tevunah* (understanding). (OJB)

The Orthodox Jewish Bible consistently defines *asher/ashrei* (same word) not as "blessed" but as "happy."

PEOPLE WHO TURN TO GOD AND PARTAKE OF HIM ARE HAPPY.
Psalm 34:8 gives a delight-filled description of what happens to people who get all they can of God:

- Oh, taste and see that the LORD is good! *Blessed* is the man who takes refuge in him! (ESV)
- *Happy* are those who take refuge in him. (NRSV)
- How *happy* is the man who takes refuge in Him! (HCSB)
- The one who takes refuge in him is *truly happy*! (CEB)

GOD'S REDEEMED ARE HAPPY PEOPLE.
The KJV translates Deuteronomy 33:29 as "*Happy* art thou, O Israel: who is like unto thee, O people saved by the LORD." The RSV and the ESV follow the KJV by rendering *asher* as "happy" in this passage.

Many other translations also use "happy," including the Holman Christian Standard Bible and the Good News Translation, as well as the Complete Jewish Bible and the Orthodox Jewish Bible. YLT renders the verse, "O thy *happiness*, O Israel!"

Other verses throughout Scripture show that happiness is the consequence of being saved by the Lord:

- *Happy* is the nation whose God is the LORD, the people whom he has chosen as his heritage. (Psalm 33:12, NRSV)
- How *happy* is the one You choose and bring near to live in Your courts! (Psalm 65:4, HCSB)
- *Happy* is he whom thus thou choosest to dwell in thy courts, close to thee. (Psalm 65:4, MNT)

THOSE PARDONED BY GOD ARE HAPPY.

In Psalm 32:1-2, we see that happiness is the natural reaction to being forgiven:

- The one whose wrongdoing is forgiven, whose sin is covered over, is *truly happy*! The one the LORD doesn't consider guilty . . . that one is *truly happy*! (CEB)
- *Happy* are those whose transgression is forgiven, whose sin is covered. *Happy* are those to whom the LORD imputes no iniquity. (NRSV)

By using the expression "truly happy," the Common English Bible translators recognized that *asher* means "happy," yet they added "truly" to give it more weight.

The New Revised Standard Version departs from the traditional RSV by consistently rendering *asher* as "happy" rather than "blessed." The introduction in the updated version says, "The word *ashre* [*asher*] . . . which is translated 'blessed' in KJV and RSV is the ordinary word for human happiness. So the OT committee voted to change 'blessed' to 'happy' wherever it translates *ashre*."[1]

Referencing Psalm 32:1, John Wesley said, "Blessed is the man (or rather, happy) whose unrighteousness is forgiven, and whose sin is covered."[2] If Wesley felt he needed to clarify that "blessed" was better rendered as "happy" more than two centuries ago, when "blessed" still conveyed the idea of happiness to so many, how much more do we need to make this point today?

GOD PROMISES HAPPINESS FOR RIGHTEOUS ACTS AND ATTITUDES.

Scripture makes it clear that our righteous actions are not just something we do for God's sake; they also bring us happiness:

- *Happy* is the man who . . . keeps the Sabbath without desecrating it, and keeps his hand from doing any evil. (Isaiah 56:2, HCSB)
- *Happy* are those whom you discipline, O LORD, and whom you teach out of your law. (Psalm 94:12, NRSV)
- *Happy* are you, O land, when your king is the son of the nobility, and your princes feast at the proper time, for strength, and not for drunkenness! (Ecclesiastes 10:17, ESV)
- All those who take refuge in Him [the Son, Messiah] are *happy*. (Psalm 2:12, HCSB)
- All who wait patiently for Him are *happy*. (Isaiah 30:18, HCSB)

THOSE WHO ARE KIND TO THE NEEDY FIND HAPPINESS.

According to Scripture, being kind to the poor glorifies God, does good for others, and brings happiness to us:

- He who despises his neighbor sins, but *happy* is he who is gracious to the poor. (Proverbs 14:21, NASB)
- If you want to be *happy*, be kind to the poor. (GNT)

Of forty-two translations I checked, there's an even split between those rendering *asher* "happy" and those using "blessed." Unfortunately, most people reading "blessed" will miss the intended sense of a flourishing happiness.

In Western cultures, if we tell people to care for the poor so they will be blessed, it appears to be an encouragement to be more pious. However, Scripture is saying we'll be *happier* if we're gracious to the poor! It's not only right, but smart. It's good for others and brings happiness to us. What could be better? Do we have a responsibility to obey God and help the poor? Absolutely, and many passages make that clear. But this verse, properly understood, appeals to our desire for happiness.

God indicates he will normally intervene when those who meet needs are themselves in need: "*Happy* is one who cares for the poor; the LORD will save him in a day of adversity" (Psalm 41:1, HCSB).

Again and again we see in God's Word that our motivation need not be limited to the desire to *do right for God*. We are also encouraged to *be motivated by happiness in God*. This may seem less spiritual, but it's God who's appealing to our longing for happiness, so obviously it isn't. Don't we need every motivation to obey God that he offers us . . . including happiness?

HAPPY PEOPLE FOLLOW THE SPIRITUAL GUIDANCE OF THEIR GODLY PARENTS.

Proverbs is full of references about the happiness that comes to sons and daughters who follow their parents' wisdom. Proverbs 8:32 says,

- Children, listen to me [Wisdom]: *happy* are those who keep my ways. (CJB)
- Do as I say, and you will be *happy*. (GNT)

The RSV, the HCSB, and more than a dozen other translations render *asher* as "happy" in this verse, while the KJV, the NASB, the NIV, and the ESV translate it "blessed."

Does it really matter which word is used? I believe it does. In Proverbs, Solomon is explaining to his son that obeying his father's instructions—which are based on God's instructions—is the way of happiness.

Keep in mind that there are Hebrew words that correspond to the English words *holy* and *sanctified*. Had the father in this passage intended to say that by obeying his instructions his son would become holy, he would have simply used a word indicating holiness. However, the word he used instead was *asher*. Hebrew children would have understood their parents' meaning: "You will be made happy if you follow my instruction."

God further appeals to parents based on their universal desire that their children be happy. Proverbs 20:7 says,

- The righteous live a life of integrity; *happy* are their children after them. (CJB)
- The one who lives with integrity is righteous; his children who come after him will be *happy*. (HCSB)

- The righteous is walking habitually in his integrity, O the *happiness* of his sons after him! (YLT)

When parents live righteously (not self-righteously), their children will typically be happy. Yet despite Scripture's clear statement, if parents were asked, "How can you make your children happier?" how many would answer, "By living my life more righteously"?

WHAT DOES *ASHER* MEAN FOR US TODAY?

The Holman Christian Standard Bible, which is more literal than dynamic, is one of a number of translations criticized for rendering *asher* as "happy" rather than "blessed." Saying that the word *happy* "does not belong in the Bible," someone commented, "Because the HCSB replaces blessed with happy, I will not be using that translation."[3]

An interviewer asked Edwin Blum, an editor of the HCSB, a question about its second edition: "Will the Psalms still use happy instead of blessed? If so, what is the reason for choosing that translation? This seems to be a pretty dramatic (and perhaps unnecessary) break from other translations."

Dr. Blum's response was, "*Happy* reflects the Hebrew text. This is more accurate than blessed, which translates a different Hebrew word. See the NRSV translation. Happy has been correctly translated since the 1930s in the Moffatt translation, in the 1930 American translation by Goodspeed and in the New English Bible of 1970. So we would ask why some translations do not carefully check the original languages."[4]

I've heard mature Christians say they're uncomfortable with "changing" blessed to happy. Remember, the original writers didn't speak English—they never used the words "blessed," "joyful," or "happy." As the old joke goes, "The King James Bible was good enough for the apostle Paul, so it's good enough for me." But it isn't as funny when you encounter sincere Christians who appear to believe that *blessed* is the inspired word while *happy* is a modern attempt to alter Scripture.

Since the KJV renders *asher* as "happy" 39 percent of the time, clearly its translators had no prejudice against the word. Furthermore, departing from the wording of the King James tradition in trying to be more faithful to the original meaning is not the same as departing from God's Word. Indeed, were the King James translators rendering *asher* into modern English—knowing that *blessed* has lost the connotation of happiness it had in 1611—I'm convinced they would translate it "happy" today far more than 39 percent of the time. Given its change in meaning, they likely wouldn't use "blessed" at all.

The ESV, which I use frequently, employs the word *happy* fewer times (thirteen) than any of forty-some translations I consulted. Does this mean the ESV translators didn't think *asher* means happy? Not judging by the notes in the *ESV Study Bible*, which gives this meaning for Psalm 1:1-2: "The truly happy person guides his life by God's instruction rather than by the advice of those who reject that instruction."[5] It makes similar notes throughout as to the "truly happy" meaning of the word *asher*, even though it's translated "blessed."[6]

THOSE WHO KNOW THE ONE TRUE GOD ARE A HAPPY PEOPLE!

The word *asher* appears twice in the following verses, loading them with a sense of happiness:

- *Happy* is the person who trusts the LORD, who doesn't turn to those who are proud or to those who worship false gods. (Psalm 40:4, NCV)
- *Happy* the people to whom such blessings fall! *Happy* the people whose God is the LORD! (Psalm 144:15, RSV)
- O the *happiness* of the people that is thus, O the *happiness* of the people whose God [is] Jehovah! (YLT)

Reading these passages and many more, I find myself perplexed by such statements as this: "Happiness isn't found in the Bible. . . . There is nothing about happiness."[7]

Puritan scholar Thomas Brooks knew the true meaning of *asher*. His comments on Psalm 144:15 capture the heart of the word:

All the happiness and blessedness of the people of God consists in this—that God is their God, and that He is their portion, and that they are His inheritance! Oh, the heaped up happiness of those whose God is the Lord! The happiness of such is so great and so glorious—as cannot be conceived, as cannot be uttered! Nothing can make that man truly miserable, who has God for his portion; nor can anything make that man truly happy, who lacks God for his portion. God is the author of all true happiness. God is the donor of all true happiness. God is the maintainer of all true happiness. God is the center of all true happiness and blessedness. Therefore, he who has Him for his God, for his portion, is the only happy man in the world![8]

If we came to terms with God's obvious desire for his people's happiness, as conveyed by the word *asher*, it would go a long way toward our becoming the happiest people on Earth.

To understand Scripture, we must understand what the original authors intended when, by divine inspiration, they used specific Hebrew and Greek words. Typically our English translations get those right, but *asher* and *makarios* are, in many cases, notable exceptions. From the Pentateuch through the prophets, *asher* repeatedly portrays the true, heartfelt happiness in being redeemed by God and in pursuing a relationship with him. *Makarios* in the New Testament does the same.

Experiencing *asher* or *makarios* doesn't mean all our problems go away. It *does* mean that in God, true happiness is available to us—the happiness our souls have always longed for.

WE CAN BE HAPPY NOW . . . AND FOREVER: A CLOSER LOOK AT THE GREEK WORD *MAKARIOS*

Those who are hungry and thirsty to be right with God are happy, because they will be filled. . . . Those who have a pure heart are happy, because they will see God. Those who make peace are happy, because they will be called the sons of God.

JESUS (MATTHEW 5:6, 8-9, NLV)

I wish we were brave enough to write in our Bibles, "Happy," instead of "Blessed," for that is the right translation.

G. CAMPBELL MORGAN

⸮

A FABLE TELLS OF an ancient prophecy about a princess who would become the wisest and fairest queen—but only after she found a palace. When a wise man gave her a key that would open palace doors, she searched relentlessly, trying countless doors, but the key never fit. Exhausted and broke, she arrived at a poor village to work the fields.

The villagers' love made her so happy that she forgot about her search, until one day she was drawn to a small cabin. Once there, she tried the key. To her surprise, the door opened to a beautiful little room brimming with life and color and a spectacular view.

Now a queen, she discovered happiness she'd once thought didn't exist.

This is the nature of the happiness people find in Christ even in the midst of suffering. It's surprising and counterintuitive—and hence all the more delightful.

WHAT DO SCHOLARS SAY *MAKARIOS* MEANS?

The *Exegetical Dictionary of the New Testament* defines *makarios* as "happy, blessed."[1] (Dictionaries typically give the primary meaning first.)

Friedrich Hauck writes that *makarios* in the New Testament "refers overwhelmingly to the distinctive religious joy which accrues to man from his share in the salvation of the kingdom of God."[2]

The Anchor Bible Dictionary says *makarios* is "the condition of happiness resulting from being favored."[3]

Regarding *makarios*, the *Theological Lexicon of the New Testament* says, "It is God alone who grants humans happiness. . . . Happy are those who hope in him, count on him, take shelter and find their strength in him!"[4]

The *HCSB Harmony of the Gospels* states, "*Makarios* . . . speaks of a happiness and contentment of heart, a peace and joy in knowing someone is doing God's will."[5]

New Testament scholar William Hendriksen said that Christ's use of *makarios* in the Beatitudes means "'happy' in the most exalted sense of the term."[6]

Pastors known for being serious Bible students say the same. John MacArthur says, "*Makarios* means happy, fortunate, blissful."[7] John Piper says *makarios* "means 'happy' or 'fortunate.'"[8] (What does a fortunate person feel but happiness and gratitude?)

Warren Wiersbe says of *makarios* in the Beatitudes, "This was a powerful word to those who heard Jesus that day. To them it meant 'divine joy and perfect happiness.'"[9]

If it seems that I'm quoting an unusually large number of scholars and Bible teachers to establish that *makarios* means "happy," you're right! There's such strong resistance to this vital point that I'm summoning substantial evidence to support this definition.

Consider scholar and pastor G. Campbell Morgan's statement I quoted in the epigraph to this chapter: "I wish we were brave enough to write in our Bibles, 'Happy,' instead of 'Blessed,' for that is the right translation." This is a remarkable statement. Morgan suggests that we lack not knowledge but courage to go against the grain of translation tradition.

Morgan says of *makarios* in the Beatitudes, "'*Happy* are they'—there is something in the sound of it which arrests our attention at once, that must have at once arrested the attention of the hearers of Jesus on that day long ago when He spoke these blessed words. For all the world is seeking for this gift of happiness."[10]

Don't miss his point. When Jesus looked at the crowds and said that poor, discredited, and persecuted people who honor God are not just holy but actually *happy*, his words were (and are) absolutely startling. Yet in English, because the word *happy* usually isn't used, we fail to recognize the surprise—and appeal—of his words.

Philip Schaff's monumental work on the church fathers cites one of Chrysostom's AD 400 sermons, translated from the Greek (which Chrysostom spoke). Chrysostom used *makarios* from the biblical text, and Schaff's work translates it, "Blessed are they that mourn." Following the word *blessed* is the translator's footnote: "'Happy' would be more exact, but 'blessed' has a fixed association with the passage quoted from the Sermon on the Mount."[11]

Chrysostom wrote six hundred years before there was an English language. But instead of using the "more exact" word *happy*, his translator felt obligated to render *makarios* with what he admits is the less accurate *blessed*. Why? Because of the "fixed association" of translation tradition! But that association of *makarios* with "blessed" wasn't fixed until the King James Version was translated twelve hundred years after Chrysostom. The association has only become stronger since then because scholars perpetuate use of the word *blessed*, necessitating repeated explanations that asher really means "happy."

While *happy* isn't always an exact equivalent of *makarios*—"truly happy" or "happy in God's favor" might sometimes be closer—I've never seen a credible argument that for today's English speaker, "blessed" is the closest equivalent of either *makarios* or *asher*.

ANCIENT TEXTS DEMONSTRATE THAT *MAKARIOS* MEANT "HAPPY" TO THE ORIGINAL NEW TESTAMENT AUDIENCE.

Asher is consistently used in Old Testament beatitude sayings that begin with "Blessed are . . ." or "Happy are . . ." (see Psalm 1:1; 33:12; 34:8; 40:4; 41:1-2; 84:4-5, 12; 89:15; 94:12; 119:1-2; 127:5; 144:15; 146:5; Proverbs 3:13; 8:32, 34). Since these passages are understood by nearly all scholars to mean "Happy are . . . ," the fact that *makarios* is used for the equivalent words of Jesus in the New Testament strongly suggests that they, too, should be understood as "Happy are . . ."

The apostles and the early church were accustomed to seeing *asher* translated as *makarios* throughout the Greek Old Testament. The book of Sirach, in the Apocrypha, not part of the universally accepted canon of Scripture, was written about 175 BC. It uses *makarios* to convey happiness: "I can think of nine men I count *happy*. . . . *Happy* the husband of a sensible wife. . . . *Happy* the man who has found a friend, and the speaker who has an attentive audience! . . . *Happy* the man who fixes his thoughts on wisdom and uses his brains to think" (Sirach 25:7-9).[12]

John Broadus's 1886 classic commentary on Matthew says of the Beatitudes, "*Happy* more nearly expresses the sense of the Greek word than 'blessed.' . . . The shock which many persons feel at the introduction of 'happy' here, is partly a reproduction of the surprise felt by our Lord's hearers—*happy* the *poor, happy* the mourners, etc.—the paradox is really part of the meaning."[13]

It's certainly conceivable to think that one might suffer and be blessed in the sense of being holy, set apart, or purified. But how can one suffer and be *happy*? That's exactly what's most striking about the passage to anyone who understands its meaning.

ENGLISH BIBLES ARE AMONG THE SMALL MINORITY IN WHICH *ASHER* AND *MAKARIOS* AREN'T TRANSLATED BY WORDS THAT MEAN "HAPPY."

The United Bible Societies' New Testament Handbook Series is a twenty-volume set of commentaries filled with linguistic insights designed to assist people worldwide in translating the New Testament.

UBS handbooks don't stop at analyzing a passage's meaning. They suggest to translators how best to convey that meaning in target languages.

The bestselling Bible versions translate John 13:17 something like this: "Now that you know these things, you will be *blessed* if you do them" (NIV). Here's what the UBS handbook says about *makarios* in this verse:

> In biblical thought the ideas of "blessed" and "happy" are related, but there is a slight difference in focus. "Blessed" focuses attention on the source of the benefit, that it has come from God, while "happy" describes the state of the person who receives the benefit.

In the present passage, as in most other New Testament passages where this Greek word [*makarios*] occurs, the focus is upon the subjective state of happiness shared by persons who have received God's blessing. For this reason, the translation "happy" is preferable to "blessed."[14]

Dozens of similar comments in the UBS handbooks instruct translators worldwide to find the common word for "happy" in their target language. These guidelines have been followed for decades by thousands of translators. The result is that people groups all over the world know what relatively few English readers know—that the passages containing *asher* and *makarios* are talking about happiness in God.

In the original French, when Pascal said, "All men seek happiness," he used the term *heureux*. This word, found ninety-three times in Pascal's *Pensées*, is translated in every French-English dictionary as "happy." All four French translations of the Bible I found online use *heureux* to translate *makarios* in the Beatitudes. Hence, each line of Matthew 5:3-11 beginning with *heureux* shows French readers that Jesus offers the very happiness Pascal says all people seek.

Since this word is translated as the equivalent of "happy" in French and countless other languages, why not English? Of the top seven bestselling English translations, all seven usually translate *makarios* as "blessed," not "happy." This is why English-speaking believers are vulnerable to the myth that most other Bible-reading believers in the world are immune to: that the Bible says nothing about happiness.

"HAPPINESS" IS THE PREDOMINANT TRANSLATION OF *MAKARIOS* IN A NUMBER OF VERSIONS.

As indicated in the tables in chapter 22, a number of modern translations, most of them not widely used, have departed from the traditional rendering of *makarios* as "blessed." One example is God's Word Translation, described here:

GW's publishers believe that communicating the original meaning of the Hebrew, Aramaic, and Greek texts that comprise the Scriptures such that everyone can comprehend requires taking a completely new look at the original languages. Many modern translations . . . have chosen simply to follow the traditions of older accepted translations, though the traditional words and grammar may no longer mean what they once did, or are not understood.[15]

GW uses the word *happy* or *happiness* 141 times—two to ten times more frequently than more traditional translations. Ironically, however, it still translates both Psalm 1 and the Beatitudes with the traditional "blessed" (illustrating how strong translation tradition can be, even among those who state their opposition to it).

Some say it's not enough to say that *asher* or *makarios* mean "happy," because that word leaves out the favor of God. But it's certainly not enough to say that *asher* and *makarios* mean "favored by God," because that leaves out the happiness connotation. In my opinion, the English word *blessed* does a fair job of capturing the favored part but a poor job capturing the happy part.

The solution might be to find an English word that means "God's favor resulting in happiness" or "happiness resulting from God's favor." But there's no such word. One option is "truly happy," which is preferred by some scholars.[16] This phrase is often used by the Common English Bible and affirmed as *asher*'s meaning in the notes of the *ESV Study Bible.* (The J. B. Phillips New Testament translates *makarios* as "truly happy" in James 1:12.)

I believe most translators would agree that any English word should be carefully chosen for how well it transmits the meaning the writer intended—and updated when necessary. But when passages are so firmly established and widely known in their traditional wording, it can be costly to go against that current.

The source language never loses its potency, but target words used in translation can and sometimes do.

SOME ARGUE THAT THE HISTORY OF THE WORD *HAPPINESS* DISQUALIFIES IT AS A TRANSLATION OF *MAKARIOS.*

It's common to hear objections to the word *happy* based on its etymology or on history. The most frequent objection is articulated by a commentator: "Happy comes from the word 'hap,' meaning 'chance.' It is therefore incorrect to translate [*makarios*] as 'happy.'"[17]

However, our language is full of words long ago detached from their original meanings. Enthusiasm originally meant "in the gods," but if I commend you for being enthusiastic, I am not suggesting that you are a polytheist. Our word *nice* comes from the Latin *nescius,* which means "ignorant." But if I say you're nice, I'm not calling you ignorant.

D. A. Carson argues in *Exegetical Fallacies,* "The meaning of a word cannot be reliably determined by etymology."[18] When people say they want to be happy, they are typically making no statement whatsoever about "chance."

The translators of the King James Version wouldn't have used *happy* and other forms of the root word *happiness* thirty-six times or translated *makarios* as some form of "happy" seventeen times if they thought its etymology disqualified it as a credible biblical word. The fact that the Puritans, Jonathan Edwards, John Wesley, Charles Spurgeon, and many others used the words *happy* and *happiness* frequently in theological and Christ-centered contexts indicates that they weren't troubled about their history but employed them because of their meaning, pointing to a glad and universally desired state of mind.

THE VERY HAPPINESS PEOPLE SEEK IS THE HAPPINESS JESUS CAME INTO THE WORLD TO BRING!

Bible translators often speak of reaching people in their heart language, rather than secondary languages not their own. The word *happiness* is a central word in our "heart language."

English is spoken as a first or second language by two billion people throughout the world, and "one in four of the world's population speaks English with some level of competence."[19] In 2012, all 193 United Nations member states adopted a resolution calling for happiness to be given greater priority. They established March 20 as the official International Day of Happiness.[20] Not only is happiness a worldwide concept, but the word *happiness* is one of the most familiar and desirable ones on the planet.

We do both the church and the world a great disservice if we abandon ourselves to the sanctimonious-sounding *blessed*. We end up speaking a foreign language most believers don't understand and most unbelievers don't appreciate.

HOW WOULD WE VIEW SCRIPTURE DIFFERENTLY IF *MAKARIOS* WERE TRANSLATED "HAPPY"?

I'll use just one book, Revelation, as an example of how readers would be affected if *makarios* were translated as "happy."

In its third sentence, Revelation would read, "*Happy in God* is the one who reads aloud the words of this prophecy, and *truly happy* are those who hear, and who keep what is written in it, for the time is near" (Revelation 1:3).

The corresponding bookend in the final chapter would be, "*Happy in God* is the one who keeps the words of the prophecy of this book" (Revelation 22:7). Seven verses later, the text would read, "*Truly happy* are those who wash their robes, so that they may have the right to the tree of life and that they may enter the city by the gates" (Revelation 22:14).

Verses in between would say,

- I heard a voice from heaven saying, "Write this: *Happy in God* are the dead who die in the Lord from now on." "*Truly happy* indeed," says the Spirit. (Revelation 14:13)
- The angel said to me, "Write this: *Happy* are those who are invited to the marriage supper of the Lamb." (Revelation 19:9)

Do you resonate with the sense of celebration and delight at attending the greatest marriage supper in history *and* being the object of love of the King of the universe? The meaning of *makarios* isn't that we'll be blessed or privileged or set apart to be there but that we'll be overwhelmed with happiness!

SPIRITUALIZING *MAKARIOS* UNDERCUTS ITS MEANING.

A pastor writes that many people have thought him to be unhappy:

> "Cheer up," people would say. "Why are you so serious all the time?" My many and varied explanations over the years may have faltered, but could have been summed up in one word: *makarios*. To these myopic observers I may not have appeared happy, because I had long since moved past "happy" to the more substantial state of Spiritual "joy." There is a deep, profound Spiritual joy that is far superior to any amount of superficial happiness.[21]

Certainly we should seek a deep joy, but is happiness something we are to "move past" to reach an unemotional "joy" that others actually mistake for unhappiness? Attempts to make *makarios* lofty and super-spiritual can rob happiness in God of its rich, emotional warmth and delight. When Jesus used the word, it meant *deep* happiness, not *deeply hidden* happiness.

The two necessary conditions for true *makarios* for believers are:

1. Objective happiness: knowing we've been chosen by God, favored by him, and relocated from the kingdom of darkness into the kingdom of light. We've been freed from bondage to sin, which is the source of unhappiness.

2. Subjective happiness: realizing the truths of our real spiritual status. We're covered by and share in the righteousness of Christ, but sometimes old habits persist. We're indwelt by the Holy Spirit, but we still battle unholiness. We're guaranteed eternal life, health, prosperity, and pleasures forevermore in God's presence. Here and now life can be hard, yet happiness in Christ is possible.

The primary reality is our standing and status in Christ and our relationship with God. Understanding this is necessary for our salvation but not sufficient for our happiness. Like prisoners who have been declared free and whose cells are unlocked, we can still act as if we're imprisoned. We must change the way we think and walk out the door to the freedom bought for us by Jesus.

What we should see in the real Beatitudes is not merely that the words of Jesus exalt good character instead of bad but that good character brings happiness and bad character brings misery.

BY ANTICIPATING THE ETERNAL HAPPINESS GOD PROMISES, WE CAN FIND *MAKARIOS*-HAPPINESS HERE AND NOW.

The impoverished man, though notified that he's the heir to a great fortune, can benefit from it only when he acts in accordance with his new identity as an heir. To experience the happy Christian life, we need to see others around us who are genuinely happy because they recognize God's grace in their lives. We need models of happiness; it's easier to follow footprints than commands. When heartfelt happiness is not seen frequently among God's people, the next generation will certainly seek it elsewhere. But when happiness is woven into our marriages, our families, and our churches, the effects will be contagious.

Anne Frank wrote in her diary, "Whoever is happy will make others happy too."[22] If this could be said by a Jewish girl hiding for fear of her life during the German occupation of the Netherlands, shouldn't the rest of us concur—especially those of us who have embraced Christ?

Makarios is more than knowing we'll be happy someday. It's knowing we'll be eternally happy, and therefore we can be happy now. And not just because eventually we'll be with God, but because here and now *God is with us—and he is happy!*

We often find happiness in things that haven't yet happened. Anticipating marriage, thinking about a new home, or planning an upcoming vacation—looking forward to future happiness brings us present joy. So why do so many Christians fail to find joy in the biblical promise of eternal happiness, resurrection, and life on the New Earth? Perhaps because they fail to exercise their God-given imaginations concerning how truly happy-making these things will be.

Makarios is built on our redemption, justification, and reconciliation to God, and the experience of right relationship with him. Those who know they're favored by God are happy about it, and those who know that God's favor is eternal can be happy in him when every outward circumstance argues against being happy. This is what David experienced when he wrote, "When the cares of my heart are many, your consolations cheer my soul" (Psalm 94:19). It's what Paul knew when he said from prison, "Rejoice in the Lord always." It's what James and Peter were saying when they told believers to be glad when facing hardships (see James 1:2; 1 Peter 4:13).

Nowhere in Scripture is happiness reserved for when life seems to be going our way. Life's dramas constantly conspire to rob us of joy. But these circumstances, and our shortcomings, aren't nearly as big or as permanent or as powerful as God and his happiness, which in his grace he offers his beloved children. And this offer is not just for "then and there," after we die, but for "here and now," while we still live in a fallen world, in and with and by the grace of a risen Jesus.

GOD TELLS HIS CHILDREN TO SPEND TIME AND MONEY PARTYING: THE HEBREW WORD *SAMACH*, PART 1

You shall rejoice before the LORD your God, you and your son and your daughter.
DEUTERONOMY 16:11

If the solemnity and feasting of such a day as this should be the greatest matter of your joy,
the day will have a night, and the feast an end, and so will your joy. But if heaven be the
matter of your joy, you may go on in your rejoicing, and every day may be your festival.
RICHARD BAXTER

E VANGELIST AND PASTOR George Müller (1805–1898) oversaw the care of ten thousand orphans. He started 117 schools, giving a Christian education to more than 120,000 children. Though Müller's daily administrative, teaching, and ministry responsibilities were staggering, he saw the key to his life and ministry as being "happy in the Lord." Müller wrote,

I might seek to set the truth before the unconverted, I might seek to benefit believers, I might seek to relieve the distressed, I might in other ways seek to behave myself as it becomes a child of God in this world; and yet, not being happy in the Lord, and not being nourished and strengthened in my inner man day by day, all this might not be attended to in a right spirit.[1]

Müller said, "Above all things see to it that your souls are happy in the Lord. . . . It is of supreme and paramount importance that you should seek above all things to have your souls truly happy in God Himself!"[2]

But what does it mean to be "happy in the Lord"? Is this actually a biblical concept? The answer is yes.

Samach is the most common Hebrew word for rejoicing and happiness. It's used of the delight God's people experience when they celebrate him and his gifts. It involves not just the mind but also the body, including references to people drinking and feasting, and newlyweds enjoying each other's hearts and bodies.

Swanson's *Dictionary of Biblical Languages with Semantic Domains* defines *samach* as "rejoicing, glad, delight . . . a feeling or attitude of joy, happiness or contentment . . . making an outward expression of that joy."[3] A Hebrew vocabulary defines *samach* as "to rejoice, be merry; to gladden, make someone merry; to cause to be happy, to help to rejoice."[4] Hence, it's entirely appropriate to translate the word as "happiness," "joy," or their synonyms.

Using the Hebrew verb *samach* and its adjective counterpart 176 times, Scripture records God's repeated call for his people to be happy. Rejoicing is commanded by God when his people gather for a feast and celebration to the Lord (see Deuteronomy 16:11, 14). They are to happily commemorate his works (see Deuteronomy 27:1-7). The Israelites were to rejoice at the fulfillment of God's promise (see Deuteronomy 12:7, 10-12, 18). They were instructed to rejoice in God's provision (see Deuteronomy 14:26). To be "happy in the Lord" is to acknowledge what he has done and then celebrate it.

SINCE GOD REPEATEDLY COMMANDS HIS PEOPLE TO BE HAPPY, OUR HAPPINESS IS A MEASURE OF OUR OBEDIENCE.

Don't rush past that statement: *our happiness is a measure of our obedience*. Reread it. Ponder it. And consider that God in his grace would never command us to be happy without providing us the necessary resources to do so.

Sameach is the adjective form of *samach*. It indicates something that's felt on an emotional level, and involves a warm feeling of satisfaction. This can be caused by the experience of God's goodness in small and large events and relationships. *Sameach* is consistent with the common use of the English word *happy*.

The following are ways *samach* and *sameach* are used in the Old Testament:

- the gladness that comes in reuniting with loved ones (see Exodus 4:14)
- the Lord's desire for a joyful response to his blessings and provision (see Deuteronomy 16:15; 26:11; 1 Kings 8:66; 2 Chronicles 7:10; Jonah 4:6; Zechariah 10:7)
- a happy heart (see Proverbs 15:13; 17:22)
- a father's joy in his son (see Proverbs 27:11; Jeremiah 20:15)
- the wicked (wrongly) rejoicing in calamity (see Psalm 35:26; Proverbs 2:14; 17:5; Micah 7:8)

As you read this chapter, remind yourself, *This is God, the one who created me and loves me, talking to me about the thing I most long for: happiness!*

We should come to God's Word the way hungry people come to the dinner table. Reading these passages isn't a cold, scholarly exercise for our heads; it's a feast for our hearts!

GOD'S DESIGN FOR MARRIAGE PROVIDED A FOUNDATION FOR HAPPINESS.

In Israel, despite the near-constant threats of attack by surrounding nations, a new husband was exempt from military service. Why? Because God commanded, "He shall be free at home one year to be *happy* with his wife" (Deuteronomy 24:5, emphasis added). The verb used here is causative, meaning not only "to *be* happy" but also "to *make* happy." In many people's minds, duty and happiness are contradictory, but God said the young husband's duty was to create happiness with his wife!

While God's happy-making purpose is explicitly stated here, how many other places in God's law is it not stated but nonetheless present? God's laws are often seen as burdensome, but they're intended to secure our happiness.

Following are examples of how *samach* is used, grouped into categories. In the remainder of this chapter, italics will indicate the words used to render *samach*. When multiple synonyms for *happiness* and *joy* are used, the other Hebrew words will appear in brackets. Don't think of this as an academic exercise that requires an understanding of Hebrew or Greek. It doesn't. Instead, view it as an opportunity to focus on the breadth and richness of happiness words in the original languages.

THE BIBLICAL FEASTS WERE GOD'S GRACIOUS GIFTS TO HIS CHILDREN.

If asked, "What does the book of Leviticus tell you about being happy?" most believers would probably say, "Nothing." But consider the instructions for the Feast of Booths, a celebration intended to commemorate Israel's departure from Egypt and journey to Sinai (see Leviticus 23:41-43): "You shall take on the first day the fruit of splendid trees, branches of palm trees and boughs of leafy trees and willows of the brook, and you shall *rejoice* before the LORD your God seven days" (verse 40).

The Israelites camped in homemade lean-tos for a week. Were they expected to fast, work hard, or memorize the law? No. God commanded, "You shall rejoice for seven days"! Apparently a few hours or even several days wasn't enough—God intended this to be *a full week* of joy! It's like parents telling their children, "For the next week, I expect you to do nothing but celebrate, have a good time, and be happy! Have I made myself clear?" Wouldn't most children, once they got over the shock, respond, "Okay—sure, we can do that!"?

WORSHIPING GOD INCLUDES EATING AND REJOICING.

Deuteronomy 12 opens with God commanding the Israelites to "destroy all the places where the nations whom you shall dispossess served their gods" (verse 2). God's people were to bring to him burnt offerings, sacrifices, tithes, freewill offerings, and the firstborn of their herds. It seems demanding and dutiful, doesn't it?

Pay attention to verse 7, where God says, "You will eat there in the presence of the LORD your God and *rejoice* with your household in everything you do, because the LORD your God has blessed you" (HCSB). Two commands: eat and rejoice. The God we know in Jesus is the same God who told his people to take a week off to eat a lot, have fun with their families and friends, and rejoice in everything they did. Doesn't that speak to your heart?

But God wasn't done. Verse 12 records this command: "You shall *rejoice* before the LORD your God, you and your sons and your daughters, your male servants and your female servants, and the Levite that is within your towns." Then he said, "You may . . . eat meat within any of your towns, as much as you desire, according to the blessing of the LORD your God that he has given you" (verse 15).

How's that for a memory verse? "Eat as much as you desire"! I wouldn't recommend this as a life verse, but it's just as inspired as John 3:16. It was a command God's people were happy to obey!

Of the offerings of their meat, God says, "You shall eat them before the LORD your God. . . . And you shall *rejoice* before the LORD your God in all that you undertake" (Deuteronomy 12:18).

For countless Christians, being happy carries with it an uneasy guilt. It's as if being holy is something we can do in God's presence but being happy is something we're more comfortable doing behind his back (as if that were possible). But in this Scripture, God's children are told to be happy "before the LORD," in the presence of their Father who provides for, approves of, participates in, and enjoys their happiness.

Picture it. This isn't God sending his children off to camp and saying, "Have a good time; see you next week." God is saying, "This feast is my idea, and I'm right here with you, enjoying the party more than anyone!"

GOD INSTRUCTED HIS PEOPLE TO SPEND SOME OF THE TITHE FOR WHATEVER THEIR APPETITE CRAVED.

No, this heading isn't a mistake. After stipulating that tithes and offerings should be brought to a certain location, God added,

> If the way is too long for you, so that you are not able to carry the tithe, when the LORD your God blesses you . . . then you shall turn it into money and bind up the money in your hand and go to the place that the LORD your God chooses and spend the money for whatever you desire—oxen or sheep or wine or strong drink, whatever your appetite craves. And you shall eat there before the LORD your God and *rejoice*. DEUTERONOMY 14:24-26

Wasn't the tithe supposed to belong to the Lord alone and never kept for oneself? That was true of the tithe given to the priests and Levites to support their work of ministry. To use that tithe otherwise would be to rob God (see Malachi 3:9-10). But in this case, God designated a completely different tithe that was specifically intended to put on a party for his people to enjoy!

Imagine the delight it must have brought the hardworking Israelites! And if you've read the Bible for many years but this seems new, ask yourself, *How have I missed it?*

The answer may be that our deeply ingrained tendency, reinforced through countless sermons, books, and conversations, is to read the Bible always through the lens of holiness and solemn obligation, causing us to miss even its emphatic statements about happiness and delight.

FOR THE HAPPINESS AND GOOD OF HIS PEOPLE, GOD COMMANDED TIMES OF REST AND CELEBRATION.

Sometimes we envision a production-oriented God who gives his people orders, then tells them to get back to work. But in Scripture, we often see God ordering them to stop working—and not just for the weekly Sabbath.

The Old Testament records a remarkable number of God-ordained celebrations for the Israelites. God built into Israel's calendar seven holidays, amounting to about thirty days per year. Add the weekly Sabbaths, and the total comes to around eighty days of feasting and rest annually. Add the later feasts of Purim (one day) and Hanukkah (eight days), plus weddings and birth celebrations, and the amount of time off for celebration and worship exceeded three months annually!

The Bible uses *samach* and other words of delight to communicate this message from God: "Rest and relax; enjoy me and my provisions; enjoy your families!" Note that God didn't merely say, "If you think you can afford it, you can take some time off." No, God *mandated* this time off for celebrating.

The Israelites were raised knowing how to work *and* celebrate. They watched their industrious parents walk away from life's demands to savor good food and drink good wine, all "before the LORD." They learned to laugh not outside but *inside* God's family. They grew up knowing they didn't have to choose between God and happiness or leave God's family to find it.

This theme continues throughout Deuteronomy: "You shall *rejoice* in all the good that the LORD your God has given to you and to your house, you, and the Levite, and the sojourner who is among you" (Deuteronomy 26:11). Again: "You shall sacrifice peace offerings and shall eat there, and you shall *rejoice* before the LORD your God" (Deuteronomy 27:7).

Instructions for annual feasts were accompanied by the declaration that outstanding debts were to be forgiven every seven years to prevent perpetual poverty in Israel (see Deuteronomy 15:1-4). Financial freedom—another great reason to be happy.

Our study of the Old Testament culture of celebration, surrounding the word *samach*, raises an important question for us today: Is the next generation growing up knowing that the greatest joy is in God and that they don't need to turn their backs on God, their family, and the church to find laughter, fun, and happiness? Are they seeing in their parents, grandparents, and role models not just dutiful obedience but true happiness in their relationship with God?

SACRIFICES AND CELEBRATIONS FILL GOD'S PEOPLE WITH SO MUCH GLADNESS THEY DON'T WANT THE PARTY TO END!

Many of us tend to associate sacrifices with fear and dread, but Scripture takes another position:

> The people of Israel who were present at Jerusalem kept the Feast of Unleavened Bread seven days with *great gladness*, and the Levites and the priests praised the

LORD day by day, singing with all their might to the LORD. . . . So they ate the food of the festival for seven days, sacrificing peace offerings and giving thanks to the LORD, the God of their fathers. 2 CHRONICLES 30:21-22

This God-centered celebration was so worshipful and, yes, fun that something remarkable happened:

Then the whole assembly agreed together to keep the feast for . . . another seven days with gladness [*simchah*]. . . . So there was *great joy* in Jerusalem, for since the time of Solomon the son of David king of Israel there had been nothing like this in Jerusalem. 2 CHRONICLES 30:23, 26

The people spontaneously decided a week wasn't enough for this party. So they extended it—and it's clear that God fully approved!

By modern Western standards, the Israelite culture was at a great economic disadvantage. There were constant chores to be done, crops to be tended and harvested, and no modern machinery to lighten the load. Yet God insisted that the people save for and spend time and money on these celebrations.

Such a weeklong, God-centered party is unprecedented by our standards. But spontaneously extending it for a second week would be unthinkable in our schedule-oriented culture. Imagine the equivalent of a godly Mardi Gras, celebrating not sin but redemption, taking pleasure in God, family, friends, and creation! Surely our need to experience celebration is just as great as Israel's. We should celebrate—and put Christ at the center of our parties!

WHY SHOULD WE PARTY?

Scripture's main reason for celebrations is to help us recognize and enjoy God's goodness.

- Let your priests, O LORD God, be clothed with salvation, and let your saints *rejoice* in your goodness. (2 Chronicles 6:41)
- May your holy people be *happy* because of your goodness. (NCV)
- Hezekiah and all the people were *happy* about what God had done for them. (2 Chronicles 29:36, NET)
- Let those who are happy [*chaphets*] when my name is cleared shout with joy [*ranan*] and *gladness*. Let them always say, "May the LORD be honored. He is pleased [*chaphets*] when everything goes well with the one who serves him." (Psalm 35:27, NIrv)

When the world looks at Christians, they may not think of us as prime candidates to invite to a party. But Scripture shows that we have more reason to celebrate and should be the first to do so. The fact that our partying honors God and makes him happy should serve to increase our happiness!

God is the source of his people's grateful, happy response to what he has done:

You have multiplied the nation; you have increased its joy [*simchah*]; they *rejoice* before you as with joy [*simchah*] at the harvest, as they are glad [*gil*] when they divide the spoil.   ISAIAH 9:3

The people openly celebrated—before God, not under the radar—making obvious his participation in their gladness. Joy is not something God merely permits; it's something he commands, sponsors, and facilitates! He's the source and object of our pleasure.

This joy is like "joy at the harvest," when people see God's bountiful provision. There are riches in God that gladden the heart as much as material riches, the difference being the enduring satisfaction of God's riches!

God's people anticipate their coming happiness when he'll fulfill his promises to rescue them: "Oh, that salvation for Israel would come out of Zion! When the LORD restores the fortunes of his people, let Jacob rejoice [*gil*], let Israel be *glad*" (Psalm 14:7).

The Good News Translation ends the verse with these words: "How *happy* the people of Israel will be." The New English Translation says, "May Jacob rejoice, may Israel be *happy!*"

GOD'S PEOPLE REJOICE OVER HIS PROVISION.

God takes care of people in countless ways, from rain for crops to relief from the heat to satisfaction in relationships. Joel 2:21, 23 says,

- Fear not, O land; be glad [*gil*] and *rejoice*, for the LORD has done great things! . . . Be glad [*gil*], O children of Zion, and *rejoice* in the LORD your God, for he has . . . poured down for you abundant rain.
- Be happy and *full of joy*, because the LORD has done a wonderful thing. . . . So be happy, people of Jerusalem; *be joyful* in the LORD your God. (NCV)

Jonah the prophet's first response to the plant that gave him shade was *samach*: "Now the LORD God appointed a plant and made it come up over Jonah, that it might be a shade over his head, to save him from his discomfort. So Jonah was *exceedingly glad* because of the plant" (Jonah 4:6). At least sixteen Scripture versions say that the plant put in place by God made Jonah "extremely happy" (e.g., NASB) or "very happy" (e.g., NIV).

God wants married couples to find great pleasure in each other, including in their sexual relationship: "Be *happy* with your wife and find your *joy* with the woman you married. . . . Let her charms keep you happy [*ahabah*]; let her surround you with her love" (Proverbs 5:18-19, GNT).

GOD SUPPLIES EVERYTHING WE NEED FOR LAUGHTER-FILLED CELEBRATIONS.

It's hard to imagine a celebration without food and drink:

You make grass grow for the cattle and plants for us to use, so that we can grow our crops and produce wine *to make us happy*, olive oil to make us cheerful, and bread to give us strength.   PSALM 104:14-15, GNT

Ecclesiastes, contemplating the futility of life "under the sun" and at times limiting its perspective to this life, is nonetheless an inspired work that should help us avoid begrudging this life as unworthy of our enjoyment. Ecclesiastes 8:15 says,

- I commend joy [*simchah*], for man has nothing better under the sun but to eat and drink and be *joyful*, for this will go with him in his toil through the days of his life that God has given him under the sun.
- I recommend having fun, because there is nothing better for people in this world than to eat, drink, and *enjoy* life. That way they will experience some happiness along with all the hard work. (NLT)
- I commended mirth, because a man hath no better thing under the sun, than to eat, and to drink, and to *be merry*. (KJV)

The following verse, in which *samach* is accompanied by a word for laughter, reflects a dinner table surrounded by fun, celebration, storytelling, relaxation, and reflections on the day's events, including the humorous ones.

Bread is made for laughter, and wine *gladdens* life.   ECCLESIASTES 10:19

In *The Two Towers* by J. R. R. Tolkien, Frodo's sidekick, Sam, spoke of stories that would be told about Frodo. Then Frodo "laughed, a long clear laugh from his heart. Such a sound had not been heard in those places since Sauron came to Middle-earth. To Sam suddenly it seemed as if all the stones were listening and the tall rocks leaning over them. But Frodo did not heed them; he laughed again."[5]

Frodo was in the sanctuary of the Enemy, weighed down by the dark power of the ring he carried. And yet he could listen to his friend and laugh—and rise above the darkness of evil. Such is the power of *samach*—heartfelt happiness—and the laughter it brings. It stands in defiance of the devil, who is humorless. Good-hearted laughter is a tribute to the happy God, who created laughter and delights to enter into it with us.

CHAPTER 26

GOD DESIRES OUR HAPPINESS NOW AND FOREVER: THE HEBREW WORD *SAMACH,* PART 2

*Sing and rejoice, O daughter of Zion, for behold, I come and I
will dwell in your midst, declares the LORD.*

ZECHARIAH 2:10

*How close, how infinitely closer yet / Must I come to thee, ere I can pay one
debt / Which mere humanity has on me set! / "How close to thee!"—no wonder,
soul, thou art glad! / Oneness with him is the eternal gladness.*

GEORGE MACDONALD

⟶ ⟵

Puritan bible commentator Matthew Henry experienced considerable suffering, including the death of his first wife in childbirth and the loss of three children in infancy. Yet it was said of him:

> [Henry] possessed the desirable disposition and power of looking on the bright
> side of everything. . . . There was a loveliness in his spirit, and a gladness in
> his heart, which caused others to feel "how happy a thing it must be to be a
> Christian." . . . [This cheerfulness] pervaded his entire life. . . . One reason of the
> great power of his life over many who were not decidedly religious men, lay in
> the constancy of that happy spirit which they saw and coveted.[1]

Where did that happy spirit come from in a Puritan who lived three centuries ago? The same place it has come from for countless others—Jesus.

Frederick Buechner says, "The place God calls you is the place where your deep gladness and the world's deep hunger meet."[2] Our deep happiness—not superficial pretense—offers the one thing everyone longs for.

Let's continue exploring God's gift of *samach,* which is indicated by the italicized English translations. In all these cases, note that God is the one who makes people happy.

233

PEOPLE REJOICE AT THE WORKS OF GOD.

Four times in the following verse, a form of the word *samach* is used: "They offered great sacrifices that day and *rejoiced,* for God had made them *rejoice* with great joy; the women and children also *rejoiced.* And the *joy* of Jerusalem was heard far away" (Nehemiah 12:43).

The Good News Translation and the Contemporary English Version both say that God had made the people "very happy"—perfectly good translations of *samach*—while the English Standard Version prefers to repeat the word *joy* throughout. The New Century Version renders it, "The people offered many sacrifices that day and were happy because God had given them great *joy.* The women and children were *happy.* The sound of *happiness* in Jerusalem could be heard far away."

Scripture brims with references to happiness about God's work:

- There is a river whose streams make *glad* the city of God, the holy habitation of the Most High. (Psalm 46:4) (Note that this river flows directly from God, the fountainhead of happiness.)
- He turned the sea into dry land; they passed through the river on foot. There did we *rejoice* in him. (Psalm 66:6)
- You, O LORD, have made me *happy* by your work. I will sing for joy [*ranan*] because of what you have done. (Psalm 92:4, NET)
- This is the day that the LORD has made; let us rejoice [*gil*] and be *glad* in it. (Psalm 118:24)

God's entire creation is called upon to rejoice in him:

- Let the sky *rejoice,* and the earth be happy [*gil*]! Let the sea and everything in it shout! (Psalm 96:11, NET)
- The LORD reigns! Let the earth be happy [*gil*]! Let the many coastlands *rejoice!* (Psalm 97:1, NET)

As the highest of God's creatures, we, too, have the happy privilege of rejoicing in our Creator.

GOD'S PRESENCE AND PROTECTION ARE GREAT REASONS TO REJOICE.

The Bible records many prayers and affirmations by people who give thanks for the Lord's intervention:

- You make me strong and *happy,* LORD. You rescued me. Now I can be *glad* and laugh at my enemies. (1 Samuel 2:1, CEV)
- I will be happy [*gil*] and *rejoice* in your faithfulness, because you notice my pain and you are aware of how distressed I am. (Psalm 31:7, NET)
- He is our God! We have put our trust in him, and he has rescued us. He is the LORD! We have put our trust in him, and now we are happy [*gil*] and *joyful* because he has saved us. (Isaiah 25:9, GNT) (The ESV says, "Be glad and *rejoice*"; the NCV says, "Rejoice and *be happy.*")

- They returned, every man of Judah and Jerusalem, and Jehoshaphat at their head, returning to Jerusalem with *joy*, for the LORD had made them *rejoice* over their enemies. (2 Chronicles 20:27) (Wycliffe renders *samach* here as "great gladness"; the CEV as "very happy.")
- O LORD, in your strength the king *rejoices*, and in your salvation how greatly he exults [*gil*]! (Psalm 21:1)

The following passage contains not only two instances of *samach*, but also *tismah* and *sasson*—all words in the semantic domain of "happiness." Appropriately, translators have chosen a rich variety of ways to render this verse, including the varying combinations of *rejoice, joy, joyful, happy, happiness, merry, glad,* and *gladness.*

- Then shall the young women rejoice [*tismah*] in the dance, and the young men and the old shall be *merry*. I will turn their mourning into joy [*sasson*]; I will comfort them, and give them *gladness* for sorrow. (Jeremiah 31:13)
- Then the young women will dance and be happy, and men, young and old, will *rejoice*. I will comfort them and turn their mourning into joy, their sorrow into gladness. (GNT)

The words for "dancing" and "comfort" also convey a sense of happiness. No less than six of the Hebrew words in this verse express fun and merriment. God goes to great lengths to help us feel the overflowing happiness he promises!

GIVING AWAY MONEY AND POSSESSIONS BRINGS HAPPINESS.
Note the contagious nature of giving in this verse:

The people had given willingly to the LORD, and they were *happy* that so much had been given. King David also was extremely *happy*.   I CHRONICLES 29:9, GNT

Seeing their joy, King David rejoiced over his people's generosity, and his joy no doubt enhanced theirs. God's people throughout the ages have discovered the same truth: benevolence begets happiness.

Hudson Taylor, a nineteenth-century missionary to China, lived a simple life, giving away two-thirds of his income. He said, "My experience was that the less I spent on myself and the more I gave to others the fuller of happiness and blessing did my soul become."[3]

A friend asked me recently, "Do you know any generous person who's unhappy?" I gave it a lot of thought. I know many generous people. Some have been through great tragedies. Some have dealt with seasons of depression and anxiety. But would I, overall, describe any of them as unhappy? No. Their generosity infuses joy into their lives and eclipses their many reasons to be sad.

So I asked myself another question, "Do I know any stingy person who's happy?" The answer came quickly: "Not a single one." And I have yet to think of an exception. Stingy people imagine they're better off not giving, but their failure to give costs them dearly.

Playwright Henrik Ibsen (1828–1906) said, "Money may be the husk of many things, but not the kernel. It brings you food, but not appetite; medicine, but not health; acquaintances, but not friends; servants, but not faithfulness; days of joy, but not peace or happiness."[4]

We all need money, but the greatest happiness comes not in spending but in wise and generous giving.

THOSE WHO SEEK GOD FIND HAPPINESS.

When our priorities are in order, with God in first position, happiness is bound to follow. Psalm 16:8-9 says,

- I have set the LORD always before me; because he is at my right hand, I shall not be shaken. Therefore my heart is *glad*, and my whole being rejoices [*gil*].
- I constantly trust in the LORD; because he is at my right hand, I will not be upended. So my heart *rejoices* and I am happy. (NET)

Psalm 40:16 echoes this idea that our gladness and rejoicing should be centered in God:

- May all who seek you rejoice [*sus*] and be *glad* in you. (ESV)
- Let those who follow you be happy and *glad*. (NCV)
- May all those who seek you be happy and *rejoice* in you! (NET)

The rejoicing described here is not about a particular course of events or temporary good fortune. Instead, it speaks of what other passages further reveal: God's children rejoicing in their unchanging Savior, who promises he'll be forever present with us and in us (see Malachi 3:1; Matthew 28:20; Colossians 1:27; Hebrews 13:8).

The following verses are but a small number of those pointing to the happiness of God-seekers:

- Glory in his holy name; let the hearts of those who seek the LORD *rejoice*! (Psalm 105:3) (The NCV says, "Let those who seek the LORD be *happy*.")
- Let my meditation be pleasing to Him; as for me, I shall be *glad* in the LORD. (Psalm 104:34, NASB)
- Give me *happiness*, O Lord, for I give myself to you. O Lord, you are so good, so ready to forgive, so full of unfailing love for all who ask for your help. (Psalm 86:4-5, NLT)

GOD'S PEOPLE REJOICE IN WISDOM.

The book of Proverbs draws a strong connection between wisdom and happiness:

- Children with good sense make their parents *happy*, but foolish children make them sad. (Proverbs 10:1, CEV)
- The father of the righteous will be very happy [*gil*]; the one who gives life to the wise will *rejoice*. Your father and your mother will *rejoice*; she who gave you birth will be happy [*gil*]. (Proverbs 23:24-25, CEB)

Proverbs 23:15 says, "My son, if your heart is wise, my heart too will be *glad*." Notice the word *too* here. This verse assumes that the child's wisdom will bring gladness to the child, as well as to the parent.

WE CAN FIND JOY IN A JOB WELL DONE.
The book of Ecclesiastes talks about work, and our satisfaction in it:

- I withheld not my heart from any joy [*simchah*]; for my heart *rejoiced* in all my labour. (2:10, KJV)
- I perceived that there is nothing better for them than to be *joyful* and to do good as long as they live. (3:12, ESV)
- I have seen that nothing is better than that man should be *happy* in his activities, for that is his lot. (3:22, NASB)
- When God gives someone wealth and possessions, and the ability to enjoy them, to accept their lot and be *happy* in their toil—this is a gift of God. (5:19, NIV)

All these passages are expressions of the perspective of life "under the sun" (Ecclesiastes 1:9), which ultimately proves vain. They express the truth that work, activities, and possessions can bring real joy, but apart from Christ they can't bring lasting, eternal joy.

ENCOURAGING WORDS SPREAD GLADNESS.
Proverbs 15:30 describes the power words have to evoke happiness:

- A cheerful look brings *joy* to the heart; good news makes for good health. (NLT)
- Smiling faces make you *happy*, and good news makes you feel better. (GNT)

Proverbs 12:25 says,
- Anxiety in a man's heart weighs him down, but a good word makes him *glad*.
- Worry can rob you of happiness, but kind words will *cheer* you up. (GNT)

THE GODLY LIFE IS A JOY-FILLED LIFE.
Although our culture today rarely traces a straight line from godliness to happiness, Scripture is emphatic about the connection:

- I was *glad* when they said to me, "Let us go to the house of the LORD!" (Psalm 122:1)
- Let me share in the prosperity of your chosen ones. Let me *rejoice* in the *joy* of your people; let me praise you with those who are your heritage. (Psalm 106:5, NLT)

In 1 Samuel 19:5, Jonathan reminds his father, Saul, who now wished to kill David, that he had once been happy with David: "He risked his life when he struck down the Philistine and the LORD gave all Israel a great victory. When you saw it, you were *happy*. So why would you sin against innocent blood by putting David to death for no reason?" (NET). The ESV translates the phrase, "You saw it, and *rejoiced*"; the New International Version says, "You saw it and were *glad*"; the New Living Translation says, "You were certainly *happy* about it." Each translation is merited, because to rejoice, to be glad, and to be happy have essentially the same meaning.

Saul's deep-seated bitterness and resentment toward David reminds us of our need for perspective in our own relationships when they become overshadowed by unhappiness. Jonathan's words to his father suggest that remembering the former happiness we had in a relationship can be a catalyst for restoring it.

The *American Journal of Psychiatry* issued the findings from a forty-five-year study of 173 men who had been scrutinized at five-year intervals since they graduated from Harvard in the early 1940s.[5]

The results show that "the secret of emotional health among older men is not a successful career, a happy marriage, or a stable childhood. . . . It lies instead in an ability to handle life's blows without passivity, blame, or bitterness."[6]

These results may have seemed revolutionary in the world of psychiatry, but they are perfectly in keeping with what Scripture has claimed for centuries:

- The life of the godly is full of light and *joy*, but the light of the wicked will be snuffed out. (Proverbs 13:9, NLT)
- An evil man is caught by sin, but the righteous one sings and *rejoices*. (Proverbs 29:6, HCSB)
- Evil people are trapped by their own sin, but good people can sing and be *happy*. (NCV)
- The precepts of the LORD are right, *rejoicing* the heart. (Psalm 19:8)
- The laws of the LORD are right, and those who obey them are *happy*. (GNT)

It's no overstatement to say that happiness and joy are products of our God-centered immersion in his Word.

THE FREQUENT USE OF *SAMACH* REFLECTS GOD'S HEART AND DESIRE FOR HIS PEOPLE.

We've examined only a sampling of the 176 biblical appearances of *samach*. In the Psalms especially, people experience *samach* when they sense God's presence and see his provision. Sometimes happiness comes when we contemplate his truth; other times it's evident when we behold his sovereign works. Always God is the source of that happiness. *Samach* typically involves a sense of conscious celebration stemming from a spirit of deep gratitude toward God.

William P. Brown summarizes well the Psalms' use of *samach*:

Happiness in the Psalms is a matter of anguished, confident trust in God. . . .
The joy-filled presence of God is embodied in the joy-filled imitation of God.
Happiness, moreover, points to . . . a refuge that rests upon God's providential
care. . . .
For the righteous in the Psalms, the need for the Lord is the beginning of

happiness, a distinctly wise happiness. The abject need mentioned so often in the Psalms reflects a world wracked by misery and disillusionment, finitude and deprivation, in other words, a *real* world. And real happiness charts a rocky path through that pain, never around it.[7]

It's not only God's people who experience *samach*; God himself does. His people pray that he would be *samach*—happy and pleased with what he sees on Earth and in them: "May the Lord be *happy* with what he has made!" (Psalm 104:31, GNT); "Do not despise these small beginnings, for the Lord *rejoices* to see the work begin" (Zechariah 4:10, NLT).

Clearly, *samach* is joy or happiness that is experienced in human feelings—indeed, what other kind of joy or happiness is there? In these passages, God expects his people to be happy as a healthy response to all the pleasures he provides—pleasures that begin and end with himself.

In concert with more than twenty other words of joy in the Old Testament, *samach* is a happiness that rings with exuberance, one God enthusiastically calls his people to. It's used here—in a great passage for anyone looking for a mood swing toward joy—in conjunction with three other words expressing mirth, glad singing, and shouting:

Sing [*rinnah*], Jerusalem. Israel, shout for joy [*ruah*]! Jerusalem, *be happy* and rejoice [*alaz*] with all your heart. ZEPHANIAH 3:14, NCV

The Message paraphrases this verse, "Sing, Daughter Zion! Raise the rafters, Israel! Daughter Jerusalem, be happy! celebrate!"

Let's join our glad voices with the great chorus of God-followers who have gone before us. We are loved, watched over, and provided for by an unfathomably great and beautiful Creator and Redeemer. Give thanks! Sing! Celebrate! Be happy!

GOD'S PEOPLE CAN AND SHOULD REJOICE AND CELEBRATE: *CHARA* AND *CHAIRO* IN THE GOSPELS AND ACTS

Your father Abraham was overjoyed that he would see my day. He saw it and was happy.
JESUS (JOHN 8:56, CEB)

Choose God for your portion; remember that he is the only happiness of a rational and immortal soul. The soul that was made for God can find no happiness but in God.
JOHN MASON

OSHO, A MYSTIC and guru once known as Bhagwan Shree Rajneesh, said, "Joy is spiritual. It is different, totally different from pleasure or happiness. It has nothing to do with the outside, with the other."[1] While his worldview dramatically conflicts with the Bible's, many Christians similarly spiritualize the word *joy*, contrasting it with happiness and portraying it as independent of emotion or pleasure.

The Greek noun *chara* is normally translated "joy," and the verb *chairo* is rendered "rejoice." Together they appear 133 times in the New Testament. Contrary to popular stereotypes, these words, viewed in context, commonly convey happiness, including powerful and pleasurable emotions.

CHARA AND *CHAIRO* SPEAK OF BOTH HAPPINESS AND JOY.

According to the Louw and Nida's *Greek-English Lexicon*, *chara* means "a state of joy and gladness—joy, gladness, great happiness." It adds, "In a number of languages 'joy' is expressed idiomatically, for example, 'my heart is dancing' or 'my heart shouts because I am happy.'"[2]

Louw and Nida's lexicon says that *chairo* means "to enjoy a state of happiness and well-being—'to rejoice, to be glad.'"[3] Another lexicon defines *chara* as "literally joy, as a feeling of inner happiness . . . a state or condition of happiness."[4]

Mounce's Complete Expository Dictionary says, "As an antonym of grief and sorrow (Jn. 16:20), *chara* denotes 'joy, happiness, gladness.'"[5]

According to the scholars, these words could be translated "to be happy" as readily as "to rejoice." With that in mind, and in keeping with various translations, I use these English terms interchangeably.

Christians are often taught that joy (translated from *chara*) is fundamentally spiritual, not secular. Yet an extensive history of *chara*, written by Hans Conzelmann, begins by saying it is "intrinsically a secular term."[6]

Conzelmann provides examples of *chara* from the Septuagint (the Greek translation of Hebrew Scripture). It's used about receiving news (see Genesis 45:16), meeting friends or relatives (see Exodus 4:14), and hearing about a trade treaty proposal (see 1 Kings 5:7). These favorable circumstances prompt rejoicing—and none of them has a spiritual dimension.

In the Apocrypha (written between the Old and New Testaments), *chara* describes joy at a wedding (see Tobit 11:17) and the happiness of victory (see 2 Maccabees 15:28).

The verb *chairo* is frequently found in the opening address of secular letters.[7] *Chara* was used commonly by both believers and unbelievers. Its secular origins and widespread use among unbelievers didn't stop the Holy Spirit from placing it in a spiritual context, infusing it with new vitality. The New Testament writers freely use other words with common secular meanings. Until recently, the church has exercised the same freedom with the word *happiness*.

CHARA AND *CHAIRO* HAVE FAR MORE BREADTH THAN OUR ENGLISH WORDS *JOY* AND *REJOICE*.

Chairo is sometimes translated "greetings," the equivalent of "happy to see you," as when people recognized Jesus in Matthew 26:49 and Matthew 28:9. In Matthew 27:29, we see the same word used by soldiers who are mocking Jesus, saying, "*Hail*, King of the Jews!" In these cases, the context makes it obvious that "rejoice" is an inappropriate interpretation.

In Luke 1:14, the angel announces John the Baptist's birth to his father, Zechariah. Most translations use "joy" and "rejoice." The full verse says, "And you will have joy [*chara*] and gladness [*agalliasis*] and many will rejoice [*chairo*] at his birth." So here *chara* is translated "joy," while its synonym *agalliasis* is translated "gladness." *Chara* could have been translated "glad" here, just as the New American Standard Bible translates it several other times in the Gospels. Similarly, *agalliasis* could easily be translated "rejoice," as it's rendered in 1 Peter 1:6, 8 (NASB).

There's no exact, one-to-one equivalency in translation. The King James translators could have justly rendered *chairo* as "be glad" in Philippians 4:4, as it reads in the Common English Bible: "Be glad in the Lord always! Again I say, be glad!" Or they could have rendered it, "Be happy in the Lord always: and again I say, be happy."

The KJV usually renders *chairo* as "rejoice"—it's a great word and a good translation. When people get a new job, become engaged, or have a baby, they can say, "I'm happy," "I'm glad," or "I'm joyful." All these terms fit. It's appropriate that the Hebrew and Greek words, with their overlapping meanings, are rendered by various English words that also have overlapping meanings.

THE COMING OF THE MESSIAH PROMPTED OVERWHELMING HAPPINESS.

Luke 1 and 2 are remarkably joy-filled chapters. The angel promises Zechariah regarding his son John's birth, "You will have *joy* and gladness [*agalliasis*], and many will *rejoice* at his birth" (Luke 1:14).

Mary, Elizabeth, the shepherds, the angels, Simeon, and Anna were overcome with happiness at the Messiah's arrival. When the preborn John was filled with God's Spirit, he jumped for joy (*agalliasis*) at the presence of Jesus (see Luke 1:44). The one whose advent caused such happiness in the hearts of so many is the same Jesus who is the source of our eternal happiness. Since we're now indwelt by the Spirit of this incarnate God, who has promised to be with us always, surely we have even greater reason to experience joy!

We're told when the wise men "saw the star, they *rejoiced* exceedingly with *great joy*" (Matthew 2:10, emphasis added). Both the verb *chairo* and the noun *chara* are used, plus the adjective *megas* (great), intensifying the happiness even further. Since this was the magi's overwhelming response to the star pointing toward Jesus, imagine their joy in the presence of Jesus himself!

Jesus' miracles and great deeds brought delight wherever he went: "All the people *rejoiced* at all the glorious things that were done by him" (Luke 13:17). The Complete Jewish Bible translates, "By these words, Yeshua put to shame the people who opposed him; but the rest of the crowd were *happy* about all the wonderful things that were taking place through him."

The world is still cursed with sin and suffering, but these obstacles can't trump joy. Christ has already come, and with him came light, hope, and redemption—the down payment of this world's final transformation.

Outbursts of happiness at Christ's first coming should inspire us to joyfully anticipate his second coming.

CHARA IS USED OF CHRIST'S HAPPINESS.

Though I dealt with Jesus' happiness in chapter 18, the topic is worthy of further consideration in relation to *chairo* and *chara*.

I recently heard someone say, "Nowhere does the Bible say that Jesus was happy." But Jesus said to his disciples, "These things I have spoken to you, that my *joy* may be in you, and that your *joy* may be full" (John 15:11). If we understand that joy and happiness are synonymous and that *chara* can be translated either way, as the lexicons attest, then John 15:11 reveals Jesus' happiness even more directly than John 11:35 ("Jesus wept") reveals his sadness. Imagine someone arguing, "The Bible doesn't say that Jesus was sad, only that he wept." It's even sillier to suggest that when Christ declared his joy he wasn't affirming his happiness.

Teams of Greek scholars render *chara* in John 15:11 as "happy": "I have told you these things so that you can have the *true happiness* that I have. I want you to be *completely happy*" (ERV).

J. B. Phillips translates the two appearances of *chara* as "joy" and "happiness": "I have told you this so that you can share my *joy*, and that your *happiness* may be complete."

Jesus surely thought of himself, the Good Shepherd, when he spoke of the shepherd recovering his lost sheep: "He *rejoices* over it more than over the ninety-nine that never went astray" (Matthew 18:13). Luke 15:5-6 records him saying, "When you find it, you are *so happy* that you put it on your shoulders and carry it back home. Then you call your friends and neighbors together and say to them, 'I am *so happy* I found my lost sheep. Let us celebrate!'" (GNT).

As we saw in chapters 18 and 19, the Jesus of the Gospels is joyful.

BEING NEAR JESUS MAKES PEOPLE HAPPY.

The Common English Bible says, "Zacchaeus came down at once, *happy* to welcome Jesus" (Luke 19:6). Imagine how this tax collector, despised by Romans for being Jewish and despised by Jews for serving Romans, felt when Jesus invited himself to his home!

> As [Jesus] was drawing near . . . the whole multitude of his disciples began to *rejoice* and praise God with a loud voice for all the mighty works that they had seen. LUKE 19:37

The presence of Jesus—his nearness, friendship, and compassion—was the key to the disciples' happiness. But he promises something even greater: "I will never leave you and I will never abandon you" (Hebrews 13:5, NET).

Being with Jesus will bring eternal joy to all who know him. But we can experience a foretaste of that joy now. We can rejoice in Jesus as John the Baptist did:

> The one who has the bride is the bridegroom. The friend of the bridegroom, who stands and hears him, *rejoices* greatly at the bridegroom's voice. Therefore this *joy* of mine is now complete. JOHN 3:29

Christ's glorification heightens and fulfills the gladness of his people. The Good News Translation concludes the verse, "This is how my own *happiness* is made complete." The New Century Version says, "In the same way, I am really *happy*."

THE STORY OF THE PRODIGAL SON CAPTURES GREAT GLADNESS.

Jesus laces this parable with happiness words. Here's what the father tells his older son:

> It was fitting to celebrate [*euphraino*] and be *glad*, for this your brother was dead, and is alive; he was lost, and is found. LUKE 15:32

Here Jesus uses two powerful happiness synonyms: *euphranthenai*, "to be glad or delighted, enjoy oneself, rejoice, celebrate,"[8] and *chairo*.[9] When two different words for joy, gladness, or happiness are used in the same sentence, the delight is unmistakable.

Consider the rich combinations of English words used to translate these synonyms.

More than six hundred years ago, in the first English Bible, Wycliffe translated the verse, "It behooved to make feast, and to have *joy*" (Luke 15:32). Here's how some translators who followed rendered the key words in this verse:

- It was meet that we should make merry, and *be glad*. (KJV, YLT)
- It was fitting to celebrate and *be glad*. (ESV, NIV, CEB, NET)
- It was right to make merry and *rejoice*. (DARBY, WNT)
- This was a day to be happy and *celebrate*. (ERV)
- We had to celebrate and be *happy*. (GNT, NCV, GW, VOICE)
- We had to celebrate and *rejoice*. (HCSB, CJB, NRSV, NASB)
- Now we should have a good time and *be happy*. (WE)

After reading all these iterations of "joy" or "rejoice," would you conclude the father wasn't happy over his son's return? Obviously not! In every one of these translations—not just the seven that use the word *happy*—Scripture clearly tells us that the father (representing God) was happy!

THE PHARISEES REJOICED WHEN JUDAS BETRAYED JESUS.

Righteous joy and unrighteous joy differ not in their emotional nature but in their object, foundation, and duration. Puritan Thomas Brooks said, "All the joys, delights, and pleasures that holiness debars men of, are sinful joys, delights and pleasures."[10]

Consider this description of the Pharisees' response when Judas handed over Jesus:

When they heard it, [the Pharisees] were *glad* and promised to give [Judas] money. And he sought an opportunity to betray [Jesus]. MARK 14:11

This is the same word, *chairo*, used to describe the happiness of believers. Though the King James Version, the New American Standard Bible, the English Standard Version, the New International Version, and the New Living Translation usually translate *chairo* as "rejoice," they don't here. Had they done so, it might have prevented the false notion that *joy* in the Bible is an inherently spiritual term.

Had the King James translation team chosen "be happy" for "good" *chairo* (as in Philippians 3:1) and "rejoice" for "bad" *chairo* (as in the Pharisees' rejoicing over Judas's betrayal) and subsequent translations followed its lead, today some people would be saying, "Happiness is only for believers" and "Joy is only for unbelievers." (Of course, they would still be missing the point.)

JESUS-FOLLOWERS REJOICE IN THE LORD.

Shortly before his crucifixion, Jesus said to his disciples, "Remember what I told you: I am going away, but I will come back to you again. If you really loved me, you would be *happy* that I am going to the Father, who is greater than I am" (John 14:28, NLT).

In John 16, Jesus speaks to their emotional response to his coming death: "You will be sorrowful, but your sorrow will turn into *joy*" (verse 20). He explains that a woman in labor experiences sorrow, "but when she has delivered the baby, she no longer remembers the anguish," which is replaced by "joy" over her child (verse 21). He says, "So also you have sorrow now, but I will see you again, and your hearts will *rejoice*, and no one will take your *joy* from you" (verse 22). The latter part of the verse is also rendered, "Then you will be *happy*, and no one will take that *happiness* away from you" (GW).

In the space of three verses, Jesus uses the terms *chairo* and *chara* five times. His suffering and sorrow, and theirs, would be temporary. His happiness, and theirs, would be eternal. *Chara* is characterized as being similar to a woman's state of mind after childbirth, as she holds her newborn. Is the joy of a mother holding her baby for the first time emotional? It's hard to imagine anything *more* emotional! Does this joy involve happiness? Of course! *Chara*, the primary New Testament word translated "joy," should never be viewed as something that's unemotional or devoid of happiness.

SEEING THE RISEN JESUS WAS THE ULTIMATE HAPPINESS FOR THE DISCIPLES; SO IT WILL BE FOR US.

The women at the tomb responded to news of the Resurrection with great happiness:

- They departed quickly from the tomb with fear and great *joy*, and ran to tell his disciples. (Matthew 28:8)
- The women were frightened and yet very *happy* . . . (Matthew 28:8, CEV)
- While they still could not believe it because they were amazed and *happy* . . . (Luke 24:41, NCV)

Similarly, the disciples in the upper room were delighted when they encountered the risen Christ (John 20:20):

- When he had said this, he showed them his hands and his side. Then the disciples were *glad* when they saw the Lord.
- . . . When the disciples saw the Lord, they became very *happy*. (CEV)

The formerly despondent disciples responded with immense happiness as they beheld their Lord.

We might suppose that their joy wouldn't last, but in fact it continued after Jesus ascended (Luke 24:51-52):

- While he blessed them, he parted from them and was carried up into heaven. And they worshiped him and returned to Jerusalem with great *joy*.
- . . . They returned to Jerusalem and were very *happy*. (CEV)

Because Jesus was alive, and because he promised to be with his followers always and return for them one day, their joy went deep and overflowed the banks of their lives.

SHARING THE GOSPEL AND BELIEVING IN JESUS BRING HAPPINESS.

Both those who offer the gospel and those who receive it naturally experience happiness:

- Now the people who plant can be *happy together* with those who harvest. (John 4:36, ERV)
- After they had come out of the water, the Lord's Spirit took Philip away. The official never saw him again, but he was *very happy* as he went on his way. (Acts 8:39, CEV)
- When those who were not Jewish heard Paul say this, they were *happy* and gave honor to the message of the Lord. (Acts 13:48, NCV)

THE JOY OF ANTICIPATING LIVING WITH GOD TRUMPS HAVING SPIRITUAL POWER.

Jesus told his disciples, "Do not *rejoice* in this, that the spirits are subject to you, but *rejoice* that your names are written in heaven" (Luke 10:20). The NCV translates the verse, "You should not be *happy* because the spirits obey you but because your names are written in heaven."

Our source of joy is the God of all happiness and our never-ending relationship with him. The spiritual power and gifts he gives are matters of real but secondary enjoyment; he's the primary object of our delight.

SEEING GOD AT WORK MAKES PEOPLE HAPPY IN ANY CIRCUMSTANCE.

Here's how believers responded to a letter about a potentially divisive issue in the early church: "When the people read it, they were filled with *joy* by the message of encouragement" (Acts 15:31, GNT).

The *chara* experienced here was due to positive circumstances involving the uplifting contents of the letter. Other times the word is associated with negative circumstances: "When [Barnabas] went to Antioch and saw how God had blessed the believers there [who were facing persecution], he was very *happy*" (Acts 11:23, ERV).

Sometimes *chairo* appears in combination with synonyms:

- *Rejoice* and be glad [*agalliao*], for your reward is great in heaven, for so they persecuted the prophets. (Matthew 5:12)
- *Be happy* about it! Be very glad! (Matthew 5:12, NLT)
- *Rejoice* in that day, and leap for joy [*skirtao*], for behold, your reward is great in heaven; for so their fathers did to the prophets. (Luke 6:23)
- *Be happy* and jump for joy! (Luke 6:23, CEV)

THE PRIVILEGE OF SUFFERING FOR JESUS MAKES HIS FOLLOWERS HAPPY.

When believers in the early church faced persecution for following Jesus, this was their response: "They left the presence of the council, *rejoicing* that they were counted worthy to suffer dishonor for the name" (Acts 5:41). The Contemporary English Version and five others translate it, "They were *happy*." How could anyone be happy in suffering? Because they found joy in being enough like Jesus to be treated as he had been. Note that they rejoiced *not* because they suffered (self-glorifying masochism) but because they were considered *worthy* to suffer for Jesus (God-glorifying grace).

We see this same supernatural reality in other passages (see Matthew 5:12; Romans 5:3; James 1:2-3; 1 Peter 4:13). It's as if our eternal happiness works its way backward into the suffering of the present moment, washing over us as a foretaste of our imminent, unending joy.

Consider what happened to Paul and Silas in Philippi: "The crowd joined in attacking them, and the magistrates tore the garments off them and gave orders to beat them with rods. And when they had inflicted many blows upon them, they threw them into prison.... [The jailer] put them into the inner prison and fastened their feet in the stocks" (Acts 16:22-24).

Sadly, God's people have been treated this way throughout history, but the next verse is astonishing: "About midnight Paul and Silas were praying and singing hymns to God, and the prisoners were listening to them" (verse 25). Why were the prisoners listening? Because to sing hymns is to express praise and joy and focus on God, not oneself.

Such actions speak powerfully to unbelievers. Words alone are cheap, but joy in suffering gets people's attention—it demands a supernatural explanation! Countless believers have used their platform of suffering, combined with Christ-centered happiness, to attract people to the gospel.

Aleksandr Solzhenitsyn came to know himself, Christ, and in turn joy through his suffering in Russian prisons. His observations are counterintuitive, yet biblical:

> In the intoxication of my youthful successes I had felt myself to be infallible, and I was therefore cruel. In the surfeit of power I was a murderer, and an oppressor. In my most evil moments I was convinced that I was doing good, and I was well supplied with systematic arguments. And it was only when, in the Gulag Archipelago, on rotting prison straw that I sensed within myself the first stirrings of good. Gradually it was disclosed to me that the line separating good and evil passes, not through states, nor between classes, nor between political parties either—but right through every human heart and through all human hearts. And that is why I turn back to the years of my imprisonment and say, sometimes to the astonishment of those about me: "Bless you, prison!"[11]

In his book *Cancer Ward*, Solzhenitsyn wrote, "A man is happy so long as he chooses to be happy, and no one can stop him."[12] Most who have seen and experienced happiness in the midst of suffering will testify that while it does indeed involve a choice, it often comes as an infusion of grace in our hearts, a gift from the God of happiness. Suffering, by its nature, is never easy, but no one has greater cause for joy than those who know Christ and believe his promise that present suffering will be followed with eternal glory and happiness.

ENJOYING GOD'S GRACE: THE GREEK WORDS *CHARA* AND *CHAIRO* IN THE APOSTLES' LETTERS

Base your happiness on your hope in Christ.

ROMANS 12:12, PHILLIPS

Grace will devastate your selfish dreams while it secures for you an eternal future far better than your wildest dreams.

PAUL DAVID TRIPP

A ROUND 1525, TWO students bound for pastoral training stopped at an inn in Germany and encountered a knight wearing breeches, a doublet, and a red hat. His hand rested on a sword as he read the book of Psalms in Hebrew. He invited the young men to join him for a drink and advised them to study the original languages. They told him they were excited that they'd soon be meeting the professor who had started the whole Reformation movement.

Upon reaching Wittenberg and meeting Martin Luther, they recognized him as that knight from the inn.[1]

With all his flaws, Luther, the father of the Protestant Reformation, loved good humor and made a daily practice of sharing his happiness with others. Do we, as Christ-followers, embody such fun-loving joy? Scripture suggests we should.

GOD'S GIFT OF JOY IS ALSO OUR SOURCE OF HOPE.

Nothing robs us of happiness faster than hopelessness, and nothing encourages it more than hope. The day or even the season of life can be dark, but hope still shines a light. Samuel Johnson wrote, "Hope is itself a species of happiness, and, perhaps, the chief happiness which this world affords."[2]

Of course, there is false hope and true hope. Scripture offers solid ground for our hope in Christ. Knowing his redemptive design, God assures his children, "I know the plans I have for you . . . plans for welfare and not for evil, to give you a future and a hope" (Jeremiah 29:11).

"The hope of the righteous brings joy" (Proverbs 10:28). In the New Testament, *chairo* and *chara* are closely connected with hope: "*Rejoice* in hope, be patient in tribulation, be constant in prayer" (Romans 12:12). Three chapters later we read, "May the God of hope fill you with all *joy* and peace in believing, so that by the power of the Holy Spirit you may abound in hope" (Romans 15:13).

According to the most authoritative translators' handbook, "fill you with all joy" here may be rendered as "cause you to be completely happy" or even "cause your hearts to burst because of happiness."[3]

Meditating on Christ and his redemptive work will cultivate our hope and thereby produce happiness.

GOD CALLS US TO SHARE BOTH THE JOY AND SORROW OF OTHERS.

God doesn't intend for us to keep our experiences and emotions to ourselves; instead, the Bible speaks of both happiness and mourning as communal activities.

- *Rejoice* with those who *rejoice*, weep with those who weep. (Romans 12:15)
- Be *happy* with those who are *happy*. . . . (Romans 12:15, NLT)
- Share the *happiness* of those who are *happy*. . . . (Romans 12:15, PHILLIPS)
- You also should be *happy* and full of joy with me. (Philippians 2:18, NCV)

Phillips translates Philippians 2:16-18, "If it should happen that my life-blood is . . . poured out . . . then I can still be very happy, and I can share my happiness with you all. I should like to feel that you could be *glad* about this too, and could share with me the happiness I speak of."

WITNESSING POSITIVE CHANGES AND GROWTH IN THOSE WE LOVE CAUSES HAPPINESS.

In order to rejoice in the obedience of those we love, we must be close enough to them to see their growth in Christ. If we remain distant, we'll miss the happiness God intends for us. The New Testament is full of examples of people who rejoiced over the transformed lives of their fellow believers:

- Though I am absent in body, yet I am with you in spirit, *rejoicing* to see your good order and the firmness of your faith in Christ. (Colossians 2:5)
- . . . I'm *happy* to see the discipline and stability of your faith in Christ. (Colossians 2:5, CEB)
- We are glad when we are weak and you are strong. Your restoration is what we pray for. (2 Corinthians 13:9) (Sixteen versions I consulted translate *chairo* here as "rejoice," twenty-three as "are glad," and four as "are happy." All three choices are good translations.)

- Your obedience is known to all, so that I *rejoice* over you. (Romans 16:19)
- Everyone knows that you are obedient to the Lord. This makes me very *happy*. (Romans 16:19, NLT)
- The news of your obedience has reached everybody, so I'm *happy* for you. (Romans 16:19, CEB)
- What thanksgiving can we return to God for you, for all the *joy* that we feel for your sake before our God. (1 Thessalonians 3:9)
- How can we possibly thank God enough for all the *happiness* you have brought us? (1 Thessalonians 3:9, CEV)

LIKE PAUL, WE SHOULD REJOICE IN OUR FRIENDS AND THEIR HAPPINESS.

Paul called the Philippians "my brothers, whom I love and long for, my *joy* and crown" (Philippians 4:1).

Those who say joy isn't an emotion need to carefully read biblical texts such as 2 Corinthians 7:13:

- Besides our own comfort, we *rejoiced* still more at the *joy* of Titus, because his spirit has been refreshed by you all.
- We were especially *delighted* to see how *happy* Titus was. . . . (NIV)
- How *happy* Titus made us with his *happiness* over the way in which all of you helped to *cheer* him up! (GNT)

Here again, *chara* describes an emotional experience prompted by a positive circumstance. Titus's happiness about what the Corinthians had done for him in turn made Paul and his companions happy. This is the contagious nature of happiness. By cheering up Titus, Corinthian believers cheered up Paul! These passages are shot through with glad feelings. Paul's happiness no doubt brought happiness to others, who brought happiness to others, who in turn did the same.

It's also true of us: if God works in our lives to make us happier in him, this happiness will spill over into the lives of our family and friends—we can count on it. Joy in Christ is God's gift not only to us but also to all those around us. And it's our gift to others too. This is why parents and grandparents, for instance, don't just owe it to themselves to be happy in Christ; they owe it to their children and grandchildren and everyone else whose lives they touch.

HAPPINESS IN THE NEW TESTAMENT IS A FRUIT OF THE HOLY SPIRIT.

What's our greatest source of joy? Paul pointed to the Holy Spirit: "The fruit of the Spirit is love, *joy*, peace, patience, kindness, goodness, faithfulness, gentleness, self-control" (Galatians 5:22-23).

Commenting on *chara*, usually rendered "joy" in this passage, the United Bible Societies' translation handbook advises, "In some languages joy is essentially equivalent to 'causes people to be very happy.' In order to indicate that this joy is not merely some passing experience, one may say 'to be truly happy within their hearts.' In some languages joy is expressed idiomatically as 'to be warm within one's heart,' or 'to dance within one's heart.'"[4]

Translating the fruit of the Spirit as adjectives rather than nouns, the Contemporary English Version reads, "God's Spirit makes us loving, happy, peaceful, patient, kind, good, faithful, gentle, and self-controlled."

If it seems that the translators are taking liberties by saying "happy" instead of "joyful," note that the other eight adjectives perfectly correspond to the nouns used in the English Standard Version and the New American Standard Bible. *Chara* is the only Greek word in this passage rendered differently by the CEV translators. Their goal was faithfulness to the original language. "Joy" is a good translation of *chara*, but so too is its synonym "happiness."

Some suggest that the order of the ninefold fruit of the Spirit is significant and that love is named first because "the greatest . . . is love" (1 Corinthians 13:13). If this is true, then joy's position as the second listed might imply it's the second greatest.

Why does Paul emphasize joy and the other eight components of the Spirit's fruit in the context of his attack on legalism in Galatians? Reading between the lines, we might surmise that joy was too rare among the Christians there, as it often is today.[5]

Paul's argument in Galatians suggests that self-righteous legalism chokes out the fruit of the Spirit, leading believers to become killjoys. Killjoys find pleasure in always being right and showing that others are wrong. Their false joy comes from thinking, *I'm the smartest, purest, and most doctrinally, behaviorally, or politically correct person in the room.* Unfortunately, no one wants to be in the room with them . . . including Jesus.

Joy, along with the fruit of the Spirit, stands in contrast to the works of the flesh (see Galatians 5:19-21). Only new life in Christ equips the believer to walk in the Spirit (see Galatians 5:16-18, 24-25).

The presence of *chara* on the list, whether it's rendered as "joy" or "happiness," raises the question, What really makes me happy or joyful? If the Father and the Son make the Spirit happy, then the joy that's the fruit of the Spirit must be God centered and God originated.

It's easy to recite the fruit of the Spirit as if it's a list of virtues or a badge of honor. But *all* the qualities are ingredients of happiness. Not just joy, which *is* happiness, but the whole list.

The permanence of the Holy Spirit's indwelling in our lives allows us to continually access a supernatural happiness. To be robbed of the ability to rejoice or of the source of joy, a believer would have to be robbed of our happy God's indwelling.

WHEN WE LOVE AS GOD LOVES, WE FIND HAPPINESS IN WHAT MAKES GOD HAPPY.

First Corinthians 13, the "love chapter," links love to rejoicing in what's right and true (verse 6):

- [Love] does not *rejoice* at wrongdoing, but rejoices with the truth.
- Love is not *happy* with evil, but is happy with the truth. (GNT)

WITH AN ETERNAL PERSPECTIVE, WE CAN FIND REASONS TO REJOICE EVEN WHEN SUFFERING.

Hardship and reasons for sorrow don't have to keep us from experiencing happiness. Apparently contradictory emotions can coexist, and indeed they should in a world that is rich in God's goodness yet also remains under the Curse:

- We are treated . . . as sorrowful, yet always *rejoicing*; as poor, yet making many rich; as having nothing, yet possessing everything. (2 Corinthians 6:8, 10)
- . . . and we are always *happy*, even in times of suffering. . . . (verse 10, CEV)

Fanny Crosby (1820–1915) composed "To God Be the Glory," "Blessed Assurance," and more than eight thousand other gospel songs. She was one of the most prolific hymn writers in history, and many of her hymns are still sung today in churches of various denominations.

When she was six weeks old, Crosby was accidentally blinded by a doctor. At age eight, she wrote one of her first poems:

> *Oh, what a happy child I am,*
> *Although I cannot see!*
> *I am resolved that in this world,*
> *Contented I will be.*[6]

Her resolution to be content was more than mere words. She told her mother that if given the choice, she'd choose to remain blind so that upon death, the first face she'd see would be Christ's. (Like many Christ-followers with disabilities, she knew God sometimes chooses to heal in this life and sometimes he doesn't.)

The apostle Paul not only accepted God's sovereignty in physical disabilities but also embraced suffering for Christ's sake (Colossians 1:24).

- I *rejoice* in my sufferings for your sake, and in my flesh I am filling up what is lacking in Christ's afflictions for the sake of his body, that is, the church.
- I am *happy* in my sufferings for you. . . . (ERV)
- I am *glad* when I suffer for you in my body. . . . (NLT)

GOD LOVES TO SURPRISE US WITH HAPPINESS.

Earlier in this chapter we looked at Paul's happiness concerning Titus in 2 Corinthians 7:13. Several verses earlier, Paul said, "God, who encourages those who are discouraged, encouraged us by the arrival of Titus. His presence was a *joy*, but so was the news he brought of the encouragement he received from you. When he told us how much you long to see me, and how sorry you are for what happened, and how loyal you are to me, I was filled with *joy!*" (2 Corinthians 7:6-7, NLT).

The Good News Translation puts it this way: "It was not only his coming that *cheered* us. . . . He told us how much you want to see me, how sorry you are, how ready you are to defend me; and so I am even *happier* now" (verse 7).

Note that *chairo* at the end of verse 7, translated "joy" (NLT) and "happier" (GNT), is triggered by Titus's arrival. *Chairo* is clearly an emotional response of great gladness. While not all biblical joy—or happiness or gladness—comes out of favorable circumstances, many times in Scripture it does.

In verse 9, we read that Paul has been caused to *chairo* as a result of their repentance, another change in circumstances:

- I *rejoice*, not because you were grieved, but because you were grieved into repenting.
- I am *happy*, not because you were made sorry, but because your sorrow led you to repentance. (NIV)

OUR FRIENDS' FAVORABLE CIRCUMSTANCES BRING US JOY.

The world tells us that happiness comes from gratifying our own desires, but the Bible turns that idea upside down. Paul says in Philippians 2:17,

- I will *rejoice* even if I lose my life, pouring it out like a liquid offering to God, just like your faithful service is an offering to God. And I want all of you to share that *joy*. (NLT)
- . . . I will be *happy* and full of *joy* with all of you. (NCV)

C. S. Lewis said, "Affection is responsible for nine-tenths of whatever solid and durable happiness there is in our natural lives."[7]

Note the emotion in Paul's words:

I think it is necessary to send back to you Epaphroditus, my brother, co-worker and fellow soldier, who is also your messenger, whom you sent to take care of my needs. For he longs for all of you and is distressed because you heard he was ill. Indeed he was ill, and almost died. . . . Therefore I am all the more eager to send him, so that when you see him again you may be *glad* and I may have less anxiety. So then, welcome him in the Lord with *great joy*, and honor people like him, because he almost died for the work of Christ. PHILIPPIANS 2:25-30, NIV

The New Century Version translates verse 28, "I want very much to send him to you so that when you see him you can be *happy*, and I can stop worrying about you."

Though the Philippians were distressed when their dear friend Epaphroditus nearly died, they rejoiced in his deliverance and would rejoice to see him face to face. Positive life circumstances can prompt deep and emotional joy and happiness.

This is an important correction to the modern sentiment that being happy due to positive circumstances, including the welfare of loved ones, is somehow unspiritual. True, circumstances change and our happiness should be grounded on Christ, who doesn't change, but that doesn't make it inappropriate to rejoice in favorable circumstances.

GOD DOESN'T RECOMMEND THAT WE FIND JOY IN HIM; HE COMMANDS IT.

- Finally, my brothers, *rejoice* in the Lord. (Philippians 3:1)
- Whatever happens, my dear brothers and sisters, *rejoice* in the Lord. (NLT)
- So now, my Christian brothers, be *happy* because you belong to Christ. (NLV)
- Be glad in the Lord always! Again I say, be glad! (Philippians 4:4, CEB)
- Delight yourselves in God, yes, find your joy in him at all times. (PHILLIPS)

Does God mean it when he says "always"? Yes. The reasons for gladness in Christ are constant, like an ocean tide. The water doesn't remain in the same place, always lapping over our feet. But even at low tide, it's still there, poised to move in again.

Paul followed verse 4 with this encouragement: "The Lord is at hand," which itself is a reason to rejoice. God is with us, never abandons us, and will deliver us soon, whether by death or by his return.

THERE'S A VITAL CONNECTION BETWEEN *CHARA* (JOY) AND *CHARIS* (GRACE).

The word for God's unmerited favor demonstrated in Christ is *charis*, from the same Greek root as *chara*.

Theologian Karl Barth (1886–1968) argued that joy and grace are virtually inseparable: "To be joyful is to expect that life will reveal itself as God's gift of grace. . . . To be joyful means to look out for opportunities for gratitude."[8]

It's beyond the scope of this book to study *charis*, grace, but to do so would fall within the larger sphere of happiness. Grace is more than happiness—indeed, it is more than nearly everything—but there's no greater reason for our happiness than God's grace.

William Morrice writes, "Christianity is a message of joy from beginning to end."[9] Passages that use *chara* and *chairo* represent a small fraction of the many conveying biblical joy, but even on their own, they'd be enough to prove that the gospel is inherently a message of joy.

Paul closed a lengthy letter, and I'll close this chapter, with a statement worth acting on (2 Corinthians 13:11):

- Finally, brothers, *rejoice*.
- And that's about it, friends. *Be cheerful.* (MSG)
- Dear brothers and sisters, I close my letter with these last words: *Be joyful.* (NLT)

CHAPTER 29

THE BIBLE LEAVES NO ROOM FOR DOUBT: OUR HAPPINESS MATTERS TO GOD

⟨❧⟩

T HE PREVIOUS NINE chapters are devoted to biblical passages containing words for happiness and joy. Yet, remarkably, we've examined only the Hebrew words *asher* and *samach* and the Greek words *makarios* and *chara*. This is only a small sampling of the Bible's happiness-related words—about one-eighth of them. And of that fraction, we've seen only a portion of their occurrences! I chose the words and examples I considered most important, but there simply wasn't room to cite a majority of them.

If you desire to dig deeper, and I hope you will, you'll find further word studies at the back of this book: Appendix 1, "Nineteen More Happiness Words in the Old Testament," and Appendix 2, "Fourteen More Happiness Words in the New Testament."

Whether you wish to look at that content now or later, I recommend that you see for yourself how much more the Bible says about joy and gladness.

THE SHEER QUANTITY OF HAPPINESS PASSAGES TELLS US HOW IMPORTANT THIS SUBJECT IS TO GOD.

Reflecting back on his life without Christ, Augustine framed his conversion in terms of happiness: "How sweet all at once it was for me to be rid of those fruitless joys which I had once feared to lose! . . . You drove them from me, you who are the true, the sovereign joy. You drove them from me and took their place, you who are sweeter than all pleasure."[1]

The fact that there are so many different words for happiness throughout Scripture powerfully attests to this topic's significance. The more we understand that true, lasting joy and delight can only be found in God, the greater our motivation will be to seek and love him with all our hearts, souls, minds, and strength.

God's unmistakable desire, so repeatedly evident in his Word, is that we be happy in him.

THERE ARE A NUMBER OF OTHER WORDS INVOLVING HAPPINESS THAT AREN'T COVERED IN THIS BOOK.

Louw and Nida's lexicon of semantic domains specifies a large category of words under domain 25, "Attitudes and Emotions." Among the subdomains are words for desire and wanting; love and compassion; hope and anticipation; contentment and satisfaction, being pleased with, thankful, and grateful; enjoying and taking pleasure in; being fond of; laughing; encouraging and consoling; and patience.

If we had unlimited space, we could easily study a thousand passages using these words, with great benefit and relevance to our subject.

Here are just three examples:

- *korennumi*: to be happy or content with what one has, with the implication of its being abundant—"to be content, to be satisfied"[2]
- *arkeomai*: to be happy or content as the result of having what one desires or needs—"to be content, to be satisfied"[3]
- *autarkes*: pertaining to being happy or content with what one has[4]

MANY PASSAGES THAT DON'T MENTION HAPPINESS CALL US TO BELIEFS AND ACTIONS THAT RESULT IN IT.

The Bible teems with commands that don't contain happiness words but which, when we obey them, bring happiness.

For instance, God calls us to contentment: "Godliness with contentment is great gain" (1 Timothy 6:6) and "Be content with what you have" (Hebrews 13:5). Contentment means being happy with what we have. Hence, every biblical reference to contentment is a reference to happiness.

Or consider the many biblical references to peace, including these:

- Seek peace and pursue it. (Psalm 34:14)
- Come to me, all you who are weary and burdened, and I will give you rest. (Matthew 11:28, NIV)
- Peace I leave with you; my peace I give you. I do not give to you as the world gives. Do not let your hearts be troubled and do not be afraid. (John 14:27, NIV)
- Do not be anxious about anything. . . . And the peace of God, which transcends all understanding, will guard your hearts and your minds in Christ Jesus. (Philippians 4:6-7, NIV)

When the Bible says, "Don't be afraid," "Don't worry," "Give thanks always," and "I am with you always," God is saying to us, "Be happy." And when Jesus said to his disciples, "Do not let your hearts be troubled," wasn't he saying, "Don't be unhappy"? (And wasn't he also implying that we have a choice as to whether to let our hearts be troubled and unhappy?)

Contemplate these words: "The LORD make his face to shine upon you and be gracious to you; the LORD lift up his countenance upon you and give you peace" (Numbers 6:25-26). Isn't this a call for God to endow his people with happiness?

Jonathan Edwards wrote, "*Peace* . . . as it is used in the Scriptures, signifies happiness; and includes all comfort, joy, and pleasure."[5] Peace is inextricably tied to happiness.

So when someone says, as many have, "Happiness isn't in the Bible," it's not even slightly true. Even in versions that don't frequently use the words *happy* and *happiness*, the concept is conspicuously present, not only in its many synonyms, but in words such as *contentment, peace, delight,* and dozens of others in every translation.

Consider this verse: "Who is a God like you, pardoning iniquity and passing over transgression for the remnant of his inheritance? He does not retain his anger forever, because he delights in steadfast love" (Micah 7:18). Such a passage may not seem to be about happiness, yet if we understand its meaning, won't we be flooded with happiness?

"Oh sing to the LORD a new song, for he has done marvelous things! His right hand and his holy arm have worked salvation for him. The LORD has made known his salvation" (Psalm 98:1-2). There are no joy-related words in this verse, yet doesn't it make you joyful?

Consider the lame man who leaped and praised God (see Acts 3:1-10). His story won't appear in a study of words related to happiness, but he was obviously overwhelmed with happiness.

"We have an advocate with the Father, Jesus Christ the righteous" (1 John 2:1). No word for happiness is mentioned here, but how does it make you feel to know that Jesus is your advocate, your defense attorney? Can you imagine Jesus standing between you and your accuser, Satan (see Revelation 12:10)? The thought makes me smile, rejoice, and praise God.

Every passage that mentions our redemption; our new nature in Christ; and God's love, grace, and mercy also makes a profound statement about our grounds for happiness.

What about eternal life? Puritan David Clarkson wrote, "Eternal life and happiness are reciprocal, and used as convertible terms in Scripture."[6]

Revelation 7:16-17 offers a description of the eternal Heaven on the New Earth. It doesn't mention any of the synonyms for joy and happiness. Yet happiness is exactly what it communicates:

> They shall hunger no more, neither thirst anymore; the sun shall not strike them, nor any scorching heat. For the Lamb in the midst of the throne will be their shepherd, and he will guide them to springs of living water, and God will wipe away every tear from their eyes.

When the Bible says that God is for us and that nothing shall separate us from Christ's love (see Romans 8:31, 39), no words for happiness are used, but the reasons for it jump off the page.

Even in the darkest portions of Scripture, such as Job or Lamentations, we're hard pressed to find any chapter that doesn't offer reasons for happiness.

Love, peace, contentment, kindness, grace, mercy, comfort, singing, praise, worship, favor, prosperity, deliverance, rescue, salvation, thanksgiving, satisfaction, chosen, redemption, gospel, trust, goodness, beauty, wonder, awe, excellence, and hope: don't all these words evoke happiness? If we added these to the happiness words described in this book and the appendices, they would more than quadruple the number of verses included, swelling the total to more than eight thousand.

If we grasp how happiness-saturated Scripture is, it will radically affect our perspective as God's children and greatly expand our outreach to the world. Whatever else the plan of God and the gospel of Jesus encompasses, without question it includes our happiness.

PART 4

Understanding and Experiencing Happiness in God

CHAPTER 30

THE EMOTIONAL SATISFACTION IN HAPPINESS AND JOY

Let all those who seek You rejoice and be glad in You; and let those who love Your salvation say continually, "Let God be magnified!"

PSALM 70:4, NKJV

Living for others is really the Christ life after all. Oh, the satisfaction, happiness and joy one gets out of it.

GEORGE WASHINGTON CARVER

NOW THAT WE'VE examined God's revelation of happiness throughout Scripture, we can complete the discussion about why the words *happiness* and *joy* are virtually interchangeable.

Over the course of two years, I examined, in a variety of translations, every passage of Scripture that uses the English words *happiness* and *joy*, as well as all their synonyms. Joni Eareckson Tada's words correspond perfectly to what I discovered in my research:

The terms [joy and happiness] are synonymous in their effect and too difficult to distinguish when we experience either one. Would you, for example, respond to the wedding of your daughter with joy or with happiness? . . .

To rob joy of its elated twin, happiness, is to deprive our soul of God's feast. Seek both as part and parcel in all circumstances. When your soul is stirred by a deep contentment, be happy. When a delightful moment strikes that is quite outside yourself, be joyful. Don't think about which one you are supposed to feel. Accept them both as a gift from a God who is rich in all such emotions.[1]

It's needless, distracting, and misleading to make fine distinctions between joy, happiness, gladness, merriment, and delight. They all speak of a heart experiencing the goodness of God and his countless gifts.

WHY ARE MANY CHRISTIANS TODAY DETERMINED TO DISCREDIT HAPPINESS?

After you finish this book, you'll continue to encounter numerous books, articles, and sermons telling you that joy is spiritual and happiness is secular,[2] that happiness is an emotion dependent on circumstances,[3] that joy is not an emotion but a choice,[4] that joy is the opposite of happiness,[5] and that happiness is fleeting and temporal while joy is eternal.[6] You'll see articles and sermons with titles such as "Happiness Is Not Joy"[7] and "Happiness Is the Enemy of Joy."[8] And despite hundreds of biblical statements to the contrary, you'll hear, "There is absolutely nothing in the Bible that says that God wants you to be happy."[9]

An e-mail I received from a Christian leader said, "In Scripture we find that God is not about the pursuit of happiness. . . . What, then, of the widespread ambition to be happy? Is it, perhaps, an ultimate idol meant by God's Enemy to distract us from joy?"

So what's our problem with happiness? Does it stem from the anti-world Christoplatonism we discussed in chapter 7? Are we suspicious that someone who is happy must be sinning? If so, what does that say about our worldview?

William Shakespeare wrote, "And this our life . . . finds tongues in trees, books in the running brooks, sermons in stones, and good in every thing."[10] Do we happily listen to the trees, read the brooks, hear the stones preach, and see good all around us in this world God made? Why would we ignore such calls to happiness or think them unworthy of him?

Perhaps we marginalize happiness because something inside us testifies that we—who were snatched from the jaws of Hell to Heaven's eternal delights, who are indwelt and empowered by a happy God—should be happier than we are. Maybe by defining joy as unemotional, positional, or transcendental, we can justify our unhappiness, in spite of God's command to rejoice always in him. Maybe saying that joy isn't happiness allows us to lower the bar and accept a downtrodden, cheerless Christian life.

In light of the hundreds of verses in part 3 and the appendices, we need to abandon the idea that we can't be happy in a sin-stained culture and that it's unspiritual to be cheerful in a hurting world. God's Word says otherwise.

Do we really wish to distance the gospel and church from happiness? If we succeed, we'll distance them from the world, too, for the world will go right on wanting happiness.

Christians shouldn't abandon happiness—we should *embrace* happiness, the true happiness Scripture freely offers through God's persistent and everlasting love.

THERE'S TRUE AND FALSE JOY, JUST AS THERE'S TRUE AND FALSE HAPPINESS.

Isaac Watts (1674–1748), who wrote "Joy to the World," spoke of "carnal joys."[11] Joy can be spiritual or unspiritual, as can happiness. Charles Spurgeon recognized the difference between false and true joy:

> Christ would not have us rejoice with the false joy of presumption, so He bares the sharp knife and cuts that joy away. Joy on a false basis would prevent us from

having true joy, and therefore, . . . the joy we may get may be worth having—not the mere surf and foam of a wave that is driven with the wind and tossed, but the solid foundation of the Rock of Ages![12]

Someone can have Christ-centered happiness or Christ-denying happiness. The former will last forever; the latter has an exceedingly short shelf life.

Notice A. W. Tozer's negative use of *joy* and positive use of *happiness* more than sixty years ago: "Human beings are busy trying to work up a joy of some sort. They try it in dance halls, . . . they turn to television programs. But we still don't see the truly happy faces."[13]

Tozer realized that artificial attempts at creating joy can't create the happiness that only comes from Christ.

When God calls us to rejoice in him, does he care only about what we think and do, not how we *feel* about him? No. He commands us to love him not just with all our minds but all our *hearts* (see Matthew 22:37). God rebukes people for serving him joylessly (see Deuteronomy 28:47). Yes, it's possible to obey and serve God without feeling joy. But God emphatically says he *wants* us to feel joy! Feelings are not the entirety of joy, but since God's joy involves his emotions, shouldn't our joy involve ours?

The psalmist said, "I will go to the altar of God, to God my exceeding joy, and I will praise you with the lyre, O God, my God" (Psalm 43:4). Can you imagine saying to someone, "You are my exceeding joy," without feeling strong emotion?

Mike Mason writes,

> When I'm joyful, I'm happy, and when I'm happy, I'm joyful. What could be plainer? Why should I want anything to do with a joy that isn't coupled with happiness, or with a kind of happiness that is without joy? Happiness without joy is shallow and transient because it's based on outward circumstances rather than an attitude of the heart. As for joy without happiness, it's a spiritualized lie. The Bible does not separate joy and happiness and neither should we.[14]

THE PURITANS USED *JOY* AND *HAPPINESS* INTERCHANGEABLY.

Richard Sibbes wrote, "We do all for joy. . . . It is the centre of the soul. . . . Heaven itself is termed by the name of joy, happiness itself."[15]

Jonathan Edwards frequently used the words *joy* and *happiness*—sometimes in the same sentence. In the compiled works of Jonathan Edwards, the words *happiness* or *happy* appear in 309 sermons or articles—a total of 3,722 times. The words *joy*, *joyful*, and *enjoy* appear almost as frequently.

Edwards cited Jesus' words in John 15:11 (KJV)—"that my joy might remain in you"— and 17:13 (KJV)—"that they might have my joy fulfilled in themselves"—to prove that "the happiness Christ gives to his people, is a participation of his own happiness."[16]

Edwards wrote of "the joy and happiness that the church shall have in her true bridegroom."[17] The nouns are synonyms, as are the adjectives: "these joyful happy persons shall be as the stones of a crown lifted up."[18] Edwards used *joyful* and *happy*, as well as *glad*, to reinforce one another, saying, "The work of God promised to be affected, is plainly an accomplishment of the joy, gladness, and happiness of God's people."[19] Edwards obviously didn't share the modern evangelical misperception that joy is spiritual and deep while happiness is secular and shallow.

In *Paradise Lost*, John Milton (1608–1674) referred to "our two first Parents" living in a "happie Garden," with its "uninterrupted joy" and "blissful solitude," with "happie hours in joy and hymning spent."[20] To Milton, happiness, joy, and bliss were synonymous.

Richard Baxter said, "The day of death is to true believers a day of happiness and joy."[21]

William Law said believers should never lack "the happiness of a lively faith, a joyful hope, and well-grounded trust in God."[22]

Law wrote, "What gross nonsense and stupidity is it, to give the name of joy or happiness to any thing but that which carries us to this joy and happiness in God?"[23]

Thomas Doolittle (1632–1707) said, "We take not so much heed, nor are we so full of care, about these visible, transitory things, as we are of the eternal joys of heaven, and the unseen happiness of the saints above."[24] If he'd exchanged the words *joys* and *happiness*, his statement would have had exactly the same meaning.

Thomas Woodcock (1888–1918) stated, "We shall come within the verge of God's own happiness, when we shall 'enter into our Master's joy' (Matt. 25:21), when we shall joy more in his happiness than in our own."[25]

Thomas Vincent (1634–1678) wrote of the apostle John, "He seems to be in an ecstasy of joy at the greatness of this privilege [being called God's son], and the happiness of such as had attained it."[26]

Thomas Ridgley (1667–1734) spoke of the Mount of Transfiguration as "a glorious scene of joy and happiness."[27]

Proving that not all Puritan preachers were named Thomas, Henry Wilkinson (1610–1675) said of God's people, "Whatever title they have to a future happiness, whatever hopes of it, whatever rest and peace and joy they expect in it, they owe all to Christ."[28]

Stephen Charnock wrote, "Upon every fresh discovery, new joys disclose themselves. The search after God is a greater happiness than the fruition of anything in the world can be.[29] . . . The happiness of heaven could not be eternal, nor the joy pure, that is mixed with those fears of falling and losing it."[30] Clearly he wouldn't use these words in parallel fashion if he regarded happiness as inferior to joy.

Richard Sibbes wrote, "We may joy in afflictions, because there is a blessing in the worst things, to further our eternal happiness."[31] Sibbes also said pastors are to be "helpers of [church people's] joy." He said that happiness is termed in the Scripture "joy" and that "joy is a principal part of happiness."[32]

English evangelical Charles Simeon wrote of the believer who dies: "Now, to his unutterable joy, he hears his Saviour say to him, 'Well done, good and faithful servant; enter thou into the joy of thy Lord.' Now, then, his utmost desires are all satisfied; and he is completely happy in the bosom of his God."[33]

Thomas Jefferson was no Puritan, but like all educated people of his time, he lived in a world filled with Puritan influence. When Jefferson wrote the Declaration of Independence, he included these now-famous words: "We hold these truths to be self-evident, that all men are created equal, that they are endowed by their Creator with certain unalienable Rights, that among these are Life, Liberty and the pursuit of Happiness." He borrowed from the preamble to Virginia's constitution, which spoke of "the enjoyment of life and liberty."

THE WESLEYS SAW COMPLETE HARMONY BETWEEN HAPPINESS AND JOY.

Six dozen of John Wesley's sermons refer to happiness, and some are dedicated entirely to it. His contemporaries Samuel Johnson (1709–1784) and Alexander Pope (1688–1744) wrote about happiness, as did many other educated people of that day. Wesley spoke of happiness not only because the Bible does but also because his audiences were intensely interested.

Wesley often told his listeners that God is the sole source of happiness. He wrote, "It is impossible, in the nature of things, that wickedness can consist [coexist] with happiness."[34]

Contemporary theologian Fred Sanders writes, "Wesley would never have distinguished between a shallow, merely emotional happiness on the one hand and a deep, settled joy on the other, because the word happiness did not connote frivolity or shallowness to him. Happy is a good word in his vocabulary, and he uses it freely, interchangeably with the word joy."[35]

Wesley wrote, "When we first know Christ . . . then it is that happiness begins; happiness real, solid, substantial."[36] He said, "None but a Christian is happy; none but a real inward Christian. A glutton, a drunkard, a gamester, may be *merry*; but he cannot be happy. The beau, the belle, may eat and drink, and rise up to play; but still they feel they are not happy. . . .They may hasten from one diversion to another: but happiness is not there."[37]

We might have expected Wesley to say, "None but a Christian is joyful" or "A drunkard may be happy, but not joyful." But he didn't, because there's no essential difference. Wesley didn't deny the value of physical pleasures, but he knew that God's children "need none of these things to make them happy; for they have a spring of happiness within. They see and love God."[38]

Wesley said, "Every Christian is happy; . . . he who is not happy is not a Christian."[39] He wasn't saying that a Christian is never sad or never faces great hardships. He was saying that part of being a Christian is experiencing the underlying and overarching happiness in Christ that goes beyond circumstances.

John Wesley wrote in his journal that a truly converted person "knows there can be no happiness on earth, but in the enjoyment of God, and in the foretaste of those 'rivers of pleasure which flow at his right hand for evermore.'"[40]

Charles Wesley (1707–1788), John's brother, was one of history's greatest hymn writers. Consider the opening lines from several of his hymns:

Happy soul, that free from harms,
Rests within the Shepherd's arms![41]

Happy the souls to Jesus joined,
And saved by grace alone.[42]

Happy the man that finds the grace,
The blessing of God's chosen race.[43]

The latter hymn goes on to speak repeatedly of being happy, and stanza 5 reads:

To purest joys she [Wisdom] all invites,
Chaste, holy, spiritual delights.[44]

Charles Wesley didn't change the subject when he used *joy* instead of *happiness.*

CHARLES SPURGEON ROUTINELY INTERMIXED THE WORDS *HAPPINESS* AND *JOY.*

A hundred years after the Wesleys called all believers to happiness, Charles Spurgeon did likewise, saying, "A happy Christian attracts others by his joy."[45] He used *happiness* or *happy* more than 23,000 times in his sermons.

Spurgeon said, "Where is the joy and happiness of the gospel?"[46] He was asking one question, not two. Here are some quotations from sermons he preached:

- Let us come to His Table, happy and joyful, through Jesus Christ our Lord.[47]
- The God of salvation, the God of the Covenant, is to be worshipped with joy! He is the happy God and He loves happy worshippers.[48]
- I commend to you who are happy, to you who are full of joy, this blessed method of securing to yourselves a continuance of that happiness.[49]
- A child of light is one who, by God's Grace, is *bright, happy, restful, full of joy.*[50]

Pastor Spurgeon declared, "Joy is a delightful thing. You cannot be too happy, Brothers and Sisters! No, do not suspect yourself of being wrong because you are full of delight. . . . Provided that it is joy in the Lord, you cannot have too much of it!"[51]

Spurgeon gave that single qualification—"in the Lord"—when it comes to our joy or happiness. Happiness to Spurgeon was biblical and God honoring, not suspect or second class.

JOY AND HAPPINESS WERE USED BROADLY AS SYNONYMS IN THE NINETEENTH AND TWENTIETH CENTURIES.

Anglican bishop J. C. Ryle said,

To be truly happy *a man must have sources of gladness which are not dependent on anything in this world.* . . . The man whose happiness depends entirely on things here below, is like him who builds his house on sand, or leans his weight on a reed. Tell me not of your happiness, if it daily hangs on the uncertainties of earth. . . . Your rivers of pleasure may any day be dried up. Your joy may be deep and earnest, but it is fearfully short-lived. It has no root. It is not true happiness.[52]

Notice how Ryle contrasted short-lived "joy" with "true happiness." Consider his reference to "happy feelings"—something often dismissed today as unspiritual. He spoke of these feelings as utterly compatible with joy: "Above all, Christ can give us peace of conscience, inward joy, bright hopes, and happy feelings."[53]

Ryle said what we all need to understand: "To be truly happy your joy must be founded on something more than this world can give you."[54]

The Christian's Secret of a Happy Life was published in 1875, during an era when Christians gladly embraced the term "happy." It became the most widely read devotional of its time.

Prior to the mid-twentieth century, nearly all commentators equated the biblical passages referring to joy with happiness. For instance, theologian and commentator Charles Hodge (1797–1878) wrote of Paul, "He was assured that if he was happy, [the Corinthians] would share in his joy (verses 1-4)."[55]

Alfred Plummer (1841–1926) explained the joy of 1 John 1:4 as "that serene happiness, which is the result of conscious union with God."[56]

A. W. Pink wrote, "The devil cannot bear to see one of Christ's people *happy*, so he tries constantly to disturb their *joy*" (italics mine).[57]

Martyn Lloyd-Jones said, "There had been nothing . . . more characteristic of all the great revivals in the history of the church than this desire on the part of God's people to give expression to the joy, the happiness, the peace which they have experienced."[58]

A. W. Tozer sometimes contrasted happiness and joy and seemed critical of happiness. Yet other times he recognized that there is God-centered joy and self-centered joy, godly happiness and ungodly happiness. Tozer said of the disciples after Pentecost, "The joy and happiness of these disciples was now the joy and blessing and delight of the Holy Spirit."[59]

Various choruses popular in the 1960s use *happiness* and *joy* as synonyms. For example, "Happiness Is to Know the Savior" (1968) includes the lyrics, "Real joy is mine."[60]

Some associate the modern evangelical suspicion about happiness with the fundamentalist movement. Yet in 1971, elderly fundamentalist John R. Rice wrote: "It is a sin for Christians not to be happy, not to be joyful."[61] Rice said, "The Christian whose roots are deep in God's Word . . . like a tree planted by the rivers of water, will have leaves that do not wither! Surely this means a happy, happy Christian life. Christians ought to win souls, but Christians ought also to be happy, joyful, sweet-tempered."[62]

DELIGHT, LOVE, JOY, AND HAPPINESS ARE INSEPARABLY LINKED.

Scripture connects love with delight, which surely involves emotion. "I will delight myself in Your commandments, which I love" (Psalm 119:47, AMP).

Similarly, rejoicing and love are often intertwined:

- Let all those who seek You rejoice and be glad in You; let such as love Your salvation say continually, "The LORD be magnified!" (Psalm 40:16, NKJV)
- He will show how much he loves you and how happy he is with you. He will laugh and be happy about you. (Zephaniah 3:17, ERV)

Such passages refute the false dichotomy that it's more important to love God than to be happy in God. To enjoy God—to be happy in God—*is* to love God.

Reducing joy to an unemotional, otherworldly state of being strips it of the delight that God and the writers of Scripture intended.

Throughout the 1987 movie *The Princess Bride*, the Sicilian mastermind Vizzini repeatedly uses the word *inconceivable* to describe event after event that actually happens. Finally, Inigo Montoya tells Vizzini, "You keep using that word. I do not think it means what you think it means."

His statement also applies to that frequently used but terribly misunderstood word *joy*. It doesn't mean what many people think and say it means: something unemotional. It means something far richer and better: delight, pleasure, and emotional satisfaction. It means *happiness*.

GOD'S COMMON GRACE OFFERS UNBELIEVERS A TASTE OF HIS HAPPINESS AND JOY.

Psalm 145:9 says, "The Lord is good to everyone and everything; God's compassion extends, to all his handiwork!" (CEB).

Speaking to unbelievers, Paul said of God, "He did not leave Himself without a witness, since He did what is good by giving you rain from heaven and fruitful seasons and satisfying your hearts with food and happiness [*euphrosune*, see appendix 2]" (Acts 14:17, HCSB). Eight translations render this Greek word "happiness," fourteen others use "joy," and more than twenty others say "gladness." All the terms are applicable to believers and unbelievers alike. Paul was building a bridge to the gospel through identifying God as the universal source of happiness.

However, there's a significant difference between the happiness of believers and unbelievers. First, the happiness of the unconverted is limited to the present. King David spoke of people whose reward is in this life (see Psalm 17:14). Abraham spoke to the rich man in Hell, saying, "Remember that in your lifetime you received your good things" (Luke 16:25, NET).

Second, the happiness of this life enjoyed by the unconverted is largely dependent on favorable circumstances (see Psalm 73:18-19; Matthew 19:22).

David Murray identifies six kinds of happiness available to unbelievers and believers alike:

- nature happiness
- social happiness
- vocational happiness
- physical happiness
- intellectual happiness
- humor happiness

The one remaining component, available only to believers, is spiritual happiness. Murray calls it "a joy that at times contains more pleasure and delight than the other six put together."[63]

Spiritual happiness comes in contemplating God and drawing close to him. Of course, the other six aren't "unspiritual" forms of happiness. Because they're God given, they're spiritual, though not redemptive.

But without the seventh kind of happiness, the first six are temporary. A reconciled relationship with God, in concert with an understanding of the biblical teaching of a resurrected Heaven and Earth, assures us that all happiness will be ours forever.

Jesus experienced all forms of happiness, and so can we. With an eternal perspective, only the righteous enjoy *true* happiness (see Psalm 16:11; 21:6; 36:7-10; 37:16; 43:4; 73:28; John 10:10). The forever that awaits us should color our lives now. We should daily backload eternity's joys into our present experience.

Spurgeon said it well:

Are there not periods of life when we feel so glad that we would fain dance for joy? Let not such exhilaration be spent upon common themes, but let the name of God stir us to ecstasy. . . . There is enough in our holy faith to create and to justify the utmost degree of rapturous delight. If men are dull in the worship of the Lord our God they are not acting consistently with the character of their religion.[64]

CHAPTER 31

HAPPINESS IS OUR CHOICE

I concluded there is nothing better than to be happy and enjoy ourselves as long as we can.

ECCLESIASTES 3:12, NLT

There is no automatic joy. Christ is not a happiness capsule; he is the way to the Father. But the way to the Father is not a carnival ride in which we sit and do nothing while we are whisked through various spiritual sensations.

CALVIN MILLER

ONCE UPON A time, a widow had two sons who provided for her. One sold umbrellas; the other, fans. Every morning the mother checked the weather. Sunshine brought her misery, because no umbrellas would sell. Rain brought her misery, because no fans would sell. Both conditions caused her to fret.

One day her friend remarked, "If the sun is shining, people buy fans. If it rains, they buy umbrellas. Change your attitude; be happy!"

It's a simple story, but it illustrates a potentially life-changing reality. Our happiness is dependent not on circumstances but on perspective. The Greek philosopher Epictetus said, "Men are disturbed not by the things which happen, but by the opinions about the things."[1]

PERSPECTIVE IS DETERMINED BY OUR FOCUS.

Helen Keller (1880–1968) wrote, "When one door of happiness closes, another opens; but often we look so long at the closed door that we do not see the one which has been opened for us."[2] At nineteen months old, Helen Keller contracted an illness that left her deaf and blind. Alexander Graham Bell, who worked with deaf children, advised her parents to contact Boston's Perkins Institute for the Blind, and as a result, former student Anne Sullivan became Keller's instructor. Keller walked through the open door of training with her teacher and eventually began to learn at an astonishing rate. Everything hinged on her attitude and perspective. She looked for open doors instead of obsessing about closed ones.

David Brainerd (1718–1747) served as a missionary to the Delaware Indians of New Jersey. He was orphaned at fourteen, and in college he suffered from debilitating tuberculosis. Having endured great suffering while serving in a fruitful ministry, he died at age twenty-nine. His biography inspired many, including pioneer missionary William Carey, as well as missionary martyr Jim Elliot. During Brainerd's final illness, he was nursed by Jonathan Edwards's daughter Jerusha, who may have contracted tuberculosis from him and who died four months after he did. Depressing story, right? But in fact, the story involved much happiness.

Understandably, Brainerd's diary frequently references his pain, using the word 78 times and *suffer* or *suffering* 30 times. Yet the most striking thing about his writing is how many more references he makes to his happiness in God and others: he uses *happy* and *happiness* 60 times, *delight* 50 times, *pleased* and *pleasure* 177 times, *joy* and *enjoy* 350 times. He also uses *blessed* more than 200 times, often meaning "happy."

Though his life was not typical, like all of us Brainerd experienced both sorrow and joy: "This morning the Lord was pleased to lift up the light of His countenance upon me. . . . Though I have been so depressed of late, respecting my hopes of future serviceableness in the cause of God, yet now I had much encouragement. . . . I felt exceedingly calm and quite resigned to God, respecting my future employment. . . . My faith lifted me above the world and removed all those mountains that I could not look over."[3]

On his twenty-fourth birthday, racked with pain, Brainerd wrote, "This has been a sweet, a happy day to me."[4]

Honesty about his illness and periodic depression demonstrated Brainerd's sincerity about his happiness. He wrote, "It appeared such a happiness to have God for my portion that I had rather be any other creature in this lower creation than not come to the enjoyment of God. . . . Lord, endear Thyself more to me!"[5]

Brainerd spoke of "the absolute dependence of a creature upon God the Creator, for every crumb of happiness it enjoys."[6] He said of God, "He is the supreme good, the only soul-satisfying happiness."[7]

One painful day he "found some relief in prayer; loved, as a feeble, afflicted, despised creature, to cast myself on a God of infinite grace and goodness, hoping for no happiness but from Him. . . . Toward night, I felt my soul rejoice that God is unchangeably happy and glorious."[8]

A terribly sick young man was able to rejoice that God is happy—always has been and always will be! How many Christians today, in times of suffering, take such solace in the happiness of God?

Brainerd made the daily choice to meditate on God, see him all around, listen to his Word and God's people, and behold him in his creation. He looked for happiness in God. He wrote, "If you hope for happiness *in* the world, hope for it from God, and not *from* the world."[9]

If a young man devoid of modern medicine and dying of an excruciating disease could make choices that brought him happiness in Christ, surely we can too.

GOD GRANTS SUPERNATURAL RESOURCES TO TRANSFORM OUR HEARTS AND MINDS WITH HAPPINESS.

Peter said of Jesus, "His divine power has granted to us all things that pertain to life and godliness, through the knowledge of him who called us to his own glory and excellence, by which he has granted to us his precious and very great promises, so that through them you may become partakers of the divine nature" (2 Peter 1:3-4).

What do God's children lack in order to live godly, happy lives? Absolutely nothing. All we need has already been granted to us—not only life and godliness but also "his precious and very great promises," which enable us, through his Holy Spirit, to access God's own nature, including his happiness.

If you believe in the God of the Bible, if you've placed your faith in Jesus Christ as your Redeemer, then the following things are true:

- The price for your happiness has been paid.
- The basis for your happiness is secure.
- The resources for your happiness are provided daily.
- The assurance of your eternal happiness is absolute, providing an objective reason for your happiness today.

To better know, follow, worship, and love Christ *produces happiness in Christ.* We can't skip these steps in order to get to happiness. It doesn't work that way. We must choose to meditate and build daily upon the foundations of our happiness, not wait for happiness to magically arrive.

Many of us divide our lives between (1) obeying and following Christ and (2) finding happiness by reading, listening to music, watching a ball game, or having fun with friends. But life isn't divided into the sacred and the secular. It all belongs to God. We find happiness as we do the things he has graciously provided for us to do.

WE CONSTANTLY CHOOSE WHETHER WE'LL THINK AND ACT IN WAYS THAT MAKE US HAPPY.

Psychologist Henry Cloud writes, "Just like your body needs certain nutrients to make it healthy, your heart, mind, and soul need certain practices to make them happy."[10]

Happiness researchers have found that circumstances can contribute about 10 percent to our happiness—a remarkably small percentage. Next comes our internal makeup, including genetic factors and temperament, which can account for 50 percent of our happiness level.[11] The final 40 percent is entirely within our control: our choices, behaviors, and thoughts.[12] Yes, we *can* control our thoughts. They're not foreign invaders against which we have no defense. Those who believe they can't help the way they think and feel are simply wrong.

Why are some people happier than those in far better circumstances? The answer is *perspective.*

We're commanded in Scripture, "Do not be conformed to this world, but be transformed by the renewal of your mind" (Romans 12:2). This change in thinking is our responsibility.

Our thought life is a choice. Martin Luther is credited with saying, "You can't stop the birds from flying over your head, but you can keep them from making a nest in your hair." What we choose to think about leads us either toward or away from Christ, and therefore toward or away from happiness in Christ.

None of the three sets of factors identified by happiness researchers takes into account the power of God's Word and the transforming work of the Holy Spirit indwelling God's children. God is sovereign over circumstances, genetics, background, and temperaments. So even the 60 percent of happiness factors we can't change are used by God to accomplish his purpose. And the 40 percent under our control are subject to the Holy Spirit's influence.

Sometimes small, easy choices bring happiness—flipping through a photo album, riding a horse, reading an inspirational book, baking cookies, or going out for dinner. Today I played about a dozen popular songs Nanci and I grew up with, and we were both smiling for an hour.

Sometimes life involves such sadness and stress that we must go through multiple steps and the passing of time before joy can emerge. David began a psalm with these words: "Be gracious to me, O LORD, for I am languishing; heal me, O LORD, for my bones are troubled. . . . I am weary with my moaning; every night I flood my bed with tears" (Psalm 6:2-3, 6). Near the end of the psalm, he says, "The LORD has heard the sound of my weeping. The LORD has heard my plea; the LORD accepts my prayer" (verses 8-9). This realization lays the groundwork for moving David toward the kind of powerful joy that is so evident in other psalms.

TO BECOME HAPPY, WE MUST DO WHAT HAPPY PEOPLE DO.

Both modern research and Scripture put the ball in our court. Happy people give generously, serve others, and seek to make others happy. Happiness doesn't precede giving and serving; it *accompanies* and *follows* it. Those who sit around waiting to be happy shouldn't hold their breath—it will likely be a long wait!

The studies are unequivocal. A 2010 survey of 4,500 American adults revealed that of Americans who volunteered an average of one hundred hours a year, 68 percent reported that volunteering made them feel physically healthier, 73 percent said it "lowered my stress levels," and 89 percent reported that it "has improved my sense of well-being."[13]

Arthur Brooks says, "Research has proven that if you want to be happy . . . serve others. People who volunteer and give become happier as a result, because the key to happiness is to labor for the happiness of others. . . . Those who feel happy are also more productive, effective and successful."[14]

This idea that happiness requires action isn't controversial. Research corresponds perfectly with Scripture. Speaking of our spiritual gifts, Paul said, "Let us use them. . . . The one who does acts of mercy, with cheerfulness" (Romans 12:6, 8). We're not just told to be cheerful but to use our gifts to foster cheerfulness.

As a young pastor, I led our church's counseling ministry. I said to a number of married couples, "You meet with me and then have the illusion that you did something to help your marriage—but coming here means nothing unless you actually make the changes we talk about." When it comes to happiness, the same principle applies: speaking about it doesn't make it happen.

I've heard people talk about their hopes or plans to *one day* read the Bible regularly, give generously, volunteer for children's ministry, or go on a mission trip. God's gift of happiness isn't based on what we'd like to do or hope to do or even plan to do—only on what we actually do.

Simply recognizing that happiness comes from knowing, loving, and serving God isn't enough. Open God's Word; go to the Bible study; join a church; volunteer at a homeless shelter; write a check to support Bible translation for unreached people groups. If we want new and better results when it comes to our happiness, we must *act*!

In 2009, researchers from the University of Rochester conducted a study tracking the success of 147 recent graduates in reaching their stated goals after graduation. Some had "intrinsic" goals, such as deep, enduring relationships. Others had "extrinsic" goals, such as achieving reputation or fame. The scholars found that intrinsic goals were associated with happier lives. But the people who pursued extrinsic goals experienced more negative emotions, such as shame and fear. They even suffered more physical maladies.[15]

It's no oversimplification to say the solution to our problems is Jesus. Of course, trusting Jesus, studying God's Word, and working alongside God's people isn't simple in the sense of being *easy*. But it's simple in the sense that it lies within our power to make daily choices that further those ends.

The practical experience of happiness requires our sustained effort. When Nanci and I bought our house, it didn't become ours in any meaningful sense until we took possession. Likewise, our happiness was bought and paid for by Christ. But until we actually take hold of it, it's not really ours.

GOD'S SOVEREIGNTY AND OUR ABILITY TO CHOOSE HAPPINESS ARE COMPLETELY COMPATIBLE.

On the one hand, God provides everything we need to be happy. On the other hand, he leaves it to us to take hold of his provisions, adopt a broader perspective, and make the choices that result in happiness.

Scripture repeatedly shows that when we come to Christ, we are no longer in bondage to sin (see Romans 6:18). Yes, we still can and do sin, but in any given moment we don't have to—we have a new nature in Christ and the enablement of the Spirit (see 2 Corinthians 5:17). However, God doesn't force us to obey him; he gives us a choice.

Consider Philippians 2:12-13: "Work out your own salvation with fear and trembling [our actions], for it is God who works in you [God's actions], both to will and to work for his good pleasure [God's actions]." We don't have to choose between God's sovereignty and human will; this passage teaches participation by both parties.

This partnership occurs when two beings genuinely work together, without any implication of equality in intellect, authority, or resolve. (Any partnership between the infinite Creator God and finite, fallen human beings is obviously unequal!)

Human choice is real and meaningful, yet that doesn't mean God is "hands off"—he still has the power to transform the human will. So God empowers us through his Spirit to believe in him and obey him. He calls upon us to genuinely cooperate with him, which requires effort and discipline on our part, yet we do so by drawing on his strength and grace.

God doesn't "make us happy" in the sense of forcing us to make choices that produce happiness. As all great teachers do, God gives us the resources we need to help us learn. (The beauty of God's sovereignty and our meaningful choice is something I discuss thoroughly in my book *hand in Hand*.[16])

WE DON'T MAKE OURSELVES HAPPY, BUT WE CAN MAKE CHOICES THAT LEAD TO HAPPINESS.

We can't make ourselves happy in God any more than a seed can make itself grow. But we're not just seeds. We're greenhouse farmers who can make sure the seed is planted, watered, and fertilized.

Paul said to the church in Corinth, "I planted, Apollos watered, but God gave the growth" (1 Corinthians 3:6). While God makes the crop grow, the people who raise the largest and best produce, winning ribbons at the county fair, do their part too.

We should never flippantly say, "Happiness is a choice." It's not always easy to choose what brings ultimate lasting happiness over what brings instant temporary happiness. Choosing happiness is not merely working harder to pull up our minds and moods, as we would our bootstraps. Rather, it's gratefully receiving God's grace and happiness.

Still, there's a lot to be said for "Just do it." Harvard psychologist Jerome Bruner says, "You more likely act yourself into feeling than feel yourself into action."[17]

Too many of us wait for sufficient motivation before making wise and joy-producing choices. But whether it's exercise, eating right, or volunteering to serve others, when we take those first steps, we overcome inertia and establish new habits. Once we see the positive happiness that results, we're much more motivated to keep up those new patterns.

WE CAN TRAIN OUR BRAINS TOWARD CHRIST-CENTERED HAPPINESS.

When a physical action is repeated over time, long-term muscle memory is formed. Biking, typing, and playing musical instruments all utilize muscle memory.

This is similar to how happiness works: the brain has its own muscle memory. We choose to follow Christ by taking a certain action, we find happiness in it, and then we do it again.

Both happiness and unhappiness are states of mind that self-perpetuate. The more delighted we are, the more delight becomes our default. The angrier we are, the more anger becomes our default.

Paul said, "Fix your thoughts on what is true. . . . Think about things that are excellent and worthy of praise" (Philippians 4:8, NLT). This doesn't happen automatically. But once we develop the habit and experience its rewards, we instinctively turn our minds to what makes us happy in Christ.

Everyone who has dieted knows that nearly any diet works when habitually followed, but no diet works when repeatedly violated. It's not the inherent virtue of a diet or exercise plan but the hour-by-hour choices related to diet or exercise that determine results.

Happiness researcher David Myers writes, "Act happy. We can sometimes act ourselves into a happier frame of mind. Manipulated into a smiling expression, people feel better; when they scowl, the whole world seems to scowl back. So put on a happy face. Talk *as if* you feel positive self-esteem, are optimistic, and are outgoing. Going through the motions can trigger the emotions."[18]

This may seem phony, but it needn't be—particularly for believers who remind themselves of their solid foundation for happiness in Christ. If happiness is a desirable state, then it's worth the effort to obtain it. Those taught to say "thank you" become more thankful. Those who teach themselves to smile become happier. By choosing Christ-pleasing actions, we cultivate Christ-pleasing attitudes.

DELIBERATE, BIBLICAL THINKING WILL MAKE US HAPPIER.

Some believers become obsessed with everything that's wrong with the world. We're continually bombarded by "news" (which is sometimes more sensational than informative) that dwells on the sufferings and tragedies of life. It's easy for this unceasing avalanche of bad news to bury the Good News.

I don't favor living in a cave, blissfully ignorant of the world's woes. Rather, we're to focus our thoughts on true eternal realities. Remembering God's presence, praying, and feeding our minds with good things that honor our King—these practices will increase our joy while starving our anxiety.

When I'm snorkeling for hours on end, taking underwater photos, I don't think about being cold, hungry, or tired—not because I'm in denial, but because I'm so focused on the magnificent and praiseworthy creativity of my Father, who made the ocean's wonders.

When I was a boy, I collected rocks. There were lots of plain stones, as well as muddy ones, with worms and bugs all around and under them. But this didn't deter me, because I wasn't collecting worms or bugs; I was collecting beautiful stones. Even when they didn't appear beautiful, I saw the hidden beauty.

As I collected rocks, and as others collect coins and stamps, we can collect reasons to praise God. We can develop an eye for beauty in God, his world, and the people and man-made objects in it. That's not denying the Curse; it's cultivating the happiness of a God-centered worldview.

Even in a fallen world, God invites us to happiness in him. Why would we say no?

FIND INNOCENT THINGS THAT ENRICH YOUR LIFE AND MAKE YOU HAPPY.

Hundreds of small choices can bring happiness—giving thanks, serving others, visiting a friend or neighbor, volunteering to work with children at church, counseling in a pregnancy center, volunteering for a ministry that opposes sex trafficking. Yes, even if these things made us miserable, we should do them anyway to love others and obey God. But God has graciously wired us to become happy by doing the very things he wants us to do!

Contentment is found not only in learning to enjoy things in life but also in choosing to replace some things with better ones. We can expand the horizons of our happiness by taking up hiking, learning to play the piano, or joining a book club while making friends and serving others in the process. We can also find happy people who love Jesus and spend time with them regularly. Nanci is one of the happy people in my life, as are our family and closest friends.

There are countless people whose depression has been lifted through having a pet. Therapy dogs are now a regular part of hospitals, care centers, and veterans' programs. Every dog can be a therapy dog. I heard someone say, "I thank God daily for the dog I never wanted . . . until I had him."

I've experienced great joy from each of the six dogs I've had in my life, from childhood to the present. By delighting in one another, animals and humans can take joy in God. Gladness multiplies in the sharing.

Dean Koontz, writing from his golden retriever's viewpoint, conveys a unique and healthy perspective:

> Hello again. Am back, me, Trixie Koontz, dog and author and happy cookie-eater. . . .
>
> Why is so hard for humans learn to . . . see beauty everywhere?
>
> One reason: desire. Humans mostly think about what they want next. Always thinking what is wanted next, you live in future, never in *now*. Can't see beauty of world, which is now, if you are full of desire for what you want next Tuesday.
>
> Dogs never know what comes next. Always surprised. Might be skin infection, might be entire meatloaf dropped on floor. . . .
>
> Want to know secret? You can't control future, either. Here it comes, skin infection or meatloaf.
>
> Is rhythm of life: meatloaf, skin infection, bag of potato chips left open on low table, meteor through roof. Good thing about life is, there's always lots more meatloaf than meteors.[19]

See your life as it is—filled with gifts from God. Find these gifts, enjoy them, and be quick to give thanks for them, multiplying God's joy and yours.

WHEN YOU CHOOSE HAPPINESS IT OVERFLOWS TO OTHERS.

A study of more than 4,700 people who were followed for more than twenty years proved the infectious nature of happiness. The *Washington Post* reported,

> Happiness is contagious, spreading among friends, neighbors, siblings and spouses like the flu, according to a large study that for the first time shows how

emotion can ripple through clusters of people who may not even know each other. . . . The study . . . found that people who are happy or become happy boost the chances that someone they know will be happy. The power of happiness, moreover, can span another degree of separation, elevating the mood of that person's husband, wife, brother, sister, friend or next-door neighbor.[20]

Scripture speaks to this same principle. Job recounted his past relationships, saying, "I *smiled* on them when they had lost confidence; my cheerful face encouraged them" (Job 29:24, GNT, emphasis added). "A cheerful look brings joy to the heart, and good news gives health to the bones" (Proverbs 15:30, NIV). The Good News Translation begins the verse this way: "Smiling faces make you happy."

When others are cheerful in our presence, our spirits are lifted, and when we in turn are cheerful, our happiness brings joy and life to them. The entrance of one cheerful person, with his or her smile and laughter and happiness, can infuse a room with joy. We can and should invest time to minister to negative, unhappy people—but for everyone's sake, we need to be around happy people too.

CHOOSE TO SAY NO TO WORRY AND YES TO TRUSTING GOD.

Just after instructing us to rejoice in the Lord, Paul writes in Philippians 4:6, "Do not be anxious about anything." Worry is a killjoy. It specializes in worst-case scenarios when God tells his children there is much that should make us rejoice:

1. He has already rescued us from the worst, which is eternal Hell.
2. Even if something terrible happens, he'll use it for our eternal good.
3. Often bad things don't happen, and our worry proves groundless.
4. Whether or not bad things happen, our worry generates no positive change.
5. The cause for all our worries—sin and the Curse—is temporary, and will soon be behind us. Forever.

The command to rejoice is not mere pretense or positive thinking. Rather, it's embracing our present life, which includes suffering. But even before God wipes it all away, he gives us compelling reasons to rejoice.

Paul continues, "In everything by prayer and supplication with thanksgiving let your requests be made known to God. And the peace of God, which surpasses all understanding, will guard your hearts and your minds in Christ Jesus" (Philippians 4:6-7).

Instead of worrying, we're to take our concerns to God, choosing to thank him—for his goodness, sovereignty, and promise to work everything together for good.

GO OUT AND ENJOY GOD'S CREATION.

Joy is like the stars. Some nights they blaze in glory; other nights they're covered by clouds. But they're always there. Since childhood, I've loved the stars. I loved them before I loved the God who made them. Loving God causes me to delight in the stars not less but more—partly because I can't look at them without thinking of him and partly because I know he loves his creation. When I enjoy the stars, I pay him a compliment and join in his enjoyment.

It won't matter whether stars are visible if you don't put yourself in a position to see them. Walk away from the Internet, open the door, step outside, and look at God's creative productions—most of which are free to behold.

Ralph Waldo Emerson (1803–1882) wrote, "If the stars should appear one night in a thousand years, how would men believe and adore. . . . But every night come out these envoys of beauty, and light the universe with their admonishing smile."[21]

Clyde Kilby (1902–1986) wrote a list of personal resolutions to help him stay alive to the beauty of God's world around him.[22] Here are two of them:

At least once every day I shall look steadily up at the sky and remember that I, a consciousness with a conscience, am on a planet traveling in space with wonderfully mysterious things above and about me. . . . I shall open my eyes and ears. Once every day I shall simply stare at a tree, a flower, a cloud, or a person. I shall not then be concerned at all to ask *what* they are, but simply be glad *that* they are. I shall joyfully allow them the mystery of what Lewis calls their "divine, magical, terrifying, and ecstatic" existence.[23]

As I write this, I'm looking up from my computer at a photo I took underwater. It reminds me of the sheer delight of my unforgettable ninety-minute encounter with a wonderful monk seal I named Molly. Whenever I look at Molly's photo, my heart fills with joyful memories and longing for the New Earth's joy and the days that await us. That anticipation gives me a harvest of happiness today.

Charles Spurgeon said,

I confess I have no sympathy with the good man, who, when he went down the Rhine, dived into the cabin that he might not see the river and the mountains lest he should be absorbed in them and forget his Savior. I like to see my Savior on the hills and by the shores of the sea! I hear my Father's voice in the thunder and listen to the whispers of His love in the cadence of the sunlit waves. These are my Father's works and, therefore, I admire them and I seem all the nearer to Him when I am among them.[24]

Spurgeon went on to say these profound words about finding happiness in this world:

If I were a great artist, I would think it a very small compliment if my son came into my house and said he would not notice the pictures I had painted because he only wanted to think of *me*. He therein would *condemn* my paintings, for if they were good for anything, he would be rejoiced to see my hand in them! Oh, but surely, everything that comes from the hand of such a Master Artist as God has something in it of Himself! The Lord rejoices in His works and shall not His people do so?[25]

DESPITE OUR CHOICES AND PREFERENCES, GOD SOMETIMES REVEALS HIS HAPPINESS IN SUBTLE WAYS.

The prophet Elijah was depressed and despondent. He desperately needed a direct self-revelation from God. Earlier, God had sent fire to consume his offering and strike down the false prophets of Baal. Though incredible, this event had no lasting effect on Elijah. Then Scripture says something remarkable:

> Behold, the LORD passed by, and a great and strong wind tore the mountains and broke in pieces the rocks before the LORD, but the LORD was not in the wind. And after the wind an earthquake, but the LORD was not in the earthquake. And after the earthquake a fire, but the LORD was not in the fire. And after the fire the sound of a low whisper. I KINGS 19:11-12

God's self-revelation was called "a low whisper" or a "still, small voice" (KJV). He often appeals to our faith by gently persuading rather than overpowering. Sometimes he bowls us over with the joy of this presence—sometimes we have to look and listen carefully to perceive him.

In his book *The Lion, the Witch and the Wardrobe*, C. S. Lewis reveals the lion, Aslan, gradually. Like the lion, God decides when to be seen. This suggests a God who is always there but doesn't foist himself upon us. The lion's name is finally mentioned when the beaver says, "Aslan is on the move—perhaps already landed."[26]

Lewis's next words capture the subtle power and wonder of Jesus, the source of all true happiness:

> And now a very curious thing happened. None of the children knew who Aslan was any more than you do; but the moment the Beaver had spoken these words everyone felt quite different. Perhaps it has sometimes happened to you in a dream that someone says something which you don't understand but in the dream it feels as if it had some enormous meaning. . . . It was like that now. At the name of Aslan each one of the children felt something jump in its inside.[27]

Had the roaring lion appeared suddenly, the wonder would have been lost. So it is in our lives. People gradually and beautifully awaken to who Jesus is. And then we feel something jump inside.

At last, Aslan appears to the children in his glory, alarming them with his redemptive suffering, followed by the wonder of his resurrection. This unveiling is much like the biblical story and our lives in the present world—gradual and beautiful. This slow unfolding of God's person and plan ultimately brings satisfying fulfillment and abiding happiness.

CHAPTER 32

WAYS TO CULTIVATE HAPPINESS

Let me hear the sounds of joy and gladness; and though you have
crushed me and broken me, I will be happy once again.

PSALM 51:8, GNT

It is impossible for any rational creature to be happy without acting all for
God: God himself could not make him happy any other way.

DAVID BRAINERD

S TELLA'S FIRST CHRISTMAS as a widow brought incredible loneliness. One day her
doorbell rang and she was greeted by a messenger holding a box.

"What's in the box?" she asked.

The messenger opened the flap to reveal a Labrador retriever puppy. "For you, ma'am."

Puzzled, Stella asked, "But . . . who sent the puppy?"

Turning to leave, he said, "Your husband. Merry Christmas."

She opened the letter from her husband, full of love and encouragement. He'd purchased the puppy shortly before he died and requested that it be delivered for Christmas.

As Stella wiped away tears, she picked up the eager puppy, which licked her face while
"Joy to the World" played on her radio. Suddenly, she felt incredible delight.[1]

This dying man's thoughtful choice brought present happiness for him, future happiness for her, and happiness to all who hear their story.

HAPPINESS IS NATURAL BUT NOT AUTOMATIC.

The book of Nehemiah records God's sovereign plan to rebuild Jerusalem. Yet it repeatedly
shows Nehemiah's strategic positioning of his people to counter the building project's many
enemies: "We prayed to our God and posted a guard day and night to meet this threat"
(Nehemiah 4:9, NIV). Their prayer acknowledged God's sovereignty. Their preparations
recognized their responsibility to act wisely.

Likewise, our actions should be in concert with our prayers—we should pray to find happiness in God and then take the kind of actions that will help us find happiness in God.

Some say, "I thought I would experience joy in the Christian life, but I never have." Is that because we spend hours a day on social media but "don't have time" to join a home Bible study? Do we schedule lunches and tennis matches but not regular times with God? Why do we expect to be happy in God when we're not choosing to do what we can to learn, study, and discuss who God is, what he has done, and what he's doing?

The Christian life is supernatural but not enchanted. God doesn't magically make us happy despite the fact that we make work, sports, leisure, or sex into our idols. If we choose to seek happiness elsewhere, God won't force himself on us. And he certainly won't give us happiness in what's not from him or what's distanced from him.

Happiness comes naturally in the same sense that fruit comes naturally from a tree. If the tree gets sufficient sunshine and water, if the ground is rich in nutrients, if the tree doesn't contract diseases, then yes, it "naturally" produces fruit. We must plant ourselves in the rich soil of God's Word, soak in the living water of God and his people, and bask in the radiant sunlight of his grace. And then happiness will come naturally.

MAKING WISE CHOICES PRODUCES ONGOING HAPPINESS.

Research psychologist Martin Seligman says pessimism and depression result from our thought habits. Pessimists believe that bad events will last a long time and will undermine everything they do. Optimists believe that defeat is just a temporary setback and that its causes are confined to this one circumstance. Confronted by a bad situation, optimists perceive it as a challenge and try harder.[2]

Seligman claims that we can change from pessimistic thinking to optimistic thinking. One of the most significant findings in psychology in the past twenty years is that individuals can choose the way they think. This corresponds with Scripture, which tells us we are to "be transformed by the renewing of [our] minds" (Romans 12:2, CEB), and that we should think about things that are good and praiseworthy (see Philippians 4:8).

Suppose a mean dog runs loose. He has attacked you three times on your way to work and bitten you twice. What are your options? Well, you can hope for the best. You can push aside the bad memories and tell yourself that maybe the dog is no longer there. You can even come equipped with pepper spray. But there's another option. You can find a different route to work.

So often we thwart our own holiness and happiness by going where we don't need to go.

Do not enter the path of the wicked,
 and do not walk in the way of the evil.
Avoid it; do not go on it;
 turn away from it and pass on.
PROVERBS 4:14-15

This passage has everything to do with happiness. After all, what does sin do? It brings calamity, terror, distress, and anguish (see Proverbs 1:26-27)—in a word, *unhappiness*. The fruit of sin is self-destruction and fatality (see Proverbs 1:31-33). It brings death and loss (see Proverbs 2:19, 22) and great disgrace (see Proverbs 3:35).

Notice how this argument against adultery is an appeal to self-interest:

Can a man carry fire next to his chest
 and his clothes not be burned? . . .
So is he who goes in to his neighbor's wife;
 none who touches her will go unpunished. . . .
He who commits adultery lacks sense;
 he who does it destroys himself.
He will get wounds and dishonor,
 and his disgrace will not be wiped away.
PROVERBS 6:27, 29, 32-33

These verses could be summed up this way: making unwise, God-neglecting choices makes us extremely unhappy.

If we comparison-shop between sin and Jesus, the difference is obvious. One brings you misery; the other, happiness.

WE DON'T *FALL* INTO SIN, RIGHTEOUSNESS, OR HAPPINESS; WE WALK INTO THEM.

I've heard people say, "I don't understand; I prayed for purity, but I fell back into watching Internet pornography. Why didn't God answer my prayer?"

My response? Your choices incapacitated your prayers. Did you set up a program that restricts your access or informs your friend or pastor when you access pornography? Did you get rid of your computer or move your screen in full view of others?

Or did you expect God to do everything for you?

"If a man is lazy," the book of Ecclesiastes says, "the rafters sag; if his hands are idle, the house leaks" (10:18, NIV). Proverbs 20:4 says, "Sluggards do not plow in season; so at harvest time they look but find nothing" (NIV). These verses don't attribute sagging rafters, leaking houses, and empty pantries to God's sovereignty. They lay responsibility for action on us.

I vividly remember a particular counseling appointment as a young pastor. Eric stormed into my office and flopped into a chair. "I'm really mad at God."

I was startled because Eric was one of the happiest young men I knew. He grew up in a strong churchgoing family, married a Christian woman, and seemed to have a sincere love for Christ.

I asked him why he was mad at God. He explained that for months he'd felt a strong attraction to a woman at his office. She felt the same. He'd prayed earnestly that God would keep him from immorality.

"Did you ask your wife to pray for you?" I said. "Did you stay away from the woman?"

"Well . . . no. We went out for lunch almost every day. And . . . we committed adultery."

I looked at Eric and slowly pushed a big book across my desk. As it inched closer to the edge, I prayed aloud, "Lord, please keep this book from falling!"

I kept pushing and praying. Sure enough, God didn't suspend the law of gravity, and the book fell.

"I'm mad at God," I said to Eric. "I asked him to keep my book from falling . . . but he didn't answer my prayer!"[3]

I can still hear the sound of that book hitting the floor. It was a symbol of Eric's life. Instead of calling on God to empower him as he took decisive steps to resist temptation, he kept making unwise choices while asking to be delivered from their natural consequences.

Eric went from genuine happiness to misery in a period of just a few years, and eventually he went to jail for sexual crimes. His immorality and sexual abuse didn't come out of the blue. They were the cumulative product of minuscule daily compromises and choices that sabotaged his righteousness and happiness.

Contrast Eric with his friend Rocky. Raised in an unbelieving home, he'd had sex with many women and later came to faith in Christ. Rocky made new choices in keeping with his new nature: immersing himself in the daily meditation of God's Word, joining Bible studies, learning to pray, sharing his faith, and reading great Christian books. He fled from sexual temptations that came his way and guarded his heart and mind. In the process of knowing Christ and following him, he became one of the happiest and most Christ-honoring people I've ever known. His marriage, family, church involvement, and service to others display the fruit of his wise choices.

Both Eric and Rocky showed a sincere love for Jesus. Both asked God to help them live righteously. But Eric expected God to save him from the consequences of his wrong choices, while Rocky called on God for strength as he did all he could to make right choices.

Both men were defined by their daily choices, which cumulatively produced sin and misery for one, and righteousness and happiness for the other.

CONTRARY TO WHAT OUR CULTURE PROMISES, SELF-CONTROL IS ESSENTIAL TO HAPPINESS.

A website for a resort called Hedonism 2 makes this invitation:

Sleep in. Stay up late. Give up counting calories. Have a drink before noon. Give up mineral water. Dine in shorts. Talk to strangers. Don't make your bed. Go skinny dipping. Don't call your mother. Let your hair down. Don't pay for anything. Don't leave a tip. Be your beautiful self in spectacular Jamaica. . . . Hedonism II is now more Super-Inclusive than ever with an enticing menu of hedonistic amenities & services to suit all your guilty pleasures.[4]

Every sentence screams, "This will make you happy." Of course, there's a time to sleep in, stay up late, and not make your bed. Vacations can be good and refreshing. But the term "guilty pleasures" should be one of many clues that if you consistently lived this way, you'd be irresponsible, unloving, and categorically unhappy. This invitation is merely an extreme and expensive form of the same philosophy countless people in our culture—and churches—live by.

In contrast, Scripture warns, "A man without self-control is like a city broken into and left without walls" (Proverbs 25:28). Such a city, and such a person, will be left unhappy. God commands us, "Make every effort to supplement your . . . knowledge with self-control" (2 Peter 1:5-6).

COMPARISON WITH OTHERS BRINGS UNHAPPINESS.

Comparison is deadly. Believing that other people are happier than we are is unproductive and unrealistic. We don't know their struggles, private pains, and secrets. Dennis Prager speaks of those caught in the comparison trap: "They suffer from what can be called compound unhappiness—just as compound interest is interest on interest, compound unhappiness is unhappiness over being unhappy."[5]

Early in our marriage, Nanci suffered guilt feelings when we visited friends and saw how neat and clean everything was, even though they, too, had young children.

One night when our friends spent the evening with us, we realized how neat and clean we'd made our house by throwing debris into our bedroom closet. We didn't let them see our messes, just as they didn't let us see theirs. So the answer to "How does she do it?" is often, "She doesn't. She shoves it into a closet!"

Once we admitted this to our friends, we all laughed. Stress levels dropped and happiness rose! We realized we're on the same battlefield. Life isn't easy, but it becomes easier when we enjoy camaraderie rather than comparison and competition.

REJECT THE NOTION THAT SUCCESS MAKES US HAPPY.

When megaselling novelist Jack Higgins was asked what he knows now that he wished he'd known when he was younger, he said, "I wish somebody had told me then that when you get to the top there's nothing there."[6]

After a few days of happiness at a new job or after finalizing a big sale, we raise the bar to the next level. But we can only go so high. Someone is always above us; some deal falls through; someone else is a better doctor, CEO, carpenter, painter, or volleyball player. Always. (And if you ever do arrive at number one, it won't be for long!)

Dennis Prager says,

> *If you equate happiness with success, you will never achieve the amount of success necessary to make you happy.* There is always more success that can be achieved. Identifying success with happiness is like moving the goalposts back 10 yards every time your football team has a first down—your team may be more and more successful, but the goalposts will always remain unreachable.[7]

I know a lot of writers, some of whom are extremely successful. But most are never satisfied. If your book sells ten thousand copies, you wish it were one hundred thousand.

If you sell a million, you want it to be ten million. If your book lands on the bestseller list, you wish it were number one; if it makes number one, you want it to stay there. If we get what we wish for, instead of being happy, we usually wish for more.

If God is the source of happiness, our happiness is based on solid ground. He has made us and knows our limitations (see Psalm 103:14). We can cultivate our trust in God without having to be the best. When one of us wins, we can all celebrate, because happiness isn't a limited commodity we have to fight over.

JOB SATISFACTION IS ABOUT MORE THAN FINDING THE PERFECT CAREER.

Writing in the *New York Times*, Arthur Brooks summarizes modern happiness research: "It turns out that choosing to pursue four basic values of faith, family, community and work is the surest path to happiness."[8]

It's possible to maximize our happiness in whatever work God gives us by doing it with excellence.

Martin Luther King Jr. said, "If a man is called to be a street sweeper, he should sweep streets even as Michelangelo painted, or Beethoven composed music or Shakespeare wrote poetry. He should sweep streets so well that all the hosts of heaven and earth will pause to say, 'Here lived a great street sweeper who did his job well.'"[9]

This is a biblically grounded statement, in keeping with the words of Paul: "Whatever you do, work heartily, as for the Lord and not for men" (Colossians 3:23). When we work out of duty alone, we likely won't experience happiness. When we're trying to please people, we become unhappy if they're displeased with us. If we labor to earn God's favor, we'll either imagine we've earned it and become proud and unhappy, or we'll realize we can't and become depressed and unhappy. Working for minimum wage, or for no pay at all, when done honestly and for God's glory, can bring more joy than any million-dollar salary (see Proverbs 10:9; Proverbs 11:1; 1 Corinthians 4:2; 1 Corinthians 10:31; Hebrews 13:18).

If you're truly dissatisfied in your work, consider changing jobs, if you can—even if it means living on a lower income. But seeming drudgery can become fulfilling when our perspectives change. If we believe in God's sovereign plan, we'll work at our jobs to please him, grow in character and Christlikeness, and use our unique sphere of influence to share the gospel.

Though I haven't seen them for twenty years, I've never forgotten the father and son who picked up our trash each week. I could hear them singing and laughing. If I was outside when they came by, they'd say, "Have a great day!"—and it was obvious that's what they were having! Likewise, God the Father loves Jesus. It showed in his work, and his Son entered into his Father's happiness.

English architect Sir Christopher Wren (1632–1723) supervised the construction of a number of magnificent cathedrals in London. According to one story, a journalist interviewed some of the workers at a building site. He asked three of them, "What are you doing?"

The first replied, "I'm cutting stone for 10 shillings a day."

The next answered, "I'm putting in 10 hours a day on this job."

The third said, "I'm helping Sir Christopher Wren construct one of London's greatest cathedrals."[10]

It's pretty obvious which of these people was the happiest! There's nothing wrong with working to be paid. But if we see the greater significance of our work—no matter how menial—and we do it all to God's glory, it changes everything.

THE STRAIGHTEST PATH TO HAPPINESS IS DEVOTING OURSELVES TO THE HAPPINESS OF OTHERS.

At a seminar, fifty people who knew each other were given five minutes to find the balloon with their name on it. Everyone searched, but no one found theirs in the allotted time. Then they were asked to collect any balloon and give it to the right person. Within minutes, each person had his or her own balloon.

The speaker began by saying, "Our happiness lies in the happiness of other people. Give them their happiness; you will get your own happiness."[11]

Psychologist Bernard Rimland conducted a study in which participants were asked to list ten people they knew best and to label them as happy or not happy. When they finished, they were to go through their lists and this time label each person as selfish or unselfish, using the following definition of selfishness: "A stable tendency to devote one's time and resources to one's own interests and welfare—an unwillingness to inconvenience one's self for others."[12]

What did Rimland discover? According to his research paper "The Altruism Paradox," *everyone who was labeled happy was also labeled unselfish.* Those "whose activities are devoted to bringing themselves happiness . . . are far less likely to be happy than those whose efforts are devoted to making others happy." In a remarkable conclusion, he said, "Do unto others as you would have them do unto you."[13]

It's not every day that we see a direct quote from Jesus in a psychological study! But the Golden Rule (see Luke 6:31) sums up Rimland's findings perfectly. This idea of selflessness appears in other Scripture passages as well, such as Philippians 2:3-4, NASB: "Do nothing from selfishness or empty conceit, but with humility of mind regard one another as more important than yourselves; do not merely look out for your own personal interests, but also for the interests of others."

According to the study, looking out for the interests of others is in our best interests!

Selflessness seems to be strangely counterintuitive to us, perhaps because we imagine that sacrificing for others is an act of holiness that's contrary to happiness. But consider this striking passage, which appeals to us to help the hungry and needy by promising great happiness if we do:

> If you give yourself to the hungry and satisfy the desire of the afflicted, then
> your light will rise in darkness and your gloom will become like midday. And
> the LORD will continually guide you, and satisfy your desire in scorched places,
> and give strength to your bones; and you will be like a watered garden, and like a
> spring of water whose waters do not fail. ISAIAH 58:10-11, NASB

What is gloom but unhappiness? What will satisfy our desires, give us strength, and make us like a watered garden (in short, make us happy)? Giving of ourselves to help others. This is no abstract spiritual blessing—it's a concrete promise of personal happiness!

The "spiritualized" thinking goes, *Care nothing about your happiness; devote your life to making others happy.* The biblical and realistic thinking is, *You can make others, God, and yourself happy at the same time—by serving others.* When we invest ourselves in others, everyone wins.

IT'S POSSIBLE TO ENJOY WATCHING OTHERS WIN.

It's not always easy to witness the success of others without pangs of envy creeping in. I heard one story of a fortunate woman who won an extreme home makeover but whose neighbors were outraged at the invasion of their space by construction workers and film crews. They spoke critically of their neighbor, saying she probably didn't know how to take care of a decent home. They called the police because of the disturbance, even though they knew it would be short lived. Jealousy surfaced. Those who didn't directly benefit from her good fortune didn't rejoice with her—they resented her.

Suppose you and a friend entered a store and your friend was awarded $100,000 for being the store's 100,000th customer. Would you be hounded by the wish that it had been you instead? Would you expect your friend to split it with you since you held the door open and otherwise would have won? Or would you have simply rejoiced for her?

I've heard people admit that looking at others' Facebook pages depresses them because they see new houses or fun vacations they'll never have. Envy undermines the opportunity for shared joy.

The degree to which we can be happy for other people without envying or resenting them determines how happy we'll truly be. Why? Because if we can only rejoice when positive things happen to us, the number of things that can make us happy is greatly reduced.

I enjoy winning. But by God's grace, I've become a gracious loser, which makes me a happier person. When coaching high school tennis, I was playing against our team's number one singles player. We'd played a couple of times a week for three years, and he'd never beaten me. But he kept getting better . . . and I didn't. That day, though I tried my best, he beat me for the first time (and not the last).

Spontaneously, when he won the final point, we both ran to the net and hugged each other, smiling, laughing, and celebrating. I realized, to my surprise, that I was as genuinely happy as he was.

Why was I so happy? I had invested myself in him and developing his skills. His success was my success.

"Rejoice with those who rejoice" (Romans 12:15, NIV) had new meaning for me. I realized that when we pour our lives into others, we truly want them to succeed.

Our happiness will always be small as long as we can only be happy for ourselves. But when we can be genuinely happy for our spouse, children, grandchildren, neighbors, and friends—and those who live thousands of miles away but are benefiting from the prayers we offer and the money we give to help build wells or translate the Bible into their language—there will be no end to our happiness.

GIVING IS A GREAT SOURCE OF HAPPINESS.

Arthur Brooks says, "Our brains are actually wired to serve others. When we give charitable money and service to others, our brain releases several stress hormones which elevate our mood and cause us to feel happy. Serving and giving help to others makes us happier, healthier, more prosperous, and therefore greatly blessed and more successful than non-givers."[14]

Jesus said, "It is more blessed [*makarios*: happy-making] to give than to receive" (Acts 20:35). Yes, we should give because it's right but also because it's smart. When we give, everyone but Satan wins. God is happy, those who receive our gifts are happy, and we're happy.

God's grace to us is the lightning; our giving to him is the thunder. As lightning precedes thunder, so God's grace precedes and causes our giving. In 1 Chronicles 29, David and the people of Israel experience great joy in giving to the Temple. And 2 Corinthians 8–9 addresses giving as a joyful, reflexive response to God's grace.

Secular studies are emphatic in their assertion that giving makes people happier. A survey of thirty thousand American households showed that "people who gave money . . . to all types of religious and secular causes were far happier than non-givers."[15] Most of the people who conduct these studies don't realize they're agreeing with Jesus.

When the classic Dickens story *A Christmas Carol* begins, we meet Ebenezer Scrooge. This wealthy miser is caustic, complaining, horrendously greedy . . . and profoundly unhappy. (His life illustrates how the word *miser* is connected with *miserable*.)

Scrooge's loyal, joyful nephew says of his stingy uncle, "His offences carry their own punishment, and I have nothing to say against him. . . . Who suffers by his ill whims? Himself, always."[16]

After a radical transformation from his three visions, Scrooge walks through the streets of London freely distributing his wealth to the needy. He's giddy with delight. This man who only one day earlier scoffed at the idea of charity now takes his greatest pleasure in giving. The most miserable human being you could imagine suddenly erupts with joy.

Had Ebenezer Scrooge decided to give away money only out of a guilt-driven sense of obligation, he wouldn't have been full of gladness. The story's greatness is in the inseparability of his newfound generosity and his happiness.

What caused Scrooge's joy-filled transformation? Gaining an eternal perspective. Through supernatural intervention, he was allowed to see his past, present, and still-changeable future through the eyes of eternity. (Let's ask God for the same insight!)

On the story's final page, Dickens says of Scrooge, "Some people laughed to see the alteration in him, but he let them laugh, and little heeded them. . . . His own heart laughed: and that was quite enough for him. . . . And it was always said of him, that he knew how to keep Christmas well, if any man alive possessed the knowledge."[17]

THE GOOD NEWS CAUSES OVERFLOWING HAPPINESS.

Sister Act 2, starring Whoopi Goldberg, contains scenes that powerfully illustrate the happiness of the gospel message that's sometimes buried under organized religion.[18] When the Catholic school assembles to hear the choir, some of the nuns, priests, and even students in the audience look stern. While the choir had fun during practices, now that they are facing the austere audience, they're nervous.

Finally Goldberg's character, Deloris, prompts them to let loose. Now they sing powerfully, with broad smiles. It's contagious—everyone present becomes more animated as the choir sings, "Oh happy day, when Jesus washed my sins away."

When the song ends, the audience jumps to its feet, applauding enthusiastically. Yes, it's only a movie, but what's portrayed is true to life. A largely dry and joyless religious community is infused with life and happiness. Intuitively, everyone watching the scene knows that this is how it should be! Why? Because the Good News of Jesus is supposed to make us happy!

CELEBRATION IS GOD'S IDEA: FEASTS, FESTIVALS, SABBATHS, SINGING, AND DANCING IN THE BIBLE

Celebrate the Festival of Shelters for seven days. Also invite the poor, including
Levites, foreigners, orphans, and widows. . . . You will be completely happy,
so celebrate this festival in honor of the LORD your God.

DEUTERONOMY 16:13-15, CEV

As long as that word [holiday] remains, it will always answer the ignorant
slander which asserts that religion was opposed to human cheerfulness; that word
will always assert that when a day is holy it should also be happy.

G. K. CHESTERTON

───────── ☙ ─────────

CECIL RHODES, FOR whom Rhodesia (now Zimbabwe) was named, was a famous and wealthy businessman, politician, and power broker in South Africa. One evening he sat on a train with Bramwell Booth. Booth could see how depressed Rhodes was and asked him, "Are you a happy man?"

Rhodes responded, "Happy? No!"

Booth then told the influential world figure there was only one place to find real happiness: "That is at the feet of the crucified Savior, because it is only there we can be freed from our sins."

Rhodes responded, pointing toward where Booth's father, General William Booth, founder of the Salvation Army, was sitting: "I would give all I possess to believe what that old man in the next carriage believes!"[1]

He saw in a Christ-follower the happiness he lacked.

PARTYING IS RARELY ASSOCIATED WITH THE BIBLE AND CHRIST-FOLLOWERS . . . BUT IT SHOULD BE!

The Bible's many references to singing, dancing, celebrations, feasts, and festivities depict not only worship but also fun, laughter, and pleasure.

Part of what blinds us to God's emphasis on happiness is our knowledge that pagans worshiped pleasure deities and their celebrations centered on drunkenness and immorality. Today celebrating suffers from guilt by association.

295

The logic goes like this:

- Since immorality is bad, sex is bad.
- Since drunkenness is bad, alcohol is bad.
- Since laziness is bad, rest is bad.
- Since greed is bad, money is bad.

We might as well say that since gluttony is bad, food is bad; and since drowning is bad, water is bad. Because sin often happens at parties, some conclude that parties must be sinful. (Of course, sin happens at work and church, too, but people seldom conclude work and church are sinful.)

The partying described in Scripture reveals the happiness of the God who invented feasts and festivals, and who commands and encourages singing, dancing, eating, and drinking.

FEASTS AND FESTIVALS WERE FUN WAYS TO WORSHIP GOD, LEARN ABOUT HIM, AND REMEMBER HIS PROVISION.

In times of celebration, the people of Israel publicly indulged in the good gifts God had blessed them with. Those gifts included food, wine, music, dance, and fun—all with the understanding that God is the source of everything good and that the enjoyment of his blessings is a happy privilege.

In worship settings today, "fellowship" has been scaled back dramatically. It may involve subdued laughter, but rarely does it reflect the great happiness described in the Bible. Indeed, the difference between the grand feast of the Lord's Supper in the New Testament and the symbolic wafers and grape juice offered by most modern churches at Communion is the difference between a great celebration on the one hand and a minimalist ritual on the other. (The symbolic modern Communion is effective only insofar as it calls up the vision of actual feasting to celebrate the work of Christ. If we rarely engage in such celebratory feasts, we leave ourselves with a mere shadow of the real celebrations God's people once enjoyed.)

Spurgeon said this about the most sacred rituals of the church, particularly Communion: "Gospel ordinances are choice enjoyments, enjoined upon us by the loving rule of Him whom we call Master and Lord. We accept them with joy and delight.... The Lord's own Supper is a joyful festival, a feast."[2]

Celebrations in the Bible weren't held quietly at home; rather, they were enjoyed publicly, with family, friends, and neighbors. By building these festivities into Israel's calendar, God integrated joy into the lives of his people. Biblical accounts show that feasts and festivals gave them a sense of identity and unity, and provided opportunities for parents to instruct their children about God. These feast days also served to link happiness with holiness—two concepts that have become tragically separated from each other in not only the world's thinking but also the church's.

Festivals such as the Feast of Tabernacles included sacrifices for sin (see Leviticus 23:37-41). Sorrow over sin and its redemptive price was real but momentary. Once the sacrifices were complete, the festival became all about being happy in God and one another.

Feasts that recognized repentance, forgiveness, and redemption included more joy than any party pagans could host, because the participants' delight was God centered, deeper, and reality based. "Happy are those whose transgression is forgiven, whose sin is covered!" (Psalm 32:1, NRSV). In light of such good news, who wouldn't want to celebrate?

There are passages in which various prophets condemned God's people because of how they observed the feasts (e.g., Isaiah 1:13-20). God wasn't displeased with the feasts—they were *his* idea. His displeasure came when people lost sight of the real purpose: celebrating the person and work of the God from whom all happiness flows and whom we obey out of great privilege.

As the church father Chrysostom said, "All life is a festival since the Son of God has redeemed you from death."[3]

CELEBRATIONS WERE PART OF THE LIFEBLOOD OF GOD'S PEOPLE.

The Passover, or Pesach, commemorates the night the angel of death destroyed all the firstborn of Egypt (see Exodus 12:3-14), resulting in the Israelites' release from captivity. It's a festival of freedom. Deuteronomy 16:11 commands, "You shall rejoice before the LORD your God."

The Feast of Weeks, or Shavuot, celebrates God giving his law on Mount Sinai and the fruitfulness associated with obedience (see Deuteronomy 16:9-12). It's one of the three feasts celebrated in Jerusalem, including the Feast of Harvest and the Day of Firstfruits (see Exodus 23:16; 34:22; Leviticus 23:10, 16; Numbers 28:26). Later, the Feast of Firstfruits was called Pentecost, the Greek word for "fifty," because it was celebrated fifty days after the Sabbath that began Passover.

The Day of Atonement, or Yom Kippur, follows Rosh Hashanah, which celebrates the creation of Adam and Eve. Both feasts concern God's salvation of his people (see Leviticus 23:26-32). Even in ancient times, people anticipated the Creator's redemptive plan.

The Feast of Booths, or Sukkot (see Deuteronomy 16:13-15), is also known as the Feast of Tabernacles. It's a seven-day feast, commonly referred to in Jewish writings as "the season of our rejoicing." It begins five days after Yom Kippur.

The Feast of Purim is a two-day celebration of God's deliverance of the Jewish captives in Persia from extermination at the hand of their enemies (see Esther 9:27-28). Purim is preceded by a minor fast, commemorating Esther's three days of fasting to prepare to meet with the king, but it ultimately moves to great feasting and gladness.

The Feast of Hanukkah, the Festival of Lights, is an extrabiblical event that invites people to rejoice over God's intervention. It commemorates the 164 BC recovery and cleansing of the Temple by Judas Maccabeus after its desecration by Antiochus Epiphanes. In John 10:22, it is referred to as the Feast of Dedication.

The point of all the feasts was to honor God with gratitude and gladness—to celebrate him and his acts of love and to be happy together in his presence. In modern cultures that don't have such feasts, we should look for ways to incorporate some of their elements into both our holidays and our church and family gatherings.

THE SABBATH WAS DESIGNED TO BE A DAY OF RESTFUL CELEBRATION—AND THE HIGHLIGHT OF EVERY WEEK.

Israel's day of rest was a central part of life for God's people: "Six days shall work be done, but on the seventh day is a Sabbath of solemn rest, a holy convocation. You shall do no work. It is a Sabbath to the LORD in all your dwelling places" (Leviticus 23:3).

The Sabbath day is also called a feast (see Leviticus 23:2, NKJV). It included a solemn assembly (see Isaiah 1:13) but was also a day of joy. Note the words of pleasure and delight God uses in relation to the Sabbath:

> If you turn back your foot from the Sabbath,
>   from doing your pleasure on my holy day,
> and call the Sabbath a delight
>   and the holy day of the LORD honorable;
> if you honor it, not going your own ways,
>   or seeking your own pleasure, or talking idly;
> then you shall take delight in the LORD . . .
>   for the mouth of the LORD has spoken.   ISAIAH 58:13-14

A quick reading of this passage might appear to suggest that God is saying, "Stop enjoying pleasure on the Sabbath." Rather, his message is, "Turn back to the Sabbath. Start enjoying the largest of all pleasures I offer you, which is to delight in me."

An outsider might think of the Sabbath as an overly restrictive day in which happiness is subdued. On the contrary, the regulations in Scripture (which were later taken by the Pharisees far beyond their original intent) were meant to free people from work obligations.

The Sabbath day typically involved the week's best meal, best wine, and best celebrating. It was a holy day in which happiness was unleashed!

FOOD IS GOD'S PROVISION TO NOURISH BOTH BODY AND SOUL.

Proverbs 15:15 says, "The cheerful of heart has a continual feast." A feast is the ultimate picture of happiness—and the Sabbath meant there was at least one feast per week.

Words describing eating, meals, and food appear more than a thousand times in Scripture, with the English translation "feast" occurring an additional 187 times. Feasting is profoundly relational, marked by conversation, storytelling, and laughter. Biblical feasts were spiritual gatherings that drew attention to God, his greatness, and his redemptive purposes.

We, too, have occasions for happiness every time we eat. Why did God make a strawberry startlingly delicious? Why did he make the cocoa tree so that, with a little ingenuity, people could make chocolate? Why is chocolate meltable, and why does it solidify around that strawberry when dipped? Why does it do what it does to our taste buds and bring extravagant delight? The answer is that not only in big things but also in a myriad of little ones, a creative, happy God wanted to make his image bearers happy.

People who love each other love to share meals. In ancient Jewish culture, eating was a thoughtful and deliberate joy. Meals were leisurely times of relationship-enriching celebration.

Historically, God's people always celebrated *more* than the surrounding nations, never less! Why shouldn't we do the same, since the gospel gives us even more reason to celebrate? Jesus repeatedly mentioned to his disciples that after we're resurrected, we'll eat together, enjoying the company of familiar biblical figures. He said, "Many will come from east and west and recline at table with Abraham, Isaac, and Jacob in the kingdom of heaven" (Matthew 8:11). This must have delighted his listeners.

He said to his apostles, "I confer on you a kingdom, just as my Father conferred one on me, so that you may eat and drink at my table in my kingdom" (Luke 22:29-30, NIV). Jesus not only ate with his disciples after his resurrection (see Luke 24:40-43), he even cooked breakfast for them (John 21:9-14).

Isaiah 25:6 prophesied, "On this mountain the LORD Almighty will prepare a feast of rich food for all peoples, a banquet of aged wine—the best of meats and the finest of wines" (NIV). God is portrayed in Scripture as the ultimate and immediate source of tangible physical happiness. Not only will he provide food in a general way, but he will be the chef who will prepare the food *for us*. And it won't just be any food; it will be the best food and the finest wine!

Close your eyes and imagine what it will be like to enjoy a feast handmade by God for all his children! If anticipating that doesn't make us smile, what will?

GOD PROVIDES WINE AS A SECONDARY SOURCE OF HAPPINESS.

Judges 9:13 mentions "wine that cheers both God and people" (NLT). How could wine make God happy? Apparently he takes pleasure in the fact that it makes people happy. Obviously he doesn't approve of its abuse, since he warns against drunkenness (see Ephesians 5:18).

The psalmist praises God for providing "plants for man to cultivate, that he may bring forth food from the earth and wine to gladden the heart of man" (Psalm 104:14-15).

Christ's first miracle was turning water to wine, and the response was great happiness on the part of the wedding guests, who said it was the best wine served that evening (see John 2:10).

Scripture offers strong condemnation for drinking too much and multiple warnings against doing so (see Proverbs 20:1; 23:19-21, 29-35). Yet Scripture records many people experiencing happy times while drinking wine together. Jesus informed his disciples at the Last Supper, "I tell you I will not drink again of this fruit of the vine until that day when I drink it new with you in my Father's kingdom" (Matthew 26:29). Surely the disciples lived the rest of their lives looking forward to eating and drinking with Jesus in his eternal Kingdom.

Isaac Watts wrote in a hymn:

Let us indulge a cheerful frame,
For joy becomes a feast;
We love the memory of his name
More than the wine we taste.[4]

Wine is a secondary pleasure that was never meant to be primary. The taste of the wine is meant to draw us to a higher sensory experience—that of tasting and seeing that God is the best, happiest, finest, and most worthy of celebrating (see Psalm 34:8).

Certainly the wine Jesus created wasn't called the best wine (see John 2:10) because it didn't contain alcohol. Could guests have gotten drunk on the wine Jesus made? Of course—just as they could overeat with the food he made and commit adultery with the sex he made. But that doesn't change the fact that he made food, sex, and everything else in his creation for our happiness and his glory!

I'd never encourage anyone who struggles with addiction to drink alcohol, any more than I'd encourage my fellow insulin-dependent diabetics to eat freely from the dessert table. But even when I can't eat dessert, I can still celebrate the fact that others find happiness in doing so and that God finds happiness in their happiness. Likewise, someone who abstains from alcohol can still rejoice that for others there is "wine that cheers both God and people."

SINGING CAN BE A MEANS TO PRAISE GOD.

Scripture is full of references to people singing joyfully to the Lord. At every feast and celebration, in public and private worship, singing filled the air:

- Let all who take refuge in you rejoice; let them ever sing for joy, and spread your protection over them, that those who love your name may exult in you. (Psalm 5:11)
- Clap your hands, all peoples! Shout to God with loud songs of joy! (Psalm 47:1)
- My soul will be satisfied as with fat and rich food, and my mouth will praise you with joyful lips . . . for you have been my help, and in the shadow of your wings I will sing for joy. (Psalm 63:5, 7)
- Shout, and sing for joy, O inhabitant of Zion, for great in your midst is the Holy One of Israel. (Isaiah 12:6)
- Sing, O heavens, for the LORD has done it; shout, O depths of the earth; break forth into singing, O mountains, O forest, and every tree in it! (Isaiah 44:23)

John Calvin, apparently a student of nature, commented on the last verse, "The little birds that sing, sing of God; the beasts clamor for him; the elements dread him, the mountains echo him, the fountains and flowing waters cast their glances at him, and the grass and flowers laugh before him."[5]

DANCING CAN BE A WAY TO EXPRESS RIGHTEOUS, EXUBERANT JOY.

David, the chief songwriter of the Psalms, not only sang and played musical instruments; he also danced:

It was told King David, "The LORD has blessed the household of Obed-edom and all that belongs to him, because of the ark of God." So David went and brought up the ark of God from the house of Obed-edom to the city of David with rejoicing. And when those who bore the ark of the LORD had gone six steps, he sacrificed an ox and a fattened animal. And David danced before the LORD with all his might. 2 SAMUEL 6:12-14

Psalm 150:4 says, "Praise him with tambourine and dance." There are eleven Hebrew words for dancing used in the Old Testament. They can mean "to twist or to whirl about in circular motions" or "spring about, jump, leap, or skip."[6]

According to Ecclesiastes 3:4, there is "a time to mourn, and a time to dance." People danced and sang to musical instruments to celebrate great events, including the crossing of the Red Sea (see Exodus 15:20-21) and David's victories (see 1 Samuel 18:6). They danced at weddings (see Song of Solomon 6:13). Children danced while playing games (see Job 21:11), often accompanied by an instrument (see Matthew 11:17; Luke 7:32). Dancing was part of celebrating the Prodigal Son's return (see Luke 15:25).[7] And since Jesus said there is rejoicing in Heaven when someone repents (see Luke 15:7), it's no stretch to suppose there will be dancing on the New Earth, too.

Festivities were commanded by God! Certainly it was possible to lose self-control at the parties, although most made sure they didn't. But the primary way to offend a holy God was to *decline to join his party*. (Indeed, in the story of the Prodigal Son, the elder brother's sin is refusing to participate in the father-ordained party to celebrate his brother's redemption.)

Some might object, saying that pagans danced to worship their false gods (see 1 Kings 18:26). And Salome danced immorally before Herod, who lusted after her (see Matthew 14:6; Mark 6:22). True. But what does that prove? Only what we already know—that humans twist what God intended for good, including eating, drinking, dancing, and making music.

THE FEASTS AND FESTIVALS IN SCRIPTURE REFLECT A BEAUTIFUL INTERSECTION OF HOLINESS AND HAPPINESS.

The early church enjoyed both the Lord's Supper (breaking bread) and "love feasts" (Jude 1:12). Acts 2:46 describes the gatherings of the believers: "Day after day they met together in the temple. They broke bread together in different homes and shared their food happily and freely" (CEV).

Paul spoke of the Lord's Supper in a way that suggested both a ceremony and a full meal eaten together (see 1 Corinthians 11:17-34). By the second century, the delightful term "love feast" was applied to the fellowship meal of believers, which was distinguished from the ceremony observing the Lord's Supper.[8] The early church celebrated the Lord's Supper as a communal act of holiness and happiness. This contrasts starkly with today's common notion of church as a joyless gathering—a place where we check off the box marked "holiness," then go out in the world to enjoy the happiness of good food, racquetball, hiking, or a campout.

REGULAR, GOD-CENTERED, HAPPINESS-FILLED CELEBRATIONS SHOULD CHARACTERIZE OUR FAMILIES AND CHURCHES.

In Dostoevsky's *The Brothers Karamazov*, Alyosha—a monastery novice—hears a priest read John 2, about Jesus turning water into wine at the wedding. Aloysha ponders, "I love that passage; it's Cana of Galilee, the first miracle. . . . Ah, that miracle! Ah, that sweet miracle! It was not men's grief, but their joy Christ visited, He worked His first miracle to help men's gladness. . . . 'He who loves men loves their gladness, too.'"[9]

Do you really believe God loves for his children to be glad? If so, how does your daily life, your family, and your church reflect that truth for all to see? Theologian Robert Hotchkins wrote, "Christians ought to be celebrating constantly. We ought to be preoccupied with parties, banquets, feasts, and merriment. We ought to give ourselves over to celebrations of joy because we have been liberated from the fear of life and the fear of death. We ought to attract people to the church quite literally by the sheer pleasure there is in being a Christian."[10]

One of the church's great challenges is to reintroduce and cultivate the spirit of happiness that should characterize God's people. We have national holidays, certainly, but when appropriate, believers can integrate into them more biblical and Christ-centered aspects. For instance, instead of just celebrating Thanksgiving with a big meal, we can take time to share with others, adults and children alike—all thanking God for specific things he has done in the previous year.

The observances of Christ's birth and resurrection have been commandeered by our culture and distanced from their true biblical and historical meanings. Rather than abandon these holidays, we can infuse them with their biblical significance. We can also celebrate other "holy and happy days" that our culture doesn't recognize and therefore won't distort.

Many nondenominational evangelical churches, my own included, don't have the benefit of long-standing church tradition. Perhaps there's merit in reestablishing biblical and distinctly Christian observances such as All Saints' Day, All Souls' Day, Ascension Day, Epiphany, Pentecost, or Reformation Sunday. We could also practice modified versions of Old Testament holidays such as Passover and Yom Kippur. Can you see the benefit in observing celebrations that have been long abandoned or trivialized in our culture?

A Feast of Saint Francis, in which churches invite the community to celebrate animals in a way that's God honoring, not pantheistic, could be a joyful and powerful outreach to people who otherwise would never connect with a church. (Regardless of our varying political persuasions, Christians should agree that the God who created the world and placed it under our management expects us to show gratitude and respect for the animals and natural resources he has entrusted to us.)

What if evangelical churches annually celebrated March 20 as the International Day of Happiness, a day officially recognized by all 192 countries of the United Nations? What an opportunity to tell each other *and* the world about the happiness of God and the happiness Christ came to bring all nations. Wouldn't it be refreshing for Christians to lead the way in making positive statements about happiness and directing people toward the happy God they desperately need to know?

Wouldn't it be great if children growing up in Christian homes looked forward to additional God-centered holidays—ones they could invite their unbelieving friends to join? Wouldn't it be fitting if church was known as the place that celebrates *more* than the world, rather than less? Worship, camaraderie, and unity would be hallmarks of such events. But one of the greatest payoffs would be reestablishing followers of Jesus as people of profound happiness who are quick to celebrate the greatness, goodness, love, grace, and happiness of our God.

God's people ought to say, "Let us eat, drink, and be merry to celebrate the time when we'll eat, drink, and be merry in a world without suffering and without end!"

Were we to do more of this kind of celebrating, and do it better, surely fewer of our children, and the next generation, would fall for the enemy's deadly lie—that the gospel of Jesus doesn't offer happiness and that people must go elsewhere to find it.

CHAPTER 34

HAPPINESS COMES FROM MEDITATING ON GOD'S WORD

How sweet Your word is to my taste—sweeter than honey in my mouth.

PSALM 119:103, HCSB

The Bible is not an end in itself, but a means to bring men to an intimate and satisfying knowledge of God, that they may enter into Him, that they may delight in His Presence, may taste and know the inner sweetness of the very God Himself in the core and center of their hearts.

A. W. TOZER

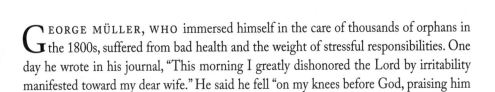

GEORGE MÜLLER, WHO immersed himself in the care of thousands of orphans in the 1800s, suffered from bad health and the weight of stressful responsibilities. One day he wrote in his journal, "This morning I greatly dishonored the Lord by irritability manifested toward my dear wife." He said he fell "on my knees before God, praising him for having given me such a wife."[1]

Müller didn't excuse his irritability. He knew his unhappiness and bad mood had displeased God and hurt his wife. He owned up to it.

But George Müller couldn't eliminate stress or occasional bad health. So what was his solution? He wrote,

I saw more clearly than ever that the first great and primary business to which I ought to attend every day was, to have my soul happy in the Lord. The first thing to be concerned about was, not how much I might serve the Lord, but how I might get my soul into a happy state, and how my inner man might be nourished. . . . I saw that the most important thing I had to do was to give myself to the reading of the Word of God, and to meditation on it.[2]

On another occasion Müller said, "In what way shall we attain to this settled happiness of soul? How shall we learn to enjoy God? . . . This happiness is to be obtained through the study of the holy Scriptures."[3]

OUR HAPPINESS IS PROPORTIONATE TO OUR INVESTMENT IN STUDYING GOD'S WORD.

My conversion to Christ didn't just make me a better person; it made me a happier person. As I've grown closer to Jesus, he has produced in me a deeper and greater happiness. Not because I've seen less evil and suffering—indeed, I've seen far more than I did when I was less happy.

My intellectual life and spiritual life aren't on different tracks. They're inseparable— Jesus said we're to love the Lord our God with our hearts *and* our minds (see Matthew 22:37). Had I not taken time to go deep and ponder God and his truth and his ways, all the spiritual inclinations in the world wouldn't have left me with a settled happiness. "As your words came to me I drank them in, and they filled my heart with joy and happiness because I belong to you, O LORD, the God who rules over all" (Jeremiah 15:16, NET).

There's nothing wrong with things such as sports and politics. But being an expert in those areas doesn't prepare us to live wisely, make Christ-centered decisions, lead our families through hard times, or prepare us to die well. Time in God's Word does.

Popular culture is so shallow, glitzy, and gossipy, it can never bring happiness. Because we're made in God's image, we're deeper than all the glitter thrown at us.

People are unhappy because they listen to the thousands of unhappy voices clamoring for attention. Joy comes from listening to and believing words of joy from the source of joy. Jesus said, "My sheep hear my voice, and I know them, and they follow me" (John 10:27). When we follow him, we are happy. When we don't, we're not.

GOD'S WORDS HAVE THE POWER TO BRING HEART-HAPPINESS.

Augustine said, "By hearing Thee I am happy; because of Thy voice I am happy."[4] There's no place we can go to hear God speak authoritatively, to hear his voice with complete confidence, other than the Bible itself.

When we're right with God, we're delighted with his words, because they're an extension of himself—his majesty, his beauty, and his happiness.

"The law of the LORD is perfect, restoring the soul. . . . The precepts of the LORD are right, rejoicing the heart" (Psalm 19:7-8, NASB). As we listen to, meditate on, and respond to God's Word, our souls are restored from sin and unhappiness to righteousness and happiness.

As a new believer in Christ, I couldn't get enough of God's Word. At night I sometimes fell asleep with my face on an open Bible. Other times I would listen to Scripture on cassette tapes (remember those?). As I drifted off to sleep, my last waking memories were of God's words.

When Jeremiah said that God's Word "became to me a joy and the delight of my heart" (Jeremiah 15:16), he was suggesting that Scripture has a cumulative effect that increases over time. Happily, by God's grace, I can attest to this.

BELIEVERS RELY ON GOD'S WORD AS THE ONLY TRUSTWORTHY REVELATION OF HIS CHARACTER AND WILL.

Tozer wrote, "The yearning to know What cannot be known, to comprehend the Incomprehensible, to touch and taste the Unapproachable, arises from the image of God in the nature of man."[5]

But *how* can we know what God is really like? We can't know without an authoritative revelation from God. Everything else is guesswork.

Anselm wrote, "Intelligent nature . . . finds its happiness, both now and forever, in the contemplation of God."[6] But we can only contemplate God with confidence if we have a source of information about God we can trust: the Bible.

Scripture says this about its own nature:

- Every scripture is inspired by God and useful for teaching, for reproof, for correction, and for training in righteousness. (2 Timothy 3:16, NET)
- No prophecy of scripture ever comes about by the prophet's own imagination, for no prophecy was ever borne of human impulse; rather, men carried along by the Holy Spirit spoke from God. (2 Peter 1:20-21, NET)

The people in Berea were commended for subjecting the apostle Paul's words to God's Word: "Now these were more noble-minded than those in Thessalonica, for they received the word with great eagerness, examining the Scriptures daily to see whether these things were so" (Acts 17:11, NASB).

Everything the Bible says about God is true; everything anyone says about God that contradicts the Bible is false. Apart from a belief in the authority of God's Word—as well as a growing knowledge of what it says—we'll be vulnerable to deception. This is why one of the greatest needs in churches today is the consistent teaching of sound doctrine. Without it, and without people reading good books that reinforce a biblical worldview, God's people will drift along, swept away by the current of popular opinion.

Faith is not inherently virtuous. Its value depends on the worth of its object. The Bible, understood in context and given precedent over our own instincts and preferences, is our dependable guide for faith and practice.

We should be wary of trendy reinterpretations of Scripture that just happen to correspond with popular culture's latest ideas. Culture, with its always-changing opinions, is not worthy of our trust. *I* am not worthy of your trust. *You* are not worthy of your trust. God is.

Only by learning what Scripture says about God can we know what's true about him—and experience the truth-based happiness that overflows from him.

GOD'S CHILDREN SHOULD VIEW SCRIPTURE AS JOY GIVING AND LIBERATING, NOT HOSTILE AND CONDEMNING.

On the one hand, the law points out our unrighteousness, leading to our condemnation (see Romans 7:7). On the other hand, the life-giving aspect of the law caused David to happily celebrate it:

- I delight in your commands because I love them. (Psalm 119:47, NIV)
- I deeply love your Law! I think about it all day. (Psalm 119:97, CEV)

Spurgeon said, "There is nothing in the Law of God that will rob you of happiness—it only denies you that which would cost you sorrow!"[7]

God tells us his laws and enforces them because he loves us—the same reason parents tell children their rules and enforce them. Children think the rules rob them of happiness. But they couldn't be more wrong.

As a young man, Samson chased what he thought would make him happy. After going where he probably shouldn't have, he came home to his father and mother saying, "I saw one of the daughters of the Philistines at Timnah. Now get her for me as my wife" (Judges 14:2). They asked why he should go to a godless nation to find a wife. But Samson insisted, "Get her for me, for she is right in my eyes" (verse 3). Wanting their boy to be happy, his parents gave in. The utter ruin and misery that followed, like one domino falling into the next, is a warning against our imagining that we and our children can be trusted to know better than God what will make us happy.

Parents who say, "I just want my children to be happy" should actually want more for them—such as to be God loving, respectful, virtuous, and generous. Children want to stay up late, eat cookies before bed, play video games for hours, and avoid their homework, imagining those things will bring them happiness. But wise parents know better. They, too, want their children to be happy—the difference is, they know what will keep them happy in the long run.

God's rules, and those of parents, are like guardrails. They appear restrictive but offer safety, freedom, and life.

WE FIND OUR DEEPEST HAPPINESS WHEN GOD'S WORD SATURATES OUR MINDS.

To meditate on God's Word is to read it and mull it over, asking God for insight and direction and letting it point out our sins so we may repent and experience God's forgiveness. Bible meditation is reflecting on God's attributes—including his love and holiness, grace and justice, happiness and wrath.

When we copy Scripture and carry it with us throughout the day, reading it and memorizing it, we make God's Word a part of us. As Paul said, "Let the word of Christ dwell in you richly" (Colossians 3:16).

John Calvin wrote, "It is the word of God alone which can first and effectually cheer the heart of any sinner. There is no true or solid peace to be enjoyed in the world except in the way of reposing upon the promises of God."[8] To repose means to recline and relax upon. We can rest upon God's promises as on a comfy bed after a hard journey.

John Piper says,

> God is glorified in his people by the way we experience him, not merely by the way we think about him. Indeed the devil thinks more true thoughts about God

in one day than a saint does in a lifetime, and God is not honored by it. The problem with the devil is not his theology, but his desires. Our chief end is to glorify God, the great Object. We do so most fully when we treasure him, desire him, delight in him so supremely that we let goods and kindred go and display his love to the poor and the lost.[9]

We all fill our minds with something. Choosing to fill our minds with God's Word is choosing to know and love him more.

David said of God's words, "More to be desired are they than gold, even much fine gold; sweeter also than honey and drippings of the honeycomb" (Psalm 19:10). You'll find abiding happiness as you go back to God's Word again and again.

READING THE BIBLE OUT OF DUTY ISN'T BAD, BUT IT'S BETTER WHEN ACCOMPANIED BY JOY.

Recently a friend told me his pastor preached, "God doesn't care about your happiness, only your obedience." In contrast, Scripture says, "Blessed is the person who fears the LORD and is happy to obey his commands" (Psalm 112:1, GW). Yes, God wants us to fulfill our duty to obey him, but we're to do so *happily*.

We're told that God "loves a cheerful giver" (2 Corinthians 9:7). Of course, he also loves an *obedient* giver, and usually the obedience comes before the happiness. So it is with Bible study. If we wait to study the Bible until we think it'll make us happy, our wait may be long. But once we get into Scripture, happiness follows. When duty is a joy and not a burden, love transcends obligation, and what's right becomes what's pleasing.

God loves this happiness-giving cycle, and so should we. David says of the godly, "His *delight* is in the law of the LORD, and on his law he meditates day and night" (Psalm 1:2, emphasis added).

As a new believer, I was told I should have "daily devotions." Unfortunately, some of my church friends thought this was an obligation to get out of the way, like brushing their teeth. I couldn't understand this, because having grown up without it, God's Word was my treasure and the compass by which I charted my life.

"Like newborn infants, long for the pure spiritual milk, that by it you may grow up into salvation" (1 Peter 2:2). Crying infants aren't concerned about doing their duty; they simply want to be fed. They crave milk because they need it.

Any day I haven't contemplated Scripture and worshiped my Lord, my happiness invariably diminishes. I tend to be impatient, critical, self-centered, and unhappy. Something's wrong—and that something is the lack of God's fresh infusion of grace through his Word.

You could read this book about happiness from cover to cover, but if you don't go to Scripture frequently to meet God and delight in him, then you can't expect to experience true, deep, and lasting happiness.

One caution: all of us will have times in Bible study that feel joyless. George Müller said, "It is a common temptation of Satan to make us give up the reading of the Word and prayer when our enjoyment is gone; as if it were of no use to read the Scriptures when we do not enjoy them, and as if it were of no use to pray when we have no spirit of prayer."[10] The key in such times isn't to give up on God's Word and prayer but to stay with it and ask him to give us joy.

WHEN WE DELIGHT IN GOD'S WORD, WE ARE DELIGHTING IN HIM.

Imagine this scenario, from an age before e-mail and Skype: a young woman is in love with a soldier serving overseas. Every day she checks her mailbox. Whenever a letter arrives, she opens it and eagerly reads and rereads every word.

Wouldn't it be accurate to say she delights in her fiancé's love letters? Would anyone correct her, "No, you should only take delight in *him*, not his letters"? That would be a meaningless distinction. Why? Because his love letters are an extension of him.

Yet I've heard people say, "Don't take pleasure in the Bible; take pleasure in *God*." But to study God's words *is* to take pleasure in God, because his Word is an expression of his very being.

Anyone who finds happiness in God must find happiness in God's words:

- In the way of your testimonies I delight as much as in all riches. (Psalm 119:14)
- I find my delight in your commandments, which I love. (Psalm 119:47)
- Oh how I love your law! It is my meditation all the day. (Psalm 119:97)

Scripture affirms that to delight in and to meditate upon God's Word is to delight in God himself.

BIBLICAL SELF-TALK, FUELED BY SCRIPTURE MEDITATION, CAN ALLEVIATE UNHAPPINESS.

Psychologists speak of self-talk—the art of telling ourselves certain things that influence our attitude, actions, and speech.

We all talk to ourselves. Whether or not self-talk is a good practice depends on what we're saying and whether it's true and helpful. For instance, Israel's judge Deborah said to herself, "O my soul, march on in strength!" (Judges 5:21, NKJV).

David was dethroned and banished by a traitorous son, and Psalms 42–43 record the words he spoke to himself: "Why are you cast down, O my soul? And why are you disquieted within me? Hope in God; for I shall yet praise Him, the help of my countenance and my God" (Psalm 42:11; 43:5).

Our tendency when we find ourselves in desperate situations is to rehearse all the causes of our self-pity and regret. However, David said to himself: "Bless the LORD, O my soul; and all that is within me, bless His holy name! Bless the LORD, O my soul, and forget not all His benefits" (Psalm 103:1-2, NKJV). Notice what David did: he gave himself a directive based upon what he knew to be right and God honoring. He rehearsed the reasons he should be joyful.

What are these benefits David told himself not to forget? He was specific: God is the one "who forgives all your iniquities, who heals all your diseases, who redeems your life from destruction, who crowns you with loving-kindness and tender mercies, who satisfies your mouth with good things, so that your youth is renewed like the eagle's" (Psalm 103:3-5, NKJV).

David went on to rehearse God's attributes: "The LORD is merciful and gracious, slow to anger and abounding in steadfast love" (Psalm 103:8). He contemplated the wonders of God's grace: "He does not deal with us according to our sins, nor repay us according to our iniquities" (verse 10).

Aware of his sin, David reminded himself (and us), "As far as the east is from the west, so far does he remove our transgressions from us" (Psalm 103:12). He told himself, "As a father shows compassion to his children, so the LORD shows compassion to those who fear him" (verse 13). Remembering his limits and frailty, David said, "He knows our frame; he remembers that we are dust" (verse 14).

David's God-centered self-talk gave him perspective—but not his own! We already have our own perspective; what we need is God's, and we get that from his Word. He ended with a final word to himself: "Bless the LORD, O my soul!" (Psalm 103:22).

Those who suffer from clinical depression will not find biblically grounded self-talk a cure-all. But all of us can be helped, to some degree, by practicing it. We can and should follow David's perspective-changing example by meditating on God's Word and engaging in Christ-honoring self-talk. If we keep telling ourselves there's no hope, we'll believe it and be profoundly unhappy. To have hope, we must draw from God's Word to tell ourselves the reasons for our hope, which all rest in God!

In his classic book *Spiritual Depression*, Martyn Lloyd-Jones wrote,

> Most of your unhappiness in life is due to the fact that you are listening to yourself instead of talking to yourself. . . . You have to take yourself in hand, you have to address yourself, preach to yourself, question yourself. You must say to your soul: "Why art thou cast down"—what business have you to be disquieted? You must turn on yourself, upbraid yourself, condemn yourself, exhort yourself, and say to yourself: "Hope thou in God"—instead of muttering in this depressed, unhappy way.[11]

When we memorize, meditate upon, and quote to ourselves biblical passages about joy, happiness, and gladness, we break out of the ruts of hopelessness, despair, and pride. We dig new channels for the rivers of our thoughts. If you took the hundreds of verses I cite throughout this book and contemplated them every week, I'm confident you would become a happier person.

If we tell ourselves we deserve better, we'll be unhappy, and we'll spread our unhappiness. If we tell ourselves the truth—that God constantly gives us better than we deserve—we'll be grateful. Instead of being continually disappointed, we'll often be pleasantly surprised. Our cheerfulness will spread.

Feeding on God's thoughts in his Word nourishes our souls and feeds our joy. Such well-fed and well-exercised minds will become repositories of worship, thanksgiving, and praise, which will overflow into conversations—breathing in joy from our Lord and breathing out praise to him. A life saturated in the Bible—seeing doctrine as a basis for humble worship, not prideful posturing—will in turn infuse others with an eternal perspective and God's happiness.

LIKE EVERY OTHER HAPPINESS-PRODUCING PRACTICE, MEDITATION ON SCRIPTURE MUST ACTUALLY BE DONE.

I've spoken with people who have known for years, even decades, that they should meditate daily on God's Word. But there are always compelling reasons not to do it today. Then today becomes yesterday, and a hundred yesterdays pile up, with Bible study undone.

Excuses come easily, but those excuses will rob us of joy. If you hope to start spending daily time in God's Word, drop everything—yes, including this book. Open God's Word and meditate on it. If you need a plan, fine. Search online for "Bible reading plans," and you'll find some great ones.[12] But you must start. Not next week, not tomorrow—*now*.

Joni Eareckson Tada says, "Great faith isn't the ability to believe long and far into the misty future. It's simply taking God at his word and taking the next step."[13] But just as we can't follow road signs unless we get on the road, we can't take God at his Word unless we take the time to read, hear, and contemplate it.

Wilhelmus à Brakel said, "The soul is either joyful or sorrowful in relation to whether he is far from God or close to Him."[14] Through Bible meditation, prayer, group Bible study, and sitting under the teaching of God's Word, we get to know our Lord better and draw closer to him. In the process, we cultivate overflowing happiness.

THE FAILURE OF CHRISTIAN MEN TO STUDY GOD'S WORD HAS CONTRIBUTED TO THEIR LOSS OF HAPPINESS.

Everything I'm talking about in this section pertains to women also, but I know more women than men who study God's Word, and I believe men are missing out on joy as a result. Many Christian men would agree that they're experts in business, hunting, fishing, football, or cars. Sadly, however, even those who attend Bible-teaching churches may know very little about the Bible and theology.

Why? It's simple. Every week, men invest hours watching sports and listening to radio talk shows. They visit car dealerships, read car repair manuals, and spend extended time under the hood. They go fishing or hunting. None of these activities is sinful, but any and all can dominate our spare time and the thoughts that occupy our minds. We're all experts in what we do and think about, and novices in everything else.

Suppose men dedicated even half the time invested in those activities to reading and listening to the Bible and great Christian books. What if they took half the time now devoted to political talk shows and hobbies and invested it in learning solid Bible doctrine? Soon they could converse theologically with as much knowledge and pleasure as they can about sports, hunting, fishing, cars, or politics. And the activities they engage in will be that much more happiness-producing because they'll know better the one who made all these other pastimes possible! Put God first, and everything else falls into place.

We all talk about what we know best—what's most important to us. That means we need to change what's important to us by investing more time in it.

How many men have frequent God-centered conversations today—with each other, their wives, and their children? How much pleasure and happiness are we depriving ourselves of by talking about everything except what matters most?

Calvin Miller lamented, "Never have there been so many disciples who did so little studying. . . . Our day is plagued by hordes of miserable Christians whose pitiful study habits give them few victories and much frustration. Serious students will develop dynamic minds and a confident use of the gifts God has given to them."[15]

HAPPINESS IS PUTTING GOD AT THE CENTER OF OUR THINKING.

Charles Spurgeon wrote, "The Promises are the Christian's Magna Charta of liberty. They are the title deeds of his heavenly estate! Happy is he who knows how to read them well and call them all his own."[16]

Frank Laubach (1884–1970) devoted his life to encouraging literacy around the world, with the goal that people everywhere would read the Bible. He wrote an influential pamphlet entitled "The Game with Minutes." In it, Laubach encouraged Christians to keep God in their minds at least one second of every minute each day.[17]

Laubach wrote,

Humble folks often believe that walking with God is above their heads, or that they may "lose a good time" if they share all their joys with Christ. What a tragic misunderstanding to regard Him as a killer of happiness! A chorus of joyous voices round the world fairly sing that spending their hours with the Lord is the most thrilling joy ever known, and that beside it a ball game or a horse race is stupid. Spending time with the Lord is not a grim duty. And if you forget Him for minutes or even days, do not groan or repent, but begin anew with a smile. We live one day at a time. Every moment can be a fresh beginning.[18]

Most days (I wish I could say all), I go to God expecting to be fed and encouraged, to be given joy and perspective. I sense God more in some moments than others, but I know he's always with me and therefore I'm with him. His wisdom, insight, grace, and love sometimes overwhelm me and nearly always encourage me. And if today isn't one of those days, I don't have to wait for tomorrow. He's still with me as I go about my day. I can still think, pray, and meditate on Scripture even as I do other things, including—even especially—the mundane. Time with God is never wasted—it spills over into the rest of our day and colors it.

Puritan Thomas Brooks wrote:

Ah, friends, if you would but in good earnest set upon reading of the holy Scriptures, you may find in them so many happinesses as cannot be numbered, and so great happinesses as cannot be measured, and so copious happinesses as cannot be defined, and such precious happinesses as cannot be valued; and if all this won't draw you to read the holy Scriptures conscientiously and frequently, I know not what will.[19]

Almost four hundred years later, these words remain true. The copious happiness Brooks found in Scripture is freely available to us all—and the prospect of that happiness should draw us back to our Bibles every day.

CHAPTER 35

HAPPINESS IN CHRIST IS DEEPER THAN THE HEALTH-AND-WEALTH GOSPEL

If anyone teaches a different doctrine . . . he is puffed up with conceit . . . imagining that godliness is a means of gain. . . . But those who desire to be rich fall into temptation, into a snare, into many senseless and harmful desires that plunge people into ruin and destruction. For the love of money is a root of all kinds of evils. It is through this craving that some have wandered away from the faith and pierced themselves with many pangs.

I TIMOTHY 6:3-5, 9-10

He that serves God for money will serve the devil for better wages.

SIR ROBERT L'ESTRANGE

JOSEPH SCRIVEN (1820–1886) wrote "What a Friend We Have in Jesus" after his fiancée drowned. George Matheson (1842–1906) wrote "O Love That Wilt Not Let Me Go" after his fiancée rejected him because he was going blind. And Horatio Spafford (1828–1888) wrote one of our best-loved hymns under tragic circumstances.

Spafford, his wife, and his four daughters planned a trip to hear his friend D. L. Moody preach in England. Detained by business, Spafford sent his family ahead on another ship. Their ship sank, and though his wife was rescued, his daughters drowned. While traveling to meet his distressed wife, he was informed by the ship's captain that they'd nearly reached the spot where his daughters perished. As he passed over their watery grave, Spafford wrote a profound hymn that has touched millions: "It Is Well with My Soul."

In stark contrast, I watched a video featuring someone whose worldview was based on the health-and-wealth philosophy. As she lay dying of cancer, she looked into a camera and said bitterly, "I've lost my faith." She felt God had broken his promises. She correctly surmised that the god she'd followed didn't exist. But that wasn't the God of the Bible, who never made the promises she thought he'd broken. God hadn't let her down; her church and its preachers had.

Christ-followers who have learned to turn to God in their hardest times have found great comfort and solace in him. Meanwhile, under the guise of laying claim to God's guarantees of profit, the health-and-wealth gospel—also known as prosperity theology—puts God's name to the pursuit of what the world tells people will make them happy.

PROSPERITY THEOLOGY IS A POISONOUS HERESY.

I don't want to be uncharitable, but I will be blunt: I believe prosperity theology is straight from the pit of Hell. Centered on giving people what they want, this worldview treats God as a genie or a cosmic slot machine: insert a positive confession, pull the lever, catch the winnings.

God's blessing on financial giving is turned into a money-back guarantee of a hundredfold return that will look like whatever we want or claim. Prayer degenerates into coercion by which adherents "name it and claim it," pulling God's leash until he increases their comforts.

"Faith" becomes a crowbar to break down the door of God's reluctance rather than a humble attempt to lay hold of his willingness. Sadly, claiming that God *must* take away an illness or a financial hardship often means calling on him to remove the very things he has permitted and designed to make us more Christlike.

Prosperity preachers routinely quote, "Beloved, I pray that all may go well with you and that you may be in good health" (3 John 1:2). Never mind that John spent time in exile for his faith—meaning that all did not go well for him—and that he was praying for God's best for his friends as God saw fit.

Consider God's role in these words spoken by a prominent preacher of the prosperity gospel: "Put God to work for you and maximize your potential in our divinely ordered capitalist system."[1] This pragmatic use of God demonstrates a clear lack of interest in God himself. After all, genies serve one purpose: to grant our wishes. Who needs a deep relationship with his genie?

The Bible paints a radically different picture of God, in which his glory is the focal point of the universe and his sovereign purpose entitles him to do what he wills, even when it violates our preferences and expectations.

When hard times come, people should lose their faith in false doctrine, not in God. In contrast to jewelry-draped televangelists, Paul said, "We must go through many hardships to enter the kingdom of God" (Acts 14:22, NIV).

IT'S OKAY TO WANT HEALTH AND PROSPERITY AS LONG AS WE RECOGNIZE THAT GOD DETERMINES THE FINAL OUTCOME.

It isn't unspiritual to desire health over sickness, wealth over poverty, and success over failure. But if the source of our happiness isn't God, then health, wealth, and success become our false gods. God becomes a mere means to an end.

I think every Bible-believing pastor should oppose the false doctrines of the health-and-wealth gospel. But *we need to be clear on exactly what we're opposing.* Prosperity theology isn't wrong because it values happiness. It's wrong because it tries to obtain happiness in secondary things rather than in God. It lays claim to out-of-context Scriptures while ignoring all the passages that expose its errors.

We're right to look forward to perfect health and wealth, and God promises them in the right place and time—after the Resurrection, on the New Earth.

When righteous Job lost everything, even his children, he worshiped God, saying, "The LORD gave and the LORD has taken away; may the name of the LORD be praised." We're told, "In all this, Job did not sin by charging God with wrongdoing" (Job 1:21-22, NIV).

In contrast, when advocates of the prosperity gospel lose their health and wealth, they lose their happiness, demonstrating that the true object of their faith was *not* God.

Our prayers are to be earnest, unapologetic requests for what we want, uttered in willing submission to whatever God wants. True faith doesn't insist that we say, "I'll conquer this cancer." Rather, we can affirm, "I know God can heal me. But I trust him. I pray he'll accomplish his best whether through sickness and death or through healing and ongoing life."

Some will write off this kind of prayer as lacking in faith since it acknowledges the possibility of death. But aside from the return of Christ in our lifetimes (possible but far from certain), we'll all die. (Do you know any 120-year-old faith healers?)

True faith is in God, not in prosperity theology or in what we believe to be best. It shouldn't be faith in faith, but faith in the God who will keep his promise of resurrection and eternal life.

Job's wife, believing God had failed them, said, "Curse God and die." Job's response exposed the shallowness of prosperity theology: "Shall we accept good from God, and not trouble?" (Job 2:9-10, NIV).

WE'RE NEVER COMMANDED TO BE HEALTHY AND WEALTHY, BUT WE *ARE* COMMANDED TO REJOICE AND BE HAPPY.

There's an important difference between health and wealth, and happiness. The primary source of our happiness isn't our circumstances but our God, who promised he'd be with us always and who commands us to rejoice in him.

Prosperity theology can't bring happiness, because health and wealth can't bring happiness. Ed Welch says this about the health-and-wealth gospel: "As a counselor I see its wretched fruit. . . . It focuses on here-and-now benefits, leaving people unprepared for hardships. Some even feel *guilty* when they suffer because they assume they have done something wrong and have yet to figure out what it is. In the end, some are angry at God because he seems to have reneged on his promises to give us a merry life."[2]

As Christians, we'll be delivered from *eternal* suffering. And even now, God will give us joyful foretastes of living in his presence. *That's* his promise. He doesn't say we'll never have hardship or suffering—he specifically promises we will. In fact, Paul told believers in Greece who were facing adversity that he was sending Timothy to them "to strengthen and encourage [them] . . . so that no one would be unsettled by these trials. For you know quite well that we are destined for them" (1 Thessalonians 3:2-3, NIV).

So not only is suffering part of life under the Curse, but God has actually *destined* us to suffer! This means our afflictions are both inevitable and purposeful—and because these Christ-followers understood that, their trials, though difficult, did not unsettle their trust in God.

Notice that Paul saw their need to be reminded of God's purpose in their suffering—that's why he sent Timothy, whom in the same passage he called "our brother and co-worker in God's service in spreading the gospel of Christ." Part of the gospel Paul and Timothy preached was God's sovereign and loving work even in our greatest hardships. Sorrow is real, but just as resurrection outdoes death, joy in Christ always trumps sorrow in the end.

As Easter worked in reverse to make Good Friday good, so our resurrection will work in reverse to bring goodness to our most difficult days. Faith is a sort of forward memory in which we trust God's promise of eternal happiness and experience a foretaste of that happiness in severe difficulty.

By focusing only on resurrection triumph and ignoring God's call and empowerment to take up our crosses and suffer hardship, prosperity theology opposes and undercuts these truths. It robs us of a biblically grounded and reality-based trust in God, who guarantees that all sorrows will end and that although we have present sorrows, our Savior simultaneously promises us both eternal *and* present joy.

A life focused on God allows us to rejoice in whatever health and wealth God entrusts to us as stewards but reminds us that he doesn't promise these as permanent conditions in the present world. We're called to give away God's money to help the needy and to fulfill the great commission (see Matthew 6:19-21; see also 1 Timothy 6:6-10, 17-19).

Some Christians are also called upon to sacrifice their health through long hours of labor or by enduring persecution. We should be willing to lay everything on the line for Jesus because our life focus is on God, not self, health, or wealth—and not happiness either, in any form other than happiness in God, which is his command and calling. It's not that material things are bad; it's that they're impotent—they can't keep their promise of happiness. Only God can.

If our happiness is grounded in God, we won't lose the basis for it, because nothing will separate us from the love of Christ (see Romans 8:37-39).

An Iranian Christ-follower spoke at our church. His dear friend in prison, who had been separated from his family for three years, writes, "They say I'm the happiest man in this prison, and I believe they're right."

This isn't the pasted-on, fake-it-till-you-make-it "joy" of the health-and-wealth gospel, but the deep and resonant happiness of someone who knows that the God with the nail-scarred hands is truly with him in prison.

TWISTING GOD'S PROMISES FOR THE FUTURE TO FIT THIS PRESENT LIFE BRINGS FLEETING AND FALSE HAPPINESS.

The true gospel is about Jesus, and therefore a gospel that's about health and wealth is a false gospel. Part of Jesus' gospel is the promise of eternal life, guaranteed by Christ's resurrection. *That* life includes everlasting health and wealth. *That* is Good News!

Prosperity theology's promises aren't false in themselves, which is why they can be supported by many Scripture passages. The deception comes in believing that God's promises can all be claimed and enjoyed *now*.

Revelation 21:4 tells us that God will end the reasons for weeping and that pain will be a thing of the past. So why not claim this promise now? Because its fulfillment will come *after* the Resurrection, on the New Earth.

The health-and-wealth gospel is based on an over-realized eschatology, in which believers claim promises in the present age that pertain to the future. For instance, God promises that his people will reign with him (see 2 Timothy 2:12), but it's misguided to think we should be reigning here and now.

The Bible's promises about the future bring great encouragement, perspective, and happiness during this life. But we shouldn't twist them to fit our timeline.

David Brainerd, suffering from tuberculosis in the 1700s, said, "In the week past I had divers turns of inward refreshing; though my body was inexpressibly weak, followed continually with agues and fevers. Sometimes my soul centered in God, as my only portion; and I felt that I should be forever unhappy, if he did not reign: I saw the sweetness and happiness of being his subject, at his disposal. This made all my difficulties quickly vanish."[3]

By "vanish," Brainerd didn't mean his challenges disappeared but that supernatural happiness in the sovereign plan of a happy God overshadowed them.

HAD JESUS LAID CLAIM TO PROSPERITY IN THIS LIFE, THERE WOULD HAVE BEEN NO CRUCIFIXION, NO ATONEMENT, AND NO HOPE FOR US.

There's a popular saying in health-and-wealth circles: "Live like a king's kid." The ultimate "King's kid" was Jesus, God's Son—but his life looked radically different from the way that phrase is intended today.

Prosperity theology sees as our model the ascended heavenly Lord rather than the descended earthly servant. Jesus warned his disciples not to follow a lordship model, but his servant model (see Mark 10:42-45). In this life, we're to share in his cross—in the next life, we'll share in his crown.

In verses you'll never see framed or posted on refrigerators, the King promises that we'll be persecuted, betrayed, flogged, and tried for our faith (see Matthew 10:16-20). He warned, "In this world you will have trouble" (John 16:33, niv) and said, "Any one of you who does not renounce all that he has cannot be my disciple" (Luke 14:33).

GOD HAS GOOD REASONS FOR NOT GIVING US EVERYTHING WE WANT RIGHT NOW.

C. S. Lewis articulated the erroneous conclusion people come to: "If God were good, He would wish to make His creatures perfectly happy, and if God were almighty He would be able to do what He wished. But the creatures are not happy. Therefore God lacks either goodness, or power, or both."[4]

Put another way, if Jesus triumphed over sin and death, why does our world still contain so much evil and suffering? Why are we still sinners, why do many of us get sick, why are some of the godliest people in the world poor, and why do all of us die? If God is happy and wants us to be happy, why doesn't he bring us complete happiness *now*?

There are varying responses to these excellent questions, and the good ones all require trust that a good, loving, holy, and just God knows what he's doing. By delaying his final judgment on evil and waiting longer to wipe away all tears from his children's eyes, he's giving more people a chance to repent and trust Christ (see 2 Peter 3:9).

Meanwhile, God is giving his children more opportunities to grow in faith (see 1 Peter 1:6), he's developing our character through trials (see Job 23:10; Isaiah 48:10), he's increasing our perseverance and hope (see Romans 5:4), and he's bringing more ultimate good to us and glory to himself (see Romans 8:28-29).

God has redeemed us "so that in the coming ages he might show the immeasurable riches of his grace in kindness toward us in Christ Jesus" (Ephesians 2:7). Throughout eternity, God will unfold more and more of his grace and kindness. As wonderful as Eden was, without sin and suffering, would Adam and Eve have reason to praise God for his grace? No. Certainly they could see God's goodness, but grace is unmerited favor to those who deserve Hell. Therefore, they had less reason to praise him than we do.

Experiencing God's grace now will pay off in eternity, too. We may want to skip this growth process and be ushered directly into eternal happiness, but that wouldn't accomplish God's highest purpose. He plans to remake Earth into an eternal world where righteousness reigns because he has marvelously overcome evil, starting in the hearts of his beloved children.

In *The Problem of Pain*, C. S. Lewis wrote, "To ask that God's love should be content with us as we are is to ask that God should cease to be God: because He is what He is, His love must, in the nature of things, be impeded and repelled by certain stains in our present character, and because He already loves us He must labour to make us lovable."[5]

THE FOUNDATION OF OUR HAPPINESS ISN'T HEALTH AND WEALTH, BUT GOD'S SOVEREIGN LOVE.

Romans 8:28 says, "We know that for those who love God all things work together for good, for those who are called according to his purpose." By recognizing and believing in God's sovereignty, even over Satan's work, our perspective is transformed.

As a child, I sometimes watched my mom bake. Before she made a cake, she'd lay the ingredients on the kitchen counter. One day I tasted each ingredient. Flour. Baking soda. Raw eggs. Vanilla extract. I discovered that *almost everything that goes into a cake tastes terrible*. But a delicious metamorphosis took place when my mother skillfully mixed the ingredients in just the right amounts and baked them at the perfect temperature. The final product was delicious!

Similarly, the individual ingredients of trials and apparent tragedies taste bitter to us. No translation of Romans 8:28 says, "Each thing by itself is good" but "All things work together *for* good"—and not on their own, but under God's sovereign hand. I don't need to say, "It's good" if my house burns down or I'm robbed and beaten or my child dies. But God, in his wisdom, measures and mixes our circumstances, then regulates the heat in order to produce something wonderful—Christlikeness—for his glory and our ultimate joy.

The Romans 8:28 of the Old Testament is Genesis 50:20. Joseph's brothers betrayed him, selling him into slavery. Decades later Joseph told them, "As for you, you meant [plotted, premeditated] evil against me, but God *meant* [same Hebrew word] it for good, to bring it about that many people should be kept alive, as they are today" (emphasis added).

While Joseph's brothers plotted harm to Joseph, God, the author of life (see Acts 3:15), plotted good for him. God didn't just make the best of a bad situation. Rather, he *intended* all along to use evil for ultimate good. He did so as part of his eternal plan—for God's children have "been predestined according to the purpose of him who works *all things* according to the counsel of his will" (Ephesians 1:11, emphasis added).

Why isn't Good Friday called *Bad* Friday? Because *we see it in retrospect*. Out of the appallingly bad came the inexpressibly good. Had Jesus been delivered from his suffering, he couldn't have delivered us from ours. If God brought the greatest good out of his Son's suffering, can't he also bring good out of ours? To imply otherwise, as prosperity theology does, is to undermine God's truth and encourage a loss of trust in God.

The Gospel accounts of the Crucifixion and Resurrection depict Christ's deep unhappiness in Gethsemane and his anticipation of the Cross. Joy and happiness are overshadowed by sorrow and grief—until the release of death. What follows for Jesus is joy, but for the apostles it is overwhelming grief.

Resurrection happiness soon shines its light, pushing sorrow into the shadows. Death is conquered, and our eternal happiness secured. What would otherwise have been remembered as Terrible Friday is transformed into Good Friday because Christ's resurrection works in reverse upon death. The hidden purpose in Christ's suffering is no longer hidden—it becomes a spectacular cause for happiness. This is the gospel's Good News! In the end, life conquers death, joy triumphs over suffering. Happiness, not sorrow, has the last word—and it will have the last word forever.

This secure future invades our present, so that even while death and sorrow remain, the new normal in Christ isn't sorrow but happiness.

Corrie ten Boom, who survived a Nazi death camp, said, "Every experience God gives us . . . is the perfect preparation for a future only He can see."[6]

Charles Spurgeon said, "In heaven we shall see that we had not one trial too many."[7] Reveling in God's sovereign grace, Spurgeon exclaimed, "Cheer up, Christian! Things are not left to chance—no blind fate rules the world! God has purposes and those purposes are fulfilled; God has plans and those plans are wise, and never can be dislocated!"[8]

PAUL'S LIFE AND LETTERS POWERFULLY REFUTE PROSPERITY THEOLOGY.

Most Pharisees believed that God blessed the faithful with good fortune, health, and prosperity. They supposed that to be righteous was to be rich, which is why Jesus' teachings about wealth (see Matthew 19:24) were so disturbing to them. Jesus said, "Woe to you who are rich, for you have already received your comfort" (Luke 6:24, NIV). We read, "The Pharisees, who were lovers of money, heard all these things, and they ridiculed him" (Luke 16:14). After all, Jesus was a poor carpenter. Clearly he didn't enjoy God's favor like they did.

Raised a Pharisee, Paul, too, believed that God's favor included material wealth. He couldn't imagine Jesus being the Messiah because of his obvious lack of prosperity. He believed God's disapproval of the man Jesus was surely self-evident in his questionable parentage, his disreputable place of upbringing, his lack of formal education, his poverty, and above all, his shameful death. But when Paul bowed his knee to Christ, he turned his back on prosperity theology. His Lord said, "I will show [Paul] how much he must suffer for my name" (Acts 9:16, NCV).

As a result of following Christ, Paul lost everything (see Philippians 3:7-8). His daily adversity and close calls with death are described in 2 Corinthians 4:7-12. Two chapters later we read about Paul's troubles, hardships, distresses, beatings, imprisonments, sleepless nights, and hunger, as well as his experiences nearly dying and being sorrowful and poor (see 2 Corinthians 6:3-10). If you read Paul's account of how hard he labored and how often he was in prison, flogged, beaten, stoned, shipwrecked, hungry, cold, and naked (see 2 Corinthians 11:23-29), you won't find stronger evidence to refute prosperity theology.

Paul had to defend himself against the prosperity preachers of his day, who berated him because he couldn't claim their wealth and prestige (see 1 Corinthians 4:8-13). He said to them, "Already you have all you want! Already you have become rich! . . . You have become kings!" (verse 8). He added, "We are weak, but you are strong. You are held in honor, but we in disrepute" (verse 10). These prosperity preachers preempted reigning with Christ by living here as kings rather than as servants. The showmanship that often accompanies the preaching of prosperity theology is exactly the attitude Paul was correcting in 1 Corinthians 4.

PAUL'S DISABILITY SERVED A HIGHER PURPOSE.

After explaining that God had given him some special revelations, Paul added:

> To keep me from becoming conceited, I was given a thorn in my flesh, a messenger of Satan, to torment me. Three times I pleaded with the Lord to take it away from me. But he said to me, "My grace is sufficient for you, for my power is made perfect in weakness." Therefore I will boast all the more gladly about my weaknesses, so that Christ's power may rest on me.   2 CORINTHIANS 12:7-9, NIV

Paul's thorn was a daily reminder of his need to trust in God's grace rather than his own gifts. When God chose not to heal him, he didn't "name it and claim it." Instead, he acknowledged God's spiritual purpose in his adversity.

Today's health-and-wealth preachers bypass the rest of this passage and say, in essence, "Paul called this disease a 'messenger of Satan.' The devil wants us sick, but God wants us well." Yes, Paul called the ailment a messenger of Satan. But God is supreme, and Satan is just one more agent he uses to accomplish his own purpose. (Certainly Satan would wish to cultivate Paul's conceit, not prevent it.)

THOSE WHO CLAIM THAT ANYONE WITH ENOUGH FAITH CAN BE HEALED HAVE GREATER FAITH THAN PAUL.

Not only was Paul himself not healed, but he left Trophimus sick in Miletus (see 2 Timothy 4:20). His beloved friend Epaphroditus was also gravely ill (see Philippians 2:24-30). Timothy, his son in the faith, had frequent stomach disorders. Note that Paul didn't tell him to "claim healing"—instead, he told him to drink a little wine for medicinal purposes (see 1 Timothy 5:23).

Now Paul is enjoying perfect health and wealth. But like many of God's servants, while he was on Earth, God's higher plan was for him to often be sick and poor. When he was taken in chains from his filthy Roman dungeon and beheaded at the order of Nero, Paul entered into eternal happiness. But in the midst of adversity, he said, "Be happy in your faith at all times. Never stop praying. Be thankful, whatever the circumstances may be" (1 Thessalonians 5:16-18, PHILLIPS).

COUNTLESS CHRISTIANS, STRIPPED OF HEALTH, HAVE TRUSTED IN AND HONORED GOD IN THEIR SUFFERING.

My friend Jim Harrell lived one of the most striking rebukes to prosperity theology I've ever witnessed.

I met Jim after he read my book *Heaven.* He was a successful businessman—strong and athletic for most of his life, until he was stricken with ALS (Lou Gehrig's disease). He asked me if I'd send him the manuscript for my book *If God Is Good* before it was published, which I was happy to do. We discussed how God was using his disease in amazing ways.

Reflecting on how his slow death from ALS was helping him to discover real life, Jim wrote me, "Suffering is the icy cold splash that wakes us up from the complacency of living this life. We truly don't see God and his purpose and strength without suffering, because we just become too comfortable."[9]

Jim's words reminded me of Paul's: "I see that my letter hurt you, but only for a little while—yet now I am happy, not because you were made sorry, but because your sorrow led you to repentance. For you became sorrowful as God intended and so were not harmed" (2 Corinthians 7:8-9, NIV). God helped these believers by drawing them back to him *through their pain.*

Jim continued,

As I contemplate what it would be like to be healed of this disease, God has caused me to focus on my own sinfulness and human condition. If healed, I genuinely fear that within a year at the latest I would begin to forget what it was like to be in this condition. I would fall into the trap of allowing life's distractions to divert me. While I realize these distractions are not bad in and of themselves, a clear and distinct advantage of suffering is its ability to sharply focus one on what's important. . . . The wonder of being healed would be indescribable; however, I seriously question whether or not that would be the best for my soul.[10]

Jim called together family and friends to share what God was doing in him, and soon he was speaking to groups and touching lives in ways that amazed him. Realizing that suffering was both opening doors for ministry and preparing him for eternity, the phrase "eternal perspective" became part of his daily vocabulary. Jim said, "I've seen more accomplished in the time I've had ALS than in the first fifty years of my life. This illness is a blessing because God is really working on my soul. I'm going into eternity with my soul in a lot better shape than if I hadn't gotten ALS."[11]

I visited Jim in Illinois a few months before he died. By then he was unable to speak clearly. But his mouth could form a smile, and he kept performing facial antics and using his limited arm movements to tell me things. His friends and family interpreted—he was repeatedly joking with me. Amid all his suffering, he experienced profound and contagious happiness.

Am I glorifying or minimizing the ravages of disease or implying that this is the only way God can work in our lives? Certainly not. But what if the highest good and greatest happiness in life is to draw close to Jesus? And what if God can help us achieve that good through suffering?

Rather than taking him out of the game of life, suffering put Jim into it. He saw that his suffering was the training required for him to win not an Olympic medal but an eternal reward. The more demanding the training, the more he locked his eyes on the prize (see 1 Corinthians 9:24-27).

More Christians need to stop listening to the health-and-wealth gospel and listen instead to people like Jim Harrell, who "though he died, he still speaks" (Hebrews 11:4).

CHAPTER 36

HAPPINESS THROUGH CONFESSION, REPENTANCE, AND FORGIVENESS

O the happiness of him whose transgression [is] forgiven, Whose sin is covered.

PSALM 32:1, YLT

Christians are happy, real ones, because they know that their sins are all forgiven.

R. A. TORREY

─────────────── ❧ ───────────────

RUTH BELL GRAHAM told the story of Alexander Grigolia, a brilliant but unhappy immigrant to the United States from Soviet Georgia. He was struck by the demeanor of the man who shined his shoes. One day, looking down at this man who worked cheerfully and enthusiastically, and considering his own misery, Grigolia asked, "Why are you always so happy?"

Surprised, the man said, "Jesus. He loves me. He died so God could forgive my badness. He makes me happy."

Grigolia said nothing in response but could not escape those simple words. Eventually he came to faith in Christ, became a college professor, and had a strong influence on his students, one being future evangelist Billy Graham.[1]

SINCE LASTING HAPPINESS CAN'T BE FOUND APART FROM GOD, SIN WILL NEVER BE A SOURCE OF HAPPINESS.

"What is the matter with the world?" Martyn Lloyd-Jones asked. "Why . . . war and all this unhappiness and turmoil and discord amongst men? . . . There is only one answer to these questions—sin. Nothing else; it is just sin."[2]

It's common to blame the world's suffering and unhappiness on lack of education, opportunity, or resources. *If only we knew more or had more, we'd surely be better.* No. Our most basic problem is just . . . sin.

Stephen Charnock wrote, "Though the fall be the cause of all our misery, yet [recognizing] it is the first step to all our happiness."[3]

Sin must be dealt with directly through awareness, confession, and repentance. Only in forgiveness can we have relational oneness with God and, hence, enduring happiness.

Anyone unaware of his or her guilt before a holy God is in the worst possible condition. What if a person with a burst appendix couldn't feel pain? He might happily stay home and watch a movie rather than go to the hospital. And then he would die.

SIN KILLS ULTIMATE HAPPINESS.

Puritan and Cambridge University professor William Whitaker (1548–1595) spoke of "sinning away that happiness wherein we were created."[4] This is a striking description of what Adam and Eve did in Paradise and what many of us do—we sin away happiness.

William Bates said, "The most pernicious effect of sin is the separation of the soul from God; and the restoral of us to happiness, is by reunion with him."[5] These two premises—that God is the source of all happiness and that sin separates us from God—lead to this conclusion: *sin separates us from happiness.*

Satan is the enemy of God's happiness and ours. While he can't rob God of happiness, he specializes in sabotaging ours, catching us on the baited hook of pleasure. The first hit of a drug, the buzz of alcohol, or the thrill of illicit sex seems so good at the time. But then the very thing that brings us a taste of joy robs us of true and abiding joy. Sin is the ultimate killjoy.

To sin is to break relationship with God. Therefore, sin is the biggest enemy of happiness, and forgiveness its greatest friend. Confession reunites us with the God of happiness.

If we believe that sin is never in our best interests, it will clarify many otherwise hard decisions in which we imagine we must choose between helping people do right and helping them be happy.

For instance, a young woman who believed that abortion takes the life of an innocent child nonetheless told me that because she loved her friend, she was going to drive her to the clinic to get an abortion. She said, "That's what you do when you love someone, even if you disagree."

I asked, "If your friend wanted to kill her parents and had a shotgun in hand, would you drive her to her parents' house?"

"Of course not."

But other than legality, what's the difference? It's never in a mother's best interest to kill her child—it will ultimately take from her far more happiness than it brings. Too often, in the name of love, we assist people in taking wrong actions which, because they are wrong, will rob them of happiness. We may congratulate ourselves for being "loving," but what good does our love do them if it encourages their self-destruction?

BECAUSE IT DOESN'T SATISFY, SIN DEMANDS INCREASING INTENSITY.

Addiction provides a picture of all sin patterns. At first, the happiness it causes seems to outweigh the misery. But eventually the periods of misery increase while the periods of happiness fade. This is called the law of diminishing returns. Life is promised; death is delivered. Every drug, alcohol, and pornography addict is living proof that the next high is less satisfying than the last.

Heroin addicts first take the drug to be happy. In moments of clarity, they despise heroin for what it's doing to them and despise themselves for yielding to it. Yet memories of brief pleasure overpower their prevailing misery. Longing to escape, they take another hit, hoping this time will bring lasting happiness. It never does.

If insanity is doing the same thing over and over while expecting different results, sin not only leads to insanity—it *is* insanity.

Regardless of your drug of choice—materialism, cocaine, pornography, power—the nature of any sin is saying, "This time will be different." Yet it just keeps killing us—in the name of happiness.

UNRIGHTEOUS LIFESTYLE CHOICES LEAD TO DEEPER UNHAPPINESS.

Historically, our culture's fashion, film, and music industries—merchants of "happiness"—have been run largely by men. The immoral values promoted by these industries lure young girls into promiscuity, convincing them it's cool. A girl has casual sex and later feels rejection, loss of respect, and disdain from the boy she believed loved her. The dream turns into a nightmare. But hoping that next time will be different, she has sex with another boy, and another, and another, until her self-respect is completely gone.

For decades, mothers have been promised they can be happy if they "terminate the pregnancy"—the deceiver's language for "kill your child." Yet I've talked with countless women who, years later, still weep over their abortions. The adverse physical and psychological consequences of abortion are well documented, including higher levels of depression and suicide.[6] Numerous post-abortion support groups exist to help women heal after getting the abortion they were told would bring them happiness.[7]

Our culture also entices people into viewing pornography. The happiness it promises instead delivers shame, loneliness, and devastation and leads to an endless downward spiral of deeper perversion and darkness.

Similarly, some people have bought into the idea that they'll find happiness in the homosexual lifestyle. But when they surrender to their desires, they typically end up unhappy.

There's a tragic irony in the positive term *gay*, which has replaced historically negative terms, such as *sodomite*, and neutral terms, such as *homosexual*. No matter how happy *gay* may sound, these are the facts about the suicide rate among homosexuals:

- The risk of suicide among gay and lesbian youth is fourteen times higher than for heterosexual youth.
- Between 30 and 45 percent of transgenders report having attempted suicide.

I didn't get these statistics from religious conservatives, but from a secular website sympathetic to gay and lesbian issues.[8] A study that analyzed twenty-five earlier studies regarding sexual orientation and mental health showed that "homosexuals and bisexuals are about 50% more likely than their heterosexual counterparts to suffer from depression and abuse drugs."[9]

For many years, it was widely assumed that this much higher level of unhappiness was due to humiliation over others' disapproval. Though society has become much more accepting of the homosexual lifestyle, unhappiness persists even among those surrounded by affirmation. Gay marriage may be legal, but that doesn't change its nature or eliminate the harm to those engaging in it.

Likewise, countless heterosexuals' lives have been destroyed by believing the false promise of happiness in an affair. I know many people who've had affairs and have spent the rest of their lives regretting it.

King Solomon could have had any woman he wanted—"the delight of the sons of man" (Ecclesiastes 2:8). But in his countless mistresses he found only emptiness and unhappiness.

Puritan Thomas Vincent said, "Nothing doth hinder men's happiness here, nothing can deprive them of happiness in the other world, but this evil of evils, sin."[10]

We fall for Satan's lies over and over again. But God tells us the truth about what will make us happy. Our ultimate happiness hinges on whom we choose to believe.

BOTH SIN AND RIGHTEOUSNESS HAVE CONSEQUENCES.

Moses warned the Israelite tribes desiring to settle on the Jordan's east side not to break their promise to help the tribes defeat their enemies on the west side. He could have said, "God will judge you." Instead he said, "Your sins will find you out" (Numbers 32:23). It's like a spiritual form of gravity. When someone steps off a roof, God doesn't judge him by making him fall. The violation of gravity brings its own consequences. Likewise, when truth and righteousness are violated, God may not dramatically bring judgment; instead, he'll allow judgment to flow naturally from the sin itself.

Though he may not directly intervene with a reward, God also may infuse good and righteous acts with their own positive effects, including happiness. If our sins will find us out, so will our righteous deeds—which, at the very least, will follow us to Heaven when we die (see Revelation 14:13).

Spurgeon said, "Remember that if you are a child of God you will never be happy in sin! You are spoiled for the world, the flesh and the devil. In the day when you were regenerated there was put into you a vital principle which can never die nor be content to dwell in the dead world."[11]

Happiness in God also means misery in sin.

OUR NEW, REGENERATED NATURES HAVE FREE ACCESS TO GOD'S WHOLE PERSON, INCLUDING HIS HAPPINESS.

"The heart is deceitful above all things, and desperately sick" (Jeremiah 17:9). Sin requires a radical solution—salvation in Christ, which transforms our nature and dramatically affects our capacity to embrace greater happiness in God. Our justification by faith in Christ satisfies the demands of God's holiness by exchanging our sins for Christ's righteousness (see Romans 3:21-26).

God grants believers new natures that free us from sin's bondage. Now we can draw upon God's power to overcome evil. Because our hearts are changed when we become new people in Christ, we *want* a better way. "You, however, are not in the flesh but in the Spirit, if in fact the Spirit of God dwells in you" (Romans 8:9).

Regeneration empowers the formerly blind to see and comprehend the things of God (see 1 Corinthians 2:12-16; 2 Corinthians 4:4, 6; Colossians 3:10). It renews the will, enabling us to make godly choices (see Philippians 2:13; 2 Thessalonians 3:5).

God speaks of the "washing of regeneration and renewal of the Holy Spirit" (Titus 3:5). Once believers are born again, we cannot continue to sin as a lifestyle because of our new natures (see 1 John 3:9). Sin is still present in our lives (see Romans 6:11-14; 1 John 1:8–2:2), but we have supernatural power to overcome it since we've died to sin (see Romans 6:6-9). God's Holy Spirit indwells us and helps us obey him (see 2 Timothy 1:14).

The result? We're free to reject sin and its misery, and embrace righteousness, with its true and lasting happiness.

Writing to her son Frank, Hannah Whitall Smith said,

> I am so glad you are beginning to know the joys of the Christian life. For my part I don't see how anyone who is not a Christian can be happy for a single minute. Children of God, who know their sins forgiven and who cast all their cares upon the One who cares for them, certainly have a right to be joyful and lighthearted. As to being so sober and solemn, it is all wrong. The merriest people I know are the most devoted Christians.[12]

WE CAN'T BE HAPPY WITHOUT DEALING RADICALLY WITH SIN.

Jesus said, "If your right eye makes you stumble, tear it out and throw it from you; for it is better for you to lose one of the parts of your body, than for your whole body to be thrown into hell" (Matthew 5:29, NASB). In moments of strength, we need to make godly decisions in preparation for moments of weakness. For example, we shouldn't put ourselves in places and with people or objects that move us toward sin (including anything with Internet access, if pornography or social media is a problem).

I received an e-mail from a young man at college who gave up his virginity. His utter despair was palpable. Of course, an unbeliever might think his misery was due to "unnecessary" guilt feelings. But in this case, they were accurate indicators of genuine guilt.

This young man might feel temporarily happier if he denied his guilt, just as someone jumping from a plane, not realizing his parachute is defective, can be temporarily exhilarated as he falls. But the moment he understands his true condition, he'll be terrified. If there's another parachute, the man's realization will serve him well. Likewise, if this young man repents and embraces Christ's forgiveness, the crushing guilt feelings that brought him to repentance will be God's grace to him—his backup parachute.

First John 3:21 says, "If our heart does not condemn us, we have confidence before God." Without the convicting work of the Holy Spirit (see John 16:8), there's no hope for any of us to turn to God—and without repentance and forgiveness, there's no restoration to relationship with our joyful God. Someone who puts his hand in a fire feels excruciating pain, causing him to withdraw it and seek medical attention. *He is far better off because he experienced the pain.* In contrast, someone with leprosy, who feels nothing because of damaged nerve endings, might seem happier for not experiencing the agony. But he'll suffer in the long term because his body still experiences destruction, whether or not he can feel it. This world desensitizes us to evil, essentially turning us into moral lepers who become numb to healthy twinges of conscience.

"Whoever conceals his transgressions will not prosper, but he who confesses and forsakes them will obtain mercy" (Proverbs 28:13).

Spurgeon said, "It does not spoil your happiness . . . to confess your sin. The unhappiness is in not making the confession."[13]

Happiness is impossible without confession, forgiveness, and a right relationship with the source of happiness. It's like trying to turn on a light that's unplugged. You can change the bulb, put on a new lamp shade, and polish the lamp, but you'll remain in darkness.

Anselm said, "Happiness ought not to be bestowed upon any one whose sins have not been wholly put away."[14] It would be cruel of God to do so, because our happiness in sin would keep us from the ultimate happiness found only in forgiveness.

Spurgeon said, "It is no wonder that those who are dwelling upon their own corruption should wear such downcast looks; but surely if we call to mind that 'Christ is made unto us righteousness,' we shall be of good cheer."[15]

Martin Luther said, "Sin is pure unhappiness, forgiveness pure happiness."[16] It's hard to imagine a more concise and accurate statement about the nature of sin and happiness. If we believe this biblically grounded truth, our lives will be transformed.

FORGIVING OTHERS IS A GREAT PAIN RELIEVER.

One of the best-known photographs from the Vietnam War is a Pulitzer Prize–winning picture of a young burn victim running in terror, arms outstretched, after a napalm bomb was dropped on her village. After months of hospitalization and multiple surgeries, nine-year-old Phan Thi Kim Phuc returned to her family.

What doctors couldn't heal, Kim Phuc says, was her heart: "The anger inside me was like a hatred high as a mountain."

But God reached out to Kim Phuc. She found a Bible and talked with a believer who invited her to church, where Kim Phuc chose to trust in Christ: "Jesus helped me learn to forgive my enemies."

Fourteen years later, while speaking in Washington, DC, she met John Plummer, who had helped coordinate the air strike on her childhood village.

John wrote of their meeting, "She held out her arms to me and embraced me. All I could say was, 'I'm sorry; I'm so sorry,' over and over again. At the same time she was saying, 'It's all right; it's all right; I forgive; I forgive.'"[17]

Today, Kim Phuc heads up the KIM Foundation International. Its mission is "to help heal the wounds suffered by innocent children and to restore hope and happiness to their lives."[18]

I've seen families, friends, neighbors, and churches torn apart by the refusal to forgive. If we believe in the joy-giving power of forgiveness, it will transform our perspectives and help us live happier, more God-honoring lives.

Every one of us could call up a catalog of grievances done to us by our children, parents, friends, spouses, employers, neighbors, the DMV, or the IRS. Some wrongs are real and serious; others are imaginary or exaggerated, but *all can undermine happiness* . . . unless true forgiveness is demonstrated by our refusal to rehearse these wrongs.

People who want to pay back family and friends don't realize that refusing forgiveness inflicts the greatest damage on themselves. The saying is true: "Bitterness is like drinking poison and waiting for the other person to die."[19] Lewis Smedes (1921–2002) wrote, "To forgive is to set a prisoner free and discover that the prisoner was you."[20]

GOD'S FORGIVENESS RELIEVES US OF THE MISERY OF ALIENATION FROM HIM.

With these words of celebration, David described forgiveness: "Happy are those to whom the LORD imputes no iniquity, and in whose spirit there is no deceit" (Psalm 32:2, NRSV).

David then recounted his state of utter misery after his adultery with Bathsheba and the murder of her husband, Uriah:

> While I kept silence, my body wasted away through my groaning all day long. For day and night your hand was heavy upon me; my strength was dried up as by the heat of summer. PSALM 32:3-4 (NRSV)

David chose the sin of adultery and subsequent murder to cover up his sin *so he could be happy.* Yet it brought groaning and caused his body to waste away.

But his confession changed everything:

> Then I acknowledged my sin to you, and I did not hide my iniquity; I said, 'I will confess my transgressions to the LORD,' and you forgave the guilt of my sin. PSALM 32:5 (NRSV)

David went on to describe the relationship with the one who delivered him from the unhappiness of sin:

> You are a hiding place for me; you preserve me from trouble; you surround me with glad cries of deliverance. PSALM 32:7 (NRSV)

Spurgeon commented about David, "The man is encircled in song, surrounded by dancing mercies, all of them proclaiming the triumphs of grace. . . . The air resounds with joy, and all this for the very man who, a few weeks ago, was roaring all the day long. How great a change! What wonders grace has done and still can do!"[21]

David began Psalm 32 with two statements to the effect of "Happy is . . ." and ended with "Rejoice and be happy in the Lord" (verse 11). There's only one source of happiness on which everything hinges: "in the Lord."

LOVE AND HAPPINESS ALWAYS FOLLOW IN THE WAKE OF FORGIVENESS.

Forgiveness and a right relationship with God bring not just relief from misery but also a surprising infusion of delight.

After unthinkable agony on the cross, Jesus uttered the words, "It is finished" (John 19:30). These same words were commonly written across records of debt when paid in full. Moments later, Jesus—having done history's hardest task—bowed his head and died.

Whether it's our final class before graduating, a huge job we're finishing, or a big manuscript we're completing, saying "It is finished" means the end of toil and the beginning of great celebration. Nothing is more happy-making than contemplating that our separation from God is finished because of what Jesus did. But it also gladdens my heart that by his grace, others can forgive me—and that I can look at those who have sinned against me and say, because of Christ's redemptive work, "It is finished. I hold no more resentment and bitterness. You are forgiven, and I am free!"

The book and movie *Unbroken* tell the compelling story of Louis Zamperini, an Olympic athlete and airman who survived forty-seven days on the open ocean and twenty-six torturous months in Japanese POW camps.

The movie skillfully portrays the human spirit's will to survive, but it leaves untold the dramatic redemptive story that followed Zamperini's release. Known as a hero for his incredible survival skills, he was deeply scarred, full of hatred, and plagued by nightmares of "the Bird," his chief torturer in the camp. The war hero became a carousing alcoholic, abusive to his wife and neglectful of his young daughter.

In contrast to the "triumph of the human spirit" message portrayed in the movie, Zamperini did *not* have in himself what it took to put his horrific ordeals behind him and survive in normal life. He hadn't experienced forgiveness for his own sins, and therefore he couldn't forgive the Japanese guards for the abuses they'd inflicted on him. Release from the Japanese prison couldn't free the prisoner within.

Ironically, despite the title of the book and movie, Zamperini had to be broken to find redemption. In great desperation, he attended a Billy Graham crusade, confessed his sins, placed his faith in Christ, experienced forgiveness, and was delivered from the nightmare of his past.

Louis Zamperini became a new person in Christ. He wrote, "Deciding to devote your life to God . . . doesn't mean instantaneous, nonstop happiness. Hard work lay ahead. I fought despondency and doubt, and tried to come to terms with what had happened to me."[22]

A year after his conversion, Zamperini returned to Japan and visited Sugamo Prison. He wrote, "I asked to meet my prison guards—now incarcerated as war criminals—determined to forgive them all in person. The hardest thing in life is to forgive. But hate is self-destructive. If you hate somebody you're not hurting the person you hate, you're hurting yourself. Forgiveness is healing."[23]

Zamperini ran and threw his arms around his persecutors, expressed his forgiveness, and shared the Good News of Jesus. He said, "The most important thing in my Christian life was to know that I forgave them—not only verbally, but to see them face to face. That's part of conversion."[24]

At first, most of the former prison guards withdrew from Zamperini because they couldn't comprehend his forgiveness. But once he preached the gospel, all but one made a profession of faith in Jesus.

Mutsuhiro Watanabe, "the Bird," who had tortured Zamperini most brutally, wasn't there. Despite being on the most-wanted list of Japanese war criminals, he'd escaped prosecution.

When Zamperini later located Watanabe, by then a rich businessman, the former guard refused to meet with him. Zamperini then sent a letter explaining he'd given his life to Christ. "Love replaced the hate I had for you," he wrote, adding, "I hope you become a Christian."[25] He said, "I knew from my own experience that there is a twisted kind of satisfaction that comes from hating. You hate and hate and hate, and think you're getting even by hating. But it's a ruse. It's a cover-up. Hate destroys—but not the object of your hatred. It destroys you."[26]

BECOMING A NEW PERSON IN CHRIST IS THE ESSENCE OF HAPPINESS.

Conversion isn't only about deliverance from sin; it's also about becoming a new person. "If anyone is in Christ, he is a new creation. The old has passed away; behold, the new has come" (2 Corinthians 5:17). *The New Testament in Modern English* by J. B. Phillips translates this and the following as, "If a man is in Christ he becomes a new person altogether—the past is finished and gone, everything has become fresh and new. All this is God's doing, for he has reconciled us to himself through Jesus Christ."

The old self is characterized by sin, guilt, and unhappiness. The new self should be characterized by the happiness of our own forgiveness and a newfound ability to forgive others.

George Whitefield preached, "Happy, happy are all you, who put on our Lord Jesus, and with him the new man!"[27]

Martyn Lloyd-Jones said, "Why believe the devil instead of believing God? Rise up and realize the truth about yourself—that all the past has gone, and you are one with Christ, and all your sins have been blotted out once and for ever. . . . It is sin to allow the past, which God has dealt with, to rob us of our joy and our usefulness in the present and in the future."[28]

In the seventeenth century, Thomas Brooks wrote these profound words, which can be of great practical help for us today: "The saints of old have always placed their happiness, peace, and comfort in their perfect and complete justification, rather than in their imperfect and incomplete sanctification."[29]

FORGIVING OTHERS AFFECTS OUR OWN FORGIVENESS AS WELL AS OUR HAPPINESS.

Scripture instructs us, "Put on a heart of compassion, kindness, humility, gentleness and patience; bearing with one another, and forgiving each other, whoever has a complaint against anyone; just as the Lord forgave you, so also should you" (Colossians 3:12-13, NASB).

Christ tells the story of a servant who owes his master millions—a debt his master freely forgives. But when that servant refuses to forgive the debt of a fellow servant who owes him much less, the king says, "You wicked servant! I forgave you all that debt because you pleaded with me. And should not you have had mercy on your fellow servant, as I had mercy on you?" The master delivers the man to the jailers until he can pay back his entire debt. Jesus warns, "So also my heavenly Father will do to every one of you, if you do not forgive your brother from your heart" (Matthew 18:32-33, 35).

God takes our failure to forgive seriously! There's no sin that Christ didn't die for, so there's no sin that we, in his strength, can't forgive.

We may not forget all the facts of someone's offense, but *we do not have to dwell on them*. We must bury the sins of others, as God has buried ours. The prophet Micah said to God, "You will again have compassion on us; you will tread our sins underfoot and hurl all our iniquities into the depths of the sea" (Micah 7:19, NIV).

Spurgeon said, "While we are young, perhaps we are foolish enough to look elsewhere for happiness, but when we grow old and cares and sorrows increase, happy, indeed, are we if we have the happiness that comes from pardoned sin!"[30]

When we extend to others the forgiveness God has extended to us, not only do we receive happiness, we become conduits of happiness. Admitting our sin is the first step toward happiness. If happiness eludes us, it's time to consider what sin remains unconfessed.

In his autobiography, Louis Zamperini made many stunning statements that don't appear in the book or movie *Unbroken*, including this: "The one who forgives never brings up the past to that person's face. . . . True forgiveness is complete and total."[31]

Mark Roberts served with Louis Zamperini, who was then in his seventies, on the staff of Hollywood Presbyterian Church. Roberts wrote a tribute about his friend entitled "Louis Zamperini: The Happiest Man I've Ever Known." Roberts says, "Every time I saw Louie, he was bounding with enthusiasm . . . often, literally bounding. . . . He loved zipping around the church campus on his skateboard. We often referred to him as a wild man, because he skated with so much utter joy and abandon."[32]

Zamperini's amazing survival didn't buy him happiness. After the war, the can-do spirit of the old Louis wasn't enough to fill the hole in his heart, repair his deep wounds, forgive his tormentors, or fill his heart with happiness. Only the grace of Jesus could do that.

CHAPTER 37

WE NEED NOT CHOOSE BETWEEN HOLINESS AND HAPPINESS

Happy and holy is the one who shares in the first resurrection!
REVELATION 20:6, PHILLIPS

This first act of divine sovereign pleasure concerning us, was the choosing of us from all eternity unto holiness and happiness.
JOHN OWEN

A S A YOUNG pastor, I preached, as others still do, "God calls us to holiness, not happiness."[1] There's a half-truth in this. I saw Christians pursue what they thought would make them happy, falling headlong into sexual immorality, alcoholism, materialism, and obsession with success. They'd turned from holiness, and the lure of happiness appeared at odds with holiness.

I was attempting to oppose our human tendency to put preferences and convenience before obedience to Christ. It all sounded so *spiritual*, and I could quote countless authors and preachers who agreed with me.

I'm now convinced we were all dead wrong.

There were several flaws in my thinking, including inconsistency with my own experience. I'd found profound happiness in Christ; wasn't that from God? Furthermore, calling people to reject happiness in favor of holiness was ineffective. It might work for a while but not in the long run, given the reality that all people seek happiness.

Tony Reinke gets it right: "Sin is joy poisoned. Holiness is joy postponed and pursued."[2]

THE FALSE DISTINCTION THAT WE SHOULD SEEK HOLINESS INSTEAD OF HAPPINESS IS BOTH UNBIBLICAL AND IMPRACTICAL.

A. W. Tozer said, "I do not believe that it is the will of God that we should seek to be happy, but rather that we should seek to be holy."[3] But this is true only if happiness is sin.

If Tozer believed happiness is always sin, he wouldn't have said, "God is happy if nobody else is"[4] or God "desires the happiness of His creatures"[5] or "God takes pleasure in the pleasure of His people."[6]

When Tozer criticized happiness, he had a particular meaning, which is evident in this statement:

> There is an ignoble pursuit of irresponsible happiness among us. . . . Most of us would rather be happy than to feel the wounds of other people's sorrows. . . . The holy man will be the useful man and he's likely to be a happy man too; but if he seeks happiness and forgets holiness and usefulness, he's a carnal man.[7]

What Tozer was opposing was not happiness per se, but attempts to be happy without God and in ways that dishonor God.

It has become common for Christians to draw a line between the holiness we know we should seek and the happiness we do seek. We see that the world seeks happiness instead of holiness. Therefore, we assume we should do the opposite. But we're wrong.

A. T. Pierson (1837–1911) said, "He who thinks duty and delight are opposed lives a comparatively low life. If he gets high enough up for a true view, he will see that all opposition between happiness and holiness is only apparent. The roads of duty and delight never [are at odds with] each other."[8]

Octavius Winslow was a prominent evangelical preacher in the 1800s. He said of the Holy Spirit, "It is his aim . . . to increase our happiness by making us more holy."[9] Winslow's profound words capture the essence of this chapter. Let them sink into your heart: "God would make us happy, but He can only make us happy by making us holy. Happiness and holiness are cognate truths. . . . They are twin sisters. He must be happy who is holy. . . . *Sin* is the parent of all misery; *holiness* the root of all happiness."[10]

Anselm lived nearly a thousand years ago, in the Dark Ages, and saw truths that can shine light on our darkness today: "Man . . . was made holy for this end, *that he might be happy in enjoying God*" (emphasis added).[11]

CHRISTIANS FEAR HAPPINESS BECAUSE THEY THINK IT ENTAILS IRRESPONSIBILITY AND NEGLIGENCE.

Some Christians see happiness as the opposite of holiness. But Scripture says otherwise.

Richard Sibbes wrote, "It is our chief wisdom to know him, our holiness to love him, our happiness to enjoy him. There is in him to be had whatsoever can truly make us happy. . . . Everything else teaches us, by the vanity and vexation we find in them, that our happiness is not in them."[12] To Sibbes, like most of the Puritans, happiness and holiness were joined at the hip—the authentic forms of both, inseparable.

Speaking ill of the pursuit of happiness misses the point. It's like saying, "I've been eating the wrong things, so I choose not to be hungry or eat anymore." No, we *are* going to hunger and eat. The solution is to cultivate an appetite for the right foods, then find and eat them.

Paul J. Wadell, in an ethics textbook, says, "Augustine and Aquinas . . . recognized that . . . the heart of the Christian moral life is learning about happiness."[13]

How much better might students respond to Christian ethics if its principles weren't just portrayed as burdensome obligation to the God of holiness we fear, but also as a privilege and delight in the God of happiness we love?

If holiness and happiness are inseparable, why not do what many churches have done for centuries and appeal to people only on the basis of holiness? Because, though holiness is a deep need of the soul, it's not always a *felt* need. By God's grace, we can use the desire for happiness to lead people to the holiness that's woven into the gospel with happiness.

SCRIPTURE REFLECTS THE HOLINESS *AND* HAPPINESS IN GOD'S CHARACTER.

Consider Leviticus 9:24: "Fire came out from the presence of the LORD and consumed the burnt offering . . . on the altar. And when all the people saw it, they shouted for joy and fell facedown" (NIV). The radically holy God sent down fire, and they did *what?* They fell facedown . . . and "shouted for joy"!

This remarkable response flows from the utter holiness of submission combined with the utter happiness of praise. To fall facedown before the infinitely holy God *while shouting for joy* is a stunning picture of redemptive glory!

In his exegetical treatment of the Psalms, Mark Futato affirms that happiness and holiness are the book's two dominant themes. He argues, "A holy life, according to the book of Psalms, results in a happy life . . . a life lived in keeping with God's instructions."[14]

Second Chronicles 6:41 says, "May your holy people be happy because of your goodness" (NCV). To be holy is to see God as he is and to become like him, covered in Christ's righteousness. And since God's nature is to be happy (as we saw in part 2), the more like him we become in our sanctification, the happier we become.

Commenting on Psalm 37, John Calvin said of the wicked, "They are miserable, while the happiness of which they boast is cursed; whereas the pious and devoted servants of God never cease to be happy, even in the midst of their greatest calamities, because God takes care of them."[15]

The servant is invited, "Come and share your master's happiness!" (Matthew 25:21, NIV). Christ could have said *holiness* here. We'll share in that, too. But we shouldn't miss his emphasis on happiness.

Any understanding of God that's incompatible with the lofty and infinitely holy view of God in Ezekiel 1:26-28 and Isaiah 6:1-4, along with the powerful view of the glorified Christ in Revelation 1, is utterly false. God is decidedly and unapologetically anti-sin, but in no sense anti-happiness. Indeed, holiness is what *secures* our happiness.

God isn't like a LEGO lord, consisting of different pieces: a blue one called holiness, a yellow one called happiness, a green one for love, and a white one for justice. God's attributes are fully interwoven in the unity of his triune person. He is always all that he is.

JONATHAN EDWARDS REGULARLY SPOKE OF HOLINESS AND HAPPINESS INTERTWINED.

Most would assume that Jonathan Edwards, best known for his sermon "Sinners in the Hands of an Angry God," was fixated on God's holiness.

But those who have read Edwards know this wasn't the case. He saw holiness and happiness as not only compatible but virtually inseparable. More than four hundred times, he used the words within a few sentences of each other—and often within a few words of each other. Consider these instances where he emphasized both:

- [God] has real pleasure in the creature's holiness and happiness.[16]
- The work of redemption is that, by which . . . men are . . . restored to holiness and happiness.[17]
- God's work, in savingly renewing and making holy and happy a poor perishing soul [is] a most glorious work.[18]
- The great power of God appears in bringing a sinner from . . . the depths of sin and misery, to such an exalted state of holiness and happiness.[19]
- The holiness and happiness of the creature . . . are things that [God] loves. These things are infinitely more agreeable to his nature than to ours.[20]
- Those that are highest in holiness [are] necessarily highest in happiness (for holiness and happiness are all one in heaven).[21]
- The spiritual fruits of holiness and happiness are interwoven one with another, and are connected together, and depend one on another.[22]

Edwards wrote, "A life of holiness is the pleasantest life in this world, because in such a life we have the imperfect beginnings of a blessed [happy] and endless sight of God; and so they have somewhat of true happiness while here. . . . Those who do not live a holy life, they have nothing at all of true happiness, because they have nothing of the knowledge of God."[23]

John Piper summarizes Edwards, saying that "the pursuit of virtue must be, in some measure, a pursuit of happiness. . . . In all virtuous acts we pursue the enjoyment of the glory of God, and more specifically, the enjoyment of the presence and the promotion of God's glory."[24]

WHAT MAKES US BETTER MAKES US HAPPIER.

Jonathan Edwards wrote, "When any reasonable creature finds that his excellency and his joy are the same thing, then he is come to right and real happiness, and not before. . . . If he be not the more excellent for his pleasures, it is a certain sign that he is not a truly happy man."[25]

Edwards argued,

This pleasure [finding happiness in God] brings no bitterness with it. That is not the case with other delights, in which natural men are wont to place their happiness. . . . If men place their happiness in them, reason and conscience will certainly give them inward disturbance in their enjoyment. There will be the sting of continual disappointments [for] . . . the soul, that places its happiness in them, always big with expectation and in eager pursuit; while they are evermore like shadows, and never yield what is hoped for.[26]

In Western nations, popular opinion holds that high moral standards are foolish, demeaning, and narrow-minded human constructs—virtually impossible to maintain and contrary to happiness. This lie has been remarkably effective. We *seem* to have to choose between sinning to be happy and abstaining from happiness through righteous self-deprivation.

If we believe the lie that saying no to sin means saying no to happiness, then no amount of self-restraint will keep us from ultimately seeking happiness in sin. John Piper writes, "Enjoy a superior satisfaction. Cultivate capacities for pleasure in Christ. . . . You were created to treasure Christ with all your heart—more than you treasure sex or sugar or sports or shopping. If you have little taste for Jesus, competing pleasures will triumph."[27]

Holiness doesn't mean abstaining from pleasure; holiness means recognizing Jesus as the source of life's greatest pleasure.

Spurgeon said, "Holiness is the royal road to happiness. The death of sin is the life of joy."[28]

ATTEMPTING TO SEPARATE HOLINESS AND HAPPINESS DISTORTS BOTH.

In his book *The Seven Deadly Virtues,* Gerald Mann tells of his first exposure to Christianity at a revival he attended as a teenager. He writes of a man who gave "a blow-by-blow account of his former life on the 'wild side.' Graphically, he portrayed scenes of gang fights, heroin sales, and sexual liaisons with wanton sirens. . . . Then he told us of how Jesus had reached into the midst of all that muck and plucked him out of it. I am certain he didn't intend to, but he made it sound as if Jesus had spoiled a rather exciting life!"[29]

Though Mann later became a Christian and a pastor, it was a long time before he returned to church. According to his perception, Christianity meant giving up what's fun. You might end up in Heaven, but to get there you have to live a hellish present life of saying no to all pleasure!

This twisted perspective is widespread and has left not only unbelievers but also Christians thinking we have only two choices:

1. Holiness: Improperly understood to mean being somber, rejecting the enjoyment of material things, and giving up the fun unbelievers experience. If we go to church and obey the rules, holiness may pay off in Heaven . . . someday. Christians who hold to this moral standard feel superior—a small compensation for their lack of happiness.

2. Happiness: Improperly understood to mean going wherever and doing whatever we want. By saying no to righteous living—labeled as "legalism"—these

Christians redefine grace to permit whatever they imagine will make them happy (including getting drunk, experimenting with drugs, and sleeping around). Others use their forgiven status as freedom to live as unbelievers do. They might call it Christian liberty and evangelism (though it's not clear what Good News they're offering, since they're essentially no different than the world).

There's a third category: Christians who feel guilty when they're happy. They confess their sins and walk with God, but somehow they suspect their happiness dishonors him. Those taught in church that it's wrong to be happy will naturally not look to Jesus for happiness. However, make no mistake: they *will* look for it elsewhere.

Archibald Alexander was an American Presbyterian theologian and professor at Princeton Seminary. He said, "Holiness is pleasing to God, beneficial to men, and *essential to the promotion of our own happiness*" (emphasis added).[30] Notice he didn't say that desiring our own happiness is wrong but that if we're to *successfully* promote our happiness, we must embrace holiness. Being holy is not only an end but a means to the end, which is our happiness.

C. S. Lewis wrote to an American friend, "How little people know who think that holiness is dull. When one meets the real thing . . . it is irresistible. If even 10% of the world's population had it, would not the whole world be converted and happy before a year's end?"[31]

A GOSPEL THAT PROMOTES HOLINESS OVER HAPPINESS ISN'T GOOD NEWS.

Too often our message to the world becomes a false gospel that lays upon people an impossible burden: to be a Christian, you must give up wanting to be happy and instead choose to be holy. "Give up happiness; choose holiness instead" is *not* good news in any sense, and therefore it is *not* the true gospel! It bears more resemblance to the legalistic worldview of the Pharisees Jesus condemned (see Matthew 23:2-4).

After coming to Christ, Hannah Whitall Smith warned her son Frank, "There is such a thing as having just enough religion to make one miserable, and as long as you hold back from a full surrender to His will, this will be the situation. Oh, do let Jesus have all of your heart! He will give you such a fullness of joy in Himself that will far more than repay you for any earthly pleasure you think you may miss because of it."[32]

Sadly, many churches and Christian families have never experienced such a liberating blend of holiness and happiness.

Theologian and seminary professor Bruce Ware told me, "Of the eighty kids who grew up in our Bible-believing church, my sister and I can count on one hand those now walking with Jesus."

If given a choice, people who grow up in evangelical churches will predictably choose what *appears* to be the delightful happiness of the world over the dutiful holiness of church. Satan tries to rig the game by leading us to believe we can't have both happiness and holiness. Offer people a choice between being hungry and thirsty or having food and drink, and their choice is obvious. Never mind that the meal may be laced with cyanide or the drink injected with arsenic. *Any offer of happiness, with or without holiness, will always win over an offer of holiness devoid of happiness.*

HAPPINESS IS A DUTY, BUT ONE THAT MAKES THE FULFILLMENT OF ALL OTHER DUTIES MORE ENJOYABLE.

We looked at duty earlier, but it merits attention here from another angle. A duty is a moral or legal obligation—a responsibility. Though duty is a good word, when Christian duty is separated from happiness in Christ, it becomes either drudgery or a means to self-righteousness.

Sadly, many people seem to believe that a righteous act done dutifully is better than the same act done happily. We associate duty with sacrifice, and happiness with selfishness. Yet we can do our duty happily so God is pleased with our actions *and* our hearts. Sacrificial giving is an example: "God loves a cheerful giver" (2 Corinthians 9:7).

John Piper writes, "We have implied in a thousand ways that the virtue of an act diminishes to the degree you enjoy doing it and that doing something because it yields happiness is bad. The notion hangs like a gas in the Christian atmosphere."[33]

William Bates said, "Religion will make us happy hereafter in the enjoyment of God, and happy here in obedience to his holy will. Such is his goodness, that our duty and happiness are the same."[34]

It should be helpful for us to see that God commands us to rejoice always, just as he commands us to be holy.

John Wesley made a profound observation:

> How uncomfortable a condition must he be in, who, having the fear but not the love of God . . . has only the toils and not the joys of religion? He has religion enough to make him miserable, but not enough to make him happy: His religion will not let him enjoy the world, and the world will not let him enjoy God. So that, by halting between both, he loses both; and has no peace either in God or the world.[35]

How many professing Christians today, as Wesley and Smith suggested, have only enough religion to make them miserable?

Adam Clarke wrote, "Every wicked man is a miserable man. God has wedded sin and misery as strongly as he has holiness and happiness. God hath joined them together; none can put them asunder."[36] He also wrote, "Our Lord prohibits that only which, from its nature, is opposed to man's happiness."[37]

Thomas Manton said, "God is a holy and happy being."[38] If we're supposed to be like God, shouldn't we be holy and happy, too? Christian pastors and writers warn people, "Don't seek happiness outside of God's will." There's truth in that advice. But shouldn't we also say, "Don't seek holiness outside of God's will"? Isn't that exactly what the Pharisees did—and what many self-righteous people still do? Just as there's false happiness, there's false holiness.

Superficial holiness can never produce true happiness. True holiness always manifests itself in authentic happiness. Psalm 1:1 says, "Blessed [happy] is the man who walks not in the counsel of the wicked, nor stands in the way of sinners, nor sits in the seat of scoffers."

Matthew Henry commented, "When the psalmist undertakes to describe a blessed man, he describes a good man; for, after all, those only are happy, truly happy, that are holy, truly holy; . . . goodness and holiness are not only the way to happiness (Rev. 22:14), but happiness itself."[39]

Thomas Watson said, "He who hath only a painted holiness, shall have a painted happiness."[40] Watson explained, "Man has a desire to be happy, yet opposes that which should promote his happiness. He has a disgust of holiness."[41]

Richard Baxter wrote, "O wilful, wretched sinners! It is not God that is so cruel to you; it is you that are cruel to yourselves. . . . You are told, that there is no way to happiness but by holiness, and yet you will not be holy. What would you have God say more to you?"[42]

What more indeed?

HOLINESS AND HAPPINESS ARE LIKE SPIRITUAL DNA.

DNA's double helix is perfectly balanced at the core of human life. Two strands wrap around each other, forming an axis of symmetry and providing a perfect complement for each other.

God has made holiness and happiness to enjoy a similar relationship: each benefits from the other. For those of us who are Christ-centered believers, our lives should overflow with both. Neither alone will suffice; both together are essential for the truly Christ-centered life.

When Jesus says, "Be perfect" (Matthew 5:48), we should recognize that true happiness in him is part of what he intends. Our pleasure is won in the "Aha!" moments of discovering firsthand why God's ways really are best. As we grow in knowledge, we can increasingly join Paul in saying, "We have the mind of Christ" (1 Corinthians 2:16) on the things he has revealed. The more we discover God's ways and experience the goodness of his holiness, the less we try to find happiness apart from him.

CHAPTER 38

IS SEEKING HAPPINESS SELFISH?

I will sacrifice with shouts of joy; I will sing and make music to the LORD.

PSALM 27:6, NIV

Nothing that you have not given away will ever be really yours. Nothing in you that has not died will ever be raised from the dead. Look for yourself, and you will find in the long run only hatred, loneliness, despair, rage, ruin, and decay. But look for Christ and you will find Him, and with Him everything else thrown in.

C. S. LEWIS

W HEN NARCOTICS DETECTIVES raided an apartment in a depressed New York City neighborhood, they found it crowded with derelicts.

The man arrested for harboring them claimed he'd chosen to live there to provide them with food, shelter, and clothes, and he didn't realize he was breaking the law. The man was millionaire John Sargent Cram, who'd studied at Princeton and Oxford.

After his acquittal, he said to a reporter, "I'm quite happy. I'm anything but a despondent person. Call me eccentric. Call it my reason for being."[1]

What Cram did truly helped some, while perhaps enabling others. And though his actions might be considered sacrificial and unselfish, they also made him happy.

IS ALL CONCERN FOR OUR OWN HAPPINESS SELFISH?

It's possible to profoundly disagree with someone's worldview while agreeing with one aspect. Atheist Ayn Rand, in *The Virtue of Selfishness*, says something I *can* agree with when applied to the issue of happiness-seeking:

> In popular usage, the word "selfishness" is a synonym of evil; the image it conjures is of a murderous brute who tramples over piles of corpses to achieve his own ends. . . . Yet the exact meaning and dictionary definition of the word "selfishness" is: *concern with one's own interests.*

This concept does not include a moral evaluation; it does not tell us whether concern with one's own interests is good or evil; nor does it tell us what constitutes man's actual interests. . . . The ethics of altruism has created the image . . . that any concern with one's own interests is evil, regardless of what these interests might be, and . . . that the brute's activities are *in fact* to one's own interest.[2]

Hence, Rand points out, "An industrialist who produces a fortune, and a gangster who robs a bank are regarded as equally immoral, since they both sought wealth for their own 'selfish' benefit."[3]

This distorted notion that wanting to be happy is inherently selfish, and therefore immoral, is believed by many Christians. Why? Partly because we focus on one group of biblical statements without balancing them with others. The Bible warns against those who are "lovers of self," identifying them as money-loving, boastful, proud, abusive, and unholy (see 2 Timothy 3:2). The self-love spoken of here is obviously wrong. But when Jesus tells us to love our neighbors as ourselves (see Matthew 22:39), he isn't arguing that we shouldn't love ourselves, only that we should extend our instincts for self-care to caring for others.

Similarly we're told, "Husbands should love their wives as their own bodies. He who loves his wife loves himself. For no one ever hated his own flesh, but nourishes and cherishes it, just as Christ does the church" (Ephesians 5:28-29). This passage assumes that a man shouldn't hate his body and starve it; he should care for it. In the same way, he's to love his wife by providing for and protecting her.

Jonathan Edwards said, "It is not a thing contrary to Christianity that a man should love . . . his own happiness. . . . Saints, and sinners, and all alike, love happiness, and have the same unalterable and instinctive inclination to desire and seek it."[4]

It's possible for someone to act sacrificially and selflessly in the best interests of others while enjoying the fruit: feeling good about having done well and receiving God's approval and reward.

Some parents believe that looking after their children's happiness means constantly saying no to their own. But if they don't take care of themselves, failing to model happiness in God, they'll deprive their children of happiness too.

Flight crews routinely announce, "If you're traveling with a child or someone who requires assistance, in the case of an emergency, secure your own oxygen mask first before helping the other person." Those instructions may sound selfish, just as it sounds selfish to say that one of our main duties in life is to find happiness in God. But only when we're delighting in our Lord do we have *far more to offer everyone else.*

WE SHOULDN'T LIMIT OUR APPETITE FOR HAPPINESS IN THE NAME OF AVOIDING SELFISHNESS.

Jonathan Edwards said, "Persons need not and ought not to set any bounds to their spiritual and gracious appetites. Rather, they ought to be endeavoring by all possible ways to inflame their desires and to obtain more spiritual pleasures."[5]

Edwards was not an advocate of spiritual moderation. He didn't believe we should be content to be "just a little happy" in our relationship with God. He said, "Our hungerings and thirstings after God and Jesus Christ and after holiness can't be too great. . . . There is no such thing as excess in our taking of this spiritual food. There is no such virtue as temperance in spiritual feasting."[6]

Edwards believed in temperance with what's secondary but not what's primary. God is primary. We can't get too much of God; therefore, we can't be too happy in God.

God calls us not only to believe he exists but also to find our greatest pleasure and truest happiness in knowing him. Rejoice, sing, shout, jump, and dance in response to him!

My wife wouldn't be flattered if I decided I was "happy enough" with her. To refrain from seeking to know her better and delight in her more, or to restrain myself from "going overboard" in my devotion to her, would do her no honor. Likewise, God is honored by our efforts to know him better, please him more, and find our happiness in him. The more we do this, the greater delight he takes in us.

WHEN LOVE AND HAPPINESS ARE INVOLVED, *SACRIFICE* IS A MISLEADING WORD.

The pediatric surgeon who serves in remote African villages for minimal pay is by some standards making a huge sacrifice. After all, she could make ten times the money in an American hospital: better hours, higher success rates, and luxurious living.

However, while she sacrifices conveniences, she is emphatically *not* sacrificing happiness. She's happiest while using her gifts and skills to help people, knowing that by God's grace she's saving lives and improving children's quality of life. She enjoys the teary gratitude of parents who thought their child's cleft palate or inability to walk could never be corrected.

So she sacrifices something small to gain something great, which includes bringing glory to God and good to others. But it also includes furthering both her present happiness and her eternal reward.

Many Western physicians and nurses recount time spent serving in poverty-stricken areas of the world as tremendously fulfilling. Yes, there were great challenges, fatigue, and at times, danger. Still, they eagerly anticipate their next "vacation" in non-tourist destinations working day and night as volunteers. They don't dread going back; they look forward to it.

LOVE AND HAPPINESS ARE HIGHER VIRTUES THAN SELF-FOCUSED "UNSELFISHNESS."

Those self-sacrificing yet self-gratifying physicians are living examples of what Jesus says: "If anyone would come after me, let him deny himself and take up his cross daily and follow me. For whoever would save his life will lose it, but whoever loses his life for my sake will save it. For what does it profit a man if he gains the whole world and loses or forfeits himself?" (Luke 9:23-25).

Many think that Jesus' primary message here is the virtue of selflessness and self-sacrifice. But take another look: he calls us to *lose* life for his sake by appealing to our desire to *find* life! It's not "selflessness" in the sense of doing what's bad for ourselves; rather, it's honoring and following Christ and thereby *doing the best possible thing for ourselves*!

C. S. Lewis began his great sermon "The Weight of Glory" by saying this:

> If you asked twenty good men today what they thought the highest of the virtues, nineteen of them would reply, Unselfishness. But if you had asked almost any of the great Christians of old, he would have replied, Love. You see what has happened? A negative term has been substituted for a positive, and this is of more than philological importance. The negative idea of Unselfishness carries with it the suggestion not primarily of securing good things for others, but of going without them ourselves, as if our abstinence and not their happiness was the important point.[7]

We've all known the overbearing, codependent mother who does everything for her children while reminding them of all her sacrifices. Her unnecessary sacrifices are self-serving (in the sinful sense), but in fact, they don't serve her well. They end up making both her and her children miserable while she exclaims, "All I ever wanted was for you to be happy!"

Lewis went on to make this critical point: "The New Testament has lots to say about self-denial, but not about self-denial as an end in itself. We are told to deny ourselves and to take up our crosses in order that we may follow Christ; and nearly every description of what we shall ultimately find if we do so contains an appeal to desire."[8]

SINCE RIGHTEOUSNESS IS ALWAYS GOOD FOR US, WE'RE MORALLY OBLIGATED TO ACT FOR OUR TRUE SELF-INTEREST.

Should we be motivated by personal gain? Should we be motivated by a desire to be happy? If it is *genuine* gain and a desire for *true* happiness, both of which are found in Christ, then the answer is yes. It does no one any good to pretend we don't want to be happy. And who but Satan would want us to feel guilty when we're happy in God?

Paul said, "Am I now seeking the approval of man, or of God? If I were still trying to please man, I would not be a servant of Christ" (Galatians 1:10). It's a given that we will live for someone's approval—we need to determine *whose*. The more we learn of his happiness in us and his love for us, the easier it is to reorient our lives to please God more than anyone else.

A high salary and good benefits will motivate someone to accept a position only if that person values big paychecks and perks. The draw of an academic credential, a sales award, an Olympic medal, or a Super Bowl ring all depend upon one's desire for such things.

Since Christ is appealing to our yearning for reward, which is a matter of personal gain, wanting reward and gain cannot be intrinsically wrong—God would never appeal to our desire for what's sinful, becaues he never tempts us (see James 1:13). We *should* want what he offers.

We are quick to recognize that Satan tempts us through offers of happiness and gain.

However, we're slower to recognize that the only way he can tempt us is by offering us what God has made us to want. His deception is in luring us with happiness apart from God, where it can't be found.

Satan's true desire for us is not happiness, but misery. This is precisely opposite from God's desires for us: our true happiness and deliverance from misery.

When God calls upon us to deny ourselves and follow him, what appears to be our loss is in fact our gain. Should we want to gain our lives or lose our lives? Losing our lives in Christ is the *means* to the end of ultimately gaining them!

THE PURSUIT OF TRUE SELF-INTEREST IS, SURPRISINGLY, A VIRTUE.

Berkeley professor Dacher Keltner says, "Recent studies in psychology suggest that the pursuit of self-interest may not be the clearest path to the greater good or personal happiness."[9] He says research indicates it's not wealth that makes us happy but relationships and serving others.[10]

But notice the misguided phrase "the pursuit of self-interest," by which he means the pursuit of money over relationships and service. What the study shows is not that the pursuit of self-interest is wrong but rather that pursuing money above relationships and service doesn't serve our true self-interest. *Those who spend their lives serving others and cultivating personal relationships do not act against their self-interest but for it.*

In God's world, happiness is found in discovering what's truly in our self-interest: loving God and our neighbor. This profound, paradigm-shifting concept, understood correctly, makes the false dichotomy obvious in the question, "Should I serve others, or should I act in my own best interests?"

Philippians 2:4 can appear to say otherwise: "[Do] not [look] to your own interests but each of you to the interests of the others" (NIV). But other translations, including the English Standard Version, better capture Paul's intent: "Let each of you look not only to his own interests, but *also* to the interests of others" (emphasis added).

If we *only* think of our interests, we're wrong. If we think of both others and ourselves, we're right. Why should a man be a good husband? For his wife's sake? Yes. For God's sake? Yes. For his own sake? *Yes.*

Even when the subject is self-sacrifice, the Bible is full of appeals for us to do what's ultimately best for us. When Paul said, "If I give away all I have, and if I deliver up my body to be burned, but have not love, I gain nothing" (1 Corinthians 13:3), he assumed that we naturally—and appropriately—*wish to gain something*!

I believe that a desire for happiness lies behind most acts of kindness. Unhappy people, even when they try to be kind, can't spread happiness they do not possess. Truly happy individuals can perform the same acts of kindness as unhappy, duty-driven people, but in doing so, they spread the happiness of their hearts, serving others and meeting needs on a deeper and more heart-touching level.

Arthur Brooks says, "Do you want to be happy? Forget yourself and get lost in this great cause. Lend your efforts to helping people. You will come to know a happiness that you have never known before if you will do that." He goes on to say, "Selfless service is a wonderful antidote to the ills that flow from the worldwide epidemic of self-indulgence. The answer lies in helping to solve the problems of those around us rather than worrying about our own."[11]

Do you see the startling paradox? Serving others and looking after their interests is acting in our own interests. If we don't grasp this, we'll make the fatal mistake of thinking that self-service makes us happy while serving others makes us unhappy, when exactly the opposite is true!

WANTING TO BE HAPPY IN GOD AND WANTING TO PLEASE HIM GO HAND IN HAND.

After the Bible itself, one of the most insightful, soul-touching books I've ever read is *The Valley of Vision*, consisting of Puritan prayers and meditations. Here's one of them:

> *O Lord,*
> *Help me never to expect any happiness*
> *from the world, but only in thee.*
> *Let me not think that I shall be more happy*
> *by living to myself,*
> *for I can only be happy if employed for thee. . . .*
> *Teach me that if I do not live a life that satisfies thee,*
> *I shall not live a life that will satisfy myself.*[12]

The writer realized that if something won't make *God* happy, it won't make *us* happy.

Many have quoted the words of missionary martyr Jim Elliot without understanding them: "He is no fool who gives what he cannot keep to gain what he cannot lose."[13] Some see this as a statement of great sacrifice, in which a radical Christ-follower dedicated himself to giving up all gain to follow Jesus. But read his words again. Jim Elliot was saying it would be foolish not to give away what he couldn't keep anyway when it would gain him something far better that would last forever.

Elliot happily went to the mission field out of his love for God and people—and out of a desire to gain great treasure! He wanted personal gain, not loss; happiness, not misery. He understood that seeking gain and happiness in Christ honors Christ.

Jesus said, "The kingdom of heaven is like treasure, buried in a field, that a man found and reburied. Then in his joy he goes and sells everything he has and buys that field" (Matthew 13:44, HCSB). Do you feel sorry for the man's huge sacrifice? You shouldn't. He sells everything joyfully because he values what he sacrifices far less than what he gains. "But it cost him everything he owned," someone might lament. Yes. *But it gained him everything he wanted.*

When a rich young man pressed Jesus about how to gain eternal life, Jesus told him, "Sell your possessions and give to the poor, and you will have treasure in heaven. Then come, follow me" (Matthew 19:21, NIV). Jesus knew that money and possessions were the man's god. Unless he dethroned his money idol, he would never be free to serve God. Sadly, this man walked away from real treasure. Instead of embracing gain that he'd never lose, he held on to gain he couldn't keep. He wasn't just unspiritual; he was foolish.

The young man wasn't willing to give up everything for a greater treasure, but the traveler crossing the field was. Why? They both greatly valued treasure. The difference is that the traveler was happy to take short-term losses to obtain greater long-term gains.

A LIFE SPENT SEEKING AND ENJOYING GOD'S REWARDS IS A LIFE WELL SPENT.

Having researched and written on the subject of eternal rewards,[14] I'm well aware of the widespread opinion that doing anything with reward in mind is ungodly—despite the fact that Scripture regularly appeals to us to be motivated by eternal rewards (e.g., Luke 14:12-14; 1 Corinthians 3:11-15; 4:5; 9:24-25; 2 Corinthians 5:9-10; 2 Timothy 2:5; 4:8; Revelation 3:11-12; 19:8).

I encourage you to take a close look at God's Word to understand that seeking the rewards he kindly offers his children is inseparable from our happiness. (Anything that doesn't ultimately make us happy isn't a reward!)

Life will only be lived well by those who look for the rewards of a life well lived. No one grows close to God unless that person believes that drawing close to God has a payoff: "Whoever would draw near to God must believe that he exists and that he *rewards* those who seek him" (Hebrews 11:6, emphasis added). Call that payoff contentment, satisfaction, peace, or excitement—it all adds up to one word: *happiness*.

The Bible's offers of rewards for obeying and serving Jesus are all incentives for happiness. God rewards what makes him happy, and when we receive his rewards, it makes us happy. No one who offers rewards is insulted when people value those rewards.

I've had a lot of coaches, but one I had in junior high really stood out—Coach McKeel. I worked hard at football for many reasons, but most of all to please him. His obvious love for his players motivated us to do our best. My greatest reward was seeing his smile and receiving his pat on my back. Years later, my desire to practice and play hard subsided under coaches who didn't seem to care about me. When you lose the joy of playing a sport, the sacrifices are no longer worth it.

What God has done for us in Christ should make us want to please him—even if there were no other reward for doing so. But graciously, he offers us rewards anyway. If we believe it's impossible to please God, we'll stop trying.

Where is overflowing joy located? Where can we find eternal pleasures? Psalm 16:11 tells us—*in God's presence.* This verse is a treasure map where *X* marks the mother lode of happiness.

Unfortunately "the presence of God" is often a catchphrase. We know that God is omnipresent (everywhere), that Jesus lives in our hearts, and that he promised he would be with us always, but we don't always act as if that is true. Though we frequently sing and speak the jargon, we're often blind to the moment-by-moment presence of the happy God with us, and therefore we're blind to joy. It isn't enough to say that God is present; we must recognize his presence with us, within us, and around us, and credit him with all the joys and pleasures he graciously gives us.[15]

Jon Bloom calls pleasure "the whistleblower of your heart." He writes, "If something sinful gives you pleasure, it's not a pleasure problem. It's a treasure problem. Your pleasure mechanism is likely functioning just fine. It's what you love that's out of whack. And pleasure is outing you. It's revealing that, despite what your mouth says and the image you try to project to others, something evil is precious to you."[16]

In the Sermon on the Mount, Jesus presented what I've called the "treasure principle":[17]

> Do not store up for yourselves treasures on earth, where moth and rust destroy, and where thieves break in and steal. But store up for yourselves treasures in heaven, where neither moth nor rust destroys, and where thieves do not break in and steal; for where your treasure is, there your heart will be also.   MATTHEW 6:19-21, NASB

Why does Jesus command his disciples to store up treasures "for yourselves"? Does it seem strange that Jesus commands us to do what's in our own best interests? Isn't that selfish? No. God expects and commands us to act out of enlightened self-interest. He wants us to live to his glory, but what's for his glory is always for our good. As John Piper puts it, "God is most glorified in us when we are most satisfied in Him."[18]

Selfishness is when we pursue gain at the expense of others. But God's treasures have no limit. When we store up treasures for ourselves in Heaven, it doesn't reduce the treasures available to others. In fact, it's by serving God and others that we store up heavenly treasures for ourselves. When we do that, everyone wins.

Hence, as he often did, Jesus clearly appealed to us to act in the interest of our own ultimate happiness by making small temporary sacrifices to obtain large eternal gain.

WHENEVER WE SAY NO TO ONE SOURCE OF HAPPINESS, WE SAY YES TO ANOTHER.

Mark Twain said, "The only way to keep your health is to eat what you don't want, drink what you don't like, and do what you'd druther not."[19] This amusing statement is half true. The whole truth is, "To get what we want most, we must abstain from some of what we want less." In other words, we make smaller short-term sacrifices concerning our diet and exercise for the larger long-term happiness of having health and energy, and living to see our grandchildren.

To do what we want *most* demands that we don't do *all* that we want. The Olympic athlete in training wants to stay in bed, eat pancakes, and drink martinis, but there's something he wants more—to win. So he goes to work in pursuit of what he wants most.

The husband who says no to temptation and cares for his wife with Alzheimer's instead of having an affair isn't sacrificing happiness for faithfulness. Instead, he's choosing the path of greater happiness through faithfulness. Yes, he's doing the right thing, and yes, he should fulfill obligations even at great cost—but in fact, he'll be happier for doing so.

The Christian life is largely won and lost on the battlefield of ideas regarding what makes us happy.

When someone says no to the happiness of eating cookies, she isn't saying no to happiness. Rather, she's saying yes to greater happiness in achieving her goals of better health and weight control.

Of course, addicts and dieters alike know that too often, in weaker moments, we choose the immediate secondary happiness that brings about long-term unhappiness—shots, hits, pills, pecan pies, or blackberry malts seem good for the moment but leave us with unwanted consequences.

God's grace doesn't just forgive us when we sin; it empowers us not to sin. Paul said that God's grace teaches us to say no to "ungodliness and worldly passions, and to live self-controlled, upright, and godly lives" (Titus 2:12). The Christian life consists largely in relying on the empowerment of the Holy Spirit to think and act contrary to the desires ingrained in us at the Fall, and instead cultivate and act in accordance with the desires of our new nature in Christ (see Romans 6:1-14).

JESUS CALLS HIS FOLLOWERS TO SACRIFICE—BUT NEVER TO SACRIFICE LONG-TERM HAPPINESS.

Paul, writing from prison and always realistic about the harsh realities of a fallen world, nonetheless experienced happiness in Christ, which he was eager to share with his fellow believers in Philippi: "If I have to offer my own blood with your sacrifice, I will be happy and full of joy with all of you. You also should be happy and full of joy with me" (Philippians 2:17-18, NCV).

I've known profoundly unhappy people—ones who yell and curse and shake their fists when children or dogs set foot on their property. Tragically, Hell has already grabbed them by the throat. Jesus, the source of joy, can deliver them not only from future Hell but its present form. But life's timer is ticking.

Similarly, I know people who are in love with God and are quick to serve, pray, quote Scripture, and share their faith. They're also quick to laugh. The "sacrifice" of following Jesus produces the greatest, most lasting happiness. And since they're doing exactly what they want to—what God has called them to do and what they're wired to do—they're almost invariably surprised to learn that others think they've made great sacrifices. They understand that following Christ both honors him and benefits them.

UNSELFISHNESS MEANS MAKING SHORT-TERM SACRIFICES THAT RESULT IN EVERYONE'S GOOD, INCLUDING OUR OWN.

Every sacrifice we make in following Christ will always result in our long-term good—but it's more than that. It will also most often result in our short-term happiness. Listen carefully to the words of Jesus to his disciples:

> Truly, I say to you, there is no one who has left house or brothers or sisters or mother or father or children or lands, for my sake and for the gospel, who will not receive a hundredfold *now in this time*, houses and brothers and sisters and mothers and children and lands, *with persecutions*, and in the age to come *eternal life.* MARK 10:29-30, *emphasis added*

Those who have been cast out of their biological families for following Christ now have God's family to welcome them. Even if they don't own their own houses, they have hundreds of houses to stay in, where they'll be warmly welcomed. Jesus promises not only eternal happiness but a hundred times more happiness here and now. (Prosperity preachers who speak of the "hundredfold blessing" conveniently ignore Christ's balancing words: "with persecutions.")

This means that for God's children, even when we make the greatest sacrifices, *there is no pointless suffering*. Of course, much may appear pointless since we are finite and fallen, incapable of understanding the purposes of God in his infinite wisdom. But God is never pointless nor off point. That's why Job could cry out in his agony, "Though he slay me, yet will I trust in him" (Job 13:15, KJV).

C. S. Lewis wrote, "While what we call 'our own life' remains agreeable, we will not surrender it to Him. What then can God do in our interests but make 'our own life' less agreeable to us, and take away the plausible source of false happiness?"[20]

What does my suffering do for me, then, whether it is suffering for Christ or the ordinary suffering of life in a sin-stained world? It makes me see how implausible it is that I can find true happiness outside of God. That's just one of the ways my suffering is purposeful. When what I once leaned on for happiness—even if it is acceptance from my family and friends—crumbles into dust, the way is cleared for me to see that God still stands and is the one solid foundation on which to build my life and happiness.

One day God's children will look back on this life with complete clarity. When we do, I believe we'll see that our only true sacrifices were when we chose sin instead of Jesus.

In 1857, pioneer missionary to Africa David Livingstone addressed students at Cambridge University. Keep in mind that Livingstone was not attempting to sound spiritual—he was simply being honest about his experience of happily following Jesus:

> I have never ceased to rejoice that God has appointed me to such an office. People talk of the sacrifice I have made in spending so much of my life in Africa. . . . Is that a sacrifice which brings its own blest reward in healthful activity, the consciousness of doing good, peace of mind, and a bright hope of a glorious destiny hereafter?—Away with . . . such a thought! It is emphatically no sacrifice. Say rather it is a privilege. Anxiety, sickness, suffering, or danger, now and then, with a foregoing of the common conveniences and charities of this life, may make us pause, and cause the spirit to waver, and the soul to sink, but let this only be for a moment. All these are nothing when compared with the glory which shall hereafter be revealed in, and for, us. *I never made a sacrifice.* (emphasis added)[21]

When we meet Jesus face to face, behold his nail-scarred hands reaching out to us, and see the look in his eyes when he says, "Enter into your Master's happiness," I believe we will gain a new perspective on this life. Quite simply, we'll see that when it came to following Jesus, the benefits always far outweighed the costs . . . each and every time.

CHAPTER 39

HAPPINESS THROUGH SELF-FORGETFULNESS AND CHRIST-CENTEREDNESS

Whoever finds his life will lose it, and whoever loses his life for my sake will find it.

JESUS (MATTHEW 10:39)

The thing we would remember from meeting a truly gospel-humble person is how much they seemed to be totally interested in us. Because the essence of gospel-humility is not thinking more of myself or thinking less of myself, it is thinking of myself less.

TIMOTHY KELLER

───────── ❧ ─────────

G EORGE WASHINGTON CARVER (1864–1943) was born into slavery on a Missouri plantation. He was a frail and sickly baby whose father had recently died. While still an infant, George and his mother were kidnapped. He was later returned to the plantation and traded for a horse, while his mother was never heard from again.

Carver was ten when he went to Kansas and put himself through high school. In 1891, he entered the college that's now called Iowa State University. He graduated in 1894 with a bachelor's degree and two years later with a master's, becoming the first black student and professor at the university.

Carver became an internationally known botanist, educator, and agricultural researcher, famous for his innovative development of crops, including peanuts, soybeans, and sweet potatoes. He was also an accomplished musician and artist.

Carver wrote to a friend who was facing racism, "Keep your hand in that of the Master, walk daily by His side, so that you may lead others into the realms of true happiness, where a religion of hate (which poisons both body and soul) will be unknown."[1]

At the Tuskegee Institute, Carver's tombstone reads: "A Life that stood out as a gospel of Self-Forgetful Service. He could have added Fortune to Fame, but caring for neither, he found happiness and honour in being helpful to the world."

George Washington Carver is remembered for his life of brilliant, humble service. That inscription connects his happiness with his "Self-Forgetful Service" (I like that the phrase is capitalized, suggesting it has substance and importance).

SELF-OBSESSION IS A FORMULA FOR UNHAPPINESS.

On the first day of a vacation, I received a phone call that marked the worst publishing experience of my life. The book I'd worked so hard to write had been changed for the worse, and I was told I had no recourse. For the first and only time, I felt the published book would be inferior to the manuscript I submitted. Though I'd faced far more difficult circumstances, it was the low point in my professional life. I was disappointed not only by what had happened but also by how deeply it affected me. If you've ever been disappointed about your own disappointment, you understand.

We were at our friends' house on Maui. Despite the beautiful surroundings, I stewed over this writing project, even though I realized I'd eventually gain perspective. (I did, but not until after the vacation; I just wanted to fast-forward to when I knew I'd feel better!)

Meanwhile, I snorkeled for hours a day. That was the only time when the cloud dramatically lifted. Floating among the beautiful fish, turtles, eels, and sharks, and even enjoying that unforgettable ninety minutes of swimming with Molly the monk seal, I lost myself in these creatures and the God who made them. I forgot about myself, my shortcomings, others' failings, and my disappointments. I left my troubled self on the shore. As long as my face was underwater, I was free and happy. It was only when I got out of the water and came back to "Randy's world" that my happiness vaporized.

Sometimes I have that same experience of losing myself during quiet times with God. Sometimes I have it when laughing with Nanci, my family, and my friends. Other times it's when I'm riding a bike or listening to music or a great audiobook.

Over the years, I've learned not simply to think less of myself but to think about myself less. When I'm thinking most about Jesus, not me, I'm most happy.

These lines from a novel ring true:

> When you're unhappy, you get to pay a lot of attention to yourself. And you get to take yourself oh so very seriously. Your truly happy people . . . don't think about themselves very much. Your unhappy person resents it when you try to cheer him up, because that means he has to stop dwellin' on himself and start payin' attention to the universe. Unhappiness is the ultimate form o' self-indulgence.[2]

WE FIND OUR GREATEST HAPPINESS WHEN WE LOSE OURSELVES IN GOD AND OTHERS.

I spoke with a close friend who had once been one of the happiest people I've ever known. But things changed. He lamented that he hadn't been happy since a traumatic event three years earlier brought him great pain and embarrassment.

I surprised him by saying, "Actually, you're wrong. I've seen you very happy a number of times since then."

"Really?" he asked. "When?"

"Whenever you're talking about Jesus and Scripture, you're happy. Whenever you're with friends, you're happy. Whenever you're serving Christ by helping people, I've seen how happy you are."

"Then why do I just remember the unhappiness?"

"When you're by yourself, you let your mind go back to what happened three years ago, and you relive the sadness, injustice, and pain. It stays fresh, as if it happened yesterday."

He nodded his agreement. My reply was just as true of me as it was of him: whenever we're focused on God and others, we forget about ourselves, and that's when we're most happy. We can recall past pain without reexperiencing it—and that's a sign of happiness.

We almost never find happiness by thinking about ourselves—*except* as recipients of God's abundant grace.

I'm glad to say that by turning away from his toxic memories, focusing on God and his Word, and serving people, my friend has regained much of his earlier joy.

An article about unhappy writers says, "The common theory for why writers are often depressed is rather basic: writers think a lot and people who think a lot tend to be unhappy."[3]

This is a half-truth. People who think a lot about *themselves* and their plans for wealth and success—e.g., writing a bestselling novel and being mentioned in the same sentence with Hemingway—do tend to be unhappy. But people who think a lot about Christ and his grace, the great doctrines of the faith, and how to love and serve others tend to be happy people. So it's not *thinking* that's the problem; it's who or what we think about, and how we choose to think about them.

BY REDIRECTING ATTENTION FROM OURSELVES TO GOD, WE ADOPT A RIGHT PERSPECTIVE THAT BRINGS HAPPINESS.

Picture this scenario: it's time for summer vacation. Dad and Mom decide to spend two weeks driving across the country—eleven days visiting national parks and three days at Disneyland.

They say to the kids, "Be grateful for this vacation. Trust that we know best, and you'll be happy."

The youngest, believing his parents, can't wait to get in the car. Everywhere they go, he looks around with wide-eyed wonder. He's delighted to see a harlequin Great Dane at a rest stop. He loves his pancakes at Denny's. He even has fun stopping at the gas station, where he admires a Harley-Davidson.

Meanwhile, his older brother is sullen, playing games on his iPad and thinking about how he'd rather be with friends instead of being stuck in this stupid car with his stupid family. His sister inserts her earbuds, wishing she could be at her friend's party instead of on this ridiculous trip.

At every stop, the two older children mope. They don't respond to their brother or parents except with an occasional smirk, frown, grunt, or eye roll.

The younger boy loves the national parks. The Grand Canyon? "Awesome!" He and his parents share each other's delight. And when the kids get to Disneyland, guess who has the best time? The happy child, of course.

The unhappy siblings complain about the long lines, the walking, and the fact that Space Mountain is closed. "What a rip-off!"

All three children are on exactly the same vacation. But their experiences are radically different. Why? Because their perspectives are different. An unhappy person finds unhappiness in the best of circumstances, and a happy person finds happiness even when things don't go well. What we take from every experience depends on what we bring to it.

Some might think the youngest son is naive. But it's his siblings who are foolish. He chose happiness; they chose misery.

TO BE TRULY HAPPY, WE MUST REJECT SATAN'S LIES AND MEDITATE ON GOD, HIS CHARACTER, AND HIS PROMISES.

Mordor, that dark land in Tolkien's *The Lord of the Rings*, lives in many human hearts. It's a dark, desolate, and depressing wasteland, replete with long stretches of emptiness. This land is haunted by the sounds of marching Orcs, ferocious Trolls, and Nazgûl flying on their fell beasts, all under the dreadful red eye of Sauron, who constantly seeks to destroy.

The human imagination can conceive of such creatures because there are real, supernatural, evil beings in our universe. The Bible speaks of demons, anti-Christs, beasts, and Satan (see Matthew 8:29; 25:41; Ephesians 6:11-16; 1 John 2:18; Revelation 13:1-8). The devil's desire is to devour us (see 1 Peter 5:8).

Depression can be symptomatic of the deep desolation of our hearts. We are capable of fearing we'll never again know happiness, and many who love God have suffered from such dread. God's grace, his promise to never forsake us, his sustaining presence, and his promise of a plan for our good are always part of the cure; sometimes therapy and medication can also play significant roles. Having firsthand experience with depression, I feel empathy for those who suffer from it. But I do think that some—though certainly not all—long-term unhappiness is the product of unbelief and wrong beliefs.

Just as I edit my writing to make it better, I must edit my beliefs and thought habits in light of God's Word. Happiness isn't my exclusive goal, of course, but it's certainly a welcome by-product.

Mike Mason writes, "No one can be happy without believing that happiness is good, right, appropriate, and allowed. . . . The lavish abundance of God's kingdom . . . can be enjoyed only by those who believe, with a faith intense enough to lead to action."[4]

Psalm 37:4 reads, "Delight *yourself* in the LORD" (emphasis added). We aren't spoon-fed his pleasures; we need to go to the banquet, reach out our hands, and eat that delicious cuisine. As surely as it's our responsibility to put good food in our mouths, it's our responsibility to be happy in God!

While it's true that God and his Word are nourishing, the thought of nourishment alone won't bring us to the table. We need to cultivate our appetite for God: "Taste and see that the LORD is good. How happy is the man who takes refuge in Him!" (Psalm 34:8, HCSB).

REJOICING TURNS OUR ATTENTION AWAY FROM OUR DIFFICULT CIRCUMSTANCES AND TOWARD GOD.

J. D. Greear states, "When life punches you in the face, you'll say, 'But I still have the love and acceptance of God, a treasure I don't deserve.' And the joy you find in that treasure can make you rejoice even when you have a bloody nose. You have a joy that death and deprivation cannot touch."[5]

Rejoicing always in the Lord seems unrealistic at times. But we must remember that this rejoicing is centered not in a passing circumstance but in a constant reality—Christ. The text *doesn't* command us to rejoice in:

- the condition of our nation
- the direction our culture is headed
- the attitude of a spouse
- the struggles of our children
- painful events at our church
- the loss of a job
- poor health

We're to rejoice *in the midst of these things*, but of course they're not the source of our joy. We're told to rejoice *in the Lord*. Rejoicing in Christ is superior to all other joys, but it's not always separate from them. Rejoicing in a friend, a parent, a child, a spouse, a job well done, or a glorious walk in the forest can in fact be rejoicing in Christ. Jonathan Edwards depicted happiness in Christ as the ultimate experience that puts all else in perspective:

> Christ Jesus has true excellency, and so great excellency, that when they come to see it they look no further, but the mind rests there. It sees a transcendent glory and an ineffable sweetness in him; it sees that till now it has been pursuing shadows, but that now it has found the substance; that before it had been seeking happiness in the stream, but that now it has found the ocean.[6]

We should thank God for every stream of joy in our lives while recognizing that Christ is the ocean from which every stream flows. Paul said, "His glorious power will make you patient and strong enough to endure anything, and you will be truly happy" (Colossians 1:11, CEV).

In light of such Scripture passages, resignation to unhappiness is unbelief and disobedience. That may sound harsh, but I'm convinced it's true, and actually hope-giving. (Since I'm not naturally chirpy, this isn't my personality speaking!) God wouldn't command *all* his children to rejoice in him always if only the naturally gleeful could obey.

We are to "consider it all joy" when we face hardship (James 1:2, NASB). But this response requires faith that God lovingly superintends our challenges.

The more I grow in my understanding of God's sovereign grace and loyal love, the happier I become. His sovereignty isn't enough; his love isn't enough. But the combination *is* enough. I don't have an all-powerful God who doesn't care; neither do I have a caring

God who doesn't have the power to make good things happen. I have a God who loves me and is sovereign over the universe, including all evil.

Instead of saying, "My circumstances don't matter; they're not the source of my joy," we'd be better off saying this: "I know the God who created me and redeemed me and has forgiven me in Christ. God is in me and with me. He uses my best circumstances to encourage me, and he can use my worst circumstances to enrich me. He has promised me eternal life with him and a wonderful family of brothers and sisters on a New Earth in a resurrected universe. One day he'll welcome me into his never-ending happiness."

My circumstances do matter. But in the scope of eternity, they're not the main source of my joy. Rather, they are opportunities for my growth and my ultimate good. When they threaten to overwhelm me, my difficult circumstances can remind me to look to God, my Rock and my Redeemer, who is my happiness.

HAPPINESS—AND SELF-FORGETFULNESS—IS A HABIT.

Scripture calls us to actively cultivate the habit of happiness by rejoicing, praying, and giving thanks (see 1 Thessalonians 5:16-18). Do you continually open your eyes to look past yourself and see God and his hand at work? Do you regularly look for reasons to thank him?

Before taking two of our grandsons on a long bike ride on a hot day, I told them, "Drink three cups of water each." A few minutes later, I walked into the bathroom and found six cups strewn about the counter. Taking me literally, they'd each filled three cups of water instead of refilling one cup three times. I still smile when I think about those six cups, and it makes me thank God for those boys and the delights they bring—delights which, from a different perspective, could seem like aggravations.

Hanging in my office is a photograph of a primitive tribal people in Togo, watching, for the first time, a motion-picture portrayal of Jesus' crucifixion. The abject shock and horror on their faces, as well as the tears in their eyes, remind me daily of what it looks like to see the Cross through fresh eyes.

Why do most of us no longer respond to Jesus' sacrifice that way? Because to us the Good News is old news. When we tire of the gospel story—when it fails to startle and amaze us—we need to ask God to give us a renewed sense of the suffering of Jesus and his overflowing love and joy, which are at the heart of our faith.

When I contemplate Christ—when I meditate on his unfathomable love and grace—I lose myself in him—and paradoxically, I find myself. When he's the center of my thinking, before I know it, I'm happy.

Tim Keller writes,

> Don't you want to be the kind of person who, when they see themselves in a mirror or reflected in a shop window, does not admire what they see but does not cringe either? . . . Wouldn't you like to be the skater who wins the silver, and yet is thrilled about those three triple jumps that the gold medal winner did? To love it the way you love a sunrise? Just to love the fact that it was done? You are as

happy that they did it as if you had done it yourself. . . . This is gospel-humility, blessed self-forgetfulness.[7]

C. S. Lewis said of the humble person, "He will not be thinking about humility: he will not be thinking about himself at all."[8]

Keller, inspired by Lewis, says, "Gospel-humility is not needing to think about myself. . . . I stop connecting every experience, every conversation, with myself. In fact, I stop thinking about myself. The freedom of self-forgetfulness. The blessed rest that only self-forgetfulness brings."[9]

As commendable as such humility is, we can never achieve it simply by willing it to appear. Otherwise, we'll be thinking about ourselves and our valiant attempts to be humble.

What we need is to be so gripped by Jesus and his grace that we truly forget about ourselves. Why would we want to think about ourselves, the lesser, when we can think about *him*, the infinitely greater? This happens directly, when we worship and serve him, and also indirectly, when we love and serve others for his glory.

When we lose ourselves in God and his Kingdom, as Jesus says, we find ourselves—and, in doing so, we find happiness.

CHAPTER 40

HAPPINESS THROUGH GRATITUDE

Let them sacrifice thank offerings and tell of his works with songs of joy.

PSALM 107:22, NIV

*When someone continually talks about how happy they are, I tend to doubt them;
but when they talk about how grateful they are, I know they have found happiness.*

ROB HAWKINS

I HEARD A STORY of someone who asked a man why he was so happy. The man picked up a binder filled with hundreds of handwritten pages and explained, "Every time someone does something kind for me, I write it in this book. And every time I feel very good about something, I write it in this book."

The questioner said, "I wish I could be as happy as you."

"If you kept a book like this, you would be."

"But the book is so big . . . I haven't had many kind things done for me, and I haven't felt good very often."

"I might have thought that too, if I hadn't recorded them all. I've learned to see and remember and be grateful for kindness and happiness when they come. Try it. Every time you doubt, read your entries and you'll see all you have to be grateful for."

Guerric (1070–1157), the Abbot of Igny, wrote, "O happiness of these times! O unhappiness of these times! Is it not happiness, when there is such plenitude of grace, and of all good things? Is it not unhappiness, when there is so much ingratitude of those that are redeemed?"[1]

The same is true of any time in history. Happiness and unhappiness are in direct proportion to gratitude and ingratitude.

THERE ARE ALWAYS REASONS TO BE THANKFUL.

Matthew Henry, the Puritan preacher and Bible commentator, made this statement after a thief stole his money: "Let me be thankful first because I was never robbed before; second, although they took my purse, they did not take my life; third, because, although they took my all, it was not much; and fourth, because it was I who was robbed, not I who robbed."[2]

Before church, I sometimes speak with a man who has faced difficult life circumstances: his son died, he has battled cancer, he lost his job, and he's feeling the pains of old age. But the smile on his face is genuine. He speaks of the goodness of God and how grateful he is for Jesus, his Savior. He's a truly happy man. I enter the church service feeling I've already met with the Lord and heard a great message, all from my encounter with this brother.

One weekend I walked through the church parking lot and asked another man how he was doing. He launched into a litany of complaints that continued through the hallways and foyer as we headed to worship. He was profoundly unhappy.

He answered my question honestly. But just because a perspective is transparently shared doesn't mean it isn't in dire need of adjustment.

These two men taught me a lesson I've seen thousands of times: with gratitude there's happiness; without it, there's unhappiness. Every time.

John said this of the grace of Jesus: "We have all received grace after grace from His fullness" (John 1:16, HCSB). "Grace after grace" is like the tide as we walk the shoreline. It comes in and goes out, but it's always either there or about to be. Grace is a gift, and the proper response to it is gratitude. Because God's grace is constant, new, and fresh, so our gratitude should be constant, new, and fresh.

As we'll see in this chapter, gratitude toward God and others magnifies our happiness. G. K. Chesterton put it beautifully: "I would maintain that thanks are the highest form of thought; and that gratitude is happiness doubled by wonder."[3]

GRATITUDE BRINGS HAPPINESS TO EVERYONE, NOT JUST BELIEVERS.

Our thankfulness glorifies God and makes him happy: "The one who offers thanksgiving as his sacrifice glorifies me" (Psalm 50:23). But God isn't the only one affected when we give thanks.

Psychologists asked undergraduates to complete a survey that included a happiness scale and measures of thankfulness. Over six weeks, the participants wrote down, once a week, five things they were grateful for. This practice had a dramatic effect on their happiness score. The study concluded, "Students who regularly expressed gratitude showed increases in well-being over the course of the study."[4]

Secular books on happiness document gratitude's role in making people happier. But cultivating gratitude proves difficult for people whose worldview leaves them with nobody to thank! Yes, they can thank someone for loaning them a car or for being their teacher. But whom can they thank for sunshine, air to breathe, and the capacity to enjoy pleasure?

People who don't believe that a sovereign God is at work through the kindness of others must thank their "lucky stars," random circumstances, or—at best—other people. Since people are small when compared to God, the object of their gratitude is small, shrinking their capacity for happiness.

God's common grace offers unbelievers a degree of happiness that's greatly enhanced through thankfulness. As Christ-followers, however, we find gratitude multiplied when we return it to God, the ultimate and primary source of all goodness.

When others encourage me, I seek to always thank God for the encouragement. My happiness stems from my gratitude to the God of providence, who orchestrates our encounter. God sends others to humble me, and they, too, are character-building gifts. It may not be as easy to thank God for them, but God calls on me to "give thanks in all circumstances," not just some (1 Thessalonians 5:18).

In a study of 1,035 high school students, those who demonstrated high levels of gratitude and strong appreciation of other people had higher GPAs, less depression, and a more positive outlook than the less grateful teens. By contrast, the teens who equated buying and owning things with success and happiness reported having lower GPAs, more depression, and a more negative outlook.[5]

The Greek word *charis*, often translated "grace," means "that which is given freely and generously—'gift, gracious gift.'"[6] God's grace is his giving to us, at great cost, what we don't deserve (see 2 Corinthians 8:9). Second Corinthians 8–9 is the longest passage on financial giving in the New Testament; *charis* ("grace") appears ten times. The passage ends with these words from Paul: "Thanks be to God for his indescribable gift.

When we genuinely experience the good news of salvation in Christ, gratitude and happiness inevitably multiply!

GRATITUDE COUPLED WITH HUMBLE SERVICE MULTIPLIES HAPPINESS.

Dennis Prager writes, "We tend to think that it is being unhappy that leads people to complain, but it is truer to say that it is complaining that leads to people becoming unhappy. Become grateful and you will become a much happier person."[7]

When possible, we should take positive action to right what's wrong. But when we complain about circumstances beyond our control, we're telling God, "You don't know what you're doing; I know better than you."

If you've recently faced a negative situation, write out a list of what you wish others had and hadn't done for you. Use your list as a guideline to minister to those who need your wisdom and encouragement. Don't grumble about others; instead, seek to change the primary life God has entrusted to you and the one you have some control over—your own.

I've heard many amazing stories of how hurting people have experienced love shown by God's people. In hard times, Nanci and I have experienced the same. Imperfect as the local church is, we thank God for it, and our gratitude spills over into happiness.

"The LORD is close to the brokenhearted and saves those who are crushed in spirit" (Psalm 34:18, NIV). Serving others is one of the best cures for loneliness and depression. "In humility count others more significant than yourselves. Let each of you look not only to his own interests, but also to the interests of others" (Philippians 2:3-4). Helen Keller wrote, "Although the world is full of suffering, it is full also of the overcoming of it."[8] She also said, "Believe, when you are most unhappy, that there is something for you to do in the world. So long as you can sweeten another's pain, life is not in vain."[9]

Nancy Leigh DeMoss says, "*Undeniable guilt,* plus *undeserved grace,* should equal *unbridled gratitude.*"[10] Far too often, though, it's our arrogance and ingratitude and complaining spirits that are unbridled. Consequently, our relationship with God and others is hindered and our happiness diminished.

Proud, presumptuous people always think they deserve better. If the day goes well, they don't notice. If it doesn't, it's a great disappointment, and someone else is always to blame.

Good days pleasantly surprise the humble. Even on a difficult day, their hearts overflow with gratitude. They're happy because they know they've received *better* than they deserve.

HAPPY PEOPLE NEVER GET OVER GOD'S GRACE.

Happy people celebrate their conversion not just once, but over and over.

John Piper says, "Gratitude leaves no room for sin, because it comes out of humility, the opposite of sin. And for sin to flourish it must be dripping with pride."[11]

In the story of the Prodigal Son in Luke 15, when the younger brother returns home to much rejoicing, the older brother questions his father's actions. The older brother is full of complaints, revealing his proud, ungrateful heart. In the same way, whenever we believe that our heavenly Father is mismanaging our lives and treating others better, we're demonstrating arrogance. Humility fosters happiness; pride undermines it.

The older brother was as unhappy in his self-righteousness as the younger brother had been in his immorality. But because the prodigal repented and welcomed his father's grace, he was now forgiven, restored, and happy. Yet the older brother, offended by grace and poisoned by ingratitude, remained unhappy.

Bible teacher M. R. DeHaan (1891–1965) said,

> The most cheerful people I have met, with few exceptions, have been those who had the least sunshine and the most pain and suffering in their lives. The most grateful people I have met were not those who had traveled a pathway of roses all their lives through, but those who were confined, because of circumstances, to their homes, often to their beds, and had learned to depend upon God as only such Christians know how to do. The "gripers" are usually, I have observed, those who enjoy excellent health. The complainers are those who have the least to complain about.[12]

Pride is the master sin, and it's manifested in our complaints. Scripture calls upon us to grow in thankfulness:

- Give thanks in all circumstances; for this is the will of God in Christ Jesus for you. (1 Thessalonians 5:18)
- Lord my God, I will give thanks to you forever! (Psalm 30:12)
- I will thank you in the great congregation; in the mighty throng I will praise you. (Psalm 35:18)
- Do all things without grumbling or disputing. . . . I am glad and rejoice with you all. Likewise you also should be glad and rejoice with me. (Philippians 2:14, 17-18)

When I came to faith in Christ, my skeptical father said, "You'll get over it." It has now been forty-five years, and I'm grateful I've never gotten over it—it has been a daily source of happiness.

When my prodigal dad, cancer-ridden and desperate at age eighty-five, surrendered his life to Christ, I celebrated his conversion. I still rejoice every time this moment comes to mind. If I find myself wishing my dad had come to my ball games and taken me fishing and said "I love you" when I was a kid, I choose instead to be grateful for the good things about him. I thank God for using him in my life decades before he came to Jesus. My father sometimes failed me; such is life under the Curse. But my Father God has never failed me, even when I don't understand his plan.

BEING GRATEFUL FOR THE LITTLE THINGS IN LIFE CULTIVATES OUR GRATITUDE IN ALL THINGS.

While researching my novel *Dominion* in 1995, I spent time in Jackson, Mississippi, with legendary pastor, author, and civil rights activist John Perkins. At the age of sixteen, John's brother was shot on the streets by a deputy sheriff and died in John's arms. Twenty years later, John was tortured in a Mississippi jail cell while his wife and children stood outside hearing his cries. But John's heart is full of grace and forgiveness, and he has been a pioneer in racial reconciliation.

John walked me through the streets of Jackson, telling me story after story, giving credit to Jesus. He took me into a thrift store, where he found an old hat on sale for twenty-five cents. He tried it on for me, flashed his big smile, and asked how it looked. I told him it looked snazzy. John just couldn't get over finding this hat—and at such a great price. I'll never forget his sheer delight at this treasure he'd discovered. It seemed not to occur to him that this very thrift store was under the umbrella of a ministry he'd led.

John and I waited in line, and once at the counter, John handed the girl a quarter, beaming at his find. Recognizing the founder of the ministry, she said, "Dr. Perkins, there's no charge for you!"

But John refused to accept special treatment. He insisted she take the quarter and proudly put on his hat. You'd have thought he'd found $10,000 in cash!

Every time I looked at John Perkins throughout the day, it made me smile. Even now, decades later, I'm smiling. It was such a little thing, yet it brought such happiness for a man who, in all the sorrows of life and in the greatness of his cause, has never diminished his God-centered appreciation for life's smallest joys.

When life is viewed with a spirit of thankfulness, we will see the happiness and reasons for happiness that surround us. Ellen Vaughn says, "Gratitude unleashes the freedom to live content in the moment, rather than being anxious about the future or regretting the past."[13]

God isn't just in the monumental moments. His artistry makes even the ordinary exceptional: the sparkle of raindrops, the artistry of spiderwebs, and the sound of an acoustic guitar. A child's laugh, swing sets, sprinklers, the smell of split cedar, and songs about surfing. Colorful birds and exotic fish. Stars that declare God's glory. Little League, skiing, Ping-Pong, long hot showers, a slam dunk, and Disneyland. Maple syrup, fresh green beans, buttermilk biscuits, and homemade strawberry jam. Aspirin, artificial limbs, wheelchairs, and synthetic insulin (I can't live without it). Ripe oranges straight off the tree. Chocolate chip cookies hot out of the oven and a tall glass of cold milk (in my case, this would require a lot more insulin). A comfortable recliner, the smell of leather upholstery, and a dog's wagging tail.

If we disregard these and thousands of other gifts, we don't just fail to notice them, we fail to notice God. God's goodness is always evident if we look in the right place. "He is actually not far from each one of us, for in him we live and move and have our being" (Acts 17:27-28).

We might imagine that missionaries think only of things of deep importance to God's Kingdom. But listen to what Jim Elliot said of Amy Carmichael and himself (both on the short list of missionaries known for their sacrifices). In a letter to his wife, Elisabeth, Jim observed,

> Amy Carmichael writes of little joys, like flowers springing by the path unnoticed except by those who are looking for them. . . . Little things, like a quietly sinking sun, a friendly dog, a ready smile. We sang a little song in kindergarten which I've never forgotten: "The world is so full of a number of things / I'm sure we should all be as happy as kings." Simple, but such a devastating rebuke to the complaining heart! I am impressed with the joy that is ours in Christ, so that heaven above and earth below become brighter and fairer.[14]

HAPPY CHRIST-FOLLOWERS NOTICE GOD'S PRESENCE AROUND EVERY CORNER.

Alexander Maclaren (1826–1910) advised, "Seek . . . to cultivate a buoyant, joyous sense of the crowded kindnesses of God in your daily life."[15] If we fail to see God's "crowded kindnesses," it's not because they're lacking but because we're blind to them.

Letters to Malcolm was C. S. Lewis's final book, written six months before he died and published after his death. In it, Lewis wrote, "We may ignore, but we can nowhere evade the presence of God. The world is crowded with Him. He walks everywhere incognito."[16]

Lewis graphically described God's self-revelation through his creation: "Any patch of sunlight in a wood will show you something about the sun which you could never get from reading books on astronomy. These pure and spontaneous pleasures are 'patches of Godlight' in the woods of our experience."[17]

How many patches of Godlight do we not see because we spend our lives indoors? And how many do we see but fail to recognize as such?

Some seem to believe that it doesn't matter much whether we see God in little things as long as we see him in the big ones. Lewis disagreed, saying, "We—or at least I—shall not be able to adore God on the highest occasions if we have learned no habit of doing so on the lowest."[18]

It's right for Christians to be happy—not because there's no evil or because we don't care about suffering but because we know evil is unnatural and temporary. Further, we know God has done for us and the world all that's necessary to solve the problems of evil and suffering—and to bring out of it far more good and happiness than there would have been if the bad things had never existed. This is why people fighting cancer or those unjustly imprisoned can have hearts full of gratitude to God.

Lewis connected all this to both praise and gratitude. Shortly before meeting his Creator face to face, he wrote about God's self-revelation in his creation:

> This heavenly fruit is instantly redolent of the orchard where it grew. This sweet air whispers of the country from whence it blows. It is a message. We know we are being touched by a finger of that right hand at which there are pleasures for evermore. There need be no question of thanks or praise as a separate event, something done afterwards. To experience the tiny theophany is itself to adore.
>
> Gratitude exclaims, very properly, "How good of God to give me this." Adoration says, "What must be the quality of that Being . . ." One's mind runs back up the sunbeam to the sun.[19]

We live in a world of high-speed everything, and we've learned to hate slowness and lingering. We need to turn off the sounds, avert our eyes from the screens, slow down, and be silent more often, opening our eyes and ears to the world God created so we might learn about him. Or, sometimes, *closing* our eyes and taking ten-minute vacations, traveling in our minds to our favorite places, with Jesus at our side.

God gives us hundreds of reasons to be grateful every hour—and if you think I'm exaggerating, ask him to make you aware of his gracious provisions surrounding you. Developing the habit and discipline of gratitude results in greater praise to God and greater happiness for ourselves. When life's tough, we can be grateful that God is with us in our suffering, that he's using it for our good, and that he promises to end it once and for all.

Keep your own happiness journal. Record God's evident goodness around you every day. You'll find that in time, you'll see more and more gifts from him—not because there *are* more, but because you're finally seeing what has been there all along.

EXPRESSING GRATITUDE IS A HOLY HABIT THAT GIVES GOD GLORY AND SPREADS HAPPINESS.

Do we consistently acknowledge God to be the greatest source of our joy? Are we filled with discontentment over what we don't have, rather than gratitude over what we do have? Do we thank God for problems we could have but don't? (I have several medical problems, but I thank God every time I fill out a physician's form and realize how few boxes I have to check on those *pages* of diseases and disorders!)

Luke tells of ten men whom Jesus healed of leprosy. Only one of them returned to say "Thank you." Jesus asked the man a question that reflects the sadness God feels at our thanklessness: "What happened to the other nine that were also healed?" (see Luke 17:11-19).

Jesus then commended the only one who returned, saying, "Rise and go your way; your faith has made you well" (Luke 17:19). This is an example of healing—far greater than physical healing—that only comes through gratitude for God's countless kindnesses to us. (We'll never exhaust them, but the more we count them, the more grateful we'll be.)

G. K. Chesterton, one of the happiest and cleverest minds of the twentieth century, noted that children are grateful when their Christmas stockings are filled with candy or toys. But what about "the gift of two miraculous legs" inside our stockings? "We thank people for birthday presents of cigars and slippers. Can I thank no one for the birthday present of birth?"[20]

The custom of praying to thank God for each meal is a wonderful one. But why should we restrict this custom to meals? Why not thank God throughout the day for a hundred other things?

Chesterton wrote,

> *You say grace before meals.*
> *All right.*
> *But I say grace before the play and the opera,*
> *And grace before the concert and the pantomime,*
> *And grace before I open a book,*
> *And grace before sketching, . . . boxing, walking, playing, dancing;*
> *And grace before I dip the pen in the ink.*[21]

GRATITUDE TO GOD BRINGS PEACE EVEN DURING THE TOUGHEST TIMES.

Nanci and I were grateful to the surgeon who operated on our daughter to remove a mass thought to be cancer (it wasn't), but we weren't praying to the surgeon. We prayed to God and credited him for the results. We knew the surgeon's hands were under God's sovereign control, making us more grateful—not less—for his God-given skill.

Of course, not every circumstance turns out as we hope and pray. Whatever the outcome, though, our gratitude for God's sovereign plan makes us slower to blame others and less likely to become embittered against them.

Many amplify their unhappiness in the face of tragedy by casting blame. Anger impedes recovery and feeds ingratitude. "Do not be anxious about anything," the apostle Paul wrote, "but in everything *by prayer* and supplication *with thanksgiving* let your requests be made known to God. And the *peace* of God, which surpasses all understanding, will guard your hearts and your minds in Christ Jesus" (Philippians 4:6-7, emphasis added). Prayer plus thanksgiving equals the peace only God can give.

True faith submits to God's plan, whether or not it coincides with ours. So we should pray not with faith in our faith, but with faith in God. "Trust in the LORD with all your heart. Never rely on what you think you know" (Proverbs 3:5, GNT). Prayers to God that freely ask, yet trust and submit—instead of demanding and insisting—lend themselves to gratitude.

God is never obligated to do as we ask. Though we're free to ask him to deliver us from difficult or painful circumstances, the final outcome of every situation is solely in God's hands. Proverbs 19:21 declares, "Many are the plans in the mind of a man, but it is the purpose of the LORD that will stand." We should thank God no matter what, trusting in his wisdom, goodness, and love.

Dr. Helen Roseveare was a medical missionary to the Congo, where rebel armies posed a constant threat. In August of 1964, word spread that the local chief had been abducted and flayed alive. One night Helen and the other women missionaries who had not already fled the country were seized at gunpoint by guerrilla soldiers, who took over the hospital compound for five months. The women were savagely beaten, humiliated, and raped by the rebel soldiers.[22]

Helen has never forgotten that first dark night: "I felt unutterably alone. For a brief moment, I felt God had failed me. He could have stepped in and prevented this rising crescendo of wickedness and cruelty. He could have saved me out of their hands. Why didn't He speak? Why didn't He intervene?"[23]

But in the midst of that terrifying ordeal, as she cried out to the Lord, she sensed him saying to her, "Helen, can you thank Me?" Helen writes, "That healing and release began when I said, 'Lord, I'm willing to thank You for trusting me with this experience, even if You never tell me why.' No, my circumstances didn't change. But He changed me in the midst of them."[24]

A SPIRIT OF ENTITLEMENT ROBS US OF HAPPINESS, AND GOD OF GLORY.

Ann Voskamp explains, "Ultimately, in his essence, Satan is an ingrate. And he sinks his venom into the heart of Eden. Satan's sin becomes the first sin of all humanity: *the sin of ingratitude*. . . . Our fall was, has always been, and always will be, that we aren't satisfied in God and what He gives."[25]

Nothing is more poisonous than the sense of entitlement that permeates our culture and sometimes, sadly, our churches. We're disappointed with family, friends, neighbors, church, the airlines, the waiter—nearly everyone. And in the process, it becomes clear that it's God we're really disappointed with—after all, if he's sovereign, he's the one subjecting us to all these irritations. How dare he not give us everything we want, when we want it?

If only we could see our situation clearly. We deserve expulsion; he gives us a diploma. We deserve the electric chair; he gives us a parade. Anything less than overwhelming gratitude should be unthinkable. He owes us *nothing*. We owe him *everything*.

"Who has ever given to God, that God should repay them?" (Romans 11:35, NIV). The answer is *nobody*.

Christians in dire situations, undergoing persecution, are often deeply grateful for God's daily blessings. How dare we whine and pout when our latte isn't hot enough?

God, open our eyes to the wonders of your grace!

We underestimate how sinful a complaining spirit is in God's eyes: "The people complained about their hardships in the hearing of the LORD, and when he heard them his anger was aroused. Then fire from the LORD burned among them and consumed some of the outskirts of the camp" (Numbers 11:1, NIV).

A "Dear Abby" letter read, "Happiness is knowing that your parents won't almost kill you if you come home a little late. Happiness is having your own bedroom. Happiness is having parents that trust you. Happiness is getting the telephone call you've been praying for. Happiness is knowing that you're well dressed as anybody. Happiness is something I don't have. Signed, Fifteen and Unhappy."[26]

A few days later, the same column carried this response to the above letter, written by a thirteen-year-old girl: "Happiness is being able to walk. Happiness is being able to talk. Happiness is being able to see. Happiness is being able to hear. Unhappiness is reading a letter from a 15 year old girl who can do all these things and still says she isn't happy. I can talk, I can see, I can hear, but I can't walk. Signed, Thirteen and Happy."[27]

If we spend time with people whose lives exemplify contentment and gratitude, their spirit of appreciation rubs off on us. Likewise, hanging out with mostly critical and ungrateful people poisons us. Complaining becomes normal.

Many who appear to have more by earthly standards actually have less of what really matters. Indeed, the richest people in the world are those who have a deep, humble, gratitude-drenched personal relationship with Christ.

A TRUE UNDERSTANDING OF GOD'S GRACE ALWAYS RESULTS IN DEEP GRATITUDE.

If the same spirit of entitlement and ingratitude that characterizes our culture characterizes God's people, what do we have to offer? Shouldn't the gospel make us different, and shouldn't that difference manifest itself in the depth of our gratitude to God?

We should never believe anything about ourselves or God that makes his grace to us seem less than astonishing.

Perhaps the greatest heritage parents can pass on to their children is the ability to perceive God's daily blessings and to respond with continual gratitude. We should be "overflowing with thankfulness" (Colossians 2:7, NIV).

If we truly grasped God's grace—even a little—we would fall on our knees and weep. Then we would get up and dance, smile, laugh, look at each other, and say, "Can you *believe* it? We're forgiven!"

Living by grace means affirming our unworthiness daily. We're never thankful for what we think we deserve. *We are deeply thankful for what we know we don't deserve.*

IN EVERY CIRCUMSTANCE, WE CAN GIVE THANKS TO GOD AND EXPERIENCE HIS JOY.

Ephesians 5:18-20 says, "Be filled with the Spirit, addressing one another in psalms and hymns and spiritual songs, singing and making melody to the Lord with your heart, giving thanks always and for everything to God the Father in the name of our Lord Jesus Christ." Being Spirit-controlled is inseparable from giving thanks in everything.

Whether we find ourselves having reason to celebrate or to mourn, there's never a time not to express our gratitude to God. Psalm 140:13 declares, "Surely the righteous shall give thanks to your name." Giving thanks is what God's people do.

Gerard Manley Hopkins (1844–1889) wrote, "The world is charged with the grandeur of God."[28] If we're not falling over ourselves giving thanks to God, we're not seeing God's grandeur, which brings the light of hope and happiness to a fallen world.

The Curse cast a shadow over happiness; heartfelt gratitude to God is a light that cuts through the shadow. Rather than enjoying the happiness of the moment, we tend to start searching for something to make us still happier, poisoning even our happy times.

Ann Voskamp writes,

> As long as thanks is possible, then joy is always possible. *Joy is always possible.* *Whenever*, meaning—now; *wherever*, meaning—here. The holy grail of joy is not in some exotic location or some emotional mountain peak experience. The joy wonder could be here! Here, in the messy, piercing ache of now, joy might be—unbelievably—possible![29]

While it may seem hard to "make ourselves happy," it's not hard to choose to give thanks, which invariably kindles happiness. We can always list things we're grateful for and recite them to God. We can share them with friends and loved ones, including our children, grandchildren, or other relatives. No matter how difficult our circumstances, the happiness that comes with thanksgiving is always within our reach.

Try it and see! Voskamp says, "No amount of regret changes the past. No amount of anxiety changes the future. Any amount of grateful joy changes the present."[30] Even if the worst suffering of our lives still lies ahead of us, our loving God assures us it will be for only a short time. Then, either at Christ's return or at our death, our suffering will end *forever.* This eternal perspective—the constant awareness that we aren't living primarily for the here and now but rather for the world to come—is something we desperately need. That's why Scottish evangelist Duncan Matheson (1824–1869) prayed, "Lord, stamp eternity upon my eyeballs."[31]

As God's children, we should gratefully remind ourselves that our happiness is limited in this life but unlimited in the life to come. A "normal day" as resurrected people on the New Earth will be incredibly better than the best day we've ever experienced here.

Nancy Leigh DeMoss writes, "The person who has chosen to make gratitude his or her mind-set and lifestyle can view anything—*anything!*—through the eyes of thankfulness. The whole world looks different when we do."[32]

Once we experience thanksgiving as our default condition, we'll find it's inseparable from our happiness, and we'll never want to go back to the barren wasteland of ingratitude. We will stop asking God, "Why have you done this *to* me?" and instead, looking at Christ's redemptive sacrifice, we will ask God, "Why have you done this *for* me?"

CHAPTER 41

HAPPINESS AND HOPE: ADJUSTING OUR EXPECTATIONS

*Blessed are you when people hate you, when they exclude you and insult
you and reject your name as evil, because of the Son of Man. Rejoice in
that day and leap for joy, because great is your reward in heaven.*

JESUS (LUKE 6:22-23, NIV)

*Live, then, and be happy, beloved children of my heart! and never forget,
that until the day God will deign to reveal the future to man, all human
wisdom is contained in these two words—"Wait and Hope."*

ALEXANDRE DUMAS

THERE'S A STORY of a man and his granddaughter who are sitting on a park bench when a traveler asks, "Is this a friendly town? I come from a town full of conflict. Is that what I'll find here?"

The grandfather replies, "Yes, my friend, I'm certain that's what you'll find." Saddened, the traveler continues on.

Before long, another traveler stops. "I come from a village with many delightful people. I wonder, would I find such charming people here?"

The grandfather smiles in response. "Welcome, friend! Yes, you certainly will!"

As the stranger walks away, the puzzled child asks, "Grandfather, why did you give those strangers two different answers to the same question?"

The grandfather answered, "The first man was looking for conflict, while the second was looking for goodness. Each will find exactly what he expects."

It's true that when we expect the best, we usually see the best. When we look for the worst, we usually find it. Frederick Langbridge (1849–1922) put it this way: "Two men look out through the same bars: One sees the mud, and one the stars."[1]

We bring ourselves to every situation, every encounter, every relationship. The unhappy person who leaves North Dakota in search of happiness in California finds more sunshine and less snow, but not more happiness. The happy Californian who relocates finds that his happiness accompanies him.

OUR EXPECTATIONS PROFOUNDLY AFFECT OUR LIFE EXPERIENCES.

We simultaneously expect too much and too little. We need to discover what we should expect less of and what merits higher expectations.

Positive people experience adversity, just as negative people do. Their expectations don't control circumstances, but they do give perspective. Optimists see more goodness and find redemptive elements even in the bad times. Scripture says, "The hopes of the godly result in happiness, but the expectations of the wicked come to nothing" (Proverbs 10:28, NLT). Likewise, Proverbs 11:23 states, "The desire of the righteous ends only in good; the expectation of the wicked in wrath."

The novel *Pollyanna* portrays a cheerful orphan girl whose minister father died. Pollyanna played "the glad game," finding something to be glad about no matter how difficult her circumstances.

Today the story is often mischaracterized—people are derisively called "Pollyannas" if they seem foolishly optimistic. But Pollyanna's optimism was learned from her father, who fought discouragement by counting the more than eight hundred "rejoicing texts" in the Bible. She states, "[Father] said if God took the trouble to tell us eight hundred times to be glad and rejoice, He must want us to do it."[2]

Pollyanna's happiness didn't involve denying reality but affirming realities invisible to pessimists. Hers was a childlike trust in God that modern cynics should learn from, not mock.

Disneyland claims to be the happiest place on Earth, but research indicates otherwise. According to Morley Safer on *60 Minutes*, the happiest nation on Earth proves to be Denmark. The United States, despite its greater wealth, ranks twenty-third, and the United Kingdom, forty-first. Denmark's remarkable secret to topping the happiness chart? Low expectations. The interviews on *60 Minutes* demonstrate that Danes have more modest dreams than Americans and they're less distressed when their hopes don't materialize.[3]

The general view of life in Denmark is compatible with the doctrine of the Fall: instead of being surprised when life doesn't go their way, Danes are grateful that things aren't worse, and they're happily surprised by health and success. If they have food, clothing, shelter, friends, and family, life seems good.

There's a biblical basis for both realistic and positive expectations. We certainly live in a world with suffering and death. But as believers, we understand that God is with us and won't forsake us, and that one day we'll live on a redeemed Earth far happier than Denmark or Disneyland on their best days!

WHEN YOU EXPECT LESS OF A FALLEN WORLD, YOU CAN BE CONTENT WITH LESS—AND HAPPY WHEN MORE THAN EXPECTED COMES TO YOU.

We should lower our expectations concerning all the advantages we think life should bring us while raising our expectations concerning Christ and what he is daily accomplishing in us.

I have two good friends: one a pessimist, the other an optimist. Sometimes the optimist fares better because he sees the positives he expects. But he can also be emotionally devastated when life takes bad turns he never anticipated.

When things go sideways, my pessimist friend is neither surprised nor distraught; he expected nothing more. Yet because of his mind-set, he sometimes fails to see the magnificent, happy-making things God does every day.

The happy middle ground of biblical realism falls somewhere in between, allowing us to honestly face life's difficulties while trusting God's sovereignty and joyfully anticipating what lies ahead of us.

Our degree of happiness in life largely depends on:

1. the amount of happiness we believe should be rightfully ours
2. our ability to find delight in a fallen world God will redeem
3. our ability to see the little things—the ten thousand reasons for happiness that surround us that we easily ignore

C. S. Lewis said,

If you think of this world as a place intended simply for our happiness, you find it quite intolerable: think of it as a place of training and correction and it's not so bad.

Imagine a set of people all living in the same building. Half of them think it is a hotel, the other half think it is a prison. Those who think it a hotel might regard it as quite intolerable, and those who thought it was a prison might decide that it was really surprisingly comfortable. So that what seems the ugly doctrine is one that comforts and strengthens you in the end. The people who try to hold an optimistic view of this world would become pessimists: the people who hold a pretty stern view of it become optimistic.[4]

G. K. Chesterton, in *Orthodoxy*, points out a positive in what many consider a negative— our sense of unease in this present world:

The Christian optimism is based on the fact that we do *not* fit in to the world. . . . The modern philosopher had told me again and again that I was in the right place, and I had still felt depressed even in acquiescence. But I had heard that I was in the *wrong* place, and my soul sang for joy, like a bird in spring. The knowledge found out and illuminated forgotten chambers in the dark house of infancy. I knew now why grass had always seemed to me as queer as the green beard of a giant, and why I could feel homesick at home.[5]

THERE'S OFTEN A CHASM BETWEEN WHAT WE WANT AND WHAT WE HAVE.

Psychologist Richard Carlson (1961–2006) wrote *Don't Sweat the Small Stuff*, in which he argued that the narrower the gap between what we have and what we want, the happier we are. Unfortunately, the moment we get what we want, we habitually let our minds drift toward something better.

Carlson said, "Ultimately, the only way to feel happy is to stop focusing your attention on what you think would make you happy and be happy with what you have."[6] Despite how obvious this seems, "most of us do just the opposite."[7]

Here's what we think: *If only I could have [fill in the blank] . . . or If only I were [fill in the blank] . . . or If only those around me were [fill in the blank] . . . then I'd be happy.*

Here's what's true: if a sovereign God loves me, bridged the gap between himself and me, lives in me, and gives me power to love, worship, and honor him, and to share his love with others, then I have all I need to be happy.

The principle stated by Dr. Carlson is seen in the writings of the apostle Paul:

> I rejoiced in the Lord greatly that now at length you have revived your concern for me. . . . Not that I am speaking of being in need, for I have learned in whatever situation I am to be content. I know how to be brought low, and I know how to abound. In any and every circumstance, I have learned the secret of facing plenty and hunger, abundance and need. I can do all things through him who strengthens me. PHILIPPIANS 4:10-13

While he surely preferred abundance and plenty to hunger and need, Paul chose not to focus on his own wants. His contentment was in Christ (see Philippians 4:13). When our contentment is in Christ, it's as durable as he is dependable. When our happiness is in Christ, we can't lose our happiness, because we can't lose Christ.

INSTEAD OF EXPECTING THE WORST, WE SHOULD CONTROL WHAT WE CAN AND LEAVE THE REST TO GOD.

Worry is the product of high stakes and low control. There's a subtle aspect to worry: if we care, we think we should worry, as if that will help somehow. In fact, worry has absolutely no redemptive value. When good things are happening, we're worried that bad things will come. When bad things happen, we worry that worse things will come. Jesus asked, "Who of you by worrying can add a single hour to your life?" (Luke 12:25, NIV).

The beauty of the Christian worldview is that while we are encouraged to take initiative and control what's within our power, we also know that the huge part of life we can't control is under God's governance. Scripture tells us, "Our God is in the heavens; he does all that he pleases" (Psalm 115:3). It assures us, "The heart of man plans his way, but the LORD establishes his steps" (Proverbs 16:9). And since God is eternally wise and good, and we're not, *we're far better off* with him in control than if we were.

Planning is often good and necessary, but we should never plan as if we control the outcome. Scripture tells us to adjust our expectations to reality:

> Come now, you who say, "Today or tomorrow we will go into such and such a town and spend a year there and trade and make a profit"—yet you do not know what tomorrow will bring. What is your life? For you are a mist that appears for a little time and then vanishes. Instead you ought to say, "If the Lord wills, we will live and do this or that." As it is, you boast in your arrogance. All such boasting is evil. JAMES 4:13-16

GOD GIVES DAILY GRACE TO DEAL WITH WHAT *DOES* HAPPEN, NOT THE THOUSAND BAD THINGS THAT DON'T.

French Renaissance philosopher Michel de Montaigne (1533–1592) said, "My life has been full of terrible misfortunes, most of which never happened."[8] Worrying over things that have never happened (and may never happen) robs us of happiness. If what I worry about doesn't happen (as is usually the case), I wasted my time. If it does happen, I still wasted my time.

American poet James Russell Lowell (1819–1891) wrote, "Let us be of good cheer, remembering that the misfortunes hardest to bear are those which never come."[9]

Worry works against not only happiness but also God's sustaining grace. Jesus assures us that if we put God and his Kingdom first, he'll sovereignly take care of us: "Do not worry about tomorrow, for tomorrow will worry about itself. Each day has enough trouble of its own" (Matthew 6:34, NIV).

The *American Journal of Medical Genetics* documents the results of a remarkable study of a particular people group that is not generally characterized by worry: "Among those surveyed, nearly 99% . . . indicated that they were happy with their lives, 97% liked who they are, and 96% liked how they look. Nearly 99% . . . expressed love for their families, and 97% liked their brothers and sisters."[10]

Who are these extraordinary people? The answer: those with Down syndrome. "A slew of recent studies has shown that people with Down syndrome report happier lives than us 'normal' folk. Even happier than rich, good looking and intelligent people."[11]

Wouldn't you suppose we'd want more people of any group characterized by such happiness? Tragically, however, studies show that of mothers who receive a positive diagnosis of Down syndrome during the prenatal period, 89 to 97 percent choose to get abortions.[12] This means that the children most likely to be happy are also most likely to be killed before birth.

MANY SECULAR CONCLUSIONS ABOUT EXPECTATIONS AND HAPPINESS CONCUR WITH SCRIPTURE.

Actor Michael J. Fox, living with Parkinson's disease, says, "My happiness grows in direct proportion to my acceptance, and in inverse proportion to my expectations."[13]

In his book *The Question of Morale*, prestigious British educator David Watson (1949–2015) portrayed the modern university as "a deeply unhappy place with a pervasive culture of disappointment, pessimism and 'moral panic.'"[14] Watson attributed this unhappiness to unrealistic expectations. He spoke of selective memory—a nostalgia concerning a mythical golden age, the "good old days" of education, when students were supposedly bright and motivated.[15]

Watson proposed, "The preoccupation with student satisfaction . . . may, in fact, breed unhappiness." Watson said that the more students assert their right to be happy, the more they become "grumpy."[16] Why? Because when we place unrealistic expectations on our happiness, we'll always be disappointed.

German philosopher Arthur Schopenhauer (1788–1860) said, with some fatalism and some truth, "The safest way of not being very miserable is not to expect to be very happy."[17] Of course, most of us want more than to not be miserable!

In light of God-revealed reality, even in this world currently tainted by sin and suffering, we can expect to know some significant happiness and have occasions for heartfelt rejoicing (see 1 Samuel 18:6). Our current happiness is both *because of* and *in spite of*. It's because of Christ and in spite of the Curse.

Considering our sinful rebellion and the judgment we deserve, every happiness, small or large, is an undeserved gift. Not a demand or even an expectation, but the pure and simple grace of God. When we experience happiness now, we're grateful; when we don't, we know someday our happiness will be full, complete, and never-ending.

THE CONTRAST BETWEEN WHAT WE DESERVE AND WHAT GOD GIVES IS DRAMATIC AND HAPPY-MAKING.

Jesus said to his disciples, "When you do all the things which are commanded you, say, 'We are unworthy slaves; we have done only that which we ought to have done'" (Luke 17:10, NASB). He's saying, in effect, "Lower your sense of what you deserve."

God told Adam and Eve what would happen to them when they turned from him and chose sin: "You will surely die" (Genesis 2:17, NASB). Based on that text alone, all we deserve and should expect is death. Only when we acknowledge this can we rejoice in the promises of life in Jesus, who said, "I am the resurrection and the life" (John 11:25).

If we realize we're utterly undeserving, suddenly the world comes alive. *Of course* life under the Curse is hard! (That's why it's called the Curse!) Instead of whining about everything that goes wrong, we're thrilled at God's many kindnesses, and our hearts overflow with thanks that we who deserve nothing but judgment, death, and Hell are given deliverance, grace, and eternal life. Day after day, God favors us not only with leniency but also with beauties, delights, and privileges we have no right to expect.

People who receive a paycheck for services rendered can't be as grateful as those who are given a pardon they know they don't merit. Jesus said of the woman who gratefully poured oil on his feet, "Her sins, which are many, are forgiven—for she loved much. But he who is forgiven little, loves little" (Luke 7:47).

Doesn't knowing that you deserve eternal Hell but instead will live in Heaven, in unending happiness, put any "bad day" in perspective?

WHAT TRUTHS SHOULD RAISE OUR EXPECTATIONS OF HAPPINESS?
God's Immeasurable Love for Us
In Ephesians, Paul prays that the recipients of his letter may "have strength to comprehend with all the saints what is the breadth and length and height and depth, and to know the love of Christ that surpasses knowledge, that you may be filled with all the fullness of God" (Ephesians 3:18-19).

He ends the chapter saying, "To him who is able to do far more abundantly than all that we ask or think, according to the power at work within us, to him be glory in the church and in Christ Jesus throughout all generations, forever and ever" (Ephesians 3:20-21).

After reading this inspired text, how great should our expectations of God be?

God's Willingness to Completely Forgive Us Whenever We Confess Our Sins

Ironically, it's easier to be restored to a positive relationship with God than with any other being. As difficult as this is to grasp, when we do, it's happy-making in the extreme.

God is the holiest being in the universe, meaning that his standards are infinitely higher than any creature's. It would be easy to conclude, then, that God would be more prone than anyone else to hold our offenses against us. Yet the opposite is true. "If we confess our sins, he is faithful and just to forgive us our sins and to cleanse us from all unrighteousness" (1 John 1:9). Who else will forgive us of everything, absolutely and every time—even when we've deeply hurt them?

It's not the sinless God but sinful people who sometimes refuse to forgive us—just as we are sometimes slow to forgive.

Nothing we've done or can ever do will surprise God or cause him to change his mind about us. No skeletons will fall out of our closets in eternity. He has seen us at our worst and still loves us. Arms wide open, he invites our confession and repentance, which he always meets with his grace and forgiveness.

How secure are we in God's love? Jesus said, "My sheep hear my voice, and I know them, and they follow me. I give them eternal life, and they will never perish, and no one will snatch them out of my hand" (John 10:27-28).

God's Constant Presence in Us and with Us

Matthew Henry said, "Happy are those who have the Lord for their God, for they have a God that they cannot be robbed of. Enemies may steal our goods, but not our God."[18]

Joshua 1:9 offers this encouragement: "The LORD your God is with you wherever you go." Jesus promised his disciples, "I am with you always" (Matthew 28:20). Here is a source of both comfort and courage: "Fear not, for I am with you; be not dismayed, for I am your God; I will strengthen you, I will help you, I will uphold you with my righteous right hand" (Isaiah 41:10).

Our happiness is largely determined by who or what we depend on. If we depend on God, we'll be happy because God is always with us: "God's Spirit dwells in you" (1 Corinthians 3:16). Of course, sometimes we'll sense his presence more than other times. But he is there for us when life is dry, stressful, or traumatic, helping us and even praying for us: "The Spirit helps us in our weakness. . . . The Spirit himself intercedes for us with groanings too deep for words" (Romans 8:26).

The stories of many prisoners—including Corrie ten Boom, Richard Wurmbrand, and Aleksandr Solzhenitsyn—document that they survived imprisonment and torture because God's supernatural indwelling presence was their lifeline. We who know Jesus have the same.

"God has said, 'Never will I leave you; never will I forsake you'" (Hebrews 13:5, NIV). Such a promise offers us happiness in the most difficult times and places.

The Transforming Power of God's Word
Never underestimate the life-changing nature of God's inspired Word: "All Scripture is inspired by God and is useful to teach us what is true and to make us realize what is wrong in our lives. It corrects us when we are wrong and teaches us to do what is right. God uses it to prepare and equip his people to do every good work" (2 Timothy 3:16-17, NLT). As we saw in chapter 34, meditating on Scripture, which God uses to make us more like Christ, is a powerful source of personal happiness.

The Sufficiency of Christ's Work on Our Behalf
Consider this promise: "[God's] divine power has granted to us all things that pertain to life and godliness" (2 Peter 1:3).

We're also told that God has "blessed us in Christ with every spiritual blessing in the heavenly places" (Ephesians 1:3).

We can rejoice knowing that Christ has already provided all we need for salvation and eternal happiness.

The Providence of God and His Sovereign Purpose in Our Lives
We can be confident knowing that God is in control of the details of our lives: "Yours, O LORD, is the greatness and the power and the glory and the victory and the majesty, for all that is in the heavens and in the earth is yours. Yours is the kingdom, O LORD, and you are exalted as head above all. Both riches and honor come from you, and you rule over all. In your hand are power and might, and in your hand it is to make great and to give strength to all" (1 Chronicles 29:11-12).

The Undiluted and Eternal Happiness That Awaits Us
"You have endowed him with eternal blessings and given him the joy of your presence" (Psalm 21:6, NLT).

Jonathan Edwards wrote, "After they have had the pleasure of beholding the face of God millions of ages, it will not grow a dull story; the relish of this delight will be as exquisite as ever."[19]

Undiminished happiness is promised us—what other king has ever promised his people anything so great? And what other king has undergone for his subjects the ultimate sacrifice to fulfill that promise?

WHAT FALSE EXPECTATIONS WILL DIMINISH OUR HAPPINESS?
We've looked at expectations that are biblically based and can increase our happiness. The following are false expectations—those that are not grounded in Scripture and undermine our happiness.

God's Love for Us Should Look Like Just What We Want

God has promised us his undying love, but we often imagine how we'd do things differently for those we loved if we were all powerful. We'd surely keep anything bad from ever happening to them, right? That may be our understanding of love, but it's not God's.

If we ignore countless passages that promise us persecution and suffering while focusing on those that promise us God's blessing, we lose sight of his promise to discipline us, build our character, and increase our Christlikeness through suffering.

We ought to expect with the highest confidence only what God has clearly, fundamentally, and absolutely promised. And if our gratitude is lessened with such an understanding, the problem is our expectations, not God's promises. If we expect God to make our lives easy, our expectations are unbiblical.

Should we expect with the highest degree of certainty that "everyone who calls upon the name of the Lord shall be saved" (Acts 2:21)? Absolutely. Scripture says so. But has God promised to save everyone we pray for? No.

Has God promised to give us all we want? No. Has he promised to meet all our *needs*? Yes. "My God will supply every need of yours according to his riches in glory in Christ Jesus" (Philippians 4:19).

Should young couples expect that God will be there for them in their marriages? Yes. But those who expect they'll never argue or struggle set themselves up for unhappiness. They're laying claim to something God never promised.

We Won't Be Persecuted for Our Faith

Jesus said, "If the world hates you, keep in mind that it hated me first" (John 15:18, NIV). Peter said we should be firm in our faith, "knowing that the same kinds of suffering are being experienced by your brotherhood throughout the world" (1 Peter 5:9).

In spite of multiple promises of suffering throughout Scripture, many Christians seem shocked or outraged when they have to face these trials. Americans have been slow to accept the extent to which Bible-believing Christ-followers have become socially unacceptable. Though we should work to hold on to our religious liberties, it's likely they'll continue to erode. But cheer up! Opposition is nothing new for God's people, and historically the church's greatest advances have come at the lowest ebb of its popularity.

The gospel we proclaim becomes unattractive when, instead of saying, "Look at the Jesus we follow," people hear, "Look at how we're being mistreated."

I see too many long-faced Christians who seem continuously angry, disillusioned, and defensive over politics and the infringement of their rights.

The Christian faith may never return to its central public role in our culture, but Christ's gospel is bigger than every obstacle. Sometimes a less popular church becomes a more faithful, dynamic, and joyful church. We may be less powerful in establishing laws and policies, but that doesn't change the truth about God's Word, which is "living and active, sharper than any two-edged sword" (Hebrews 4:12). When he was in prison and facing execution,

Paul wrote, "Because I preach this Good News, I am suffering and have been chained like a criminal. But the word of God cannot be chained" (2 Timothy 2:9, NLT).

The Supreme Court is not supreme. A majority of nine fallen and finite people cannot change the laws of God. Any church whose happiness hinges on its popularity will either compromise its integrity or surrender its happiness—in either case failing to show the world the true and joyful gospel of Jesus.

Jesus Must Return in Our Lifetime

"Stay awake, for you do not know on what day your Lord is coming. . . . Be ready, for the Son of Man is coming at an hour you do not expect" (Matthew 24:42, 44).

Christ will surely return, just as he promised (see Luke 21:27). Since the beginning of church history, many believers have thought Christ would return in their lifetimes. So far, everyone who has died in the past two thousand years has been wrong in that expectation.

I remember, as a young Christian in the 1970s, when millions of people were reading bestselling books proclaiming Christ *had to return by 1980.* The result was a loss of credibility and a failure to focus on long-term plans to serve Christ and spread the gospel.

In recent years, I've often heard believers say, "Christ has to return within the next few years." *No, he doesn't.* He may, but he may not return for decades or centuries. That's entirely up to him. Meanwhile, it's up to us to continue living for him.

Life Will Go Smoothly and We'll Always Have Health and Wealth

M. Scott Peck opens *The Road Less Traveled*, "Life is difficult. . . . Once we truly know that life is difficult—once we truly understand and accept it—then life is no longer difficult."[20] Well, it's *less* difficult, anyway!

Paul said, "We brought nothing into the world, and we cannot take anything out of the world. But if we have food and clothing, with these we will be content" (1 Timothy 6:7-8). Food and clothing may seem like low expectations. By the standards of the health-and-wealth gospel (see chapter 35), these expectations are dismally low, but they're accompanied by dramatically high expectations of God, who gives us riches in Heaven. After all, he's the source of our joy!

Has God promised to make us healthy and wealthy? No, not in this life—only in the resurrected life on the New Earth (see chapter 43).

Life Will Be Fair and People Will Treat Us Kindly and Thoughtfully

Jesus said, "If you lend to those from whom you expect to receive, what credit is that to you? . . . But love your enemies, and do good, and lend, expecting nothing in return, and your reward will be great" (Luke 6:34-35).

All Bible passages about forgiveness involve lowering our expectations of people and not insisting they live up to our standards, or demanding perfection we don't measure up to ourselves. God's grace should calm us and cheer us.

If my saying, "Cheer up" seems naive, someone else—Jesus—said it first: "I have told you this, so that you might have peace in your hearts because of me. While you are in the world, you will have to suffer. But cheer up! I have defeated the world" (John 16:33, CEV).

Churches Owe Us Better Treatment than We've Received

I often talk with people who have been hurt by fellow believers and are ready to give up on the church. I am sadly aware that churches have contributed to much unhappiness. Nanci and I have experienced hurts in the only two churches we've ever been part of. But had we given up on church, we'd likely have become embittered and passed on that bitterness to our children. We'd also have been robbed of the great happiness of worship, fellowship, and service that has, in the long run, far outweighed all the difficulties.

When our expectations of church people, and especially pastors, are inordinately high, we become deeply disappointed, thinking that Christians should know better and have no business being imperfect (often not realizing how imperfect we ourselves are and that the problem with church people is often that they are too much like us).

Scripture tells us we shouldn't be "neglecting to meet together, as is the habit of some," but should gather together, "encouraging one another" (Hebrews 10:25). When we back away from the local church, we often engage in spiritual isolation that's likely to not only distance us from God's work but also sour us and our children to the great good churches are doing.

Though it's a growing trend, I believe that the solution isn't being "done with church." We need to fix our eyes on Jesus, raise our expectations of our personal need to obey him by being part of and serving the church, and lower our expectations of others so we'll be more understanding and forgiving. Sometimes we need to find another church that teaches God's Word and centers on Jesus. He sees all the flaws in the church, but he hasn't given up on his bride, and he won't (see Matthew 16:18). Neither should we.

BY LOWERING OUR EXPECTATIONS OF THIS LIFE AND RAISING THEM OF ETERNAL LIFE, WE CAN EXPERIENCE TRUE HAPPINESS NOW.

Max Lucado tells the story of a boy on the beach who eagerly scoops up and packs sand. Using a plastic shovel and a bright red bucket, he creates a magnificent sand castle. He works all afternoon, creating a tower, walls, and even a moat. Not far away, a man in his office shuffles papers into stacks and delegates assignments. He punches buttons on a phone and keys on a keyboard, makes profits, and builds his own castle.

In both cases, time passes, the tide rises, and the castles are destroyed. But there's a big difference. The boy expects what's coming and celebrates it. He's eager for the waves to hit his castle. He smiles as his castle erodes and turns into no more than formless lumps in the sand. The businessman's life also ebbs and flows, and the works of his hands are swept away. If his castle isn't taken from him, he'll be taken from his castle. But he chooses not to think about this. Unlike the boy, this man is unprepared for what will happen. While the boy has no sorrow and regret, the man does all he can to hold on to his castle and is inconsolable when his life or house or business slips away.[21]

God spoke all his words in Scripture to certain people in certain times, but in the larger sense, they apply to all his children, if we understand that our future in his presence will never end. No matter what comes today or tomorrow, may these words from the Lord to his people Israel become our expectation of the life God ultimately intends for all his children: "I know the plans I have in mind for you, declares the LORD; they are plans for peace, not disaster, to give you a future filled with hope" (Jeremiah 29:11, CEB).

CHAPTER 42

FINDING HAPPINESS NOW IN GOD'S PROMISES OF ETERNAL HAPPINESS

Multitudes who sleep in the dust of the earth will awake: some to everlasting life, others to shame and everlasting contempt. Those who are wise will shine like the brightness of the heavens, and those who lead many to righteousness, like the stars for ever and ever.

DANIEL 12:2-3, NIV

Christian, meditate much on heaven, it will help thee to press on, and to forget the toil of the way. This vale of tears is but the pathway to the better country: this world of woe is but the stepping-stone to a world of bliss. . . . And, after death, what cometh? What wonder-world will open upon our astonished sight?

CHARLES SPURGEON

I N THE DECLINE *and Fall of the Roman Empire*, Edward Gibbon (1737–1794) wrote about Abdalrahman, one of the most powerful and wealthy Muslim rulers of the Roman era. This exalted monarch's words appear on an ancient memorial:

I have now reigned above fifty years in victory or peace; beloved by my subjects, dreaded by my enemies, and respected by my allies. Riches and honors, power and pleasure, have waited on my call, nor does any earthly blessing appear to have been wanting to my felicity. In this situation, I have diligently numbered the days of pure and genuine happiness which have fallen to my lot: they amount to FOURTEEN. O man! Place not thy confidence in this present world![1]

Suppose over a person's lifetime, he or she has ten times the days of happiness as Abdalrahman—that would be 140 days, or less than five months. Or suppose someone has a hundred times as many days of happiness. That would still be less than four years. Suppose we're talking about the happiest person ever, who lived to be one hundred and was happy nearly all the days of his or her life. Tally those days, and compare them to eternity. By any standard, there aren't that many happy days when this is the only life in which we suppose happiness can exist.

Jonathan Edwards's daughter Jerusha and David Brainerd, whom she tended in his dying days, became very close. Edwards recalls Brainerd's words to Jerusha: "If I thought I should not see you, and be happy with you in another world, I could not bear to part with you. But we shall spend a happy eternity together!"[2]

In AD 60, Seneca, the Roman Stoic philosopher and statesman who advised Nero, wrote, "No happiness lasts for long."[3] At that same time, the apostle Paul and others were spreading the good news that happiness is in God and will last forever. About five years later, Seneca died in Rome and Paul shortly after, both by Nero's decree. Three years later, when the political tide turned against him, Nero killed himself.

Happiness in this world is short lived . . . unless death is not the end of us and the world, and a happy life in a happy world awaits us still.

A BELIEF IN A HAPPY AFTERLIFE BRINGS US GREAT HAPPINESS IN THE PRESENT.

A character in the movie *Pirate Radio* says, "You know, a few months ago, I made a terrible mistake. I realized something, and instead of crushing the thought the moment it came . . . I'm afraid it's stuck in my head forever. These are the best days of our lives. It's a terrible thing to know, but I know it."[4]

This fictional character is absolutely right: for people with no faith in God, who deny the Resurrection, these *are* the best days, and certainly they're winding down to a fixed end. But for genuine Christ-followers, these are decidedly *not* the best days of our lives. In fact, the best by far is yet to come!

J. I. Packer puts it well: "Hearts on earth say in the course of a joyful experience, 'I don't want this ever to end.' But it invariably does. The hearts of those in heaven say, 'I want this to go on forever.' And it will. There can be no better news than this."[5] Hence, the doctrine of the New Heaven and New Earth is not simply about our future happiness; it is central to our present happiness.

Puritan George Swinnock wrote, "God is the true happiness of the soul, because he is an eternal good. . . . Outward mercies, in which most place their felicity, are like land-floods, which swell high, and make a great noise, but are quickly in again, when the blessed God, like the spring-head, runneth over, and runneth ever."[6]

When we grasp this, we realize what eternal life means—the ever-continuing enjoyment of God, who will always cause his universe to overflow with his happiness.

C. S. Lewis wrote,

The settled happiness and security which we all desire, God withholds from us by the very nature of the world: but joy, pleasure, and merriment He has scattered broadcast. We are never safe, but we have plenty of fun, and some ecstasy. It is not hard to see why. The security we crave would teach us to rest our hearts in this world and oppose an obstacle to our return to God: a few moments of happy love, a landscape, a symphony, a merry meeting with our friends, a bathe or a football match, have no such tendency. Our Father refreshes us on the journey with some pleasant inns, but will not encourage us to mistake them for home.[7]

WHEN WE FAIL TO MEDITATE ON HEAVEN'S HAPPINESS, OUR LIVES ARE LESS HAPPY AND THE GOSPEL LESS ATTRACTIVE.

Paul wrote of "the faith and love that spring from the hope stored up for you in heaven . . . which you have already heard in the true message of the gospel" (Colossians 1:5, NIV). Heaven is central to the gospel message of eternal life. We can't expect to grow in faith and love without focusing on the hope stored up for us in Heaven.

Tozer wrote,

> When the followers of Jesus Christ lose their interest in heaven they will no longer be happy Christians, and when they are no longer happy Christians they cannot be a powerful force in a sad and sinful world. It may be said with certainty that Christians who have lost their enthusiasm about the Savior's promises of heaven-to-come have also stopped being effective in Christian life and witness in this world.[8]

A culturally engaged young man who's a bestselling author with a large following interviewed me concerning my book *Heaven*. Before the interview, he told me apologetically, "Truth is, I didn't read your book."

I had read his books, so I smiled and said, "Let me guess why. It's because you think Heaven will be boring, and it's the beauties and wonders of this life—the natural world and human culture—that you're *really* interested in."

Surprised, he said, "Yes!"

"That's exactly why you *should* read it," I said. "It's about the New Earth the Bible presents, with resurrected people on a resurrected planet; with resurrected nature, nations, and cultures; with resurrected art, music, literature, drama, environment, and galaxies—all for the glory of God."

His eyes brightened and then faded, as if to say, "If only that were true."

Well, it *is* true. The gospel—the Good News—is way better than we believe it to be. But if we pay attention when we read the Bible, we'll see it.

Ironically, the young man who interviewed me seeks to be relevant, to reach the world with a Christian message it can embrace. He values literature, art, music, and entertainment, and he wishes Christians valued them. Yet he hasn't embraced the biblical teaching of a resurrected Earth—a message that includes an eternal, Christ-centered enjoyment of the very cultural goodness he values, a message his audience needs and would love to hear.

HEAVEN IS NO FAIRY TALE.

Despite this modern scientific age, we're more gullible than ever about false claims of happiness, while more skeptical about God's true claims.

Cosmologist Stephen Hawking says, "I regard the brain as a computer which will stop working when its components fail. There is no heaven or afterlife for broken down computers; that is a fairy story for people afraid of the dark."[9]

In contrast, Jesus Christ says, "I have come down from heaven" (John 6:38). Shortly before going to the cross to secure our redemption, he said, "There are many rooms in my Father's house. I wouldn't tell you this, unless it was true. I am going there to prepare a place for each of you" (John 14:2, CEV).

With due respect for his remarkable accomplishments, Stephen Hawking lacks any way of knowing anything whatsoever about Heaven or the afterlife, having never experienced either. I choose instead to believe Jesus, who's no stranger to Heaven, having come from there and returned.

C. S. Lewis said,

> We are very shy nowadays of even mentioning heaven. We are afraid of the jeer about "pie in the sky," and of being told that we are trying to "escape" from the duty of making a happy world here and now into dreams of a happy world elsewhere. But either there is "pie in the sky" or there is not. If there is not, then Christianity is false, for this doctrine is woven into its whole fabric. If there is, then this truth, like any other, must be faced. . . . There have been times when I think we do not desire heaven; but more often I find myself wondering whether, in our heart of hearts, we have ever desired anything else.[10]

THE HAPPINESS WE CRAVE IS NOT MERELY FOR THIS LIFE, BUT FOR ETERNITY.

In Thornton Wilder's play *Our Town*, which won a Pulitzer Prize in 1938, a character states, "Now there are some things we all know, but we don't take'm out and look at'm very often. We all know that *something* is eternal. And it ain't houses and it ain't names, and it ain't earth, and it ain't even the stars . . . everybody knows in their bones that *something* is eternal, and that something has to do with human beings. . . . There's something way down deep that's eternal about every human being."[11]

Scripture confirms this idea, saying that God has "set eternity in the human heart" (Ecclesiastes 3:11, NIV).

In part 2, we explored the happiness that has always existed within Father, Son, and Holy Spirit. E. J. Fortman argues that the triune God's happiness is at the heart of what awaits God's people in Heaven:

> What is the *essence of heaven*? . . . In their beatific vision, love and enjoyment of the triune god. For the three divine persons have an infinitely perfect vision and love and enjoyment of the divine essence and of one another. And in this infinite knowing, loving and enjoying lies the very life of the triune God, the very essence of their endless and infinite happiness. If the blessed are to be endlessly and supremely happy, then, they must share in the very life of the triune God, in the divine life that makes Them endlessly and infinitely happy. (emphasis added)[12]

GOD'S PROMISE OF ETERNAL HAPPINESS IN A REDEEMED UNIVERSE STANDS IN STARK CONTRAST TO OTHER WORLDVIEWS.

Thirteen hundred years ago, the Venerable Bede proclaimed, "What, beloved brethren, will be the glory of the righteous; what that great gladness of the saints, when every face shall shine as the sun; when the Lord shall . . . receive them into the kingdom of His Father . . . to restore them to Paradise?"[13]

In contrast, Sigmund Freud (1856–1939) wrote, "The intention that man should be happy is not in the plan of Creation."[14] Freud, one of the architects of our prevailing cultural worldview, was wrong about many things, but he couldn't have been in greater conflict with Scripture on this point. God planned for our eternal happiness since before Creation. This happiness will be finally and fully realized in the promised culmination of his redemptive plan, in the New Heaven and New Earth.

God comforts his people in great suffering, saying to them, "Look, I am ready to create new heavens and a new earth!" (Isaiah 65:17, NET). What should be our response to this promise? God uses joy-drenched words to describe this New Earth, promising a place where his people will bring happiness not only to each other but also to him:

> Be happy and rejoice forevermore over what I am about to create! For look, I am ready to create Jerusalem to be a source of joy, and her people to be a source of happiness. Jerusalem will bring me joy, and my people will bring me happiness. The sound of weeping or cries of sorrow will never be heard in her again. ISAIAH 65:18-19, NET

Other passages reiterate the promise of coming happiness:

- Indeed, the LORD will comfort Zion; He will comfort all her waste places. And her wilderness He will make like Eden, and her desert like the garden of the LORD; joy and gladness will be found in her, thanksgiving and sound of a melody. (Isaiah 51:3, NASB)
- The ransomed of the LORD shall return and come to Zion with singing; everlasting joy shall be upon their heads; they shall obtain gladness and joy, and sorrow and sighing shall flee away. (Isaiah 35:10)

Contemplate what God has in store for you. Read and reread those verses. Memorize them. And don't ever cease to be amazed at the fantastic, everlasting happiness God promises his people in the new creation.

OUR STATED DOCTRINES AND ACTUAL BELIEFS ABOUT ETERNITY OFTEN BEAR LITTLE RESEMBLANCE TO ONE ANOTHER.

A man whose daughter died lamented, "I will never touch her face again, never put my arms around her."

But the girl loved Jesus, and so did her father. So I asked, "Do you believe in the resurrection?"

"Of course."

"The resurrection means you absolutely *will* touch your daughter's face again! You'll be able to hug your daughter in your resurrection body. Not only will she be totally and permanently healed, you'll see her in her perfect body, and you'll be in yours."

Even though this father believed in the resurrection, its meaning had escaped him. He was right to grieve, because their relationship was interrupted. But it wasn't terminated. The promise of resurrection means there will be not only a spiritual reunion in the present Heaven but also a physical reunion on the New Earth.

The grieving father is an example of many who believe in the doctrine of the resurrection yet don't think in terms of living forever in fully healthy and undying versions of their current bodies. The apostle Paul had a very short list of what was of first importance: that Christ died for our sins, was buried, and was raised on the third day. All these truths are covered in two verses (see 1 Corinthians 15:3-4). But Paul took another four verses to speak of one other thing: the appearances of Christ after his resurrection. He said the risen Christ appeared to Cephas (Peter), then the twelve, then to more than five hundred brothers at once—most of whom were still living at the time Paul wrote—then to James, then all the apostles, and finally to Paul himself (see 1 Corinthians 15:5-8).

The physical appearances of the resurrected Jesus were vitally important to Paul and foundational to what the gospel entails. They were the picture and the guarantee of our own physical resurrections. With our physical nature comes the ability to enjoy the pleasures of eating, drinking, and living in a world of wonders that God made for us to enjoy. A disembodied eternity was, to Paul, a pitiful notion (see 1 Corinthians 15:19). The gospel is good news, and from Paul's perspective, spending eternity in a ghostly state would not be good news at all!

Isaac Watts spoke of the resurrection when he said, "Our happiness is not designed to be complete till the soul and body are united in a state of perfection and glory."[15] In a hymn he called it "that eternal world of joy."[16]

MOST OF US DON'T LIVE AS IF WE BELIEVE IN HEAVEN.

When we hang on, white-knuckled, to this life, it proves our disbelief in an afterlife that is physical (with real health), material (with real wealth), social (with real culture and relationships), and personal (with real happiness and continuance of our identity).

I've heard it said, "We can't begin to imagine Heaven and what life will be like there." Certainly, our imaginations can't do it justice, but we *can* imagine it! Otherwise, it won't appeal to us and we won't anticipate it as we should: "In keeping with his promise we are looking forward to a new heaven and a new earth, where righteousness dwells" (2 Peter 3:13, NIV). If we eagerly await vacations and what we're going to see and do, how much more should we anticipate our eternal life with King Jesus!

Richard Baxter said, "Can you think that anything is fitter for the chiefest of your thoughts and cares, than the God and kingdom, which you hope for ever to enjoy? Or is there anything that can be more suitable, or should be more delightful to your thoughts, than to employ them about your highest hopes, upon your endless happiness and joy?"[17]

Some of my happiest and most hope-giving thoughts come in pondering what it will be like to live as a resurrected being on a resurrected Earth under the benevolent rule of Christ. We all use our imaginations daily—why not turn them loose on the place the Carpenter from Nazareth said he was going to build for us to live in (see John 14:2)?

Charles Spurgeon said of the resurrection,

> This is the Christian's brightest hope. Many believers make a mistake when they long to die and long for Heaven. Those things may be desirable, but they are not the ultimatum of the saints. The saints in Heaven are perfectly free from sin, and, so far as they are capable of it, they are perfectly happy; but a disembodied spirit never can be perfect until it is reunited to its body. God made man not pure spirit, but body and spirit, and the spirit alone will never be content until it sees its corporeal frame raised to its own condition of holiness and glory.
>
> Think not that our longings here below are not shared in by the saints in Heaven. They do not groan, as far as any pain can be, but they long with greater intensity than you and I long, for the "adoption, the redemption of our body" [Romans 8:23, NKJV]. . . .
>
> In Heaven it is that faith and hope have their fullest swing and their brightest sphere, for glorified saints believe in God's Promise, and hope for the resurrection of the body.[18]

NO HOPE IS GREATER OR MORE SECURE THAN ETERNAL LIFE WITH JESUS.

Hope is the light at the end of life's tunnel. Not only does it make the tunnel endurable, it fills the heart with anticipation of the world into which we will one day emerge. Not just a better world, but a new and perfect world. A world alive, fresh, beautiful, and devoid of pain, suffering, and war; a world without disease, accident, and tragedy; a world without dictators and madmen. A world ruled by the only one worthy of ruling.

This hope isn't an unrealistic dream or fantasy. Rather, it's a solid expectation secured by the blood-bought promises of our Savior and King. After making the pledge that he will end all suffering and death, Christ, "who was seated on the throne said, 'I am making everything new!' Then he said, 'Write this down, for these words are trustworthy and true'" (Revelation 21:5, NIV).

Jesus was saying, "That's my promise, permanently inscribed in the scars on my hands and feet." In a world where little seems certain, this is a promise we can take to the bank!

The happiness that's incorporated in the Christian worldview is never based on wishful thinking; it's reality-based, Christ-centered faith. Belief in Jesus and in God's Word will stand up in suffering; wishful thinking will not.

It's tragic and hope-robbing for Christ-followers to think the only place we can experience what's good is here and now! Sin, the Fall, and the Curse are *not* the norm for the created universe; they're temporary aberrations that Christ will dramatically bring to an end and permanently replace with a New Heaven and New Earth.

Meditate on what he has assured us is true. Ask God to help you envision the fulfill-ment of this magnificent promise that goes deeper and reaches higher and wider than any other ever made.

THOSE WHO UNDERSTAND THE REALITY OF THE RESURRECTION DON'T NEED "BUCKET LISTS."

The term "bucket list" was popularized by the 2007 movie of the same name. It refers to an inventory of things people want to do before they kick the bucket. The idea is that since our time on Earth is limited, we have to do important things *now*, before we die, because this is our only opportunity.

This makes sense from a naturalistic worldview—one that doesn't recognize any after-life. It also makes sense from various religious worldviews that maintain there may be existence after death but there's no physical resurrection or no continuity between this life and the next.

The one worldview in which the bucket list makes no sense at all is biblical Christianity.

Don't misunderstand. Nanci and I enjoy life; we like going to new places and doing new things. I don't believe this is wrong, nor is it wrong to list things you'd like to do if God gives you the resources and strength and guidance to do so before you die.

But the "bucket list" mentality—that this life is our only chance to ever enjoy adventure and fun—flies in the face of the biblical teaching of the resurrection:

- Your dead will live, LORD; their bodies will rise—let those who dwell in the dust wake up and shout for joy. . . . The earth will give birth to her dead. (Isaiah 26:19, NIV)
- Many of those whose bodies lie dead and buried will rise up, some to everlasting life and some to shame and everlasting disgrace. (Daniel 12:2, NLT)
- We will be changed. For the perishable must clothe itself with the imperishable, and the mortal with immortality. (1 Corinthians 15:52-53, NIV)
- The Lord Jesus Christ . . . will transform our lowly bodies so that they will be like his glorious body. (Philippians 3:20-21, NIV)

Despite the centrality of the resurrection in Scripture and church history, many Christians have never been clearly taught its meaning, so they imagine they'll live forever in a disembodied state. In fact, of Americans who believe in a resurrection of the dead, two-thirds believe they will not have bodies after the resurrection.[19]

But this predominant viewpoint is self-contradictory. A nonphysical resurrection is like a sunless sunrise. There's no such thing. Resurrection *means* we will have bodies! If we didn't have bodies, we wouldn't be resurrected.

Christ's resurrection body demonstrated what our own will be like: "See my hands and my feet, that it is I myself. Touch me, and see. For a spirit does not have flesh and bones as you see that I have" (Luke 24:39).

The resurrected Jesus walked on Earth for forty days; we will walk on the New Earth eternally. He occupied space; we will occupy space. He ate and drank with his disciples, we will eat and drink with him and each other.

A sincere believer once told me, "I hate to admit this, but I don't look forward to Heaven. I wish I could live with Jesus on this Earth. I hate sin and suffering and death, and I want it all to end, but I wish the Earth would go on forever. I don't want to stop enjoying the beauty of God's world!"

As much as this man loved Jesus, the Heaven he'd heard about seemed terribly boring and tedious. He thought eternity would mean living in an inhuman realm and that death would mark the end of his opportunity to enjoy music, literature, adventure, travel, learning, discovery, work, and service. So he hoped God would understand why he spent his time and money on his bucket list. After all, he thought, *now* was his only chance to experience what made him most happy.

Ironically, what this man wished for is exactly what the Bible promises! But as long as he failed to grasp the true biblical story—the unfolding drama of redemption culminating in the resurrection of our bodies and universe—he had no way to realize that for God's children, there's simply no need for a bucket list.

TO SOME, ETERNITY IS THE SUNSET; TO OTHERS, IT'S THE SUNRISE.

Richard Baxter, a Puritan pastor, wrote the greatest book on Heaven of his era, *The Saints' Everlasting Rest*. He said, "If your heavenly interest be the matter of your joy, you may rejoice tomorrow as well as today, and the next day as well as tomorrow, and the next year as well as this. If prosperity be your joy, your joy must be short, for your worldly prosperity will be so."[20] Baxter was saying that our happiness in anything must take into account its duration. The most intense happiness of someone's life amounts to nothing if, in the end, he's not forever happy.

If people have a worldview that doesn't include God, then trying to be happy as long as they can will be the only chance at happiness they'll ever have. *But it doesn't have to be that way.*

If our worldview is biblical, then being positive and joyful is embracing reality, not denying it. Based on what the Bible teaches, this present life is the closest unbelievers will ever come to Heaven and the closest believers will ever come to Hell.

Thomas Watson wrote, "Eternity to the godly is a day that has no sunset; eternity to the wicked is a night that has no sunrise."[21]

Scripture speaks of two eternal destinations, one characterized by everlasting happiness, the other by everlasting misery. Richard Baxter wrote, "The saints have a real happiness, and the damned a real misery; the saints are serious and high in their joy and praise, and the damned are serious and deep in their sorrow and complaints."[22]

Spurgeon preached,

In heaven there shall be no interruptions [due to] care or sin; no weeping shall dim our eyes; no earthly business shall distract our happy thoughts; we shall have nothing to hinder us from gazing forever on the Sun of Righteousness with unwearied eyes. Oh, if it be so sweet to see him now and then, how sweet to gaze on that blessed face, and never have a cloud rolling between, and never have to turn one's eyes away to look on a world of weariness and woe![23]

Teaching seminary students about preaching, Spurgeon said, "When you speak of heaven, let your face light up with a heavenly gleam. Let your eyes shine with reflected glory. And when you speak of hell—well, then your usual face will do."[24]

THE MOMENT AFTER DEATH, ALL WHO KNOW JESUS WILL EXPERIENCE A FLOOD OF HAPPINESS GREATER THAN WE'VE EVER KNOWN.

The first question we may ask ourselves in Heaven is, *Given Christ's finished work on my behalf, with the indwelling Son and Holy Spirit, why didn't I experience more of this happiness in God before I died?*

I often think about being with Jesus, Mom, my friend Jerry, and countless others who have gone before me. To join them, I'll have to die—but since I have to die anyway, the destination overshadows all the preflight inconveniences!

English Reformer and martyr John Bradford (1510–1555) wrote in a letter nearly five hundred years ago,

Let us long for our happy life, our laughing life, our joyful life; which we shall enjoy and then have in very deed, when we depart by death out of this dangerous state. . . . Therefore let us prepare ourselves accordingly, and, in misery and sorrow, be glad through hope. Now we are dispersed; but we shall be gathered together again there, where we shall never part, but [always] be together in joy eternal.[25]

Bradford's phrase "our laughing life" sings to me. Jesus said, "How happy are you who weep now, for you are going to laugh!" (Luke 6:21, PHILLIPS).

There's weeping in the present world, and there's also laughter. But there's a major difference. For believers, the first is temporary; the second is eternal. We're told that God will make our weeping end (see Revelation 21:4). But our laughter will never end.

Fortunately we don't have to die before we can know the joy of Christ! He's with us and in us here and now, so his happiness is with us and in us, if only we learn to tap into it.

Henry Martyn (1781–1812) was a brilliant English scholar who went to India as a missionary. On August 10, 1805, he sailed from his homeland knowing he wouldn't see it again. Martyn appreciated his home in England, but his longing for his home in Heaven was even greater. The sermon he preached on board that day was based on Hebrews 11:16: "They were longing for a better country—a heavenly one" (NIV).

Martyn wrote this in his journal:

In prayer I soon launched sweetly into eternity, and found joy unspeakable in thinking of my future rest, and of the boundless love and joy I should ever taste in Christ's beloved presence hereafter. I found no difficulty in stirring myself up to the contemplation of heaven; my soul through grace realized it, and I delighted to dwell by faith on those blissful scenes.[26]

Henry Martyn became like those described in the text he preached on that day:

All these people were still living by faith when they died. They did not receive the things promised; they only saw them and welcomed them from a distance, admitting that they were foreigners and strangers on earth. People who say such things show that they are looking for a country of their own. . . . They were longing for a better country—a heavenly one. Therefore God is not ashamed to be called their God, for he has prepared a city for them. HEBREWS 11:13-14, 16 (NIV)

The "country of their own" spoken of here is a real country, with a real capital city, the New Jerusalem. It's an actual place where these "foreigners and strangers on earth" will ultimately live in actual bodies. If the promises God made to them were promises regarding Earth (and they were), then the heavenly "country of their own" must ultimately include Earth. The fulfillment of these prophecies requires exactly what Scripture elsewhere promises—a resurrection of God's people *and* God's Earth.

What thrilled these expectant believers was not that God would rule in Heaven—he already did. They dreamed of the time that he would rule here on Earth, removing sin, death, suffering, poverty, and heartache. They trusted that the Messiah would come and bring Heaven with him. The early Christians believed that God would answer what has since become the most frequently prayed prayer in human history: that once and forever, God's will would be done on Earth as it is in Heaven (see Matthew 6:10).

This frequently overlooked subject is of such immense importance to our happiness that it merits another chapter to explore the nature of God's New Earth.

CHAPTER 43

FUTURE HAPPINESS ON THE NEW EARTH

*Certainly the LORD will console Zion; he will console all her ruins. He will
make her wilderness like Eden, her desert like the Garden of the Lord. Happiness
and joy will be restored to her, thanksgiving and the sound of music.*

ISAIAH 51:3, NET

O how happy is it, to have all our thoughts swallowed up in that world.

DAVID BRAINERD

───────── ◎ ─────────

A T THE END of Peter Jackson's film adaptation of Tolkien's *Return of the King*, Bilbo
Baggins—extremely old and decrepit—is invited to board an Elven ship to sail from
Middle-earth to Valinor (a sort of Heaven). He smiles, and a youthful energy returns to
his eyes as he says, "I think I'm quite ready for another adventure."[1]

For the Christian, death is not the end of our adventure but our exit from a world where
dreams and adventures shrink, and our entrance into a far better world where dreams and
adventures forever expand.

THE BEST PART OF OUR RESURRECTED LIVES ON THE NEW EARTH WILL BE SEEING GOD.

"No longer will there be any curse. The throne of God and of the Lamb will be in the city,
and his servants will serve him. *They will see his face*" (Revelation 22:3-4, NIV, emphasis
added). Based on this and other passages, ancient theologians often spoke of the "beatific
vision," from three Latin words that together mean "a happy-making sight." Because God
is the fountainhead of all happiness, and because he is forever happy in his triune oneness,
to gaze on him will be to enter into happiness.

"Without holiness no one will see the Lord" (Hebrews 12:14, NIV). For us to see God
would require us to undergo radical transformation between now and then. And that's
exactly what will happen. By faith in Christ, God's children already have his righteousness,

which will allow us into Heaven (see Romans 3:22; 2 Corinthians 5:21). Because we stand completely righteous before God in Christ, once we are glorified and forever made sinless, we'll be able to see God and live.

English poet John Donne (1572–1631) wrote beautifully of this coming day for every child of God: "I shall rise from the dead. . . . I shall see the Son of God, the sun of Glory, and shine myself, as that sun shines. I shall . . . be united to the Ancient of Days, to God himself, who had no morning, never began."[2] He also said, "No man ever saw God and lived; and yet, I shall not live till I see God; and when I have seen him I shall never die."[3]

Do you sense the happiness and wonder in Donne's words? To see God's face is the loftiest of all aspirations, but sadly, for many of us, it's not at the top of our wish lists. (When we understand its full implications, it certainly will be!)

WHAT AWAITS US ON THE NEW EARTH?

One of the greatest gifts we can give our children and grandchildren is teaching them the doctrines of the resurrection and the New Earth. Don't try to get children excited about becoming ghosts. God has made us to be physical beings living in a physical world—eating, drinking, playing, working, loving, worshiping, and laughing to God's glory. That's the promise of the resurrection—eternal delight and joy in the presence of the God who redeemed us.

Revelation 21:1-4 beautifully portrays what awaits God's children:

> I saw a new heaven and a new earth. . . . I saw the holy city, new Jerusalem, coming down out of heaven from God. . . . And I heard a loud voice from the throne saying, "Behold, the dwelling place of God is with man. He will dwell with them, and they will be his people, and God himself will be with them as their God. He will wipe away every tear from their eyes, and death shall be no more, neither shall there be mourning, nor crying, nor pain anymore, for the former things have passed away."

We normally think of going up to Heaven to live with God in his place. That's indeed what happens when we die. But the ultimate promise is that *God will come down to live with us in our place*, on the New Earth. The ultimate Heaven will not be "us with God" but "God with us" (see Revelation 21:3).

Imagine the delight of Jesus' disciples when he said to them, "At the renewal of all things, when the Son of Man sits on his glorious throne, you who have followed me will also sit on twelve thrones, judging the twelve tribes of Israel" (Matthew 19:28, NIV).

Christ did not speak of the *destruction* or *abandonment* of all things but their *renewal*. God designed humans to live on Earth to his glory. Christ's incarnation, life, death, and resurrection secured a New Earth, where life will be the way God always intended.

Similarly, Peter preached that Christ must remain in Heaven "until the time comes for God to restore everything, as he promised long ago through his holy prophets" (Acts 3:21, NIV). This cosmic restoration is not God bringing disembodied people to fellowship with him in a spirit realm. Rather, it is God returning humankind to what we once were—what he designed us to be—and to something far greater. It means that the entire physical universe will not just go back to its pre-Fall glory but forward to something even more magnificent.

God's original plan included human beings living happy and fulfilled lives. Imagine sitting around campfires on the New Earth, wide eyed at the adventures recounted. Yes, I mean telling real stories around real campfires. After all, friendship, camaraderie, laughter, stories, and campfires are all good gifts from God for physical people living in a physical world . . . and the Bible tells us that's what we'll be!

On that New Earth, we may experience adventures that make our current rock climbs, surfing, skydiving, and upside-down roller coaster rides seem tame. Why do I say this? It's an argument from design. We take pleasure in exhilarating experiences not because of sin but because God wired us this way. We weren't made to sit all day in dark rooms, doing nothing but watching actors pretend to live.

Heaven will be deeply appreciated by the disabled, who will be liberated from ravaged bodies and minds, and by the sick and elderly, who will be free from their pains and restrictions. They'll walk and run and see and hear—some for the first time.

Father Boudreaux envisioned the eternal reunion of God's people: "What outbursts of gladness among the members of his family! . . . No, no more separation! What delightful music there is in that short sentence! Death shall be no more, and therefore we shall never more be torn away from the society of our kindred and friends."[4]

Think of those "outbursts of gladness" we will experience with friends and family who loved Jesus and are with him now. Picture walking together on a redeemed Earth. We will all have powerful bodies, stronger than those of Olympic decathletes. We will laugh, play, talk, and reminisce. Now picture someone approaching. It's Jesus, with a big smile on his face. We all fall to our knees in worship. He pulls us up and embraces us. What happiness!

GOD GAVE THE PROPHET ISAIAH GLIMPSES OF LIFE ON THE NEW EARTH.

Although Isaiah 60 doesn't contain the term *New Earth* (as do nearby chapters 65 and 66), we can be certain much of the chapter describes that place, since the prophet's words are applied directly to the New Earth in Revelation 21–22. God speaks to his people of a transformed Jerusalem: "The LORD rises upon you and his glory appears over you. Nations will come to your light, and kings to the brightness of your dawn" (Isaiah 60:2-3, NIV). God's people will have a glorious future in which Earth's nations and kings will participate.

This will be a time of unprecedented rejoicing: "Then you will look and be radiant, your heart will throb and swell with joy" (Isaiah 60:5, NIV). On the renewed Earth, the nations will bring their greatest treasures into this glorified city: "The wealth on the seas will be brought to you, to you the riches of the nations will come" (verse 5, NIV).

There will be animals from various nations on the New Earth: "Herds of camels will cover your land, young camels of Midian and Ephah" (Isaiah 60:6, NIV). Redeemed people will travel from far places to the glorified Jerusalem: "All from Sheba will come, bearing gold and incense and proclaiming the praise of the LORD" (verse 6, NIV). People who dwell on islands will worship God, and ships will come from "Tarshish, bringing your children from afar, with their silver and gold, to the honor of the LORD your God, the Holy One of Israel, for he has endowed you with splendor" (verse 9, NIV).

Most of us are unaccustomed to thinking of nations, rulers, civilizations, and culture in Heaven, but Isaiah 60 is one of many passages that demonstrate that the New Earth will in fact be *earthly*.

John applied the words of Isaiah directly to the New Jerusalem (see Revelation 21:25-26): "Your gates will always stand open, they will never be shut, day or night, so that people may bring you the wealth of the nations—their kings led in triumphal procession" (Isaiah 60:11, NIV).

God promises something that has never yet been true of the earthly Jerusalem: "I will make peace your governor and well-being your ruler. No longer will violence be heard in your land, nor ruin or destruction within your borders, but you will call your walls Salvation and your gates Praise" (Isaiah 60:17-18, NIV).

Isaiah then describes another scene that John connects directly to the New Earth in Revelation 21:23; 22:5: "The sun will no more be your light by day, nor will the brightness of the moon shine on you, for the LORD will be your everlasting light, and your God will be your glory. Your sun will never set again, and your moon will wane no more; the LORD will be your everlasting light, and your days of sorrow will end" (Isaiah 60:19-20, NIV).

Of the New Jerusalem, we're told, "Nothing impure will ever enter it, nor will anyone who does what is shameful or deceitful, but only those whose names are written in the Lamb's book of life" (Revelation 21:27, NIV). Isaiah gives the same message, using inclusive language that could not apply to the old Earth under the Curse: "Then all your people will be righteous" (Isaiah 60:21, NIV). The rest of verse 21 reads, "They will possess the land [*erets*, Earth] forever." The Earth will be theirs—not for a glorious decade or century or millennium, but *forever*.[5]

Jonathan Edwards said that Isaiah 60 consists of "promises of making God's people happy, that God therein might be glorified. . . . It is wholly a promise of a future, great, and wonderful work of God's power and grace, delivering his people from all misery, and making them exceeding happy."[6]

Reflecting on Isaiah 60 as a whole, Edwards wrote, "All the preceding promises are plainly mentioned as so many parts or constituents of the great and exceeding happiness of God's people; and God's glory is mentioned rather as God's end, or the sum of his design in this happiness." He added, "The work of God promised to be effected, is plainly an accomplishment of the joy, gladness and happiness of God's people, instead of their mourning and sorrow; and the end in which the work issues . . . is obtained and summed up, is his glory." He summarizes, "The whole chapter is made up of nothing but promises of future, exceeding happiness to God's church."[7]

WHAT'S ON YOUR POST-BUCKET LIST?

Nanci and I like to talk about our post-bucket lists, which include all the things we look forward to doing *after* we die. In particular, we anticipate our eternal life on the New Earth, after the resurrection. We're told in Scripture that there will be not only a New Earth but also new heavens (see Isaiah 65:17; 66:22; Revelation 21:1)—the celestial heavens made new, presumably with new galaxies and stars and planets scattered across the new universe. Remembering the Andromeda Galaxy I first marveled at through my telescope before coming to faith in Christ, I'd love to journey to the New Andromeda Galaxy, to the praise and glory of King Jesus.

After enjoying the eternal presence of Jesus and seeing God's face, there are countless secondary items on our post-bucket lists. Nanci dreams of spending time by a lake, playing with dogs. Joni Eareckson Tada told us that, once freed from her wheelchair, she wants to run through flowering meadows on the New Earth—and she invited us to run with her. We fully expect to keep that engagement. Since we're told we'll have physical bodies and live on a physical Earth, why not?

Perhaps an alarm is going off in your head: "But that's unspiritual. We should *only* want to be with Jesus." Well, as I said, being with Jesus is at the top of the list. But that doesn't mean there shouldn't be other things that follow it—things that fully honor him and flow out of his grace and kindness to us.

Remember, while God is the primary happiness, he has filled the universe with secondary happinesses that all point back to and glorify him. He is the source of all happiness, but countless tributaries flow out from him. If that's true in a world languishing under the Fall, surely there won't be fewer of those tributaries but far more once the Curse is reversed. And surely they'll be even more wondrous and happy-making.

Would the same God who says we should eat and drink to his glory be offended if we want to play with his animals and travel to his stars for his glory?

Of course, some of the experiences on our post-bucket lists may not turn out exactly as we envision them, but I think God is honored when we let the imaginations he gave us soar as we move our eyes beyond this present fallen world to anticipate the risen world that's the climax of his redemptive plan.

WHO KNOWS ALL THAT AWAITS US IN THE NEW WORLD?

If our current lives were our only chance for happiness on Earth, God's plan would have been thwarted. But eternal happiness on Earth awaits his children. That changes everything!

Will God take us back in time and space to observe the outworking of his plan? George Whitefield said, "I believe it will be one part of our happiness in heaven, to take a view of, and look back upon, the various links of the golden chain which drew us there."[8]

But because God isn't limited by time, we may be able to study history from a front-row seat. Want to watch the crossing of the Red Sea? Or be there when Daniel's three friends emerge from the fiery furnace? It would be easy for God to open the door to the past for us.

Ephesians 2:7 unveils one of God's purposes for redemption: "in order that in the coming ages he might show the incomparable riches of his grace, expressed in his kindness to us in Christ Jesus" (NIV). The word translated *show* means "to reveal." The phrase "in the coming ages" indicates a progressive, ongoing revelation, in which we learn more and more about God's grace and kindness in Christ. We'll never stop learning about his character and affection for us.

I often learn new things about my wife, daughters, and closest friends, even though I've known them for many years. If I can always be learning something new about finite human beings, how much more will I be learning about Jesus in the ages to come? None of us will ever begin to exhaust his depths.

Jesus said to his disciples, "Learn from me" (Matthew 11:29). On the New Earth, we'll have the privilege of sitting at Jesus' feet as Mary of Bethany did, walking with him over the countryside as his disciples did, and always learning from him. In Heaven, we'll continually learn new things about God, going ever deeper in our understanding. In Christ "are hidden all the treasures of wisdom and knowledge" (Colossians 2:3). Life in the New Heaven and New Earth will be a treasure hunt, with every day yielding new and delightful discoveries in Christ.

Whatever God wants us to do in that world, we'll be equipped to do. Our service will not only bring him glory; it will also bring us joy.

At last we'll be who we were meant to be. Everywhere we go, there will be new people to meet, new places to enjoy, new things to discover. What's that smell? A feast? A party's ahead. And we're invited. Jesus will be there to welcome us!

Isn't this the ultimate happiness? And it's exactly what God promises in our eternal life on a New Earth.

IN HEAVEN, WE'LL NO LONGER BATTLE THE TEMPTATION TO SIN.

Once we're with Christ, our desires will always be pure, attending to their proper objects. We'll enjoy food without gluttony or eating disorders. We'll express admiration and affection without hatred, envy, lust, fornication, or betrayal. Those twisted desires simply won't exist. We'll be able to do as we wish and go where we wish, never wondering if our wishes are wrong!

God created us to be endlessly happy, and when sin robbed us of that prospect, he went to the cross to restore us. Once we're in our glorified condition, sin will never again have a hold on us.

Theologian Paul Helm says, "The freedom of heaven, then, is the freedom from sin; not that the believer just happens to be free from sin, but that he is so constituted or reconstituted that he cannot sin. He doesn't want to sin, and he does not want to want to sin."[9]

Thomas Manton wrote, "Whatsoever is painful and burdensome to nature, is a fruit of sin, a brand and mark of our [rebellion] against God. Therefore, when sin is done away, affliction, which is the fruit of it, is done away also. In hell there is evil, and only evil; in heaven, happiness, and only happiness."[10]

We'll worship Jesus as the Almighty and bow to him in reverence, yet we'll never experience his disapproval in Heaven—because we'll never disappoint him. He'll never be unhappy with us.

We'll be able to relax fully—the other shoe will never drop. There is no other shoe. Christ bore every one of our sins. He paid the ultimate price so we'd be forever free from sin and the dread of sin.

KNOWING THAT THE BEST IS YET TO COME SHOULD RADICALLY AFFECT OUR VIEWS OF OLD AGE AND DETERIORATING HEALTH.

As people without Christ age and experience physical and mental decline, they can only look back to when they were at their best, never to regain the health and vigor they once had. But elderly or bedridden Christians with an eternal perspective don't look back to the peak of their ability. Rather, they look *forward* to it!

John Donne had it right when he said our deliverance is "from death, in death, and by death."[11] This life ends in bodily death, but that death begins a new and superior life in the presence of Christ. So we can say with the apostle Paul, "O death, where is your victory? O death, where is your sting?" (1 Corinthians 15:55).

My waning years on a fallen planet under the Curse won't be the last my wife, daughters, grandchildren, and friends see of me, or I of them! One day all who know Jesus will have bodies and minds far better than the best we ever knew here. We'll be startled at the wonders of God's new creation. We'll find ourselves able to think and act in ways that will amaze us—unhindered by the sin that once so impaired us.

If you have good memories, by all means enjoy them. But don't spend your remaining days here looking back at your life wistfully, wishing for the better times—"the good old days." Instead, look forward to "the great new days"! Meanwhile, trust God for strength for today's challenges.

Isaac Watts wrote in his wonderful book *The World to Come*, "O happy souls, that keep themselves awake to God in the midst of this dreaming world! Happy indeed, when our Lord shall call us out of these dusky regions, and we shall answer his call with holy joy, and spring upward to the inheritance of the saints in light!"[12]

ONE OF THE MOST IMPORTANT ASPECTS OF OUR ETERNAL FUTURE IS THE DOCTRINE OF CONTINUITY.

"If anyone is in Christ, he is a new creation. The old has passed away; behold, the new has come" (2 Corinthians 5:17). This sounds like a radical change, and indeed it is. But though we undergo change and become *new* people when we come to Christ, we still remain the *same* people. (Our families still recognize us, and our dogs don't growl at us as if we were strangers.)

Memory is a basic element of personality. Heaven will cleanse us, but it will not extinguish our origins or history. The fact that we're told we'll give an account of our lives to God requires that we bring the memories from this life into the afterlife (see Romans 14:12).

Forgetting this life would undercut its meaning. All lessons learned would be forgotten;

all growth in Christ and service for him would be unimportant; all suffering would be purposeless; all happy experiences would forever disappear.

Instead, the eternal happiness of Heaven will be greatly enhanced because we'll understand with certainty what God calls us to believe by faith now: "What we suffer now is nothing compared to the glory he will reveal to us later" (Romans 8:18, NLT).

We'll each be able to say with Job, "In my flesh I will see God; I myself will see him with my own eyes—I, and not another" (Job 19:26-27, NIV).

If we don't grasp the principle of redemptive continuity, we can't possibly understand the resurrection. "There must be continuity," Anthony Hoekema writes, "for otherwise there would be little point in speaking about a resurrection at all. The calling into existence of a completely new set of people totally different from the present inhabitants of the earth would not be a resurrection."[13]

We, the same people who walk this Earth, will walk the New Earth. "*We* will be with the Lord forever" (1 Thessalonians 4:17, NIV, emphasis added).

The empty tomb is ultimate proof that Christ's resurrection body was the same body that died on the cross. If resurrection meant the creation of a previously nonexistent body, Christ's original body would have remained in the tomb. But when Jesus said to his disciples after his resurrection, "It is I myself," he emphasized that he was the same person in spirit *and* body (Luke 24:39). His disciples saw the marks of his crucifixion—unmistakable evidence that this was the same body.

Because we each have a physical body, we already have the single best reference point for envisioning a *new* body. We know what bodies are like, so we can imagine what a perfected body will be like!

C. S. Lewis spoke of the larger resurrection, which includes not just our body, but our world. He wrote, "I can now communicate to you the fields of my boyhood—they are building-estates to-day—only imperfectly, by words. Perhaps the day is coming when I can take you for a walk through them."[14]

THE RESURRECTION OF ANIMALS WILL LIKELY BE A HAPPY-MAKING PART OF THE NEW EARTH.

Those who love animals often live with profound regret that they won't be able to see fascinating creatures or beloved pets again. However, I'm convinced Scripture indicates that animals will inhabit the resurrected Earth and will be a greater source of happiness than ever before.

Someone once asked Billy Graham if his dog would be in Heaven. Graham said, "If having his dog Charlie in heaven will make him happy God will see to it his dog will be there."[15] Animals aren't nearly as valuable as people, but God is their maker and has touched many people's lives through them.

We needn't be embarrassed either to grieve the loss of our pets or to want to see them again. If we believe God created them, that he loves us and them, and that he intends to restore his creatures from the bondage they experienced because of our sin, then we have biblical grounds for not only wanting but expecting we may be happy with them again on the New Earth.

"We know that the whole creation has been groaning as in the pains of childbirth right up to the present time" (Romans 8:22, NIV). Paul explained that the redemption of our bodies won't only bring deliverance to us *but also to the rest of creation.*

Romans 8 doesn't refer to some abstract "animalkind" that cries out for deliverance. Rather, the creatures that groan and cry out for their resurrection are specific suffering people and specific animals. I believe this suggests that in the New Earth, God will likely remake certain animals that lived on the old Earth.

Many passages indicate that God will bring judgment on "men and animals" or "man and beast" because of humankind's sin (see Exodus 9:22-25; Jeremiah 7:20; 21:6; Ezekiel 14:12-13, 17). God's blessings on the righteous include blessings not only on their children but also on the offspring of their animals (see Deuteronomy 7:13-14; 28:1-4).

This fits the words anticipating Christ's coming: "All flesh will see the salvation of God" (Luke 3:6, NASB). The Greek word translated "flesh" is *sarx.* Some Bible versions translate this as "all people" or "all mankind," but the word is more inclusive. "All flesh" includes animals. No, they don't confess sins, repent, and experience forgiveness and salvation the way we do as human beings, but they, too, will behold and benefit from Christ's redemptive work.

Psalm 104 demonstrates God's intimate involvement with the lives of his animals and his purposes for them, speaking of birds, cattle, wild donkeys, rock badgers, and lions, saying, "The earth is full of your creatures" (verse 24). It speaks of "the sea, vast and spacious, teeming with creatures beyond number" (verse 25, NIV) and "Leviathan [a sea creature], which you formed to frolic there" (verse 26, NIV). The psalm goes on to say, "These all look to you" (verse 27). The psalm writer adds, "When you take away their breath, they die and return to the dust" (verse 29, NIV).

But then we're told something amazing: "You send forth Your Spirit, they are created; and You renew the face of the earth" (Psalm 104:30, NKJV). "They" seems to refer to the animals that have died and returned to the dust. What does it mean that God sends his Spirit and creates them? It appears that he's talking about re-creating animals after they've died. Why? To "renew the face of the earth." The same "they" that die are the "they" that are re-created as part of the Earth's regeneration (see Matthew 19:28).

Isaiah 11:6-9 speaks of a coming glorious era on Earth when leopards and goats, calves and lions will lie peacefully beside one another and where dangerous animals such as vipers "will neither harm nor destroy on all my holy mountain."

When will there be no more harm on Earth? Not on the old Earth or even in the Millennium, which will end in rebellion and warfare, but on the New Earth, where there will be no more sin, death, or suffering (see Revelation 21:4).

Eden was perfect. But without animals, Eden wouldn't be Eden. The New Earth is the new Eden—Paradise regained, transformed into the blessing of the second Adam (see Romans 5:14-15). Would God take away from us in Heaven what he gave to Adam and

Eve in Eden for their delight, companionship, and help? Would he revoke his earlier decision to put animals with human beings, and under humankind's care?

John Wesley spent much of his life in the company of the horses he rode from town to town, preaching the gospel. While on horseback, he wrote these reflections on animals in the resurrection:

> With their beauty their happiness will return. . . . In the new earth, as well as
> in the new heavens, there will be nothing to give pain, but everything that the
> wisdom and goodness of God can create to give happiness. As a recompense for
> what they [animals] once suffered . . . they shall enjoy happiness suited to their
> state, without alloy, without interruption, and without end. . . . What, if it should
> then please the all-wise, the all-gracious Creator to raise them higher in the
> scale of beings? What, if it should please him . . . to make them . . . capable of
> knowing and loving and enjoying the Author of their being?[16]

IN GOD'S PLAN, *ALL* CREATION WILL BE DELIVERED TO A STATE OF COMPLETE HAPPINESS.

Anthony Hoekema writes, "The kingdom of God . . . does not mean merely the salvation of certain individuals nor even the salvation of a chosen group of people. It means nothing less than the complete renewal of the entire cosmos, culminating in the new heaven and the new earth."[17]

The gospel is far greater than most of us imagine. It isn't just good news for us—it's good news for animals, plants, stars, and planets. It's good news for the sky above and the Earth below. Albert Wolters says, "The redemption in Jesus Christ means the *restoration of an original good creation*."[18]

How far will redemption reach? Isaac Watts, a great hymn writer and an accomplished theologian, nailed it in the lyrics of "Joy to the World": "He comes to make his blessings flow / Far as the curse is found." God will not abandon his creation; he'll redeem it. He doesn't give up on the Earth any more than he gives up on us. Righteous humanity will indeed rule the New Earth to the glory of God . . . forever!

Theologian A. A. Hodge (1823–1886) said it beautifully:

> The reason, the intellectual curiosity, the imagination, the aesthetic instincts, the
> holy affections, the social affinities, the inexhaustible resources of strength and
> power native to the human soul, must all find in heaven exercise and satisfaction.
> Then there must always be a goal of endeavor before us, ever future. . . . Heaven
> will prove the consummate flower and fruit of the whole creation and of all the
> history of the universe.[19]

The power of Christ's resurrection is enough not only to remake us but also to remake every square inch of the universe. God says, "The creation waits in eager expectation for the children of God to be revealed. . . . The creation itself will be liberated from its bondage to decay and brought into the freedom and glory of the children of God" (Romans 8:19, 21, NIV).

John Calvin commented, "I understand the passage to have this meaning—that there is no element and no part of the world which, being touched . . . with a sense of its present misery, does not intensely hope for a resurrection."[20] *As humankind goes, so goes all of creation.* The destiny of all creation rides on our coattails.

What possible effect could our redemption have on galaxies that are billions of light-years away? The same effect the Fall had on them. Adam and Eve's sin didn't merely create a personal catastrophe or a local, Edenic catastrophe; it was a catastrophe of cosmic proportions. And because human beings and Earth are inseparably linked, together we fell, and together we'll rise.

We'll glorify God by ruling over the physical universe with creativity and camaraderie, showing respect and benevolence for all we rule. We'll be revealed at our resurrection, when our adoption will be finalized and our bodies redeemed. We'll be fully human, with righteous spirits and incorruptible bodies.

Here and now, we talk about dealing with challenging life changes and adjusting to the "new normal." What awaits us after the resurrection is the ultimate: unmitigated happiness and praise to God for the depths of his redeeming grace. Perhaps that will require its own adjustment—a magnificent one in which we remind ourselves that for the first time, righteousness can never again be compromised by sin, happiness can never again be eclipsed, God's presence can never be questioned, peace can never be threatened, and perspective can never be lost. This will be the "new normal" of the New Heaven and New Earth.

The promise of a glorious and abundantly happy life in a redeemed universe means more to all who have lived with memories of darkness.

ALL PEOPLE, WHETHER OR NOT THEY KNOW IT, LONG FOR WHAT CAN ONLY BE FOUND IN JESUS.

When I was nine years old, dreaming of growing up to be an astronaut, I was shaken by President John F. Kennedy's assassination. I went home from school and found my mother weeping. Five months before I started high school, Martin Luther King Jr. was assassinated. His stand for peaceful nonviolent justice had touched me deeply; but in a moment, he was gone. Two months later, Robert F. Kennedy, another symbol of hope in my young mind, was murdered.

My already-fading idealism was shattered. Any hope for happiness I had because I lived in the greatest nation on Earth evaporated in the space of nine weeks. I felt not only disillusionment but also purposelessness and profound loneliness. I'd never heard the gospel or thought seriously about Jesus. I remember as if it were yesterday the emptiness I felt.

Part of my dream of becoming an astronaut was sparked by my desire to leave this world and find something better. That's why I read science fiction and comic books—I wanted something that this world and this life didn't offer.

Many children dream of being professional athletes, actors, or great musicians. As we get older, realism sinks in: it seems we'll never be able to live out most of our dreams. Plus, the few we achieve don't satisfy. We may become cynical and lose the sense of awe and wonder our dreams once brought us.

When the Curse is reversed, however, shrunken dreams will be revived and enhanced. Perhaps that's one reason Jesus said childlikeness—and the trusting nature that accompanies it—is necessary for Heaven (see Matthew 18:3; Luke 18:16). Children aren't disillusioned and hopeless. Their dreams fuel their imaginations and bring them joy.

When I came to Christ as a high school sophomore, the promise of eternal happiness and all its implications began to sink in. I can't tell you how much it meant to me, but I can tell you it means even more to me now.

Wonder is an antidepressant. Unhappiness shrivels in the white heat of worship and awe. Excitement about embarking on a great journey outshines and overshadows the sadness of what might otherwise be a dreary life.

WE WERE ALL MADE FOR A PERSON AND A PLACE; JESUS IS THE PERSON, HEAVEN IS THE PLACE.

Jonathan Edwards said of God's people, "They are not only invited to go with Christ, and to dwell with him, but to inherit a kingdom with him; to sit down with him on his throne, and to receive the honour and happiness of a heavenly kingdom. . . . God made heaven on purpose for them, and fitted it for their delight and happiness."[21]

Emmanuel Ndikumana was nineteen years old when he heard that a group of young men in Burundi planned to murder him in two weeks. He chose to stay where he was and survived the attempted murder through God's amazing providence. When telling me his story, Emmanuel made this comment: "You Americans have a strange attitude toward death; you act as if it's the end."

The truth is, we'll be far happier in this life if we understand it isn't our only chance for happiness . . . and neither is it our best chance. I've read books on happiness stressing that we must be happy right here and now, living in the moment, because *this is all we have*. But the Christian worldview is that God's people will have an eternity of present-tense happiness. This assurance of never-ending happiness is capable of front-loading joy into our lives today.

In the ages to come, we'll remember past happiness and its cause (God) and look forward to future happiness and its cause (God). So if you're not happy today, or if your happiness isn't as deep as you wish, relax. Take a deep breath. You're not missing your only opportunity to be happy! The time is coming when there will be nothing you can do except be happy. And that time will never end! Still, the Bible makes clear that God doesn't want you to wait until then to be happy in Christ.

All who know Jesus will live together in that resurrected world, with the Lord we love and the friends we cherish. We'll embark together on the ultimate adventure in a spectacular new universe awaiting our exploration and dominion.

Jesus will be the center of everything. Happiness will be the lifeblood of our resurrected lives. And just when we think, *It doesn't get any better than this*—it will!

If we come to understand the biblical doctrine of the resurrection and the New Earth, we'll find exactly what we all wish for. So let's be sure we understand it! How kind of God to provide for us exactly what he wired us to most desire—to be in his presence forever, delighting in him and each other and enjoying our lives together.

Father Boudreaux wrote, "Never can there come a day when He will frown upon us, and make us feel that His love for us has grown cold. . . . Never will there come a day when His divine beauty will fade away, or when He will lose his power of making us happy."[22]

Think of it: millions of years from now, in the presence of the happy God who will never tire of us, we'll still be young. We'll be able to say every day, "I will never be separated from my endlessly loving and creative God and Savior, the source of all happiness. Every day has been better than the one before . . . and the best is *still* yet to be!"

CHAPTER 44

DRINK DEEPLY FROM GOD'S GIFT OF HAPPINESS

Happy [are] those who do not follow the counsel of the wicked.
. . . Rather, the law of the LORD is their joy.
PSALM 1:1-2, NAB

If a man would lead a happy life, let him but seek a sure object for his trust,
and he shall be safe: his heart is fixed, trusting in the Lord.
THOMAS MANTON

M ARK TWAIN IS among history's most witty and gifted writers. Sadly, he saw Christianity as an enemy of happiness and good humor. He wrote, "I cannot see how a man of any large degree of humorous perception can ever be religious—except he purposely shut the eyes of his mind and keep them shut by force."[1]

In Twain's book *The Mysterious Stranger,* his character the devil describes the Creator as "a God who could make good children as easily as bad, yet preferred to make bad ones; who could have made every one of them happy, yet never made a single happy one . . . and finally, with altogether divine obtuseness, invites his poor, abused slave to worship him!"[2]

Late in life, Twain said in his autobiography, "Age creeps upon [people]; infirmities follow; shames and humiliations bring down their prides and their vanities; those they love are taken from them, and the joy of life is turned to aching grief. The burden of pain, care, misery, grows heavier year by year."[3]

This man who brought delight and laughter to countless people through his books and lectures lost the happiness and humor he valued above all, never understanding it was a gracious gift and a reflection of the God he rejected.

JESUS OFFERS LIGHT AND LAUGHTER TO A WORLD OF DARKNESS AND GLOOM.

One day I got a late start on a bike ride and went too far. By the time I turned around, I found myself miles from home on a trail with absolutely no light. At times I could not see the trail's edge, and I had no clue what was on either side.

I was in the dark. Alone. Or at least I thought so, until I felt a presence and realized I'd just passed someone within inches. I could easily have run into him or her. I don't remember being afraid of the dark until that night. I had no light and couldn't flip a switch or call someone to solve my problem. When I finally made it to the dim lights of civilization, I was flooded with relief . . . and sheer *happiness!*

The people Jesus spoke to lived without streetlights. If they didn't have a lamp and a means to light it, they groped in darkness, vulnerable to assailants. They understood what it meant when Jesus said, "I am the light of the world. Whoever follows me will not walk in darkness, but will have the light of life" (John 8:12).

Jesus didn't say, "I'll point you to the light" or "I'll give you the light." He said, "I am the light." The only Light.

CHRISTIANS SHOULD SEE HAPPINESS AS AN ALLY IN SPREADING THE GOSPEL.

If only today's church could grasp what God's people have always known and, instead of fighting happiness, embrace it as a partner in preaching the good news of great joy. Paul expressed his astonishment that the Galatian Christians were "turning to a different gospel—not that there is another one" (Galatians 1:6-7). The phrasing is significant—he was saying they distorted the gospel and it was therefore no longer the gospel at all. Their gospel was human centered and burdensome and misery making, not Christ centered and freedom giving and happy making. A gospel not dominated start to finish with the grace of Jesus is an unhappy gospel. And there's no such thing, since gospel means "good news."

For many years, I've been involved in teaching people about generous giving. I've learned that trying to convince people to become givers purely out of a sense of responsibility is ineffective. It's futile to appeal to God's demands when people feel unloved by him and don't believe they can be happy in him.

John Calvin said, "Unless [people] place their entire happiness in him, they will never yield up their whole selves to him in truth and sincerity."[4]

Instead of backing away from happiness or trying to correct those who love the word *happiness* (which almost everyone does, except some inside the church), we should embrace it, realizing that Jesus is inseparable from happiness.

If someone declares a desire to be happy, we should never say, "You just need to obey God and forget about being happy." Rather, we should say, "God wired you that way." Then we can ask, "Have the things you've thought would make you happy worked for you?" The answer is probably no. That's the time to suggest, "Maybe you haven't looked in the right place." We can then present the Bible's bad news, which explains the sin problem that makes them unhappy. Then we can share the good news of the gift of God that can reconcile them to their holy Creator and thereby make them eternally happy.

As sinners in rebellion against the happy God who made us, we're separated from happiness because we're separated from its source. But the staggeringly good news is that by trusting Christ's redemptive work for us, we can enter into a relationship with God. In doing so, we can enter into what we long for: the happiness found only in God.

NEARLY EVERYTHING JESUS SAID ABOUT HIMSELF WAS AN APPEAL TO OUR LONGING FOR HAPPINESS.

Jesus said to people starving for peace, hope, and happiness, and thirsting for significance, "I am the bread of life; whoever comes to me shall not hunger, and whoever believes in me shall never thirst" (John 6:35).

Jesus cried out, "If anyone thirsts, let him come to me and drink. Whoever believes in me, as the Scripture has said, 'Out of his heart will flow rivers of living water'" (John 7:37-38).

Jesus said, "Let him come to me and drink." We're not to come to any other person or thing; not to money, success, power, beauty, or religion. Just to Jesus.

Jesus quenches our thirst from the inside. The Holy Spirit indwells us so that no matter what goes on around us, no matter what hostile and heartbreaking circumstances we face, this remains true: "Out of [our] heart will flow rivers of living water." Not trickles, not creeks, but full-fledged rivers of life-giving water!

Jesus said, "I am the door" (John 10:9). The door to what? To the food and refreshment the sheep crave. "If anyone enters by me, he will be saved and will go in and out and find pasture." What is the bread, the water, the life, the door? Happiness in God that can be found nowhere else.

A physician or therapist will tell you it's not easy to convince people to do what they need to do unless it's also what they *want* to do. God offers, through Jesus, not only what people need but also what they want.

Let's remove the blinders of burdensome, happiness-minimizing Christianity so we can see the appealing offers Jesus made that were obvious to his first followers. When he says, "I am the way, and the truth, and the life. No one comes to the Father except through me" (John 14:6), he's also saying, "I am the only way to the Father's happiness. You can't get to true and eternal happiness unless you come through me."

Jesus offers us more than happiness—but nothing less.

HAPPINESS BELONGS IN A CHRISTIAN VOCABULARY.

David Clarkson wrote, "There is no essential difference betwixt happiness on earth and happiness in heaven; they differ but gradually. If a man on earth could enjoy perfect communion with God, he would be perfectly happy."[5] In other words, the closer we draw to God, the happier we become. That isn't a simplistic statement. It's biblical, true, and repeatedly affirmed and experienced by God's people throughout history.

Joy is a wonderful word, provided we don't strip it of its biblical warmth and emotion. *Blessed* is a good word, though it would be even better if most of us knew what it means (or meant). But *happy* and *happiness* resonate with people outside the church and many inside it. The world doesn't need to hear, "Stop seeking happiness, you selfish people," but "Jesus came to save you from sin and make you forever happy."

N. D. Wilson challenges Christ-followers, "Speak your joy. Mean it. Sing it. Do it. Push it down into your bones. Let it overflow your banks and flood the lives of others. At his right hand, there are pleasures forevermore. When we are truly like him, the same will be said of us."[6]

GOD THREATENS TERRIBLE THINGS IF WE WILL NOT BE HAPPY.

I'll bet that heading got your attention. Standing on its own, it sounds shocking, even outrageous. But Scripture supports it.

God's Word Translation renders Deuteronomy 28:47, "You didn't serve the LORD your God with a joyful and happy heart when you had so much." Whether we find joy and happiness in God and his abundant gifts dramatically affects how he views our service for him. He is not a master who cares only that his servants do what they're told but a Father who cares deeply about his children's love for him and the heartfelt emotional gladness we find in him as we obey.

The obedience of dutiful drudgery is better, but only marginally so, than outright disobedience. Indeed, God sometimes disciplines his people who fail to find happiness in him by sending unfavorable circumstances. Here's the whole verse I quoted with the jaw-dropping one that follows: "Because you did not serve the LORD your God with joyfulness and gladness of heart, because of the abundance of all things, therefore you shall serve your enemies whom the LORD will send against you, in hunger and thirst, in nakedness, and lacking everything. And he will put a yoke of iron on your neck until he has destroyed you" (Deuteronomy 28:47-48).

This passage prompted British clergyman Jeremy Taylor (1613–1667) to write the striking words I used in the heading: "[God] threatens terrible things if we will not be happy."[7] Read this passage, and you'll see that Taylor's statement is true. If we refuse to serve the Creator and Redeemer of our souls in happiness, we will surely end up serving the enemy of our souls in unhappiness!

God's severe mercy in bringing adversity when we don't serve him with joyfulness and gladness of heart may turn us to God, where we'll find in him the only heartfelt and lasting happiness available to us.

THE BIBLE NEVER PRETENDS THAT HAPPINESS IS EASY OR CONSTANT.

John Piper writes, "If you live gladly to make others glad in God, your life will be hard, your risks will be high, and your joy will be full."[8]

It's unrealistic to expect perpetual happiness while the Curse is in effect. But the day is coming when "there will no longer be any curse" (Revelation 22:3, HCSB). Believing this can bring us great happiness even today.

I'm not always happy, any more than I'm always holy. But by God's grace, I'm more supernaturally happy in Christ now than I've ever been. And I've also learned to make choices that increase my joy. Great pain certainly dulls—and at times even overshadows—happiness, but it can't destroy happiness that's grounded in our ever-faithful God.

Nanci and I give ourselves and each other permission to let unhappiness sink in when we hear bad news. We don't pretend all is well when it isn't. But knowing God's commands to rejoice in him and his all-sufficient power to enable us to do so, we meditate on his Word and call on him to impart his gladness to us. In time—whether minutes, hours, or days—God changes our natural responses with his supernatural, joy-giving presence. Sometimes sorrow and joy do battle; sometimes they coexist, but when our hearts and minds are on Christ, joy is never far away: "You changed my sorrow into dancing. You took away my clothes of sadness, and clothed me in happiness" (Psalm 30:11, NCV).

I can't guarantee my level of happiness tomorrow, but I believe God's rock-solid promise of never-ending happiness that can touch me here and now.

DRAWING NEAR TO GOD IS DRAWING NEAR TO HAPPINESS.

Charles Simeon, acutely aware of human depravity, nonetheless wrote, "Let us but learn to enjoy God in every thing, and every thing in God, and we shall find that this world, polluted as it is, is yet a Paradise: with God's favour, pulse [dried legumes] is better than royal delicacies, and the meanest dungeon is a palace."[9]

When Nanci and I stared up at Michelangelo's forty-seven interconnected paintings on the ceiling of the Sistine Chapel, five hundred years after it was painted, I couldn't take my eyes off the famous fresco the *Creation of Adam*. God, symbolized by a white-bearded man, has just put the breath of life into Adam, yet at the same time appears to be reaching out to him. The two aren't touching. The scene suggests that the closer Adam is to God, the greater his capacity to be who he was meant to be.

C. S. Lewis said, "If you want to get warm you must stand near the fire. . . . If you want joy, power, peace, eternal life, you must get close to . . . the thing that has them."[10] It's God who is the source of all these gifts—that's why our closeness to happiness is commensurate to our closeness to God.

Much of the battle for joy hinges on whether we believe God is happy and wants us to be too—and whether we recognize that at this very moment God is showing himself and his happiness in hundreds of ways, if only we'll look.

This is what Brother Lawrence called "practicing the presence of God." Joseph de Beaufort interviewed Lawrence, who said, "We should feed and nourish our souls with high notions of God which would yield us great joy in being devoted to Him."[11]

When we find happiness in Christ, it can't be taken from us. Lawrence, like all of us, had times of doubts and struggle. But the default of his life was to be conscious of God's loving presence, the key to his remarkable happiness. Beaufort said, "[Lawrence] is now so accustomed to that Divine presence that he receives from it continual comfort and peace. For about thirty years his soul has been filled with joy and delight so continual, and sometimes so great, that he is forced to find ways to hide their appearing outwardly to others who may not understand."[12]

Wouldn't it be great if one of our biggest problems was having *so much* happiness in God that people couldn't understand it?

CHAPTER 45

GOD PROMISES WE'LL LIVE "HAPPILY EVER AFTER"

Heavens and earth, be happy. Mountains, shout with joy, because the LORD
comforts his people and will have pity on those who suffer.

ISAIAH 49:13, NCV

He was truly God, and therefore could satisfy; he was truly man, and
therefore could obey and suffer in our stead. He was God and man in
one person, that God and man might be happy together again.

GEORGE WHITEFIELD

HANNAH WHITALL SMITH became world famous for her 1875 book *The Christian's Secret of a Happy Life*. But most readers don't know her full story.

Smith's husband struggled with what we now know as bipolar disorder. Sadly, he also followed false doctrines. She lost three of her seven children in their childhood or youth. Her other children, influenced by the universities they attended, lost their faith. One deserted her husband and children, whom Hannah then raised. Another became the first wife of Bertrand Russell, following him in his agnosticism. The other went insane toward the end of his life.[1] Hannah was no stranger to suffering. Despite this, she wrote, "I am happy in Jesus; my soul is filled with a quiet calm and peaceful rest that cannot be described."[2]

Smith said of God, "He loves me, and I can leave it all to Him. It doesn't matter much anyhow how this life is passed; it must end sometime and I can wait. And meanwhile I do find the knowledge of the fact that Jesus is mine and I am His enough to make me happy."[3]

When I came to Christ as a teenager, I found happiness like I'd never known. In the church I attended, an old Swedish Covenant congregation, we often sang the hymn "Trust and Obey," written in 1887. Though it has been many years since I sat in that church, the refrain still runs through my mind:

Trust and obey, for there's no other way
To be happy in Jesus, but to trust and obey.[4]

Some might consider that message simplistic, but I found it to be completely true. When I trusted Jesus, I was happy; when I didn't, I wasn't. When I obeyed Jesus, I was happy. When I didn't, I wasn't.

It's forty-five years later now, and I can confirm that those words are just as true now as they were then. In fact, they've proven true every day of my life since.

Note that the words aren't an appeal to trust and obey because God demands it (though he has every right to). Rather, the motive for trusting and obeying is being *happy in Jesus*.

When that hymn was written, happiness in Jesus was regarded as a righteous desire. That's how we should regard it today.

REDEMPTION INVOLVES THE RESTORATION AND EXPANSION OF THE JOY TRAGICALLY LOST IN THE GARDEN.

Nearly every myth, legend, and utopian prophecy expresses the hope that Earth and its inhabitants might be restored to the happiness we instinctively know was somehow lost. "They all lived happily ever after" is more than a fairy-tale ending. It's the deep-seated dream of the human race. Why? Because we're made in the image of a happy God who loves us and desires us to enter forever into his happiness. That reality is built into our DNA, whether or not we know it. Every fairy-tale ending is a faint reflection of what will be the true outcome of God's redemptive plan.

Spurgeon beautifully explained the gospel this way: "Now that Jesus Christ has come to restore the ruins of the Fall, He has come to bring back to us the old joy—only it shall be even sweeter and deeper than it could have been if we had never lost it! A Christian has never fully realized what Christ came to make him until he has grasped the joy of the Lord. Christ wishes His people to be happy."[5]

If the world is our main object of rejoicing, we can't "rejoice always" (1 Thessalonians 5:16) since there's so much evil and suffering. But if God himself is the primary object of our rejoicing, the foundation of our happiness always remains the same, since he always remains the same, and since he is infinitely good and loves us with an undying love.

This world under sin is in his hands, and he'll restore the world to what it should be (see Acts 3:21). Meanwhile, "we wait for the happy fulfillment of our hope in the glorious appearing of our great God and Savior, Jesus Christ" (Titus 2:13, NET). We rejoice today because he promises us an unending tomorrow, overflowing with gladness and delight.

Tim Keller writes, "The main problem . . . in the Christian life is that we have not thought out the deep implications of the gospel, we have not 'used' the gospel in and on all parts of our life."[6] One of those implications—one of those parts of life—is the arena of happiness. Many of us have failed to see and experience the repercussions of the gospel in terms of our personal gladness.

HAPPINESS IS FOUND IN THE LAST PLACE MANY PEOPLE LOOK.

John Calvin said, "While all men seek after happiness, scarcely one in a hundred looks for it from God."[7] One reason is because we're sinners. Another is because the average person wouldn't imagine that happiness could be found in God. If they know Christians, they may or may not see any evidence that God makes people happy.

Many sense that the clock is ticking, and not only are they not happy enough, but even their present happiness is winding down. There's a prevailing cynicism about whether lasting happiness can be found. Psychiatrist Thomas Szasz (1920–2012) said, "Happiness is an imaginary condition, formerly attributed by the living to the dead, now usually attributed by adults to children, and by children to adults."[8] Szasz implied that in our "enlightened" age, people no longer believe that those who have died live on in happiness. According to the naturalistic worldview, life ends at death. And even if those who reject a biblical worldview believed in an afterlife, they'd have no basis beyond wishful thinking to imagine it would be better than this one.

Unlike Szasz, Charles Spurgeon believed in Jesus and God's Word, including 1 John 1:4: "These things we write to you, that your joy may be full." Preaching on this passage, he said,

Come, let us be happy and joyful! If we have looked sad for a while, let us now be brightened by thoughts of Christ. . . . Let us not be satisfied until we have shaken off this lethargy and misery, and have once again come into the proper and healthy state in which a child of God should always be found, namely, a state of spiritual joy![9]

Jesus' words "Ask . . . that your joy may be made full" (John 16:24) are remarkable. They indicate that joy is a major motive behind prayer. The Christian worldview doesn't offer some vague, tenuous hope that there *might* be eternal happiness. It offers the solid promise of an eternal relationship with a happy God whose love is so great it sent him to the Cross to secure our eternal righteousness and thus our never-ending happiness.

English Nonconformist minister Christopher Fowler (1610–1678) said that God's children, because of "the love of God in Christ to them . . . have joy and comfort—that joy that angels cannot give, and devils cannot take."[10]

Jonathan Edwards said, "The enjoyment of [God] is the only happiness with which our souls can be satisfied. To go to heaven fully to enjoy God, is infinitely better than the most pleasant accommodations here. . . . [These] are but shadows; but the enjoyment of God is the substance. These are but scattered beams; but God is the sun. These are but streams; but God is the fountain."[11]

George Müller said, "I specially commend this point to the notice of my younger brethren and sisters in Christ. The secret of all true effectual service is joy in God."[12]

But is this "secret" known by young people being trained for church ministry and missions in Christian colleges and seminaries today? J. C. Ryle warned,

True religion . . . was intended to increase real joy and happiness among men. The servant of Christ . . . has no right to hand over innocent recreations and family gatherings to the devil and the world. The Christian who . . . walks the earth with a face as melancholy as if he was always attending a funeral, does injury to the cause of the Gospel.[13]

THE CHRISTIAN WORLDVIEW OFFERS AN OPTIMISM AND HAPPINESS NO OTHER RELIGION DOES.

Pagan worshipers always sought to make their gods happy. Paul said, "What pagans sacrifice they offer to demons and not to God" (1 Corinthians 10:20). Sacrifices were meant to appease demon-gods who are, by nature, profoundly unhappy.

How *could* they be happy? They cut themselves off from God, the source of happiness, and were banished from Heaven, the place of happiness. They know that Jesus has a time already set for their torment (see Matthew 8:29). Meanwhile, the demons exact suffering however they can: "The devil . . . is filled with fury, because he knows that his time is short" (Revelation 12:12, NIV).

Satan and demons stand in stark contrast to the true God. The gospel is that of the happy God (see 1 Timothy 1:11). God is the happy and only Sovereign (see 1 Timothy 6:15). What a radical difference between entering the presence of a happy, powerful ruler who has granted us grace and trying hopelessly to win the favor of hateful, devouring, and decidedly unhappy demons!

Remarkably, we don't need to cower and cringe before God, afraid that in his holiness he will strike us down. In Christ, we have a fully righteous standing before God—one that can't be earned and therefore can't be lost. "Let us confidently approach the throne of grace to receive mercy and find grace whenever we need help" (Hebrews 4:16, NET). Our God of happiness has made the way for us even now to come before him freely and draw deeply from his mercy, grace, and help at any and all times.

Those who believe there's a God are only halfway there in terms of happiness. Because if they don't believe in a happy God, they don't believe in a God who can make them happy. What George Swinnock said in the seventeenth century captures perfectly what's at stake: "Every person or people is happy or miserable, as the God is whom they serve, as that is in which they place their felicity; for nothing can give out more happiness to another than it hath in itself."[14] Swinnock was right—an unhappy God could never make us happy. But a happy God who loves us will forever make us happy . . . and he won't wait until we die to start the process.

Christ needs to be the foundation of our happiness—what else is sufficiently strong to keep our happiness secure? Attempting to find happiness by turning from Christ is as nonsensical as parched people turning away from cool water and heading toward a desert. If we see Jesus as the heart and soul of happiness, we'll much more effectively resist the constant temptations to turn from him.

WHAT IF CHURCHES OFFERED THE HAPPINESS THE WORLD LONGS FOR?

Imagine if our churches were known for being communities of Jesus-centered happiness, overflowing with the sheer gladness of what it means to live out the good news of great joy. Imagine if our children brought their friends to church and their comment was, "Those people seem so nice . . . and happy." Wouldn't this infuse the gospel with a meaning that most of the world has never heard and that even many of God's people have never known?

I'm not talking about contrived happiness as a pretense or a strategy for church growth, but the genuine happiness that naturally flows from God and the gospel. I'm talking about a Bible that's full of celebrations and centered on a Messiah whose first miracle was to save a party by turning water into wine.

Spurgeon told his church, "There is so much misery in this world that none of us ought to add to it. . . . Let us, on the contrary, seek to increase happiness and joy wherever we can!"[15]

Envision how contagious the doctrine of God's happiness could be if taught and grasped and lived out. Imagine if we—though tired and stressed—wanted to gather with the church not out of sheer duty but because it brings more happiness than anything else we can think to do. What if we really believed the gospel doesn't just offer us and our children and our communities and our world what we *need* but offers us what, in the depths of our hearts, we *want*?

Imagine if pastors, elders, or deacons sat down together and said, "Let's study and teach what the Bible says about God's happiness and ours."

Think of the refreshment that weary, burdened, guilt-ridden people would enjoy if the church put on regular celebrations of biblical proportions, with great food and drink and music and laughter and fun, just to say, "We love you, Lord Jesus, and we're here to celebrate who you are and all you've done for us!"

What if people understood what Augustine, transformed by the grace of Jesus, said: "When I seek Thee, my God, I seek a happy life"?[16]

What if we quoted the Reformers and Puritans and Spurgeon and took their view of happiness? What if we cited John Calvin's words: "True and solid joy in which the minds of men may rest will never be found any where else but in God. . . . Therefore, none but the faithful, who are contented with his grace alone, can be truly and perfectly happy"?[17]

What if our children and grandchildren learned from childhood that to know God is to know happiness—and to not know him is misery that propels us to search for happiness where it can't be found? What if, without having to explore the world's sin, as Augustine did, they could understand his prayer after his conversion: "There is a joy that is not given to those who do not love you, but only to those who love you for your own sake. You, yourself, are their joy"?[18] What if they understood Augustine's words, "They who think there is another, pursue some other and not the true joy"?[19]

Were God's happiness truly spilling into and out of his people, make no mistake: our children and grandchildren and communities would know it. Sure, if we believe and teach God's Word, we'll suffer and be criticized. But if the happiness of God and in God permeated us, wouldn't there be far more to attract the happiness-seeking world to Jesus?

What if we stopped critiquing the word *happiness* and embraced it? What if we stopped insisting that the only proper term is *joy*, which we describe as some vague, transcendent, unemotional state that no one understands? What if we recognized the full Hebrew and Greek vocabulary of biblical gladness and gladly embraced the many corresponding English happiness words?

What if church attenders heard fewer sermons saying that happiness is superficial and even sinful and that it is the opposite of joy, and more sermons on the hundreds of biblical passages such as this one?

> The people of Israel will come to the high points of Jerusalem and shout for joy. Their faces will shine with happiness about all the good things from the LORD: the grain, new wine, oil, young sheep, and young cows. They will be like a garden that has plenty of water, and they will not be troubled anymore. Then young women of Israel will be happy and dance, the young men and old men also. I will change their sadness into happiness; I will give them comfort and joy instead of sadness. JEREMIAH 31:12-13, NCV

What if our children saw in our families and churches a breadth of Christ-centered, ultimately optimistic happiness and were taught that this happiness originates in God, not the world? How might it fulfill these words: "That the generation to come might know, even the children yet to be born, that they may arise and tell them to their children, that they should put their confidence in God" (Psalm 78:6-7, NASB)?

What if when our families left church and went to school, work, restaurants, and musical and dramatic performances, they didn't feel they were walking away from God but toward the same happy God they've been worshiping?

What if when suffering came, we faced it with an underlying faith that erupted into genuine gladness and thanksgiving? What if instead of looking away or being paralyzed by the needs of this world, we—with humility and gladness—reached out to intervene for the hungry, the sick, the unborn, the racially profiled, and the persecuted? Wouldn't our children be less likely to leave the Christian faith, push away church as a bad memory, and pursue the world's inferior happiness substitutes that will ultimately destroy them?

THE CHRISTIAN LIFE SHOULD BE VIEWED AS INSEPARABLE FROM HEART-FILLING HAPPINESS IN JESUS.

Charles Spurgeon, a champion of strong doctrine and Bible-based preaching, described his conversion this way: "Oh, it was a joyful day, a blessed day! Happy day, happy day, when His choice was known to me, and fixed my choice on Him!"[20]

Remembering my own conversion as I do, I couldn't agree more.

At one point in my life, I wanted Jesus plus happiness. But this, I'm convinced, is wrong. What I first experienced as a young Christian was exactly right—happiness *in* Jesus. Jesus plus happiness separates the two, and when this occurs, happiness ascends the throne instead of Jesus. But happiness in Jesus recognizes that Jesus is bigger than happiness. This keeps happiness in its place. It doesn't become an idol; instead, it's seen for what it is—a natural and beautiful by-product of knowing and loving God.

Spurgeon said,

> We expect young people to be merry, and young Christians may well make merry and be glad. . . . I do not believe that spiritual decline, though it is very common,

is at all inevitable. I believe it to be as unnecessary as it is sinful. We might always retain that early joy and delight. . . .

Whatever joy I had in Christ twenty years ago, I have much more, now. Whatever I had that could delight me concerning Him was shallow and superficial, then, compared with the deeper delight my spirit finds in His service, in His work, in His people, and especially in Himself![21]

My experience has been the same. My happiness in Christ is as heartfelt—and much deeper—at age sixty than when I was a new Christian.

To those who have long been believers, Spurgeon said,

The straight way to a perpetual newness and freshness of holy youth is to go to Christ, again, just as we did at the first. . . . They that are full of the joy of the Lord never find life grows weary. . . . Getting near to Christ, you will partake in His joy and that joy shall be your strength, your freshness—the newness of your life! God grant us to drink of the Eternal Fountain, that we may forever overflow![22]

May it be said of us that because of the God we know, the Jesus we love, and the gospel we embrace, treasure, and gladly share, we are truly the happiest people in the world.

And may we see our present happiness as a down payment on the eternal happiness that awaits us, bought and paid for by the blood of Christ, who is eager to welcome us into his happiness—happiness that had no beginning and will have no end.

Spurgeon's advice seems a fitting summary for this book:

Find your joy where God would have you find it, namely, in that part of your nature which is *new*, in the *new* principles, the *new* promises, the New Covenant and the blood of the New Covenant which are yours—all of them! . . . The Kingdom of God is within you! Rejoice in it! . . .

Find your joy in the new creation of God as you see it in others. The angels rejoice over one sinner that repents [Luke 15:10]—surely you and I ought to do so! Try and do good and bring others to Christ—and when a soul shows signs of turning to its God, let that be your joy. . . .

"Be you glad and rejoice *forever*." . . . As long as you live there will be something in the new creation that shall be to you a wellspring of fresh joy and delight. Heaven will only enlarge this joy. Be glad forever because God will always be creating something fresh in which you may be glad. . . .

Ours is a heritage of joy and peace! My dear Brothers and Sisters, if anybody in the world ought to be happy, we are the people![23]

This is both our duty and our delight: to embrace and reflect the happiness of God, our Creator and Redeemer. When we find in him all the reasons that we should be the happiest people in the world, the world will notice, God will rejoice, and we, his privileged children, will begin the celebration that will never end.

NINETEEN MORE HAPPINESS WORDS IN THE OLD TESTAMENT

My people will be happy forever because of the things I will make.

ISAIAH 65:18, NCV

She was happy, she knew she was happy, and knew she ought to be happy.

JANE AUSTEN, *EMMA*

———————— ◌ ————————

H UMANS DISPLAY HAPPINESS in many ways, from quiet worship to loud singing to humble service to skateboarding. To depict these multiple facets, the Old Testament contains many Hebrew synonyms for happiness in addition to *samach* and *asher*. As you'll see from comparing the total number of times each word appears in Scripture (see chapter 22) with the examples I cite, the verses here are only a small sampling. Note that I've italicized the English translations of the particular word for happiness I'm dealing with.

TOB AND TOWB

Definition of *tob*: "festive . . . pertaining to a joyful time or feeling . . . pleasing . . . a feeling of fondness and enjoyment"[1] (486 occurrences)

Proverbs 15:15 says, "All the days of the afflicted are bad, but a *cheerful* heart has a continual feast" (NASB).

The English Standard Version, the New Revised Standard Version, and the Holman Christian Standard Bible also use "cheerful."

- A *merry* heart hath a continual feast. (KJV)
- *Gladness* of heart [is] a perpetual banquet. (YLT)
- A *happy* heart is like a continual feast. (NCV)

The Good News Translation, the Common English Bible, and the New Living Translation also render *tob* "happy." "How lovely on the mountains are the feet of him who brings good news, who announces peace and brings good news of *happiness*, who announces salvation, and says to Zion, 'Your God reigns!'" (Isaiah 52:7, NASB).

A Dictionary of Biblical Languages defines the related *towb* as "gladly . . . good of heart, i.e., a joyful, happy feeling or attitude."[2] For example, "You didn't serve the LORD your God with a joyful and *happy* heart when you had so much" (Deuteronomy 28:47, GW).

YATAB

Definition: "feeling pleasure and enjoyment"[4] (117 occurrences)

- The priest's heart was *glad*. He took the ephod and the household gods and the carved image and went along with the people. (Judges 18:20)
- A glad heart makes a *cheerful* face, but by sorrow of heart the spirit is crushed. (Proverbs 15:13)

SIMCHAH

Definition: "joy, gladness, delight, i.e., a feeling or attitude of joyful happiness and cheerfulness . . . with a focus on sensory input"[5] (94 occurrences)

- Also in the day of your *gladness* and in your appointed feasts, and on the first days of your months, you shall blow the trumpets over your burnt offerings. . . . I am the LORD your God. (Numbers 10:10, NASB)
- Also blow your trumpets at *happy* times and during your feasts.(NCV)
- All the people went up after him, playing on pipes, and rejoicing [*samach*] with great *joy*, so that the earth was split by their noise. (1 Kings 1:40)
- For seven days they celebrated the Feast of Unleavened Bread in a very *joyful* way. The LORD had made them happy [*samach*], and had turned the heart of the king of Assyria toward them to encourage them in the work of the house of God, the God of Israel. (Ezra 6:22, NCV)

Note the emphasis on the source of their joy: "The LORD had made them *happy*." The God-commanded feast and celebration were secondary means to happiness, made possible by God, the primary source.

After listening to the Bible read aloud for hours, the Jews were sad to realize they'd fallen short of God's commands. Nehemiah told them, "Do not grieve, for the joy [*chedvah*] of the LORD is your strength" (Nehemiah 8:10, NIV). Just two verses later, we're told of the Israelites' remarkable response: "All the people went their way to eat and drink and to send portions and to make great *rejoicing*, because they had understood the words that were declared to them" (verse 12).

The King James Version translates *simchah* here as "mirth"; the New American Standard Bible renders it "to celebrate a great festival." Simply put, this is a big party.

- You will make known to me the path of life; in Your presence is *fullness of joy*; in Your right hand there are pleasures [*naim*] forever. (Psalm 16:11, NASB)

- You make me *glad* by being near to me. (CEV)
- You have turned for me my mourning into dancing; you have loosed my sackcloth and girded me with *gladness*. (Psalm 30:11, NASB)
- You changed my sorrow into dancing. You took away my clothes of sadness, and clothed me in *happiness*. (NCV)
- Serve the LORD with *gladness*! Come into his presence with singing! (Psalm 110:2)
- Serve the LORD *cheerfully*. (GW)
- The hope of the righteous brings *joy*, but the expectation of the wicked will perish. (Proverbs 10:28)
- The hopes of the godly result in *happiness*. (NLT)
- You have multiplied the nation; you have increased its *joy*; they rejoice [*samach*] before you as with *joy* at the harvest, as they are glad [*gil*] when they divide the spoil. (Isaiah 9:3)
- God, you have caused the nation to grow and made the people *happy*. And they have shown their happiness to you, like the *joy* during harvest time, like the joy of people taking what they have won in war. (NCV)

Here the translators render *simchah* "happy" and "joy" in the same verse, while *samach* is rendered "happiness" and *gil* as "joy." The near interchangeability of the words in Hebrew is reflected in the English translations. We should avoid making sharp distinctions between English terms when they're translations of inspired words without such distinctions.

CHAPHETS
Definition: "delight, take pleasure in, be eager"[3] (73 occurrences)

- The steps of a man are established by the LORD, when he *delights* in his way. (Psalm 37:23)
- To do Thy pleasure, my God, I have *delighted*. (Psalm 40:8, YLT)
- Our God is in the heavens; he does all that he *pleases*. (Psalm 115:3)
- Keep me obedient to your commandments, because in them I find *happiness*. (Psalm 119:35, GNT)
- "Let him who boasts boast in this, that he understands and knows me, that I am the LORD who practices steadfast love, justice, and righteousness in the earth. For in these things I *delight*," declares the LORD. (Jeremiah 9:24)

RANAN
Definition: "shout for joy, sing for joy . . . loud public melodic and rhythmic words, with a focus on the joy it expresses"[6] (53 occurrences)

- Satisfy us in the morning with your loyal love! Then we will *shout for joy* and be happy [*samach*] all our days! (Psalm 90:14, NET)

- Good people, rejoice [*samach*] and be happy [*gil*] in the LORD. *Sing* all you whose hearts are right. (Psalm 32:11, NCV)
- Her priests also I will clothe with salvation, and her godly ones will *sing aloud for joy*. (Psalm 132:16, NASB)
- *Shout for joy*, O heavens! And *rejoice*, O earth! Break forth into joyful shouting [*rinnah*], O mountains! For the LORD has comforted His people and will have compassion on His afflicted. (Isaiah 49:13, NASB)
- Heavens and earth, *be happy*. Mountains, shout with joy. (NCV)
- Your dead shall live; their bodies shall rise. You who dwell in the dust, awake and *sing for joy*! For your dew is a dew of light, and the earth will give birth to the dead. (Isaiah 26:19)
- Your people have died, but they will live again; their bodies will rise from death. You who lie in the ground, wake up and be *happy*! (NCV)

The related noun *renanah* is a "shout of joy, i.e., to call out loudly a signal (or possibly words) that communicates joy . . . joyful song, i.e., utter words and sounds of joy by music."[7]

- You satisfy me more than the richest feast. I will praise you with *songs of joy*. (Psalm 63:5, NLT)
- My mouth shall *praise* with lips of *full out joying*. (WYC)
- Serve the LORD with gladness; come before Him with *joyful singing*. (Psalm 100:2, NASB)
- Worship the LORD with joy; come before him with *happy songs*! (GNT)

The noun *rinnah*, with thirty-three appearances in the Bible, means "rejoicing, shout of joy, an expression of a joyful state . . . singing, i.e., the making of joyful music with the voice and words."[8]

- His anger is but for a moment, His favor is for a lifetime; weeping may last for the night, but a *shout of joy* comes in the morning. (Psalm 30:5, NASB)

Here the ESV doesn't render the Hebrew word "shout" but says, "Joy comes with the morning," as essentially do the King James Version, the Revised Standard Version, the New English Translation, and the New Living Translation.

- Those who sow in tears shall reap with *joyful shouting*. (Psalm 126:5, NASB)

This time the ESV does include shouts: "Those who sow in tears shall reap with *shouts of joy!*"

Isaiah 55:12 says, "You will go out with joy and be led forth with peace; the mountains and the hills will break forth into *shouts of joy* before you, and all the trees of the field will clap their hands" (NASB). The KJV, the RSV, the ESV, and the GNT translate *rinnah* "singing" here instead of "shouts of joy." Singing is another possible understanding of verbalized joy.

GIL

Definition: "rejoice, be glad, be joyful . . . attitude or feeling of favorable circumstance"[10] (45 occurrences)

- The king celebrates [*samach*] your strength, LORD; look how *happy* he is about your saving help! (Psalm 21:1, CEB)
- This is the day the LORD has brought about. We will be *happy* and rejoice [*samach*] in it. (Psalm 118:24, NET)
- Let us be *happy*, let us celebrate! (GNT)

The prophet Habakkuk lamented as his nation was threatened by the invading armies of Babylon. At the end of his book, he says,

- Though the fig tree should not blossom, nor fruit be on the vines, the produce of the olive fail and the fields yield no food, the flock be cut off from the fold and there be no herd in the stalls, yet I will rejoice [*alaz*] in the LORD; I will take *joy* in the God of my salvation. (Habakkuk 3:17-18)
- I will rejoice because of the LORD; I will be *happy* because of the God who delivers me! (NET)

The ESV translation of *gil*, "take joy," like the NET's "I will be happy," captures Habakkuk's mind-set in the midst of horrific obstacles. He was actively grasping happiness in the Lord—determined, by God's grace and strength, not to allow his tragic circumstances to defeat him. This is one of the more dramatic proofs in Scripture that joy and happiness aren't just passive reactions but involve determined choices.

Sometimes we read Scripture about rejoicing or trusting and think, *Easy to say, but you're not facing what I am.* But few people have faced conditions as dire as Habakkuk, with the impending destruction of his nation, family, friends, and entire way of life. His statement "I will be happy because of the God who delivers me" demonstrates that delighting in God isn't dependent on favorable circumstances. Happiness in God involves an act of will toward the God who's there and who loves us, even in hunger, war, and prison cells.

RUWA

Definition: "verbal shout for joy or worship . . . shout in triumph or exaltation"[9] (44 occurrences)

- Make a *joyful noise* to the LORD, all the earth! (Psalm 100:1)
- *Shout for joy* to the LORD, all the earth. (NIV)
- The morning stars sang together and all the sons of God *shouted for joy*. (Job 38:7)

SACHAQ

Definition: "laugh, be amused, play"[11] (36 occurrences)

A Hebrew scholar defines *sachaq* as to "make acts which show joy, happiness, and positive laughter, such as dancing, playing, frolicking, or reverent but joyful worship."[12]

God used the same word when referring to Leviathan playing in the waters (see Psalm 104:26) and children playing in the streets (see Zechariah 8:5).

- David said to [his wife] Michal, . . . "I will *celebrate* before the LORD." (2 Samuel 6:21)
- I *played* before Jehovah. (YLT)
- I will go on *dancing* to honor the LORD. (GNT)
- I *smiled* on them when they had no confidence, and the light of my face they did not cast down. (Job 29:24)
- I *smiled* on them when they had lost confidence; my cheerful face encouraged them. (GNT)

Sachaq appears twice in the powerful words we discussed in chapter 18, where Wisdom, likely personified by Christ, says, "I was having fun [*sashua*], *smiling* before him all the time, *frolicking with* his inhabited earth and delighting [*sashua*] in the human race" (Proverbs 8:30-31, CEB).

Note the intense physical energy of *sachaq* evident in these translations:

- Again you shall adorn yourself with tambourines and shall go forth in the *dance of the merrymakers.* (Jeremiah 31:4)
- You will again be happy and *dance merrily* with your tambourines. (NLT)
- And hast gone out in the chorus of the *playful.* (YLT)

TERUAH

Definition: "a blast, i.e., the sound of an ancient trumpet as a signal . . . shouts of joyful acclaim"[13] (35 occurrences)

From *rua*, this noun is used to describe the great "shout" before the walls of Jericho fell down (Joshua 6:20).

- As the ark of the covenant of the LORD came into the camp, all Israel shouted with a great *shout,* so that the earth resounded. (1 Samuel 4:5, NASB)
- The army *cheered so loudly* that the ground shook. (CEV)
- The Israelites gave such a *loud shout of joy.* (GNT)
- Sing to Him a new song; play skillfully with a *shout of joy.* (Psalm 33:3, NASB)
- He will yet fill your mouth with laughter, and your lips with *shouting.* (Job 8:21)

The words *joy, joyful,* or *rejoicing* appear in at least twenty-two translations of this verse. The King James Version renders *teruah* as "rejoicing"; the New International Version, the New Revised Standard Version, the Complete Jewish Bible, the New Century Version, and at least twelve others say "shouts of joy"; and God's Word Translation says "happy shouting."

The KJV and several other versions don't use the term "shout," emphasizing the joy aspect of *teruah* over the volume as the primary intent. Other versions, including the NIV and the NCV, say "shouts of joy."

SUS

Definition: "a feeling or attitude of fondness and enjoyment in an object, implying a love or relationship to the object of delight."[14] (27 occurrences)

- May the righteous be glad [*samach*] and rejoice [*alats*] before God; may they be *happy* and joyful [*simchah*]. (Psalm 68:3, NIV)
- I *rejoice* at your word like one who finds great spoil. (Psalm 119:162)
- How *happy* I am because of your promises—as happy as someone who finds rich treasure. (GNT)
- I will greatly *rejoice* in the LORD; my soul shall exult [*gil*] in my God, for he has clothed me with the garments of salvation; he has covered me with the robe of righteousness, as a bridegroom decks himself like a priest with a beautiful headdress, and as a bride adorns herself with her jewels. (Isaiah 61:10)
- I *delight* greatly in the LORD; my soul rejoices in my God. (NIV)
- The LORD makes me *very happy*; all that I am rejoices in my God. (NCV)
- Be *glad* and rejoice [*gil*] forever in that which I create; for behold, I create Jerusalem to be a joy [*gila*], and her people to be a gladness [*masos*]. (Isaiah 65:18)
- My people will be *happy* forever because of the things I will make. (NCV)

RACHAB

Definition: "be joyful, formally, expand . . . be in a state of happiness"[15] (25 occurrences)

- Then you will see and be radiant, and your heart will thrill and *rejoice*; because the abundance of the sea will be turned to you, the wealth of the nations will come to you. (Isaiah 60:5, NASB)
- You will shine with happiness; you will be excited and *full of joy*. (NCV)
- Your heart will throb and *swell with delight*. (CJB)

SASSON

Definition: "gladness, exultation . . . with a focus on making sounds and expressions of joy"[16] (22 occurrences)

I'll break this treatment of *sasson*, a relative of *sus*, into four components.

God brings his people happiness through his favor and their righteous response.

- The Jews had light and gladness [*simchah*] and *joy* and honor. (Esther 8:16, RSV, ESV)
- There was radiant happiness and *joyous honor*. (NET)

The NIV and several other translations understand the word *orah*, elsewhere translated "light," as a third synonym for happiness in this verse: "It was a time of happiness [*orah*] and joy, *gladness* and *honor*."

Sometimes God's people need help rediscovering their former happiness.
"Restore to me the *joy* of Your salvation and sustain me with a willing spirit" (Psalm 51:12, NASB). The Contemporary English Version renders it, "Make me as *happy* as you did when you saved me; make me want to obey!"

Jesus Christ changed my life when I was fifteen; he infused me with a deep happiness centered in him. As time passed, I had to relearn to celebrate the happiness in Christ that had come so naturally as a new believer. I had to recover my first love: "You have let go of the love you had at first. So remember the high point from which you have fallen" (Revelation 2:4-5, CEB).

God promises to restore Jerusalem and live there with his people in everlasting happiness.
"The ransomed of the LORD will return and come with joyful shouting [*rinnah*] to Zion, and everlasting joy [*simchah*] will be on their heads. They will obtain *gladness* and joy [*simchah*], and sorrow and sighing will flee away" (Isaiah 51:11, NASB).

This passage promises far more than a return from exile; it promises everlasting joy and the final end of sorrow. It's found in near proximity to passages about the New Earth that include Isaiah 60, 65, and 66, and it sounds very much like the words of Jesus in Revelation 21:1-4 concerning the New Earth.

The joy-rich translations of Isaiah 51:11 bring out different shades of its meaning. Note the translation of *sasson* in these versions:

- The people the LORD has freed will return and enter Jerusalem with joy. Their happiness will last forever. They will have *joy* and gladness, and all sadness and sorrow will be gone far away. (NCV)
- Let [them] . . . come to Zion with singing and with everlasting joy upon their heads. Let *happiness* and joy overwhelm them; let grief and groaning flee. (CEB)
- They will enter Zion with a happy shout. Unending joy will crown them, *happiness* and joy will overwhelm them; grief and suffering will disappear. (NET)

Meditating on God's Word brings great happiness to the hearts of his people.
"As your words came to me I drank them in, and they filled my heart with *joy* and happiness [*simchah*] because I belong to you, O LORD, the God who rules over all" (Jeremiah 15:16, NET).

What brings joy and happiness to God's people? Drinking in his words and contemplating the fact that we belong to God, the sovereign ruler and our loving Father. What could be better than that?

MASOS

Definition: "joy, delight . . . showing celebration, gaiety, and merriment"[17] (16 occurrences)

- Beautiful in its loftiness, the *joy* of the whole earth . . . is Mount Zion, the city of the Great King. (Psalm 48:2, NIV)

- It is . . . a source of *joy* to the whole earth. (NET)
- Jerusalem, rejoice [*samach*]. All you people who love Jerusalem, be happy [*gil*]. Those of you who felt sad for Jerusalem should now feel *happy* with her. (Isaiah 66:10, NCV)
- The *joy* of our hearts has ceased; our dancing has been turned to mourning. (Lamentations 5:15)

The GNT renders this verse, "*Happiness* has gone out of our lives; grief has taken the place of our dances."

Here we see Scripture's realism. While joy and happiness are to be celebrated and cultivated, there are also times of sorrow and mourning. The New Testament takes us a step further by showing that in times of grief, we can gain perspective on even the deepest sorrow through the indwelling Holy Spirit, our ever-present resource for happiness.

ALAZ

Definition: "in a reveling state of great joy and happiness"[18] (16 occurrences)

- The LORD is my strength and my shield; in him my heart trusts, and I am helped; my heart *exults*, and with my song I give thanks to him. (Psalm 28:7)
- My heart *leaps for joy*. (NIV)
- I am *very happy*. (NCV)
- Let the field be *joyful*, and all that is therein: then shall all the trees of the wood rejoice. (Psalm 96:12, KJV)
- Let the fields be *jubilant*. (NIV)
- Let the countryside and everything in it *celebrate*! (CEB)
- My inmost being will *rejoice* when your lips speak what is right. (Proverbs 23:16, NASB)
- My innermost being will *cheer*. (HCSB)
- Everything in me will *celebrate*. (NLT)

SHASHUA

Definition: "delight . . . an object in which one finds happiness or joy"[19] (9 occurrences)

- If your law had not been my *delight*, I would have perished in my affliction. (Psalm 119:92, ESV, NIV)
- If your law had not been the source of my *joy*, I would have died from my sufferings. (GNT)
- Trouble and anguish have found me out, but your commandments are my *delight*. (Psalm 119:143)
- As pressure and stress bear down on me, I find *joy* in your commands. (NLT)
- Your commandments still make me *happy*. (GW)

ALATS

Definition: "be jubilant . . . verbal expressions of joy and praise"[20] (8 occurrences)

- Hannah prayed, and said, My heart *rejoiceth* in the LORD, mine horn is exalted in the LORD . . . because I *rejoice* in thy salvation (1 Samuel 2:1, KJV).
- Protect those who love you; because of you they are *truly happy*. (Psalm 5:11, GNT)
- When it goes well with the righteous, the city *rejoices*, and when the wicked perish there are shouts of gladness [*rinnah*]. (Proverbs 11:10)
- When good people succeed, the city is *happy*. When evil people die, there are shouts of joy. (NCV)
- I will be glad and *rejoice* in thee: I will sing praise to thy name, O thou most High. (Psalm 9:2, KJV)

ALLIYZ

Definition: "rejoicing, reveling . . . a state of great joy"[21] (7 occurrences)

- The mirth [*masos*] of the tambourines is stilled, the noise [*sasson*] of the *jubilant* has ceased, the mirth [*masos*] of the lyre is stilled. (Isaiah 24:8)

Different translations capture the loss of happiness because of impending judgment:

- The joyful timbrels are stilled, the noise of the *revelers* has stopped, the joyful harp is silent. (NIV)
- The cheerful sound of tambourines is stilled; the *happy* cries of celebration are heard no more. The melodious chords of the harp are silent. (NLT)

ALAS

Definition: "enjoy . . . take pleasure of [in] something or someone"[22] (3 occurrences)

Soon after the celebration of sexual love in marriage (see Proverbs 5:18-19) comes this account of a twisted offer of delight in sexual sin: "Come, let us take our fill of love till morning; let us *delight* ourselves with love" (Proverbs 7:18). The God-given pleasure of sex becomes an instrument of destruction: "All at once he follows her, as an ox goes to the slaughter. . . . He does not know that it will cost him his life" (verses 22-23).

CHADAH

Definition: "be delighted, rejoice . . . be in a cheerful mood"[23] (2 occurrences)

- You grant him blessings forever; you make him *happy* with the *joy* of your presence. (Psalm 21:6, CEB)

This is God conveying to us his own happiness!

- Jethro *rejoiced* for all the good that the LORD had done to Israel, in that he had delivered them out of the hands of the Egyptians. (Exodus 18:9)

- Jethro was *delighted.* (NIV, NLT)
- Jethro was very *happy.* (NCV)
- Jethro was *glad.* (CEB)

Here's another illustration of how a word in the Hebrew semantic domain of happiness can be translated by a variety of English synonyms. The NCV adds the word *very* to "happy" in an attempt to reflect the intensity of *chadah*. But what's the difference between rejoicing, delighting, or being happy or glad? They're all on the menu of the happiness semantic domain, and the choices reflect the different preferences of various teams of Hebrew scholars. The essential meaning is the same.

FOURTEEN MORE HAPPINESS WORDS IN THE NEW TESTAMENT

*These things have I spoken unto you, that in me ye may have peace. In the world
ye have tribulation: but be of good cheer; I have overcome the world.*
JESUS (JOHN 16:33, ASV)

*Plunge ye all into this sea of sweetness, dive deep into this abyss
of happiness—Christ Jesus is yours for ever and for ever. . . .
He is the most joyful man who is the most Christly man.*
CHARLES SPURGEON

⁂

LET'S LOOK AT New Testament passages using other words in the happiness family—
all rich with meaning.

KAUCHAOMAI

Definition: "to express an unusually high degree of confidence in someone or something
. . . 'to boast'"[1] (37 occurrences)

This boasting, in some contexts, involves finding happiness in what's being boasted
about. (Most of the occurrences don't appear to relate to happiness, but some clearly do.)

People can boast about their education, accomplishments, parents, spouse, children,
or grandchildren. Or they can boast about something evil. In any case, their boasting is in
what they suppose makes them happy.

- Through him we have also obtained access by faith into this grace in which we
  stand, and we *rejoice* in hope of the glory of God. (Romans 5:2)
- More than that, we also *rejoice* in God through our Lord Jesus Christ. (Romans 5:11)
- Let the one who *boasts*, *boast* in the Lord. (1 Corinthians 1:31)

The Geneva Bible (1599) translates the verse, "He that *rejoiceth*, let him *rejoice* in the
Lord."

EUDOKEO

Definition: "to be pleased with, to take pleasure in"[2] (21 occurrences)

Here are a few uses of *eudokeo* in the New Testament, each of them applying to God and reminding us of his happiness:

- Behold, a voice out of the heavens said, "This is My beloved Son, in whom I am *well-pleased*." (Matthew 3:17, NASB)
- Do not be afraid, little flock, for your Father has chosen *gladly* to give you the kingdom. (Luke 12:32, NASB)
- It is your Father's *good pleasure* to give you the kingdom. (ESV)
- It gives your Father *great happiness* to give you the Kingdom. (NLT)

This remarkable verse, Luke 12:32, speaks volumes. We aren't just told not to fear; we're told *why* we need not fear. We're a flock of seemingly insignificant sheep, but the almighty and infinitely significant God is our Shepherd, our Father, and our King. By his grace, he has *happily* chosen to give us the Kingdom, that we might be ruled by him and (as other passages show us) rule forever with him (see 2 Timothy 2:12).

It amazes me that God has gladly chosen to do this. He doesn't begrudgingly yield certain benefits to his subjects to buy their loyalty. He's a gracious, benevolent Father, and his gifts are his "good pleasure" and "great happiness"!

These aren't ideas I bring to the text—the concepts are already there. Jesus spoke the inspired term *eudokeo*, translated "gladly," "good pleasure," and "great happiness." Human fathers delight in giving their children good gifts precisely because the heavenly Father takes such pleasure in giving *his* children great gifts.

God's love for us is not detached and impersonal. It's emotional and filled with affection and delight.

AGALLIAO AND AGALLIASIS

Definition: "a state of great joy . . . often involving verbal expression and appropriate body movement"[3] (16 occurrences)

The noun *agalliasis* is used by Luke three times: twice in his Gospel and once in Acts. Mary bursts into song about the son who would be her own Redeemer:

- I am *very happy* because God is my Savior. (ERV)

Surely Mary anticipated some of the shame that would fall upon her and Joseph when others discovered she was pregnant outside marriage. Her life wouldn't be easy, but she trusted and rejoiced in her God.

When Jesus' disciples returned from sharing the Good News, here was Jesus' reaction:

- In that same hour he *rejoiced* in the Holy Spirit. (Luke 10:21)
- The Holy Spirit made Jesus feel *very happy*. (ERV)

This same word, *agalliao,* is used to describe Jesus' joy that is used in telling of Mary's joy. If we are to imitate Jesus, God's Son, we must cultivate our capacity to experience profound happiness in God's Spirit, who indwells us.

Jesus spoke of the gladness of Abraham to see his Savior bringing to pass what would become the Good News:

- Your father Abraham *rejoiced* that he would see my day. He saw it and was glad [*chairo*]. (John 8:56)
- Your father Abraham was very happy.... He saw that day and was glad. (NCV)

This significant statement speaks of an Old Testament saint living in Heaven who was apparently able to see and take pleasure in Jesus' incarnation and earthly life. Heaven may well be filled with multitudes of God's people happily beholding his unfolding drama of redemption on Earth.

- Day by day, attending the temple together and breaking bread in their homes, they received their food with *glad* and generous hearts. (Acts 2:46)
- They . . . shared their food *happily* and freely. (CEV)
- Of the Son he says, "Your throne . . . your God, has anointed you with the oil of *gladness* beyond your companions." (Hebrews 1:8-9)
- I appointed you and made you *happier* than any of your friends. (CEV)

The following summary statements and passages all center on the words *agalliasis* or *agalliao.*

The light of Christ, shining through others, can bring us great joy and gladness.

Jesus said that John the Baptist was "a burning and shining lamp, and you were willing to *rejoice* for a while in his light" (John 5:35). The New Century Version says, "You were *happy* to enjoy his light for a while."

My friend Greg Coffey, who came to Christ at seventeen, shone with a great light and then died two years later. The five young missionary martyrs who were murdered in Ecuador in 1956 were bright lights for Christ, along with their wives, who survived them. God used these Christ-followers to draw thousands of young people into missions.

I also think of Garland Gabbert, Cal Hess, Jim Spinks, and Tom Lyman—older men in our church who drew me and many others closer to Christ through their light. Rather than having hearts that shriveled as they grew older, they became more loving and ministry minded. May we all draw our light and joy from Jesus so that it's never extinguished, any more than he can be.

Our faith in Christ and our salvation are sources of great joy and gladness.

The Philippian jailer asked Paul and Silas, "Sirs, what must I do to be saved?" (Acts 16:30). They responded, "Believe in the Lord Jesus, and you will be saved, you and your household" (verse 31).

The jailer's family turned to Christ and washed Paul's and Silas's wounds, and then they were baptized (see Acts 16:32-33).

- He brought them up into his house and set food before them. And he *rejoiced* along with his entire household that he had believed in God. (Acts 16:34)
- He and his family were *very happy* because they now believed in God. (NCV)

Anticipating our eventual deliverance from all suffering can bring us great joy and gladness even in the midst of trials.

- In this you *rejoice*, though now for a little while, if necessary, you have been grieved by various trials. (1 Peter 1:6)
- This makes you *very happy*, even though now for a short time different kinds of troubles may make you sad. (NCV)

Commenting on this verse, Spurgeon said,

Unfelt trial is no trial. . . . There is a vast difference between a gracious submission to God's divine will and a callous steeling of your heart to endure anything that happens to you without any feeling whatever. . . . It is through the weeping and the lamenting, oftentimes, that the very essence of the blessing comes to us.[4]

Our relationship with Christ causes us to rejoice with great joy and gladness.

- Though you have not seen him, you love him. Though you do not now see him, you believe in him and *rejoice* with joy [*chara*] that is inexpressible and filled with glory. (1 Peter 1:8)
- You *rejoice* with a glorious, inexpressible joy. (NLT)

If in this life we gladly share in Christ's sufferings, we'll one day experience great joy and gladness in his presence.

- Rejoice [*chara*] and be *glad*, for your reward is great in heaven, for so they persecuted the prophets who were before you. (Matthew 5:12)
- Be glad and *rejoice*. (HCSB)
- Be happy and *excited*! (CEV)
- Rejoice [*chairo*] insofar as you share Christ's sufferings, that you may also rejoice [*chairo*] and be *glad* when his glory is revealed. (1 Peter 4:13)
- Be glad for the chance to suffer as Christ suffered. It will prepare you for even *greater happiness* when he makes his glorious return. (CEV)

All God's people will one day celebrate the marriage of the Lamb.

- Let us rejoice [*chairo*] and *exult* [*agalliao*] and give him the glory, for the marriage of the Lamb has come, and his Bride has made herself ready. (Revelation 19:7)

- Let us be glad and *rejoice*. (NLT)
- Let us rejoice and *celebrate*. (CEB)
- We will be glad and *happy*. (CEV)
- Let us rejoice, let us be *glad with all our hearts*. (PHILLIPS)
- Joy we, and *make we mirth*. (WYC)

We will rejoice, as will all of Heaven, at the glorious marriage of Christ to his bride—us! *Chairo* and *agalliao* aren't used to contrast each other but to reinforce the overall sense of profound happiness over Christ, the bridegroom, and the church, his bride.

The word agalliasis *has a key place in one of the greatest benedictions in all Scripture.*

- To him who is able to keep you from stumbling and to present you blameless before the presence of his glory with *great joy*, to the only God, our Savior, through Jesus Christ our Lord, be glory, majesty, dominion, and authority, before all time and now and forever. Amen. (Jude 1:24-25)
- You will be *very happy*. (WE)
- . . . without fault and with unspeakable *joy*. (PHILLIPS)
- . . . in full out *joy*. (WYC)

EUPHRAINO

Definition: "to make glad, to cheer up, to cause to be happy"[5] (14 occurrences)

- Be *happy* because of this, heaven! Be *happy*, God's holy people and apostles and prophets! God has punished her because of what she did to you. (Revelation 18:20, NCV)

Euphrosune, the related noun, is defined by Louw and Nida's lexicon as "a state of joyful happiness—'joyfulness, rejoicing.'"[6]

- He did not leave Himself without witness, in that He did good and gave you rains from heaven and fruitful seasons, satisfying your hearts with food and *gladness*. (Acts 14:17, NASB)
- He did what is good by . . . satisfying your hearts with food and *happiness*. (HCSB)

Paul brought the gospel to unbelievers with the claim that the same God who had always provided common grace now offered them the special grace of eternal happiness in his Son. This example clearly affirms that God offers happiness (not just religious joy) through the gospel. Paul used happiness as a bridge to the desires of the human heart, bringing the gospel with him.

The definition of *euphrainomai* is "to rejoice as an expression of happiness." Louw and Nida's lexicon gives instructions to Bible translators regarding Acts 2:26: "My *heart was glad*, and my tongue *rejoiced*; my flesh also will dwell in hope." The lexicon says, "In some languages it may be necessary to translate *euphrainomai* in Ac 2:26 in an idiomatic manner, for example, 'my heart sings' or 'my heart shouts because it is happy.'"[7]

The Worldwide English New Testament version translates this verse, "That made my *heart very happy*. It made my tongue *sing for joy*."

Peter quoted from Psalm 16:11 in Acts 2:28, using *euphronsune* to render the Hebrew *simchah*:

- You will make me *full of gladness* with your presence.
- Your presence will *fill me with happiness*. (CEB)

The Bible translators' handbook says of Acts 2:28, "'To be full' only specifies the completeness of the event of joy, and this in turn is only an expression of a state, that is, 'being happy.' The final clause may, therefore, be rendered as 'because you are with me I am completely happy' (or 'very very happy,' with an expression of intensive degree)."[8]

Euphraino is also used to describe both the celebration of the rich fool and the father who forgave his prodigal son.

The rich fool, who builds storehouses for earthly treasure and doesn't trust in God, advises himself to *euphraino*: "Soul, you have ample goods laid up for many years; relax, eat, drink, *be merry*" (Luke 12:19). The New English Translation says, "Relax, eat, drink, *celebrate!*"

God interrupts the man's brief celebration: "You fool! This very night your life will be demanded from you. Then who will get what you have prepared for yourself?" (Luke 12:20, NIV).

The narrative about the gracious father who forgave his prodigal son likewise uses *euphraino* multiple times:

> "Bring the fattened calf and kill it, and let us eat and *celebrate*. For this my son was dead, and is alive again; he was lost, and is found." And they began to *celebrate*. . . . "It was fitting to *celebrate* and *be glad*, for this your brother was dead, and is alive; he was lost, and is found." LUKE 15:23-24, 32

The rich fool and the gracious father are separated in Luke's narrative by only three chapters, and the identical word is used to depict their experience of joyful celebration. Both throw parties, enjoying food, drink, and laughter. The difference isn't in the food they eat and the wine they drink but in their hearts before God. A few verses earlier we see these words from Jesus: "I tell you, there is *joy* before the angels of God over one sinner who repents" (Luke 15:10). By putting on his own joyful party, this earthly father is mirroring the heavenly Father's joyful party in Heaven over a beloved image bearer entering his family. When God celebrates in Heaven, surely his people should celebrate on Earth!

As self-obsessed as the rich fool, the Prodigal Son's older brother uses the same word *euphraino* in his complaint to his father: "I never disobeyed your command, yet you never gave me a young goat, that I might *celebrate* with my friends" (Luke 15:29). The father points out that the older son could have chosen to celebrate any time. That he didn't was his own fault.

While living in the Father's house (perhaps in Christian families and churches), we can dutifully go through the motions of exterior righteousness while resenting God's extravagant grace in others' lives and refusing to enter into his happiness over them.

Instead, like the joy-filled, forgiving father who throws the party for his repentant son, we should celebrate God's grace in the lives of our fellow prodigals.

ASPASOMAI

Definition: "to be happy about, to anticipate with pleasure" (59 occurrences, most often meaning "to welcome")

- They did not get the things that God promised his people, but they saw them coming far in the future and were *glad*. (Hebrews 11:13, NCV)
- They were *glad* just to see these things from far away. (CEV)

At least seven versions translate it similarly, though most say "welcomed" (NASB) or "greeted" (ESV).

THARSEO/THARREO

Definition: "to have confidence and firmness of purpose in the face of danger or testing—'to be courageous . . . to be bold'"[9] (13 occurrences)

Tharseo occurs in the Gospels and Acts, *tharreo* in the letters. The courage depicted in these verses also implies a sense of good cheer:

- Behold, some people brought to him a paralytic, lying on a bed. And when Jesus saw their faith, he said to the paralytic, "*Take heart*, my son; your sins are forgiven." (Matthew 9:2)
- Son, be of *good cheer*; thy sins be forgiven thee. (KJV)
- *Cheer up*, my son! Your sins are forgiven. (PHILLIPS)

When Jesus came walking on the water toward the disciples' boat, "they all saw him and were terrified. But immediately he spoke to them and said, '*Take heart*; it is I. Do not be afraid'" (Mark 6:50). The King James Version says, "Be of *good cheer*."

- "*Cheer up*, my daughter," [Jesus] said, "your faith has made you well!" (Matthew 9:22, PHILLIPS)
- The following night the Lord stood by him and said, "*Be of good cheer*, Paul; for as you have testified for Me in Jerusalem, so you must also bear witness at Rome." (Acts 23:11, NKJV)
- That's why we live with such *good cheer*. You won't see us drooping our heads or dragging our feet!" (2 Corinthians 5:6, MSG)
- So always *be cheerful*! (CEV)

SUNCHAIREIN

Definition: "to enjoy a state of happiness or well-being together"[10] (7 occurrences)

Sunchairein is used of those celebrating with Elizabeth concerning her pregnancy: "Her neighbors and relatives heard that the Lord had shown great mercy to her, and they *rejoiced with her*" (Luke 1:58). The New Life Version says, "They were *happy for her*."

The man who finds his beloved animal "calls to his friends and neighbors and says, 'Be *happy with me* because I found my lost sheep'" (Luke 15:6, NCV).

This idea is reinforced a few verses later: "'*Be happy with me* because I have found the coin that I lost.' In the same way, there is *joy* in the presence of the angels of God when one sinner changes his heart and life" (Luke 15:9-10, NCV).

If anything should bring believers together in shared joy, it's witnessing God's grace in people's lives! When we hear reports of people coming to faith in Christ, are we quick to thank God and celebrate his grace?

"If one member suffers, all suffer together; if one member is honored, all *rejoice together*" (1 Corinthians 12:26). The Complete Jewish Bible says, "If one part is honored, all the parts *share its happiness.*"

HEDEOS

Definition: "experiencing happiness, based primarily upon the pleasure derived"[11] (5 occurrences)

William Morrice notes that this word "occurs very frequently in classical Greek in the sense of 'delight,' 'enjoyment,' or 'pleasure.'"[12]

It's used negatively in Titus 3:3 and James 4:1 of sensual desires. But it's used positively of people listening to Jesus: "The great throng heard him *gladly*" (Mark 12:37). The New International Version says "with *delight*"; the NCV says "with *pleasure.*"

Paul used *hedeos* twice in this verse:

- I will boast all the more *gladly* of my weaknesses, so that the power of Christ may rest upon me. . . . I will most *gladly* spend and be spent for your souls. (2 Corinthians 12:9, 15)
- I am very *happy* to brag about my weaknesses. (NCV)

SKIRTAO

Definition: "to be extremely happy . . . leaping or dancing for joy"[13] (3 occurrences)

After the newly pregnant Mary came to visit her cousin, who was also pregnant, with John the Baptist, Elizabeth said, "Behold, when the sound of your greeting came to my ears, the baby in my womb *leaped* for joy" (Luke 1:44). The Contemporary English Version says, "My baby became happy and *moved* within me." This is an astounding account of the preborn John responding joyfully to the presence of the preborn Jesus!

"Rejoice in that day, and *leap for joy*, for behold, your reward is great in heaven; for so their fathers did to the prophets" (Luke 6:23). The Good News Translation says, "Be glad when that happens and *dance for joy*"; the CEV is translated, "Be happy and *jump for joy!*"

EUTHUMEO

Definition: "to become encouraged and hence cheerful"[14] (3 occurrences)

- Is anyone among you suffering? Then he must pray. Is anyone *cheerful*? He is to sing praises. (James 5:13, NASB)

- Is any *merry*? let him sing psalms. (KJV)
- Is anyone *happy*? Let them sing songs of praise. (NIV)

HILAROS AND HILAROTES

Definition: "cheerfully happy"[15] (2 occurrences)

In the longest passage on giving in the New Testament (see 2 Corinthians 9), Paul wrote, "Each one must give as he has decided in his heart, not reluctantly or under compulsion, for God loves a *cheerful* giver" (verse 7). The NCV renders it, "God loves the person who gives *happily*." Paul also used *hilaros* to describe exercising the gift of mercy:

- Having gifts that differ according to the grace given to us, let us use them . . . the one who does acts of mercy, with *cheerfulness*. (Romans 12:6, 8)
- If someone has the gift of showing kindness to others, he should be *happy* as he does it. (12:8, NLV)

We should serve happily as we use our gifts, but the bonus is that serving others will itself enhance our happiness.

SUNEDOMAI

Definition: "pleasure derived from some experience . . . to rejoice in, to delight in"[16] (1 occurrence)

Romans 7:22 says, "I *delight* in the law of God, in my inner being." The NCV says, "In my mind, I am *happy* with God's law."

Paul affirmed God's Word as a source of happiness.

ASMENOS

Definition: "experiencing happiness, implying ready and willing acceptance—'happily, gladly'"[17] (1 occurrence)

Acts 21:17 says, "When we had come to Jerusalem, the brothers received us *gladly*." The Common English Bible says, "welcomed us *warmly*."

EUPSYCHO

Definition: "to become encouraged . . . cheerful"[18] (1 occurrence)

- I hope in the Lord Jesus to send Timothy to you soon, so that I too may be *cheered* by news of you. (Philippians 2:19)
- I will be *happy* to learn how you are. (NCV)

Here we see Paul as an ordinary person. Like all of us, he loves to hear from old friends and catch up on the latest good news about them. If he were with us today, I'm confident he'd be happy to get an e-mail or a phone call letting him know how old friends are doing—especially if they spoke of God, his grace, and the gospel of Jesus.

ACKNOWLEDGMENTS

I am indebted to Tyndale House for being a publisher with global vision and a commitment to God and his Word. Thanks especially to my friend Ron Beers, who has time and again invested himself in this book. Carol Traver has done her usual good work, and I'm grateful to her and the whole Tyndale team.

Stephanie Rische was an editorial marvel, in her great patience and willingness to go the extra mile to accommodate an author intent on getting it right. Her own commitment to care and accuracy lessened my guilt feelings at making improvements right until the end. I'm appreciative of the various fact checkers, copyeditors, and proofreaders, including Sarah Rubio, Keith Williams, Stephanie Brockway, Lisanne Kaufmann, Cheryl Warner, Lauren Lindemulder, and Katie Arnold.

Special thanks to Doreen Button at Eternal Perspective Ministries for her keen eye in editing and willingness to put in long hours, going over the manuscript with me again and again (and yes, again). Stephanie Anderson's sharp and skillful editing instincts and Bonnie Hiestand's incredibly quick turnarounds hunting down endnote material were of immense help. Thanks to Kathy Norquist for her excellent revisions and to Julia Stager for her valuable input to part 3 especially, for creating the charts and graphs I requested, and for doing it beautifully.

I'm grateful for the incredible work by the rest of our EPM staff, including Linda Jeffries, Chelsea Weber, Karen Coleman, Sharon Misenhimer, Brenda Abelein, Tami Yeager, and Dwight Myers. The work they all do frees me up to write and greatly extends the reach of these words.

Thanks to the following three brothers who are not only great thinkers and scholars but old buddies going back nearly forty-five years to when we were actually young: Jim "King James" Swanson, who was so accommodating in going over my endless questions concerning the Hebrew and Greek synonyms for happiness; John Kohlenberger, who stood with me at my wedding and I at his, forty years ago, and whose scholarly insights were very beneficial; and Larry Gadbaugh (we were also in each other's weddings), who passed on to me various articles and insights related to happiness.

I greatly appreciate Scott Lindsey of Logos Bible Software for graciously giving me the several dozen reference works I requested and for always being supportive. Thank you, Lord, for Logos 6, the best research assistant on the planet—and available to me day and night!

My friend John Piper introduced me to the doctrine of God's happiness nearly thirty years ago through *Desiring God* and *The Pleasures of God*. Scott Anderson and Tony Reinke at Desiring God Ministries both gave me encouragement and insights.

While immersed in my research, I was delighted to read an e-mail from my dear sister Joni Eareckson Tada, addressing the exaggerated difference between joy and happiness we so often hear today. Joni's words resonated perfectly with what I had discovered in two years of studying Scripture and church history, and encouraged me to press on.

Roy Peterson, formerly with Wycliffe Bible Translators and the Seed Company and now with the Bible Society, connected me with Gilles Gravelle, who was a great help with translation comparisons. So too were Roger Malstead and David Zeidan. I'm also grateful for Jung, Min-Young, Simon Crisp, and Barrie Evans, who responded to the translation survey Gilles sent out on my behalf, as well as others whose names can't be mentioned because of security issues. We will one day gather together on the New Earth and have dinner with King Jesus, where there will be no question about security!

Reinier de Blois, author of the *Semantic Dictionary of Biblical Hebrew*, was an invaluable help in dialoguing with me concerning differences in rendering Hebrew and Greek words in various languages. Thanks also to Hebrew professor Michael J. Chan and friends Ted and Linda Walker.

Bill Reeves kindly provided considerable assistance in contract-related issues. Over one thousand Facebook responders, who I will not list by name, kindly responded to my question: "What do you think of when you hear the word *blessed*?"

Steve Ziegler was with me in the recording studio for large portions of nine days as we recorded the *Happiness* audio. He alertly caught various errors along the way that helped improve the final product. Thomas Terry, aka "Odd Thomas," and the remarkable servant-hearted young men of Humble Beast Records were gracious hosts to us as we occupied their space.

I deeply appreciated and benefited from conversations with my family, not only Nanci, but also my daughters, Karina and Angela, and their husbands, Dan Franklin and Dan Stump. Thank you each for bringing me such happiness for so long!

We've had many delightful and insight-producing conversations with friends about happiness: Steve and Sue Keels, Alan and Theda Hlavka, Jim Lundy, Mike Peterson, Drew Peterson, Stu and Linda Weber, Paul and Michelle Norquist, Mark and Debbie Eisenzimmer, Lawrence and Robin Green, and Jay Echternach and Kress Drew. Also, Doug and Wendy Gabbert, Matt and Christie Engstrom, Chris and Jenny Ivester, Rod and Diane Meyer, and Don and Pat Maxwell. Todd Wagner, Grant Bowles, Trevin Wax, Greg and Cathe Laurie, Todd and Susan Peterson, Art and Kelly Ayris, Vergil and Kelsey

Brown, and Tony and Martha Cimmarrusti. Thanks to our God for graciously giving us such good and perceptive friends.

Thanks to those who did some early research and editing of chapters: Bob Schilling, Paul Conant, Josh Dear, Cathy Ramey, Bob Hoyt, and Sarah Thebarge. Todd DuBord, Doug Nichols, and Jerry Tobias all passed on helpful materials.

My writer friends among the ChiLibris vets shared their thoughts on this subject with me at two retreats. These included Bill Myers, Frank and Barb Peretti, Jim and Cindy Bell, Harry and Kris Kraus, Ken and Deb Raney, Robin Jones Gunn ("may Christy and Todd live forever"), Terri Blackstock, Angie Hunt, Robin Lee Hatcher, Brandilyn Collins, Melody Carlson, Gayle Roper, Francine Rivers, and Jerry Jenkins.

I'm grateful to Gerry Breshears at Western Seminary, who critiqued chapters of the book in their earliest (and worst) condition and also asked me to teach a seminary class on the theology of happiness. And thanks to Jim Chase, my servant-hearted friend and brother who filmed that class for us.

Thanks to Charles Steynor and the staff at Ecola Creek Lodge, where I spent several weeks working on the manuscript.

I can't convey the depth of my gratitude to the hundreds of people on our EPM prayer team. To whatever degree God chooses to touch lives through this book, and whatever else I'm involved in, you will have played a major role. One day you'll receive your reward.

Thanks, above all, to the "happy God" (1 Timothy 6:15) and to my Lord and Savior Jesus Christ, whose Father has given him a greater gladness than anyone in the universe (Hebrews 1:8-9) and who purchased my salvation for the joy set before him (Hebrews 12:2).

With heart overflowing, I join David in saying, "I constantly trust in the LORD; because he is at my right hand, I will not be upended. So my heart rejoices and I am happy" (Psalm 16:8-9, NET).

NOTES

INTRODUCTION WHAT IS HAPPINESS?

1. Rhonda Byrne, *The Secret* (New York: Atria Books, 2006), 88.
2. Frank Houghton, *Amy Carmichael of Dohnavur* (Fort Washington, PA: CLC Publications, 1953), chapter 25.
3. *Merriam-Webster Unabridged Dictionary* (Britannica Digital Learning, 2014), s.v. "happiness," http://www.merriam-webster.com/dictionary/happiness.
4. Ibid.
5. Martin H. Manser, *Dictionary of Bible Themes: The Accessible and Comprehensive Tool for Topical Studies* (London: Martin Manser, 2009), no. 5874.
6. Gavin Andrews and Scott Henderson, eds., *Unmet Need in Psychiatry: Problems, Resources, Responses* (Cambridge: Cambridge University Press, 2000), 239.
7. Dennis Prager, *Happiness Is a Serious Problem: A Human Nature Repair Manual* (New York: ReganBooks, 1998), 115.
8. J. I. Packer, *Hot Tub Religion: Christian Living in a Materialistic World* (Carol Stream, IL: Tyndale, 1987), 2.
9. Thomas Watson, *A Divine Cordial: Romans 8:28.*
10. Charles H. Spurgeon, "Titles of Honor" (Sermon #3300).

CHAPTER 1 WHY DO WE LONG FOR HAPPINESS?

1. *The Shawshank Redemption*, directed by Frank Darabont (Castle Rock Entertainment, 1994).
2. Timothy Keller, *Walking with God through Pain and Suffering* (New York: Dutton, 2013), 31.
3. Mary Roach, "Can You Laugh Your Stress Away?" *Health* 10, no. 5 (September 1996): 92.
4. Steve Turner, *The Gospel according to the Beatles* (Louisville, KY: John Knox, 2006), 187–88.
5. Thomas A. Hand, *St. Augustine on Prayer* (South Bend, IN: Newman Press, 1963), 1.
6. Augustine, "Concerning Felicity," *The City of God*, trans. Marcus Dods, book 4.
7. Hand, *St. Augustine on Prayer*, chapter 1.
8. Blaise Pascal, *Pensées*, number 425.
9. Thomas Manton, "Twenty Sermons on Important Passages of Scripture," *The Complete Works of Thomas Manton*, vol. 2.
10. Richard Sibbes, "A Breathing after God," *The Complete Works of Richard Sibbes*, vol. 2.
11. Robert Crofts, *The Terrestriall Paradise, or, Happinesse on Earth.*
12. Thomas Boston, *The Whole Works of the Late Reverend and Learned Mr. Thomas Boston*, vol. 1.
13. Jonathan Edwards, "Christian Happiness," *The Works of Jonathan Edwards: Sermons and Discourses, 1720–1723*, vol. 10.

14. George Whitefield, "Worldly Business No Plea for the Neglect of Religion," *Selected Sermons of George Whitefield*.

15. George Whitefield, "The Folly and Danger of Parting with Christ for the Pleasures and Profits of Life," *Selected Sermons of George Whitefield*.

16. Augustine, "We Should Not Seek for God and the Happy Life Unless We Had Known It," *The Confessions of St. Augustine*, trans. J. G. Pilkington.

17. Pascal, *Pensées*, number 425.

18. Patrick J. Geary, ed., *Readings in Medieval History*, vol. 2, 4th ed. (Toronto: University of Toronto Press, 2010), 330.

19. J. C. Ryle, *Happiness: The Secret of Happiness as Found in the Bible* (Cedar Lake, MI: Waymark Books, 2011), 7.

20. Anugrah Kumar, "LifeChurch.tv Pastor Craig Groeschel Says God Doesn't Want You Happy," *Christian Post*, February 9, 2015, http://www.christianpost.com/news/lifechurch-tv-pastor-craig -groeschel-says-god-doesnt-want-you-happy-133795/.

21. David P. Gushee and Robert H. Long, *A Bolder Pulpit: Reclaiming the Moral Dimension of Preaching* (Valley Forge, PA: Judson Press, 1998), 194.

22. Brian McGreevy, *Hemlock Grove: A Novel* (New York: Farrar, Straus and Giroux, 2012), 243.

23. John A. Broadus, *On the Preparation and Delivery of Sermons*, 4th ed., rev. by Vernon L. Stanfield (San Francisco: Harper & Row, 1979), 117.

24. Thomas Williams, ed., *Anselm: Basic Writings* (Indianapolis: Hackett, 2007), 392.

25. Pascal, *Pensées*, number 409.

26. A. W. Tozer, *Who Put Jesus on the Cross?* (Camp Hill, PA: WingSpread, 2009), e-book.

CHAPTER 2 WHAT DOES OUR LONGING FOR HAPPINESS REVEAL ABOUT US?

1. "John Littig and Lynne Rosen, NYC Self-Help Couple, Die in Suicide Pact, Police Say," CBS News, June 7, 2013, http://www.cbsnews.com/news/john-littig-and-lynne-rosen-nyc -self-help-couple-die-in-suicide-pact-police-say/.

2. For this example and for some of the wording, I am indebted to Dan Franklin, *Life Bible Fellowship Update*, June 26, 2014.

3. Aristotle, *Nicomachean Ethics*, book 1, section 7.

4. Denis Diderot, as quoted in Francis Elijah Ndunagum, *Building an Altar of Sacrifice* (London: Global Gospel Empowerment Commission, 2013), 157.

5. Charles Darwin, *Charles Darwin: His Life Told in an Autobiographical Chapter, and in a Selected Series of His Published Letters*, ed. Francis Darwin (London: John Murray, 1892), 59.

6. William James, "The Religion of Healthy Mindedness," *The Varieties of Religious Experience*.

7. Anne Frank, *Anne Frank: The Diary of a Young Girl* (New York: Bantam Books, 1997), 325.

8. L. K. Washburn, "Helps to Happiness," *Freethinker* 18, part 2, July 24, 1898, 474.

9. C. S. Lewis, *The Discarded Image* (New York: Cambridge University Press, 1964), 84.

10. A. A. Milne, "The House at Pooh Corner," *The World of Pooh* (New York: Dutton, 2010), 306–7.

11. C. S. Lewis, *Surprised by Joy* (Orlando, FL: Harcourt, 1955), 7.

12. A. W. Tozer, *The Pursuit of God* (Radford, VA: Wilder, 2008), 65.

13. Thomas Wolfe, "God's Lonely Man," *The Hills Beyond* (Baton Rouge: Louisiana State University Press, 2000), 186, 189.

14. Frank B. Minirth and Paul D. Meier, *Happiness Is a Choice* (Grand Rapids, MI: Baker, 1994), 13.

15. Charles H. Spurgeon, *The Fullness of Joy* (New Kensington, PA: Whitaker House, 1997), 79.

16. Charles Darwin, *The Autobiography of Charles Darwin* (Rockville, MD: Serenity, 2008), 80–81.

17. Thomas Traherne, "The First Century," *Centuries of Meditations*, no. 29.

18. George Macdonald, *An Expression of Character: The Letters of George MacDonald* (Grand Rapids, MI: Eerdmans, 1994), 18.

CHAPTER 3 DOES GOD WANT US TO BE HAPPY?

1. C. S. Lewis, as quoted in Sheldon Vanauken, *A Severe Mercy* (San Francisco: HarperSanFrancisco, 1992), 189.

2. Charles H. Spurgeon, "Joy, a Duty" (Sermon #2405).

3. A Lois Lane, "Experiment 3.3: Why I Cannot Be a Happy Single, Part 1," *The Singleness Experiments* (blog), https://singlenessexperiments.wordpress.com/category/uncategorized/.

4. William G. Morrice, *We Joy in God* (London: SPCK, 1977), 2.

5. David Kinnaman and Gabe Lyons, *UnChristian: What a New Generation Really Thinks about Christianity . . . and Why It Matters* (Grand Rapids, MI: Baker, 2007), 27.

6. Jonathan Edwards, "Resolutions," *The Works of Jonathan Edwards*, vol. 1, resolution #22.

7. Richard Sibbes, "A Breathing after God," *The Complete Works of Richard Sibbes*, vol. 2.

8. C. S. Lewis, *Mere Christianity* (New York: HarperCollins, 2001), book 2, chapter 3, "The Shocking Alternative."

9. Leonardo Blair, "Victoria Osteen Ripped for Telling Church 'Just Do Good for Your Own Self'; Worship Is Not for God, 'You're Doing it for Yourself,'" *Christian Post*, August 30, 2014, http://www.christianpost.com/news/victoria-osteen-ripped-for-telling-church-just-do-good -for-your-own-self-worship-is-not-for-god-youre-doing-it-for-yourself-125636/.

10. Mike Mason, *Champagne for the Soul: Celebrating God's Gift of Joy* (Vancouver, BC: Regent College, 2003), 15.

11. Samuel Rutherford, "To My Lady Kenmure," letter 7, *Letters of Samuel Rutherford* (Edinburgh: Banner of Truth, 1973), 26.

12. Octavius Winslow, "The Sympathy of Christ with Spiritual Joy," *The Sympathy of Christ with Man*.

13. John Flavel, *The Whole Works of the Rev. Mr. John Flavel*, vol. 2 (London: J. Mathews, 1799), 215.

CHAPTER 4 WHY DOES OUR HAPPINESS MATTER?

1. Janet Bartholomew, *Does God Care?* (Bloomington, IN: Xlibris Corporation, 2000), 153–54.

2. Hannah Whitall Smith, *The Christian's Secret of a Holy Life: The Unpublished Personal Writings of Hannah Whitall Smith*, ed. Melvin E. Dieter (Oak Harbor, WA: Logos Research Systems, 1997).

3. Ibid.

4. C. S. Lewis, *English Literature in the 16th Century* (Oxford: Oxford University Press, 1973), 187–88.

5. J. C. Ryle, "Conversion," *Old Paths: Being Plain Statements on Some of the Weightier Matters of Christianity*.

6. Ibid.

7. Charles H. Spurgeon, *The Autobiography of Charles H. Spurgeon: Compiled from His Diary, Letters, and Records*, vol. 1.

8. H. L. Mencken, *A Mencken Chrestomathy* (New York: Vintage Books, 1982), 624.

9. L. K. Washburn, "Helps to Happiness," *Freethinker* 18, part 2, July 24, 1898, 474.

10. John Piper, "Sorrowful yet Always Rejoicing," Desiring God, December 29, 2012, http://www .desiringgod.org/resource-library/sermons/sorrowful-yet-always-rejoicing.

11. "Joe Theismann's Wife Wants Him to Be Divorced," *Orlando Sentinel*, December 9, 1994.

12. Johannes P. Louw and Eugene A. Nida, eds., *Greek-English Lexicon of the New Testament: Based on Semantic Domains* (New York: United Bible Societies, 1996).

13. Algernon Swinburne, as quoted in D. H. Lawrence, *Study of Thomas Hardy and Other Essays* (Cambridge: Cambridge University Press, 1985), 113.

14. G. K. Chesterton, *Orthodoxy*, chapter 6, "The Paradoxes of Christianity."

15. C. S. Lewis, *The Weight of Glory* (New York: HarperCollins, 2001), 26.

16. Helen H. Lemmel, "Turn Your Eyes upon Jesus," 1922.

17. Jonathan Edwards, "His Early and Rapturous Sense of Divine Things."

18. Peter Kreeft, ed., *A Shorter Summa: The Most Essential Philosophical Passages of St. Thomas Aquinas* (San Francisco: Ignatius Press, 1993), 144.

19. Alexander Roberts, James Donaldson, and A. Cleveland Coxe, eds., "The Epistle of Ignatius to the Ephesians," in *The Ante-Nicene Fathers: Translations of the Writings of the Fathers down to A.D. 325*, vol. 1, *The Apostolic Fathers with Justin Martyr and Irenaeus* (Buffalo, NY: Christian Literature, 1885), 49.

20. Roberts, Donaldson, and Coxe, "The Second Epistle of Ignatius to the Ephesians," in *Ante-Nicene Fathers*, 101.

21. Roberts, Donaldson, and Coxe, "The Epistle of Ignatius to Polycarp," in *Ante-Nicene Fathers*, 93.

22. Ibid., 96.

23. Augustine, *The City of God*, book 22.

24. Vernon Joseph Burke, *Augustine's Love of Wisdom: An Introspective Philosophy* (West Lafayette, IN: Purdue University Research Foundation, 1992), 44.

25. Augustine, as quoted in Pat Killion Coate, *The Little Book of Happiness: Quotes by History's Icons, Celebrities, and Saints* (Charleston, SC: BookSurge, 2006), 8.

26. Roberts, Donaldson, and Coxe, "The Treatises of Cyprian," in *Ante-Nicene Fathers*, vol. 5, *Fathers of the Third Century: Hippolytus, Cyprian, Caius, Novatian*, 465.

27. Thomas Aquinas, *Summa Theologica*, Prima Secundae Partis, question 5, article 4.

28. Martin Luther, as quoted in Tal D. Bonham, *Humor, God's Gift* (Nashville: Broadman Press, 1988), 245.

29. John Calvin, as quoted in John Piper, *When I Don't Desire God* (Wheaton, IL: Crossway, 2004), 16.

30. Jonathan Edwards, "The Pure in Heart Blessed," *The Works of Jonathan Edwards*, vol. 2.

31. Jonathan Edwards, "Christian Happiness," *The Works of Jonathan Edwards: Sermons and Discourses, 1720–1723*, vol. 10.

32. Thomas Watson, "Man's Chief End," *A Body of Divinity*.

33. Blaise Pascal, *Pensées*, number 425.

34. Aquinas, *Summa Theologica*, Prima Secundae Partis, question 29, article 4.

35. John Wesley, *The Works of the Reverend John Wesley* (New York: J. Emory and B. Waugh, 1831), 181–82.

36. Ibid., 182.

37. John Wesley, "On Divine Providence," *Sermons on Several Occasions*, sermon #67.

38. Charles H. Spurgeon, *Morning and Evening: Daily Readings*, June 14 (morning).

CHAPTER 5 WHAT'S THE DIFFERENCE BETWEEN JOY AND HAPPINESS?

1. John Piper, "Let Your Passion Be Single," Desiring God, November 12, 1999, http://www.desiringgod .org/conference-messages/let-your-passion-be-single.

2. Brian Cromer, "Difference between Joy and Happiness," *Briancromer.com* (blog), April 28, 2008, http://briancromer.com/2008/04/28/difference-between-joy-and-happiness/.

3. Jonathan Edwards, "The Church's Marriage to Her Sons, and to Her God," *The Works of Jonathan Edwards*, vol. 2.

4. Edwards, "Wherein the Zealous Promoters of This Work Have Been Injuriously Blamed," *Works of Jonathan Edwards*, vol. 1.

5. Richard Baxter and William Orme, "The Character of a Sound, Confirmed Christian," *The Practical Works of the Rev. Richard Baxter*, vol. 8.

6. William Law, *A Serious Call to a Devout and Holy Life* (Mahwah, NJ: Paulist Press, 1978), 158.

7. Charles H. Spurgeon, *C. H. Spurgeon's Autobiography, Compiled from His Diary, Letters, and Records*, vol. 2.

8. Charles H. Spurgeon, "Heaven Above and Heaven Below" (Sermon #2128).

9. Spurgeon, "The Sweet and the Sweetener" (Sermon #2403).

10. Spurgeon, "A Happy Christian" (Sermon #736).

11. Susanna Wesley, *The Complete Writings* (Oxford: Oxford University Press, 1997), 172.

12. Oswald Chambers, *Biblical Ethics* (Great Britain: Oswald Chambers Publications, 1947), 14.

13. Oswald Chambers, *My Utmost for His Highest* (Grand Rapids, MI: Discovery House, 2006), 31.

14. Oswald Chambers, *God's Workmanship and He Shall Glorify Me* (Grand Rapids, MI: Discovery House, 1997), 346.

15. "In Your Opinion, What's the Difference between Joy and Happiness?" Yahoo! Answers, https://answers.yahoo.com/question/index?qid=20070926074249AAEJsKt.

16. Oswald Chambers, *The Oswald Chambers Devotional Reader* (Nashville: Thomas Nelson, 1990), 128.

17. A. W. Tozer, *Who Put Jesus on the Cross?* (Camp Hill, PA: WingSpread, 2009), e-book.

18. A. W. Tozer, *The Attributes of God*, vol. 1 (Camp Hill, PA: WingSpread, 2007), 78–79.

19. Greg Forster, *The Joy of Calvinism: Knowing God's Personal, Unconditional, Irresistible, Unbreakable Love* (Wheaton, IL: Crossway, 2012), 147–48.

20. Ricardo Sanchez, *It's Not Over* (Lake Mary, FL: Charisma House Book Group, 2012), 144.
21. Elizabeth George, *Walking with the Women of the Bible: A Devotional Journey through God's Word* (Eugene, OR: Harvest House, 1999), 28.
22. Hannah Whitall Smith, *The Christian's Secret of a Holy Life: The Unpublished Personal Writings of Hannah Whitall Smith*, ed. Melvin E. Dieter (Oak Harbor, WA: Logos Research Systems, 1997).
23. George Vaillant, "The Difference Joy Makes: Finding Contentment through Psychotherapy and Christian Faith," Conference at the Institute of Religion, Houston, October 8–9, 1998.
24. Dorcas Willis, *The Journey Called Ministry* (Bloomington, IN: AuthorHouse, 2013), 41.
25. Celeste P. Walker, *Joy: The Secret of Being Content* (Hagerstown, MD: Review and Herald, 2005), 65.
26. S. D. Gordon, quoted in Billy Graham, *Peace with God: The Secret Happiness* (Nashville: Thomas Nelson, 2000), 202.
27. Kristin Jack, "Jesus Doesn't Want You to Be Happy," Urbana Student Missions Conferences blog, October 11, 2005, http://urbana.org/go-and-do/missional-life/jesus-doesnt-want-you-be-happy.
28. *Merriam-Webster Unabridged Dictionary* (Britannica Digital Learning, 2014), s.v. "joy," http://www.merriam-webster.com/dictionary/joy.
29. *American Heritage Dictionary of the English Language*, 4th ed., s.v. "joy."
30. *Collins English Dictionary*, 6th ed., s.v. "joy."
31. *Evangelical Dictionary of Biblical Theology*, ed. Walter A. Elwell (Grand Rapids, MI: Baker, 1996), s.v. "joy."
32. Ibid.
33. Martin H. Manser, *Dictionary of Bible Themes: The Accessible and Comprehensive Tool for Topical Studies* (London: Martin Manser, 2009), s.v. "happiness."
34. Ibid., s.v. "joy."
35. Jonathan Edwards, *A Jonathan Edwards Reader* (New Haven, CT: Yale University Press, 1995), 37.
36. Joni Eareckson Tada, *Joni and Friends Daily Devotional*, November 28, 2013.

CHAPTER 6 DO MODERN STUDIES CONFIRM THE BIBLICAL PERSPECTIVES ON HAPPINESS?

1. Gary A. Haugen, *Just Courage: God's Great Expedition for the Restless Christian* (Downers Grove, IL: InterVarsity Press, 2009), 16–17.
2. Will Willimon, as quoted by Matthew Mobley, SermonCentral, March 2008, http://www.sermoncentral.com/illustrations/sermon-illustration-matthew-mobley-stories-65603.asp.
3. Gallup-Healthways Well-Being Index, 2008, referenced in "Poll: Unhappy Workers Take More Sick Days," Associated Press, June 18, 2008.
4. Sonja Lyubomirsky, *The How of Happiness: A Scientific Approach to Getting the Life You Want* (New York: Penguin, 2008).
5. "Peace of Mind," Duke University sociological study, cited in Rudy A. Magnan, *Reinventing American Education* (Bloomington, IN: Xlibris Corporation, 2010), 23.
6. Sonja Lyubomirsky, "Happiness and Religion, Happiness as Religion," *How of Happiness* (blog), *Psychology Today*, June 25, 2008, http://www.psychologytoday.com/blog/how-happiness/200806/happiness-and-religion-happiness-religion.
7. Lyubomirsky, *How of Happiness*, 234.
8. David Powlison, *Seeing with New Eyes* (Phillipsburg, NJ: Presbyterian & Reformed Publishing, 2003), 43.
9. J. C. Ryle, *Expository Thoughts on the Gospels, St. John*, vol. 1.
10. J. Gresham Machen, *What Is Faith?* rev. ed. (Edinburgh: Banner of Truth, 1991), 153.
11. Thomas Watson, "Man's Chief End," *A Body of Divinity*.
12. Paul Smith, "What Made Jesus Happy?" *Instrument Rated Theology* (blog), October 10, 2011, http://instrument-rated-theology.com/2011/10/10/what-made-jesus-happy/.
13. Fred Sanders, *The Deep Things of God: How the Trinity Changes Everything* (Wheaton, IL: Crossway, 2010), 106.
14. Jerry Bridges, *Respectable Sins: Confronting the Sins We Tolerate* (Colorado Springs: NavPress, 2007), 36.

15. Elton Trueblood, *The Humor of Christ* (New York: Harper & Row, 1964), 32.
16. Octavius Winslow, "The Sympathy of Christ with Spiritual Joy," *The Sympathy of Christ with Man.*
17. Some of my thoughts here are inspired by William Morrice, *Joy in the New Testament* (Grand Rapids, MI: Eerdmans, 1985), 11.
18. Ibid., 12.
19. Ibid.

CHAPTER 7 IS HAPPINESS UNSPIRITUAL?

1. Randy Alcorn, *Heaven* (Carol Stream, IL: Tyndale, 2004), 52.
2. Plato, *Phaedo*, (65–68; 91–94), quoted in Walter A. Elwell, ed., *Evangelical Dictionary of Theology* (Grand Rapids, MI: Baker, 1984), 859.
3. Plato, *Gorgias*, 493a.
4. John A. Sarkett, "How Did We Lose the Rest of the Story?" in *After Armageddon: A Bible Study on the World Wide Web*, 1996, http://sarkett.com/aa/9.shtml.
5. C. S. Lewis, *The Screwtape Letters* (New York: Macmillan, 1982), 41–42.
6. C. S. Lewis, *Mere Christianity* (New York: HarperCollins, 2001), "The Practical Conclusion," "Sexual Morality."
7. *Babette's Feast*, directed by Gabriel Axel (Panorama Films, 1987).
8. C. S. Lewis, *The Four Loves* (New York: Harcourt, Brace, 1960), "Charity."

CHAPTER 8 CAN GOOD THINGS BECOME IDOLS THAT STEAL OUR HAPPINESS?

1. Walter B. Knight, *Knight's Treasury of 2,000 Illustrations* (Grand Rapids, MI: Eerdmans, 1995), 448.
2. Timothy Keller, *Counterfeit Gods: The Empty Promises of Money, Sex, and Power, and the Only Hope That Matters* (New York: Dutton, 2009), xi–xii.
3. Thomas Boston, *The Whole Works of the Late Reverend and Learned Mr. Thomas Boston*, vol. 1.
4. Timothy Keller, "How Can I Know God?" Reedemer Presbyterian Church, June 1991, http://www.redeemer.com/learn/skeptics_welcome/how_can_i_know_god/.
5. John Calvin, as quoted in Andy Park, *The Worship Journey: A Quest of Heart, Mind, and Strength* (Woodinville, WA: Augustus Ink Books, 2010), 40.
6. C. S. Lewis, *The Screwtape Letters* (New York: HarperCollins, 2001), 118.
7. J. R. R. Tolkien, *The Hobbit* (New York: Random House, 1982), 217.
8. Augustine, *The Confessions of Saint Augustine*, trans. Edward B. Pusey, book 10, chapter 22.
9. Timothy Keller, "How to Lose Joy," *Daily Keller* (blog), October 7, 2013, http://dailykeller.com/how-to-lose-joy/.
10. Ed Diener and Robert Biswas-Diener, *Happiness: Unlocking the Mysteries of Psychological Wealth* (Malden, MA: Blackwell, 2008), chapter 7.
11. George Whitefield, "Thankfulness for Mercies Received, a Necessary Duty," *Selected Sermons of George Whitefield.*
12. John Piper, "We Want You to Be a Christian Hedonist!" Desiring God, August 31, 2006, http://www.desiringgod.org/ResourceLibrary/Articles/ByDate/2006/1797_We_Want_You.

CHAPTER 9 WHAT HAPPENS WHEN WE PUT PLEASURE IDOLS IN GOD'S PLACE?

1. Graham Noble, "The Life and Death of the Terrible Turk," *Eurozine*, May 23, 2003, http://www.eurozine.com/articles/2003-05-23-noble-en.html.
2. "The Stanley Tam Story," YouTube video, 1:01:55, posted by U.S. Plastic Corporation, April 9, 2014, https://www.youtube.com/watch?v=QxPGFlxTSro.
3. Henry Scougal, *Works of the Rev. Henry Scougal* (Glasgow: William Collins, 1830), 62.
4. Timothy Keller, "Talking about Idolatry in a Postmodern Age," Monergism.com, April 1, 2007, http://www.monergism.com/content/talking-about-idolatry-postmodern-age.
5. Author Unknown, "An AA Poem," as quoted in Raymond Goldberg, *Drugs across the Spectrum* (Independence, KY: Cengage Learning, 2013), 325.

6. Arthur C. Brooks, "Love People, Not Pleasure," *New York Times*, July 18, 2014, http://www.nytimes
   .com/2014/07/20/opinion/sunday/arthur-c-brooks-love-people-not-pleasure.html.

7. Thomas David Kehoe, *Hearts and Minds: How Our Brains Are Hardwired for Relationships* (Boulder,
   CO: University College Press, 2006), 132.

8. John Piper, *Future Grace* (Colorado Springs: Multnomah, 2012), 336.

9. "'The Drama Is Nonstop': $4 Million Powerball Winner 'Wild' Willie Steely Wants His Old Life Back
   . . . and a Break from All the TV Producers Offering Him Reality Shows," *Daily Mail*, September 25,
   2013, http://www.dailymail.co.uk/news/article-2431868/Powerball-jackpot-winner-Wild-Willie
   -Steely-wants-old-life-back.html.

10. Hannah Maundrell, "How the Lives of 10 Lottery Millionaires Went Disastrously Wrong," *Money*
    (blog), December 3, 2008, http://www.money.co.uk/article/1002156-how-the-lives-of-10-lottery
    -millionaires-went-disasterously-wrong.htm.

11. Ibid.

12. "Lottery's Biggest Losers: Big Wins Don't Equal Better Lives," Fox News, March 29, 2012,
    http://www.foxnews.com/us/2012/03/29/lotterys-biggest-losers-big-wins-dont-equal-better
    -lives/#ixzz1wsFdtP73.

13. Ibid.

14. Maundrell, "Lives of 10 Lottery Millionaires."

15. "Biggest Lottery Losers," *World of Female*, http://www.worldoffemale.com/biggest-lottery-losers-you
    -will-hate-them/.

16. Ibid.

17. John Campanelli, "For These Lottery Winners, a Dream Come True Turned into a Nightmare,"
    The Plain Dealer, February 8, 2010.

18. George Swinnock, "Heaven and Hell Epitomised," *The Works of George Swinnock*, vol. 3.

19. Edward Leigh, *A Treatise of Divinity: Consisting of Three Bookes*, Booke 2.

20. Tony Reinke, "The World's Joy-Tragedy," Desiring God, August 30, 2014, http://www.desiringgod.org
    /articles/the-world-s-joy-tragedy.

21. C. S. Lewis, *The Weight of Glory* (New York: HarperCollins, 2001), 30–31.

22. Mark A. Noll, *From Every Tribe and Nation* (Grand Rapids, MI: Baker Academic, 2014), 18.

CHAPTER 10 WHAT (OR WHO) IS OUR PRIMARY SOURCE OF HAPPINESS?

1. C. S. Lewis, *God in the Dock* (Grand Rapids, MI: Eerdmans, 1970), 280.

2. Tom Brady, interview by Steve Kroft, *60 Minutes*, CBS News, November 6, 2005, http://www.cbsnews
   .com/news/transcript-tom-brady-part-3/.

3. Samuel Rutherford, *Letters of Samuel Rutherford* (Edinburgh: Banner of Truth, 1973), 209.

4. Thomas A. Hand, *Augustine on Prayer*, rev. ed. (New York: Catholic Book, 1986), 17.

5. Augustine, "That the Platonists, Though Knowing Something of the Creator," *The City of God*, trans.
   Marcus Dods, book 10.

6. Ibid., 271.

7. Augustine, *The Works of Aurelius Augustine: A New Translation*, vol. 5, ed. Marcus Dods (Edinburgh:
   T. & T. Clark, 1872), 13.

8. Ibid.

9. Hand, *Augustine on Prayer*, 25.

10. Thomas Brooks, "An Ark for All God's Noahs," *The Complete Works of Thomas Brooks*, vol. 2.

11. Jeremiah Burroughs, *Rare Jewel of Christian Contentment* (Lafayette, IN: Sovereign Grace, 2001),
    35–36.

12. Robert Bolton, *A Discourse about the State of True Happiness*, Psalm 1.

13. John Bunyan, "Christ: A Complete Saviour," *The Works of John Bunyan*, vol. 1.

14. John Calvin, *Institutes of the Christian Religion*, trans. Henry Beveridge, Book Third, chapter 9,
    "Of Meditating on the Future Life."

15. Wilhemus à Brakel, *The Christian's Reasonable Service*, vol. 1, chapter 3, "The Essence of God."

16. John Gibbon, in James Nichols, Samuel Annesley, eds., *Puritan Sermons, 1659–1689*, repr., vol. 1 (Wheaton, IL: Richard Owen Roberts, 1981), 99.

17. Thomas Aquinas, *Summa Theologica*, Prima Pars, question 3, article 2.

18. William Bates, "Daily Scripture Readings: Thursday, May 11," *Record of Christian Work*, vol. 18, ed. W. R. Moody (New York: Fleming H. Revell, 1899), 271.

19. C. S. Lewis, *Mere Christianity* (New York: HarperCollins, 2001), book 2, chapter 3, "The Shocking Alternative."

20. Ibid.

21. Ibid.

22. C. S. Lewis, *The Complete C. S. Lewis Signature Classics* (New York: HarperCollins, 2007), 221.

23. Steve DeWitt, *Eyes Wide Open: Enjoying God in Everything* (Grand Rapids, MI: Credo House, 2012), 129.

24. Robert Crofts, *The Terrestriall Paradise, or, Happinesse on Earth*.

25. Richard L. Bushman, ed., *The Great Awakening: Documents on the Revival of Religion, 1740–1745* (Chapel Hill: University of North Carolina Press, 1989), 30.

CHAPTER 11 DO SECONDARY GIFTS HAVE REAL VALUE APART FROM THEIR SOURCE?

1. John Wesley, "The Unity of the Divine Being," *Sermons on Several Occasions*, sermon #114.

2. J. R. R. Tolkien, *The Fellowship of the Ring* (New York: Houghton Mifflin, 1966), 339.

3. Timothy Keller, *Counterfeit Gods: The Empty Promises of Money, Sex, and Power, and the Only Hope That Matters* (New York: Dutton, 2009), 172.

4. John Milton, *Complete Poems and Major Prose* (Indianapolis: Hackett, 2003), 80.

5. David Rosenfelt, *The Puppy Express: On the Road with 25 Rescue Dogs . . . What Could Go Wrong?* (UK: Little, Brown Book Group, 2014).

6. Matthew Henry, *An Exposition of the Old and New Testament*, vol. 1, Genesis 21.

7. Richard Baxter and William Orme, "Right Rejoicing," *The Practical Works of the Rev. Richard Baxter*, vol. 17.

8. John Calvin, *Institutes of the Christian Religion*, trans. Henry Beveridge, Book Second, chapter 2, "Man Now Deprived of Freedom of Will, and Miserably Enslaved."

9. Adriaan Theodoor Peperzak, *The Quest for Meaning: Friends of Wisdom from Plato to Levinas* (Bronx: Fordham University Press, 2003), 99.

10. C. S. Lewis, *Letters to Malcolm* (New York: Harcourt, 2002), 91.

11. Brother Lawrence, "Pursuing the Sense of the Presence of God," *The Practice of the Presence of God*, ed. Harold J. Chadwick (Alachua, FL: Bridge-Logos, 1999).

CHAPTER 12 IS GOD HAPPY?

1. *Chariots of Fire*, directed by Hugh Hudson (Twentieth Century Fox, 1981).

2. Armand M. Nicholi, *The Question of God: C. S. Lewis and Sigmund Freud Debate God, Love, Sex, and the Meaning of Life* (New York: Free Press, 2002), 97.

3. Terence E. Fretheim, "God, Creation, and the Pursuit of Happiness," in *The Bible and the Pursuit of Happiness*, ed. Brent A. Strawn (New York: Oxford University Press, 2012), 37.

4. Brent A. Strawn, "The Triumph of Life: Towards a Biblical Theology of Happiness," *Bible and the Pursuit of Happiness*, 314.

5. A. W. Tozer, *The Knowledge of the Holy* (New York: HarperCollins, 1961), 1.

6. Jonathan Edwards, "The Importance and Advantage of a Thorough Knowledge of Divine Truth," *Select Sermons*.

7. J. I. Packer, "God," in *New Dictionary of Theology*, ed. Sinclair Ferguson, David Wright, and J. I. Packer (Downers Grove, IL: InterVarsity Press, 1988), 277.

8. Charles H. Spurgeon, "The Reception of Sinners" (Sermon #1204).

9. Ellen T. Charry, "The Necessity of Divine Happiness: A Response from Systematic Theology," *Bible and the Pursuit of Happiness*, 239.

10. George Orwell, *George Orwell: In Front of Your Nose (1946–1950)*, ed. Sonia Orwell and Ian Angus (Boston: Nonpareil Books, 2000), 217.

11. William Bates, "Sermons on the Forgiveness of Sins: Divine Forgiveness a Powerful Motive to Thankfulness," *The Whole Works of the Rev. W. Bates*, vol. 2.

12. Thomas Fuller, as quoted in Walter A. Newport III, ed., *Lifelines: A Favorite Collection of Words of Inspiration* (Fairfax, VA: Xulon Press, 2008), 42.

CHAPTER 13 WHAT DOES THE BIBLE SAY ABOUT GOD'S HAPPINESS?

1. DK Publishing, *Off the Tourist Trail: 1,000 Unexpected Travel Alternatives* (London: DK Travel, 2009), 173.

2. Jonathan Edwards, *A Jonathan Edwards Reader* (New Haven, CT: Yale University Press, 1995), 36–37.

3. A. W. Tozer, *The Attributes of God*, vol. 1 (Camp Hill, PA: WingSpread, 2007), 10, 12–13.

4. "25 Weirdest Looking Animals," *Pagog!* August 11, 2007, http://www.pagog.com/2007/08/11/25-weirdest-looking-animals/.

5. Michael Goheen and Craig Bartholomew, *Living at the Crossroads* (Grand Rapids, MI: Baker Academic, 2008), xii.

6. Charles H. Spurgeon, "A Free Salvation" (Sermon #199).

7. W. Gesenius and S. P. Tregelles, *Gesenius' Hebrew-Chaldee Lexicon to the Old Testament* (Bellingham, WA: Logos Research Systems, 2003).

8. James Swanson, *A Dictionary of Biblical Languages with Semantic Domains: Hebrew (Old Testament)* (Oak Harbor, WA: Logos Research Systems, 1997).

9. *The A. W. Tozer Bible (King James Version)* (Peabody, MA: Hendrickson, 2012), 1086.

10. C. S. Lewis, *The Screwtape Letters* (New York: HarperCollins, 2001), 72, 38–39.

11. Lauren Barlow, ed., *Inspired by Tozer: 59 Artists, Writers and Leaders Share the Insight and Passion They've Gained from A. W. Tozer* (Ventura, CA: Regal, 2011), 94.

12. Robert Duncan Culver, "The Impassibility of God: Cyril of Alexandria to Moltmann," *Christian Apologetics Journal* 01, no. 1 (Spring, 1998).

13. Albert Barnes, *Notes, Critical, Explanatory, and Practical, on the Book of Psalms*, vol. 1 (New York: Harper & Brothers, 1868), 314.

14. Jonathan Edwards, "The Portion of the Righteous," *The Works of Jonathan Edwards*, vol. 2.

15. Oliver D. Crisp, *Jonathan Edwards on God and Creation* (New York: Oxford University Press, 2012), 132.

16. Edwards, "Portion of the Righteous," *Works of Jonathan Edwards*, vol. 2.

17. Steven M. Studebaker and Robert W. Caldwell III, *The Trinitarian Theology of Jonathan Edwards* (Surrey, UK: Ashgate, 2012), 52.

CHAPTER 14 IS GOD HAPPY, OR IS HE BLESSED?

1. Mack R. Douglas, *How to Make a Habit of Succeeding* (Gretna, LA: Pelican, 1994), 30.

2. Johannes P. Louw and Eugene A. Nida, eds., *Greek-English Lexicon of the New Testament: Based on Semantic Domains* (New York: United Bible Societies, 1996), s.v. "*makarios*."

3. Frederick William Danker, ed., *A Greek-English Lexicon of the New Testament and Other Early Christian Literature*, 3rd ed. (Chicago: University of Chicago Press, 2000), s.v. "*makarios*."

4. Horst Balz and Gerhard Schneider, eds. *Exegetical Dictionary of the New Testament*, vol. 2 (Grand Rapids, MI: Eerdmans, 1991), s.v. "*makarios*."

5. Archibald Thomas Robertson, *Word Pictures in the New Testament*, vol. 4.

6. John Phillips, *Exploring the Pastoral Epistles: An Expository Commentary* (Grand Rapids, MI: Kregel, 2004), 190.

7. George W. Knight III, *The Pastoral Epistles: A Commentary on the Greek Text* (Grand Rapids, MI: Eerdmans, 1992), 91.

8. Robert Jamieson, A. R. Fausset, and David Brown, *Commentary Critical and Explanatory on the Whole Bible*, 1 Timothy 1:11.

9. John Piper, *The Pleasures of God: Meditations on God's Delight in Being God* (Sisters, OR: Multnomah, 2000), 25.

10. John Piper, *God Is the Gospel: Meditations on God's Love as the Gift of Himself* (Wheaton, IL: Crossway, 2005), 100.

11. Charles H. Spurgeon, "Adorning the Gospel" (Sermon #2416).

12. Fred Sanders, *The Deep Things of God* (Wheaton, IL: Crossway, 2010), 94.

13. Piper, *Pleasures of God*, 26.

14. Henry Donald Maurice Spence-Jones and Joseph S. Exell, eds., *The Pulpit Commentary*, vol. 48, 1 Timothy.

15. James A. Wallace, *Preaching to the Hungers of the Heart: The Homily on the Feasts and within the Rites* (Collegeville, MN: Liturgical Press, 2002), 61.

16. Thomas C. Oden, *Classic Christianity: A Systematic Theology* (New York: HarperCollins, 2009), 141.

17. John Wesley, quoted in Terry Lindvall, *Surprised by Laughter* (Nashville: Thomas Nelson, 1996), part 6.

CHAPTER 15 WHAT MAKES THE TRIUNE GOD HAPPY?

1. "A Father's Love: The World's Strongest Dad," YouTube video, 10:00, posted by "Proud to be an Indian," December 3, 2011, https://www.youtube.com/watch?v=ax4VIVs-qsE; "Father Runs Triathlon with His Son in Tow," YouTube video, 4:14, posted by "Truth and Charity," September 20, 2008, https://www.youtube.com/watch?v=UH943Az_lPQ.

2. A. W. Tozer, *The Knowledge of the Holy* (New York: HarperCollins, 1961), 23.

3. Charles H. Spurgeon, "The Immutability of God" (Sermon #1).

4. Michael Reeves, *Delighting in the Trinity* (Downers Grove, IL: InterVarsity Press, 2012), 16.

5. William G. T. Shedd, "Trinity in Unity," *Dogmatic Theology*, vol. 1.

6. Augustus H. Strong, *Systematic Theology* (Philadelphia: American Baptist Publication Society, 1907), 347.

7. Stephen Charnock, *The Complete Works of Stephen Charnock*, vol. 4.

8. Quran 4:171–172, Yusuf Ali.

9. Quran 19:88–93, Yusuf Ali.

10. Reeves, *Delighting in the Trinity*, 40.

11. Steve DeWitt, *Eyes Wide Open: Enjoying God in Everything* (Grand Rapids, MI: Credo House, 2012), 46–47.

12. William Bates, "The Everlasting Rest of the Saints in Heaven," *The Whole Works of the Rev. W. Bates*, vol. 3.

13. Matthew Fox, *Meditations with Meister Eckhart* (Rochester, VT: Bear, 1983), 129.

14. Jonathan Edwards, "Notes on the Bible: Exodus," *The Works of Jonathan Edwards*, vol. 2.

15. James M. Houston, *The Fulfillment: Pursuing True Happiness* (Colorado Springs: David C. Cook, 2007), 270–71.

16. Robert L. Dabney, "The General Judgment and Eternal Life," *Syllabus and Notes of the Course of Systematic and Polemic Theology*, 2nd ed.

CHAPTER 16 IS GOD HAPPY WITH HIMSELF? (AND SHOULD HE BE?)

1. Norman Cousins, *Anatomy of an Illness* (New York: W. W. Norton, 1979).

2. C. S. Lewis, *Reflections on the Psalms* (New York: Harcourt, Brace, 1958), 93–95.

3. Ibid., 95, 97.

4. Charles H. Spurgeon, "Faith" (Sermon #107).

5. John Piper, "Is Jesus an Egomaniac?" Desiring God, January 4, 2010, http://www.desiringgod.org/conference-messages/is-jesus-an-egomaniac.

6. Jonathan Edwards, in John Piper, "Undoing the Destruction of Pleasure," Desiring God, April 10, 2001, http://www.desiringgod.org/conference-messages/undoing-the-destruction-of-pleasure.

7. William H. Goold, ed., *The Works of John Owen*, vol. 1 (Cambridge, MA: Harvard University Press, 1862), 144–45.

8. Dictionary.com, s.v. "serendipity," http://dictionary.reference.com/browse/serendipity.

9. Victor Hugo, *Les Misérables*, chapter 4.
10. John Bunyan, "Christ: A Complete Saviour," *The Works of John Bunyan*, vol. 1.
11. Randy Alcorn, "More on Depression in the Christian Life and Ministry," *Eternal Perspective Ministries* (blog), September 11, 2007, http://www.epm.org/blog/2007/Sep/11/more-on-depression-in-the -christian-life-and-minis.
12. Charles H. Spurgeon, *Lectures to My Students* (Grand Rapids, MI: Zondervan, 1954), 156.
13. Spurgeon, "The Fruit of the Spirit—Joy" (Sermon #1582).
14. *The A. W. Tozer Bible (King James Version)* (Peabody, MA: Hendrickson, 2012), 1117.
15. Archibald Alexander, *A Manual of Devotion for Soldiers and Sailors* (Philadelphia: Presbyterian Board of Publication, 1847), 25–26.
16. C. S. Lewis, *The Four Loves* (New York: Harcourt, Brace, 1960), "Charity."
17. Charles H. Spurgeon, *The Sword and the Trowel* (London: Passmore & Alabaster, 1866), 99.
18. Robert William Dale, *Week-day Sermons* (London: Hodder & Stoughton, 1895), 117–18.

CHAPTER 17 HAS THE CHURCH HISTORICALLY SEEN GOD AS UNHAPPY OR HAPPY?
1. Mark Twain, *The Adventures of Huckleberry Finn* (New York: Fawcett Columbine, 1996), 6.
2. See Samuel Clemens, "Letter to Olivia Clemens," July 17, 1889; Mark Twain, *The Mysterious Stranger* (Berkeley: University of California Press, 1969), 186–87; Albert Bigelow Paine, *Mark Twain: A Biography*, vol. 1 (New York: Harper & Brothers, 1912), 412–13.
3. Michael William Holmes, ed., *The Apostolic Fathers: Greek Texts and English Translations*, rev. ed. (Grand Rapids, MI: Baker, 1999), 291.
4. Gregory of Nyssa, "Hom. Beat. 1.80," in *Gregory of Nyssa: Homilies on the Beatitudes*, ed. Hubertus R. Drobner and Albert Viciano (Leiden: Brill, 2000), 24–25.
5. Arthur Hyman, James J. Walsh, and Thomas Williams, eds., *Philosophy in the Middle Ages* (Indianapolis: Hackett, 2010), 158.
6. Peter Abelard, *Peter Abelard: Collationes*, trans. and ed. John Marenbon and Giovanni Orlandi (Oxford: Oxford University Press, 2003), cix.
7. Thomas Aquinas, *Summa Theologica*, Prima Pars, question 3, article 2.
8. Thomas Aquinas, *Summa Contra Gentiles*, book 1, chapter 100.
9. Thomas Aquinas, "Happiness," chapter 14, *Grace: The Gift of Happiness*, http://www.catholictradition.org /Christ/happiness14.htm.
10. Aquinas, *Summa Theologica*, Prima Secundae Partis, question 3, article 1.
11. Thomas Aquinas, *Of God and His Creatures: An Annotated Translation* (London: Burns & Oates, 1905), 224.
12. Aquinas, *Summa Theologica*, Prima Secundae Partis, question 3, article 1.
13. Aquinas, *Summa Contra Gentiles*, book 3, chapter 63. See Lawrence F. Hundersmarck, "Thomas Aquinas on Beatitude," in *Imagining Heaven in the Middle Ages: A Book of Essays*, ed. Jan Swango Emerson and Hugh Feiss (New York: Garland, 2000), 165–83.
14. Thomas à Kempis, *The Imitation of Christ* (Milwaukee: Bruce, 1940), 68.
15. Martin Luther, *Luther's Works: Sermons on the Gospel of St. John* (St. Louis: Concordia, 1986), 107.
16. John Calvin, *Institutes of the Christian Religion*, trans. Henry Beveridge, Book Third, chapter 9, "Of Meditating on the Future Life."
17. Presbyterian Church in the US General Assembly, *Memorial Volume of the Westminster Assembly, 1647–1897* (Richmond, VA: Presbyterian Committee of Publication, 1897), 144.
18. Stephen Charnock, "A Discourse upon God's Knowledge," *The Existence and Attributes of God*.
19. Charnock, "A Discourse upon the Goodness of God," *Existence and Attributes of God*.
20. Benedict Pictet, *Christian Theology*, trans. Frederick Reyroux (London: R. B. Seeley and W. Burnside, 1834), 76.
21. Matthew Henry, *Matthew Henry's Commentary on the Whole Bible*, vol. 1, Genesis 2:1-3.
22. William Bates, "The Four Last Things: On Heaven," *The Whole Works of the Rev. W. Bates*, vol. 3.
23. Bates, "The Everlasting Rest of the Saints in Heaven," *Whole Works of the Rev. W. Bates*, vol. 3.
24. Ibid.

25. Edward Leigh, *A Treatise of Divinity: Consisting of Three Bookes* (London: E. Griffin, 1646), 123, http://goo.gl/55K5Q5.

26. Ibid., 120.

27. Ibid.

28. Ibid., 122.

29. John Gill, "Of the Blessedness of God," *A Body of Doctrinal Divinity*, book 1.

30. Jonathan Edwards, "Nothing upon Earth Can Represent the Glories of Heaven," *The Works of Jonathan Edwards: Sermons and Discourses, 1723–1729*, vol. 14.

31. Jonathan Edwards, "The Pure in Heart Blessed," *The Works of Jonathan Edwards*, vol. 2.

32. Edwards, "God's Last End Is But One," *Works of Jonathan Edwards*, vol. 1.

33. Charles Hodge, *Essays and Reviews* (New York: Robert Carter & Brothers, 1857), 265.

34. Charles H. Spurgeon, "Encouragements to Prayer" (Sermon #2380).

35. Spurgeon, "The Fruit of the Spirit—Joy" (Sermon #1582).

36. Charles H. Spurgeon, *God Will Bless You* (New Kensington, PA: Whitaker House, 1997), 18.

37. William G. T. Shedd, "Divine Attributes," *Dogmatic Theology*, vol. 1.

38. H. D. M. Spence-Jones, ed., *The Pulpit Commentary: Jeremiah*, vol. 2.

39. A. W. Pink, *Gleanings from Paul: Studies in the Prayers of the Apostle* (Bellingham, WA: Logos Research Systems, 2005), 344.

40. Cornelius Van Til, *Christian Theistic Ethics* (Phillipsburg, NJ: Presbyterian & Reformed Publishing, 1980).

41. D. M. Lloyd-Jones, *God the Father, God the Son* (Wheaton, IL: Crossway, 1996), 68.

42. A. W. Tozer, *The Attributes of God*, vol. 1 (Camp Hill, PA: WingSpread, 2007), 8–13.

43. Wayne A. Grudem, *Systematic Theology: An Introduction to Biblical Doctrine* (Grand Rapids, MI: Zondervan/InterVarsity Press, 1994, 2000), 218.

44. Ibid., 218–19.

45. Thomas C. Oden, *The Living God: Systematic Theology*, vol. 1 (San Francisco: HarperSanFrancisco, 1992), 128.

46. Terence E. Fretheim, "God, Creation, and the Pursuit of Happiness," in *The Bible and the Pursuit of Happiness*, ed. Brent A. Strawn (New York: Oxford University Press, 2012), 34.

47. John McReynolds, "The Happiness of God," Global Jesus Christ Network, August 17, 2010, http://www.gjcn.org/2010/08/basics-15-the-happiness-of-god/.

CHAPTER 18 WAS JESUS HAPPY?

1. Sherwood E. Wirt, *Jesus, Man of Joy* (Eugene, OR: Harvest House, 1999), 10–11.

2. "Amanda's Reason to Remember," About.com, http://christianity.about.com/od/miraculousintervention /a/amandatestimony.htm.

3. John Gill, "Commentary on Proverbs," *John Gill's Exposition of the Bible*.

4. Charles Bridges, *An Exposition of the Book of Proverbs* (New York: Robert Carter & Brothers, 1850), 64.

5. Ralph Wardlaw, *Lectures on the Book of Proverbs*, vol. 1.

6. Derek Kidner, *The Proverbs: An Introduction and Commentary*, The Tyndale Old Testament Commentaries (Downers Grove, IL: InterVarsity Press, 1984), 79.

7. Tremper Longman III, *How to Read Proverbs* (Downers Grove, IL: InterVarsity Press, 2002), 107.

8. Dylan Demarsico, "In the Beginning Was Laughter," *Behemoth*, Christianity Today, www. christianitytoday.com/behemoth/2014/issue-5/in-beginning-was-laughter.html.

9. Ibid.

10. John Piper, *Seeing and Savoring Jesus Christ* (Wheaton, IL: Crossway, 2004), 36.

11. Oswald Chambers, *My Utmost for His Highest*, August 31 (New York: Dodd, Mead, 1963), 178.

12. David Clarkson, "The Love of Christ," *The Practical Works of David Clarkson*, vol. 3.

13. Johannes P. Louw and Eugene A. Nida, eds., *Greek-English Lexicon of the New Testament: Based on Semantic Domains* (New York: United Bible Societies, 1996), s.v. "*chara*."

14. Charles H. Spurgeon, "Christ's Joy and Ours" (Sermon #2935).

15. James Martin, *Between Heaven and Mirth: Why Joy, Humor, and Laughter Are at the Heart of the Spiritual Life* (New York: HarperCollins, 2012), 46.
16. Piper, *Seeing and Savoring Jesus Christ*, 35–36.
17. William Morrice, *Joy in the New Testament* (Grand Rapids, MI: Eerdmans, 1985), 86.
18. A. W. Tozer, *The Pursuit of God* (Ventura, CA: Regal, 2013), 40.
19. E. Stanley Jones, "We Turn to Our Resources," *Abundant Living: 364 Daily Devotions* (Nashville: Abingdon Press, 2014).
20. Paul J. Wadell, *Happiness and the Christian Moral Life: An Introduction to Christian Ethics* (Lanham, MD: Rowman & Littlefield, 2012), 19.
21. Francis de Sales, "Spiritual Life," *Christian Register*, December 28, 1916.
22. Spurgeon, "The Special Call and the Unfailing Result" (Sermon #616).

CHAPTER 19 DID JESUS LAUGH, PLAY, AND HAVE A SENSE OF HUMOR?

1. Charles Dickens, *A Christmas Carol*, stave 3, "The Second of the Three Spirits."
2. Samuel Lamerson, "Jesus Never Laughed?" *Bible Study Magazine* (blog), November 19, 2014, http://www.biblestudymagazine.com/bible-study-magazine-blog/2014/11/19/jesus-never-laughed.
3. Mike Abendroth, "NoCo90 Episode11: Jesus Never Laughed?" YouTube video, 1:34, posted by No Compromise Radio, March 27, 2013, http://www.youtube.com/watch?v=Kp6_enc3Sg0.
4. Elton Trueblood, *The Humor of Christ* (New York: Harper & Row, 1964), 10.
5. Leland Ryken, James C. Wilhoit, and Tremper Longman III, eds., "Humor—Jesus as Humorist," *Dictionary of Biblical Imagery* (Downers Grove, IL: InterVarsity Press, 1998), 410.
6. Ibid.
7. See footnote on Matthew 25:15, *ESV Study Bible* (Wheaton, IL: Crossway, 2008).
8. See note on Matthew 18:24, *The NET Bible* (Biblical Studies Press, 2006).
9. Trueblood, *Humor of Christ*, 9.
10. Viktor E. Frankl, *Man's Search for Meaning* (New York: Washington Square Press, 1959), 16–17.
11. Jeremiah Burroughs, *Learning to Be Happy* (London: Grace Publications Trust, 1988), 9.
12. Charles H. Spurgeon, "The Believer's Heritage of Joy" (Sermon #2415).

CHAPTER 20 HAPPINESS, JOY, AND GLADNESS IN THE BIBLE

1. "Tribe Hears the Gospel of Jesus for First Time and Goes Wild!" YouTube video, 00:56, posted by SelflessEmpire, June 29, 2010, https://www.youtube.com/watch?v=RnXX3HPFPoc.
2. "Kimyal New Testament Launch in Indonesia," Vimeo video, 5:23, posted by United Bible Societies, 2011, http://vimeo.com/16493505.
3. James Swanson, *A Dictionary of Biblical Languages with Semantic Domains: Hebrew (Old Testament)* (Oak Harbor, WA: Logos Research Systems, 1997), 116–34; personal correspondence with the author, January 3, 2014.
4. William Morrice, *Joy in the New Testament* (Grand Rapids, MI: Eerdmans, 1985), 15.
5. Robert J. Dean, "Joy," *Holman Bible Dictionary*, ed. Trent C. Butler (Nashville: Holman Bible, 1991).
6. Charles H. Spurgeon, "Strange Things" (Sermon #2614).
7. James Barr, *The Semantics of Biblical Language* (London: Oxford University Press, 1961), 233.
8. See Reinier de Blois, ed., with Enio R. Mueller, *Semantic Dictionary of Biblical Hebrew*, United Bible Societies, http://www.sdbh.org/.
9. Dr. Reinier de Blois, personal correspondence with the author, August 10, 2013.

CHAPTER 21 WHY DOES IT MATTER WHETHER WE TRANSLATE THE ORIGINAL WORDS AS "BLESSED" OR "HAPPY"?

1. See *asher* in Francis Brown, ed., with S. R. Driver and Charles A. Briggs, *A Hebrew and English Lexicon of the Old Testament*, trans. Edward Robinson (Oxford: Clarendon, 1952); David J. A. Clines, ed., *Dictionary of Classical Hebrew*, vol. 1 (Sheffield, UK: Sheffield Phoenix Press, 1993); Ludwig Koehler, Walter Baumgartner, and Johan Jakob Stamm, *The Hebrew and Aramaic Lexicon of the Old Testament*, vol. 1 (Leiden, Netherlands: E. J. Brill, 1994).

2. *Random House Webster's Unabridged Dictionary* (New York: Random House Reference, 2005), s.v. "blessed."

3. J. Orr, ed., *The International Standard Bible Encyclopaedia*, vol. 1 (Chicago: Howard-Severance, 1915), s.v. "blessedness."

4. John F. Walvoord and Roy B. Zuck, eds., *The Bible Knowledge Commentary: Old Testament* (Wheaton, IL: Victor Books, 1985), 966.

5. Thesaurus.com, s.v. "blessed," http://thesaurus.com/browse/blessed.

6. *Merriam-Webster Unabridged Dictionary* (Britannica Digital Learning, 2014), s.v. "blessed," http://www.merriam-webster.com/thesaurus/blessed?show=0&t=1374098168.

7. *Oxford English Dictionary*, OED Online, http://www.oed.com, s.v. "blessed."

8. Personal conversation with James Swanson, author of *A Dictionary of Biblical Languages with Semantic Domains*, August 20, 2013.

9. Mark David Futato, *Interpreting the Psalms: An Exegetical Handbook* (Grand Rapids, MI: Kregel, 2007), 63, 67.

10. Ibid., 66–67.

11. Ibid., 67.

12. Tokunboh Adeyemo, ed., *Africa Bible Commentary* (Grand Rapids, MI: Zondervan, 2006), 609.

13. Roger Ellsworth, *Opening up Psalms* (Leominster: Day One, 2006), 24.

14. Robert Jamieson, A. R. Fausset, and David Brown, *Commentary Critical and Explanatory on the Whole Bible*, Psalm 1:1.

15. Robert G. Bratcher and William D. Reyburn, *A Handbook on Psalms*, UBS Handbook Series (New York: United Bible Societies, 1991), 16.

16. Robert B. Hughes and J. Carl Laney, *Tyndale Concise Bible Commentary* (Carol Stream, IL: Tyndale, 2001), 208.

17. James H. Waltner, *Psalms: Believers Church Bible Commentary* (Scottdale, PA: Herald Press, 2006), 31.

18. Charles H. Spurgeon, "The Truly Blessed Man" (Sermon #3270).

19. John Nielson and Royal Skousen, "How Much of the King James Bible Is William Tyndale's?: An Estimation Based on Sampling," *Reformation* 3 (1998): 73; Ray L. Huntington and W. Jeffrey Marsh, "Revisiting William Tyndale, Father of the English Bible," https://ojs.lib.byu.edu/spc/index.php/RelEd/article/viewFile/20668/19150.

20. Using the Logos Bible Software's Text Comparison Tool, my research assistant Julia Stager compared the KJV, NASB, and ESV texts of Genesis 1, Psalm 1, Ezekiel 36, Matthew 2, Romans 8, and Revelation 21. The results showed an average variation of 30 percent from the KJV by the NASB and 32 percent by the ESV, meaning a correspondence of 70 percent and 68 percent respectively. A table showing the full results, chapter by chapter, can be found at www.epm.org/textcomparison.

21. Miles Coverdale, ed., *The Letters of the Martyrs: Collected and Published in 1564*, letters of Bishop Ridley.

22. Thomas Brooks, "A Memoir," *The Complete Works of Thomas Brooks*, vol. 1.

23. Ibid., "A String of Pearls."

24. William Shakespeare, *King Henry VIII*, Act 4, Scene 2.

25. Charles Simeon, "Deuteronomy 29:4," *Horae Homileticae: Numbers to Joshua*, vol. 2.

26. Noah Webster, *An American Dictionary of the English Language*, vol. 1 (New York: S. Converse, 1828), 273.

27. Francis R. Brown, S. R. Driver, and Charles A. Briggs, *Enhanced Brown-Driver-Briggs Hebrew and English Lexicon* (Oak Harbor, WA: Logos Research Systems, 2000).

28. James Swanson, *A Dictionary of Biblical Languages with Semantic Domains: Hebrew (Old Testament)* (Oak Harbor, WA: Logos Research Systems, 1997), s.v. "*barak*."

29. Leon Morris, *The Gospel according to Matthew* (Grand Rapids, MI: Eerdmans, 1992), 277.

30. Gary Holloway, *James and Jude* (Joplin, MO: College Press, 1996), James 1:12.

31. John W. Stott, *The Message of the Sermon on the Mount: Christian Counter-Culture* (Downers Grove, IL: InterVarsity Press, 1978), 33.

32. Ibid.

33. See John R. Kohlenberger, "Author Page," Amazon.com, http://www.amazon.com /John-R.-Kohlenberger/e/B001IGHPGM.

34. Paul Smith, "Blessed or Happy?" *Instrument Rated Theology* (blog), September 14, 2011, http://instrument-rated-theology.com/2011/09/14/blessed-or-happy/.

35. Paul Smith, "What Made Jesus Happy?" *Instrument Rated Theology* (blog), October 10, 2011, http://instrument-rated-theology.com/2011/10/10/what-made-jesus-happy/.

36. Ibid.

37. *Semantic Dictionary of Biblical Hebrew*, United Bible Societies, http://www.sdbh.org.

38. Dr. Reinier de Blois, personal correspondence with the author, August 12, 2013.

CHAPTER 22 GOD FAVORS HIS PEOPLE WITH HAPPINESS: AN OVERVIEW OF *ASHER* AND *MAKARIOS*

1. David Jeremiah, *Signs of Life: Back to the Basics of Authentic Christianity* (Nashville: Thomas Nelson, 2007), 235–36.

2. V. P. Hamilton, "רָשֵׁא" in the *Theological Wordbook of the Old Testament* (Chicago: Moody Press, 1980), 183.

3. Francis Brown, S. R. Driver, and Charles Briggs, *The Brown-Driver-Briggs Hebrew and English Lexicon* (Peabody, MA: Hendrickson, 1994), s.v. "רָשֵׁא."

4. James Swanson, personal correspondence with the author, March 26, 2015.

5. Johannes P. Louw and Eugene A. Nida, eds., *Greek-English Lexicon of the New Testament: Based on Semantic Domains* (New York: United Bible Societies, 1996).

6. Carl R. Holladay, "The Beatitudes: Happiness and the Kingdom of God," *The Bible and the Pursuit of Happiness: What the Old and New Testaments Teach Us about the Good Life* (New York: Oxford University Press, 2012), 144.

7. Gilles Gravelle, personal correspondence with the author, August 3, 2013.

8. "Version Information:Young's Literal Translation," Bible Gateway, http://www.biblegateway.com /versions/Youngs-Literal-Translation-YLT-Bible/.

9. Paul Franklyn, quoted by John Meunier, "Common English Bible: Happy or Blessed?" *An Arrow through the Air* (blog), December 9, 2010, https://johnmeunier.wordpress.com/2010/12/09 /common-english-bible-happy-or-blessed/.

10. Gerald R. McDermott, ed., *Understanding Jonathan Edwards: An Introduction to America's Theologian* (Oxford: Oxford University Press, 2009), 94.

11. William Barclay, *The New Daily Study Bible: The Gospel of Matthew*, vol. 1 (Louisville: John Knox, 2001), 102.

12. Dr. Reinier de Blois, personal correspondence with the author, August 12, 2013.

CHAPTER 23 WE FIND LASTING HAPPINESS IN GOD: A CLOSER LOOK AT THE HEBREW WORD *ASHER*

1. Robert C. Dentan, "The Story of the New Revised Standard Version," Bible Research, http://www .bible-researcher.com/dentan1.html.

2. John Wesley, "The Way to the Kingdom," *Sermons on Several Occasions*, sermon #7.

3. Chris Land, October 30, 2008, comment on Brent Kercheville, "NLT Study Bible, ESV Study Bible, and 'Blessed' (Psalm 1:1)," Christian Monthly Standard, October 6, 2008, http://www .christianmonthlystandard.com/index.php/nlt-study-bible-esv-study-bible-and-blessed-psalm-11/.

4. Edwin Blum, as quoted in Gibbs, February 22, 2009, comment on Kercheville, "NLT Study Bible, ESV Study Bible, and 'Blessed' (Psalm 1:1)."

5. See footnote on Psalm 1:1-2, *ESV Study Bible* (Wheaton, IL: Crossway Bibles, 2008).

6. *ESV Study Bible* (Wheaton, IL: Crossway Bibles, 2008).

7. Pastor Jono, Tumblr repost by "forevertaketheworld," *Just Another Day*, July 1, 2012, http://forevertaketheworld.tumblr.com/post/26288260926.

8. Thomas Brooks, "The Only Happy Man in the World!" SermonIndex.net, http://www.sermonindex .net/modules/articles/index.php?view=article&aid=22002.

CHAPTER 24 WE CAN BE HAPPY NOW . . . AND FOREVER: A CLOSER LOOK AT THE GREEK WORD *MAKARIOS*

1. Horst Balz and Gerhard Schneider, eds. *Exegetical Dictionary of the New Testament*, vol. 2 (Grand Rapids, MI: Eerdmans, 1991), s.v. "*makarios.*"
2. Gerhard Kittel, ed., *Theological Dictionary of the New Testament*, vol. 4, trans. Geoffrey W. Bromiley (Grand Rapids, MI: Eerdmans, 1967), s.v. "*makarios.*"
3. David Noel Freedman, *The Anchor Bible Dictionary, K–N*, vol. 4 (New Haven, CT: Yale University Press, 1992), s.v. "*makarios.*"
4. Ceslas Spicq, *Theological Lexicon of the New Testament*, ed. and trans. James D. Ernest (Peabody, MA: Hendrickson, 1994), s.v. "*makarios.*"
5. Steven L. Cox and Kendell H. Easley, *HCSB Harmony of the Gospels* (Nashville: Holman Bible, 2007), 68.
6. William Hendriksen, *New Testament Commentary: Exposition of the Gospel according to Matthew*, vol. 9 (Grand Rapids, MI: Baker Academic, 1982), 265.
7. John MacArthur, *The MacArthur New Testament Commentary: Matthew 1–7* (Chicago: Moody Press, 1985), 142.
8. John Piper, *When I Don't Desire God: How to Fight for Joy* (Wheaton, IL: Crossway, 2004), 240.
9. Warren W. Wiersbe, *The Bible Exposition Commentary* (Wheaton, IL: Victor Books, 1996), Matthew 5:1.
10. G. Campbell Morgan, in Sunday School Commission, Diocese of New York, *Teachers' Notes on The Teachings of Jesus Christ the Messiah Concerning the Kingdom of God*, part 1 (Milwaukee, WI: Young Churchman, 1913), 27.
11. Philip Schaff, *Nicene and Post-Nicene Fathers*, series 1, vol. 13, "Saint Chrysostom: Homilies on Philippians" (Homily 14).
12. "Ecclesiasticus (Sirach)," *New English Bible*, Christian Research and Apologetics Ministry, https://carm.org/ecclesiasticus.
13. John A. Broadus, *Commentary on the Gospel of Matthew* (Philadelphia: American Baptist Publication Society, 1886), 87–88.
14. Barclay M. Newman and Eugene A. Nida, *A Handbook on the Gospel of John*, UBS Handbook Series (New York: United Bible Societies, 1980), 437.
15. "God's Word Translation," *Wikipedia*, http://en.wikipedia.org/wiki/God's_Word_Translation.
16. Mark David Futato, *Interpreting the Psalms: An Exegetical Handbook* (Grand Rapids, MI: Kregel, 2007), 66–67.
17. Spiros Zodhiates, *The Pursuit of Happiness: An Exegetical Commentary on the Beatitudes*, rev. ed. (Chattanooga, TN: AMG, 1976).
18. D. A. Carson, *Exegetical Fallacies* (Grand Rapids, MI: Baker Academic, 1996), 32.
19. Mike Gould and Marilyn Rankin, *Cambridge International AS and A Level English Language Coursebook* (Cambridge: Cambridge University Press, 2014), 218.
20. "International Day of Happiness," United Nations, http://www.un.org/en/events/happinessday/.
21. David S. Lampel, "A Better Way to Live," *Aspects* 87 (February 1998), Internet Christian Library, http://www.iclnet.org/pub/resources/text/aspects/asp-087.txt.
22. Anne Frank, *The Diary of Anne Frank* (New York: Random House, 2003), 542.

CHAPTER 25 GOD TELLS HIS CHILDREN TO SPEND TIME AND MONEY PARTYING: THE HEBREW WORD *SAMACH*, PART 1

1. George Müller, *A Narrative of Some of the Lord's Dealings with George Müller*, part 3.
2. Ibid.
3. James Swanson, *A Dictionary of Biblical Languages with Semantic Domains: Hebrew (Old Testament)* (Oak Harbor, WA: Logos Research Systems, 1997), s.v. "*samach.*"
4. George M. Landes, *Building Your Biblical Hebrew Vocabulary: Learning Words by Frequency and Cognate*, vol. 41 (Atlanta: Society of Biblical Literature, 2001), 68.
5. J. R. R. Tolkien, *The Two Towers* (New York: Houghton Mifflin, 1966), 697.

CHAPTER 26 GOD DESIRES OUR HAPPINESS NOW AND FOREVER: THE HEBREW WORD
SAMACH, PART 2
1. Charles Chapman, *Matthew Henry: His Life and Times* (London: Arthur Hall, Virtue, 1859), 114–17.
2. Frederick Buechner, *Wishful Thinking: A Theological ABC* (New York: Harper & Row, 1973), 118.
3. Howard Taylor and Geraldine Taylor, *Hudson Taylor in Early Years: The Growth of a Soul* (New York: Hodder & Stoughton, 1912), 121.
4. Henrik Ibsen, quoted in Diane K. Dean, *From Ordinary to Extraordinary* (Mustang, OK: Tate, 2009), 12.
5. Daniel Goleman, "Men at 65: New Findings on Well-Being," *New York Times*, January 16, 1990.
6. Richard Flaste, ed., *The New York Times Book of Science Literacy* (New York: HarperPerennial, 1992), 165.
7. William P. Brown, "Happiness and Its Discontents in the Psalms," *The Bible and the Pursuit of Happiness*, ed. Brent A. Strawn (New York: Oxford University Press, 2012), 115.

CHAPTER 27 GOD'S PEOPLE CAN AND SHOULD REJOICE AND CELEBRATE: *CHARA*
AND *CHAIRO* IN THE GOSPELS AND ACTS
1. Osho (Bhagwan Shree Rajneesh), *Joy: The Happiness That Comes from Within*, 2nd ed. (New York: St. Martin's Griffin, 2009), 9.
2. Johannes P. Louw and Eugene A. Nida, eds., *Greek-English Lexicon of the New Testament: Based on Semantic Domains* (New York: United Bible Societies, 1996), 25.123.
3. Ibid., 25.125.
4. Timothy Friberg, Barbara Friberg, and Neva F. Miller, *Analytical Lexicon of the Greek New Testament* (Grand Rapids, MI: Baker, 2000), s.v. "*chara*."
5. William D. Mounce, *Mounce's Complete Expository Dictionary of Old and New Testament Words* (Grand Rapids, MI: Zondervan, 2006), s.v. "*chara*."
6. Ibid.
7. William Morrice, *Joy in the New Testament* (Grand Rapids, MI: Eerdmans, 1985), 68.
8. Frederick William Danker, ed., *A Greek-English Lexicon of the New Testament and Other Early Christian Literature*, 3rd ed. (Chicago: University of Chicago Press, 2000).
9. Ibid.
10. Thomas Brooks, "The Crown and Glory of Christianity," *The Complete Works of Thomas Brooks*, vol. 4.
11. Aleksandr I. Solzhenitsyn, *The Gulag Archipelago: 1918–1956*, vol. 2 (New York: Harper & Row, 1974), 615–17.
12. Aleksandr Solzhenitsyn, *Cancer Ward* (New York: Farrar, Straus and Giroux, 1991), 270.

CHAPTER 28 ENJOYING GOD'S GRACE: THE GREEK WORDS *CHARA* AND *CHAIRO* IN
THE APOSTLES' LETTERS
1. Martin Brecht, *Martin Luther: Shaping and Defining the Reformation, 1521–1532* (Minneapolis: Fortress Press, 1990), 43–44.
2. James Boswell, *The Life of Samuel Johnson*, ed. David Womersley (New York: Penguin Classics, 2008), 197.
3. Barclay M. Newman and Eugene A. Nida, *A Handbook on Paul's Letter to the Romans*, UBS Handbook Series (New York: United Bible Societies, 1973), 277.
4. Daniel C. Arichea and Eugene A. Nida, *A Handbook on Paul's Letter to the Galatians*, UBS Handbook Series (New York: United Bible Societies, 1976), 140.
5. I am indebted here to some thoughts and words shared with me by my friend Larry Gadbaugh.
6. Fanny Crosby, *Fanny Crosby's Life-Story* (New York: Every Where Publishing, 1903), 27.
7. C. S. Lewis, *The Four Loves* (New York: Harcourt, Brace, 1960), "Affection."
8. Karl Barth, *Church Dogmatics: The Doctrine of Creation*, vol. 3, part 4 (Edinburgh: T. & T. Clark, 2004), 378.
9. William Morrice, *Joy in the New Testament* (Grand Rapids, MI: Eerdmans, 1985), 75.

CHAPTER 29 THE BIBLE LEAVES NO ROOM FOR DOUBT: OUR HAPPINESS MATTERS TO GOD

1. Augustine, *Confessions*, trans. R. S. Pine-Coffin (New York: Penguin Classics, 1961), book 9, chapter 1.
2. Johannes P. Louw and Eugene A. Nida, eds., *Greek-English Lexicon of the New Testament: Based on Semantic Domains* (New York: United Bible Societies, 1996), 25.80–25.84.
3. Ibid., 25.81.
4. Ibid., 25.80.
5. Jonathan Edwards, "The Portion of the Righteous," *The Works of Jonathan Edwards*, vol. 2.
6. David Clarkson, "Believers' Communion with the Father and Son," *The Practical Works of David Clarkson*, vol. 3.

CHAPTER 30 THE EMOTIONAL SATISFACTION IN HAPPINESS AND JOY

1. Joni Eareckson Tada, *More Precious Than Silver: 366 Daily Devotional Readings* (Grand Rapids, MI: Zondervan, 1998), November 28.
2. George E. Vaillant, *Spiritual Evolution: A Scientific Defense of Faith* (New York: Broadway Books, 2008), 124.
3. Dawn Wyant, "One Word 2013," *Thoughts and Ponderings* (blog), January 7, 2013, http://morningstardawn.blogspot.com/2013/01/one-word-2013.html.
4. Ibid.
5. C. Hollis Crossman, "The Opposite of Happiness," *The 300 (Judges 7): Lay Theology for the Faithful* (blog), August 7, 2012, http://cholliscrossman.blogspot.com/2012/08/the-opposite-of-happiness.html.
6. Jackie Lopina, "Loving Your Friend through Infertility: What to Pray For," *Hoping in God* (blog), May 2, 2011, http://jackielopina.wordpress.com/2011/05/02/loving-your-friend-through-infertility-what-to-pray-for-part-3/.
7. Amy H., "Happiness Is Not Joy: Joy Is Better," *The Rusk and Bannock Project* (blog), March 4, 2015, http://ruskandbannock.com/2015/03/04/happiness-is-not-joy-joy-is-better/.
8. Steve Austin, "Happiness Is the Enemy of Joy," *Grace Is Messy* (blog), December 5, 2011, http://graceismessy.com/2011/12/05/happiness-is-the-enemy-of-joy/.
9. Amy Pardue, "What's Wrong with Pursuing Happiness?" *Hunger for Him* (blog), February 25, 2010, http://hungerforhim.blogspot.com/2010/02/whats-wrong-with-pursuing-happiness.html.
10. William Shakespeare, *As You Like It*, Act 2, Scene 1.
11. Isaac Watts, *The Psalms and Hymns of Isaac Watts* (Oak Harbor, WA: Logos Research Systems, 1998).
12. Charles H. Spurgeon, "Christ's Joy and Ours" (Sermon #2935).
13. A. W. Tozer, *Life in the Spirit* (Peabody, MA: Hendrickson, 2009), 153.
14. Mike Mason, *Champagne for the Soul: Celebrating God's Gift of Joy* (Vancouver, BC: Regent College, 2003), 31.
15. Richard Sibbes, "Commentary on 2 Corinthians Chapter 1, Verse 12," *The Complete Works of Richard Sibbes*, vol. 3.
16. Jonathan Edwards, "The Peace Which Christ Gives His True Followers," *The Works of Jonathan Edwards*, vol. 2.
17. Ibid.
18. Edwards, "Thoughts on Revival," *Works of Jonathan Edwards*, vol. 1.
19. Edwards, "Dissertation on the End for Which God Created the World," *Works of Jonathan Edwards*, vol. 1.
20. John Milton, *Paradise Lost*, book 3.
21. Richard Baxter and William Orme, "The Character of a Sound, Confirmed Christian," *The Practical Works of the Rev. Richard Baxter*, vol. 8.
22. William Law, *A Serious Call to a Devout and Holy Life* (Mineola, NY: Dover, 2013), 113.
23. Ibid., 133.
24. Thomas Doolittle, in James Nichols, Samuel Annesley, eds., *Puritan Sermons: 1659–1689*, repr., vol. 4 (Wheaton, IL: Richard Owen Roberts, 1981), 3.
25. Thomas Woodcock, in *Puritan Sermons*, vol. 5, 499.

26. Thomas Vincent, in *Puritan Sermons*, vol. 2, 620.

27. Thomas Ridgley, *A Body of Divinity*, vol. 2 (Philadelphia: William W. Woodward, 1815), 467.

28. Henry Wilkinson, in *Puritan Sermons*, vol. 6, 218.

29. Stephen Charnock, "The Knowledge of God," *The Complete Works of Stephen Charnock*, vol. 4.

30. Charnock, "Weak Grace Victorious," *The Complete Works of Stephen Charnock*, vol. 5.

31. Sibbes, "Divine Meditations," *The Complete Works of Richard Sibbes*, vol. 7.

32. Sibbes, "Commentary on 2 Corinthians Chapter 1, Verse 24," *The Complete Works of Richard Sibbes*, vol. 3.

33. Charles Simeon, "The Blessedness of Departed Saints," *Horae Homileticae: Revelation*, vol. 21.

34. John Wesley, "The Doctrine of Original Sin," *The Works of the Reverend John Wesley*, vol. 5.

35. Fred Sanders, "John Wesley as a Happy Puritan," *The Seedbed Blog*, August 13, 2012, http://seedbed .com/feed/wesley-as-a-happy-puritan/.

36. Wesley, "Spiritual Worship" (Sermon #82).

37. Ibid.

38. John Wesley, "A Plain Account of Christian Perfection," *The Works of the Rev. John Wesley*, vol. 11.

39. Wesley, "Spiritual Worship."

40. John Wesley, *The Journal of the Rev. John Wesley*, vol. 1.

41. Charles Wesley, "Christ, the Good Shepherd," *The Church of England Hymn-Book: New Edition*, ed. D. T. K. Drummond and Robert Greville (Edinburgh: William Oliphant and Sons, 1840), no. 117.

42. Ibid., no. 374.

43. Charles Wesley, "Describing the Pleasantness of Religion," *John and Charles Wesley: Selected Prayers, Hymns, Journal Notes, Sermons, Letters and Treatises* (Mahwah, NJ: Paulist Press, 1981), 181.

44. Ibid.

45. Spurgeon, "The Keynote of the Year" (Sermon #2121).

46. Spurgeon, "The Two Effects of the Gospel" (Sermon #26).

47. Spurgeon, "A Peculiar People" (Sermon #2530).

48. Spurgeon, "Encouragements to Prayer" (Sermon #2380).

49. Spurgeon, "The Sweet and the Sweetener" (Sermon #2403).

50. Spurgeon, "Despised Light Withdrawn" (Sermon # 2413).

51. Spurgeon, "Joy, A Duty" (Sermon #2405).

52. J. C. Ryle, "Are You Happy?" *Home Truths, Miscellaneous Addresses and Tracts*.

53. J. C. Ryle, *Expository Thoughts on the Gospels: St. Matthew*.

54. Ryle, "Are You Happy?" *Consider Your Ways*.

55. Charles Hodge, *2 Corinthians*, The Crossway Classic Commentaries (Wheaton, IL: Crossway, 1995), 2 Corinthians 2:1-4.

56. Alfred Plummer, *Epistles of St. John*, 1 John 1:4-5.

57. A. W. Pink, *The Nature of God* (Bellingham, WA: Logos Research Systems, 2005), 273.

58. D. Martyn Lloyd-Jones, *Joy Unspeakable: Power and Renewal in the Holy Spirit* (Wheaton, IL: Harold Shaw, 1984), 101.

59. Tozer, *Life in the Spirit*, 153.

60. Ira F. Stanphill, "Happiness Is to Know the Savior" (1968).

61. John R. Rice, *A Christian's Wells of Joy* (Murfreesboro, TN: Sword of the Lord, 1971), 7.

62. Ibid., 75.

63. David Murray, "7 Kinds of Happiness," *HeadHeartHand* (blog), September 17, 2014, http://headhearthand.org/blog/2014/09/17/7-types-of-happiness/.

64. Charles H. Spurgeon, *The Treasury of David*, Psalm 150.

CHAPTER 31 HAPPINESS IS OUR CHOICE

1. Epictetus, *Enchiridion* (New York: Dover, 2004), 3.

2. Helen Keller, as quoted in Amy E. Dean, *Peace of Mind: Daily Meditations for Easing Stress* (New York: Bantam, 1995), 364.

3. David Brainerd, as quoted in Jonathan Edwards, *Life and Diary of David Brainerd* (New York: Cosimo, 2007), 78–79.

4. Ibid., 81.
5. Ibid., 90.
6. Ibid., 112.
7. Ibid., 151.
8. Ibid., 153, 183.
9. David Brainerd, as quoted in Jonathan Edwards, *The Life of the Rev. David Brainerd, Missionary to the Indians* (Edinburgh: H. S. Baynes, 1824), 302.
10. Henry Cloud, *The Law of Happiness: How Spiritual Wisdom and Modern Science Can Change Your Life* (New York: Howard Books, 2011), 10.
11. Sonja Lyubomirsky, *The How of Happiness: A Scientific Approach to Getting the Life You Want* (New York: Penguin Books, 2007), 20–21.
12. Ibid., 20–23.
13. Therese J. Borchard, "How Giving Makes Us Happy," *World of Psychology* (blog), PsychCentral.com, December 22, 2013, http://psychcentral.com/blog/archives/2013/12/22/how-giving-makes-us-happy/.
14. Arthur C. Brooks, as quoted in "Those Who Serve Others Are *Happier, Healthier,* and More *Prosperous,*" Spokane Cares, http://www.spokanecares.org/index.php?c_ref=160.
15. Arthur C. Brooks, "Love People, Not Pleasure," *New York Times,* July 18, 2014, http://www.nytimes.com/2014/07/20/opinion/sunday/arthur-c-brooks-love-people-not-pleasure.html.
16. Randy Alcorn, *hand in Hand* (Colorado Springs: Multnomah, 2014).
17. Jerome Bruner, *On Knowing: Essays for the Left Hand* (Cambridge, MA: Belknap Press, 1979), 24.
18. David G. Myers, "Want a Happier Life?" http://www.davidmyers.org/Brix?pageID=46.
19. Trixie Koontz, dog, as told to Dean R. Koontz, *Bliss to You: Trixie's Guide to a Happy Life* (New York: Hyperion, 2008), 36–39.
20. Rob Stein, "Happiness Can Spread among People like a Contagion, Study Indicates," *Washington Post,* December 5, 2008.
21. Ralph Waldo Emerson, *Nature and Selected Essays* (New York: Penguin, 1982), 37.
22. Clyde Kilby's resolutions, as cited in John Piper, *The Pleasures of God* (Colorado Springs: Multnomah, 2000), 95–96.
23. Ibid., 95.
24. Charles H. Spurgeon, "God Rejoicing in the New Creation" (Sermon #2211).
25. Ibid.
26. C. S. Lewis, *The Lion, the Witch and the Wardrobe* (New York: HarperCollins, 2003), chapter 8.
27. Ibid., chapter 7.

CHAPTER 32 WAYS TO CULTIVATE HAPPINESS

1. Cathy Miller, "Delayed Delivery," as quoted in Joe Wheeler, *The Best of Christmas in My Heart,* vol. 2 (Brentwood, TN: Howard, 2008).
2. Martin E. P. Seligman, *Learned Optimism* (New York: Knopf, 1991), 4–5.
3. Randy Alcorn, *The Purity Principle* (Sisters, OR: Multnomah, 2003), 9–10.
4. "Hedonism 2," Exotic Travel Dream, 2008, http://exotictraveldream.eu/index.php?option=com_content&view=article&id=32&Itemid=29.
5. Dennis Prager, *Happiness Is a Serious Problem: A Human Nature Repair Manual* (New York: ReganBooks, 1998), 24.
6. Ravi Zacharias, *Cries of the Heart* (Nashville: Thomas Nelson, 1998), 129.
7. Prager, *Happiness Is a Serious Problem,* 37–38.
8. Arthur C. Brooks, "A Formula for Happiness," *New York Times,* December 14, 2013.
9. Martin Luther King Jr., *MLK Quote of the Week: "All labor that uplifts humanity has dignity and importance and should be undertaken with painstaking excellence"* (blog), The King Center, April 9, 2013, http://www.thekingcenter.org/blog/mlk-quote-week-all-labor-uplifts-humanity-has-dignity-and-importance-and-should-be-undertaken.
10. Lou Nicholes, *Romans: A Roadmap for the Christian Life* (Fairfax, VA: Xulon Press, 2004), 113.

11. "Our Happiness Lies in the Happiness of Others," *Real Life Times*, April 15, 2014, http://reallifetimesnews.com/our-happiness-lies-in-the-happiness-of-others/.
12. Bernard Rimland, "The Altruism Paradox," *Psychological Reports* 51, no. 2 (October 1982): 521–22, http://www.amsciepub.com/doi/abs/10.2466/pr0.1982.51.2.521.
13. Ibid.
14. Arthur C. Brooks, as quoted in "Those Who Serve Others Are *Happier, Healthier*, and More *Prosperous*," Spokane Cares, http://www.spokanecares.org/index.php?c_ref=160.
15. Daniel M. Oppenheimer and Christopher Y. Olivola, eds., *The Science of Giving* (New York: Psychology Press, 2011), 8.
16. Charles Dickens, *A Christmas Carol*, stave 3, "The Second of the Three Spirits."
17. Dickens, *Christmas Carol*, stave 5, "The End of It."
18. *Sister Act 2*, directed by Bill Duke (Touchstone Pictures, 1993).

CHAPTER 33 CELEBRATION IS GOD'S IDEA: FEASTS, FESTIVALS, SABBATHS, SINGING, AND DANCING IN THE BIBLE
1. Warren Wiersbe, *The Wycliffe Handbook of Preaching and Preachers* (Chicago: Moody Press, 1984), 187.
2. Charles H. Spurgeon, "To Those Who Feel Unfit for Communion" (Sermon #2131).
3. William G. Morrice, *We Joy in God* (London: SPCK, 1977), 52.
4. Isaac Watts, *Psalms and Hymns of Isaac Watts*, "Pardon and Strength from Christ" (Hymn #24).
5. John Calvin, *Calvin: Commentaries* (London: S.C.M. Press, 1958), 60.
6. Chad Brand, Archie England, and Charles W. Draper, eds., *Holman Illustrated Bible Dictionary* (Nashville: Holman Bible Publishers, 2003).
7. Ibid., 384–85.
8. Ibid., 1055–56.
9. Fyodor Dostoevsky, *The Brothers Karamazov*, chapter 4, "Cana of Galilee."
10. Robert Hotchkins, as quoted in Philip Graham Ryken, *Jeremiah and Lamentations: From Sorrow to Hope* (Wheaton, IL: Crossway, 2001), 271.

CHAPTER 34 HAPPINESS COMES FROM MEDITATING ON GOD'S WORD
1. Arthur T. Pierson, *George Müller of Bristol (1805–1898)* (Peabody, MA: Hendrickson, 2008), 130–31.
2. George Müller, "How to Be Happy and Strong in the Lord," in *Guide to Holiness*, vol. 18–19 (New York: Walter C. Palmer, 1871), 78.
3. George Müller, "Joyfulness and Usefulness," in *The Advocate of Christian Holiness* (January, 1880), 7.
4. Philip Schaff, *Nicene and Post-Nicene Fathers*, series 1, vol. 7, "Augustine: Homilies on the Gospel of John" (Tractate #25).
5. A. W. Tozer, *The Knowledge of the Holy* (New York: HarperCollins, 1961), 9.
6. E. V. Gerhart, "The Doctrine of Anselm on the Death of Christ," *The Reformed Quarterly Review*, vol. 29 (Philadelphia: Reformed Church Publication Board, 1882), 308–9.
7. Charles H. Spurgeon, "Repentance After Conversion" (Sermon #2419).
8. John Calvin, *Commentary on the Book of Psalms*, vol. 2, Psalm 51.
9. John Piper, *When I Don't Desire God* (Wheaton, IL: Crossway, 2004), 30–31.
10. Pierson, *George Müller of Bristol*, 462.
11. D. Martyn Lloyd-Jones, *Spiritual Depression: Its Causes and Cure* (Grand Rapids, MI: Eerdmans, 1965), 20–21.
12. See "Bible Reading Plan," BibleStudyTools.com, http://www.biblestudytools.com/bible-reading-plan/.
13. Joni Eareckson Tada, as quoted by Gladys Haynes Green, *God's Faithfulness: The Greens' Journey* (Bloomington, IN: CrossBooks, 2012), 74.
14. Wilhelmus à Brakel, *The Christian's Reasonable Service*, vol. 1, chapter 17, "The Necessity of Satisfaction by the Surety Jesus Christ."
15. Calvin Miller, *The Taste of Joy: Recovering the Lost Glow of Discipleship* (Downers Grove, IL: InterVarsity Press, 1983), 18.

16. Spurgeon, "Obtaining Promises" (Sermon #435).
17. Frank C. Laubach, *The Game with Minutes* (Eastford, CT: Martino Fine Books, 2012).
18. Brother Lawrence and Frank Laubach, *Practicing His Presence* (Sargent, GA: The SeedSowers, 1973), 36.
19. Thomas Brooks, "The Crown and Glory of Christianity," *The Complete Works of Thomas Brooks*, vol. 4.

CHAPTER 35 HAPPINESS IN CHRIST IS DEEPER THAN THE HEALTH-AND-WEALTH GOSPEL
1. Norman Vincent Peale, quoted in "Quick Quotes on Money," *Christian History*, April 1987, http://www.christianitytoday.com/ch/1987/issue14/1404.html.
2. Ed Welch, "Death to Healthy, Wealthy and Happy," Christian Counseling and Educational Foundation, February 3, 2014, http://www.ccef.org/resources/blog/death-healthy-wealthy-and-happy.
3. David Brainerd, *An Account of the Life of the Late Rev. Mr. David Brainerd*, ed. Jonathan Edwards, part 8.
4. C. S. Lewis, quoted in Clyde S. Kilby, *The Christian World of C. S. Lewis* (Grand Rapids, MI: Eerdmans, 1964), 66.
5. C. S. Lewis, *The Problem of Pain* (New York: Macmillan, 1962), 19.
6. Corrie ten Boom, *The Hiding Place* (Peabody, MA: Hendrickson, 2009), x.
7. Charles H. Spurgeon, *The Treasury of David*, Psalm 38.
8. Charles H. Spurgeon, "A Basket of Summer Fruit" (Sermon #343).
9. Randy Alcorn, *If God Is Good* (Colorado Springs: Multnomah, 2009), 417.
10. Ibid., 387.
11. Randy Alcorn, "Jim Harrell: Perspectives in Suffering, Part 2," YouTube video, 9:40, Eternal Perspective Ministries, December 10, 2008, http://www.epm.org/blog/2008/Dec/10/jim-harrell -perspectives-in-suffering-part-2.

CHAPTER 36 HAPPINESS THROUGH CONFESSION, REPENTANCE, AND FORGIVENESS
1. Ruth Bell Graham, *Legacy of a Pack Rat* (Nashville: Thomas Nelson, 1989), 187.
2. D. Martyn Lloyd-Jones, *Studies in the Sermon on the Mount* (Grand Rapids, MI: Eerdmans, 1976), 102.
3. Stephen Charnock, "The Necessity of Regeneration," *The Complete Works of Stephen Charnock*, vol. 3.
4. William Whitaker, in James Nichols and Samuel Annesley, eds., *Puritan Sermons, 1659–1689*, repr., vol. 1 (Wheaton, IL: Richard Owen Roberts, 1981), 511.
5. William Bates, *Select Practical Works of Rev. John Howe and Dr. William Bates*, ed. James Marsh (New York: G. & C. & H. Carvill, 1830), 455.
6. Randy Alcorn, *Why ProLife?* (Peabody, MA: Hendrickson, 2012), chapter 11.
7. Ibid.
8. Natasha Tracy, "Homosexuality and Suicide: LGBT Suicide: A Serious Issue," HealthyPlace.com, April 12, 2013, http://www.healthyplace.com/gender/glbt-mental-health/homosexuality-and -suicide-lgbt-suicide-a-serious-issue/.
9. Nancy Schimelpfening, "Homosexuality Strongly Linked to Depression and Suicide," About.com, October 30, 2014, http://depression.about.com/b/2008/09/23/homosexuality-strongly-linked-to -depression-and-suicide.htm.
10. Thomas Vincent, in *Puritan Sermons*, vol. 2, 619.
11. Charles H. Spurgeon, "Your Rowers Have Brought You into Great Waters" (Sermon #1933).
12. Hannah Whitall Smith, *The Christian's Secret of a Holy Life: The Unpublished Personal Writings of Hannah Whitall Smith*, ed. Melvin E. Dieter (Oak Harbor, WA: Logos Research Systems, 1997).
13. Spurgeon, "Sorrow and Sorrow" (Sermon #2691).
14. Anselm, *Cur Deus Homo*, Book First, chapter 24.
15. Charles H. Spurgeon, *Morning and Evening: Daily Readings*, January 31 (morning).
16. Martin Luther, "Sermon for the 19th Sunday after Trinity," *Sermons of Martin Luther*.
17. Ruth Schenk, "Napalm Attack Begins 36-year Journey to Faith and Forgiveness," *Southeast Outlook*, September 11, 2008.
18. Kim Phuc Foundation International, http://www.kimfoundation.com.

19. Ron McManus, as quoted in Craig Brian Larson and Phyllis Ten Elshof, *1001 Illustrations That Connect* (Grand Rapids, MI: Zondervan, 2008), 504.

20. Lewis B. Smedes, as quoted in Alex A. Lluch and Helen Eckmann, *Simple Principles to Enjoy Life and Be Happy* (San Diego: WS Publishing, 2008), 46.

21. Charles H. Spurgeon, *The Treasury of David*, Psalm 32.

22. Louis Zamperini and David Rensin, *Don't Give Up, Don't Give In: Lessons from an Extraordinary Life* (New York: HarperCollins, 2014), xxiv.

23. Ibid.

24. "Olympian, World War II Veteran Dies at 97," Baptist Press, July 7, 2014, http://townhall.com/news /religion/2014/07/07/olympian-world-war-ii-veteran-dies-at-97-n1859735.

25. "Faith: Louis Zamperini Reads His Letter to the Bird," YouTube video, 1:39, posted by Faith Community Church, September 11, 2011, https://www.youtube.com/watch?v=_rHWZQdjfHQ.

26. Zamperini and Rensin, *Don't Give Up, Don't Give In*, 73, 75.

27. George Whitefield, "A Preservative against Unsettled Notions, and Want of Principles, in Regard to Righteousness and Christian Perfection," *Selected Sermons of George Whitefield*.

28. D. Martyn Lloyd-Jones, *Spiritual Depression: Its Causes and Cure* (Grand Rapids, MI: Eerdmans, 1965), 76.

29. Thomas Brooks, "The Golden Key to Open Hidden Treasures," *The Complete Works of Thomas Brooks*, vol. 5.

30. Spurgeon, "The Secret of Happiness" (Sermon #3227).

31. Zamperini and Rensin, *Don't Give Up, Don't Give In*, 219.

32. Mark D. Roberts, "Louis Zamperini: The Happiest Man I've Ever Known," Patheos, July 3, 2014, http://www.patheos.com/blogs/markdroberts/2014/07/03/louis-zamperini-the-happiest-man-ive -ever-known/#ixzz3MT5Cl7sJ.

CHAPTER 37 WE NEED NOT CHOOSE BETWEEN HOLINESS AND HAPPINESS

1. Richard Mansel, "God Calls Us to Holiness, Not Happiness," *Forthright Magazine*, March 4, 2008, http://forthright.net/2008/03/04/god_calls_us_to_holiness_not_happiness_1/.

2. Tony Reinke, "The World's Joy-Tragedy," Desiring God, August 30, 2014, http://www.desiringgod.org /articles/the-world-s-joy-tragedy.

3. A. W. Tozer, *Man: The Dwelling Place of God*, comp. Anita M. Bailey (Camp Hill, PA: WingSpread, 1997), chapter 25, "Three Faithful Wounds," e-book.

4. *The A. W. Tozer Bible (King James Version)* (Peabody, MA: Hendrickson, 2012), 1086.

5. Ibid., 861.

6. A. W. Tozer, *The Attributes of God*, vol. 1 (Camp Hill, PA: WingSpread, 2007), 78.

7. Tozer, *Man: The Dwelling Place of God*, chapter 25.

8. A. T. Pierson, *The Westminster Budget*, February 9, 1893.

9. Octavius Winslow, "The Guidance of the Spirit," *No Condemnation in Christ Jesus*.

10. Octavius Winslow, "Reason 10: Trial Is Precious Because It Assimilates Us to Divine Holiness," *The Precious Things of God*.

11. Anselm, *Cur Deus Homo*, Book Second, chapter 1.

12. Richard Sibbes, "The Soul's Conflict and Victory Over Itself by Faith," *The Complete Works of Richard Sibbes*, vol. 1.

13. Paul J. Wadell, *Happiness and the Christian Moral Life: An Introduction to Christian Ethics* (Lanham, MD: Rowman & Littlefield, 2012), 19.

14. Mark David Futato, *Interpreting the Psalms: An Exegetical Handbook* (Grand Rapids, MI: Kregel, 2007), 67.

15. John Calvin, *Commentary on the Book of Psalms*, vol. 2, Psalm 37.

16. Jonathan Edwards, "A Dissertation concerning the End for Which God Created the World," *Works of Jonathan Edwards*, vol. 1.

17. Ibid.

18. Edwards, "Religious Affections," *Works of Jonathan Edwards*, vol. 1.

19. Edwards, "God Glorified in Man's Dependence," *Works of Jonathan Edwards*, vol. 2.

20. Edwards, "Concerning the Divine Decrees in General, and Election in Particular," *Works of Jonathan Edwards*, vol. 2.

21. Edwards, "Heaven," *Works of Jonathan Edwards*, vol. 2.

22. Edwards, "Notes on the Bible," *Works of Jonathan Edwards*, vol. 2.

23. Edwards, "The Pure in Heart Blessed," *Works of Jonathan Edwards*, vol. 2.

24. John Piper, "Was Jonathan Edwards a Christian Hedonist?" Desiring God, September 29, 1987, http://www.desiringgod.org/articles/was-jonathan-edwards-a-christian-hedonist.

25. Edwards, "The Pure in Heart Blessed," *Works of President Edwards*, vol. 8.

26. Ibid.

27. John Piper, "Lust," in *Killjoys: The Seven Deadly Sins*, ed. Marshall Segal (Minneapolis: Desiring God, 2015), 96.

28. Charles H. Spurgeon, "The Christian's Badge," *Able to the Uttermost: Twenty Gospel Sermons*.

29. Gerald Mann, "On Eating Drinking and Being Merry (Luke 5:27-39)," Bible.org, https://bible.org/seriespage/17-eating-drinking-and-being-merry-luke-527-39.

30. Archibald Alexander, *A Treatise on Justification by Faith*, section 9.

31. C. S. Lewis, *Letters to an American Lady* (Grand Rapids, MI: Eerdmans, 1967), 19.

32. Hannah Whitall Smith, quoted in Robert J. Morgan, *My All in All* (Nashville: B&H, 2008), August 17.

33. John Piper, *Desiring God* (Colorado Springs: Multnomah, 2011), 100.

34. William Bates, "The Four Last Things: On Heaven," *The Whole Works of the Rev. W. Bates*, vol. 3.

35. John Wesley, "Upon Our Lord's Sermon on the Mount: Discourse Nine" (Sermon #29), Wesley Center Online, http://wesley.nnu.edu/john-wesley/the-sermons-of-john-wesley-1872-edition/sermon-29-upon-our-lords-sermon-on-the-mount-discourse-nine/.

36. Adam Clarke, *The Holy Bible Containing the Old and New Testaments: With a Commentary and Critical Notes*, vol. 3, "Notes on Psalm 32:10."

37. Adam Clarke, *Adam Clarke's Commentary on the New Testament*, vol. 1, "Notes on Matthew 5:44."

38. Thomas Manton, "Twenty Sermons on Important Passages of Scripture," *The Complete Works of Thomas Manton*, vol. 2.

39. Matthew Henry, *Matthew Henry's Commentary on the Whole Bible*, vol. 3, Psalm 1:1-3.

40. Thomas Watson, "The Godly Man's Picture," *Discourses on Important and Interesting Subjects*, vol. 1.

41. Thomas Watson, *A Body of Divinity*, chapter 4, "The Fall," section 3, "Original Sin."

42. Richard Baxter and William Orme, "A Call to the Unconverted to Turn and Live," *The Practical Works of the Rev. Richard Baxter*, vol. 7.

CHAPTER 38 IS SEEKING HAPPINESS SELFISH?

1. Hallowell Bowser, "The Long, Shrill City," *Saturday Review*, January 27, 1962, 24.

2. Ayn Rand, *The Virtue of Selfishness* (New York: New American Library, 1964), vii–viii.

3. Ibid., viii.

4. Jonathan Edwards, "The Spirit of Charity: The Opposite of a Selfish Spirit," *Christian Love, as Manifested in the Heart and Life*.

5. Jonathan Edwards, "The Spiritual Blessings of the Gospel Represented by a Feast," *The Works of Jonathan Edwards: Sermons and Discourses, 1723–1729*, vol. 14.

6. Ibid.

7. C. S. Lewis, *The Weight of Glory* (New York: HarperCollins, 2001), 25.

8. Ibid., 25–26.

9. Dacher Keltner, "The Evolution of Compassion," University of California, Berkeley, http://www.altruists.org/static/files/The%20Evolution%20of%20Compassion%20%28Dacher%20Keltner%29.pdf.

10. Ibid.

11. Arthur C. Brooks, as quoted in "Those Who Serve Others Are *Happier, Healthier*, and More *Prosperous*," Spokane Cares, http://www.spokanecares.org/index.php?c_ref=160.

12. Arthur G. Bennett, *The Valley of Vision* (Edinburgh: Banner of Truth, 1975), 168.

13. Elisabeth Elliot, *Shadow of the Almighty* (Peabody, MA: Hendrickson, 2008), 11.

14. Randy Alcorn, *The Law of Rewards* (Carol Stream, IL: Tyndale, 1989).
15. In this regard I recommend Ryan Lister's *The Presence of God* (Wheaton, IL: Crossway, 2015).
16. Jon Bloom, "Why Your Happiness Is So Important to God," Desiring God, September 15, 2014, http://www.desiringgod.org/articles/why-your-happiness-is-so-important-to-god.
17. Randy Alcorn, *The Treasure Principle* (Colorado Springs: Multnomah, 2001).
18. John Piper, *When I Don't Desire God* (Wheaton, IL: Crossway, 2004), 254.
19. Mark Twain, *Tales, Speeches, Essays, and Sketches* (New York: Penguin, 1994), 204.
20. C. S. Lewis, *The Joyful Christian*, repr. (New York: Touchstone, 1996), 210.
21. David Livingstone, *Cambridge Lectures*, Lecture I.

CHAPTER 39 HAPPINESS THROUGH SELF-FORGETFULNESS AND CHRIST-CENTEREDNESS

1. George Washington Carver, *George Washington Carver: In His Own Words*, ed. Gary R. Kremer (Columbia: University of Missouri Press, 1991), 135.
2. Tom Robbins, *Jitterbug Perfume* (New York: Bantam, 2003), 261.
3. Cody Delistraty, "The Neurological Similarities between Successful Writers and the Mentally Ill," *Thought Catalog* (blog), March 18, 2014, http://thoughtcatalog.com/cody-delistraty/2014/03/the-neurological-similarities-between-successful-writers-and-the-mentally-ill.
4. Mike Mason, *Champagne for the Soul: Celebrating God's Gift of Joy* (Vancouver, BC: Regent College, 2003), 53–54.
5. J. D. Greear, *Gospel: Recovering the Power That Made Christianity Revolutionary* (Nashville: B&H, 2011), 81.
6. Jonathan Edwards, "Sermon 12: Isaiah 32," *The Works of Jonathan Edwards*, vol. 2.
7. Timothy Keller, *The Freedom of Self-Forgetfulness* (Denver: 10Publishing, 2012), 32–33.
8. C. S. Lewis, *Mere Christianity* (New York: HarperCollins, 2001), book 3, chapter 8, "The Great Sin."
9. Keller, *The Freedom of Self-Forgetfulness*, 32.

CHAPTER 40 HAPPINESS THROUGH GRATITUDE

1. Guerric of Igny, *Mediæval Preachers and Mediæval Preaching: A Series of Extracts, Translated from the Sermons of the Middle Ages, Chronologically Arranged*, ed. J. M. Neal (London: J. Masters, 1856), 152.
2. Matthew Henry, quoted in James S. Hewett, ed., *Illustrations Unlimited* (Carol Stream, IL: Tyndale, 1988), 264.
3. G. K. Chesterton, *The Collected Works of G. K. Chesterton*, vol. 20 (San Francisco: Ignatius Press, 2001), 463.
4. S. Lyubomirsky, K. M. Sheldon, and D. Schkade, "Pursuing Happiness: The Architecture of Sustainable Change," *Review of General Psychology* 9, no. 2 (2005): 111–31.
5. "Grateful People Are Happier and Better Students than Materialistic People," FYI Living, August 8, 2011, http://fyiliving.com/research/grateful-people-are-happier-and-better-students-than-materialistic-people/.
6. Johannes P. Louw and Eugene A. Nida, eds., *Greek-English Lexicon of the New Testament: Based on Semantic Domains* (New York: United Bible Societies, 1996).
7. Dennis Prager, *Happiness Is a Serious Problem: A Human Nature Repair Manual* (New York: ReganBooks, 1998), 59.
8. Helen Keller, *Optimism* (Whitefish, MT: Kessinger, 2003), 17.
9. Helen Keller, *We Bereaved* (New York: Leslie Fulenwider, 1929).
10. Nancy Leigh DeMoss, *Choosing Gratitude: Your Journey to Joy* (Chicago: Moody Press, 2009), 35.
11. John Piper, "A Tribute to Gratitude," Desiring God, November 27, 2008, http://www.desiringgod.org/articles/a-tribute-to-gratitude.
12. M. R. DeHaan, *Broken Things* (Grand Rapids, MI: Zondervan, 1948), 21.
13. Ellen Vaughn, *Radical Gratitude* (Grand Rapids, MI: Zondervan, 2005), 203.
14. Elisabeth Elliot, *Shadow of the Almighty* (Peabody, MA: Hendrickson, 2008), 113–14.
15. Alexander Maclaren, "Requiting God," *Expositions of Holy Scripture: Psalms*.

16. C. S. Lewis, *Letters to Malcolm* (New York: Harcourt, 2002), 75.
17. Ibid., 91.
18. Ibid., 91.
19. Ibid., 90.
20. G. K. Chesterton, as quoted in *The Inspirational Christmas Almanac* (Colorado Springs: Cook Communications Ministries, 2006), 87.
21. Chesterton, *Collected Works of G. K. Chesterton*, vol. 10, 43.
22. Dan Graves, "Congo Rebels Reached Helen Roseveare," Christianity.com, August 2014, http://www.christianhistorytimeline.com/DAILYF/2002/08/daily-08-15-2002.shtml.
23. Helen Roseveare, *Living Sacrifice* (Minneapolis: Bethany House, 1979), 20–21.
24. Helen Roseveare, *Digging Ditches* (Tain, Scotland: Christian Focus, 2005), 76–77.
25. Ann Voskamp, *One Thousand Gifts: A Dare to Live Fully Right Where You Are* (Grand Rapids, MI: Zondervan, 2010), 15.
26. Charles Allen McClain, *Good News for Off Seasons* (Nashville: Abingdon Press, 1979), 49.
27. Ibid.
28. Gerard Manley Hopkins, *"God's Grandeur" and Other Poems* (New York: Dover, 1995), 15.
29. Voskamp, *One Thousand Gifts*, 33.
30. Ann Voskamp, Twitter post, July 14, 2014, 4:39 a.m., http://twitter.com/AnnVoskamp.
31. Duncan Matheson, as quoted in C. R. Hurditch, ed., *Footsteps of Truth*, vol. 1 (London: J. F. Shaw, 1883), 393.
32. DeMoss, *Choosing Gratitude*, 62.

CHAPTER 41 HAPPINESS AND HOPE: ADJUSTING OUR EXPECTATIONS

1. Frederick Langbridge, "A Cluster of Quiet Thoughts," *The Oxford Dictionary of Quotations*, 2nd ed. (London: Oxford University Press, 1966), 310.
2. Eleanor H. Porter, *Pollyanna*, chapter 22, "Sermons and Woodboxes."
3. Morley Safer, "The Pursuit of Happiness," CBS News video, 12:06, from *60 Minutes*, June 15, 2008, http://www.cbsnews.com/video/watch/?id=4181996n.
4. C. S. Lewis, "Answers to Questions on Christianity," *God in the Dock* (Grand Rapids, MI: Eerdmans, 1972), 52.
5. G. K. Chesterton, *Orthodoxy*, chapter 5, "The Flag of the World."
6. Richard Carlson, *Shortcut through Therapy: Ten Principles of Growth-Oriented, Contented Living* (New York: Plume, 1995), 158–59.
7. Ibid., 158.
8. Michel de Montaigne, as quoted in Paul McKenna, *Change Your Life in Seven Days* (London: Transworld, 2004), 159.
9. James Russell Lowell, as quoted in Tryon Edwards, ed., *A Dictionary of Thoughts* (Detroit: F. B. Dickerson, 1908), 23.
10. Brian Skotko, Susan Levine, and Richard Goldstein, "Self-Perceptions from People with Down Syndrome," *American Journal of Medical Genetics* 155, no. 10 (October 2011): 2360–69.
11. Jevan, "People with Down Syndrome Are Happier than Normal People," *The Tribal Way* (blog), October 2, 2012, http://thetribalway.com/?p=273.
12. H. Choi, M. Van Riper, and S. Thoyre, "Decision Making Following a Prenatal Diagnosis of Down Syndrome: An Integrative Review," *Journal of Midwifery and Women's Health* 57, no. 2 (March/April 2012): 156–164.
13. Michael J. Fox, as quoted in H. S. Lim, *Living Well: Quenches Thirst in Life's Voyage* (Singapore: Partridge, 2012), 98.
14. Gail Kinman, "How Can the Academy Get Over Its Gloom? Just Grow Up, Gail Kinman Hears," *Times Higher Education*, November 5, 2009, http://www.timeshighereducation.co.uk/408898.article. See also David Watson, *The Question of Morale* (Open University Press, 2009).
15. Ibid.
16. Ibid.

17. Arthur Schopenhauer, *Councils and Maxims*, trans. T. Bailey Saunders (London: Swan Sonnenschein, 1891), 9.
18. Matthew Henry, *Matthew Henry's Commentary on the Whole Bible*, vol. 1, Genesis 31:25-35.
19. Jonathan Edwards, "The Pure in Heart Blessed," *The Works of Jonathan Edwards*, vol. 2.
20. M. Scott Peck, *The Road Less Traveled* (New York: Simon & Schuster, 1978), 15.
21. Max Lucado, *And the Angels Were Silent* (Nashville: Thomas Nelson, 2013), 105–6.

CHAPTER 42 FINDING HAPPINESS NOW IN GOD'S PROMISES OF ETERNAL HAPPINESS
1. Edward Gibbon, *The Decline and Fall of the Roman Empire* (New York: Random House, 2003), 969.
2. Jonathan Edwards, *The Works of President Edwards*, vol. 1 (New York: Leavitt, Trow, 1844), 655.
3. Seneca, as quoted by David G. Myers, *Psychology*, 6th ed. (New York: Worth, 2001), 484.
4. *Pirate Radio*, directed by Richard Curtis (Universal Studios, 2009).
5. J. I. Packer, *Concise Theology* (Carol Stream, IL: Tyndale, 1993), 267.
6. George Swinnock, "The Fading of the Flesh," *The Works of George Swinnock*, vol. 4.
7. C. S. Lewis, *The Problem of Pain* (New York: Macmillan, 1962), 115.
8. A. W. Tozer and H. Verploegh, *The Quotable Tozer II: More Wise Words with a Prophetic Edge* (Camp Hill, PA: Christian Publications, 1997), 103.
9. David Morgan, "Stephen Hawking: Heaven Is 'a Fairy Story,'" CBS News, May 17, 2011, http://www.cbsnews.com/news/stephen-hawking-heaven-is-a-fairy-story/.
10. Lewis, *Problem of Pain*, 144–48.
11. Thornton Wilder, *Our Town* (New York: HarperCollins, 2003), 87–88.
12. E. J. Fortman, *Everlasting Life after Death* (New York: Alba House, 1976), 309.
13. Venerable Bede, "Sermon on All Saints," *Orators of the Early and Mediaeval Church* (New York: G. P. Putnam's Sons, 1900), 304.
14. Sigmund Freud, as quoted in Neal Ranzoni, *The Book on "Happiness Quotes"* (CreateSpace Independent Publishing Platform, 2013), 5.
15. Isaac Watts, *The World to Come*, vol. 1 (section 5, objection 8).
16. Isaac Watts, "Delight in the Worship of the Sabbath," *Church Psalmody* (Boston: Perkins, Marvin, 1834), 163.
17. Richard Baxter and William Orme, "The Divine Life: Walking with God," *The Practical Works of the Rev. Richard Baxter*, vol. 13.
18. Charles H. Spurgeon, "Creation's Groans and the Saints' Sighs" (Sermon #788).
19. *Time* (March 24, 1997): 75, quoted in Paul Marshall with Lela Gilbert, *Heaven Is Not My Home: Learning to Live in God's Creation* (Nashville: Word, 1998), 234.
20. Baxter and Orme, "Right Rejoicing," *Practical Works of the Rev. Richard Baxter*, vol. 17.
21. Thomas Watson, as quoted in Warren W. Wiersbe, *The Wiersbe Bible Commentary: Old Testament* (Colorado Springs: David C. Cook, 2007), 1119.
22. Baxter and Orme, "The Saints' Everlasting Rest," *Practical Works of the Rev. Richard Baxter*, vol. 22.
23. Charles H. Spurgeon, *Morning and Evening: Daily Readings*, December 10 (morning).
24. Charles H. Spurgeon, quoted in Paul Lee Tan, *Encyclopedia of 7700 Illustrations* (Garland, TX: Bible Communications, 1996).
25. Miles Coverdale, ed., *The Letters of the Martyrs: Collected and Published in 1564*, the letters of John Bradford.
26. John Sargent, *Life and Letters of the Rev. Henry Martyn* (London: Seeley, Jackson, and Halliday, 1862), 101.

CHAPTER 43 FUTURE HAPPINESS ON THE NEW EARTH
1. *The Lord of the Rings: Return of the King*, directed by Peter Jackson (New Line Cinema, 2003).
2. John Donne, "Preached on Midsummer Day" (Sermon #118, John 1:8).
3. Donne, "Preached at Lincoln's Inn" (Sermon #95, Job 19:26).
4. F. J. Boudreaux, *The Happiness of Heaven*, chapter 11.
5. In my summary of Isaiah 60, I am indebted to Richard Mouw's *When the Kings Come Marching In* (Grand Rapids, MI: Eerdmans, 1983).

6. Jonathan Edwards, "End in Creation," *The Works of President Edwards*, vol. 2.
7. Ibid.
8. George Whitefield, "Walking with God," *Selected Sermons of George Whitefield*.
9. Paul Helm, *The Last Things* (Carlisle, PA: Banner of Truth, 1989), 92.
10. Thomas Manton, "The Transfiguration of Jesus Christ in Matthew 17 and Luke 9," *The Works of Thomas Manton*, vol. 1.
11. John Donne and Henry Alford, *The Works of John Donne*, vol. 6 (London: John W. Parker, 1839), 280.
12. Isaac Watts, *The World to Come* (Discourse 3, Motive 5).
13. Anthony Hoekema, *The Bible and the Future* (Grand Rapids, MI: Eerdmans, 1979), 251.
14. C. S. Lewis, *Letters to Malcolm* (New York: Harcourt, 2002), 122.
15. Arch Stanton, *Animals in Heaven: Fantasy or Reality?* (Victoria, BC: Trafford, 2004), 264.
16. From John Wesley's sermon "The General Deliverance" (Sermon #60). See John Wesley, "General Deliverance Sermon 60," ed. Randy Alcorn, Eternal Perspective Ministries, February 21, 2010, http://www.epm.org/resources/2010/Feb/21/general-deliverance-sermon-60.
17. Hoekema, *Bible and the Future*, 53.
18. Albert M. Wolters, *Creation Regained: Biblical Basics for a Reformational Worldview* (Grand Rapids, MI: Eerdmans, 1985), 11.
19. A. A. Hodge, *Evangelical Theology: A Course of Popular Lectures* (Edinburgh: Banner of Truth, 1976), 400–401.
20. John Calvin, *Commentary on Romans*, Romans 8:19-22.
21. Jonathan Edwards, "The Final Judgment," *The Works of Jonathan Edwards*, vol. 1.
22. Boudreaux, *Happiness of Heaven*, chapter 21.

CHAPTER 44 DRINK DEEPLY FROM GOD'S GIFT OF HAPPINESS

1. Mark Twain, as quoted in Robert Andrews, *The Columbia Dictionary of Quotations* (New York: Columbia University Press, 1993), 778.
2. Mark Twain, *The Mysterious Stranger and Other Stories* (New York: Harper & Brothers, 1922), 139.
3. Mark Twain, *Autobiography of Mark Twain: Reader's Edition*, vol. 1 (Berkeley and Los Angeles, CA: University of California Press, 2012), 182.
4. John Calvin, *Institutes of the Christian Religion*, trans. Henry Beveridge, Book First, chapter 2, "What It Is to Know God—Tendency of This Knowledge."
5. David Clarkson, "Believers' Communion with the Father and Son," *The Practical Works of David Clarkson*, vol. 3.
6. N. D. Wilson, "Lighten Up, Christians: God Loves a Good Time," Christianity Today, May 7, 2014, http://www.christianitytoday.com/ct/2014/april/lighten-up-christians-god-loves-good -time.html?start=2.
7. Jeremy Taylor, as quoted in C. S. Lewis, *George MacDonald: An Anthology* (New York: HarperCollins, 2001), xxxv.
8. John Piper, *Don't Waste Your Life* (Wheaton, IL: Crossway, 2003), 10.
9. Charles Simeon, "Genesis 2:16-17," *Horae Homileticae: Genesis to Deuteronomy*, vol. 1.
10. C. S. Lewis, *Mere Christianity* (New York: HarperCollins, 2001), book 4, chapter 4, "Good Infection."
11. Brother Lawrence and Frank Laubach, *Practicing His Presence* (Sargent, GA: The SeedSowers, 1973), 10.
12. Ibid.

CHAPTER 45 GOD PROMISES WE'LL LIVE "HAPPILY EVER AFTER"

1. Hannah Whitall Smith, *The Christian's Secret of a Holy Life: The Unpublished Personal Writings of Hannah Whitall Smith*, ed. Melvin E. Dieter (Oak Harbor, WA: Logos Research Systems, 1997).
2. Ibid.
3. Ibid.
4. John H. Sammis, "Trust and Obey," *Church Hymnal* (Cleveland, TN: Tennessee Music and Printing, 1951), 157.

5. Charles H. Spurgeon, "Christ's Joy and Ours" (Sermon #2935).

6. Timothy Keller, "The Centrality of the Gospel," http://download.redeemer.com/pdf/learn/resources/Centrality_of_the_Gospel-Keller.pdf.

7. John Calvin, *Commentary on the Book of Psalms*, vol. 2, Psalm 37:27-29.

8. Thomas Szasz, quoted in *Oxford Treasury of Sayings and Quotations*, ed. Susan Ratcliffe, 4th ed. (Oxford: Oxford University Press, 2011), 201.

9. Spurgeon, "How to Become Full of Joy" (Sermon #3272).

10. Christopher Fowler, "How a Christian May Get Such a Faith That Is Not Only Saving, But Comfortable and Joyful at Present," *The Morning Exercises at Cripplegate, St. Giles in the Fields and in Southwark*, notes and trans. James Nichols, vol. 2.

11. Jonathan Edwards, "The Christian Pilgrim," *The Works of President Edwards*, vol. 7.

12. George Müller, "Effectual Service to God," in *Fireside Readings: A Collection of Essays, Poems and Sentences*, comp. H. A. Mumaw (Elkhart, IN: Mennonite Publishing, 1881), 20.

13. J. C. Ryle, *Expository Thoughts on the Gospels, St. John*, vol. 1, John 2.

14. George Swinnock, "The Incomparableness of God," *The Works of George Swinnock*, vol. 4.

15. Spurgeon, "A Message to the Glad and the Sad" (Sermon #2546).

16. Augustine, *Confessions*, trans. by R. S. Pine-Coffin (New York: Penguin Classics, 1961), book 10, chapter 20.

17. Calvin, *Commentary on the Book of Psalms*, vol. 1, Psalm 16:11.

18. Augustine, *Augustine's Confessions* (Oxford: Oxford University Press, 2014), 52.

19. Augustine, *The Confessions of Saint Augustine* (New York: E. P. Dutton, 1900), 255.

20. Spurgeon, "Two Immutable Things" (Sermon #2438).

21. Spurgeon, "Our Youth Renewed" (Sermon #3417).

22. Spurgeon, "Sermon for New Year's Day" (Sermon #1816).

23. Spurgeon, "God Rejoicing in the New Creation" (Sermon #2211).

APPENDIX 1 NINETEEN MORE HAPPINESS WORDS IN THE OLD TESTAMENT

1. James Swanson, *A Dictionary of Biblical Languages with Semantic Domains: Hebrew (Old Testament)* (Oak Harbor, WA: Logos Research Systems, 1997), s.v. "*tob*" and "*towb*."

2. Ibid., s.v. "*towb*."

3. Ibid., s.v. "*hapes*."

4. Ibid., s.v. "*yaal*."

5. Ibid., s.v. "*simchah*."

6. Ibid., s.v. "*ranan*."

7. Ibid., s.v., "*renanah*."

8. Ibid., s.v., "*rinnah*."

9. Ibid., s.v., "*ruwa*."

10. Ibid., s.v. "*gil*."

11. Ibid., s.v. "*sachaq*."

12. Ibid.

13. Ibid., s.v. "*teruwah*."

14. Ibid., s.v. "*sus*."

15. Ibid., s.v. "*rachab*."

16. Ibid., s.v. "*sasson*."

17. Ibid., s.v. "*masos*."

18. Ibid., s.v. "*alaz*."

19. Ibid., s.v. "*shashua*."

20. Ibid., s.v. "*alats*."

21. Ibid., s.v. "*alliyz*."

22. Ibid., s.v. "*alas*."

23. Ibid., s.v. "*chadah*."

APPENDIX 2 FOURTEEN MORE HAPPINESS WORDS IN THE NEW TESTAMENT

1. James Swanson, *A Dictionary of Biblical Languages with Semantic Domains: Hebrew (Old Testament)* (Oak Harbor, WA: Logos Research Systems, 1997), s.v. "*kauchaomai.*"
2. Johannes P. Louw and Eugene A. Nida, eds., *Greek-English Lexicon of the New Testament: Based on Semantic Domains* (New York: United Bible Societies, 1996), 25.87.
3. Ibid., 25.133.
4. Charles H. Spurgeon, *The Fullness of Joy* (New Kensington, PA: Whitaker House, 1997), 106.
5. Louw and Nida, *Greek-English Lexicon of the New Testament*, 13.127.
6. Ibid., 25.121.
7. Ibid., 25.122.
8. Barclay M. Newman and Eugene A. Nida, *A Handbook on the Acts of the Apostles*, UBS Handbook Series (New York: United Bible Societies, 1972), 52.
9. Louw and Nida, *Greek-English Lexicon of the New Testament*, 25.156.
10. Ibid., 25.125.
11. Ibid., 21.17.25.
12. William Morrice, *Joy in the New Testament* (Grand Rapids, MI: Eerdmans, 1985), 33.
13. Louw and Nida, *Greek-English Lexicon of the New Testament*, 15.243.
14. Ibid., 25.146.
15. Ibid., 25.117.
16. Ibid., 25.127.
17. Ibid., 25.128.
18. Ibid., 25.146.

ABOUT THE AUTHOR

RANDY ALCORN is an author and the founder and director of Eternal Perspective Ministries (EPM), a nonprofit organization dedicated to teaching principles of God's Word and assisting the church in ministering to unreached, unfed, unborn, uneducated, unreconciled, and unsupported people around the world. His ministry focus is communicating the strategic importance of using our earthly time, money, possessions, and opportunities to invest in need-meeting ministries that count for eternity. He accomplishes this by analyzing, teaching, and applying biblical truth.

Before starting EPM in 1990, Randy served as a pastor for fourteen years. He has a bachelor of theology and a master of arts in biblical studies from Multnomah University and an honorary doctorate from Western Seminary in Portland, Oregon, and has taught on the adjunct faculties of both. A *New York Times* bestselling author, Randy has written more than forty books, including *Heaven*, *The Treasure Principle*, and the award-winning novel *Safely Home*. His books have sold more than nine million copies and have been translated into more than sixty languages.

Randy has written for many magazines, including EPM's *Eternal Perspectives*. He is active on Facebook and Twitter, and has been a guest on more than seven hundred radio, television, and online programs.

Randy resides in Gresham, Oregon, with his wife, Nanci. They have two married daughters and are the proud grandparents of five grandsons. Randy enjoys time spent with his family, biking, playing tennis, researching, and reading.

You may contact Eternal Perspective Ministries at www.epm.org or 39085 Pioneer Blvd., Suite 206, Sandy, OR 97055 or 503-668-5200.

Follow Randy on Facebook: www.facebook.com/randyalcorn, on Twitter: www.twitter.com/randyalcorn, and on his blog: www.epm.org/blog.

BOOKS BY RANDY ALCORN

FICTION

Deadline

Dominion

Deception

Edge of Eternity

Eternity

Lord Foulgrin's Letters

The Ishbane Conspiracy

Safely Home

Courageous

The Chasm

CHILDREN'S

Heaven for Kids

Wait Until Then

Tell Me About Heaven

STUDY GUIDES

The Grace and Truth Paradox Study Guide

The Treasure Principle Study Guide

The Treasure Principle Bible Study

The Purity Principle Study Guide

If God Is Good Study Guide

The Heaven Small Group Discussion Guide

The Heaven Workbook

NONFICTION

Happiness

God's Promise of Happiness

Heaven

Touchpoints: Heaven

50 Days of Heaven

In Light of Eternity

Managing God's Money

Money, Possessions, and Eternity

The Law of Rewards

ProLife Answers to ProChoice Arguments

Sexual Temptation: Guardrails for the Road to Purity

The Goodness of God

The Grace and Truth Paradox

The Purity Principle

The Treasure Principle

Why ProLife?

If God Is Good . . .

The Promise of Heaven

We Shall See God

90 Days of God's Goodness

Life Promises for Eternity

Eternal Perspectives

Everything You Always Wanted to Know about Heaven

hand in Hand

Help for Women Under Stress

The Resolution for Men

Seeing the Unseen

Does the Birth Control Pill Cause Abortions?

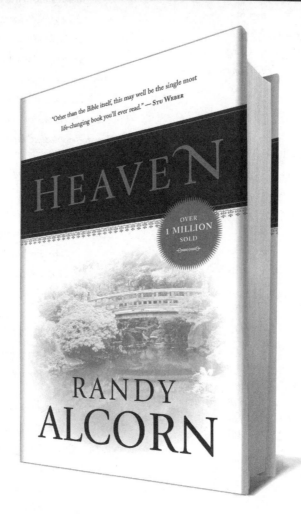